THE LAW AND WORKING OF THE CONSTITUTION: DOCUMENTS 1660–1914

Vol. I   1660–1783

THE CONSTITUTIONAL HISTORY
OF MEDIEVAL ENGLAND
J. E. A. Jolliffe
Third edition

THE CONSTITUTIONAL HISTORY
OF MODERN BRITAIN
Sir David Lindsay Keir
Sixth edition

*

SELECT DOCUMENTS OF
ENGLISH CONSTITUTIONAL HISTORY
1307–1485. S. B. Chrimes and A. L. Brown

THE LAW AND WORKING OF
THE CONSTITUTION

Documents 1625–1660. I. A. Roots and
D. H. Pennington. *In preparation*

Documents 1660–1914. Two vols.
W. C. Costin and J. Steven Watson

THE LAW AND WORKING OF THE CONSTITUTION: DOCUMENTS 1660–1914

BY

W. C. COSTIN, M.A., D.LITT.
PRESIDENT OF ST JOHN'S COLLEGE, OXFORD

AND

J. STEVEN WATSON, M.A.
STUDENT AND TUTOR OF CHRIST CHURCH, OXFORD

IN TWO VOLUMES

VOLUME I
1660–1783

ADAM & CHARLES BLACK
LONDON

FIRST PUBLISHED 1952
SECOND EDITION 1961

A. AND C. BLACK LIMITED
4, 5 AND 6 SOHO SQUARE, LONDON W.1

PRINTED IN GREAT BRITAIN
BY R. AND R. CLARK, LTD., EDINBURGH

THOMAE WHITE EQUITI AURATO
OLIM SCHOLARI REDINGENSI
DEINDE SODALITATIS MERCATORUM SCISSORUM
MAGISTRO
COLLEGII DIVI JOHANNIS BAPTISTAE
FUNDATORI
TANTI BENEFICII MEMORES
JOHANNENSES DUO

INTRODUCTION

THE present selection of documents illustrating the development of the British Constitution since 1660 has, we make bold to claim, two novel features. The first is a negative one. We have not, in the manner of some of our predecessors in this field, prefaced each of our documents, or groups of documents, with a set of notes, commentaries, or asides of praise and blame; at the most our notes are designed to make the reader able to understand the circumstances of the case as well as if he had the whole of the original document, instead of an excerpt, before him. Nor have we, as others of such predecessors have preferred, attempted to write the constitutional history of two hundred and fifty years in some century—or score— of breathless pages, and attached it to the front of the selections by way of guide or précis of what is to follow. We have chosen rather to use all the available space for the inclusion of original materials, intending by our presentation to make it possible for them to speak for themselves. But the student in need of a general commentary will, we trust, make use of some full-scale modern work such as Sir David Keir's *Constitutional History of Modern Britain*, for which these volumes should present *pièces justificatives*; for information on some particular topics he would do well to consult the appropriate sections of Sir William Holdsworth's *History of English Law*.

In the second place, we have taken seriously the observation that the British Constitution is not written down in books but is flexible in the sense of being found in the minds and practice of each generation.

Those who have confined their attention to the great constitutional milestones have not been able to show the whole, nor indeed some of the most interesting aspects, of the constitution. To do so one must go behind the Statutes and the Judgements known to lawyers. These are but the " bones cast in a little low dry garret " which we desire to clothe with flesh and blood and bring out into the world. We have been anxious—if we may vary the metaphor— to show the wheels turning, the driver at the controls, and the direction of the journey, as well as the authorized stopping-places. To do this we have drawn upon more varied sources, correspondence, commission reports, novels, memoranda, and so on (as has only been done tentatively by others for earlier periods and on a much smaller scale, and by none, to our knowledge, for this). We hope thus to vivify as well as to extend the range of information. This has been the hardest part of the work : for statesmen, in dealing with some practical problem, but rarely put their reflections whole upon paper (even when the solution can only be reached from constitutional first principles), or if they do, they seldom achieve that brevity for which we had perforce to look in making this selection. Nevertheless, we hope that we have been able to bring into the foreground institutions of such paramount importance as the Cabinet, for which one might search the Statutes of these years in vain. It is hoped also that the Statutes and the great decisions of the Courts will, in this company, reveal more of their true significance.

Our emphasis, in fact, has throughout been upon showing the constitution in working order, and not as a collection of exhibits in a museum. This, we hope, will avoid error. In the first volume, for example, the study of the relationship of the King and his Ministers under the first two Hanoverians should make the cruder Whig misinterpretations of the reigns of George II and George III impossible, even for those who have neither taste nor time to study the work of modern scholars who have so drastically altered old conceptions of the eighteenth century. In this volume the Statutes themselves emphasize the contrast between the seventeenth and eighteenth centuries. In the former the great Acts establishing the framework of a system come thick upon us. In the latter, when the mass of local legislation is cleared out of the way (upon which, together with foreign affairs, the bulk of Parliamentary time was consumed), there remains a small group of Acts aiming at electoral reform and the independence of members. However ineffective, these deserve the increased notice which here they must attract. But in the comparative dearth of major change, the need to show how habit and custom were the real factors of weight is increased. Nowhere is this more true than in local government. And it must be done by seeing men at work.

Apart from this attempt to broaden the sources of such a collection we can claim that in our second volume (mainly of the nineteenth century) we had, even in the use of Statutes, to break new ground. In treating this century of change we have borne in mind Maitland's claim that constitutional history must be concerned with all the many and various fragments of government and authority of the modern world. Thus to show the extension of the franchise by successive Reform Acts is necessary but not enough : we have tried to show something of the treatment of groups within the state (trade unions as well as churches), the development of delegated legislation, the appearance of the modern Civil Service, the reform of the Judicature, and the enormous but chaotic growth of local government. Difficulties arise from the amount of the material and the verbosity of modern Statutes, so that we can often give the student only a single specimen. But in this part of the work we have remained no less anxious to state general principles in concrete terms : we have preferred to illustrate, for example, freedom of the individual in terms of street-corner meetings or housing regulations, rather than to reproduce some set-piece oration by an elder statesman. Consider, for instance, the immense constitutional significance, and the importance to every citizen, of the change in ideas revealed between Sir William Erle's memorandum on restraint of trade, and the opinions expressed in the case of Vacher *v.* the London Compositors or in the Osborne Judgement. Or take the doctrine of the control of finance by the Commons ; does this not emerge more vividly when it is examined in connection with the establishment of the Public Accounts Committee and the discussion of the shortage of parliamentary time ? It emerges indeed not as a platitude but as a problem, and one with which men of flesh and blood have to deal as best they can, interpreting for themselves the spirit of the constitution.

To find the space for all the material we have been discussing we have felt it right to keep rigidly to the constitution of the United Kingdom. Indian and overseas affairs have been excluded : Ireland is included only in respect of her connection—and the dissolution of that connection—with the United Kingdom. We have not attempted any detailed illustration of the local differences between England and Scotland.

In each volume the material has been arranged in four main groups, by origins rather than by subject-matter. These groups are Statutes, Parliamentary Proceedings (including Select Committees and Resolutions as well as debates), Judicial Proceedings, and the Miscellaneous Section to which we have referred above. This division is no more perfectly satisfactory than the attempted classification of powers in our constitution. Necessarily some parts, even successive stages, of the same subject are to be found in more than one section ; we have endeavoured by means of full cross-references in footnotes to enable the reader to bring all these together with ease. This, in conjunction with an index which includes topics and offices as well as proper names, should make it simpler to trace selected subjects through different sources and periods. Within each section the documents are printed simply in chronological order. The text of the Statutes quoted is that of the Statutes of the Realm to the end of that series (the death of Queen Anne) and thereafter the printed editions of the Statutes at Large. In all sections we have retained the capitalization and punctuation of the documents as given in the sources to which reference is made. Omissions are marked by dots except where, as in some of the Statutes, the numeration of sections or paragraphs makes an omission sufficiently obvious.

As legal terms—some commonplace and current but some obsolete and obscure—necessarily occur in both volumes, we have provided the reader with a glossary which, it is our hope, will not prove the least useful portion of this work. Our aim has been to explain technical phrases in words exact enough to satisfy lawyers but yet plain enough to be understood by historians.

We would like to express our thanks to the many colleagues and friends with whom we have discussed these volumes in their formation and from whose suggestions and criticism we have derived benefit. In particular we would acknowledge our debt of gratitude to Sir David Keir and to Professor F. H. Lawson for their sympathetic advice and encouragement, and to Mr. D. R. E. Hopkins of Christ Church for the preparation of the index.

The issue of a second edition of this volume has given us the opportunity to correct some errors in the text and we are grateful to friends who have called our attention to these. We have also revised some of the footnotes.

W. C. C.
J. S. W.

OXFORD,
TRINITY, 1961

ACKNOWLEDGEMENTS

FOR permission to print in this volume extracts from works still under copyright we would thank G. Bell & Sons, Ltd. (Wheatley's edition of *The Diary of Samuel Pepys*); the Cambridge University Press (*The Life and Correspondence of Philip Yorke, Earl of Hardwicke*, by Philip C. Yorke); the Clarendon Press, Oxford (*The Continuation of the Life of Edward, Earl of Clarendon*); Eyre & Spottiswoode, Ltd. (Lord Hervey's *Memoirs of the Reign of George II*); the Controller of H.M. Stationery Office (*The Diary of the First Earl of Egmont*: Historical Manuscripts Commission); Longmans Green & Co., Ltd. (Dykes' *Source Book of Constitutional History from 1660* and Foxcroft's *Life and Letters of Sir G. Saville*); Macmillan & Co., Ltd. (Fortescue's *Correspondence of George III*); and the Nottingham City Council (Nottingham Borough Records).

CONTENTS OF VOLUME I

SECTION A: STATUTES

PAGE

I. Legalization of the Convention Parliament, 1660   I

II. Act abolishing Feudal Tenures, 1660   2

III. An Act to preserve the Person and Government of the King, 1661   5

IV. Act restoring the Temporal Authority of Ecclesiastical Persons, 1661   9

V. Act against Tumultuous Petitioning, 1661   9

VI. Confirmation of Acts of Convention Parliament, 1661   10

VII. The Naval Discipline Act, 1661   11

VIII. The Ecclesiastical Causes Act, 1661   13

IX. The Corporation Act, 1661   15

X. The Militia Act, 1662   17

XI. The Act of Uniformity, 1662   20

XII. The Licensing Act, 1662   29

XIII. The Triennial Act, 1664   33

XIV. The Five Mile Act, 1665   34

XV. The Second Conventicle Act, 1670   36

XVI. The First Test Act, 1673   39

XVII. The Second Test Act, 1678   43

XVIII. Habeas Corpus Amendment Act, 1679   46

XIX. Legalization of the Convention Parliament, 1689   54

XX. The Mutiny Act, 1689   55

XXI. Coronation Oath Act, 1689   57

XXII. The Oaths of Supremacy and Allegiance, 1689   60

XXIII. Expulsion of Papists from London, 1689   61

XXIV. The Toleration Act, 1689   63

XXV. The Bill of Rights, 1689   67

PAGE

XXVI. Confirmation of William & Mary and of the   74
Convention Parliament, 1689

XXVII. Restoration of the Charters of the City of London,   75
1689

XXVIII. Establishment of the Bank of England, 1694   77

XXIX. The Triennial Act, 1694   79

XXX. The Trial of Treasons Act, 1696   80

XXXI. An Act against Corrupt Elections, 1696   83

XXXII. Continuance of Parliament on Demise of the   84
Sovereign, 1696

XXXIII. Procedure in Parliamentary Elections, 1696   85

XXXIV. Act for the Security of the Crown, 1696   87

XXXV. An Act against Popery, 1700   90

XXXVI. The Act of Settlement, 1701   92

XXXVII. An Act for Attainder of the Pretended Prince of   96
Wales, 1701

XXXVIII. An Act imposing the Abjuration Oath, 1701   97

XXXIX. Act for the Union with Scotland, 1707   98

XL. Further Act for the Union with Scotland, 1707   110

XLI. The Regency Act, 1707   111

XLII. Act imposing Property Qualifications on Mem-   117
bers of the House of Commons, 1710

XLIII. The Occasional Conformity Act, 1711   118

XLIV. The Schism Act, 1714   121

XLV. The Riot Act, 1715   123

XLVI. The Septennial Act, 1716   126

XLVII. An Act to ease Officers of Corporations, 1718   127

XLVIII. The Dependency of Ireland Act, 1719   128

XLIX. The Use of English only in the Law Courts, 1731   129

L. Act imposing Qualifications on Justices of the   130
Peace, 1732

LI. A Place Act, 1743   131

LII. Protection of Justices and Constables, 1751   133

LIII. The Militia Act, 1757   135

LIV. Crown Revenue Act, 1760   138

PAGE

LV. Judges and the Demise of the Crown, 1760   139

LVI. Electoral Qualification of Freemen, 1762   140

LVII. Trial of Controverted Elections, 1770   140

LVIII. The Royal Marriages Act, 1772   143

LIX. A Place Act (Electors), 1782   145

LX. A Place Act (Members), 1782   146

LXI. Repeal of the Dependency of Ireland Act, 1782   147

LXII. A Civil Establishment Act, 1782   147

LXIII. The Legislative and Judicial Independence of   150
the Irish Parliament and Courts, 1783

SECTION B: PARLIAMENTARY PROCEEDINGS

I. Money Bills, 1661–78   153

II. Impeachment of Clarendon, 1667   155

III. Skinner v. The East India Company, 1666–70   157

IV. Suspending Power, 1673   163

V. Dispute between the Two Houses over Shirley   167
v. Fagg, 1675

VI. Dispute between the Two Houses over the Four   172
Barristers, 1675

VII. Charles II and Royal Prerogative of Peace and   179
War, 1677

VIII. Impeachment of Danby, 1678–79   180

IX. The Exclusion Bill, 1680   183

X. Publication of Votes of the Commons, 1681   184

XI. Impeachment for Crimes cognizable in Common   185
Law Courts, 1681

XII. Summoning the Convention Parliament, 1688   186

XIII. The Legality of Impeachment for Treason, 1689   188

XIV. Refusal of Royal Assent to Bills, 1693   189

XV. The House of Commons and Petitions, 1701   191

XVI. Lords' Protests against Tacking, 1700–1702   192

XVII. Commons Insistence on adjudicating on Elec-   193
toral Matters, 1704

PAGE

XVIII. Voting of Funds for the Public Service,   197
1706

XIX. The Impeachment of Henry Sacheverell, 1710   197

XX. Expulsion of Robert Walpole, 1712   207

XXI. Procedure on Bills imposing Local Taxation,   208
1716

XXII. Protest against the Septennial Act, 1716   208

XXIII. Standing Army, 1717   210

XXIV. Protest against the Mutiny Act, 1718   210

XXV. Peerage Bill, 1719   213

XXVI. The King's Councils, 1738   216

XXVII. Publication of Proceedings of the House of   217
Commons, 1738

XXVIII. Ministry dependent on Commons, 1739   217

XXIX. Double Cabinet, 1740   218

XXX. Legislation affecting the Crown, 1743   218

XXXI. Arrest of John Wilkes, M.P., for Seditious Libel,   219
1763

XXXII. General Warrants, 1766   227

XXXIII. Wilkes and the Middlesex Election, 1768–69   229

XXXIV. The Case of Brass Crosby, 1771   236

XXXV. The House of Lords and the House of Commons,   238
1778

XXXVI. Collective Responsibility of Ministers, 1778   238

XXXVII. Power of the Crown, 1780   239

XXXVIII. King's Prerogative of choosing Ministers, 1782–   240
1783

XXXIX. Irish and English Parliaments, 1782   241

SECTION C: JUDICIAL PROCEEDINGS

I. Bushell's Case, 1670   245

II. Thomas v. Sorrell, 1674   249

III. The Case of Anthony, Earl of Shaftsbury, 1677   251

IV. The Common Law and the Press, 1680   252

PAGE

v. *Quo Warranto* : to the Charters of the City of London, 1681–83 — 254

vi. Godden *v.* Hales, 1686 — 256

vii. The Seven Bishops' Case, 1688 — 258

viii. The Bankers' Case, 1696–1700 — 271

ix. Ashby *v.* White and Others, 1704 — 278

x. Case of the Aylesbury Men, 1704 — 279

xi. The Case of John Tutchin, 1704 — 285

xii. The Case of Dammaree, 1710 — 286

xiii. The King against the Chancellor, Masters, and Scholars of the University of Cambridge, 1724 — 288

xiv. Rex *v.* Broadfoot, 1743 — 289

xv. Wilkes *v.* Lord Halifax, 1763 — 291

xvi. Wilkes *v.* Wood (Case of General Warrants), 1763 — 294

xvii. Leach *v.* John Money, James Watson, and Robert Blackmore, Three of the King's Messengers, 1765 — 295

xviii. Entick *v.* Carrington and Others (Case of Search Warrants), 1765 — 297

xix. The Case of Brass Crosby, 1771 — 311

xx. Sommersett's Case, 1772 — 314

xxi. Rex *v.* Tubbs, 1776 — 316

SECTION D: MISCELLANEA

i. A First Minister, 1660–67 — 317

ii. The Privy Council and its Committees, 1660–67 — 318

iii. Management of the Commons, 1663 — 322

iv. The Declaration of Indulgence, 1672 — 324

v. Party Origins and Parliament, 1673 — 325

vi. Money Bills : Lords and Commons, 1677 — 326

vii. Crown and Foreign Policy, 1677 — 327

viii. King's Approval of the Speaker, 1679 — 328

PAGE

IX. Charles II and Temple's Scheme for a Privy   329
Council, 1679

X. The Cabinet, *circa* 1680   330

XI. The Powers of the Privy Council, 1681   331

XII. Surrender by Bristol Corporation to Charles II   332
of its Charters, 1683

XIII. Charles II's New Charter to the City of Bristol,   333
1685

XIV. A Balanced Constitution, 1685   340

XV. An Election : City of York, 1685   342

XVI. The Declaration of Indulgence, 1687   343

XVII. James II and Borough Corporations, 1688   347

XVIII. Invitation to William, Prince of Orange, June   352
30, 1688

XIX. Locke on " Federative Power ", 1689   354

XX. The Cabinet, 1694   355

XXI. The Convocation Controversy, 1697   357

XXII. The Privy Council, 1701   358

XXIII. Party Government, 1706-14   359

XXIV. Queen Anne's Charter to the City of Bristol, 1711   362

XXV. Administration of Justices, 1724   364

XXVI. The Independent Member and the Ministry,   365
1729

XXVII. The Court—the Member—the Constituents,   366
1732

XXVIII. Harwich Election, 1734   367

XXIX. A Principal Minister, 1733   369

XXX. The King's Influence, 1735-37   369

XXXI. The Conduct of Administration, 1740   371

XXXII. Duty of a Cabinet Minister, 1742   374

XXXIII. Minutes of a Cabinet Meeting, 1743   374

XXXIV. The King and the Ministry, 1744-46   375

XXXV. County Election, 1747   377

XXXVI. De la Constitution d'Angleterre, 1748   378

XXXVII. Formation of a Ministry, 1754   382

PAGE

XXXVIII. The Ministry and the Commons, 1754–55   385

XXXIX. Departmental Ministers, 1755   387

XL. Opposition, 1757   388

XLI. Commission of the Peace   389

XLII. Representative Theory   392

XLIII. Secretary of State, 1761   393

XLIV. Local Government : *ad hoc* Bodies   394

XLV. Blackstone on Parliament and Prerogative   395

XLVI. Burke on Party, 1770   396

XLVII. Prime Minister, 1778   398

XLVIII. Supremacy of Commons, 1782   398

XLIX. The King and the Cabinet, 1782   399

L. The Treasury and Election Expenses, 1782   399

LI. The King seeks a Government, 1783   401

LII. The King intervening to defeat a Ministry, 1783   403

LIII. Local Government, 1783   404

GLOSSARY   406

INDEX   427

ABBREVIATIONS
IN VOLUME I

Add. MSS. = Additional Manuscripts, British Museum.

C.J. = Commons Journals.

Cowper = Cowper's Reports.

E.H.R. = English Historical Review.

Gardiner = S. R. Gardiner, *The Constitutional Documents of the Puritan Revolution.* Third Edition, 1906.

Grey's Debates = The Hon. A. Grey, *Debates of the House of Commons, 1667–1694.* 10 vols. 1769.

Hatsell, J. = *Precedents of Proceedings in the House of Commons, 1818.*

H.M.C. = Historical Manuscripts Commission.

Holdsworth = *History of English Law.*

L.J. = Lords Journals.

North MSS. = Manuscripts of Lord North, Bodleian Library.

Parl. Hist. = W. Cobbett, *Parliamentary History of England, 1808-14.*

Prothero = G. W. Prothero, *Select Statutes,* etc. Fourth Edition, 1913.

S.T. = Howell, *State Trials, 1814-16.*

Statutes at Large = The King's Printers, vols. v-xiv.

Statutes of the Realm = vols. v-ix, 1819–1822.

Vaughan's Reports = Common Pleas, 1666–1673.

SECTION A

STATUTES

I

LEGALIZATION OF THE CONVENTION PARLIAMENT, 1660 [1]

12 Car. II, c. 1.

For the preventing all Doubts and Scruples concerning the Assembling, Sitting, and Proceeding of this present Parliament: Bee it Declared and Enacted, and it is Declared and Enacted by the King Our Soveraigne Lord, and by the Lords and Commons in Parliament assembled and by Authoritie of the same That the Parliament begun and holden at Westminster the third day of November in the Sixteenth yeare of the Raigne of the late King Charles of Blessed Memory is fully dissolved and determined ; And that the Lords and Commons now sitting at Westminster in this present Parliament are the two Houses of Parliament, and soe shalbe, and are hereby Declared Enacted and Adjudged to be to all Intents Constructions and Purposes whatsoever, notwithstanding any want of the Kings Majesties Writt or Writts of Summons or any Defect or Alteration of or in any Writt or Writts of Summons or any other Defect or Default whatsoever ; as if this Parliament had beene summoned by Writt or Writts in His Majesties Name according to the usuall Forme, and as if His Majestie had beene present in person at the Assembling, and Commencement of this present Parliament. Provided alwaies That this present Parliament may be dissolved by His Majestie after the usuall manner as if the same had beene summoned by Writt or Writts in his Majesties Name. Provided alsoe and it is hereby enacted That His Majesties Royall Assent to this Bill shall not determine this present Session of Parliament.

[1] See Sect. A, No. VI, p. 10, Sect. A No. XIX, p. 54, Sect. A, No. XXVI, p. 74.

II

ACT ABOLISHING FEUDAL TENURES,[1] 1660

12 Car. II, c. 24.

*An Act for takeing away the Court of Wards and Liveries and
Tenures in Capite and by Knights Service and Purveyance, and for
setling a Revenue upon his Majesty in Lieu thereof.*

Whereas it hath beene found by former experience that the
Courts of Wards and Liveries and Tenures by Knights service
either of the King or others, or by Knights service in Capite
or Soccage in Capite of the King and the consequents upon the
same have beene much more burthensome . . . to the Kingdome
then they have beene beneficiall to the King, And whereas since
the Intermission of the said Court[2] . . . many persons have by
Will and otherwise made disposall of their Lands held by Knights
service whereupon diverse Questions might possibly arise unlesse
some seasonable remedy be taken to prevent the same Bee it therefore Enacted . . . That the Court of Wards and Liveries and
all Wardships Liveries Primer-Seizins and Ouster-le-mains values
and forfeitures of Marriages by reason of any Tenure of the Kings
Majesty or of any other by Knights service and all meane Rates and
all other Gifts Grants Charges incident or ariseing for or by reason
of Wardships Liveries Primer Seizins or Ouster-le-main, be taken
away and discharged . . . from the said twenty fourth day of
February One thousand six hundred forty five, any Law, Statute
Custome or Usage to the contrary hereof in any wise notwithstanding,
And that all Fines for Alienation Seizures and Pardons for Aliena-
tions Tenure by Homage and all Charges incident or ariseing for or
by reason of Wardship Livery Primer-Seizin or Ouster-le-main or
Tenure by Knights service Escuage and also Aide pur file marrier
et pur faier fitz Chivalier and all other Charges incident therunto be
likewise taken away and discharged from the said twenty fourth day
of February One thousand six hundred forty and five, Any Law
Statute Custome or Usage to the contrary hereof in any wise notwithstanding, And that all Tenures by Knights service of the King,
or of any other person and by Knights service in Capite, and by
Soccage in Capite of the King and the fruits and consequents thereof
happened . . . thereupon or thereby be taken away and discharged Any Law Statute Custome or Usage to the contrary hereof
any wise notwithstanding, And all Tenures of any Honours Mannours

[1] See Gardiner, No. 65.   [2] Feb. 24, 1645 (O.S.).

Lands Tenements or Hereditaments of any Estate of Inheritance at the common Law held either of the King or of any other person or persons Bodyes Pollitique or Corporate are hereby Enacted to be turned into free and common Soccage to all intents and purposes, from the said twenty-fourth day of February One thousand six hundred forty five, and shall be soe . . . deemed to be from the said twenty fourth day of February One thousand six hundred forty five, and for ever thereafter turned into free and common Soccage, any Law Statute Custome or Usage to the contrary hereof any wise notwithstanding ;

II. And that the same shall for ever hereafter stand and be discharged of all Tenure by Homage Escuage Voyages Royall and charges for the same Wardships incident to Tenure by Knights service and values and forfeitures of marriage and all other charges incident to tenure by Knights service And of and from Aide pur file marrier & Aide pur faier fitz Chivalier Any Law Statute Custome or Usage or to the contrary in any wise notwithstanding. And that all conveyances and devises of any Mannours Lands Tenements and Hereditaments made since the said twenty fourth of February shall be expounded to be of such effect as if the same Mannours Lands tenements and Hereditaments had beene then held and continued to be holden in free and common Soccage onely Any Law Statute Custome or usage to the contrary hereof any wise notwithstanding.

[§ III. Repeals 23 Hen. VIII, c. 6, establishing the Court of Wards and 33 Hen. VIII, c. 22, concerning the officers of that Court.]

IV. And bee it further Enacted . . . that all tenures hereafter to be created by the Kings Majestie His Heires or Successors upon any gifts or grants of any Mannours Lands Tenements or Hereditaments of any Estate of Inheritance at the common Law shall be in free and common Soccage onely. . . .

[§§ V-VII. Certain rents, heriots, fines for alienation, tenures in frankalmoin, copyhold and grand sergeanty, belonging to King or private persons, to be retained.]

VIII. And bee it further Enacted . . . that where any person hath or shall have any Child or Children under the age of twenty one yeares and not married at the time of his death that it shall be . . . lawfull to and for the Father of such child or children whether borne at the time of the decease of the Father or at that time in ventre sa mere, or whether such Father be within the age of twenty one yeares or of full age by his deed executed in his life time, or by his last Will and Testament in writeing, . . . to dispose of the custody and tuition of such child or children for and dureing such

time as he or they shall respectively remaine under the age of
twenty one yeares . . . to any person or persons in possession or
remainder other then Popish Recusants, And that such disposition of
the custodie of such childe or children . . . shall be good and
effectuall against all and every person or persons claiming the
custodie or tuition of such childe or children as Guardian in
soccage or otherwise . . .

[§ IX deals with the estates of minors and § X preserves all rights to
a seat in the Lords' House.]

XI. And whereas diverse oppressions have beene still continued
and severall Countyes have submitted themselves to sundry Rates
and Taxes and Compositions to redeeme themselves from such
vexations and oppressions [in regard to purveyance] And forasmuch
as the Lords and Commons assembled in Parliament doe finde that
the said Remedies are not fully effectuall, and that noe other remedy
will be soe effectuall and just as to take away the occasion thereof
especially if satisfaction and recompence shall be therefore made to
His Majesty His Heires and Successors which is hereby provided to
His Majestyes good likeing and content, His Majestie is therefore
gratiously pleased that it may be enacted ; . . . That from henceforth noe summe or summes of money or other thing shall be taken
raised taxed rated imposed paid or leavyed for or in regard of any
provision Carriages or purveyance for His Majestie His Heires or
Successors And that henceforth noe person or persons by any
Warrant Commission or Authoritie under the Great Seale or otherwise by colour of buying or makeing provision or purveyance for His
Majestie, or any Queene of England for the time being, or of any
the Children of any King or Queene of England for the time being
or that shall be or for his their or any of their Household shall take
any Timber Fewell, Catle Corne, Grain Mault Hay Straw Victuall
Cart Carriage or other thing whatsoever of any the Subjects of
His Majestie His Heires or Successors without the free and full
consent of the Owner or Owners thereof had and obtained without
menace or enforcement, nor shall summon warne take use or
require any of the said Subjects to furnish or finde any Horses Oxen
or other Cattell Carts Ploughs Waines or other carriages for the use
of his Majestie His Heires or Successors or of any Queene of
England, . . . for the carrying the Goods of His Majestie His
Heires or Successors or the said Queenes or Children or any of them
without such full and free consent as aforesaid Any Law Statute
Custome or Usage to the contrary notwithstanding.

[§ XII. No pre-emption allowed on behalf of the King and Royal
Family. Persons making purveyance to be committed to gaol and

tried on indictment. Party aggrieved to have treble damages. Such action and execution after judgement not to be delayed except by writ of error under penalty of Premunire.]

[§ XIII. King's rights to tin in the Stannaries, and to Butlerage and Prizage of wines not to be prejudiced.]

XIV. And now to the intent and purpose that His Majesty His Heires and Successors may receive a full and ample Recompence and Satisfaction as well for the proffits of the said Court of Wards . . . as alsoe for all manner of Purveyance and Provisions . . . taken away and abolished . . . Bee it enacted . . . That there shall be paid unto the Kings Majestie His Heires and Successors for ever hereafter in recompense as aforesaid the severall Rates Impositions Dutys and Charges herein after expressed[1] . . .

[Details of Excise Duties on Beer, Cider, Meade, Strong Water, Spirits, Coffee, Chocolate, Sherbet, and Tea.]

[§§ XV-XLII deal with administration of these duties, including (§ 33) the erection of a principal Head Office of Excise in London with branch offices depending.]

III

AN ACT TO PRESERVE THE PERSON AND GOVERNMENT OF THE KING,[2] 1661

13 Car. II, St. I, c. 1.

The Lords and Commons assembled in Parliament deeply weighing and considering the miseries and calamities of well nigh twenty yeares before your Majesties happy Return and withall reflecting upon the causes & occasions of soe great and deplorable confusions do in all humility and thankfulnes acknowledge Your Majesties incomparable Grace and Goodnes to Your People in Your Free and Generall Pardon Indempnity and Oblivion by which Your Majestie hath beene pleased to deliver Your Subjects not only from the Punishment but alsoe from the Reproach of their former miscarriages which unexampled Piety and Clemency of Your Majesty hath enflamed the hearts of us Your Subjects with an ardent desire to expresse all possible zeal and duty in the care and preservation of your Majesties Person in whose Honour and Happines consists the good and welfare of Your People and in preventing (as much as

[1] See Sect. C, No. VIII, p. 271, Sect. A, No. LIV, p. 138.
[2] See Sect. A, No. XXXIV, p. 87, and Vol. II, Sect. A, No. VII, p. 10, and No. XXIX, p. 98.

may be) all Treasonable and Seditious Practices and Attempts for the time to come And because the growth and increase of the late troubles & disorders did in a very great measure proceed from a multitude of seditious Sermons Pamphlets and Speeches dayly preached printed and published with a transcendent boldnes defaming the Person and Government of your Majestie and your Royall Father wherein men were to much encouraged and (above all) from a wilfull mistake of the Supreame and lawfull Authoritie whilst men were forward to cry up and maintaine those Orders and Ordinances Oathes and Covenants to be Acts legall and warrantable which in themselves had not the least colour of Law or Justice to support them from which kind of distempers as the present Age is not yet wholly freed so Posterity may be apt to relapse into them if a timely remedy be not provided Wee therefore the Lords and Commons in Parliament assembled having duly considered the premisses and remembering that in the Thirteenth yeare of the Reigne of Queene Elizabeth [1] of ever blessed memory a right good and profitable law was made for preservation of Her Majesties Person Do most humbly beseech Your most Excellent Majesty that it may be Enacted . . . That if any person or persons whatsoever . . . during the naturall life of our most Gracious Soveraigne Lord the King, (whom Almighty God preserve and blesse with a long and prosperous Reigne) shall within the Realme or without compass imagine invent devise or intend death or destruction or any bodily harm tending to death or destruction maim or wounding imprisonment or restraint of the Person of the same our Soveraigne Lord the King or to deprive or depose him from the Stile Honour or Kingly Name of the Imperiall Crowne of this Realme or of any other His Majesties Dominions or Countreys or to levy war against His Majestie within this Realme or without or to move or stirr any Foreiner or Strangers with force to invade this Realme or any other His Majesties Dominions or Countreys being under His Majesties Obeysance and such Compassings Imaginations Inventions Devices or Intentions or any of them shall express utter or declare by any Printing Writing Preaching or Malicious and advised speaking being legally convicted thereof upon the Oaths of two lawfull and credible Witnesses upon triall or otherwise convicted or attainted by due course of Law then every such person and persons soe as aforesaid offending shall be deemed declared and adjudged to be Traitors and shall suffer paines of death and alsoe loose and forfeit as in cases of High Treason.

    II. And be it further Enacted by the Authority aforesaid That if any person . . . during his Majesties life shall malitiously and advisedly

---

[1] See 13 Eliz., c.1, Prothero, p. 57.

publish or affirm the King to be an Heretick or a Papist or that he endeavours to introduce Popery or shall maliciously and advisedly by writing printing preaching or other speaking expresse publish utter or declare any Words Sentences or other thing or things to incite or stir up the people to hatred or dislike of the Person of His Majestie or the established Government then every such person . . . being thereof legally convicted shall be disabled to have or enjoye and is hereby disabled and made incapable of having holding enjoying or exercising any place Office or promotion Ecclesiasticall Civill or Military or any other Imployment in Church or State other then that of his Peerage and shall likewise be liable to such further and other punishments as by the Common Laws or Statutes of this Realm may be inflicted in such cases

III. And to the end that no man hereafter may be misled into any seditious or unquiet demeanour . . . Be it therefore further Enacted by the Authority aforesaid That if any person . . . shall maliciously and advisedly by Writing Printing Preaching or other speaking express publish utter declare or affirm That the Parliament begun at Westminster upon the third day of November in the yeare of our Lord One thousand six hundred and forty is not yet dissolved or is not determined or that it ought to be in being or hath yet any continuance or existence or that there lies any Obligation upon him or any other person from any Oath Covenant or Engagement whatsoever to endeavor a change of Government either in Church or State or that both Houses of Parliament or either House of Parliament have or hath a Legislative Power without the King [1] or any other words to the same effect That then every such person . . . shall incurr the danger and penalty of a Premunire mentioned in a Statute made in the sixteenth yeare of the Reigne of King Richard the Second And it is hereby alsoe declared That the Oath usually called the Solemn League and Covenant was in it selfe an unlawfull Oath and imposed upon the Subjects of this Realm against the Fundamentall Laws and Liberties of this Kingdome and that all Orders and Ordinances or pretended Orders and Ordinances of both or either Houses of Parliament for imposing of Oathes Covenants or Engagements Leavying of Taxes or Raising of Forces and Armes to which the Royall Assent either in Person or by Commission was not expresly had or given were in theire first creation and making and still are and soe shall be taken to be null and void to all intents and purposes whatsoever Provided neverthelesse that all and every person and persons Bodies Politique and Corporate who have beene or shall att any time hereafter be questioned for any thing acted or done by colour of any the Orders or Ordinances herein before

[1] See Vol. II, Sect. B, No. III, p. 157.

mencioned and declared to be null and void and are indempnified by an Act[1] entituled An Act of Free and Generall Pardon Indempnity and Oblivion made in the twelfth yeare of His Majesties Reign that now is or shall be indempnified by any Act of Parliament shall and may make such use of the said Orders and Ordinances for theire Indempnity according to the true intent and meaning of the said Act and no other as he or they might have done if this Act had not beene made Any thing in this Act contained to the contrary notwithstanding.

IV. Provided alwaies That noe person be prosecuted for any of the offences in this Act mentioned (other then such as are made and declared to be high Treason) unlesse it be by Order of the Kings Majestie His Heires or Successors under his or theire Signe Manual or by Order of the Councell Table of His Majesty His Heires or Successors directed unto the Attorney Generall for the time being or some other of the Council learned[2] to His Majesty His Heires or Successors for the time being nor shall any person or persons by vertue of this present Act incur any of the penalties herein before mencioned unlesse he or they be prosecuted within six moneths next after the Offence committed and indicted thereupon within three moneths after such prosecucion Any thing herein contained to the contrary notwithstanding

[§ V. Testimony of two witnesses openly avowed is required.]

VI. Provided likewise and be it Enacted That this Act or any thing therein contained shall not extend to deprive either of the Houses of Parliament or any of theire Members of theire just ancient Freedome and priviledge of debating any matters or busines which shall be propounded or debated in either of the said Houses or att any Conferences or Committees of both or either of the said Houses of Parliament or touching the repeal or alteracion of any old or preparing any new Lawes or the redressing any publique griev-ance but that the said Members of either of the said Houses and the Assistants of the House of Peers and every of them shall have the same freedome of speech and all other Priviledges whatsoever as they had before the making of this Act Any thing in this Act to the contrary thereof in any wise notwithstanding

VII. Provided alwaies and be it Ordained and Enacted That no Peer of this Realm shall be tried for any offence against this Act but by his Peers and further That every Peer who shall be convicted of any offence against this Act after such conviction be disabled during his life to sit in Parliament unlesse His Majesty shall graciously be pleased to pardon him And if His Majesty shall

---

[1] 12 Car. II, c. 11.   [2] *i.e.* King's Counsel.

grant his pardon to any Peer of this Realm or Commoner convicted
of any offence against this Act after such Pardon granted the Peer
or Commoner so pardoned shall be restored to all intents and
purposes as if he had never beene convicted Any thing in this Law
to the contrary in any wise notwithstanding.

IV

ACT RESTORING THE TEMPORAL AUTHORITY OF ECCLESIASTICAL PERSONS, 1661

13 Car. II, St. I, c. 2.

Whereas at the Parliament begun at Westminster the third day
of November in the sixteenth yeare of the Reign of our late
Soveraign Lord King Charles of blessed memory since deceased
an Act of Parliament was made Entituled An Act for disinabling
all persons in Holy Orders to exercise any Temporall Jurisdiction
or Authority [1] Which Act hath made severall alterations prejudiciall
to the constitution and ancient Rights of Parliament and contrary
to the Laws of this Land and is by experience found otherwise
inconvenient Be it Enacted . . . That the said Act . . . and every
clause matter and thing therein conteyned shall be and is hereby
from hence forth repealed annulled and made void to all intents
and purposes whatsoever.

V

ACT AGAINST TUMULTUOUS PETITIONING,[2] 1661

13 Car. II, St. I, c. 5.

Whereas it hath beene found by sad experience that Tumultuous
and other Disorderly solliciting and procuring of Hands by private
persons to Petitions Complaints Remonstrances & Declarations
and other Addresses to the King or to both or either Houses of
Parliament for alteration of matters established by Law redresse
of pretended grievances in Church or State or other publique
Concernments have beene made use of to serve the ends of Factious

[1] 17 Car. I, c. 27 (Gardiner, No. 48). Cf. Vol. II, Sect. A, No. XIII,
p. 28.
[2] See Sect. B, No. XV, p. 191, and Vol. II, Sect. A, No. VIII, p. 12.

& Seditious persons gotten into power to the violation of the publique
Peace and have beene a great meanes of the late unhappy Wars
Confusions and Calamities in this Nation For preventing the like
mischiefe for the future Be it enacted . . . That no person or
persons whatsoever shall . . . solicite labor or procure the getting
of Hands or other consent of any persons above the number of
twenty or more to any Petition Complaint Remonstrance Declaration or other Addresses to the King or both or either Houses of
Parliament for alteration of matters established by Law in Church
or State unlesse the matter thereof have beene first consented unto
and Ordered by three or more Justices of that County or by the
Major part of the Grand Jury of the County or division of the County
where the same matter shall arise at theire publique Assizes or
Generall Quarter Sessions or if arising in London by the Lord Maior
Aldermen and Commons in Common Councell assembled And
that no person or persons whatsoever shall repaire to His Majesty
or both or either of the Houses of Parliament upon pretence of
presenting or delivering any Petition . . . accompanied with excessive
number of people nor att any one time with above the number of ten
persons upon pain of incurring a penalty not exceeding the sum of
One hundred pounds in money and three months Imprisonment . . .

II. Provided[1] alwaies That this Act . . . shall not . . . extend
to debar or hinder any person or persons not exceeding the number
of Ten aforesaid to present any publique or private Grievance or
Complaint to any Member or Members of Parliament after his
Election . . . or to the Kings Majesty for any remedy to bee
thereupon had nor to extend to any Address whatsoever to His
Majesty by all or any the Members of both or either Houses of
Parliament during the sitting of Parliament but that they may
enjoye theire freedome of Accesse to His Majesty as heretofore
hath beene used.

VI

CONFIRMATION OF ACTS OF CONVENTION PARLIAMENT,[2] 1661

13 Car. II, St. I, c. 7.

Whereas during the late Difficulties and Exigences of Affaires
in the absence of His most Excellent Majesty and in reference to his
returne from beyond the Seas into these His Majesties Dominions

[1] Sect. C, No. VII, p. 258, and Sect. D, No. XVI (c), p. 346.
[2] See Sect. A, No. I, p. 1, No. XIX, p. 54, and No. XXVI, p. 74.

The Lords and Commons being assembled att Westminster the five and twentieth day of Aprill in the Twelfth yeare of His Majesties Reigne were from thence and after His Majesties returne continued untill the nine and twentieth day of December then next following and now last past and then dissolved by His Majesty In which time severall Acts were passed by His Majesty by and with the Advice and Consent of the said Lords and Commons assembled as aforesaid which being of necessary use are fitt to be continued & confirmed although the manner of the said assembling enforced by the difficulties and exigencies aforesaid which then lay upon the Nation is not to be drawne into example Be it therefore enacted . . . That all & singuler the Acts made or mentioned to be made by His said Majesty by and with the advice or Consent of the Lords and Commons upon or since the said five and twentieth day of Aprill herein after particularly mentioned and expressed That is to say [Here follows a schedule of 20 such Acts.[1]] and all and every the Clauses Sentences and Articles . . . hereby are ratified and confirmed and enacted and declared to have the full Force and Strength of Acts of Parliament. . . .

VII

THE NAVAL DISCIPLINE ACT,[2] 1661

13 Car. II, St. I, c. 9.

An Act for the Establishing Articles and Orders for the regulateing and better Government of His Majesties Navies Ships of Warr & Forces by Sea.

For the regulating and better Government of his Majesties Navies Ships of War and Forces by Sea wherein under the good Providence and protection of God the Wealth Safety and Strength of this Kingdome is soe much concerned Bee it Enacted . . . That all and every the Articles and Orders in this Act mentioned shall be duely and respectively put in Execution observed and obeyed in manner hereafter mentioned.

1. That all Comanders Captaines and other Officers att Sea shall cause the publique Worshipp of Almighty God according to the Liturgy of the Church of England established by Law . . . to be performed in theire respective Ships And that prayers and preachings by the respective Chaplaines in holy Orders be

---

[1] Some temporary Acts were not re-enacted.

[2] Contrast with Sect. A, No. X, p. 17, and Sect. A, No. XX, p. 55.

performed diligently and that the Lords Day be observed according to Law. . . .

34. And it is hereby further Enacted That the Lord High Admirall for the time being shall by vertue of this Act have full power and authority to grant Commissions to Inferior Vice Admiralls or Commander in Cheife of any Squadron of Ships to call and assemble Court marshalls consisting of Commanders and Captaines and no Court martiall where the paines of death shall bee inflicted shall consist of lesse then Five Captaines at least the Admiralls Lieutennant to be as to this purpose esteemed as a Captaine and in no case wherein sentence of death shall passe by vertue of the Articles aforesaid or any of them (except in case of mutiny) there shall be execution of such Sentence of Death without the leave of the Lord High Admirall if the offence be committed within the Narrow Seas But in case any of the Offences aforesaid be committed in any Voyage beyond the Narrowe Seas whereupon Sentence of Death shall be given in pursuance of the aforesaid Articles or of any of them then Execution shall not be done but by Order of the Commander in Cheife of that Fleete or Squadron wherein Sentence of Death was passed.

35. And be it further Enacted and Declared That the Judge Advocate of any Fleete for the time being shall have full power and authority to administer an Oath to any person or witnes in order to the Examination or Tryall of any of the Offences aforesaid and in the absence of a Judge Advocate the Court marshall shall have full power and authority to appoint any person to administer an Oath to the purpose aforesaid.

II. Provided alsoe and bee it further Enacted . . . That this Act or any thing or things therein conteyned shall not in any manner of wise extend to give unto the Lord Admirall of England for the time being or to any his Vice Admiralls Judge or Judges of the Admiralty his or theire Deputy or Deputies or to any other the Officers or Ministers of the Admiralty or to any others having or claiming any Admirall Power Jurisdiction or Authority within this Realme and Wales or any other the Kings Dominions any other Power Right Jurisdiction Preheminence or Authority then he or they or any of them lawfully have hath or had or ought to have and enjoye before the making of this Act other then for such of the Offences specified in the severall Articles conteyned in this Act as hereafter shall be done upon the main Sea or in Ships or Vessells being and hovering in the maine Streame of great Rivers onely beneath the Bridges of the same Rivers nigh to the Sea within the Jurisdiction of the Admiralty and in none other places whatsoever and comitted only by such persons as shall be in actuall Service and Pay in his Majesties Fleete or Ships of War.

VIII

THE ECCLESIASTICAL CAUSES ACT, 1661

13 Car. II, St. I, c. 12.

An Act for Explanation of a Clause contained in an Act of Parliament made in the seventeenth yeare of the late King Charles Entituled An Act for Repeal of a Branch of a Statute Primo Elizabethe concerning Commissioners for Causes Ecclesiasticall.

Whereas in an Act of Parliament made in the seaventeenth yeare of the late King Charles Entituled An Act[1] for Repeal of a Branch of a Statute Primo Elizabethe concerning Commissioners for Causes Ecclesiasticall it is amongst other things Enacted[2] That no Archbishop Bishop nor Vicar Generall nor any Chancellor nor Commissary of any Archbishop Bishop or Vicar Generall nor any Ordinary whatsoever nor any other Spirituall or Ecclesiasticall Judge Officer or Minister of Justice nor any other person or persons whatsoever exerciseing Spirituall or Ecclesiasticall Power Authority or Jurisdiction by any Grant Licence or Commission of the Kings Majestie His Heirs or Successors or by any Power or Authority derived from the King His Heirs or Successors or otherwise (shall from and after the first day of August which then should be in the yeare of our Lord God One thousand six hundred forty one) award impose or inflict any Pain Penalty Fine Amercement Imprisonment or other corporall punishment upon any of the Kings Subjects for any contempt misdemeanor crime offence matter or thing whatsoever belonging to Spirituall or Ecclesiasticall Cognizance or Jurisdiction whereupon some doubt hath beene made that all ordinary power of Coertion and Proceedings in Causes Ecclesiasticall were taken away whereby the ordinary course of Justice in Causes Ecclesiasticall hath been obstructed Be it therefore declared and enacted . . . That neither the said Act nor any thing therein contained doth or shall take away any ordinary Power or Authority from any of the said Archbishops Bishops or any other person or persons named as aforesaid but that they and every of them exercising Ecclesiasticall Jurisdiction may proceed determine sentence execute and exercise all manner of Ecclesiasticall Jurisdiction and all Censures and Coertions apperteyning and belonging to the same before the makeing of the Act before recited in all causes and matters belonging to Ecclesiasticall Jurisdiction according to the Kings Majesties Ecclesiasticall Lawes used and practised in this Realme in as ample manner and

---

[1] See 17 Car. I, c. 11 (Gardiner, No. 35).   [2] § 2 of 17 Car. I, c. 11.

forme as they did and might lawfully have done before the makeing
of the said Act.

II. And be it further Enacted . . . That the afore recited Act of
Decimo septimo Caroli and all the matters and Clauses therein
contained (excepting what concernes the High Commission Court
or the new erection of some such like Court by Commission)[1] shall
be and is hereby repealed to all intents and purposes whatsoever
Any thing clause or sentence in the said Act contained to the contrary notwithstanding.

III. Provided alwaies and it is hereby Enacted That neither
this Act nor any thing herein contained shall extend or be construed
to revive or give force to the said Branch of the said Statute made
in the said first yeare of the Reigne of the said late Queen Elizabeth
mentioned in the said Act of Parliament made in the said seaventeenth
yeare of the Reigne of the said King Charles but that the said Branch
of the said Statute made in the said first yeare of the Reigne of the
said Queene Elizabeth shall stand and be repealed in such sort
as if this Act had never beene made

IV. Provided alsoe and it is hereby further Enacted That it
shall not be lawfull for any Archbishop Bishop Vicar Generall
Chancellor Commissary or any other Spirituall or Ecclesiasticall
Judge Officer or Minister or any other person having or exercising
Spirituall or Ecclesiasticall Jurisdiction to tender or administer unto
any person whatsoever the Oath usually called the oath Ex Officio
or any other Oath whereby such person to whom the same is tendred
or administred may be charged or compelled to confesse or accuse
or to purge him or her selfe of any criminall matter or thing whereby
he or she may be lyable to any censure or punishment Any thing in
this Statute or any other Law Custome or Usage heretofore to the
contrary hereof in any wise notwithstanding.

V. Provided alwaies that this Act or any thing therein contained shall not extend or be construed to extend to give unto
any Archbishopp Bishop or any other Spirituall or Ecclesiasticall
Judge Officer or other person or persons aforesaid any power or
authority to exercise execute inflict or determine any Ecclesiasticall
Jurisdiction Censure or Coertion which they might not by Lawe
have done before the yeare of our Lord One thousand six hundred
and thirty nine nor to abridge or diminish the Kings Majesties
Supremacy in Ecclesiasticall matters[2] and affaires nor to confirm
the Canons made in the yeare One thousand six hundred and forty
nor any of them nor any other Ecclesiasticall Lawes or Canons not
formerly confirmed allowed or enacted by Parliament or by the
established Lawes of the Land as they stood in the yeare of the Lord
One thousand six hundred thirty and nine.

[1] See Sect. A, No. XXV, p. 69.   [2] See Sect. A, No. XV, § xvii, p. 39.

IX

THE CORPORATION ACT,[1] 1661

13 Car II, St. II, c. 1.

Whereas questions are likely to arise concerning the validity of Elections of Magistrates and other Officers and Members in Corporations as well in respect of removing some as placing others during the late troubles contrary to the true intent and meaning of theire Charters and Liberties And to the end that the succession in such Corporations may be most probably perpetuated in the hands of persons well affected to His Majesty and the established Government it being to well knowne that notwithstanding all His Majesties endeavors and unparaleld Indulgence in pardoning all that is past neverthelesse many evill spirits are still working Wherefore for prevention of the like mischeife for the time to come and for preservation of the Publique Peace both in Church and State Bee it Enacted . . . That Commissions shall before the twentieth day of February next be issued forth under the Great Seale of England unto such persons as his Majestie shall appoint for the executing of the Powers and Authorities herein after expressed And that all and every the . . . Commissioners . . . shall . . . be Commissioners respectively for and within the severall Cities Corporations and Burroughs and Cinque Ports and theire Members and other Port Townes within the Kingdome of England Dominion of Wales and Towne of Berwicke upon Tweed for which they shall be respectively nominated and appointed

II. And be it further Enacted . . . That no Charter of any Corporation Cities Townes Burroughs Cinque Ports and their Members and other Port Towns in England or Wales or Towne of Berwicke upon Tweed shall at any time hereafter be avoided for or by reason of any act or thing done or omitted to be done before the First day of this present Parliament

III. And be it further Enacted . . . That all persons who upon the Foure and twentieth day of December One thousand six hundred sixty and one shall be Maiors Aldermen Recorders Bailiffes Towne=Clerks Common Councel men and other persons then bearing any Office or Offices of Magistracy or Places or Trusts or other Imployment relating to or concerning the Government of the said respective Cities Corporations and Burroughs and Cinque Ports and theire Members and other Port Towns shall at any time

[1] Repealed 9 Geo. IV, c. 17. See Vol. II, Sect. A, No. XIX, p. 42.

before the Five and twentieth day of March One thousand six
hundred sixtie and three . . . be required by the said respective Commissioners . . . to take the Oathes of Allegiance and
Supremacy and this Oath following.[1]

I A. B. do declare and beleive That it is not lawfull upon any
pretence whatsoever to take Arms against the King and that I do
abhor that Traiterous Position of taking Arms by His Authority
against His Person or against those that are commissioned by Him
So helpe me God.

And alsoe att the same time shall publiquely subscribe before the
said Commissioners or any Three of them this following Declaration.

I, A.B. do declare That I hold that there lyes no Obligation
upon me or any other person from the Oath commonly called The
Solemn League and Covenant and that the same was in it selfe an
unlawfull Oath and imposed upon the Subjects of this Realm
against the knowne Laws and Liberties of the Kingdome.

IV. And that all such of the said Maiors and other the persons
aforesaid . . . who shall refuse to take and subscribe the same
. . . shall . . . be by Authority of this Act (ipso facto) removed
and displaced of and from the said Offices and Places respectively
and the said Offices and Places . . . shall be . . . void to all intents
and purposes as if the said respective persons so refusing were
naturally dead

V. And neverthelesse Be it further enacted . . . That the said
Commissioners or any Five or more of them shall have full power
. . . by Order and Warrant . . . to displace or remove any of the
persons aforesaid from the said respective Offices and Places or
Trusts aforesaid if the said Commissioners . . . shall deem it
expedient for the publique safety although such persons shall have
taken and subscribed or be willing to take and subscribe the said
Oathes and Declaration

[§ VI. Commissioners may restore any Magistrate unduly removed.]

[§§ VII-VIII define various procedural duties of the Commissioners in respect to Oaths.]

IX.[2] Provided alsoe, . . . That from and after the expiration of
the said Commissions no . . . person shall for ever hereafter be
placed elected or chosen in or to any the Offices or Places aforesaid

---

[1] The oath and declaration were repealed 5 Geo. I, c. 6, see below,
Sect. A, No. XLVII, p. 127.

[2] See Sect. A, No. XLIII, p. 118, and No. XLVII, p. 127. The Indemnity Act of 16 Geo. II, c. 30, renewed from time to time, virtually removed
the Sacramental Text. See Vol. II, Sect. A, No. XIX, p. 42.

that shall not have within one yeare next before such Election or Choice taken the Sacrament of the Lords Supper according to the Rites of the Church of England and that every such person . . . so placed elected or chosen shall likewise take the aforesaid three Oathes and subscribe the said Declaration att the same time when the Oath for the due execution of the said Places and Offices respectively shall be administred And in default hereof every such placing election and choice is hereby Enacted and Declared to bee void.

X. Provided alwaies . . . That every person who shall be placed in any Corporation by vertue of this Act shall upon his admission take the Oath or Oaths usually taken by the Members of such Corporation.

[§§ XI, XII define further the powers of the Commissioners and terminate them on 25 March 1663.]

[§ XIII exempts the reversions of offices in London granted before the civil wars from the operation of the Act.]

X

THE MILITIA ACT,[1] 1662

14 Car. II, c. 3.

An Act declaring the sole right of the Militia to be in the King, and for the present ordering and disposing the same.

Forasmuch as within all His Majesties Realmes and Dominions the sole and supreame Power Government Command and Disposition of the Militia and of all Forces by Sea and Land and of all Forts and places of Strength is and by the Laws of England ever was the undoubted Right of His Majesty and His Royall Predecessors Kings and Queenes of England and that both or either of the Houses of Parliament cannot nor ought to pretend to the same nor can nor lawfully may raise or levy any War offensive or defensive against His Majesty His Heires or lawfull Successors and yet the contrary thereof hath of late yeares beene practised almost to the ruine and destruction of this Kingdome and during the late usurped Governments many evil and rebellious principles have beene instilled into the minds of the people of this Kingdome which may breake forth unless prevented to the disturbance of the peace and quiet thereof Bee it therefore enacted . . . That the Kings most Excellent Majestie His Heires and Successors shall and may from time

---

[1] A statute, 13 Car. II, St. I, c. 6, had made temporary provision for the Militia, declaring the sole right thereof to be in the King. See also Sect. A, No. LIII, p. 135, and Vol. II, Sect. A, No. XIV, p. 29, and No. XXX, p. 100.

to time as occasion shall require issue forth severall Commissions of
Leiutenancy to such persons as His Majesty . . . shall thinke fit
to be His Majesties Leiutenants for the severall & respective
Counties Cities and places of England & Dominion of Wales and
Town of Berwick upon Tweed which Leiutenants shall have full
power and authority to call togeather all such persons at such times
and to arm and array them in such manner as is hereafter expressed
and declared and to form them into Companies Troops and Regiments and in case of Insurrection Rebellion or Invasion them to
lead conduct and imploy . . . as well within the said severall
Counties Cities and places for which they shall be commissionated
respectively as alsoe into any other the Counties and places . . .
according as they shall from time to time receive directions from
His Majesty His Heires and Successors and that the said respective
Leiutenants shall have full power and authority from time to time
to constitute appointe and give Commissions to such persons as they
shall thinke fitt to be Colonels Majors Captaines and other Commission Officers of the said persons so to be armed arrayed and
weaponed and to present to His Majestie . . . the names of such
person and persons as they shall thinke fitt to be Deputy Leiutenants
and upon His Majesties approbation of them shall give them
Deputations accordingly Alwaies understood that His Majesty . . .
have power and authority to direct and order otherwise and accordingly att His pleasure may appoint and commissionate or displace
such Officers . . . And that the said Leiutenants respectively
and . . . by theire directions the said Deputy Leiutenants . . . or
any two or more of them shall have power from time to time to
train exercise and put in readines and alsoe to lead and conduct the
persons so to be armed arrayed and weaponed by the directions and
to the intents and purposes as is hereafter expressed and declared

II. And for the providing Horse and Armes and Furniture
thereunto belonging for the arming and weaponing the persons
aforesaid and alsoe for the defraying and paying the necessary
charges thereunto belonging in manner as hereafter followeth Be it
further Enacted That the said respective Leiutenants . . . or the
maior part of such Leiutenants and Deputy Leiutenants then
present . . . which maior part shall bee three att the least have
hereby full Power and Authority to charge any person with Horse
Horsman and Armes or with Foot Souldier and Armes in the same
County Shire City . . . where his her or theire Estates lie . . .
not exceeding the limitations and proportions hereafter mentioned
(that is to say) No person shall be charged with finding a Horse
Horseman and Armes unless such person . . . have a Revenue of
Five hundred pounds by the yeare in possession or have an Estate

of Six thousand pounds in goods or money besides the furniture of his or theire houses and so proportionably. . . . And they are not to charge any person with finding a Foot Souldier and Armes that hath not a yearely Revenue of Fifty pounds in possession or a personal Estate of Six hundred pounds in goods or moneys (other then the stocke upon the ground) and after the aforesaid rate proportionably . . . Nor shall they charge any person with the finding both of Horse and Foot in the same County. . . .

VI. And for furnishing Ammunition and other Necessaries the said respective Leiutenants . . . shall have power to lay fitting Rates upon the respective Counties. . . . And in case of Invasions Insurrections or Rebellions whereby occasion shall be to draw out such Souldiers into actuall Service the persons so charged as aforesaid shall provide each theire Souldier respectively with pay in hand not exceeding one moneths pay . . . and for satisfaction of the Officers for theire pay during such time not exceeding one moneth . . . provision shall be made for the same by His Majesty . . . out of His Publique Treasury or Revenue

VII. And be it Enacted that the said Leiutenants . . . may [impress carts horses etc. and pay compensation for same] . . . upon occasion of Invasion Insurrection or Rebellion And that the said Leiutenants or Deputies or the Chiefe Officers upon the place shall and may imprison Mutineers and such Souldiers as doe not theire Duties as Souldiers at the day of theire Musters and Training and shall and may inflict for punishment for every such Offence any pecuniary Mulct not exceeding five shillings or the penalty of Imprisonment without Bail or Mainprise not exceeding twenty dayes . . .

XX.[1] And it is hereby declared and enacted That the ordinary times for training exerciseing and mustering the Forces to be raised by vertue of this Act shall be these following (that is to say) the General Muster and Exercise of Regiments not above once a Yeare the training and exerciseing of single Companies not above foure times a Yeare unlesse speciall Directions be given by His Majestie or His Privy Council And that such single Companies and Troopes shall not att any one time be continued in Exercise above the space of two dayes And that att a Generall Muster and Exercise of Regiments no Officer or Souldier shall be constrained to stay for above foure dayes togeather from theire respective habitations And that att every such Muster and Exercise every Musqueteer shall bring with him [powder, arms etc. as specified]. . . .

XXIV. Provided alwaies . . . That no person charged with

---

[1] The limit of days of service repealed by 15 Car. II, c. 4, § VIII. A maximum of 14 days a year substituted, § IX.

the finding of Horse or Foote . . . shall be compellable to serve in his or theire proper person but may . . . find one or more fitt or sufficient man or men . . . to be approved by his Captain. . . . And that every such person or persons so found and provided . . . shall and hereby are required to serve as Souldier and Souldiers . . . and such person departing from the said service without leave . . . shall forfeit the sum of Twenty pounds. . . .

XXXI. Provided that neither this Act nor any matter or thing therein contained shall be deemed . . . to extend to the giveing . . . any power for the transporting of any the Subjects of this Realme or any way compelling them to march out of this Kingdome otherwise then by the Lawes of England ought to be done . . .

XI

THE ACT OF UNIFORMITY, 1662

14 Car. II, c. 4.

Whereas in the first yeare of the late Queene Elizabeth there was one uniforme Order of Common Service and Prayer and of the Administration of Sacraments Rites and Ceremonies in the Church of England (agreeable to the Word of God and usage of the Primitive Church) compiled by the Reverend Bishopps and Clergy set forth in one Booke entituled The Book of Common Prayer and Administration of Sacraments and other Rites and Ceremonies in the Church of England and enjoyned to be used by Act of Parliament holden in the said First yeare of the said late Queene entituled An Act [1] for the Uniformity of Common Prayer and Service in the Church and Administration of the Sacraments very comfortable to all good people desirous to live in Christian conversation and most profitable to the Estate of this Realme upon the which the Mercy Favour and Blessing of Almighty God is in no wise so readily and plentifully poured as by Common Prayers due useing of the Sacraments and often preaching of the Gospell with Devotion of the Hearers And yet this notwithstanding a great number of people in divers parts of this Realm following theire own sensualitie and liveing without knowledge and due feare of God do willfully and schismatically abstaine and refuse to come to theire Parish Churches and other Publique places where Common Prayer Administration of the Sacraments and preaching of the Word of God is used upon the Sundayes and other dayes ordained & appointed to be kept and

[1] 1 Eliz. c. 2 (Prothero, p. 13).

observed as Holy dayes And whereas by the great and scandalous
neglect of Ministers in using the said Order or Liturgy so set forth
and enjoyned as aforesaid great mischeifs & inconveniencies during
the times of the late unhappy troubles have arisen and grown and
many people have beene led into Factions and Schismes to the great
decay and scandall of the Reformed Religion of the Church of
England and to the hazard of many souls For prevention whereof
in time to come for setling the Peace of the Church and for allaying
the present distempers which the indisposition of the time hath
contracted The Kings Majestie according to His Declaration of the
Five and twentieth of October One thousand six hundred and
sixty granted His Commission under the great Seale of England to
severall Bishops and other Divines to review the Booke of Common
Prayer and to prepare such Alterations and Additions as they
thought fitt to offer And afterwards the Convocations of both the
Provinces of Canterbury and Yorke being by His Majesty called
and assembled and now sitting His Majestie hath beene pleased to
authorize and require the Presidents of the said Convocations and other
the Bishopps and Clergy of the same to reveiw the said Booke . . .
And that after mature consideration they should make such Additions
and Alterations in the said Bookes respectively as to them should
seeme meet and convenient and should exhibit and present the
same to His Majesty in writing for his further allowance or confirmation since which time upon full and mature deliberation they
the said Presidents Bishops and Clergy of both Provinces have
accordingly reviewed the said Bookes and have made some Alterations . . . And have exhibited and presented the same unto His
Majestie in writing in one Booke entituled The Booke of Common
Prayer and Administration of the Sacraments and other Rites and
Ceremonies of the Church according to the use of the Church of
England togeather with the Psalter or Psalmes of David pointed as
they are to be sung or said in Churches and the forme and manner
of making ordaining and consecrating of Bishopps Preists and
Deacons All which His Majesty haveing duly considered hath fully
approved and allowed the same . . . Now in regard that nothing
conduceth more to the setling of the Peace of this Nation (which
is desired of all good men) nor to the honour of our Religion and the
propagation thereof then an universall agreement in the Publique
Worshipp of Almighty God and to the intent that every person
within this Realme may certainely knowe the rule to which he is to
conforme in Publique Worship . . . Be it enacted . . . That all
and singuler Ministers in any Cathedrall Collegiate or Parish Church
or Chappell or other place of Publique Worship within this Realme
of England Dominion of Wales and Town of Berwick upon Tweed

shall be bound to say and use the Morning Prayer Evening Prayer Celebration and Administration of both the Sacraments and all other the Publique and Common Prayer in such order and forme as is mentioned in the said Booke annexed and joyned to this present Act and entituled The Booke of Common Prayer and Administration of the Sacraments and other Rites and Ceremonies of the Church according to the use of the Church of England togeather with the Psalter or Psalmes of David pointed as they are to be sung or said in Churches and the forme or manner of making ordaining and consecrating of Bishops Preists and Deacons. And that the Morning and Evening Prayers therein contained shall upon every Lords day and upon all other dayes and occasions and att the times therein appointed be openly and solemnly read by all and every Minister or Curate in every Church Chappell or other place of Publique Worshipp within this Realme of England and places aforesaid.

II. And to the end that Uniformity in the Publique Worshipp of God (which is so much desired) may be speedily effected bee it further enacted . . . That every Parson Vicar or other Minister whatsoever who now hath and enjoyeth any Ecclesiasticall Benefice or Promotion within this Realme of England or places aforesaid shall . . . before the Feast of Saint Bartholomew which shall be in the yeare of our Lord God One thousand six hundred sixty and two openly publiquely and solemnely read the Morneing and Evening Prayer appointed to be read by and according to the said Booke of Common Prayer att the times thereby appointed and after such reading thereof shall openly and publiquely before the Congregation there assembled declare his unfeigned assent & consent to the use of all things in the said Booke contained and prescribed in these words and no other :

I A. B. doe declare my unfaigned assent and consent to al and every thing contained and prescribed in and by the Booke intituled The Booke of Common Prayer and Administration of the Sacraments and other Rites and Ceremonies of the Church according to the use of the Church of England togeather with the Psalter or Psalmes of David pointed as they are to be sung or said in Churches and the form or manner of making ordaining and consecrating of Bishops Preists and Deacons.

III. And that all and every such person who shall (without some lawfull Impediment to be allowed and approved of by the Ordinary of the place) neglect or refuse to doe the same within the time aforesaid (or in case of such Impediment) within one Moneth after such Impediment removed shall (ipso facto) be deprived of all his Spirituall Promotions And that from thence forth it shall be lawfull to and for all Patrons and Donors of all and singuler the said Spirituall Promotions or of any of them according to theire respective Rights and Titles to present or collate to the same as though the person or persons so offending or neglecting were dead.

IV.[1] And . . . That every person whoe shall hereafter be presented or collated or put into any Ecclesiasticall Benefice or Promotion within this Realme of England and places aforesaid shall . . . upon some Lords day openly publiquely and solemnly read the Morning and Evening Prayers appointed to be read by and according to the said Booke of Common Prayer att the times thereby appointed and after such reading thereof shall openly and publiquely before the Congregation there assembled declare his unfeigned assent and consent to the use of all things therein contained and prescribed according to the forme before appointed And that all and every such person who shall . . . refuse to doe the same within the time aforesaid . . . shall (ipso facto) be deprived of all his said Ecclesiasticall Benefices and Promotions And that from thenceforth it shall and may be lawfull to and for all Patrons . . . to present or collate to the same as though the person or persons so offending or neglecting were dead

V. And . . . That in all places where the proper Incumbent of any Parsonage or Vicaridge or Benefice with Cure doth reside on his Living and keepe a Curate the Incumbent himselfe in person (not haveing some lawfull Impediment to be allowed by the Ordinary of the place) shall once (at the least) in every moneth openly and publiquely read the Comon prayers and Service in and by the said Booke prescribed and (if there be occasion) administer each of the Sacraments and other Rites of the Church in the Parish Church . . . upon pain to forfeit the summ of Five pounds to the use of the poore . . . and in default of payment within ten dayes to be levied by distresse and sale of the goods and Chattells . . .

VI. And . . . That every Deane Canon and Prebendary of every Cathedrall or Collegiate Church and all Masters and other Heads Fellowes Chaplaines and Tutors of or in any Colledge Hall House of Learning or Hospitall and every Publique Professor and Reader in either of the Universities [2] and in every Colledge elsewhere and every Parson Viccar Curate Lecturer and every other person in Holy Orders and every School master keeping any publique or private Schoole & every person instructing or teaching any Youth in any House or private Family as a Tutor or School master who upon the First day of May which shall be in the yeare of our Lord God

---

[1] An Indemnity for those who had failed to read Morning and Evening Prayers or to declare their assent to the Prayer Book was passed 16 Geo. II, c. 30, § 2, and was renewed from time to time, e.g. 18 Geo. II, c. 11.

[2] See Vol. II, Sect. B, No. XVII, p. 190.

One thousand six hundred sixty two or at any time thereafter shall be Incumbent or have possession of any Deanry Canonry Prebend Mastershipp Headshipp Fellowshipp Professors place or Readers place Parsonage Vicarage or any other Ecclesiasticall Dignity or Promotion or of any Curates place Lecture or School or shall instruct or teach any Youth as Tutor or Schoolmaster shall before the Feast day of St. Bartholomew which shall be in the yeare of our Lord One thousand six hundred sixty two or at or before his or theire respective admission to be Incumbent or have possession aforesaid subscribe the Declaration or Acknowledgement following scilicet

I A. B. do declare that it is not lawfull upon any pretence whatsoever to take Armes against the King and that I do abhorr that traiterous Position of taking Armes by His Authority against His Person or against those that are commissionated by him And that I will conforme to the Liturgy of the Church of England as it is now by Law established And I do declare that I do hold there lies no Obligacion upon me or on any other person from the Oath commonly called the Solemne League and Covenant to endeavour any change or alteration of Government either in Church or State And that the same was in it selfe an unlawfull Oath and imposed upon the Subjects of this Realme against the knowne Lawes and Liberties of this Kingdome

Which said Declaration and Acknowledgment shall be subscribed by every of the said Masters and other Heads Fellowes [etc.] . . . upon pain that all and every of the persons aforesaid failing in such Subscription shall loose and forfeit such respective Deanary Canonry Prebend Mastershipp Headship Fellowship Professors place Readers place Parsonage Viccarage Ecclesiasticall Dignity or Promotion Curates place Lecture and School and shall be utterly disabled and (ipso facto) deprived of the same And that every such respective Deanry Canonry Prebend Mastership Headship Fellowship Proffessors Place Readers Place Parsonage Viccarage, Ecclesiasticall Dignity or Promotion Curates place Lecture and Schoole shall be void as if such person so failing were naturally dead

VII. And if any Schoolmaster or other person instructing or teaching Youth in any private House or Family as a Tutor or School master shall instruct or teach any Youth as a Tutor or School master before Licence obtained from his respective Archbishop Bishop or Ordinary of the Diocesse according to the Lawes and Statutes of this Realme (for which he shall pay twelve pence onely) and before such subscription and acknowledgement made as aforesaid then every such Schoolmaster and other instructing and teaching as aforesaid shall for the first offence suffer three monthes Imprisonment without bail or mainprize and for every second and other such offence shall suffer three moneths Imprisonment without baile or mainprize and alsoe forfeit to His Majesty the sum of Five pounds . . .

VIII. Provided alwaies that from and after the Twenty fifth day of March which shall be in the yeare of our Lord God One thousand six hundred eighty two there shall be omitted in the said Declaration or Acknowledgment so to be subscribed and read these words following scilicet

And I do declare that I do hold there lies no Obligacion on me or any other person from the Oath comonly called the Solemne League and Covenant to endeavor any change or alteration of Government either in Church or State and that the same was in it selfe an unlawfull Oath and imposed upon the Subjects of this Realme against the knowne Lawes and Liberties of this Kingdome.

So as none of the persons aforesaid shall from thence forth be at all obliged to subscribe or read that part of the said Declaration or Acknowledgement.

IX. Provided alwaies . . . that from and after the Feast of St. Bartholomew which shall be in the yeare of our Lord One thousand six hundred sixty and two no person who now is Incumbent and in possession of any Parsonage Vicarage or Benefice and who is not already in Holy Orders by Episcopall Ordination or shall not before the said Feast day of St. Bartholomew be ordained Preist or Deacon according to the forme of Episcopall Ordination shall have hold or enjoye the said Parsonage Vicaradge Benefice with Cure or other Ecclesiasticall Promotion within this Kingdome of England or the Dominion of Wales or Town of Berwick upon Tweed but shall be utterly disabled and (ipso facto) deprived of the same And all his Ecclesiastical Promotions shall be void as if he was naturally dead.

X. And bee it further enacted . . . that no person whatsoever shall thenceforth be capable to bee admitted to any Parsonage Vicarage Benefice or other Ecclesiastical Promotion or Dignity whatsoever nor shall presume to consecrate & administer the Holy Sacrament of the Lords Supper before such time as he shall be ordained Preist . . .

XI. Provided that the penalties in this Act shall not extend to the Forreiners or Aliens of the Forrein Reformed Churches allowed or to be allowed by the Kings Majestie His Heires and Successors in England.

XII. Provided alwaies that no title to conferre or present by lapse shall accrewe by any avoydance or deprivation (ipso facto) by vertue of this Statute but after six moneths after notice of such voidance or deprivation given by the Ordinary to the Patron or such sentence of deprivation openly and publiquely read in the Parish

Church of the Benefice Parsonage or Vicarage becomeing void or whereof the Incumbent shall be deprived by vertue of this Act.

XIII. And . . . that no Form or Order of Common Prayers Administracion of Sacraments Rites or Ceremonies shall be openly used in any Church Chappell or other publique place of or in any Colledge or Hall in either of the Universities the Colledges of Westminster Winchester or Eaton or any of them other then what is prescribed and appointed to be used in and by the said Booke And that the present Governour or Head of every Colledge and Hall in the said Universities and of the said Colledges of Westminster Winchester and Eaton within one moneth after the Feast of St. Bartholomew which shall be in the yeare of our Lord One thousand six hundred sixty and two And every Governour or Head of any of the said Colledges or Halls hereafter to be elected or appointed within one moneth next after his Election or Collation and Admission into the same Government or Headshipp shall openly and publiquely in the Church Chappell or other publique place of the same Colledge or Hall and in the presence of the Fellowes and Scholars of the same or the greater part of them then resident subscribe unto the Nine and thirty Articles of Religion mentioned in the Statute made in the thirteenth yeare of the Reigne of the late Queene Elizabeth And unto the said Booke and declare his unfeigned . . . approbation of the said Articles and of the same Booke . . . And that all such Governours or Heads of the said Colledges and Halls or any of them as are or shall be in Holy Orders shall once (at least) in every quarter of the yeare (not having a lawfull Impediment) openly and publiquely read the Morning Prayer and Service . . . upon pain to loose and be suspended of and from all the Benefitts and Profitts belonging to the same Government or Headshipp by the space of six moneths by the Visitor or Visitors of the same Colledge or Hall And if any Governour or Head of any Colledge or Hall suspended for not subscribing unto the said Articles and Booke or for not reading of the Morning Prayer and Service as aforesaid shall not att or before the end of Six monthes next after such suspension subscribe unto the said Articles and Booke and declare his consent thereunto as aforesaid or read the Morning Prayer and Service as aforesaid then such Government or Headshipp shall be (ipso facto) void

XIV. Provided alwaies that it shall and may be lawfull to use the Morning and Evening Prayer and all other Prayers and Service prescribed in and by the said Booke in the Chappells or other publique places of the respective Colledges and Halls in both the Universities in the Colledges of Westminster Winchester and Eaton and in the Convocations of the Clergies of either Province in Latine Any thing in this Act contained to the contrary notwithstanding

XV. And . . . that no person shall be or be received as a
Lecturer or permitted suffered or allowed to preach as a Lecturer
or to preach or read any Sermon or Lecture in any Church Chappell
or other place of Publique Worshipp . . . unlesse . . . licensed
by the Archbishopp of the Province or Bishopp of the Diocesse or
(in case the See be void) by the Guardian of the Spiritualties under
his Seale and shall in the presence of the same Archbishop or Bishop
or Guardian read the nine and thirty Articles of Religion . . . with
declaration of his unfeigned assent to the same . . . And alsoe shall
upon the first Lecture day of every moneth afterwards so long as he
continues Lecturer or Preacher there at the place appointed for his
said Lecture or Sermon before his said Lecture or Sermon openly
publiquely and solemnly read the Common Prayers and Service in
and by the said Booke appointed . . . And that all and every such
person and persons who shall neglect or refuse to do the same shall
from thenceforth be disabled to preach the said or any other Lecture
or Sermon . . .

XVI. Provided alwaies That if the said Sermon or Lecture be
to be preached or read in any Cathedrall or Collegiate Church or
Chappell it shall be sufficient for the said Lecturer openly at the
time aforesaid to declare his assent and consent to all things contained in the said Booke according to the form aforesaid

XVII. And . . . That if any person who is by this Act disabled
to preach any Lecture or Sermon shall during the time that he shall
continue and remaine so disabled preach any Sermon or Lecture
that then for every such offence the person and persons so offending
shall suffer Three Monthes Imprisonment . . .

XIX. Provided nevertheless that this Act shall not extend to
the University Churches . . . but that the same Sermons and
Lectures may be preached or read in such sort and manner as
the same have been heretofore preached or read This Act or anything herein contained to the contrary thereof in any wise notwithstanding. . . .

XXI. Provided alwaies . . . That in all those Prayers Letanies
and Collects which doe any way relate to the King Queene or Royall
Progeny the Names be altered and changed from time to time and
fitted to the present occasion according to the direction of lawfull
Authority.

XXII. Provided alsoe . . . that a true printed Copy of the
said Booke . . . shall att the costs and charges of the parishoners of
every Parish Church and Chappelry Cathedrall Church Colledge and
Hall be attained and gotten before the Feast day of St. Bartholomew
in the yeare of our Lord One thousand six hundred sixty and two
upon pain of forfeiture of three pounds by the moneth for so long

time as they shall then after be unprovided thereof by every Parish or Chapelry Cathedrall Church Colledge and Hall making default therein.

[XXIII. The Bishops of Hereford St. Davies Asaph Bangor and Landaff shall cause a Welsh translation to be made, one copy of which to be deposited in each Church by 1665. Service to be said in Welsh.]

And one other Booke of Common Prayer in the English Tongue shall be bought and had in every Church throughout Wales in which the Booke of Common Prayer in Welsh is to be had by force of this Act before the First day of May One thousand six hundred sixty and foure and the same Booke to remaine in such convenient places within the said Churches that such as understand them may resort at all convenient times to read and peruse the same and alsoe such as do not understand the said Language may by conferring both Tongues togeather the sooner attaine to the knowledge of the English Tongue . . .

XXIV. And to the end that the true and perfect Copies of this Act and the said Booke [1] hereunto annexed may be safely kept and perpetually preserved and for the avoiding of all disputes for the time to come Be it therefore enacted . . . That the respective Deanes and Chapters of every Cathedrall or Collegiate Church within England and Wales shall at theire proper costs and charges before the Twenty fifth day of December One thousand six hundred sixty & two obtain under the Great Seale of England a true and perfect printed Copy of this Act and of the said Booke annexed hereunto to be by the said Deanes and Chapters and theire Successors kept and preserved in safety for ever and to be alsoe produced and shewed forth in any Court of Record as often as they shall be thereunto lawfully required And alsoe there shall be delivered true and perfect Copies of this Act and of the same Booke into the respective Courts at Westminster and into the Tower of London to be kept and preserved for ever among the Records of the said Courts and the Records of the Tower to be alsoe produced and shewed forth in any Court as need shall require which said Bookes soe to be exemplified under the Great Seale of England shall be examined by such persons as the Kings Majestie shall appoint under the Great Seale of England for that purpose and shall be compared with the Originall Booke hereunto annexed . . . printing of the same Booke or of any thing therein contained and shall certifie . . . that they have examined and compared the same Booke and find it to be a true and perfect Coppy . . .

XXVII. Provided alsoe That the Booke of Common Prayer . . .

[1] The authentic version of the Prayer Book was annexed as a schedule to this Act.

established by Act of Parliament in the First and Eighth yeares of Queene Elizabeth shall be still used and observed in the Church of England untill the Feast of Saint Bartholomew which shall be in the yeare of our Lord God One thousand six hundred sixty and two.

XII

THE LICENSING ACT,[1] 1662

13 & 14 Car. II, c. 33.

Whereas the well-government and regulating of Printers and Printing Presses is matter of Publique care and of great concernment especially considering that by the general licentiousnes of the late times many evil disposed persons have been encouraged to print and sell heretical schismatical blasphemous seditious and treasonable Bookes Pamphlets and Papers and still doe continue such theire unlawfull and exorbitant practice to the high dishonour of Almighty God the endangering the peace of these Kingdomes and raising a disaffection to His most Excellent Majesty and His Government For prevention whereof no surer meanes can be advised then by reducing and limiting the number of Printing Presses and by ordering and setling the said Art or Mystery of Printing by Act of Parliament in manner as herein after is expressed. . . . Be it enacted That no person or persons whatsoever shall presume to print or cause to be printed either within this Realm of England or any other His Majesties Dominions or in the parts beyond the Seas any heretical seditious schismatical or offensive Bookes or Pamphlets wherein any Doctrine or Opinion shall be asserted or maintained which is contrary to Christian Faith or the Doctrine or Discipline of the Church of England or which shall or may tend or be to the scandall of Religion or the Church or the Government or Governors of the Church State or Common wealth or of any Corporation or particular person or persons whatsoever nor shall import publish sell or dispose any such Booke or Books or Pamphlets nor shall cause or procure any such to be published or put to sale or to be bound stitched or sowed togeather

II. And be it further ordained . . . That no private person or persons whatsoever shall att any time hereafter print or cause to be printed any Booke or Pamphlet whatsoever unlesse the same Booke

[1] Continued by 16 & 17 Car. II, c. 7, for seven years. Revived by 1 Jac. II, c. 17, for another seven years and continued for one further year by 4 & 5 Will. & Mar. c. 24. See also Sect. C, No. IV, p. 252, No. XI, p. 285, Nos. XVI, XVII and XVIII, pp. 294-310. Cf. Vol. II, Sect. A, No. X, p. 17.

and Pamphlet togeather with all and every the Titles Epistles Prefaces Proems Preambles Introductions Tables Dedications and other matters and things thereunto annexed be first entered in the Booke of the Register of the Company of Stationers of London except Acts of Parliament Proclamations and such other Books and Papers as shall be appointed to be printed by vertue of any Warrant under the Kings Majesties Sign Manual or under the hand of one or both of His Majesties Principal Secretaries of State and unlesse the same Booke and Pamphlet and also all and every the said Titles Epistles Prefaces Proems Preambles Introductions Tables Dedications and other matters and things whatsoever thereunto annexed or therewith to be imprinted shall be first lawfully licensed and authorized to be printed by such person and persons only as shall be constituted and appointed to license the same according to the direction and true meaning of this present Act herein after expressed and by no other (that is to say) That all Books concerning the Common Lawes of this Realm shall be printed by the special allowance of the Lord Chancellor or Lord Keeper of the Great Seal of England for the time being the Lords Cheife Justices and Lord Cheife Baron for the time being or one or more of them or by theire or one or more of theire appointments And that all Books of History concerning the State of this Realm or other Books concerning any Affaires of State shall be licensed by the Principal Secretaries of State for the time being or one of them . . . And that all Bookes to bee imprinted concerning Heraldry Titles of Honour and Armes or otherwise concerning the Office of Earle Marshal shall be licensed by the Earl Marshal for the time being or by his appointment or in case there shall not then be an Earl Marshal shall be licensed by the Three Kings of Armes Garter. Clarenceux and Norroy or any two of them whereof Garter Principal King of Armes to be one And that all other Bookes to bee imprinted or reprinted whether of Divinity Phisick Philosophy or whatsoever other Science or Art shall be first licensed and allowed by the Lord Arch Bishop of Canterbury and the Lord Bishop of London for the time being or one of them or by theire or one of theire appointments or by either one of the Chancellors or Vice-Chancellors of either of the Universities of this Realme for the time being Provided alwaies that the said Chancellors or Vice Chancellors of either of the said Universities shall only license such Bookes as are to be imprinted or reprinted within the limits of the said Universities respectively but not in London or else where not medling either with Bookes of the Common Lawes or matters of State or Government nor any Booke or Bookes the right of printing whereof doth solely and properly belong to any particular person or persons without his or theire Consent first obtained in that behalfe

III. And be it enacted . . . That every person and persons who . . . are . . . authorized to license the imprinting of Bookes or reprinting thereof with any Additions or Amendments as aforesaid shall have one written Copy of the same Booke or Bookes which shall be soe licensed . . . with the Titles Epistles Prefaces Tables Dedications and all other things whatsoever thereunto annexed which said Copy shall be delivered by such Licenser or Licensers to the Printer or Owner for the imprinting thereof and shall be safely and intirely returned by such Printer or owner after the imprinting thereof unto such Licenser or Licensers to be kept in the publick Registrys of the said Lord Archbishop or Lord Bishop of London respectively or in the Office of the Chancellor or Vice Chancellor of either the said Universities or with the said Lord Chancellor or Lord Keeper of the Great Seal for the time being or Lord Cheife Justices or Cheif Baron or one of them or the said Principal Secretaries of State or with the Earle Marshall or the said Kings of Armes or one of them of all such Books as shall be licensed by them respectively and if such Booke so to be licensed shall be an English Booke or of the English Tongue there shall be twoe Written Copies thereof delivered to the Licenser or Licensers (if he or they shall so require) one Copy whereof so licensed shall be delivered back to the said Printer or Owner and the other Copy shall be reserved and kept as is aforesaid to the end such Licenser or Licensers may be secured that the Copy so licensed shall not be altered without his or theire privity And upon the said Copy licensed to be imprinted he or they who shall so license the same shall testifie under his or their hand or hands That there is not any thing in the same contained that is contrary to Christian Faith or the Doctrine or Discipline of the Church of England or against the State or Government of this Realme or contrary to good life or good manners or otherwise as the nature and subject of the Worke shall require which License or Approbation shall be printed in the beginning of the same Booke with the Name or Names of him or them that shall authorize or license the same for a Testimony of the allowance thereof

.   .   .   .   .

[§§ IV-VIII. Merchants to import books into London only, to present a catalogue to the Archbishop, and not to open packages except in presence of a duly appointed person and a member of the Stationers' Company. Protects copyright granted by Letters Patent, and attaches penalties to violation of this; printers of books, under penalty, are to put their names on their books; the persons who may sell books are limited and placed under regulation; and no English books printed abroad are, in the interests of the printing trade, to be imported without special licence.]

IX. And be it further enacted . . . That no person or persons
within the City of London or the Liberties thereof or elsewhere
shall erect or cause to be erected any Presse or Printing House
nor shall knowingly demise or let or willingly suffer to be held or
used any House Vault Cellar or other Room whatsoever to or by
any person or persons for a Printing House . . . unlesse he or
they who erect such Presse . . . shall first give notice to the Master
or Wardens of the said Company of Stationers for the time being
of the erecting of such Presse . . . [Penalty £5].

[§§ X-XIII. Maximum number of Master Printers to be 20, each
to give surety of £300. No master to have more than 2 presses, nor
more than 2 apprentices each. Regulation of journeymen.]

XIV. And for the better discovering of printing in Corners
without License Be it further enacted . . . That one or more
Messengers [1] of his Majesties Chamber by Warrant under His
Majesties Sign Manual or under the Hand of one or both of His
Majesties principal Secretares of State or the Master and Wardens
of the said Company of Stationers or any one of them shall have
power and authority with a Constable to take unto them such
assistance as they shall thinke needfull . . . to search all Houses
and Shops where they shall knowe or upon some probable reason
suspect any Books or Papers to be printed bound or stitched especially Printing Houses Booksellers Shops and Warehouses and Book-
binders Houses and Shops and to view there what is imprinting
binding or stitching and to examine whether the same be licensed
and to demand a sight of the said License and if the said Booke . . .
shall not be licensed then to seize upon so much thereof as shall be
found imprinted togeather with the several Offenders and to bring
them before one or more Justices of the Peace whoe are hereby . . .
required to commit such Offenders to Prison there to remaine untill
they shall be tried and acquitted or convicted and punished for the
said Offences And case the said Searchers shall . . . find any Booke
or Bookes . . . which they shall suspect to contain matters therein
contrary to the Doctrine or Discipline of the Church of England
or against the State and Government Then upon such suspition
to seise upon such Book or Books . . . and to bring the same
unto the said Lord Archbishop of Canterbury and Lord Bishop of
London . . . or to the Secretaries of State . . . who shall take
such further course for the suppressing thereof as to them or any
of them shall seeme fit. . . .

[§ XV. Penalties, &c, for offenders.]

[1] See Sect. C, No. XVI, p. 294, and No. XVIII, p. 297, and Sect. D,
No. XLIII, p. 393.

XVI. And be it further enacted . . . That every Printer shall reserve three printed Copies of the best and largest Paper of every Book new printed or reprinted by him with Additions and shall before any publick venting of the said Book bring them to the Master of the Company of Stationers and deliver them to him one whereof shall be delivered to the Keeper of his Majesties Library and the other two to be sent to the Vice-Chancellors of the two Universities respectively for the use of the Publique Libraries of the said Universities

XVII. Provided alwaies That nothing in this Act shall . . . extend to the prejudice or infringing of any the just Rights and Priviledges of either of the two Universities of this Realm touching and concerning the licensing or printing of Books in either of the said Universities

XVIII. Provided alwaies That no search shall be att any time made in the House or Houses of any the Peers of this Realm or of any other person or persons not being free of or using any of the Trades in this Act before mentioned but by special Warrant from the Kings Majestie under his Sign Manual or under the Hand of one or both of His Majesties principal Secretaries of State or for any other Books then such as are in printing or shall be printed after the Tenth of June One thousand six hundred and sixty two Any thing in this Act to the contrary thereof in any wise notwithstanding

[§§ XIX-XXIII deal with certain temporary and personal cases, notably a proviso for a printing press in York.]

XXIV. Provided That this Act shall continue and be in force for two yeares to commence from the Tenth of June One thousand six hundred sixty and two and no longer.

XIII

THE TRIENNIAL ACT,[1] 1664

16 Car. II, c. 1.

An Act for the assembling and holding of Parliaments once in Three yeares at the least, And for the repeale of an Act entituled An Act for the preventing of Inconveniencies happening by the long Intermission of Parliaments.

Whereas the Act made in the Parliament begun at Westminster the Third day of November in the Sixteenth Yeare of the Raigne of our late Soveraigne Lord King Charles of blessed Memory entituled

[1] See Sect. A, No. XXIX, p. 79, No. XLVI, p. 126, and Vol. II, Sect. A, No. XLII, § 7, p. 143.

An Act for the preventing of Inconveniencies happening by the long Intermission of Parliaments [1] is in Derogation of His Majestyes just Rights and Prerogative inherent to the Imperiall Crowne of this Realme for the calling and assembling of Parliaments, And may be an occasion of manifold mischeifes and inconveniences, and much endanger the Peace and Safety of His Majestie, and all His Leidge People of this Realme, Be it therefore enacted . . . That the said Act . . . all and every the Articles Clauses and Things therein contained, . . . shall be . . . declared to be null and void to all intents and purposes whatsoever, . . .

II. And because by the auntient Lawes and Statutes of this Realme made in the Raigne of King Edward the Third Parliaments are to be held very often [2]; . . . bee it declared and enacted . . . That hereafter the sitting and holding of Parliaments shall not be intermitted or discontinued above three yeares at the most, but that within three yeares from and after the determination of this present Parliament and soe from time to time within three yeares after the determination of any other Parliament or Parliaments, or if there be occasion more often, Your Majestie Your Heires and Successors doe issue out Your Writts for calling assembling and holding of another Parliement to the end there may be a frequent calling assembling and holding of Parliaments once in Three yeares at the least.

XIV

THE FIVE MILE ACT,[3] 1665

17 Car. II, c. 2.

Whereas diverse Parsons Vicars Curates Lecturers and other persons in Holy Orders have not declared their unfaigned assent and consent to the use of all things contained and prescribed in the Booke of Common Prayer and Administration of the Sacraments and other Rites and Ceremonies of the Church according to the use of the Church of England, or have not subscribed the Declaration or Acknowledgement contained in a certaine Act of Parlyament made in the Fowerteenth yeare of His Majestyes Raigne and Intituled An Act [4] for the Uniformity of Publique Prayers and Administration of Sacraments . . . according to the said Act or any other subsequent Act. And whereas they or some of them and diverse other person & persons not ordained according to the Forme of the Church of England, and as have since the Act of Oblivion ||

[1] 16 Car. I, c. 1 (Gardiner, No. 27).   [2] 4 Edw. III, c. 14 and 36 Edw. III, c. 10.
[3] See Sect. A, No. XXIV, § VI, p. 65.   [4] See Sect. A, No. XI, p. 20.

taken upon them to preach in unlawfull Assemblyes Conventicles or
Meeteings under colour or pretence of Exercise of Religion contrary to the Lawes and Statutes of this Kingdome have setled themselves in diverse Corporations in England sometimes Three or more
of them in a place thereby takeing an oportunity to distill the
poysonous Principles of Schisme and Rebellion into the hearts of
His Majestyes Subjects to the great danger of the Church and
Kingdome. Bee it therefore enacted . . . That the said Parsons
Viccars Curates Lecturers and other persons in holy Orders, or pretended holy Orders, or pretending to holy Orders, and all Stipendaryes
and other persons who have beene possessed of any Ecclesiasticall or
Spiritual Promotion and every of them who have not declared their
unfaigned assent and consent as aforesaid and subscribed the Declaration aforesaid and shall not take and subscribe the oath following :

I A B doe sweare That it is not lawfull upon any pretence
whatsoever to take Armes against the King And that I doe abhorr
that Traiterous Position of takeing Armes by His Authoritie against
His Person or against those that are commissionated by Him in
pursuance of such Commissions And that I will not at any time
endeavour any Alteration of Goverment either in Church or State.

II. And all such person and persons as shall take upon them
to preach in any unlawfull Assembly Conventicle or Meeting
under colour or pretence of any Exercise of Religion contrary to
the Lawes and Statutes of this Kingdome shall not unlesse onely
in passeing upon the Road come or be within Five miles of any
Citty or Towne Corporate or Burrough that sends Burgesses to the
Parlyament within His Majesties Kingdome of England Principallitie
of Wales or of the Towne of Berwicke upon Tweede or within Five
miles of any Parish Towne or Place wherein he or they have since
the Act of Oblivion beene Parson Viccar Curate Stipendary or
Lecturer or taken upon them to preach in any unlawfull Assembly
Conventicle or Meeting under colour or pretence of any Exercise
of Religion contrary to the Lawes and Statutes of this Kingdome
before he or they have taken and subscribed the Oath aforesaid . . .
in open Court . . . upon forfeiture for every such offence the
summe of Forty pounds of lawfull English money, the one Third
part thereof to His Majestie and His Successors, the other Third
part to the use of the poore of the Parish where the offence shall
be committed and the other Third part thereof to such person or
persons as shall or will sue for the same . . .

III. Provided alwayes . . . That it shall not be lawfull for any
person or persons restrained from comeing to any Citty Towne
Corporate Burrough Parish Towne or Place as aforesaid or for any
other person or persons as shall not first take and subscribe the said

Oath and as shall not frequent Divine Service established by the Lawes of this Kingdome and carry him or herselfe reverently decently and orderly there to teach any Publick or Private School or take any Boarders or Tablers that are taught or instructed by him or herselfe or any other upon paine for every such offence to forfeit the sum of Forty pounds to be recovered and distributed as aforesaid.

IV. Provided alsoe . . . That it shall be lawfull for any two Justices of the Peace of the respective County upon Oath to them of any offence against this Act which Oath they are hereby impowered · to administer to committ the Offender for Six Monethes without Baile or Maineprize, unlesse upon or before such Commitment he shall before the said Justices of the Peace sweare and subscribe the aforesaid Oath and Declaration.

[§ V. This Act not to be pleaded to prevent appearance in court required by judicial process.]

XV

THE SECOND CONVENTICLE ACT,[1] 1670

22 Car. II, c. 1.

For providing further and more speedy Remedies against the growing and dangerous practices of Seditious Sectaries and other disloyall Persons who under pretence of tender Consciences have or may at their Meetings contrive Insurrections (as late experience hath shewen) Bee it enacted . . . That if any person of the Age of Sixteene yeares or upwards being a Subject of this Realme at any time after the Tenth day of May next shall be present at any Assembly Conventicle or Meeteing under colour or pretence of any Exercise of Religion in other manner then according to the Liturgy and practice of the Church of England in any place within the Kingdome of England, Dominion of Wales or Towne of Berwicke upon Tweede, at which Conventicle, Meeting or Assembly there shall be five persons or more assembled together over and besides

---

[1] The First Conventicle Act is 16 Car. II, c. 4. (This Act was to remain in force for three years and to expire at the end of the first session of the next Parliament. It made no distinction between a preacher and a member of the congregation. For the first offence of being present at an illegal conventicle (defined as above) a convicted person was to be imprisoned for three months, for a second offence for six months, for a third offence he was to be transported for seven years, unless he paid fines of £5, £10, and £100 respectively. The penalties could only be inflicted after indictment at Quarter Sessions or Assizes. The First Conventicle Act also inflicted the penalty of transportation on a Quaker who refused to take an oath lawfully tendered.) See also Sect. A, No. XXIV, p. 63.

those of the same Household, if it be in a House where there is
a Family inhabiting, or if it be in a House, Feild or place where
there is noe Family inhabiting then where any five persons or more
are soe assembled as aforesaid, it shall . . . be lawfull . . . for any
one or more Justices of the Peace of the County Limitt, Division,
Corporation or Liberty . . . and he and they are hereby required
and enjoyned upon proofe . . . made of such offence either by
Confession of the partie or Oath of two Witnesses (which Oath
the said Justice and Justices of the Peace . . . are hereby . . .
required to administer), or by notorious Evidence and Circumstance
of the Fact to make a Record of every such offence . . . which
Record . . . shall to all intents and purposes be in Law . . . a full
and perfect Conviction of every such Offender for such Offence,
and thereupon the said Justice, Justices and cheife Magistrate
respectively shall impose on every such Offender soe convict as
aforesaid a Fine of Five shillings for such first Offence which Record
and Conviction shall be certifyed . . . at the next Quarter Sessions of
the Peace for the County or place where the Offence was committed,

II. And bee it further enacted . . . That if such Offender . . .
shall at any time againe committ the like Offence or Offences contrary to this Act and be thereof in manner aforesaid convicted, then
such Offender . . . shall for every such Offence incurr the penaltie
of Ten shillings. which Fine and Fines shall be leavyed by Distresse
and Sale. . . .

III. And bee it further enacted . . . That every peison who
shall take upon him to preach or teach in any such Meeting,
Assembly or Conventicle and shall thereof be convicted as aforesaid shall forfeite for every such first offence the Summe of Twenty
pounds . . . And if the said Preacher or Teacher . . . be a
Stranger, and his Name and Habitation not knowne, or is fled and
cannot be found, or in the judgment of the Justice Justices or cheife
Magistrate . . . shall be thought unable to pay the same, the said
Justice, Justices or cheife Magistrate respectively are hereby impowered and required to leavy the same . . . upon the Goods and
Chattells of any such persons who shall be present at the same Conventicle. . . .

IV. And bee it further enacted . . . That every person who
shall wittingly and willingly suffer any such Conventicle, Meeteing
or unlawfull Assembly aforesaid to be held in his or her House,
Outhouse Barne Yard or Backeside and be convicted thereof in
manner aforesaid shall forfeite the summe of Twenty pounds. . . .

[§ V. No person to pay more than £10 on account of the poverty
of other persons.]

[§§ VI-VII. Provisions for Appeals.]

VIII. And bee it further enacted . . . That the Justice, Justices of the Peace and cheife Magistrate respectively, or the respective Constables Head-boroughs and Tythingmen by Warrant . . . shall and may with what aide force and assistance they shall thinke fitt for the better execution of this Act after refusall or denyall to enter, breake open and enter into any House or other place where they shall be informed any such Conventicle as aforesaid is or shall be held as well within Liberties as without and take into their custody the persons there unlawfully assembled to the intent they may be proceeded against according to this Act, And that the Lieutenants or Deputy Lieutenants or any Commissionated Officer of the Militia or other of his Majesties Forces with such Troopes or Companies of Horse and Foote, and alsoe the Sheriffes and other Magistrates and Ministers of Justice or any of them jointly or severally . . . with such other Assistance as they shall thinke meete or can gett in readines with the soonest on Certificate . . . of any one Justice of the Peace or cheife Magistrate of his perticular Information or Knowledge of such unlawfull Meeting or Conventicle held or to be held in their respective Countyes or places, and that he with such assistance as he can gett together is not able to suppresse and dissolve the same . . . are hereby required and enjoyned to repaire unto the place . . . and by the best meanes they can to dissolve, dissipate or prevent all such unlawfull Meetings, and take into their Custody such and soe many of the said persons soe unlawfully assembled as they shall thinke fitt to the intent they may be proceeded against according to this Act.

IX. Provided alwayes That noe Dwelling house of any Peere of this Realme where he or his Wife shall be then resident shall be searched by vertue of this Act, but by immediate Warrant from his Majestie under his Signe Manuall, or in the presence of the Lieutenant or one Deputy Lieutenant or two Justices of the Peace whereof one to be of the Quorum of the same County or Rideing.

X. And bee it further enacted . . . That if any Constable Headborough Tythingman Churchwarden or Overseer of the Poore who shall know or be credibly informed of any such Meeteings or Conventicles held within his Precincts Parish or Limitts and shall not give information thereof to some Justice of the Peace or the cheife Magistrate and endeavour the conviction of the partyes according to his duty, . . . and be thereof convicted in manner aforesaid he shall forfeite for every such offence the summe of Five pounds . . . And that if any Justice of the Peace or cheife Magistrate shall wilfully and wittingly ommitt the performance of his duty in the execution of this Act he shall forfeite the summe of One hundred pounds. . . .

[§ XI. Those sued under this Act may plead the general issue, and a successful defendant to have treble costs.]

XII. And bee it further enacted . . . That this Act and all Clauses therein contained shall be construed most largely and beneficially for the suppresseing of Conventicles and for the justification and encouragement of all persons to be employed in the execution thereof, And that noe Record, Warrant or Mittimus to be made by vertue of this Act, or any proceedings thereupon shall be reversed avoided or any way impeached by reason of any defaulte in forme . . .

XIII. Provided alsoe That noe person shall be punished for any offence against this Act unlesse such Offender be prosecuted for the same within three moneths after the Offence committed, And that noe person who shall be punished for any offence by vertue of this Act shall be punished for the same offence by vertue of any other Act or Law whatsoever.

[§ XIV. Aldermen of London to have all powers and duties of a Justice of the Peace under this Act.]

[§ XV. Penalties incurred by a married woman to be levied on her husband.]

XVI. . . . Provided alsoe That noe Peere of this Realme shall be attached or imprisoned by vertue or Force of this Act. Any thing matter or clause therein to the contrary notwithstanding.

XVII. Provided alsoe That neither this Act nor any thing therein contained shall extend to invalidate or avoid his Majesties Supremacy in Ecclesiasticall Affaires,[1] But that his Majestie and his Heires and Successors may from time to time and at all times hereafter exercise and enjoy all powers and authorities in Ecclesiasticall Affaires as fully and as amply as himselfe or any of his Predecessors have or might have done the same. Any thing in this Act notwithstanding.

XVI

THE FIRST TEST ACT,[2] 1673

25 Car. II, c. 2.

For preventing dangers which may happen from Popish Recusants and quieting the minds of his Majestyes good Subjects Bee it enacted . . . That all and every person or persons as well

---

[1] See Sect. A, No. VIII, § V, p. 14.

[2] From the passing of the Indemnity Act, 16 Geo. II, c. 30, the Sacramental Text was virtually removed. See also Sect. A, No. XXIV, p. 63, and Vol. II, Sect. A, No. XIX, p. 42. See also Sect. D, No. XVI, p. 344.

Peeres as Commoners that shall beare any Office or Offices Civill or
Military or shall receive any Pay, Salary, Fee or Wages by reason
of any Patent or Grant from his Majestie or shall have Command
or Place of Trust from, or under his Majestie or from any of his
Majestyes Predecessors or by his or their authority, or by authoritie
derived from him or them within the Realme of England, Dominion
of Wales or Towne of Berwicke upon Tweede, or in his Majestyes
Navy or in the severall Islands of Jersey and Guernsey or shall be
of the Household or in the Service or imployment of his Majestie,
or of his Royall Highnesse the Duke of Yorke who shall inhabite,
reside or be within the Citty of London or Westminster or within
thirty miles distant from the same on the first day of Easter Terme
that shall be in the yeare of our Lord one thousand six hundred
seaventy three . . . all and every the said person and persons
shall personally appeare before the end of the said Terme or of
Trinity Terme next following in his Majestyes High Court of
Chancery or in his Majestyes Court of Kings Bench and there in
publique and open Court betweene the houres of nine of the Clocke
and twelve in the Forenoone take the severall Oathes of Supremacy
and Allegiance which Oath of Allegiance is contained in a Statute
made in the third yeare of King James [1] by Law established, . . .
And that all and every of the said . . . Officers not haveing taken
the said Oathes in the said respective Courts aforesaid shall on or
before the first day of August one thousand six hundred seaventy
three at the Quarter Sessions for that County or place where he or
they shall be, inhabite or reside on the twentyeth day of May take
the said Oathes in open Court betweene the said houres of nine and
twelve of the Clocke in the Forenoone, and the said respective Officers
aforesaid shall alsoe receive the Sacrament of the Lords Supper
according to the Usage of the Church of England at or before the
first day of August in the yeare of our Lord one thousand six
hundred and seaventy three in some Parish Church upon some
Lords day commonly called Sunday immediately after Divine
Service and Sermon.

II. Bee it further enacted . . . That all and every person or
persons . . . taken into any Office or Offices Civill or Military or
shall receive any Pay, Salary, Fee or Wages by reason of any Patent
or Grant of his Majestie or shall have Command or place of Trust
from or under his Majestie His Heires or Successors or by his or
their authority or by authoritie derived from him or them within
this Realme of England [etc.] . . . or in his Majestyes Navy, or
in the severall Islands of Jersey and Guernsey, or that shall be
admitted into any Service or imployment in his Majesties or Royall

[1] 3 & 4 Jac. I, c. 4 (Prothero, p. 256).

Highnesses Household or Family after the first day of Easter Terme aforesaid and shall inhabite, . . . within the Cittyes of London or Westminster or within thirty miles of the same shall take the said Oathes aforesaid in the said respective Court or Courts aforesaid in the next Terme after such his or their admittance or admittances into the Office or Offices Imployment or Imployments aforesaid betweene the houres aforesaid. . . . And all and every such person . . . shall alsoe receive the Sacrament of the Lords Supper according to the Usage of the Church of England within three moneths after his or their admittances in, or receiving their said authority and imployment in some publique Church upon some Lords day commonly called Sunday immediately after Divine Service and Sermon, And every of the said persons . . . shall first deliver a Certificate of such his receiving the said Sacrament as aforesaid under the Hands of the respective Minister and Churchwarden and shall then make proofe of the truth thereof by two credible Witnesses at the least upon Oath, All which shall be inquired of and putt upon Record in the respective Courts.

III. And bee it further enacted . . . That all . . . that doe . . . refuse to take the said Oathes and Sacrament . . . shall be ipso facto adjudged uncapeable and disabled in Law to all intents and purposes whatsoever to have occupy or enjoy the said Office or Offices Imployment or Imployments or any part of them or any matter or thing aforesaid or any proffitt or advantage appertaining to them or any of them, and every such Office and Place Imployment and Imployments . . . is hereby adjudged void.

IV. And bee it further enacted That all . . . that shall . . . refuse to take the said Oathes or the Sacrament as aforesaid, . . . and yet after such neglect and refusal shall execute any of the said Offices or Imployments after the said times expired . . . and being thereupon lawfully convicted, . . . every such person . . . shall be disabled from thenceforth to sue, or use any Action, Bill, Plaint or Information in course of Law, or to prosecute any Suite in any Court of Equity or to be Guardian of any Childe or Executor or Administrator of any person, or capeable of any Legacie or Deed of Gift or to beare any Office within this Realme of England, Dominion of Wales or Towne of Berwicke upon Tweede and shall forfeite the Summe of five hundred pounds. . . .

V. And bee it further enacted . . . That the Names of all and singular such persons and Officers aforesaid that . . . shall take the Oathes aforesaid shall be in the respective Courts of Chauncery and Kings Bench and the Quarter Sessions inrolled, . . . for every one to resort to and looke upon, without Fee or Reward, and likewise none of the person or persons aforesaid shall give or pay as any Fee or Reward to any Officer or Officers belonging to any of the Courts as aforesaid above the Summe of twelve pence for his or their Entry of his or their takeing of the said Oathes aforesaid.

[§ VI. Courts required to administer the Oaths.]

VII. And bee it further enacted That if any person or persons, not bred up by his or their Parent or Parents from their Infancy in the Popish Religion and professing themselves to be Popish Recusants shall breed up, instruct or educate his or their Childe or Children . . . in the Popish Religion; every such person being thereof convicted shall be from thenceforth disabled of bearing any Office or place of Trust or Proffitt in Church or State; And all such Children as shall be soe brought up instructed or educated, are and shall be hereby disabled of bearing any such Office or place of Trust or Proffitt, untill he and they shall bee perfectly reconciled and converted to the Church of England and shall take the Oathes of Supremacy and Alleigiance aforesaid before the Justices of the Peace . . . and thereupon receive the Sacrament of the Lords Supper after the Usage of the Church of England, and obtaine a Certificate thereof under the Hands of two or more of the said Justices of the Peace.

VIII. And bee it further enacted . . . That at the same time when the persons concerned in this Act shall take the aforesaid Oathes of Supremacy and Alleigiance, they shall likewise make and subscribe this Declaration[1] following under the same Penalties and Forfeitures as by this Act is appointed;

I A.B. doe declare That I doe beleive that there is not any Transubstantiation in the Sacrament of the Lords Supper, or in the Elements of Bread and Wine, at, or after the Consecration thereof by any person whatsoever.

Of which Subscription there shall be the like Register kept as of the takeing the Oathes aforesaid. . .

[§ IX saves the rights of the peerage and of certain officers, and requires " Popish officers " to appoint deputies who shall take the oath.]

[§ X provides that peers may take the oath in Parliament.]

[§ XI. A saving proviso for married women, persons under 18 years of age, etc.]

[§ XII. A person forfeiting under the Act may receive back his office on compliance with the statutory requirements.]

[§ XIII exempts non-commissioned officers in the navy who subscribe the Declaration.]

[§ XIV exempts the pensions of the Earl and Countess of Bristol.]

[§ XV exempts constables, tithingmen, churchwardens, and various private officers.]

[1] See Sect. A, No. XLIV, § II, p. 122.

XVII

THE SECOND TEST ACT, 1678

30 Car. II, St. II, c. 1.

An Act for the more effectuall preserving the Kings Person and Government by disableing Papists from sitting in either House of Parlyament.

Forasmuch as diverse good Lawes have beene made for preventing the Increase and Danger of Popery in this Kingdome, which have not had the desired Effects by reason of the free accesse which Popish Recusants have had to his Majestyes Court and by reason of the Liberty which of late some of the Recusants have had and taken to sitt and vote in Parliament. Wherefore and for the Safety of His Majestyes Royall Person and Government Bee it enacted . . . That . . . noe Person that now is or hereafter shall be a Peere of this Realme or Member of the House of Peeres shall vote or make his Proxie in the House of Peeres or sitt there dureing any Debate in the said House of Peeres, Nor any person that now is or hereafter shall be a Member of the House of Commons shall vote in the House of Commons or sitt there dureing any Debate in the said House of Commons after their Speaker is chosen untill such Peere or Member shall from time to time respectively and in manner following first take the severall Oathes of Allegiance and Supremacy and make subscribe and audibly repeate this Declaration [1] following ;

I A. B. doe solemnely and sincerely in the presence of God professe testifie and declare That I doe believe that in the Sacrament of the Lords Supper there is not any Transubstantiation of the Elements of Bread and Wine into the Body and Blood of Christ at or after the Consecration thereof by any person whatsoever ; And that the Invocation or Adoration of the Virgin Mary or any other Saint, and the Sacrifice of the Masse as they are now used in the Church of Rome are superstitious and idolatrous, And I doe solemnely in the presence of God professe testifie and declare That I doe make this Declaration and every part thereof in the plaine and ordinary sence of the Words read unto me as they are commonly understood by English Protestants without any Evasion, Equivocation or Mentall Reservation whatsoever and without any Dispensation already granted me for this purpose by the Pope or any other Authority or Person whatsoever or without any hope of

---

[1] This Declaration was virtually suspended by the Act of 16 Geo. II, c. 30, renewed from time to time. See also Sect. A, No. XXIV, p. 63, and Vol. II, Sect. A, No. XX, p. 45. See also Sect. D, No. XVI, p. 344.

any such Dispensation from any person or authority whatsoever or without thinking that I am or can be acquitted before God or Man or absolved of this Declaration or any part thereof although the Pope or any other Person or Persons or Power whatsoever should dispence with or annull the same, or declare that it was null and void from the begining. . . .

II. And bee it further enacted That . . . every Peere of this Realme and Member of the House of Peeres, and every Peere of the Kingdome of Scotland or of the Kingdome of Ireland being of the Age of One and twenty yeares or upwards not haveing taken the said Oathes and made and subscribed the said Declaration, and every Member of the said House of Commons not haveing as aforesaid taken the said Oathes and made and subscribed the said Declaration, and every Person now or hereafter convicted of Popish Recusancy who hereafter shall . . . come advisedly into or remaine in the presence of the Kings Majestie or Queens Majestie or shall come into the Court or House where they or any of them reside as well dureing the Raigne of His present Majestie (whose Life God long preserve) as dureing the Raigns of any His Royall Successors Kings or Queens of England shall incurr and suffer all the paines, penalties forfeitures and disabilities in this Act mentioned or contained, unlesse such Peere Member or Person soe convicted doe respectively in the next Terme after such his comeing or remaineing take the said Oathes and make and subscribe the said Declaration in his Majestyes High Court of Chauncery betweene the houres of Nine and Twelve in the Forenoone.

III. And bee it further enacted by the Authoritie aforesaid That if any Person that now is or hereafter shall be a Peere of this Realme or Member of the House of Peeres or Member of the House of Commons shall presume to doe any thing contrary to this Act or shall offend in any of the Cases aforesaid That then every such Peere and Member soe offending shall from thenceforth bee deemed and adjudged a Popish Recusant Convict to all intents and purposes whatsoever and shall forfeite and suffer as a Popish Recusant Convict and shall be disabled to hold or execute any Office or Place of Proffitt or Trust Civill or Military . . . and shall be disabled from thenceforth to sitt or vote in either House of Parlyament or make a Proxy in the House of Peeres or to sue or use any Action Bill Plaint or Information in course of Law or to prosecute any Suite in any Court of Equity or to be Guardian of any Childe or Executor or Administrator of any person or capeable of any Legacie or Deed of Gift and shall forfeite for every wilfull Offence against this Act the summe of Five hundred pounds to be recovered and received by him or them that shall sue for the same, and to be prosecuted by any Action of Debt Suite Bill Plaint or Information in any of His Majestyes Courts at Westminster where noe Essoigne Protection or Wager of Law shall lye.

IV. And bee it further enacted by the Authority aforesaid That . . . it shall and may be lawfull to and for the House of Peeres and House of Commons or either of them respectively as often as they or either of them shall see occasion either in this present Parlyament or any other hereafter to be holden to order and cause all or any of the Members of their respective Houses of Parlyament openly in their respective Houses of Parlyament to take the said Oathes and to make and subscribe the said Declaration at such times and in such manner as they shall appoint. And if any Peere shall contrary to such Order made by their said House wilfully presume to sitt therein without takeing the said Oathes and subscribeing the said Declaration according to the said Order, Every such Peere or Member of the House of Peeres soe presumeing to sitt shall be adjudged and is hereby declared to be uncapeable and disabled in Law to all intents and purposes whatsoever to sitt in the said House of Peeres and give any Voice therein either by Proxie or otherwise howsoever dureing that Parlyament. And if any Member or Members of the House of Commons shall contrary to such Order made by their House wilfully presume to sitt therein without takeing the said Oathes and makeing and subscribeing the said Declaration Every such Member or Members of the House of Commons soe presumeing to sitt shall be adjudged and is hereby declared to be uncapeable and disabled in Law to all intents and purposes whatsoever to sitt in the said House of Commons or give any Voice therein dureing that Parlyament.

V. And bee it enacted That in every case where any Member or Members of the House of Commons shall by vertue of this Act be disabled to sitt or vote in the House of Commons Then and in every such Case without any further Conviction or other Proceeding against such Member or Members the Place or Places for which they or any of them were elected is hereby declared void, and a new Writt or Writts shall issue out of the High Court of Chauncery by Warrant or Warrants from the Speaker of the House of Commons for the time being and by Order of the said House for the Election of a new Member or Members to serve in the House of Commons in the Place or Places of such Member or Members soe disabled to all intents and purposes as if such Member or Members were naturally dead.

VI. And bee it further enacted by the Authoritie aforesaid That . . . every Person . . . who . . . shall be a sworne Servant to the Kings or Queens Majestie not haveing before that time duely taken the Oathes and made and subscribed the Declaration contained in an Act entituled An act for preventing Dangers which may happen from Popish Recusants shall take the said Oathes and make and subscribe the Declaration before expressed in His Majestyes High Court of Chauncery in the manner aforesaid . . . And if any such Person shall refuse or neglect to doe the same, and yet after such refusall or neglect shall advisedly come into or remaine in the presence of the Kings or Queens Majestie or shall come into the Court or House where they or any of them reside as well dureing the Raigne of His present Majestie as dureing the Raigns of His and their Royall Successors Kings or Queens of England and every of them, Every such Person shall be disabled to hold any Place as such sworne Servant and shall incurr and suffer all the Paines Penalties Forfeitures and Disabilities in this Act mentioned or contained.

VII. Provided That nothing in this Act shall relate to or have any effect upon any person being a Naturall borne Subject of the King of Portugall who now is or hereafter shall be a sworne Servant to the Queens Majestie not exceeding Nine in number at any one time, nor to such Women Servants as her Majestie shall under her Hand and Seale from time to time for that purpose be pleased to nominate the said Women Servants soe nominated not exceeding the number of Nine at any one time.

[§ VIII. Regulations concerning taking of Oaths and Declaration.]

[§ IX. Licence for temporary visits to Court not exceeding ten days at a time may be given by six Privy Councillors.]

[§ X. An offender subsequently taking Oaths, etc., to be discharged from penalties and incapacities, but not from the forfeiture of £500.]

XI.[1] Provided alwayes That nothing in this Act contained shall extend to His Royall Highnesse the Duke of Yorke.

XVIII

HABEAS CORPUS AMENDMENT ACT,[2]
1679
31 Car. II, c. 2.

An Act for the better secureing the Liberty of the Subject and for Prevention of Imprisonments beyond the Seas.

Whereas great Delayes have beene used by Sheriffes Gaolers and other Officers to whose Custody any of the Kings Subjects have

---

[1] This proviso was added by the House of Lords and passed by the Commons with a majority of two. See also Sect. A, No. XXV, p. 67, and Sect. A, No. XXXVI, § III, p. 94.

[2] See Vol. II, Sect. A, No. XVII, p. 38.

beene committed for criminall or supposed criminall Matters in makeing Returnes of Writts of Habeas Corpus to them directed by standing out an Alias and Pluries Habeas Corpus and sometimes more and by other shifts to avoid their yeilding Obedience to such Writts contrary to their Duty and the knowne Lawes of the Land whereby many of the Kings Subjects have beene and hereafter may be long detained in Prison in such Cases where by Law they are baylable to their great charge and vexation. For the prevention whereof and the more speedy Releife of all persons imprisoned for any such criminall or supposed criminall Matters Bee it enacted . . . That whensoever any person or persons shall bring any Habeas Corpus directed unto any Sheriffe or Sheriffes Gaoler Minister or other Person whatsoever for any person in his or their Custody and the said Writt shall be served upon the said Officer or left at the Gaole or Prison with any of the Under Officers Underkeepers or Deputy of the said Officers or Keepers that the said Officer or Officers his or their Under Officers Under-Keepers or Deputyes shall within Three dayes after the Service thereof as aforesaid (unlesse the Committment aforesaid were for Treason or Fellony plainely or specially expressed in the Warrant of Committment) upon Payment or Tender of the Charges of bringing the said Prissoner to be ascertained by the Judge or Court that awarded the same and endorsed upon the said Writt not exceeding Twelve pence per Mile and upon Security given by his owne Bond to pay the Charges of carrying backe the Prisoner if he shall bee remanded by the Court or Judge to which he shall be brought according to the true intent of this present Act and that he will not make any escape by the way make Returne of such Writt or bring or cause to be brought the Body of the Partie so committed or restrained unto or before the Lord Chauncellor or Lord Keeper of the Great Seale of England for the time being or the Judges or Barons of the said Court from whence the said Writt shall issue or unto and before such other person and persons before whome the said Writt is made returnable according to the Command thereof, and shall likewise then certifie the true causes of his Detainer or Imprisonment unlesse the Committment of the said Partie be in any place beyond the distance of Twenty miles from the place or places where such Court or Person is or shall be resideing and if beyond the distance of Twenty miles and not above One hundred miles then within the space of Ten dayes and if beyond the distance of One hundred miles then within the space of Twenty dayes after such delivery aforesaid and not longer.

II. And to the intent that noe Sheriffe Gaoler or other Officer may pretend ignorance of the import of any such Writt Bee it

enacted (by the Authoritie aforesaid) That all such Writts shall be
marked in this manner Per Statutum Tricesimo primo Caroli Secundi
Regis and shall be signed by the person that awards the same And
if any person or persons shall be or stand committed or detained as
aforesaid for any Crime unlesse for Treason or Fellony plainely
expressed in the Warrant of Committment in the Vacation time and
out of Terme it shall and may be lawfull to and for the person or
persons soe committed or detained (other then persons Convict or
in Execution) by legall Processe or any one in his or their behalfe
to appeale or complaine to the Lord Chauncellor or Lord Keeper
or any one of His Majestyes Justices either of the one Bench or of
the other or the Barons of the Exchequer of the Degree of the Coife
and the said Lord Chauncellor Lord Keeper Justices or Barons or
any of them upon view of the Copy or Copies of the Warrant or
Warrants of Committment and Detanier or otherwise upon Oath
made that such Copy or Copyes were denyed to be given by such
person or persons in whose Custody the Prisoner or Prisoners is or
are detained are hereby authorized and required upon Request made
in Writing by such person or persons or any on his her or their
behalfe attested and subscribed by two Witnesses that were present
at the delivery of the same to award and grant an Habeas Corpus
under the Seale of such Court whereof he shall then be one of the
Judges to be directed to the Officer or Officers in whose Custodie
the Party soe committed or detained shall be returnable immediate
before the said Lord Chauncellor or Lord Keeper or such Justice
Baron or any other Justice or Baron of the Degree of the Coife of
any of the said Courts . . . and thereupon within two dayes after
the Partie shall be brought before them the said Lord Chauncellor
or Lord Keeper or such Justice or Baron before whome the Prisoner
shall be brought as aforesaid shall discharge the said Prisoner from
his Imprisonment takeing his or their Recognizance with one or
more Suretie or Sureties in any summe according to their discretions
haveing reguard to the quality of the Prisoner and nature of the
Offence for his or their appearance in the Court of Kings Bench the
Terme following or at the next Assizes Sessions or Generall Gaole-
Delivery of and for such County City or Place where the Committment was or where the Offence was committed or in such other
Court where the said Offence is properly cognizable as the Case
shall require and then shall certifie the said Writt with the Returne
thereof and the said Recognizance or Recognizances into the said
Court where such Appearance is to be made unlesse it shall appeare
unto the said Lord Chauncellor or Lord Keeper or Justice or
Justices or Baron or Barons that the Party soe committed is detained
upon a legall Processe Order or Warrant out of some Court that

hath Jurisdiction of Criminall Matters or by some Warrant signed and sealed with the Hand and Seale of any of the said Justices or Barons or some Justice or Justices of the Peace for such Matters or Offences for the which by the Law the Prisoner is not Baileable.

III. Provided alwayes and bee it enacted That if any person shall have wilfully neglected by the space of two whole Termes after his Imprisonment to pray a Habeas Corpus for his Enlargement such person soe wilfully neglecting shall not have any Habeas Corpus to be granted in Vacation time in pursuance of this Act.

IV. And bee it further enacted by the Authoritie aforesaid That if any Officer or Officers his or their Under-Officer or Under-Officers Under-Keeper or Under-Keepers or Deputy shall neglect or refuse to make the Returnes aforesaid or to bring the Body or Bodies of the Prisoner or Prisoners according to the Command of the said Writt within the respective times aforesaid or upon Demand made by the Prisoner or Person in his behalfe shall refuse to deliver or within the space of Six houres after demand shall not deliver to the person soe demanding a true Copy of the Warrant or Warrants of Committment and Detayner of such Prisoner, which he and they are hereby required to deliver accordingly all and every the Head Gaolers and Keepers of such Prisons and such other person in whose Custodie the Prisoner shall be detained shall for the first Offence forfeite to the Prisoner or Partie grieved the summe of One hundred pounds and for the second Offence the summe of Two hundred pounds and shall and is hereby made incapeable to hold or execute his said Office . . .

V. And for the prevention of unjust vexation by reiterated Committments for the same Offence Bee it enacted by the Authoritie aforesaid That noe person or persons which shall be delivered or sett at large upon any Habeas Corpus shall at any time hereafter bee againe imprisoned or committed for the same Offence by any person or persons whatsoever other then by the legall Order and Processe of such Court wherein he or they shall be bound by Recognizance to appeare or other Court haveing Jurisdiction of the Cause and if any other person or persons shall knowingly contrary to this Act recommitt or imprison or knowingly procure or cause to be recommitted or imprisoned for the same Offence or pretended Offence any person or persons delivered or sett at large as aforesaid or be knowingly aiding or assisting therein then he or they shall forfeite to the Prisoner or Party grieved the summe of Five hundred pounds Any colourable pretence or variation in the Warrant or Warrants of Committment notwithstanding to be recovered as aforesaid.

VI. Provided alwayes and bee it further enacted That if any

person or persons shall be committed for High Treason or Fellony plainely and specially expressed in the Warrant of Committment upon his Prayer or Petition in open Court the first Weeke of the Terme or the first day of the Sessions of Oyer and Terminer or Generall Gaole Delivery to be brought to his Tryall shall not be indicted sometime in the next Terme Sessions of Oyer and Terminer or Generall Gaole Delivery after such Committment it shall and may be lawfull to and for the Judges of the Court of Kings Bench and Justices of Oyer and Terminer or Generall Gaole Delivery and they are hereby required upon motion to them made in open Court the last day of the Terme Sessions or Goale-Delivery either by the Prisoner or any one in his behalfe to sett at Liberty the Prisoner upon Baile unlesse it appeare to the Judges and Justices upon Oath made that the Witnesses for the King could not be produced the same Terme Sessions or Generall Goale-Delivery. And if any person or persons committed as aforesaid upon his Prayer or Petition in open Court the first weeke of the Terme or first day of the Sessions of Oyer and Terminer or Generall Goale Delivery to be brought to his Tryall shall not be indicted and tryed the second Terme Sessions of Oyer and Terminer or Generall Goale Delivery after his Committment or upon his Tryall shall be acquitted he shall be discharged from his Imprisonment.[1]

VII. Provided alwayes That nothing in this Act shall extend to discharge out of Prison any person charged in Debt or other Action or with Processe in any Civill Cause but that after he shall be discharged of his Imprisonment for such his Criminall Offence he shall be kept in Custodie according to Law for such other Suite.

VIII. Provided alwaies and bee it enacted by the Authoritie aforesaid That if any person or persons Subject of this Realme shall be committed to any Prison or in Custodie of any Officer or Officers whatsoever for any Criminall or supposed Criminall matter That the said person shall not be removed from the said Prison and Custody into the Custody of any other Officer or Officers unlesse it be by Habeas Corpus or some other Legall Writt or where the Prisoner is delivered to the Constable or other inferiour Officer to carry such Prisoner to some Common Goale or where any person is sent by Order of any Judge of Assize or Justice of the Peace to any common Worke-house or House of Correction or where the Prisoner is removed from one Prison or place to another within the same County in order to his or her Tryall or Discharge in due course of Law or in case of suddaine Fire or Infection or other necessity and if any person or persons shall after such Committ-

---

[1] Cf. Vol. II, Sect. A, No. V, p. 7, for an example of statutory extension of time during which a prisoner could be held in gaol.

ment aforesaid make out and signe or countersigne any Warrant or Warrants for such removeall aforesaid contrary to this Act as well he that makes or signes or countersignes such Warrant or Warrants as the Officer or Officers that obey or execute the same shall suffer and incurr the Paines and Forfeitures in this Act beforementioned both for the first and second Offence respectively to be recovered in manner aforesaid by the Partie grieved.

IX. Provided alsoe and bee it further enacted by the Authoritie aforesaid That it shall and may be lawfull to and for any Prisoner and Prisoners as aforesaid to move and obtaine his or their Habeas Corpus as well out of the High Court of Chauncery or Court of Exchequer as out of the Courts of Kings Bench or Common Pleas or either of them And if the said Lord Chauncellor or Lord Keeper or any Judge or Judges Baron or Barons for the time being of the Degree of the Coife or any of the Courts aforesaid in the Vacation time upon view of the Copy or Copies of the Warrant or Warrants of Committment or Detainer or upon Oath made that such Copy or Copyes were denyed as aforesaid shall deny any Writt of Habeas Corpus by this Act required to be granted being moved for as aforesaid they shall severally forfeite to the Prisoner or Partie grieved the summe of Five hundred pounds to be recovered in manner aforesaid.

X. And bee it enacted and declared by the Authority aforesaid That an Habeas Corpus according to the true intent and meaning of this Act may be directed and runn into any County Palatine The Cinque Ports or other priviledged Places within the Kingdome of England Dominion of Wales or Towne of Berwicke upon Tweede and the Islands of Jersey or Guernsey Any Law or Usage to the contrary notwithstanding.

XI. And for preventing illegall Imprisonments in Prisons beyond the Seas Bee it further enacted by the Authoritie aforesaid That noe Subject of this Realme that now is or hereafter shall be an Inhabitant or Resiant of this Kingdome of England Dominion of Wales or Towne of Berwicke upon Tweede shall or may be sent Prisoner into Scotland Ireland Jersey Gaurnsey Tangeir or into other Parts Garrisons Islands or Places beyond the Seas which are or at any time hereafter shall be within or without the Dominions of His Majestie His Heires or Successors and that every such Imprisonment is hereby enacted and adjudged to be illegall and that if any of the said Subjects now is or hereafter shall bee soe imprisoned every such person and persons soe imprisoned shall and may for every such Imprisonment maintaine by vertue of this Act an Action or Actions of false Imprisonment in any of His Majestyes Courts of Record against the person or persons by whome he or she shall be soe committed detained imprisoned sent Prisoner or transported contrary to the true meaning of this Act and against all or any person or persons that shall frame contrive write seale or countersigne any Warrant or Writeing for such Committment Detainer Imprisonment or Transportation or shall be adviseing aiding or assisting in the same or any of them and the Plaintiffe in every such Action shall have Judgement to recover his treble Costs besides Damages which Damages soe to be given shall not be lesse then Five hundred pounds in which Action noe delay stay or stopp of Proceeding by Rule Order or Command nor noe Injunction Protection or Priviledge whatsoever nor any more then one Imparlance shall be allowed excepting such Rule of the Court wherein the Action shall depend made in open Court as shall bee thought in Justice necessary for speciall cause to be expressed in the said Rule and the person or persons who shall knowingly frame contrive write seale or countersigne any Warrant for such Committment Detainer or Transportation or shall soe committ detaine imprison or transport any person or persons contrary to this Act or be any wayes adviseing aiding or assisting therein being lawfully convicted thereof shall be disabled from thenceforth to beare any Office of Trust or Proffitt within the said Realme of England Dominion of Wales or Towne of Berwicke upon Tweede or any of the Islands Territories or Dominions thereunto belonging and shall incurr and sustaine the Paines Penalties and Forfeitures limitted ordained and provided in and by the Statute of Provision and Premunire made in the Sixteenth yeare of King Richard the Second and be incapeable of any Pardon from the King His Heires or Successors of the said Forfeitures Losses or Disabilities or any of them.

XII. Provided alwayes That nothing in this Act shall extend to give benefitt to any person who shall by Contract in writeing agree with any Merchant or Owner of any Plantation or other person whatsoever to be transported to any parts beyond the Seas and receive earnest upon such Agreement although that afterwards such person shall renounce such Contract.

XIII. Provided alwayes and bee it enacted That if any person or persons lawfully convicted of any Felony shall in open Court pray to be transported beyond the Seas and the Court shall thinke fitt to leave him or them in Prison for that purpose such person or persons may be transported into any parts beyond the Seas This Act or any thing therein contained to the contrary notwithstanding.

XIV. Provided alsoe and bee it enacted That nothing herein contained shall be deemed construed or taken to extend to the Imprisonment of any person before the First day of June One thousand six hundred seaventy and nine or to any thing advised procured or otherwise done relateing to such Imprisonment Any thing herein contained to the contrary notwithstanding.

XV. Provided alsoe That if any person or persons at any time resiant in this Realme shall have committed any Capitall Offence in Scotland or Ireland or any of the Islands or Forreigne Plantations of the King His Heires or Successors where he or she ought to be tryed for such Offence such person or persons may be sent to such place there to receive such Tryall in such manner as the same might have beene used before the makeing of this Act Any thing herein contained to the contrary notwithstanding.

XVI. Provided alsoe and bee it enacted That noe person or persons shall be sued impleaded molested or troubled for any Offence against this Act unlesse the Partie offending be sued or impleaded for the same within Two yeares at the most after such time wherein the Offence shall be committed in case the partie grieved shall not be then in Prison and if he shall be in Prison then within the space of Two yeares after the decease of the Person imprisoned or his or her delivery out of Prison which shall first happen.

XVII. And to the intent noe person may avoid his Tryall at the Assizes or Generall Gaole-Delivery by procureing his Removeall before the Assizes at such time as he cannot be brought backe to receive his Tryall there Bee it enacted That after the Assizes proclaimed for that County where the Prisoner is detained noe person shall be removed from the Common Gaole upon any Habeas Corpus granted in pursuance of this Act but upon any such Habeas Corpus shall be brought before the Judge of Assize in open Court who is thereupon to doe what to Justice shall appertaine.

XVIII. Provided neverthelesse That after the Assizes are ended any person or persons detained may have his or her Habeas Corpus according to the Direction and Intention of this Act.

XIX. And bee it also enacted by the Authoritie aforesaid That if any Information Suite or Action shall be brought or exhibited against any person or persons for any Offence committed or to be committed against the Forme of this Law it shall be lawfull for such Defendants to pleade the Generall Issue that they are not guilty or that they owe nothing and to give such speciall matter in Evidence to the Jury that shall try the same which matter being pleaded had beene good and sufficient matter in Law to have discharged the said Defendant or Defendants against the said Information Suite or Action and the said matter shall be then as availeable to him or them to all intents and purposes as if he or they had sufficiently pleaded sett forth or alledged the same matter in Barr or Discharge of such Information Suite or Action.

XX. And because many times Persons charged with Petty Treason or Felony or as Accessaries thereunto are committed upon Suspicion onely whereupon they are Baileable or not according as the Circumstances makeing out that Suspicion are more or lesse weighty which are best knowne to the Justices of Peace that committed the persons and have Examinations before them or to other Justices of the Peace in the County Bee it therefore enacted That where any person shall appeare to be committed by any Judge or Justice of the Peace and charged as Accessary before the Fact to any Petty Treason or Felony or upon Suspicion thereof or with Suspicion of Petty Treason or Felony which Petty Treason or Felony shall be plainely and specially expressed in the Warrant of Committment that such Person shall not be removed or bailed by vertue of this Act or in any other manner then they might have beene before the makeing of this Act.

XIX

LEGALIZATION OF THE CONVENTION PARLIAMENT,[1] 1689

1 Will. & Mar., c. 1.

For preventing all Doubts and Scruples which may in any wise arise concerning the Meeting Sitting and Proceeding of this present Parlyament Bee it Declared and Enacted . . . That the Lords Spirituall and Temporall and Commons Convened at Westminster the Two and twentyeth day of January in the Yeare of Our Lord One thousand six hundred eighty eight and there Sitting on the Thirteenth day of February following are the Two Houses of Parlyament and soe shall be and are hereby Declared Enacted and Adjudged to be to all Intents Constructions and Purposes whatsoever Notwithstanding any want of Writt or Writts of Summons or any other defect of Forme or Default whatsoever as if they had beene Summoned according to the usuall Forme, And that this present Act and all other Acts, to which the Royall Assent shall at any time be given before the next Prorogation after the said Thirteenth of February shall be Understood Taken and Adjudged in Law to Beginne and Commence upon the said Thirteenth of February on which Day Their said Majestyes at the Request and by the Advice of the Lords and Commons Did

[1] See Sect. A, No. I, p. 1, and No. VI, p. 10, and No. XXVI, p. 74. For Summons see Sect. B, No. XII, p. 186.

Accept the Crowne and Royall Dignity of King and Queene of England France and Ireland and the Dominions and Territories thereto belonging.

. . . . . .

[§ II repeals 30 Car. II, St. II, c. 1[1] and other Acts in so far as they required Members of either House to take oaths therein prescribed.]

[§ III provides that the taking of the oaths prescribed by this Act shall be as effectual as taking the oaths prescribed by the Act repealed, and that members of future Parliaments shall take the oaths prescribed by this Act.]

IV. And it is hereby further Enacted [2] . . . That the Oathes above appointed by this Act to be taken in the stead and place of the Oathes of Allegiance and Supremacy, shall be in the Words following and noe other.

I, A B Doe sincerely Promise and Sweare that I will be Faithfull and beare true Allegiance to Their Majestyes King William and Queene Mary Soe helpe me God.

I, A B Doe Sweare that I doe from my Heart Abhorr Detest and Abjure as Impious and Hereticall that damnable Doctrine and Position That Princes Excommunicated or Deprived by the Pope or any Authoritie of the See of Rome may be Deposed or Murthered by their Subjects or any other whatsoever And I doe Declare that noe Forreigne Prince, Person, Prelate State or Potentate hath or ought to have any Power Jurisdiction Superiority Preeminence or Authoritie Ecclesiasticall or Spirituall within this Realme Soe helpe me God.

V. Provided alwayes and be it Declared That this present Parlyament may be Dissolved after the usuall manner as if the same had been Summoned and called by Writt.

XX

THE MUTINY ACT,[3] 1689

1 Will. & Mar., c. 5.

Whereas the raising or keeping a Standing Army within this Kingdome in time of Peace unlesse it be with Consent of Parlyament is against Law And whereas it is judged necessary by Their

[1] Sect. A, No. XVII, p. 43.

[2] See Sect. A, No. XXII, p. 60, and No. XXIV, p. 63.

[3] See Sect. A, No. VII, p. 11, and Sect. B, No. XXIV, p. 210.   See also Vol. II, Sect. A, No. XXXVII, p. 124, and Sect. B, No. XX, p. 194, and Sect. C, No. II, p. 237.

Majestyes and this present Parliament That dureing this time of Danger severall of the Forces which are now on foote should be continued and others raised for the Safety of the Kingdome for the Common Defence of the Protestant Religion and for the reduceing of Ireland

And whereas noe Man may be forejudged of Life or Limbe or subjected to any kinde of punishment by Martiall Law or in any other manner then by the Judgement of his Peeres and according to the knowne and Established Laws of this Realme Yet nevertheless it being requisite for retaineing such Forces as are or shall be raised dureing this Exigence of Affaires in their Duty an exact Discipline be observed And that Soldiers who shall Mutiny or stirr up Sedition or shall desert Their Majestyes Service be brought to a more Exemplary and speedy Punishment then the usuall Forms of Law will allow

II. Bee it therefore Enacted . . . That from and after the Twelfth day of Aprill in the Yeare of our Lord One thousand six hundred eighty nine every Person being in Their Majestyes Service in the Army and being Mustered and in Pay as an Officer or Soldier who shall at any time before the Tenth Day of November in the Yeare of our Lord One thousand six hundred eighty nine Excite Cause or Joyne in any Mutiny or Sedition in the Army or shall desert Their Majestyes Service in the Army shall suffer Death or such other Punishment as by a Court-Martiall shall be Inflicted

III. And it is hereby further Enacted and Declared That Their Majestyes or the Generall of Their Army for the time being may by vertue of this Act have full Power and Authority to grant Commissions to any Lieftenants Generall or other Officers not under the Degree of Collonells from time to time to Call and Assemble Court Martialls for Punishing such Offences as aforesaid

IV. And it is hereby further Enacted and Declared That noe Court Martiall which shall have power to inflict any punishment by vertue of this Act for the Offences aforesaid shall consist of fewer then thirteene whereof none to be under the degree of Captaines.

V. Provided alwayes That noe Field Officer be Tryed by other then Field Officers And that such Court Martiall shall have Power and Authoritie to administer an Oath to any Witnesse in order to the Examination or Tryall of the Offences aforesaid

VI. Provided alwayes that nothing in this Act contained shall extend or be construed to Exempt any Officer or Soldier whatsoever from the Ordinary Processe of Law

VII. Provided alwayes That this Act or any thing therein contained shall not extend or be any wayes construed to extend to or concerne any the Militia Forces of this Kingdome [1]

[1] See, however, Sect. A, No. LIII, § XLV, p. 137.

VIII. Provided alsoe that this Act shall continue and be in Force untill the said Tenth day of November in the said Yeare of our Lord One thousand six hundred eighty nine and noe longer [1]

IX. Provided alwayes and bee it enacted That in all Tryalls of Offenders by Courts Martiall to be held by vertue of this Act where the Offence may be punished by death every Officer present at such Tryall before any Proceeding be had thereupon shall take an Oath upon the Evangelists before the Court (and the Judge Advocate or his Deputy shall and are hereby respectively Authorized to Administer the same) in these words That is to say

You shall well and truely Try and Determine according to your Evidence the Matter now before you betweene Our Soveraigne Lord and Lady the King and Queens Majestyes and the Prisoner to be Tryed.   Soe helpe you God.

X. And noe Sentence of Death shall be given against any Offender in such Case by any Court Martiall unlesse nine of Thirteene Officers present shall concurr therein And if there be a greater number of Officers present then the Judgment shall passe by the concurrence of the greater part of them soe Sworne and not otherwise and noe Proceedings Tryall or Sentence of Death shall be had or given against any Offender but betweene the houres of Eight in the Morning and One in the Afternoone.

Why ? co people drunk & incapable then [handwritten marginal note]

XXI

CORONATION OATH ACT, 1689

1 Will. & Mar., c. 6.

Whereas by the Law and Ancient Usage of this Realme the Kings and Queens thereof have taken a Solemne Oath upon the Evangelists at Their respective Coronations to maintaine the Statutes Laws and Customs of the said Realme and all the People and Inhabitants thereof in their Spirituall and Civill Rights and Properties But forasmuch as the Oath itselfe on such Occasion Administred hath heretofore beene framed in doubtfull Words and Expressions with relation to ancient Laws and Constitutions at this time unknowne To the end therefore that One Uniforme Oath may be in all Times to come taken by the Kings and Queens of this Realme and to Them respectively Administred at the times of Their and every of Their Coronation.

[1] This Act was annually renewed with additions such as the statutory power to make Articles of War (1 Anne, St. II, c. 20) which (4 Geo. I, c. 4) operated within the Kingdom as well as in overseas dominions. Articles of War for troops in foreign territories continued to rest on Prerogative until 53 Geo. III, c. 17.

II. May it please Your Majesties That it may be Enacted And bee it Enacted . . . That the Oath herein Mentioned and hereafter Expressed shall and may be Administered to their most Excellent Majestyes King William and Queene Mary (whome God long preserve) at the time of Their Coronation in the presence of all Persons that shall be then and there present at the Solemnizeing thereof by the Archbishop of Canterbury or the Archbishop of Yorke or either of them or any other Bishop of this Realme whome the King's Majesty shall thereunto appoint and who shall be hereby thereunto respectively Authorized which Oath followeth and shall be Administred in this Manner that is to say,

[§ III. For the text of the Coronation Oath as here enacted see under.]

IV. And bee it further Enacted That the said Oath shall be in like manner Administred to every King or Queene that shall Succeede to the Imperiall Crowne of this Realme at their respective Coronations . . .

THE CORONATION OATH

1660.	1689.
(*From The Forms of Prayers (etc.) at the Coronation . . . London, Printed for Randal Taylor, 1689.*)	(*As prescribed by the Act 1 Will. & Mar., c. 6.*)

The Arch-Bishop or Bishop shall say,

Sir, Will you grant and keep, and by your Oath Confirm to the People of *England* the Laws and Customs to them granted by the Kings of *England* your Lawful and Religious predecessors, and namely, the Laws, Customs and Franchises granted to the Clergy by the Glorious King *St. Edward* your Predecessor, according to the Laws of God, the true Profession of the Gospel Established in this Kingdom, and agreeable to the Prerogative of the Kings thereof, and the Ancient Customs of the Realm?	Will You solemnely Promise and Sweare to Governe the People of this Kingdome of England and the Dominions thereto belonging according to the Statutes in Parlyament Agreed on and the Laws and Customs of the same?

King. I grant and promise to keep them.

The King and Queene shall say,

I solemnly Promise soe to doe.

Archbp. Sir, will you keep peace and Godly Agreement (according to your Power) both to God, the Holy Church, the Clergy and the People?

King. I will keep it.

Archbp. Sir, will you (to your

Arch Bishop or Bishop, Will

power) cause Law, Justice and Discretion to Mercy and Truth to be executed to your Judgment?

King. I will.

Archbp. Sir, Will you grant to hold and keep the Laws and Rightful Customs which the Commonalty of this your Kingdom have? And will you defend and uphold them to the Honour of God, so much as in you lyeth?

King. I grant and promise so to do.

Then one of the Bishops read this passage to the King

Our Lord and King, We beseech you to pardon and to grant and to preserve unto us, and to the Churches committed to your Charge all Canonical Priviledges, and due Law and Justice, and that you would protect and defend us, as every good King in his Kingdoms ought to be Protector and Defender of the Bishops and the Churches under their Government.

The King answereth. With a willing and Devout Heart I promise and grant my pardon; and that I will preserve and maintain to you, and the Churches committed to your Charge, all Canonical priviledges, and due Law and Justice, and that I will be your Protector and Defender to my power, by the assistance of God, as every good King in his Kingdom in right ought to Protect and Defend the Bishops and Churches under their Government.

Then the King arose, and was led to the Communion Table, where he takes a Solemn Oath in sight of all the People, to observe all the Premisses and laying his hand upon the Bible, said,

The things which I have here Promised, I shall perform and keep; So Help me God, and the Contents of this Book.

You to Your power cause Law and Justice in Mercy to be Executed in all Your Judgments

King and Queene. I will.

Arch Bishop or Bishop. Will You to the utmost of Your power Maintaine the Laws of God the true Profession of the Gospell and the Protestant Reformed Religion Established by Law? And will You Preserve unto the Bishops and Clergy of this Realme and to the Churches committed to their Charge all such Rights and Priviledges as by Law doe or shall appertaine unto them or any of them.

King and Queene. All this I Promise to doe.

After this the King and Queene laying His and Her Hand upon the Holy Gospells, shall say

The things which I have here before promised I will performe and Keepe, Soe help me God.

Then the King and Queene shall kisse the Booke.

XXII

THE OATHS OF SUPREMACY AND ALLEGIANCE, 1689

1 Will. & Mar., c. 8.

[§ I recites Oaths of Supremacy and Allegiance mentioned in 1 Eliz. c. 1 : 3 & 4 Jac. I, c. 4.[1]]

[§ II abrogates these oaths.]

[§§ III and IV provides the new oaths to be taken by all Bishops and Peers, and before whom.]

[§ V that all persons in office are to take the oath, on penalty.]

[§ VI of voiding the office.]

VII. And bee it further Enacted . . . That if any ArchBishop or Bishop or any other Person now haveing any Ecclesiasticall Dignitie Benefice or Promotion shall neglect or refuse to take the Oathes by this Act appointed . . . Every such Person . . . is . . . Suspended from the Execution of his . . . Office by the Space of Six months . . . And if the said Person . . . shall not within the said space of Six months take the said Oathes . . . then he . . . shall be ipso facto deprived of his . . . Office Benefice Dignity and Promotion Ecclesiasticall.

[§ VIII. The same procedure and penalty of suspension and deprivation provided for any master, governor, head or fellow of any college or hall, in either of the two universities, or of any other college, or master of any hospital or school, or professor of divinity, law, physic or other science in either of the universities, or in the city of London.]

[§ IX. Penalties for refusal to take the oath duly tendered. A third refusal to do so shall render the person refusing incapable of holding any office, and liable, if he refuses the Declaration in 30 Car. II, St. II, c. 1, to be deemed a " popish recusant convict ".]

[§ X. Land and sea officers to take the oath.]

XI. And bee it further enacted That the Oath appointed by the Statute [2] made in the Thirteenth Yeare of King Charles the Second, . . . The Forme and Words of which Oath are in the same Statute expressed And alsoe soe much of a Declaration prescribed in another Act made in the same Yeare Entituled An Act for the Uniformity of Publick Prayers . . . as is expressed in these Words (viz)

I A B Declare That it is not Lawfull upon any Pretence whatsoever to take Arms against the King and that I doe abhor that Traiterous Position of takeing Arms by His Authority against His

---

[1] See Prothero, pp. 1 and 256.

[2] Sect. A, No. IX, p. 15, and Sect. A, No. XI, § VIII, p. 25.

Person or against those that are Commissioned by Him. Shall not from henceforth be required or enjoyned nor any Person suffer any Forfeiture Penalty or Losse by the not takeing subscribeing or makeing the said Oath or the said recited part of the said Declaration The last forementioned Statutes or any other Law or Statute to the contrary notwithstanding.

XII. And bee it Enacted That the Oathes that are intended and required to be taken by this Act are the Oathes in these expresse Words hereafter following ; . . .

[For the terms of the oaths see 1 Will. & Mar., c. 1.[1]]

[§ XIII. The names of all persons taking the oaths shall be inrolled in rolls kept only for that purpose.]

[§§ XIV and XV. Provision for members of corporations and officers who could not take the abrogated oaths.]

XVI. Provided alwayes . . . That it be left to the King to allow to such of the Clergy as shall refuse the Oaths prescribed by this Act as he shall thinke fitt not exceeding the number of Twelve an Allowance out of their Ecclesiasticall Benefices or Promotions for their Subsistance not exceeding a Third Part and to continue dureing His Majesties Pleasure and noe longer.

XXIII

EXPULSION OF PAPISTS FROM LONDON, 1689 [2]

1 Will. & Mar., c. 9.

Whereas the great numbers of Papists resorting to the Cityes of London and Westminster are and for a long time have beene found dangerous to the Peace and Safety of this Kingdome For the better Preservation of the Common Safety and avoiding their mischievous Practices and Designes

II. Bee it enacted . . . That for the better discovering and amoveing all Papists and reputed Papists out of the said Cities and Ten miles of the same it shall and may be lawfull and it is hereby Required that the Lord Mayor of London for the time being and every Justice of the Peace of the City of London and for the City and Liberties of Westminster and Burrough of Southwarke and of the Countyes of Midlesex Surrey Kent and Sussex within their respective Countyes Cityes Boroughes and Limitts doe from time

---

[1] Sect. A, No. XIX, p. 54.   [2] See Sect. A, No. XXXV, p. 90.

to time cause to be Arrested and brought before him every person or persons not being a Merchant Forreigner within the said Cities or within Ten miles of the same as are or are reputed to be Papists and tender unto him the Declaration mentioned in the Statute made in the Thirtyeth Yeare of King Charles the Second Entituled An Act for the more effectuall preserveing the Kings Person and Government by disableing Papists from Sitting in either House of Parlyament And in case such person upon such tender refuse audibly and solemnly to repeate make and subscribe the said Declaration and shall after such refusall remaine continue or be within the said City or Cityes or Ten miles distance from the same That in every such Case he or she shall forfeite and suffer as a Popish Recusant Convict by the Lawes already established shall or may forfeit or suffer

III. And it is hereby further Enacted That every Justice of Peace shall and doe certifie all and every Subscription before him by vertue of this Act taken and likewise the Names of all and every Person refuseing to repeate take make or subscribe as aforesaid . . . And if the said Person soe refuseing and certifyed shall not . . . in open Court audibly and solemnly repeate take make and subscribe the Declaration aforesaid and Indorse or Enter his soe doeing upon the Certificate soe returned shall be from the time of such his neglect or refusall taken esteemed and adjudged a Popish Recusant Convict and as such to forfeite and be proceeded against.

IV. Provided alwayes That this Act shall not extend to such person or persons as now use any Trade Mistery or Manuall Occupation within the said Liberties of London and Westminster or within ten miles of the same Nor to such as within Six months before the Thirteenth day of February One thousand six hundred eighty eight had their Dwellings or Places of abode within the said Cities or ten miles compasse of the same not haveing any Dwelling or Place of abode elsewhere soe as he or they before the First day of August One thousand six hundred eighty nine doe certifie his or their Names Additions and Places of abode at the Sessions of the Peace . . .

V. Provided that nothing in this Act shall relate to or have any effect upon any Forreigner that is or shall be a Meniall Servant to any Ambassador or Publicke Agent.

VI. Provided That nothing in this Act shall relate to or have any effect upon any person being a naturall borne Subject of the King of Portugall who now is or hereafter shall be a sworne Servant to the Queene Dowager nor to any other Servants being naturall borne Subjects of Their Majestyes . . . not exceeding the number of Thirty at any one time soe as none of the said Servants being naturall borne Subjects of their Majestyes be a Jesuite Priest Monke or Fryer Any Law or Statute to the contrary notwithstanding.

XXIV

THE TOLERATION ACT, 1689 [1]

1 Will. & Mar., c. 18.

An Act for Exempting their Majestyes Protestant Subjects dissenting from the Church of England from the Penalties of certaine Lawes.

Forasmuch as some ease to scrupulous Consciences in the Exercise of Religion may be an effectuall meanes to unite their Majestyes Protestant Subjects in Interest and Affection Bee it enacted . . . That neither the Statute made in the three and twentieth yeare of the Raigne of the late Queene Elizabeth Entituled An Act [2] to Retaine the Queens Majestyes Subjects in their due Obedience, Nor the Statute made in the twenty ninth yeare of the said Queene Intituled An Act [3] for the more speedy and due Execution of certaine Branches of the Statute made in the three and twentyeth yeare of the Queens Majestyes Raigne viz The aforesaid Act, nor that Branch or Clause of a Statute made in the first yeare of the Raigne of the said Queene Intituled An Act [4] for the Uniformity of Common Prayer and Service in the Church . . . whereby all persons haveing noe lawfull or reasonable excuse to be absent are required to resort to their Parish Church or Chappell or some usuall place where the Common Prayer shall be used upon paine of Punishment by the Censures of the Church and alsoe upon paine that every person soe offending shall forfeite for every such Offence twelve pence Nor the Statute [5] made in the third year of the Raigne of the late King James Intituled An Act for the better discovering and repressing Popish Recusants Nor that other Statute [6] made in the same yeare Intituled An Act to Prevent and Avoid Dangers which may grow by Popish Recusants Nor any other Law or Statute of this Realme made against Papists or Popish Recusants Except the Statute made in the five and twentyeth yeare of King Charles the

---

[1] See Sect. A, No. XLIII, § VII, p. 119.
[2] 23 Eliz., c. i. (Prothero, p. 74).
[3] 28 & 29 Eliz., c. 6 (Prothero, p. 88).
[4] 1 Eliz., c. 2 (Prothero, p. 13).
[5] 3 & 4 Jac. I, c. 4 (Prothero, p. 256).
[6] 3 & 4 Jac. I, c. 5 (Prothero, p. 262).

Second, Intituled An Act[1] for preventing Dangers which may happen from Popish Recusants And except alsoe the Statute made in the thirtyeth yeare of the said King Charles the Second Intituled An Act[2] for the more effectuall preserveing the Kings Person and Government by disableing Papists from sitting in either House of Parlyament Shall be construed to extend to any person or persons dissenting from the Church of England that shall take the Oaths mentioned in a Statute[3] made by this present Parliament . . . And shall make and subscribe the Declaration mentioned in a Statute made in the thirtyeth yeare of the Raigne of King Charles the Second[4] . . . Which Oaths and Declaration the Justices of Peace at the generall Sessions of the Peace . . . are hereby required to tender and administer to such persons as shall offer themselves to take make and subscribe the same and thereof to keepe a Register And likewise none of the persons aforesaid shall give or pay as any Fee or Reward to any Officer or Officers belonging to the Court aforesaid above the summe of six pence nor that more then once for his or their Entry of his takeing the said Oaths and makeing and subscribeing the said Declaration Nor above the further summe of six pence for any Certificate of the same to be made out and signed by the Officer or Officers of the said Court.

II. And bee it further enacted . . . That all . . . persons already convicted or prosecuted in order to Conviction of Recusancy . . . grounded upon the aforesaid Statutes or any of them that shall take the said Oaths mentioned in the said Statute made this present Parliament and make and subscribe the Declaration aforesaid . . . and to be thence respectively certified into the Exchequer shall be thenceforth exempted and discharged from all the Penalties Seizures Forfeitures Judgements and Executions incurred by force of any the aforesaid Statutes without any Composition Fee or further Charge whatsoever

III. And bee it further enacted . . . That all . . . persons that shall . . . take the said Oathes and make and subscribe the Declaration aforesaid shall not be lyable to any Paines Penalties or Forfeitures mentioned in an Act[5] made in the five and thirtyeth yeare of the Raigne of the late Queene Elizabeth . . . Nor in an Act[6] made in the two and twentyeth yeare of the Raigne of the late King Charles the Second . . . Nor shall any of the said persons be prosecuted in any Ecclesiasticall Court for or by reason of their Nonconforming to the Church of England

[1] 25 Car. II, c. 2 (see Sect. A, No. XVI, p. 39).
[2] 30 Car. II, St. II, c. 1 (see Sect. A, No. XVII, p. 43).
[3] 1 Will. & Mar., c. 1 (see Sect. A, No. XIX, p. 54).
[4] 30 Car. II, St. II, c. 1 (see Sect. A, No. XVII, p. 43).
[5] 35 Eliz., c. 1. (Prothero, p. 89).
[6] 22 Car. II, c. 1. (see Sect. A, No. XV, p. 36).

IV. Provided alwayes . . . That if any Assembly of persons dissenting from the Church of England shall be had in any place for Religious Worship with the doores locked barred or bolted dureing any time of such Meeting together all and every person or persons that shall come to and be at such Meeting shall not receive any benefitt from this Law but be lyable to all the Paines and Penalties of all the aforesaid Laws recited in this Act for such their Meeting notwithstanding his takeing the Oaths and his makeing and subscribing the Declaration aforesaid Provided alwayes That nothing herein contained shall . . . exempt any of the persons aforesaid from paying of Tythes or other Parochiall Duties or any other Duties to the Church or Minister nor from any Prosecution in any Ecclesiasticall Court or elsewhere for the same

[§ V allows local officers " scrupling the oaths " to act by deputy.]

VI. And bee it further enacted . . . That noe person dissenting from the Church of England in Holy Orders or pretended Holy Orders or pretending to Holy Orders nor any Preacher or Teacher of any Congregation of dissenting Protestants that shall make and subscribe the Declaration aforesaid and take the said Oaths . . . and shall alsoe declare his approbation of and subscribe the Articles of Religion mentioned in the Statute[1] made in the thirteenth yeare of the Raigne of the late Queene Elizabeth Except the thirty fourth thirty fifth and thirty sixth and these words of the twentyeth Article viz. (the Church hath power to decree Rights or Ceremonies and Authority in Controversies of Faith and yet) shall be lyable to any of the paines or penalties mentioned in an Act[2] made in the seventeenth yeare of the Raigne of King Charles the Second . . . Nor the penalties mentioned in the aforesaid Act[3] made in the two and twentyeth yeare of his said late Majesties Raigne for or by reason of such persons preaching at any Meeting for the Exercise of Religion Nor to the penalty of one hundred pounds mentioned in an Act made in the thirteenth and fourteenth of King Charles the Second[4] . . . for officiating in any Congregation for the Exercise of Religion permitted and allowed by this Act

. . . .

VII. And whereas some dissenting Protestants scruple the baptizeing of Infants Bee it enacted . . . That every person in pretended Holy Orders or pretending to Holy Orders or Preacher or Teacher that shall subscribe the aforesaid Articles of Religion Except before excepted and alsoe except part of the seven and

[1] 13 Eliz. c. 12. (Prothero, p. 64).
[2] 17 Car. II, c. 2 (see Sect. A, No. XIV, p. 34).
[3] 22 Car. II, c. 1 (see Sect. A, No. XV, p. 36).
[4] 14 Car. II, c. 4 (see Sect. A, No. XI, p. 20).

twentyeth Article touching Infant Baptisme and shall take the said Oathes and make and subscribe the Declaration aforesaid . . . every such person shall enjoy all the Privileges Benefitts and Advantages which any other dissenting Minister as aforesaid might have or enjoy by vertue of this Act

VIII. And bee it further enacted . . . That every Teacher or Preacher in Holy Orders or pretended Holy Orders that is a Minister Preacher or Teacher of a Congregation that shall take the Oathes herein required and make and subscribe the Declaration aforesaid And alsoe subscribe such of the aforesaid Articles of the Church of England as are required by this Act . . . shall be thenceforth exempted from serveing upon any Jury or from being chosen or appointed to beare the Office of Churchwarden Overseer of the Poore or any other Parochiall or Ward Office or other Office in any Hundred of any Shire City Towne Parish Division or Wapentake

[§ IX permits a justice of the peace to tender the oath to any person who attends a religious meeting and prescribes a penalty if the oath so tendered is not taken.]

X. And whereas there are certaine other persons Dissenters from the Church of England who scruple the takeing of any Oath Bee it enacted . . . That every such person shall make and sub- scribe the aforesaid Declaration and alsoe this Declaration of Fidelity following viz

I A. B. doe sincerely promise and solemnly declare before God and the World that I will be true and faithfull to King William and Queene Mary And I doe solemnly professe and Declare That I doe from my Heart Abhor Detest and Renounce as Impious and Hereticall that damnable Doctrine and Position That Princes Excommunicated or Deprived by the Pope or any Authority of the See of Rome may be Deposed or Murthered by their Subjects or any other what- soever And I doe declare that no Forreigne Prince Person Prelate State or Potentate hath or ought to have any Power Jurisdiction Superiority Preeminence or Authoritie Ecclesiasticall or Spirituall within this Realme.

And shall subscribe a Profession of their Christian Beliefe in these Words

I A B professe Faith in God the Father and in Jesus Christ His Eternall Sonne the true God and in the Holy Spirit one God blessed for evermore And doe acknowledge the Holy Scriptures of the Old and New Testament to be given by Divine Inspiration,

[The remainder of the section exempts all who make the subscrip- tion from penalties prescribed by 5 Eliz., c. 1 : 13 Car. II, St. II, c. 1, p. 15, and enables them to enjoy all other benefits conferred on Dissenters by this Act.]

[§§ XI and XII prescribe for " purging " after refusal of the oaths.]

XIII. Provided alwayes and it is the true intent and meaning of this Act That all the Laws made and provided for the frequenting of Divine Service on the Lords day commonly called Sunday shall be still in force and executed against all persons that offend against the said Laws except such persons come to some Congregation or Assembly of Religious Worship allowed or permitted by this Act

XIV. Provided alwayes . . . That neither this Act nor any Clause Article or Thing herein contained shall . . . extend to give any ease benefitt or advantage to any Papist or Popish Recusant whatsoever, or any person that shall deny in his Preaching or Writeing the Doctrine of the Blessed Trinity as it is declared in the aforesaid Articles of Religion

[§ XV prescribes penalties for disturbance of religious worship permitted by law.]

XVI. Provided alwayes That noe Congregation or Assembly for Religious Worship shall be permitted or allowed by this Act untill the place of such Meeting shall be certified to the Bishop of the Diocesse or to the Arch-Deacon of that Archdeaconry or to the Justices of the Peace at the Generall or Quarter Sessions of the Peace for the County City or Place in which such Meeting shall be held and registred in the said Bishops or Archdeacons Court respectively or recorded at the said Generall or Quarter Sessions the Register or Clerke of the Peace whereof respectively is hereby required to register the same and to give Certificate thereof to such person as shall demand the same for which there shall be none greater Fee nor Reward taken then the Summe of six pence.

XXV

THE BILL OF RIGHTS, 1689
1 Will. & Mar., Sess. 2, c. 2.

An Act declareing the Rights and Liberties of the Subject and Setleing the Succession of the Crowne.

I. Whereas the Lords Spirituall and Temporall and Commons assembled at Westminster lawfully fully and freely representing all the Estates of the People of this Realme did upon the thirteenth day of February in the yeare of our Lord one thousand six hundred eighty eight present unto their Majesties then called and known by the Names and Stile of William and Mary Prince and Princesse of Orange being present in their proper Persons a certaine Declaration in Writeing made by the said Lords and Commons in the Words following viz

Whereas the late King James the Second by the Assistance of diverse evill Councellors Judges and Ministers imployed by him did endeavour to subvert and extirpate the Protestant Religion and the Lawes and Liberties of this Kingdome

By Assumeing and Excerciseing a Power of Dispensing [1] with and Suspending [2] of Lawes and the Execution of Lawes without Consent of Parlyament.

By Committing and Prosecuting diverse Worthy Prelates for humbly Petitioning to bee excused from Concurring to the said Assumed Power.

By issueing and causeing to be executed a Commission under the Great Seale for Erecting a Court called The Court of Commissioners for Ecclesiasticall Causes.

By Levying Money for and to the Use of the Crowne by pretence of Prerogative for other time and in other manner then the same was granted by Parlyament.

By raising and keeping a Standing Army within this Kingdome in time of Peace without Consent of Parlyament and Quartering Soldiers contrary to Law.

By causing severall good Subjects being Protestants to be disarmed at the same time when Papists were both Armed and Imployed contrary to Law.

By Violating the Freedome of Election of Members to Serve in Parlyament.[3]

By Prosecutions in the Court of Kings Bench for Matters and Causes cognizable onely in Parlyament and by diverse other Arbitrary and Illegal Courses.

And whereas of late yeares Partiall Corrupt and Unqualifyed Persons have beene returned and served on Juryes in Tryalls and Particularly diverse Jurors in Tryalls for High Treason which were not Freeholders,

And excessive Baile hath beene required of Persons committed in Criminall Cases to elude the Benefitt of the Lawes made for the Liberty of the Subjects.

And excessive Fines have beene imposed.

And illegall and cruell Punishments inflicted.

And severall Grants and Promises made of Fines or Forfeitures before any Conviction or Judgement against the Persons upon whome the same were to be levyed.

All which are utterly and directly contrary to the knowne Lawes and Statutes and Freedome of this Realme.

[1] See Sect. C, No. VI, p. 256.
[2] See Sect. C, No. VII, p. 258, and Sect. D, No. XVI, p. 343.
[3] See Sect. D, No. XVII (C), p. 348.

And whereas the said late King James the Second haveing Abdicated the Government and the Throne being thereby Vacant His Highnesse the Prince of Orange (whome it hath pleased Almighty God to make the glorious Instrument of Delivering this Kingdome from Popery and Arbitrary Power) did (by the Advice of the Lords Spirituall and Temporall and diverse principall Persons of the Commons) cause Letters[1] to be written to the Lords Spirituall and Temporall being Protestants and other Letters to the severall Countyes Cityes Universities Burroughs and Cinque Ports for the Choosing of such Persons to represent them as were of right to be sent to Parlyament to meete and sitt at Westminster upon the two and twentyeth day of January in this Yeare One thousand six hundred eighty and eight in order to such an Establishment as that their Religion Lawes and Liberties might not againe be in danger of being Subverted, Upon which Letters Elections haveing beene accordingly made.

And thereupon the said Lords Spirituall and Temporall and Commons pursuant to their respective Letters and Elections being now assembled in a full and free Representative of this Nation takeing into their most serious Consideration the best meanes for attaining the Ends aforesaid Doe in the first place (as their Auncestors in like Case have usually done) for the Vindicating and Asserting their auntient Rights and Liberties, Declare

That the pretended Power of Suspending of Laws or the Execution of Laws by Regall Authority without Consent of Parlyament is illegall.

That the pretended Power of Dispensing with Laws or the Execution of Laws by Regall Authoritie as it hath beene assumed and exercised of late is illegall.

That the Commission for erecting the late Court of Commissioners for Ecclesiasticall Causes and all other Commissions and Courts of like nature are Illegall and Pernicious.[2]

That levying Money for or to the Use of the Crowne by pretence of Prerogative without Grant of Parlyament for longer time or in other manner then the same is or shall be granted is Illegall.

That it is the Right of the Subjects to petition the King and all Commitments and Prosecutions for such Petitioning are Illegall.

That the raising or keeping a standing Army within the Kingdome in time of Peace unlesse it be with Consent of Parlyament is against Law.

That the Subjects which are Protestants may have Arms for their Defence suitable to their Conditions and as allowed by Law.

That Election of Members of Parlyament ought to be free.

[1] Sect. B, No. XII (B), p. 187.   [2] See Sect. A, No. VIII, § II, p. 14.

That the Freedome of Speech and Debates or Proceedings in Parlyament ought not to be impeached or questioned in any Court or Place out of Parlyament.

That excessive Baile ought not to be required nor excessive Fines imposed nor cruell and unusuall Punishments inflicted.

That Jurors ought to be duely impannelled and returned and Jurors which passe upon Men in Trialls for High Treason ought to be Freeholders.

That all Grants and Promises of Fines and Forfeitures of particular persons before Conviction are illegall and void.

And that for Redresse of all Grievances and for the amending strengthening and preserving of the Lawes Parlyaments ought to be held frequently.

And they doe Claime Demand and Insist upon all and singular the Premises as their undoubted Rights and Liberties and that noe Declarations Judgements Doeings or Proceedings to the Prejudice of the People in any of the said Premisses ought in any wise to be drawne hereafter into Consequence or Example. To which Demand of their Rights they are particularly encouraged by the Declaration of his Highnesse the Prince of Orange as being the onely meanes for obtaining a full Redresse and Remedy therein. Haveing therefore an intire Confidence That his said Highnesse the Prince of Orange will perfect the Deliverance soe farr advanced by him and will still preserve them from the Violation of their Rights which they have here asserted and from all other Attempts upon their Religion Rights and Liberties. The said Lords Spirituall and Temporall and Commons assembled at Westminster doe Resolve That William and Mary Prince and Princesse of Orange be and be declared King and Queene of England France and Ireland and the Dominions thereunto belonging to hold the Crowne and Royall Dignity of the said Kingdomes and Dominions to them the said Prince and Princesse dureing their Lives and the Life of the Survivour of them And that the sole and full Exercise of the Regall Power be onely in and executed by the said Prince of Orange in the Names of the said Prince and Princesse dureing their joynt Lives And after their Deceases the said Crowne and Royall Dignitie of the said Kingdoms and Dominions to be to the Heires of the Body of the said Princesse And for default of such Issue to the Princesse Anne of Denmarke and the Heires of her Body And for default of such Issue to the Heires of the Body of the said Prince of Orange. And the Lords Spirituall and Temporall and Commons doe pray the said Prince and Princesse to accept the same accordingly.

And that the Oathes hereafter mentioned be taken by all Persons of whome the Oathes of Allegiance and Supremacy might be required by Law instead of them And that the said Oathes of Allegiance and Supremacy be abrogated.

I A B doe sincerely promise and sweare That I will be faithfull and beare true Allegiance to their Majestyes King William and Queene Mary   Soe helpe me God.

I A B doe sweare That I doe from my Heart Abhorr, Detest and Abjure as Impious and Hereticall this damnable Doctrine and Position That Princes Excommunicated or Deprived by the Pope or any Authority of the See of Rome may be deposed or murdered by their Subjects or any other whatsoever. And I doe declare That noe Forreigne Prince Person Prelate, State or Potentate hath or ought to have any Jurisdiction Power Superiority Preeminence or Authoritie Ecclesiasticall or Spirituall within this Realme   So helpe me God.

Upon which their said Majestyes did accept the Crowne and Royall Dignitie of the Kingdoms of England France and Ireland and the Dominions thereunto belonging according to the Resolution and Desire of the said Lords and Commons contained in the said Declaration. And thereupon their Majestyes were pleased That the said Lords Spirituall and Temporall and Commons being the two Houses of Parlyament should continue to sitt and with their Majestyes Royall Concurrence make effectuall Provision for the Setlement of the Religion Lawes and Liberties of this Kingdome soe that the same for the future might not be in danger againe of being subverted, To which the said Lords Spirituall and Temporall and Commons did agree and proceede to act accordingly. Now in pursuance of the Premisses the said Lords Spirituall and Temporall and Commons in Parlyament assembled for the ratifying confirming and establishing the said Declaration and the Articles Clauses Matters and Things therein contained by the Force of a Law made in due Forme by Authority of Parlyament doe pray that it may be declared and enacted That all and singular the Rights and Liberties asserted and claimed in the said Declaration are the true auntient and indubitable Rights and Liberties of the People of this Kingdome and soe shall be esteemed allowed adjudged deemed and taken to be and that all and every the particulars aforesaid shall be firmly and strictly holden and observed as they are expressed in the said Declaration And all Officers and Ministers whatsoever shall serve their Majestyes and their Successors according to the same in all times to come. And the said Lords Spirituall and Temporall and Commons seriously considering how it hath pleased Almighty God in his marvellous Providence and mercifull Goodness to this Nation to provide and preserve their said Majestyes Royall Persons most happily to Raigne over us upon the Throne of their Auncestors for which they render unto him from the bottome of their Hearts

their humblest Thanks and Praises doe truely firmely and assuredly
and in the Sincerity of their Hearts thinke and doe hereby recognize
acknowledge and declare That King James the Second haveing
abdicated the Government and their Majestyes haveing accepted
the Crowne and Royall Dignity as aforesaid Their said Majestyes
did become were are and of right ought to be by the Lawes
of this Realme our Soveraigne Liege Lord and Lady King and
Queene of England France and Ireland and the Dominions thereunto belonging in and to whose Princely Persons the Royall State
Crowne and Dignity of the said Realmes with all Honours Stiles
Titles Regalities Prerogatives Powers Jurisdictions and Authorities
to the same belonging and appertaining are most fully rightfully
and intirely invested and incorporated united and annexed And for
preventing all Questions and Divisions in this Realme by reason
of any pretended Titles to the Crowne and for preserveing a Certainty in the Succession thereof in and upon which the Unity Peace
Tranquillity and Safety of this Nation doth under God wholly
consist and depend The said Lords Spirituall and Temporall and
Commons doe beseech their Majestyes That it may be enacted
established and declared That the Crowne and Regall Government
of the said Kingdoms and Dominions with all and singular the
Premisses thereunto belonging and appertaining shall bee and continue to their said Majestyes and the Survivour of them dureing
their Lives and the Life of the Survivour of them And that the
entire perfect and full Exercise of the Regall Power and Government
be onely in and executed by his Majestie in the Names of both their
Majestyes dureing their joynt Lives And after their deceases the said
Crowne and Premisses shall be and remaine to the Heires of the
Body of her Majestie and for default of such Issue to her Royall
Highnesse the Princess Anne of Denmarke and the Heires of her
Body and for default of such Issue to the Heires of the Body of his said
Majestie [1] And thereunto the said Lords Spirituall and Temporall and
Commons doe in the Name of all the People aforesaid most humbly
and faithfully submitt themselves their Heires and Posterities for
ever and doe faithfully promise That they will stand to maintaine and
defend their said Majesties and alsoe the Limitation and Succession
of the Crowne herein specified and contained to the utmost of their
Powers with their Lives and Estates against all Persons whatsoever
that shall attempt any thing to the contrary.   And whereas it hath
beene found by Experience that it is inconsistent with the Safety
and Welfaire of this Protestant Kingdome to be governed by a Popish
Prince or by any King or Queene marrying a Papist the said Lords
Spirituall and Temporall and Commons doe further pray that it

[1] See Act of Settlement: Sect. A, No. XXXVI, p. 92.

may be enacted That all and every person and persons that is are or shall be reconciled to or shall hold Communion with the See or Church of Rome or shall professe the Popish Religion or shall marry a Papist shall be excluded and be for ever uncapeable to inherit possesse or enjoy the Crowne and Government of this Realme and Ireland and the Dominions thereunto belonging or any part of the same or to have use or excercise any Regall Power Authoritie or Jurisdiction within the same [And in all and every such Case or Cases the People of these Realmes shall be and are hereby absolved of their Allegiance[1]] And the said Crowne and Government shall from time to time descend to and be enjoyed by such person or persons being Protestants as should have inherited and enjoyed the same in case the said person or persons soe reconciled holding Communion or Professing or Marrying as aforesaid were naturally dead [And that every King and Queene of this Realme who at any time hereafter shall come to and succeede in the Imperiall Crowne of this Kingdome shall on the first day of the meeting of the first Parlyament next after his or her comeing to the Crowne sitting in his or her Throne in the House of Peeres in the presence of the Lords and Commons therein assembled or at his or her Coronation before such person or persons who shall administer the Coronation Oath to him or her at the time of his or her takeing the said Oath (which shall first happen) make subscribe and audibly repeate the Declaration mentioned in the Statute[2] made in the thirtyeth yeare of the Raigne of King Charles the Second Entituled An Act for the more effectuall Preserveing the Kings Person and Government by disableing Papists from sitting in either House of Parlyament. But if it shall happen that such King or Queene upon his or her Succession to the Crowne of this Realme shall be under the Age of twelve yeares then every such King or Queene shall make subscribe and audibly repeate the said Declaration at his or her Coronation or the first day of the meeting of the first Parlyament as aforesaid which shall first happen after such King or Queene shall have attained the said Age of twelve yeares.[3]] All which their Majestyes are contented and pleased shall be declared enacted and established by authoritie of this present Parliament and shall stand remaine and be the Law of this Realme for ever And the same are by their said Majestyes by and with the advice and consent of the Lords Spirituall and Temporall and Commons in Parlyament assembled and by the authoritie of the same declared enacted and established accordingly

II. And bee it further declared and enacted by the Authoritie

---

[1] Annexed to the Original Act in a separate Schedule.
[2] See Sect. A, No. XVII, p. 43.
[3] Annexed to the Original Act in a separate Schedule.

aforesaid That from and after this present Session of Parlyament noe Dispensation by Non obstante of or to any Statute or any part thereof shall be allowed but that the same shall be held void and of noe effect Except a Dispensation be allowed of in such Statute and except in such Cases as shall be specially provided for by one or more Bill or Bills to be passed dureing this present Session of Parliament.

III. Provided[1] that noe Charter or Grant or Pardon granted before the three and twentyeth Day of October in the yeare of our Lord one thousand six hundred eighty nine shall be any wayes impeached or invalidated by this Act but that the same shall be and remaine of the same force and effect in Law and noe other then as if this Act had never beene made.

XXVI

CONFIRMATION OF WILLIAM & MARY AND OF THE CONVENTION PARLIAMENT, 1689

2 Will. & Mar., Sess. 1, c. 1.

Wee your Majestyes most humble and loyall Subjects the Lords Spirituall and Temporall and Commons in this present Parlyament assembled doe beseech your most excellent Majestyes that it may be published and declared in this High Court of Parlyament and enacted by authoritie of the same That we doe recognize and acknowledge your Majestyes were are and of Right ought to be by the Laws of this Realme our Soveraigne Liege Lord and Lady King and Queene of England France and Ireland and the Dominions thereunto belonging in and to whose Princely Persons the Royall State Crowne and Dignity of the said Realms with all Honours Stiles Titles Regalities Prerogatives Powers Jurisdictions and Authorities to the same belonging and appertaining are most fully rightfully and intirely invested and incorporated united and annexed. And for the avoiding of all Disputes and Questions concerning the Being and Authority of the late Parliament assembled at Westminster the thirteenth day of February one thousand six hundred eighty eight Wee doe most humbly beseech your Majestyes that it may be enacted And bee it enacted . . . That all and singular the Acts made and enacted in the said Parlyament were and are Laws and Statutes of this Kingdome and as such ought to be reputed taken and obeyed by all the People of this Kingdome.[2]

[1] See Sect. D, No. XVII (D), p. 349.
[2] See Sect. A, No. I, p. 1 ; No. VI, p. 10 ; No. XIX, p. 54.

XXVII

RESTORATION OF THE CHARTERS OF THE CITY OF LONDON,[1] 1689

2 Will. & Mar., c. 8.

An Act for Reversing the Judgment in a Quo Warranto against the City of London and for Restoreing the City of London to its antient Rights and Priviledges.

Whereas a Judgement was given in the Court of Kings Bench in or about Trinity Terme in the five and thirtyeth yeare of the Raigne of the late King Charles the Second upon an Information in the nature of a Quo Warranto exhibited in the said Court against the Mayor and Commonalty and Citizens of the City of London That the Liberty Priviledge and Franchise of the said Mayor and Commonalty and Citizens being a Body Politicke and Corporate should be seized into the Kings Hands as forfeited. And forasmuch as the said Judgement and the Proceedings thereupon is and were illegall and arbitrary And for that the Restoreing of the said Mayor and Commonalty and Citizens to their antient Liberties of which they had beene deprived tends very much to the Peace and good Setlement of this Kingdome Bee it declared and enacted . . . That the said Judgement . . . for the seizing into the said late Kings Hands the Liberty Priviledge or Franchise of the Mayor and Commonaltie and Citizens of the City of London of being of themselyes a Body Corporate and Politick by the Name of The Mayor and Commonalty and Citizens of the City of London and by that Name to plead and be impleaded and to answere and to be answered or in what manner or words soever such Judgement was entred is shall be and are hereby reversed annulled and made void to all intents and purposes whatsoever and that Vacats be entred upon the Rolls of the said Judgement for the Vacating and Reversall of the same accordingly

II. And be it further . . . enacted . . . That the Mayor and Commonaltie and Citizens of the City of London shall and may for ever hereafter remaine continue and be and prescribe to be a Body Corporate and Politick in re facto et nomine by the Name of Mayor and Commonaltie and Citizens of the City of London . . . And the said Mayor and Commonaltie and Citizens of the said City shall and may as by Law they ought peaceably have and enjoy all and every their Rights Gifts Charters Grants Liberties Priviledges Franchises

[1] See also Sect. C, No. V, p. 254. Sect. D, Nos. XII, XIII, XVII and XXIV, pp. 332-39, 347-52, 362-64.

Customs Usages Constitutions Prescriptions Immunities Markets Duties Tolls Lands Tenements Estates and Hereditaments whatsoever which they lawfully had or had lawfull Right Title or Interest of in or to at the time of the recording or giveing the said Judgment or at the time or times of the said pretended Forfeitures

III. And bee it enacted . . . That all Charters Letters Patents and Grants for incorporating the Citizens and Commonaltie of the said City or any of them and all Charters Grants Letters Patents and Commissions touching or concerning any of their Liberties or Franchises or the Liberties Priviledges Franchises Immunities Lands Tenements and Hereditaments Rights Title or Estates of the Mayor and Commonaltie and Citizens of the City of London made or granted to any person or persons whatsoever by the late King Charles the Second since the said Judgement given or by the late King James the Second be and are hereby declared and adjudged null and void to all intents and purposes whatsoever

[§§ IV-XI confirm proceedings in mayoral court, etc., since the Quo Warranto proceedings, officers already chosen, leases made, judgements obtained by the City and Freedoms granted. Arrangements prescribed for choice of new Mayor and other officers and Common Council.]

XII. And Bee it enacted . . . That all and every of the severall Companies and Corporations of the said City shall from henceforth stand and be incorporated by such Name and Names and in such sort and manner as they respectively were at the time of the said Judgment given and every of them are hereby restored to all and every the Lands Tenements Hereditaments Rights Titles Estates Liberties Powers Priviledges Precedences and Immunities which they lawfully had and enjoyed at the time of giveing the said Judgment . . .

[§§ XIII, XV confirm leases and Freedoms granted by City Companies since the judgement.]

XVI. Provided alwayes . . . That this present Act of Parlyament shall be accepted taken and reputed to be a Generall and Publick Act of Parliament Of which all and every the Judge and Judges of this Kingdome in all Courts shall take notice on all Occasions whatsoever as if it were a publick Act of Parlyament relating to the whole Kingdome any thing herein contained to the contrary thereof in any wise notwithstanding.

XXVIII

ESTABLISHMENT OF THE BANK OF ENGLAND, 1694

5 & 6 Will. & Mar., c. 20.

An Act for granting to theire Majesties severall Rates and Duties upon Tunnage of Shipps and Vessells and upon Beere Ale and other Liquors for Secureing certaine Recompenses and Advantages in the said Act mentioned to such Persons as shall voluntary advance the Sūme of Fifteene hundred thousand pounds towards the carrying on the Warr against France.

XVII. . . . And be it further enacted by the Authority aforesaid That for the better raiseing and paying into the Receipte of the Exchequer the sūme of Twelve hundred thousand pounds parte of the sūme of Fifteene hundred thousand pounds the yearely sūme of One hundred and forty thousand pounds ariseing by and out of the Duties and Imposicōns granted by this Act shall be kepte separate and aparte in the said Receipte of Exchequer to be paid over from time to time unto such person and persons and in such manner proporcōn and forme as is herein after directed.

XVIII. And be it further enacted by the authority aforesaid That it shall and may be lawfull to and for theire Majesties by cōmission under the Greate Seale of England to authorize and appointe any number of persons to take and receive all such voluntary subscripcōns as shall be made on or before the first day of August which shall be in the yeare of our Lord One thousand six hundred ninety four by any person or persons Natives or Foreigners Bodies Politicke or Corporate for and towards the raiseing and paying into the Receipte of Exchequer the said sūme of Twelve hundred thousand pounds . . . and that the yearely sūme of One hundred thousand pounds . . . ariseing by and out of the said Duties and Imposicōns before mencōned shall be applyed issued and directed and is hereby appropriated to the use and advantage of such person and persons Bodies Politicke and Corporate as shall make such voluntary subscripcōns . . .

XIX. And be it further enacted That it shall and may be lawfull to and for theire Majesties by Letters Patents under the Greate Seale of England to limitt directe and appointe how and in what manner and proporcōns and under what rules and direccōns the said sūme of Twelve hundred thousand pounds . . . and the said yearely sūme of One hundred thousand pounds . . . may be assigneable or transferrable assigned or transferred to such person or persons only as shall freely and voluntarily accepte of the same and not otherwise and to incorporate all and every such Subscribers and Contributors theire Heires Successors or Assignes to be one Body Corporate and Politick by the name of The Governor and Company of the Banke of England and by the same name of The Governor and Company of the Banke of England to have perpetuall succession and a Cōmon Seale . . .

XX. . . . And that att any time upon Twelve months notice after the First day of August which shall be in the yeare of our Lord One thousand seven hundred and five upon repayment by Parliament of the said sūme of Twelve hundred thousand pounds . . . then and from thenceforward the said yearely payments and every of them of One hundred thousand pounds . . . and the said Corporačon shall absolutely cease and determine, . . .

XXV. And it is hereby further enacted by the authority aforesaid That the said Corporačon soe to be made shall not borrowe or give security by Bill Bond Covenant or Agreement under theire Cōmon Seale for any more further or other sūme or sūmes of money exceedeing in the whole the sūme of Twelve hundred thousand pounds soe that they shall not owe at any one time more then the said sūme unlesse it be by Act of Parliament upon Fonds agreed in Parliament ; and in such case only such further sūmes as shall be soe directed and allowed to be borrowed by Parliament and for such time only untill they shall be repaid such further sūmes as they shall borrowe by such authority and if any more or further or other sūme or sūmes of money shall be borrowed taken up lent or advanced under theire Cōmon Seale or for payment of which any Bond Bill Covenant or Agreement or other Writeing shall be made sealed or given under the Cōmon Seale of the said Corporačon soe to be made then and in such case all and every person and persons who shall be a member or members of the said Corporačon his and theire respective Heires Executors and Administrators shall in his and theire respective private and personall capacities be chargeable with and lyable in proporčon to theire severall Shares or Subscripčons to the repayment of such moneyes . . .

XXVI. And to the intent that theire Majesties Subjects may not be oppressed by the said Corporačon by theire monopolizing or ingrosseing any sort of Goods Wares or Merchandizes Be it further Declared and Enacted by the authority aforesaid That the said Corporačon . . . shall not att any time dureing the continuance thereof deale or trade . . . with any of the Stock-moneyes or Effects of or any wise belonging to the said Corporačon in the buying or selling of any Goods Wares or Merchandizes whatsoever and every person or persons who shall soe deale or trade or by whose order or direccons such Dealeings or Tradeing shall be made prosecuted or managed shall forfeite for every such Dealeing or Tradeing and every such order and direccons treble the value of the Goods and Merchandize soe traded for to such person or persons who shall sue for the same by Accon of Debt . . .

XXVII. Provided that nothing herein conteined shall any wayes be construed to hinder the said Corporacon from dealeing in Bills of Exchange or in buying or selling Bullion Gold or Silver or in selling any goods wares or merchandize whatsoever which shall really and bona fide be left or deposited with the said Corporacon for money lent and advanced thereon and which shall not be redeemed att the time agreed on or within three moneths after or from selling such goods as shall or may be the produce of Lands purchased by the said Corporacon.

XXVIII. [Provided [1] alwaies and be it enacted by the authority aforesaid That all and every Bill or Bills obligatory and of creditt under the Seale of the said Corporacon made or given to any person or persons shall and may by Indorsement thereon under the hand of such person or persons be assigneable and assigned to any person or persons who shall voluntarily accepte the same and soe by such Assignee toties quoties by indorsement thereupon and that such Assignement and Assignements soe to be made shall absolutely vest and transferre the Right and Property in and unto such Bill or Bills Obligatory and of Creditt and the moneyes due upon the same and that the Assignee or Assignees shall and may sue for and mainetaine an accon thereupon in his owne name.] . . .

XXIX

THE TRIENNIAL ACT,[2] 1694

6 & 7 Will. & Mar., c. 2.

An Act for the frequent Meeting and calling of Parliaments.

Whereas by the ancient Laws and Statutes of this Kingdome frequent Parliaments ought to bee held And whereas frequent and new Parliaments tend very much to the happy union and good agreement of King and People Wee Your Majesties most loyal and

[1] § XXVIII is annexed to the Original Act in a separate Schedule.
[2] See Sect. A, No. XIII, p. 33, No. XLVI, p. 126, and Vol. II, Sect. A, No. XLII, § 7, p. 143.

obedient Subjects the Lords Spiritual and Temporal and Commons in this present Parliament assembled doe most humbly beseech your most excellent Majesties that it may bee declared and enacted in this present Parliament and it is hereby declared and enacted . . . That from henceforth a Parliament shall bee holden once in Three years att the least.

II. And bee it further enacted . . . That within Three yeares att the farthest from and after the Dissolution of this present Parliament and soe from time to time for ever hereafter within Three yeares att the farthest from and after the determination of every other Parliament Legal Writts under the Great Seal shall bee issued by directions of your Majesties your Heires and Successors for calling assembling and holding another new Parliament.

III. And be it further enacted . . . That from henceforth noe Parliament whatsoever that shall att any time hereafter bee called assembled or held shall have any continuance longer then for Three yeares onely att the farthest to bee accounted from the day on which by the Writts of Summons the said Parliament shall bee appointed to meet.

IV. And bee it further enacted by the authority aforesaid That this present Parliament shall cease and determine on the First day of November which shall bee in the yeare of our Lord One thousand six hundred ninety six unlesse their Majesties shall think fitt to dissolve it sooner.

XXX

THE TRIAL OF TREASONS ACT, 1696

7 & 8 Will. III, c. 3.

Whereas nothing is more just and reasonable than that Persons prosecuted for High Treason and Misprision of Treason whereby the Liberties Lives Honour Estates Bloud and Posterity of the Subjects may bee lost and destroyed should bee justly and equally tried and that Persons accused as Offenders therein should not bee debarred of all just and equal Means for Defence of their Innocencies in such Cases In order thereunto and for the better Regulation of Tryals of Persons prosecuted for High Treason and Misprision of such Treason Bee it enacted . . . That . . . all and every Person and Persons whatsoever that shall bee accused and indicted for High Treason whereby any Corruption of Blood may or shall bee made . . . or for Misprision of such Treason shall have a true Copy of the whole Indictment but not the Names of the Witnesses delivered unto them or any of them Five Days att the least before hee or they shall bee tryed for the same whereby to enable them and any of them respectively to advise with Counsell thereupon to plead and make their Defence his or their Attorney or Attorneys Agent or Agents or any of them requiring the same and paying the Officer his reasonable Fees for writing thereof not exceeding Five Shillings for the Copy of every such Indictment And that every Person soe accused and indicted arraigned or tryed for any such Treason as aforesaid or for Misprision of such Treason . . . shall bee received and admitted to make his and their full Defence by Counsel learned in the Law and to make any Proof that hee or they can produce by lawfull Witnesse or Witnesses who shall then bee upon Oath for his and their just Defence in that behalfe And in case any Person or Persons so accused or indicted shall desire Counsel the Court before whom such Person or Persons shall bee tryed or some Judge of that Court shall and is hereby authorized and required immediately upon his or their request to assigne to such Person and Persons such and soe many Counsel not exceeding Two as the Person or Persons shall desire to whom such Counsel shall have free Accesse at all seasonable Houres Any Law or Usage to the contrary notwithstanding.

II. And bee it further enacted That . . . noe Person or Persons whatsoever shall bee indicted tryed or attainted of High Treason . . . or of Misprision of such Treason but by and upon the Oaths and Testimony of Two lawfull Witnesses either both of them to the same Overtact or one of them to one and another of them to another Overtact of the same Treason unlesse the Party indicted and arraigned or tryed shall willingly without violence and in open Court confesse the same or shall stand Mute or refuse to plead or in cases of High Treason shall peremptorily challenge above the Number of Thirty five of the Jury Any Law Statute or Usage to the contrary notwithstanding.

III. Provided always that any Person or Persons being indicted as aforesaid for any the Treasons or Misprisions of the Treasons aforesaid may bee outlawed and thereby attainted of or for any of the said Offences of Treason or Misprision of Treason And in Cases of the High Treasons aforesaid where by the Law after such Outlawry the Party outlawed may come in and bee tryed hee shall upon such Tryal have the Benefitt of this Act.

IV. And bee it further enacted . . . That if Two or more distinct Treasons of diverse Heads or Kinds shall bee alledged in one Bill of Indictment one Witnesse produced to prove one of the said Treasons and another Witnesse produced to prove another of the said Treasons shall not bee deemed or taken to bee

Two Witnesses to the same Treason within the meaning of this Act.

V. And to the intent that the Terror and Dread of such Criminal Accusations may in some reasonable time bee removed Bee it further enacted . . . That . . . noe Person or Persons whatsoever shall bee indicted tryed or prosecuted for any such Treason as aforesaid or for Misprision of such Treason that shall bee committed or done within the Kingdome of England Dominion of Wales or Towne of Berwick upon Tweed . . . unlesse the same Indictment bee found by a Grand Jury within Three years next after the Treason or Offence done and committed. . . .

VI. Always provided and excepted that if any Person or Persons whatsoever shall bee guilty of designing endeavouring or attempting any Assassination on the Body of the King by Poyson or otherwise such Person or Persons may bee prosecuted at any time notwithstanding the aforesaid Limitation ;

VII. And that all and every Person and Persons who shall bee accused indicted or tryed for such Treason as aforesaid or for Misprision of such Treason . . . shall have Copies of the Pannel of the Jurors who are to try them duely returned by the Sheriff and delivered unto them and every of them soe accused and indicted respectively Two Days at the least before hee or they shall bee tryed for the same And that all Persons soe accused and indicted for any such Treason as aforesaid shall have the like Processe of the Court where they shall bee tryed to compell their Witnesses to appeare for them att any such Tryal or Tryals as is usually granted to compell Witnesses to appeare against them.

VIII. And bee it further enacted That noe Evidence shall bee admitted or given of any Overt Act that is not expresly laid in the Indictment against any Person or Persons whatsoever.

IX. Provided alsoe . . . [Indictment may not be quashed for verbal errors] But neverthelesse any Judgement given upon such Indictment shall and may bee liable to bee reversed upon a Writt of Error in the same manner and noe other than as if this Act had not been made.

X. . . . And whereas upon the Tryals of Peers or Peeresses a Major Vote is sufficient either to acquitt or condemn Bee it further enacted . . . That upon the Tryal of any Peer or Peeresse either for Treason or Misprision all the Peers who have a Right to sitt and vote in Parliament shall bee duely summoned Twenty Days att least before every such Tryal to appearee att every such Tryal And that every Peere soe summoned and appeareing att such Tryal shall vote in the Tryal of such Peer or Peeresse soe to bee tryed every such Peere first takeing the Oaths mentioned in an Act of Parliament

made in the First Yeare of the Reign of King William and Queene
Mary [1] . . . And alsoe every such Peer subscribing and audibly
repeating the Declaration mentioned in An Act [2] for the more
effectual preserving the Kings Person and Government by disabling
Papists from sitting in either House of Parliament and made in the
Thirtieth Yeare of the Reigne of the late King Charles the Second.

XI. Provided always That neither this Act nor any thing therein
contained shall any ways extend to or bee construed to extend to
any Impeachment or other Proceedings in Parliament in any kind
whatsoever.

XII. Provided alsoe That this Act nor any thing therein contained shall any ways extend to any Indictment of High Treason
nor to any Proceedings thereupon for counterfeiting His Majesties
Coyn His Great Seale or Privy Seale His Signe Manual or Privy
Signett.

XXXI

AN ACT AGAINST CORRUPT ELECTIONS, [3]
1696
7 & 8 Will. III, c. 4.

Whereas grievous Complaints are made and manifestly appeare
to bee true in the Kingdome of undue Elections of Members to
Parliament by excessive and exorbitant Expences contrary to the
Laws and in Violation of the Freedom due to the Election of Representatives for the Commons of England in Parliament to the great
Scandal of the Kingdome dishonorable and may bee destructive
to the Constitutions of Parliaments wherefore for Remedy therein
and that all Elections of Members to Parliament may bee hereafter
freely and indifferently made without Charge or Expence Bee it
enacted . . . That noe Person or Persons hereafter to bee elected
to serve in Parliament . . . shall or doe hereafter by himselfe or
themselves or by any other Ways or Means on his or their behalfe
or att his or their Charge before his or their Election to serve in
Parliament . . . directly or indirectly . . . make any Present Gift
Reward or Entertainment . . . to or for any such Person or
Persons in particular or to any such County City . . . or Place in

[1] Sect. A, No. XXII, p. 60.   [2] Sect. A, No. XVII, p. 43.
[3] See also Sect. A, No. XXXIII, p. 85, No. XLII, p. 117, No. LI,
p. 131, No. LVI, p. 140, No. LIX, p. 145, Sect. D, No. V, p. 325, No. XV,
p. 342, No. XXVII, p. 366, No. XXXV, p. 377, and No. L, p. 399, and
Vol. II, Sect. A, No. XXXIII, p. 107.

general . . . in order to bee elected or for being elected to serve in Parliament . . .

II. And it is hereby further enacted and declared That every Person and Persons soe giving presenting or allowing makeing promising or engageing doeing acting or proceeding shall bee and are hereby declared & enacted disabled and incapacitated upon such Election to serve in Parliament . . . and shall not act sitt or have any Vote or Place in Parliament but shall bee and are hereby declared and enacted to bee to all Intents Constructions & Purposes as if they had been never returned or elected Members for the Parliament.

XXXII

CONTINUANCE OF PARLIAMENT ON DEMISE OF THE SOVEREIGN,[1] 1696

7 & 8 Will. III, c. 15.

Whereas this Kingdome of England may be exposed to great Dangers by the Invasion of Foreigners or by the traiterous Conspiracies of wicked and ill disposed Persons whenever itt shall please God to afflict these Realmes by the Death of our Gracious Sovereigne King William (whome God long preserve) or by the Death of any of His Heires and Successors before a Parliament can bee summoned and called by the next Heire and Successor to the Crowne For Prevention whereof bee itt enacted . . . That this present Parliament or any other Parliament which shall hereafter bee summoned and called by His Majesty King William His Heirs and Successors shall not determine or bee dissolved by the Death or Demise of His said Majesty His Heirs and Successors but such Parliament shall and is hereby enacted to continue and is hereby impowered and required immediately to meete convene and sitt and to act notwithstanding such Death or Demise for and dureing the Time of Six Moneths and noe longer unlesse the same shall bee sooner prorogued or dissolved by such Person who shall be next Heire to the Crowne of this Realme of England in Succession according to an Act[2] of Parliament made in the first Yeare of the Reigne of King William and Queene Mary intituled An Act declareing the Rights and Liberties of the Subject and settling the Succession of the Crowne And if the said Parliament shall bee soe prorogued then itt shall

[1] See 6 Anne, c. 41, § iv, Sect. A, No. XLI, p. 112, and Sect. A, No. LV, p. 139, and Vol. II, Sect. A, No. IX, p. 16, No. XXXII, § 51, p. 106, No. XL, p. 136.

[2] See Sect. A, No. XXV, p. 67.

meete and sitt on and upon the Day unto which itt shall be prorogued
and continue for the Residue of the said Time of Six Months unlesse
sooner prorogued or dissolved as aforesaid.

II. And itt is hereby further enacted by the Authority aforesaid
That in case there shall be noe Parliament in being att the time of
the Death or Demise of His Majesty or any of His Heirs and
Successors then the last preceding Parliament shall immediately
convene and sitt and is hereby impowered and required to act as
aforesaid to all Intents and Purposes as if the said Parliament had
never beene dissolved.

III. Provided always and itt is hereby declared That nothing
in this Act contained shall extend or bee construed to extend to
alter or abridge the Power of the King His Heires and Successors
to prorogue or dissolve Parliaments nor to repeale or make voyd
one Act[1] of Parliament made in the Sixth and Seventh Yeares of
the Reigne of His present Majesty King William intituled An Act
for the frequent Meeting and calling of Parliaments but that the
said Act shall continue in force in every thing that is not contrary
to or inconsistent with the Direction of this Act.

XXXIII

PROCEDURE IN PARLIAMENTARY ELECTIONS,[2] 1696

7 & 8 Will. III, c. 25.

Whereas by the evill Practices and irregular Proceedings of
Sheriffs . . . and other Officers in the Execution of Writts and
Precepts for electing of Members to serve in Parliament as well
the Freeholders and others in their Right of Election as alsoe the
Persons by them elected to bee theire Representatives have hereto-
fore beene greatly injured and abused . . . Bee it enacted . . .
That when any new Parliament shall att any Time hereafter bee
summoned or called there shall bee Forty Dayes betweene the
Teste and Returnes of the Writts of Summons And that the Lord
Chancellor Lord Keeper or Lords Commissioners of the Great
Seale for the tyme being shall issue out the Writts for Election of
Members to serve in the same Parliament with as much Expedition

---

[1] See Sect. A, No. XXIX, p. 79.
[2] See also Sect. A, No. XXXI, p. 83, No. XLII, p. 117, No. LI, p. 131,
No. LVI, p. 140, No. LIX, p. 145. (See note 3, p. 83, for other refs.)

as the same may bee done . . . And that every such Officer upon
the Receipt of the same Writt shall upon the Back thereof indorse
the Day hee received the same and shall forthwith upon Receipt
of the Writt make out the Precept or Precepts to each Borough
Towne Corporate Port or Place within his Jurisdiction where
any Member or Members are to bee elected to serve in such New
Parliament or to supply any vacancy dureing the present or any
future Parliament And within Three dayes after the Receipt of the
said Writt of Election shall by himselfe or proper Agent deliver or
cause to bee delivered such Precept or Precepts to the proper Officer
of every such Borough Towne Corporate Port or Place within his
Jurisdiction to whom the Execution of such Precept doth belong
or appertaine and to noe other Person whatsoever And every such
Officer upon the Back of the same Precept shall indorse the Day of
his Receipt thereof in the presence of the Party from whom hee
received such Precept and shall forthwith cause publick Notice to
bee given of the Tyme and Place of Election and shall proceed
to Election thereupon within the space of Eight Dayes next after
his Receipt of the same Precept and give Foure Dayes notice att
least of the Day appointed for the Election.

II. And bee itt further enacted by the Authority aforesaid That
neither the Sheriffe or his Under-Sheriffe in any County or City
nor the Mayor Bayliffe Constable Port-Reeve or other Officer or
Officers of any Borough Towne Corporate Port or Place to whom
the Execution of any Writt or Precept for electing Members to serve
in Parliament doth belong or appertaine shall give pay receive or
take any Fee Reward or Gratuity whatsoever for the makeing out
Receipt Delivery Returne or Execution of any such Writt or Precept.

III. And bee itt further enacted by the Authority aforesaid That
the Sheriffe . . . shall hold his County Court for the same Election
att the most publick and usuall Place of Election . . . giveing
Tenne Dayes Notice of the Tyme and Place of Election And in case
the said Election bee not determined upon the View with the Consent
of the Freeholders there present but that a Poll shall bee required
for Determination thereof then the said Sheriffe . . . shall forthwith there proceed to take the said Poll . . . And every Freeholder
before hee is admitted to Poll at the same Election shall if required
by the Candidates or any of them first take the Oath herein after
mentioned [that he has a freehold at such a place worth 40/- yearly,
and that he has not before been polled at that election].

[Penalty for perjury or subornation.]
[§ IV. The Sheriff not to adjourn the County Court without the
consent of the candidates.]
[§ V. Election officer to give to any one a copy of the Poll for a

reasonable charge. Every wilful offence contrary to this Act shall entail forfeiture of five hundred pounds to aggrieved party.]

VI. And bee itt also enacted That noe Person or Persons shall bee allowed to have any Vote . . . for or by reason of any Trust Estate or Mortgage unlesse such Trustee or Mortgagee be in actuall possession or receipt of the Rents and Profitts of the same Estate, but that the Mortgagor or Cestui que trust in possession shall and may vote for the same Estate notwithstanding such Mortgage or Trust And that all Conveyances of any Mesuages Lands Tenements or Hereditaments in any County City Borough Towne Corporate Port or Place in order to multiply Voices or to splitt and divide the Interest in any Houses or Lands among severall Persons to enable them to vote att Elections . . . are hereby declared to bee void and of none Effect and that noe more than one single Voice shall bee admitted for one and the same House or Tenement.

[§ VII. Voters and candidates not to be under 21 years of age.]

[§§ VIII and IX. Special arrangements for Yorkshire and Southamptonshire.]

XXXIV

ACT FOR THE SECURITY OF THE CROWN,[1]
1696
7 & 8 Will. III, c. 27.

Whereas the Welfare and Safety of this Kingdom and the Reformed Religion do next under God intirely depend upon the Preservation of Your Majesties Royal Person and Government which by the mercifull Providence of God of late have been delivered from the bloody and barbarous Attempts of Traytors and other Your Majesties Enemies who there is just Reason to believe have been in great measure encouraged to undertake and prosecute such their wicked Designs partly by Your Majesties great and undeserved Clemency towards them and partly by the want of a sufficient Provision in the Law for the securing Offices and Places of Trust to such as are well affected to Your Majesties Government and for the repressing and punishing such as are knowne to be disaffected to the same For Remedy whereof may it please Your Majesty that it may be enacted and be it enacted . . . That . . . all and every Person and Persons who shall refuse to take the Oaths

[1] See also Sect. A, No. III, p. 5, and Vol. II, Sect. A, No. VII, p. 10, and No. XXIX, p. 198.

mentioned and appointed to be taken in an Act [1] of Parliament made in the First Yeare of the Reigne of His present Majestie and the late Queen of Blessed Memory intituled An Act for the abrogating of the Oaths of Supremacy and Allegiance and appointing other Oaths or either of them . . . shall until he or they have duly taken the said Oaths be liable to incurr forfeit pay and suffer all and every the Penalties Forfeitures Sums of Money Disabilities and Incapacities which by the Laws and Statutes of this Realme now in Force or any of them are inflicted upon Popish Recusants duely convict of Recusancy

[Records of refusal to be transmitted through Assize Judges to the Exchequer which will proceed against lands and goods as in the case of a Popish Recusant Convict.]

II. And be it further enacted by the Authority aforesaid That if any Person or Persons shall from and after the said First Day of May maliciously by writing printing preaching teaching or advised speaking utter publish or declare that His present Majesty is not the lawfull and rightfull King of these Realms or that the late King James or the pretended Prince of Wales hath any Right or Title to the Crown of these Realms or that any other Person or Persons hath or have any Right or Title to the same otherwise than according to an Act [2] of Parliament made in the First Yeare of the Reigne of His present Majesty and the late Queen intituled An Act declaring the Rights and Liberties of the Subject and settling the Succession of the Crown such Person or Persons being thereof lawfully convicted shall incurr the Danger and Penalty of Premunire mentioned in the Statute of Premunire made in the Sixteenth Yeare of the Reigne of King Richard the Second.

III. And whereas for the better Preservation of His Majesties Royal Person and Government against the aforesaid wicked and traiterous Designs upon a full Discovery thereof great Numbers of His Majesties good Subjects have entred into and subscribed an Association [3] in the Words following . . . Wee whose Names are hereunto subscribed doe heartily sincerely and solemnly professe testifie and declare That His present Majesty King William is rightfull and lawfull King of these Realmes   And wee doe mutually promise and engage to stand by and assist each other to the utmost of our Power in the Support and Defence of His Majesties most Sacred Person and Government against the late King James and all his Adherents And in case His Majesty come to any violent or untimely Death (which God forbid) Wee doe hereby further freely and unanimously oblige ourselves to unite associate and stand by each other in

---

[1] Sect. A, No. XXII, p. 60.   [2] Sect. A, No. XXV, p. 67.
[3] Cf. 27 Eliz., c. 1. (Prothero, p. 80).

revenging the same upon His Enemies and their Adherents and in supporting and defending the Succession of the Crowne according to an Act . . . declaring the Rights and Liberties of the Subject and settling the Succession of the Crowne Be itt therefore enacted . . . That the said Association shall be . . . good and lawfull . . . according to the true Meaning . . . of the same.

[§§ IV-XVII provide for compulsory subscription to the Association by civil and military officers, members of Parliament, etc., and penalties for failure to do so, and also provide penalties for persons returning from France without licence who shall be adjudged guilty of high treason.]

XVIII. And be it further enacted by the Authority aforesaid That no Person who shall refuse to take the Oaths directed by an Act made in the First Yeare of the Reigne of his present Majesty and the late Queen Mary,[1] . . . or being Quakers shall refuse to subscribe the Declaration of Fidelity directed by one other Act of Parliament[2] . . . shall be admitted to give any Vote for the Election of any Knight of the Shire Citizen Burgesse or Baron of the Cinque Ports to serve in Parliament.

[§ XIX allows the temporary retention in custody of persons charged with High Treason.]

XX. And for the better securing of the Succession of the Crowne in such manner as in and by an Act made in the First Yeare of the Reigne of King William and Queen Mary intituled An Act[3] declaring the Rights and Liberties of the Subject and settling the Succession of the Crowne is provided limited and appointed Be it further enacted by the Authority aforesaid That no Commission either Civil or Military shall cease determine or be void by reason of the Death or demise of His present Majesty or of any of His Heirs or Successors Kings or Queens of this Realme but that every such Commission shall bee continue and remaine in full force and virtue for the space of Six Months next after any such Death or Demise unlesse in the meane Time superseded determined or made void by the next and immediate Successor to whom the Imperial Crowne of this Realme according to the Act of Settlement herein before mentioned is limitted and appointed to go remaine or descend.

[§ XXI provides that Offices of Inheritance are not to be made void by reason of non-subscription to the Association, provided deputies are appointed who will so subscribe.]

---

[1] Sect. A, No. XXII, p. 60.   [2] Sect. A, No. XXIV, p. 63.
[3] Sect. A, No. XXV, p. 67.

XXXV

AN ACT AGAINST POPERY,[1] 1700

11 Will. III, c. 4.

Whereas there has beene of late a much greater Resort into this Kingdom than formerly of Popish Bishops Priests and Jesuits and they doe very openly and in insolent Manner affront the Laws and daily endeavour to pervert His Majesties naturall borne Subjects which has beene occasioned by Neglect of the due Execution of the Laws already in Force For preventing the further Growth of Popery and of such treasonable and execrable Designes and Conspiracies against His Majesties Person and Government and the Established Religion as have lately as well as frequently heretofore been brought to Light and happily defeated by the wonderfull Providence of God Be it enacted . . . That . . . all and every Person and Persons who shall apprehend and take One or more Popish Bishop Priest or Jesuite and prosecute him or them soe apprehended and taken untill he or they be convicted of saying Mass or of exerciseing any other Part of the Office or Function of a Popish Bishop or Priest within these Realmes shall have and receive from the Sheriffe or Sheriffs of the County where such Conviction shall be made (without paying any Fee for the same) for every such Offender soe convicted the Summe of One hundred Pounds within Four Months after such Conviction and Demand thereof made by tendring a Certificate to the said Sheriffe or Sheriffs under the Hand or Hands of the Judge or Justices before whom such Conviction shall be made certifying the Conviction . . .

[§ II. Sheriffs to be repaid by the Treasury.]

III. And for a further Remedy against the Growth of Popery over and beyond the good Laws already made Be it further enacted by the Authority aforesaid That if any Popish Bishop Priest or Jesuit whatsoever shall say Masse or exercise any other Part of the Office or Function of a Popish Bishop or Priest within these Realmes or the Dominions thereunto belonging or if any Papist or Person makeing Profession of the Popish Religion shall keepe Schoole or take upon themselves the Education or Government or Boarding of Youth in any Place within this Realme or the Dominions thereto belonging and such Person or Persons being thereof lawfully convicted that then every such Person shall on such Conviction be adjudged to perpetuall

---

[1] See Sect. A, No. XXIII, p. 61.

Imprisonment in such Place or Places within this Kingdome as the King by Advice of His Privy Councill shall appoint

IV. And be it alsoe further enacted by the Authority aforesaid That . . . if any Person educated in the Popish Religion or professing the same shall not within Six Months after he or she shall attaine the Age of Eighteene Yeares take the Oaths of Allegiance and Supremacy and alsoe subscribe the Declaration sett downe and exprest in an Act[1] of Parliament made in the Thirtieth Yeare of the Reigne of the late King Charles the Second intituled An Act for the more effectuall preserveing the Kings Person and Government by disabling Papists from sitting in either House of Parliament to be by him or her made repeated and subscribed in the Courts of Chancery or Kings Bench or Quarter Sessions of the County where such Person shall reside every such Person shall in respect of him or herselfe only and not to or in respect of any of his or her Heires or Posterity be disabled and made incapable to inherit or take by Discent Devise or Limittation in Possession Reversion or Remainder any Lands Tenements or Hereditaments within this Kingdome of England Dominion of Wales or Towne of Berwick upon Tweed And that during the Life of such Person or untill he or she doe take the said Oaths and make repeate and subscribe the said Declaration in Manner as aforesaid the next of his or her Kindred which shall be a Protestant shall have and enjoy the said Lands Tenements and Hereditaments without being accountable for the Profitts by him or her received during such Enjoyment thereof as aforesaid but in case of any wilfull Wast . . . the Party disabled his or her Executors and Administrators shall and may recover Treble Damages . . . And every Papist or Person makeing Profession of the Popish Religion shall be disabled and is hereby made incapable to purchase either in his or her owne Name or in the Name of any other Person or Persons to his or her Use or in Trust for him or her any Mannors Lands Profitts out of Lands Tenements Rents Termes or Hereditaments . . .

[§ V. The Act not to extend to masses said in a foreign minister's house, if the priest is not a natural born subject.]

[§§ VI and VII. Penalties for sending Roman Catholic children abroad, or for refusing maintenance to a Protestant child.]

[1] Sect. A, No. XVII, p. 43.

XXXVI

THE ACT OF SETTLEMENT, 1701

12 & 13 Will. III, c. 2.

An Act for the further Limitation of the Crown and better securing the Rights and Liberties of the Subject

Whereas in the First Year of the Reign of Your Majesty and of our late most gracious Sovereign Lady Queen Mary (of blessed Memory) An Act of Parliament was made intituled An Act [1] for declaring the Rights and Liberties of the Subject and for setling the Succession of the Crown wherein it was (amongst other things) enacted established and declared That the Crown and Regall Government of the Kingdoms of England France and Ireland and the Dominions thereunto belonging should be and continue to Your Majestie and the said late Queen during the joynt Lives of Your Majesty and the said Queen and to the Survivor And that after the Decease of Your Majesty and of the said Queen the said Crown and Regall Government should be and remain to the Heirs of the Body of the said late Queen And for Default of such Issue to Her Royall Highness the Princess Ann of Denmark and the Heirs of Her Body And for Default of such Issue to the Heirs of the Body of Your Majesty And it was thereby further enacted That all and every Person and Persons that then were or afterwards should be reconciled to or shall hold Communion with the See or Church of Rome or should professe the Popish Religion or marry a Papist should be excluded and are by that Act made forever incapable to inherit possess or enjoy the Crown and Government of this Realm and Ireland and the Dominions thereunto belonging or any part of the same or to have use or exercise any regall Power Authority or Jurisdiction within the same And in all and every such Case and Cases the People of these Realms shall be and are thereby absolved of their Allegiance And that the said Crown and Government shall from time to time descend to and be enjoyed by such Person or Persons being Protestants as should have inherited and enjoyed the same in case the said Person or Persons so reconciled holding Communion professing or marrying as aforesaid were naturally dead After the making of which Statute and the Settlement therein contained Your Majesties good Subjects who were restored to the full and free Possession and Enjoyment of their Religion Rights and Liberties by the Providence of God giving Success to Your Majesties just Under-

[1] Sect. A, No. XXV, p. 67.

takings and unwearied Endeavours for that Purpose had no greater
temporall Felicity to hope or wish for then to see a Royall Progeny
descending from Your Majesty to whom (under God) they owe
their Tranquility and whose Ancestors have for many Years been
principall Assertors of the reformed Religion and the Liberties of
Europe and from our said most gracious Sovereign Lady whose
Memory will always be precious to the Subjects of these Realms
And it having since pleased Almighty God to take away our said
Sovereign Lady and also the most hopefull Prince William Duke of
Gloucester (the only surviving Issue of Her Royall Highness the
Princess Ann of Denmark) to the unspeakable Grief and Sorrow of
Your Majesty and Your said good Subjects who under such Losses
being sensibly put in mind that it standeth wholly in the Pleasure
of Almighty God to prolong the Lives of Your Majesty and of Her
Royall Highness and to grant to Your Majesty or to Her Royall
Highness such Issue as may be inheritable to the Crown and Regall
Government aforesaid by the respective Limitations in the said
recited Act contained doe constantly implore the Divine Mercy for
those Blessings And Your Majesties said Subjects having Daily
Experience of Your Royall Care and Concern for the present and
future Wellfare of these Kingdoms and particularly recommending
from Your Throne a further Provision to be made for the Succession
of the Crown in the Protestant Line for the Happiness of the Nation
and the Security of our Religion And it being absolutely necessary
for the Safety Peace and Quiet of this Realm to obviate all Doubts
and Contentions in the same by reason of any pretended Titles to
the Crown and to maintain a Certainty in the Succession thereof to
which Your Subjects may safely have Recourse for their Protection
in case the Limitations in the said recited Act should determine
Therefore for a further Provision of the Succession of the Crown in
the Protestant Line We Your Majesties most dutifull and Loyall
Subjects the Lords Spirituall and Temporall and Commons in this
present Parliament assembled do beseech Your Majesty that it may
be enacted and declared and be it enacted and declared . . . That
the most Excellent Princess Sophia Electress and Dutchess Dowager
of Hannover Daughter of the most Excellent Princess Elizabeth
late Queen of Bohemia Daughter of our late Sovereign Lord King
James the First of happy Memory be and is hereby declared to be
the next in Succession in the Protestant Line to the Imperiall Crown
and Dignity of the said Realms of England France and Ireland
with the Dominions and Territories thereunto belonging after His
Majesty and the Princess Ann of Denmark and in Default of
Issue of the said Princess Ann and of His Majesty respectively and
that from and after the Deceases of His said Majesty our now

Sovereign Lord and of Her Royall Highness the Princess Ann of Denmark and for Default of Issue of the said Princess Ann and of His Majesty respectively the Crown and Regall Government of the said Kingdoms of England France and Ireland and of the Dominions thereunto belonging with the Royall State and Dignity of the said Realms and all the Honours Stiles Titles Regalities Prerogatives Powers Jurisdictions and Authorities to the same belonging and appertaining shall be remain and continue to the said most Excellent Princess Sophia and the Heirs of her Body being Protestants And thereunto the said Lords Spirituall and Temporall and Commons shall and will in the Name of all the People of this Realm most humbly and faithfully submitt themselves their Heirs and Posterities and do faithfully promise That after the Deceases of His Majesty and Her Royall Highness and the failure of the Heirs of their respective Bodies to stand to maintain and defend the said Princess Sophia and the Heirs of her Body being Protestants according to the Limitation and Succession of the Crown in this Act specified and contained to the utmost of their Powers with their Lives and Estates against all Persons whatsoever that shall attempt any thing to the contrary.

II. Provided always and it is hereby enacted That all and every Person and Persons who shall or may take or inherit the said Crown by vertue of the Limitation of this present Act and is are or shall be reconciled to or shall hold Communion with the See or Church of Rome or shall profess the Popish Religion or shall marry a Papist shall be subject to such Incapacities as in such Case or Cases are by the said recited Act provided enacted and established and that every King and Queen of this Realm who shall come to and succeed in the Imperiall Crown of this Kingdom by vertue of this Act shall have the Coronation Oath administred to him her or them at their respective Coronations according to the Act of Parliament[1] made in the First Year of the Reign of His Majesty and the said late Queen Mary intituled An Act for establishing the Coronation Oath and shall make subscribe and repeat the Declaration in the Act first above recited mentioned or referred to in the Manner and Form thereby prescribed

III. And whereas it is requisite and necessary that some further Provision be made for securing our Religion Laws and Liberties from and after the Death of His Majesty and the Princess Ann of Denmark and in default of Issue of the Body of the said Princess and of his Majesty respectively Be it enacted . . .

That whosoever shall hereafter come to the Possession of this Crown shall joyn in Communion with the Church of England as by Law established

[1] Sect. A, No. XXI, p. 57.

That in case the Crown and Imperiall Dignity of this Realm shall hereafter come to any Person not being a Native of this Kingdom of England this Nation be not obliged to ingage in any Warr for the Defence of any Dominions or Territories which do not belong to the Crown of England without the Consent of Parliament That no Person who shall hereafter come to the Possession of this Crown shall go out of the Dominions of England Scotland or Ireland without Consent of Parliament.[1]

repeal in 1st years of Hanovers.

That from and after the Time that the further Limitation by this Act shall take Effect all Matters and Things relating to the well governing of this Kingdom which are properly cognizable in the Privy Councill by the Laws and Customs of this Realme shall be transacted there and all Resolutions taken thereupon shall be signed by such of the Privy Councill as shall advise and consent to the same.[2]

That after the said Limitation shall take Effect as aforesaid no Person born out of the Kingdoms of England Scotland or Ireland or the Dominions thereunto belonging (although he be naturalized and made a Denizen) (except such as are born of English Parents) shall be capable to be of the Privy Councill or a Member of either House of Parliament or to enjoy any Office or Place of Trust either Civill or Military or to have any Grant of Lands Tenements or Hereditaments from the Crown to himself or to any other or others in Trust for him [3]

That no Person who has an Office or Place of Profit under the King or recieves a Pention from the Crown shall be capable of serving as a Member of the House of Commons.[4]

constant worry during Georgian

That after the said Limitation shall take Effect as aforesaid Judges Commissions be made Quam diu se bene Gesserint and their Salaries ascertained and established but upon the Address of both Houses of Parliament it may be lawfull to remove them.[5]

That no Pardon under the Great Seal of England be pleadable to an Impeachment by the Commons in Parliament.[6]

IV. And whereas the Laws of England are the Birthright of the People thereof and all the Kings and Queens who shall ascend the Throne of this Realm ought to administer the Government of the same according to the said Laws and all their Officers and Ministers ought to serve them respectively according to the same

[1] Repealed by 1 Geo. I, St. II, c. 51.
[2] Repealed by 4 & 5 Anne, c. 20, § xxvii. See Sect. D, No. XXII, p. 358.
[3] 1 Geo. I, St. II, c. 4, makes it clear that this incapacity is not retrospective to persons naturalized before the accession of Geo. I. Repealed 7 & 8 Vict. c. 66.
[4] See Sect. A, No. XLI, § XXIV, p. 115, No. LI, p. 131, No. LX, p. 146, and Vol. II, Sect. A, No. XXXII, § 52, p. 107. See also Re-election of Ministers Act, 9 Geo. V, c. 2 (G. Le May, *British Government, 1914–53*, p. 14).
[5] See Sect. A, No. LV, p. 139.   [6] See Sect. B, No. VIII (C), p. 182.

The said Lords Spirituall and Temporall and Commons do therefore further humbly pray That all the Laws and Statutes of this
Realm for securing the established Religion and the Rights and
Liberties of the People thereof and all other Laws and Statutes of
the same now in Force may be ratified and confirmed   And the same
are by His Majesty by and with the Advice and Consent of the said
Lords Spirituall and Temporall and Commons and by Authority of
the same ratified and confirmed accordingly.

XXXVII

AN ACT FOR ATTAINDER OF THE PRETENDED PRINCE OF WALES, 1701

13 and 14 Will. III, c. 3.

Whereas the pretended Prince of Wales since the Decease of
the late King James by the Incitation and Encouragement of the
French King (being bred up and instructed to introduce the Romish
Superstition and French Government into these Your Majesties
Kingdoms) openly and traiterously with design to dethrone Your
Majesty assumed the Name and Title of James the Third King of
England Scotland and Ireland and caused himself to be so pro-
claimed in the Kingdom of France in manifest Violation of Your
Majesties most lawfull and rightful Title to the Crown of these
Realms and of the several Acts of Parliament made as well for recog-
nizing of the same as for settling the Succession of the Crown contrary to the Duty of his Allegiance and to the disturbing of the Peace
of these Your Majesties Kingdoms to the End therefore that Your
Majesties good and loyal People of England assembled in Parliament
may in the most solemn Manner express their utmost Resentment
of so great an Indignity done to Your Majesties most sacred Person
and Government and that the said Traitor may be brought more
certainly and speedily to condign Punishment May it please Your
Majesty that it may be enacted . . . That the said pretended Prince
of Wales stand and be convicted and attainted of High Treason and
that he suffer Pains of Death and incurr all Forfeitures as a Traitor
convicted and attainted of High Treason

II. And for preventing traiterous Correspondence between
Your Majesties Subjects and the said pretended Prince of Wales
or his Adherents Be it further enacted . . . That if any of the
Subjects of the Crown of England . . . shall within this Realm
or without hold entertain or keep any Intelligence or Correspondence
in Person or by Letters Messages or otherwise with the said pre-

tended Prince of Wales or with any Person or Persons imployed by him knowing such Person to be so imployed or shall by Bill of Exchange or otherwise remitt or pay any Sum or Sums of Money for the Use or Service of the said pretended Prince of Wales knowing such Money to be for such Use or Service such Person so offending being lawfully convicted shall be taken deemed and adjudged to be guilty of High Treason and shall suffer and forfeit as in Cases of High Treason.

III. And be it further enacted That where any of the Offences against this Act shall be committed out of this Realm the same may be alledged and laid enquired of and tryed in any County of this Kingdom of England.

XXXVIII

AN ACT IMPOSING THE ABJURATION OATH, 1701

13 & 14 Will. III, c. 6.

[The Preamble and § I recite the various statutes establishing the succession, and impose on all office-holders, ecclesiastical persons, Foundation members of Colleges and teachers in the Universities and Schools, and all lawyers the subjoined oath of abjuration.]

I A. B. do truly and sincerely acknowledge profess testify and declare in my Conscience before God and the World That our Sovereign Lord King William is lawfull and rightful King of this Realm and of all other His Majesties Dominions and Countries thereunto belonging And I do solemnly and sincerely declare That I do believe in my Conscience that the Person pretended to be the Prince of Wales during the Life of the late King James and since his Decease pretending to be and taking upon himself the Stile and Title of King of England by the Name of James the Third hath not any Right or Title whatsoever to the Crown of this Realm or any other the Dominions thereto belonging   And I do renounce refuse and abjure any Allegiance or Obedience to him   And I do swear that I will bear Faith and true Allegiance to His Majesty King William and Him will defend to the utmost of my Power against all Traiterous Conspiracies and Attempts whatsoever which shall be made against His Person Crown or Dignity   And I will do my best endeavour to disclose and make known to His Majesty and His Successors all Treasons and Traiterous Conspiracies which I shall know to be against Him or any of them   And I do faithfully promise to the utmost of my Power to support maintain and defend the Limitation and Succession of the Crown against him the said James and all other Persons whatsoever as the same is and stands limited (by an Act [1] intituled An Act declaring the Rights and Liberties of the Subject and setling the Succession of the Crown) to His Majesty during His Majesties Life and after His Majesties Decease to the Princess Ann of Denmark and the Heirs of Her Body being Protestants and for default of such Issue to the Heirs of the Body of His Majesty being Protestants And as the same by one other Act [2] intituled An Act for the further Limitation of the Crown and better securing the Rights and Liberties of the Subject is and stands limitted after the Decease of His Majesty and the Princess Ann of Denmark and for default of Issue of the said Princess and of His Majesty respectively to the Princess Sophia Electoress and Dutchess Dowager of Hanover and the Heirs of Her Body being Protestants And all these Things I do plainly and sincerely acknowledge and swear according to these express Words by me spoken and according to the plain and common Sense and Understanding of the same Words without any Equivocation mental Evasion or secret Reservation whatsoever And I do make this Recognition Acknowledgment Abjuration Renunciation and Promise heartily willingly and truly upon the true Faith of a Christian

[§§ II-IX define the office-holders who must take the oath, the authorities to administer it, and the penalties (loss of the office or place) for failure to take the oath.]

[§§ X-XI. provide that all members of both Houses of Parliament shall take the oath and may not sit or vote unless they do, with heavy legal disabilities if they fail to do so.]

[§§ XII-XIV provide the machinery of administration.]

[§ XV makes it high treason to compass or imagine the death of the Princess Anne of Denmark.]

XXXIX

ACT FOR THE UNION WITH SCOTLAND, [3]

1707

6 Anne, c. 11.

Most gracious Sovereign

Whereas Articles of Union were agreed on the Twenty second Day of July in the Fifth Year of Your Majesties Reign by the

---

[1] Sect. A, No. XXV, p. 67. [2] Sect. A, No. XXXVI, p. 92.
[3] Cf. The Irish Union, Vol. II, Sect. A, No. XII, p. 20.

Commissioners nominated on Behalf of the Kingdom of England under Your Majesties Great Seal of England . . . in pursuance of an Act of Parliament made in England . . . and the Commissioners nominated on the Behalf of the Kingdom of Scotland under Your Majesties Great Seal of Scotland . . . in pursuance of the Fourth Act of the Third Session of the present Parliament of Scotland to treat of and concerning an Union of the said Kingdoms And whereas an Act hath passed in the Parliament of Scotland at Edinburgh . . . wherein 'tis mentioned that the Estates of Parliament . . . had agreed to and approved of the said Articles of Union with some Additions and Explanations and that Your Majesty with Advice and Consent of the Estates of Parliament for establishing the Protestant Religion and Presbyterian Church Government within the Kingdom of Scotland had passed in the same Session of Parliament an Act intituled Act for securing of the Protestant Religion and Presbyterian Church Government which by the Tenor thereof was appointed to be inserted in any Act ratifying the Treaty and expresly declared to be a fundamental and essential Condition of the said Treaty or Union in all Times coming the Tenor of which Articles as ratified and approved of with Additions and Explanations by the said Act of Parliament of Scotland follows

ARTICLE I. That the Two Kingdoms of England and Scotland shall upon the First Day of May which shall be in the Year One thousand seven hundred and seven and for ever after be united into One Kingdom by the Name of Great Britain and that the Ensigns Armorial of the said United Kingdom be such as Her Majesty shall appoint and the Crosses of St. George and St. Andrew be conjoyned in such Manner as Her Majesty shall think fit and used in all Flags Banners Standards and Ensigns both at Sea and Land.

ARTICLE II. That the Succession to the Monarchy of the United Kingdom of Great Britain and of the Dominions thereto belonging after Her most Sacred Majesty and in Default of Issue of Her Majesty be remain and continue to the most Excellent Princess Sophia Electoress and Dutchess Dowager of Hanover and the Heirs of Her Body being Protestants upon whom the Crown of England is settled . . . And that all Papists and Persons marrying Papists shall be excluded from and for ever incapable to inherit possess or enjoy the Imperial Crown of Great Britain and the Dominions thereunto belonging or any Part thereof and in every such Case the Crown and Government shall from time to time descend to and be enjoyed by such Person being a Protestant as should have inherited and enjoyed the same in case such Papist or Person marrying a Papist was naturally dead

ARTICLE III. That the United Kingdom of Great Britain be

represented by One and the same Parliament to be stiled The Parliament of Great Britain.

ARTICLE IIII. That all the Subjects of the United Kingdom of Great Britain shall from and after the Union have full Freedom and Intercourse of Trade and Navigation to and from any Port or Place within the said United Kingdom and the Dominions and Plantations thereunto belonging and that there be a Communication of all other Rights Privileges and Advantages which do or may belong to the Subjects of either Kingdom except where it is otherwise expresly agreed in these Articles.

[Article V declares all ships owned by Scotsmen, even if foreign built, to be British.]

ARTICLE VI. That all Parts of the United Kingdom for ever from and after the Union shall have the same Allowances Encouragements and Drawbacks and be under the same Prohibitions Restrictions and Regulations of Trade and liable to the Same Customs and Duties on Import and Export And that the Allowances Encouragements and Drawbacks Prohibitions Restrictions and Regulations of Trade and the Customs and Duties on Import and Export settled in England when the Union commences shall from and after the Union take place throughout the whole United Kingdom excepting and reserving the Duties upon Export and Import of such particular Commodities from which any Persons the Subjects of either Kingdom are specially liberated and exempted by their Private Rights which after the Union are to remain safe and entire to them in all Respects as before the same. . . .

[Scots Cattle imported into England to be subject only to the same duties as English Cattle. Bounty on export of oats when price is less than 15/- a quarter. Victuals not to be imported into Scotland from overseas.]

[Article VII. Scotland to be liable to the English Excise, with exception of beer.]

[Article VIII. The Salt Duties : special temporary arrangements.]

[Article IX. The Land Tax : Scotland to pay £48,000 for every £1,997,763 : 8 : 4½ of England.]

[Articles X, XI, XII, XIII. Stamped Vellum, Window Tax, Coals, Culm and Cinders and Malt : special exemptions for Scotland.]

ARTICLE XIV. That the Kingdom of Scotland be not charged with any other Duties laid on by the Parliament of England before the Union except these consented to in this Treaty in regard it is agreed that all necessary Provision shall be made by the Parliament of Scotland for the Publick Charge and Service of that Kingdom for the Year One thousand seven hundred and seven Provided nevertheless that if the Parliament of England shall think fit to lay any further

Impositions by way of Customs or such Excises with which by virtue of this Treaty Scotland is to be charged equally with England in such Case Scotland shall be liable to the same Customs and Excises and have an Equivalent to be settled by the Parliament of Great Britain with this further Provision That any Malt to be made and consumed in that Part of the United Kingdom now called Scotland shall not be charged with any Imposition on Malt during this present War And seeing it cannot be supposed that the Parliament of Great Britain will ever lay any Sort of Burthens upon the United Kingdom but what they shall find of Necessity at that Time for the Preservation and Good of the Whole and with due regard to the Circumstances and Abilities of every part of the United Kingdom therefore it is agreed that there be no further Exemption insisted upon for any Part of the United Kingdom but that the Consideration of any Exemptions beyond what are already agreed on in this Treaty shall be left to the Determination of the Parliament of Great Britain.

[Article XV deals with equivalents in duties as between the two kingdoms, and provides for the spending of excess receipts in Scotland on indemnifying private persons for loss in consequence of re-coinage, repayment of capital stock of the African and Indian Company of Scotland, thereafter that all the public debts of the Kingdom of Scotland, as shall be adjusted by this present parliament, shall be paid, and that two thousand pounds per annum for the space of seven years shall be applied towards encouraging and promoting the manufacture of coarse wool. Finally any balance shall be used for the improvement of the fisheries and manufactures generally.]

ARTICLE XVI. That from and after the Union the Coin shall be of the same Standard and Value throughout the United Kingdom as now in England and a Mint shall be continued in Scotland under the same Rules as the Mint in England and the present Officers of the Mint continued subject to such Regulations and Alterations as Her Majesty Her Heirs or Successors or the Parliament of Great Britain shall think fit.

ARTICLE XVII. That from and after the Union the same Weights and Measures shall be used throughout the United Kingdom, as are now established in England and Standards of Weights and Measures shall be kept by those Burghs in Scotland to whom the keeping the Standards of Weights and Measure now in Use there does of special Right belong All which Standards shall be sent down to such respective Burghs from the Standards kept in the Exchequer at Westminster subject nevertheless to such Regulations as the Parliament of Great Britain shall think fit.

ARTICLE XVIII. That the Laws concerning Regulation of Trade Customs and such Excises to which Scotland is by virtue of this Treaty to be liable be the same in Scotland from and after the

Union as in England and that all other Laws in Use within the
Kingdom of Scotland do after the Union and notwithstanding thereof
remain in the same Force as before (except such as are contrary to or
inconsistent with this Treaty) but alterable by the Parliament of Great
Britain with this Difference betwixt the Laws concerning publick
Right Policy and Civil Government and those which concern private
Right that the Laws which concern publick Right Policy and Civil ·
Government may be made the same throughout the whole United
Kingdom But that no Alteration be made in Laws which concern
private Right except for evident Utility of the Subjects within Scotland.

ARTICLE XIX. That the Court of Session or Colledge of Justice
do after the Union and notwithstanding thereof remain in all Time
coming within Scotland as it is now constituted by the Laws of
that Kingdom and with the same Authority and Privileges as before
the Union subject nevertheless to such Regulations for the better
Administration of Justice as shall be made by the Parliament of
Great Britain [Qualifications necessary for appointment by the
Crown of Ordinary Lords of Sessions] yet so as the Qualifications
made or to be made for capacitating Persons to be named Ordinary
Lords of Session may be altered by the Parliament of Great Britain
And that the Court of Justiciary do also after the Union and not-
withstanding thereof remain in all Time coming within Scotland
as it is now constituted by the Laws of that Kingdom and with the
same Authority and Privileges as before the Union subject nevertheless to such Regulations as shall be made by the Parliament of
Great Britain and without Prejudice of other Rights of Justiciary
[An Admiralty jurisdiction to be maintained in Scotland as in
England] And that all other Courts now in being within the Kingdom
of Scotland do remain but subject to Alterations by the Parliament
of Great Britain and that all inferiour Courts within the said Limits
do remain subordinate as they are now to the supream Courts of
Justice within the same in all Time coming And that no Causes in
Scotland be cognoscible by the Courts of Chancery Queen's Bench
Common Pleas or any other Court in Westminster Hall and that
the said Courts or any other of the like Nature after the Union shall
have no Power to cognosce review or alter the Acts or Sentences
of the Judicatures within Scotland or stop the Execution of the
same [An Exchequer Court to be established in Scotland]

ARTICLE XX. That all Heretable Offices Superiorities Heretable
Jurisdictions Offices for Life and Jurisdictions for Life be reserved
to the Owners thereof as Rights of Property [1] in the same Manner
as they are now enjoyed by the Laws of Scotland notwithstanding
this Treaty.

[1] See 20 Geo. II, c. 43, "An Act for taking away and abolishing the Heretable Jurisdictions . . . and for making Satisfaction to the Proprietors thereof".

Article XXI. That the Rights and Privileges of the Royal Burghs in Scotland as they now are do remain entire after the Union and notwithstanding thereof.

Article XXII. That by virtue of this Treaty of the Peers of Scotland at the Time of the Union Sixteen shall be the Number to sit and vote in the House of Lords and Forty five the Number of the Representatives of Scotland in the House of Commons of the Parliament of Great Britain and that when Her Majesty Her Heires or Successors shall declare Her or Their Pleasure for holding the First or any subsequent Parliament of Great Britain until the Parliament of Great Britain shall make further provision therein a Writ do issue under the Great Seal of the United Kingdom directed to the Privy Council of Scotland commanding them to cause Sixteen Peers who are to sit in the House of Lords to be summoned to Parliament and Forty five Members to be elected to sit in the House of Commons of the Parliament of Great Britain according to the Agreement in this Treaty in such Manner as by an Act of this present Session of the Parliament of Scotland is or shall be settled which Act is hereby declared to be as valid as if it were a Part of and ingrossed in this Treaty And that the Names of the Persons so summoned and elected shall be returned by the Privy Council of Scotland into the Court from whence the said Writ did issue And that if her Majesty on or before the First Day of May next on which Day the Union is to take place shall declare under the Great Seal of England that it is expedient that the Lords of Parliament of England and Commons of the present Parliament of England should be the Members of the respective Houses of the First Parliament of Great Britain for and on the Part of England then the said Lords of Parliament of England and Commons of the present Parliament of England shall be the Members of the respective Houses of the First Parliament of Great Britain for and on the Part of England And Her Majesty may by Her Royal Proclamation under the Great Seal of Great Britain appoint the said First Parliament of Great Britain to meet at such Time and Place as Her Majesty shall think fit which Time shall not be less than Fifty Days after the Date of Such Proclamation and the Time and Place of the Meeting of such Parliament being so appointed a Writ shall be immediately issued under the Great Seal of Great Britain directed to the Privy Council of Scotland for the summoning the Sixteen Peers and for electing Forty five Members by whom Scotland is to be represented in the Parliament of Great Britain And the Lords of Parliament of England and the Sixteen Peers of Scotland such Sixteen Peers being summoned and returned in the Manner agreed in this Treaty and the Members of the House of Commons of the said Parliament of England and the Forty five

Members for Scotland such Forty five Members being elected and returned in the Manner agreed in this Treaty . . . shall be the Two Houses of the First Parliament of Great Britain and that Parliament may continue for such Time only as the present Parliament of England might have continued if the Union of the Two Kingdoms had not been made unless sooner dissolved by Her Majesty And that every one of the Lords of Parliament of Great Britain and every Member of the House of Commons of the Parliament of Great Britain in the First and all succeeding Parliaments of Great Britain until the Parliament of Great Britain shall otherwise direct shall take the respective Oaths appointed [1] [by 1 Will. & Mar., the declaration against Roman Catholicism [2] mentioned in 30 Car. II, Stat. II, c. 1, and the Oath required by 13 & 14 Will. III, c. 6,[3] as amended by 1 Anne, c. 16] And it is declared and agreed that these Words This Realm The Crown of this Realm and The Queen of this Realm mentioned in the Oaths and Declaration contained in the aforesaid Acts which were intended to signifie the Crown and Realm of England shall be understood of the Crown and Realm of Great Britain and that in that Sense the said Oaths and Declaration be taken and subscribed by the Members of both Houses of the Parliament of Great Britain.

ARTICLE XXIII. That the aforesaid Sixteen Peers mentioned in the last preceding Article to sit in the House of Lords of the Parliament of Great Britain shall have all Priviledges of Parliament which the Peers of England now have and which they or any Peers of Great Britain shall have after the Union and particularly the Right of Sitting upon the Trials of Peers And in case of the Trial of any Peer in Time of Adjournment or Prorogation of Parliament the said Sixteen Peers shall be summoned in the same Manner and have the same Powers and Privileges at such Trial as any other Peers of Great Britain and that in case any Tryals of Peers shall hereafter happen when there is no Parliament in being the Sixteen Peers of Scotland who sat at the last preceding Parliament shall be summoned in the same Manner and have the same Powers and Privileges at such Tryals as any other Peers of Great Britain and that all Peers of Scotland and their Successors to their Honours and Dignities shall from and after the Union be Peers of Great Britain and have Rank and Precedency next and immediately after the Peers of the like Orders and Degrees in England at the Time of the Union and before all Peers of Great Britain of the like Orders and Degrees who may be created after the Union and shall be tryed as Peers of Great Britain and shall enjoy all Privileges of Peers as fully as the Peers of

[1] Sect. A, No. XXII, p. 60.   [2] Sect. A, No. XVII, p. 43.
[3] Sect. A, No. XXXVIII, p. 97.

England do now or as they or any other Peers of Great Britain may hereafter enjoy the same except the Right and Privilege of sitting in the House of Lords and the Privileges depending thereon and particularly the Right of sitting upon the Tryals of Peers.

ARTICLE XXIV. That from and after the Union there be one Great Seal for the United Kingdom of Great Britain which shall be different from the Great Seal now used in either Kingdom And that the quartering the Arms and the Rank and Precedency of the Lyon King of Arms of the Kingdom of Scotland as may best suit the Union be left to Her Majesty And that in the mean time the Great Seal of England be used as the Great Seal of the United Kingdom and that the Great Seal of the United Kingdom be used for sealing Writts to elect and summon the Parliament of Great Britain and for sealing all Treaties with Foreign Princes and States and all Publick Acts Instruments and Orders of State which concern the whole United Kingdom and in all other Matters relating to England as the Great Seal of England is now used and that a Seal in Scotland after the Union be always kept and made use of in all Things relating to private Rights or Grants which have usually passed the Great Seal of Scotland and which only concern Offices Grants Commissions and private Rights within that Kingdom and that until such Seal shall be appointed by Her Majesty the present Great Seal of Scotland shall be used for such Purposes and that the Privy Seal Signet Casset Signet of the Justiciary Court Quarter Seal and Seals of Courts now used in Scotland be continued but that the said Seals be altered and adapted to the State of the Union as Her Majesty shall think fit and the said Seals and all of them and the Keepers of them shall be subject to such Regulations as the Parliament of Great Britain shall hereafter make And that the Crown Scepter and Sword of State the Records of Parliament and all other Records Rolls and Registers whatsoever both Publick and Private General and Particular and Warrants thereof continue to be kept as they are within that Part of the United Kingdom now called Scotland and that they shall so remain in all Time coming notwithstanding the Union.

ARTICLE XXV. That all Laws and Statutes in either Kingdom so far as they are contrary to or inconsistent with the Terms of these Articles or any of them shall from and after the Union cease and become void and shall be so declared to be by the respective Parliaments of the said Kingdoms.

As by the said Articles of Union ratified and approved by the said Act of Parliament of Scotland Relation being thereunto had may appear.

II. And the Tenor of the aforesaid Act[1] for securing the Protestant Religion and Presbyterian Church Government within the Kingdom of Scotland is as follows.

OUR Soveraign Lady and the Estates of Parliament considering that by the late Act of Parliament for a Treaty with England for an Union of both Kingdoms it is provided that the Commissioners for that Treaty should not treat of or concerning any Alteration of the Worship Discipline and Government of the Church of this Kingdom as now by Law established which Treaty being now reported to the Parliament and it being reasonable and necessary that the true Protestant Religion as presently professed within this Kingdom with the Worship Discipline and Government of this Church should be effectually and unalterably secured therefore Her Majesty with Advice and Consent of the said Estates of Parliament doth hereby establish and confirm the said true Protestant Religion and the Worship Discipline and Government of this Church to continue without any Alteration to the People of this Land in all succeeding Generations . . . And Her Majesty with Advice and Consent aforesaid expresly provides and declares that the foresaid true Protestant Religion contained in the above mentioned Confession of Faith with the Form and Purity of Worship presently in Use within this Church and its Presbyterian Church Government and Discipline (that is to say) the Government of the Church by Kirk Sessions Presbyteries Provincial Synods and General Assemblies all established by the foresaid Acts of Parliament pursuant to the Claim of Right[2] shall remain and continue unalterable and that the said Presbyterian Government shall be the only Government of the Church within the Kingdom of Scotland

And further for the greater Security of the foresaid Protestant Religion and of the Worship Discipline and Government of this Church as above established Her Majesty with Advice and Consent foresaid statutes and ordains that the Universities and Colledges of Saint Andrew's Glasgow Aberdeen and Edinburgh as now established by Law shall continue within this Kingdom for ever and that in all Time coming no Professors Principals Regents Masters or others bearing Office in any University Colledge or School within this Kingdom be capable or be admitted or allowed to continue in the Exercise of their said Functions but such as shall own and acknowledge the Civil Government in Manner prescribed or to be prescribed by the Acts of Parliament as also that before or at their Admissions they do and shall acknowledge and profess and shall

---

[1] The Act passed 16 Jan., 5 Anne in Scotland, mentioned in the Preamble.

[2] The Claim of Right was the Scottish equivalent to the English Bill of Rights.

subscribe to the foresaid Confession of Faith as the Confession of their Faith and that they will practise and conform themselves to the Worship presently in Use in this Church and submit themselves to the Government and Discipline thereof and never endeavour directly or indirectly the Prejudice or Subversion of the same and that before the respective Presbyteries of their Bounds by whatsoever Gift Presentation or Provision they may be thereto provided.

And further Her Majesty with Advice aforesaid expresly declares and statutes that none of the Subjects of this Kingdom shall be liable to but all and every one of them for ever free of any Oath Test or Subscription within this Kingdom contrary to or inconsistent with the foresaid true Protestant Religion and Presbyterian Church Government Worship and Discipline as above established and that the same within the Bounds of this Church and Kingdom shall never be imposed upon or required of them in any Sort And lastly that after the Decease of Her present Majesty (whom God long preserve) the Soveraign succeeding to Her in the Royal Government of the Kingdom of Great Britain shall in all Time coming at His or Her Accession to the Crown swear and subscribe that they shall inviolably maintain and preserve the foresaid Settlement of the True Protestant Religion with the Government Worship Discipline Right and Privileges of this Church as above established by the Laws of this Kingdom in Prosecution of the Claim of Right

And it is hereby statute and ordained that this Act of Parliament with the Establishment therein contained shall be held and observed in all Time coming as a fundamental and essential Condition of any Treaty or Union to be concluded betwixt the Two Kingdoms without any Alteration thereof or Derogation thereto in any Sort for ever As also that this Act of Parliament and Settlement therein contained shall be insert and repeated in any Act of Parliament that shall pass for agreeing and concluding the foresaid Treaty or Union betwixt the Two Kingdoms and that the same shall be therein expresly declared to be a fundamental and essential Condition of the said Treaty or Union in all Time coming which Articles of Union and Act immediately above written Her Majesty with Advice and Consent aforesaid statutes enacts and ordains to be and continue in all Time coming the sure and perpetual Foundation of a compleat and entire Union of the Two Kingdoms of Scotland and England under the express Condition and Provision that this Approbation and Ratification of the foresaid Articles and Act shall be no ways binding on this Kingdom until the said Articles and Act be ratified approved and confirmed by Her Majesty with and by the Authority of the Parliament of England as they are now agreed to approved and confirmed by Her Majesty with and by the

Authority of the Parliament of Scotland declaring nevertheless that the Parliament of England may provide for the Security of the Church of England as they think expedient to take place within the Bounds of the said Kingdom of England and not derogating from the Security above provided for establishing of the Church of Scotland within the Bounds of this Kingdom as also the said Parliament of England may extend the Additions and other Provisions contained in the Articles of Union as above insert in Favours of the Subjects of Scotland to and in Favours of the Subjects of England which shall not suspend or derogate from the Force and Effect of this present Ratification . . . in the Parliament of Scotland.

And lastly her Majesty enacts and declares that all Laws and Statutes in thïs Kingdom so far they are contrary to or inconsistent with the Terms of these Articles as above mentioned shall from and after the Union cease and become void.

．　　　．　　　．　　　．　　　．　　　．

[§ III recites 5 Anne, c. 5, an Act for securing the Church of England, 13 Eliz., c. 12,[1] an Act for the reformation of ministers of the Church, and 14 Car. 2, c. 4,[2] the Act of Uniformity, and re-enacts them as regards the Church of England.]

And be it further enacted by the Authority aforesaid That after the Demise of Her Majesty (whom God long preserve) the Sovereign next succeeding to Her Majesty in the Royal Government of the Kingdom of Great Britain and so for ever hereafter every King or Queen succeeding . . . at His or Her Coronation shall in the Presence of all Persons who shall be attending . . . take and subscribe an Oath to maintain and preserve inviolably the said Settlement of the Church of England. . . .

And be it further enacted by the Authority aforesaid That this Act and all and every the Matters and Things therein contained be and shall for ever be holden and adjudged to be a fundamental and essential Part of any Treaty of Union to be concluded between the said Two Kingdoms. . . .

IV. May it therefore please Your most Excellent Majesty that it may be enacted and be it enacted . . . That all and every the said Articles of Union as ratified and approved by the said Act of Parliament of Scotland as aforesaid and herein before particularly mentioned and inserted and also the said Act of Parliament of Scotland for establishing the Protestant Religion and Presbyterian Church Government within that Kingdom intituled Act for securing the Protestant Religion and Presbyterian Church Government and every Clause Matter and Thing in the said Articles and Act contained

---

[1] See Prothero, p. 64.　　　　　　　　[2] See Sect. A, No. XI, p. 20.

shall be and the said Articles and Act are hereby for ever ratified approved and confirmed.

V. And it is hereby further enacted by the Authority aforesaid That the said Act passed in this present Session of Parliament intituled An Act for securing the Church of England as by Law established and all and every the Matters and Things therein contained and also the said Act of Parliament of Scotland intituled Act for securing the Protestant Religion and Presbyterian Church Government with the Establishment in the said Act contained be and shall for ever be held and adjudged to be and observed as fundamental and essential Conditions of the said Union and shall in all Times coming be taken to be and are hereby declared to be essential and fundamental Parts of the said Articles and Union and the said Articles of Union so as aforesaid ratified approved and confirmed by Act of Parliament of Scotland and by this present Act and the said Act passed in this present Session of Parliament intituled An Act for securing the Church of England as by Law established and also the said Act passed in the Parliament of Scotland intituled Act for securing the Protestant Religion and Presbyterian Church Government are hereby enacted and ordained to be and continue in all Times coming the complete and intire Union of the Two Kingdoms of England and Scotland

VI. And whereas since the passing the said Act in the Parliament of Scotland for ratifying the said Articles of Union one other Act intituled Act settling the Manner of electing the Sixteen Peers and Forty five Members to represent Scotland in the Parliament of Great Britain hath likewise passed in the said Parliament of Scotland at Edinburgh the Fifth Day of February One thousand seven hundred and seven the Tenor whereof follows

Our Sovereign Lady considering that by the Twenty Second Article of the Treaty of Union . . . the said Sixteen Peers and Forty five Members in the House of Commons be named and chosen in such Manner as by a subsequent Act in this present Session of Parliament in Scotland should be settled . . . Therefore Her Majesty with Advice and Consent of the Estates of Parliament statutes enacts and ordains that the said Sixteen Peers who shall have Right to sit in the House of Peers in the Parliament of Great Britain on the Part of Scotland by virtue of this Treaty shall be named by the said Peers of Scotland whom they represent their Heires or Successors to their Dignities and Honours out of their own Number and that by open Election and Plurality of Voices of the Peers present and of the Proxies for such as shall be absent . . . and in case of the Death or legal Incapacity of any of the said Sixteen Peers that the aforesaid Peers of Scotland shall nominate another of their own Number in place of the said Peer or Peers in Manner before and after mentioned And that of the said Forty five Representatives of Scotland in the House of Commons in the Parliament of Great Britain Thirty shall be chosen by the Shires or Steuartries and Fifteen by the Royal Burrows as follows. . . .

[The remainder of the section prescribes in detail the Representation of Scotland in the United Parliament, and subjects electors and elected to the electoral laws of Scotland, together with the penal sections against Papists laid down in 8 & 9 Will. III, c. 3. It also prescribes the regulations for the election of representative peers.]

[§ VII re-enacts the Scottish Act settling the election of sixteen representative peers and forty-five members.]

XL

FURTHER ACT FOR THE UNION WITH SCOTLAND, 1707

6 Anne, c. 40.

An Act for rendring the Union of the two Kingdoms more intire and complete.

Whereas by her Majesties great Wisdom and Goodness the Union of the Two Kingdoms hath been happily effected and the whole Island is thereby subject to One Sovereignty and represented by One Parliament to the end therefore that the said Union may be rendred more complete and intire be it enacted . . . That from and after the First Day of May in the Year of our Lord One thousand seven hundred and eight the Queen's Majesty Her Heirs and Successors shall have but One Privy Council in or for the Kingdom of Great Britain to be sworn to Her Majesty her Heires and Successors as Sovereigns of Great Britain and such Privy Council shall have the same Powers and Authorities as the Privy Council of England lawfully had used and exercised at the Time of the Union and none other

II. And to the end the publick Peace may be in like manner preserved throughout the whole Kingdom be it further enacted by the Authority aforesaid That in every Shire and Stewartry within . . . Scotland and also in such Cities Boroughs Liberties and Precincts within Scotland as Her Majesty Her Heirs or Successors shall think fit there shall be appointed by Her Majesty Her Heirs or Successors under the Great Seal of Great Britain a sufficient Number of good and lawful Men to be Justices of the Peace within

their respective Shires Stewartries Cities Boroughs Liberties or
Precincts which Persons so appointed over and above the several
Powers and Authorities vested in Justices of the Peace by the Laws
of Scotland shall be further authorized to do use and exercise over all
Persons within their several Bounds whatever doth appertain to the
Office and Trust of a Justice of Peace[1] by virtue of the Laws and Acts
of Parliament made in England before the Union in relation to or for
the Preservation of the publick Peace   Provided nevertheless that
in the Sessions of the Peace the Methods of Tryal and Judgments
shall be according to the Laws and Customs of Scotland

III. Provided That nothing in this Act contained shall . . .
infringe any Rights Liberties or Privileges heretofore granted to the
City of Edinburgh or to any other Royal Borough of being Justices
of Peace within their respective Bounds.

[§ IV. The Circuit Courts to be increased from once to twice a
year.]

[§§ V-VI. Detailed regulations for electing Representatives of
Scotland to the House of Commons.]

XLI

THE REGENCY ACT, 1707

6 Anne, c. 41.[2]

*An Act for the Security of Her Majesties Person and Government
and of the Succession to the Crown of Great Britain in the Protestant
Line.*

Whereas by the happy Union of England and Scotland it is
become necessary to make divers Alterations in relation to an Act
passed in the Parliament of England in the Fourth Year of the
Reign of Her present Majesty whom God long preserve intituled
An Act[3] for the better Security of Her Majesties Person and Government and of the Succession to the Crown of England in the Protestant Line and to extend the Provisions of the said Act throughout
the whole United Kingdom for the better Security of our most
gracious Sovereigns Person and Government and of the Succession
to the Crown of Great Britain in the Protestant Line as it is now by
the Laws and Statutes of this Realm settled limited and appointed
Be it therefore enacted . . . That if any Person or Persons shall
maliciously advisedly and directly by writing or printing maintain

[1] Sect. D, No. XLI, p. 389.
[2] This Act is cited in the Stats. at Large as 6 Anne, c. 7.
[3] 4 & 5 Anne, c. 20.

and affirm that our Sovereign Lady the Queen that now is is not the lawful and rightful Queen of these Realms or that the pretended Prince of Wales who now stiles himself King of Great Britain or King of England by the Name of James the Third or King of Scotland by the Name of James the Eighth hath any Right or Title to the Crown of these Realms or that any other Person or Persons hath or have any Right or Title to the same otherwise than according to an Act [1] of Parliament made in England in the First Year of the Reign of Their late Majesties King William and Queen Mary of ever blessed and glorious Memory intituled An Act declaring the Rights and Liberties of the Subject and settling the Succession of the Crown and one other Act [2] made in England in the Twelfth Year of the Reign of His said late Majesty King William the Third intituled An Act for the further Limitation of the Crown and better securing the Rights and Liberties of the Subject And the Acts lately made in England and Scotland mutually for the Union of the Two Kingdoms or that the Kings or Queens of this Realm with and by the Authority of Parliament are not able to make Laws and Statutes of sufficient Force and Validity to limit and bind the Crown and the Descent Limitation Inheritance and Government thereof every such Person or Persons shall be guilty of High Treason and being thereof lawfully convicted shall be adjudged Traytors and shall suffer Pains of Death and all Losses and Forfeitures as in Cases of High Treason

[§§ II and III. Preachers declaring or maintaining the Queen not to be the lawful Queen to incur the penalties of premunire. Proof to be made by two witnesses and prosecution to be within three months.]

IV. And be it further enacted by the Authority aforesaid That this present Parliament or any other Parliament which shall hereafter be summoned and called by Her Majesty Queen Anne Her Heirs or Successors shall not be determined or dissolved by the Death or Demise of Her said Majesty Her Heirs or Successors [3] but such Parliament shall and is hereby enacted to continue and is hereby impowered and required if sitting at the Time of such Demise immediately to proceed to act notwithstanding such Death or Demise for and during the Term of Six Months and no longer unless the same be sooner prorogued or dissolved by such Person to whom the Crown of this Realm of Great Britain shall come remain and be according to the Acts for limiting and settling the Succession and for the Union above mentioned And if the said Parliament shall be prorogued then it shall meet and sit on and

---

[1] Sect. A, No. XXV, p. 67. [2] Sect. A, No. XXXVI, p. 92.
[2] See also Sect. A, No. XXXII, p. 84, and Vol. II, Sect. A, No. IX, p. 16, and No. XXXII, § 51, p. 106.

upon the Day unto which it shall be prorogued and continue for the Residue of the said Time of Six Months unless sooner prorogued or dissolved as aforesaid.

V. And be it further enacted by the authority aforesaid That if there be a Parliament in being at the Time of the Death of Her Majesty Her Heirs or Successors but the same happens to be separated by Adjournment or Prorogation such Parliament shall immediately after such Demise meet convene and sit and shall act notwithstanding such Death or Demise for and during the Time of Six Months and no longer unless the same shall be sooner prorogued or dissolved as aforesaid.

[§ VI. If no Parliament is in being, then the last preceding one to meet and be a Parliament and continue for six months as above.]

[§ VII. No abridgement of the royal prerogative to summon and dissolve Parliament. Triennial Act[1] of 6 & 7 Will. & Mar., c. 2, confirmed.]

VIII. And be it further enacted by the Authority aforesaid That the Privy Council of Her Majesty Her Heirs or Successors for the Kingdom of Great Britain shall not be determined or dissolved by the Death or Demise of Her Majesty Her Heirs or Successors but such Privy-Council shall continue and act as such by the Space of Six Months next after such Demise unless sooner determined by the next Successor to whom the Imperial Crown of this Realm is limited and appointed to go remain and descend nor shall the Office or Place of Lord Chancellor or Lord Keeper of the Great Seal of Great Britain or of Lord High Treasurer of Great Britain Lord President of the Council for Great Britain Lord Privy Seal of Great Britain Lord High Admiral of Great Britain or of any of the Great Officers of the Queen or Kings Household for the Time being nor shall any Office Place or Imployment Civil or Military within the Kingdoms of Great Britain or Ireland Dominion of Wales Town of Berwick upon Tweed Isles of Jersey Guernsey Alderney and Sarke or any of Her Majesties Plantations become void by reason of the Demise or Death of Her present Majesty Her Heirs or Successors Queens or Kings of this Realm but the said Lord Chancellor [etc.] shall continue in their respective Offices Places and Imployments for the Space of Six Months next after such Death or Demise unless sooner removed and discharged by the next in Succession as aforesaid

[§ IX. The Great Seal is the seal to be used until the successor to the Crown gives orders for a new seal.]

X. And be it further enacted by the Authority aforesaid That whensoever Her Majesty (whom God long preserve) shall happen to

---

[1] Sect. A, No. XXIX, p. 79.

demise and depart this Life without Issue of Her Body the Privy Council for Great Britain in being at the Time of such Demise of Her Majesty shall with all convenient Speed cause the next Protestant Successor entitled to the Crown of Great Britain by virtue of the Acts before mentioned to be openly and solemnly proclaimed in Great Britain and Ireland in such Manner and Form as the preceding Kings and Queens respectively have been usually proclaimed after the Demise of their respective Predecessors and that all and every Member and Members of the said Privy Council wilfully neglecting or refusing to cause such Proclamation to be made shall be guilty of High Treason and being thereof lawfully convicted shall be adjudged Traytors and shall suffer Pains of Death and all Losses and Forfeitures as in Cases of High Treason and also all and every Officer and Officers within the said Kingdoms of Great Britain and Ireland who shall by the said Privy Council be required to make such Proclamations and shall wilfully refuse or neglect to make the same shall be guilty of High Treason and being thereof lawfully convicted shall be adjudged Traytors and shall suffer Pains of Death and all Losses and Forfeitures as in Cases of High Treason

XI. And because it may happen that the next Protestant Successor may at the Time of such Demise of Her Majesty be out of the Realm of Great Britain in Parts beyond the Seas Be it therefore enacted by the Authority aforesaid That for the continuing of the Administration of the Government in the Name of such Protestant Successor until Her or His Arrival in Great Britain the Seven Officers herein after named who shall be in the Possession of their Offices at the Time of such Demise of Her Majesty that is to say the Archbishop of Canterbury at that Time being the Lord Chancellor or Lord Keeper of the Great Seal of Great Britain at that Time being the Lord High Treasurer of Great Britain at that Time being the Lord President of the Council for Great Britain at that Time being the Lord Privy Seal of Great Britain at that Time being the Lord High Admiral of Great Britain at that Time being and the Lord Chief Justice of the Queen's Bench at that Time being shall be and are by virtue of this Act constituted and appointed Lords Justices of Great Britain and are and shall be by virtue of this Act impowered in the Name of such Successor and in Her and His stead to use exercise and execute all Powers Authorities Matters and Acts of Government and Administration of Government in as full and ample Manner as such next Successor could use or execute the same if She or He were present in Person within this Kingdom of Great Britain until such Successor shall arrive or otherwise determine their Authority.

XII. Nevertheless be it further enacted by the Authority aforesaid That such Person who by the Limitations aforesaid is or shall be next to succeed to the Crown of this Realm in case of Her Majesties Demise without Issue shall and is hereby impowered at any Time during Her Majesties Life by Three Instruments under Her or His Hand and Seal revocable or to be altered at Her and His Will and Pleasure to nominate and appoint such and so many Persons being natural born Subjects of this Realm of Great Britain as She or He shall think fit to be added to the Seven Officers before named to the Lords Justices as aforesaid who shall be impowered by Authority of this Act to act with them as Lords Justices of Great Britain as fully and in the same Manner as if they had been herein particularly named which said Lords Justices or the major Part of them which shall assemble so as such major Part be not fewer than Five shall and may use and exercise all the Powers and Authorities before mentioned as fully and effectually to all Intents and Purposes as if all of them had been assembled together and consenting.

[§§ XIII and XIV. These three Instruments are to be transmitted sealed to, and to be held sealed by, the Successor's Resident in England, the Archbishop of Canterbury, and the Lord Chancellor. Revocations of the nominations therein to be similarly treated. On the Queen's death these three officers are to produce and open the Instruments in Privy Council. Persons violating these provisions to incur penalties enacted in statute of premunire.]

[§§ XV-XVII. Provision as to the instrument and the powers of the Lord Justices who may not dissolve Parliament nor give the Royal Assent to any Act for repealing or altering the Act of Uniformity in England nor the Act of Scotland for securing the Presbyterian Church there.]

[§§ XVIII-XXIII. Provisions as to oaths to be taken after the Queen's death, and to the use by her successor of a seal. Regulations for calling of Parliament and provision in case any of the seven offices above are in commission.]

XXIV. And be it further enacted[1] . . . That no Person who shall have in his own Name or in the Name of any Person or Persons in Trust for him or for his Benefit any new Office or Place of Profit whatsoever under the Crown which at any Time since the Five and twentieth Day of October in the Year of our Lord One thousand seven hundred and five have been created or erected or hereafter shall be created or erected nor any Person who shall be Commissioner or Sub-Commissioner of Prizes Secretary or Receiver of the Prizes nor any Comptroller of the Accompts of the Army nor any Commissioner of Transports nor any Commissioner of the sick

[1] See Sect. A, No. XXXVI, § III, p. 95, also No. LI, p. 131, and No. LX, p. 146.

and wounded nor any Agent for any Regiment nor any Commissioner for any Wine Licences nor any Governor or Deputy Governor of any of the Plantations nor any Commissioners of the Navy imployed in any of the Out Ports nor any Person having any Pension from the Crown during Pleasure shall be capable of being elected or of sitting or voting as a Member of the House of Commons in any Parliament which shall be hereafter summoned and holden.

XXV. Provided always That if any Person being chosen a Member of the House of Commons shall accept of any Office of Profit from the Crown during such Time as he shall continue a Member his Election shall be and is hereby declared to be void and a new Writ shall issue for a new Election as if such Person so accepting was naturally dead Provided nevertheless that such Person shall be capable of being again elected as if his Place had not become void as aforesaid.

XXVI. Provided also . . . That in order to prevent for the future too great a Number of Commissioners to be appointed or constituted for the executing of any Office that no greater Number of Commissioners shall be made or constituted for the Execution of any Office than have been imployed in the Execution of such respective Office at some Time before the First Day of this present Parliament.

XXVII. Provided also That nothing herein contained . . . be construed to extend to any Member of the House of Commons being an Officer in Her Majesties Navy or Army who shall receive any new or other Commission in the Navy or Army respectively.

XXVIII. And be it further enacted That if any Person hereby disabled or declared to be incapable to sit or vote in any Parliament hereafter to be holden shall nevertheless be returned as a Member to serve for any County Stewartry City Town or Cinque Port in any such Parliament such Election and Return are hereby . . . declared to be void to all Intents and Purposes whatsoever And if any Person disabled or declared incapable . . . shall after the Dissolution or Determination of this present Parliament presume to sit or vote as a Member of the House of Commons in any Parliament . . . such Person so sitting or voting shall forfeit the Sum of Five Hundred Pounds. . . .

XXIX. And be it further enacted . . . That every Person disabled to be elected, . . . in the House of Commons of any Parliament of England shall be disabled to be elected or to sit or vote in the House of Commons of any Parliament of Great Britain.

[§ XXX. Commissioners for the Equivalent for Scotland not to be disabled from sitting in Parliament.]

XLII

ACT IMPOSING PROPERTY QUALIFICATIONS ON MEMBERS OF THE HOUSE OF COMMONS,[1] 1710

9 Anne, c. 5.

For the better preserving the Constitution and Freedom of Parliament Be it enacted . . . That from and after the Determination of this present Parliament no Person shall be capable to sit or vote as a Member of the House of Commons for any County City Borough or Cinque Port within that Part of Great Britain called England the Dominion of Wales and Town of Berwick upon Tweed who shall not have an Estate Freehold or Copyhold for his own Life or for some greater Estate either in Law or Equity to and for his own Use and Benefit of or in Lands Tenements or Hereditaments over and above what will satisfie and clear all Incumbrances that may affect the same lying or being within that Part of Great Britain called England the Dominion of Wales and Town of Berwick upon Tweed of the respective annual Value hereafter limited videlicet the annual Value of Six hundred Pounds above Reprizes for every Knight of a Shire and the annual Value of Three hundred Pounds above Reprizes for every Citizen Burgess or Baron of the Cinque Ports . . .

II. Provided always That nothing in this Act contained shall extend to make the eldest Son or Heir Apparent of any Peer or Lord of Parliament or of any Person qualified by this Act to serve as Knight of a Shire uncapable of being elected and returned and sitting and voting as a Member of the House of Commons in any Parliament.

III. Provided always That nothing in this Act contained shall extend or be construed to extend to either of the Universities in that Part of Great Britain called England but that they and each of them may elect and return Members to represent them in Parliament as heretofore they have done Any thing herein contained to the contrary notwithstanding

IV. Provided always and be it enacted by the Authority aforesaid That no Person whatsoever shall be construed to be qualified to sit in the House of Commons within the Meaning of this Act by virtue of any Mortgage whatsoever whereof the Equity of Redemption is

[1] See also Sect. A, No. XXXI, p. 83, No. LI, p. 131, No. LX, p. 146, and Vol. II, Sect. A, No. XII, p. 23. (This Act was modified by 1 & 2 Vict. c. 48 and wholly repealed by 21 & 22 Vict. c. 26.)

in any other Person or Persons unless the Mortgagee shall have been in Possession of the mortgaged Premises for the Space of Seven Years before the Time of his Election Any thing herein contained to the contrary notwithstanding.

[§§ V-VIII. Oath to be taken by candidates at time of Election that they are duly qualified. Form and method of the oath.]

XLIII

THE OCCASIONAL CONFORMITY ACT,[1]

1711

10 Anne, c. 6.

An Act for preserving the Protestant Religion by better securing the Church of England as by Law established and for confirming the Toleration granted to Protestant Dissenters by an Act intituled An Act for exempting Their Majesties Protestant Subjects dissenting from the Church of England from the Penalties of certain Laws and for supplying the Defects thereof and for the further securing the Protestant Succession by requiring the Practicers of the Law in North Britain to take the Oaths and subscribe the Declaration therein mentioned.

Whereas an Act [2] was made in the Thirteenth Year of the Reign of the late King Charles the Second, . . . and another Act [3] was made in the Five and twentieth Year of the Reign of the said late King Charles the Second, . . . both which Acts were made for the Security of the Church of England as by Law established Now for the better securing the said Church and quieting the Minds of Her Majesties Protestant Subjects dissenting from the Church of England and rendring them secure in the Exercise of their religious Worship as also for the further strengthning of the Provision already made for the Security of the Succession to the Crown in the House of Hanover Be it enacted . . . That if any Person or Persons . . . either Peers or Commoners who have or shall have any Office or Offices Civil or Military or receive any Pay Salary Fee or Wages by reason of any Patent or Grant from or under Her Majesty or any of Her Majesties Predecessors or of Her Heirs or Successors or shall have any Command or Place of Trust . . . within that Part of Great

---

[1] §§ i-vi of this Act, repealed by 5 Geo. I, c. 4, § i. But § ii of that Act disables a Mayor or other officer from holding such positions who attends a Dissenting Chapel clothed with the insignia of his office.

[2] Sect. A, No. IX, p. 15.   [3] Sect. A, No. XVI, p. 39.

Britain called England the Dominion of Wales or Town of Berwick upon Tweed or in the Navy or in the several Islands of Jersey or Guernsey . . . or if any Mayor Alderman Recorder Bayliff Town Clerk Common Council Man or other Person bearing any Office of Magistracy [in England, Wales etc.] . . . who by the said recited Acts . . . are obliged to receive the Sacrament of the Lords Supper according to the Rites and Usage of the Church of England . . . shall at any Time after their Admission into their respective Offices . . . knowingly or willingly resort to or be present at any Conventicle Assembly or Meeting [within England Wales etc.] . . . for the Exercise of Religion in other Manner than according to the Liturgy and Practice of the Church of England . . . or shall knowingly and willingly be present at any such Meeting . . . although the Liturgy be there used, where Her Majesty . . . shall not there be prayed for in express Words according to the Liturgy . . . shall forfeit Forty Pounds to be recovered by him or them that shall sue for the same . . . in any of Her Majesties Courts. . . .

II. And be it further enacted That every Person convicted . . . shall be disabled from henceforth to hold such Office . . . and shall be adjudged incapable to bear any Office or Employment whatsoever. . . .

III. Provided always and be it further enacted . . . That if any Person . . . who shall have been convicted . . . shall after such Conviction conform to the Church of England for the Space of One Year without having been present at any Conventicle Assembly or Meeting . . . and receive the Sacrament of the Lords Supper according to the Rites and Usage of the Church of England at least Three Times in the Year every such Person . . . shall be capable of the Grant of any the Offices or Employments aforesaid.

[§ IV. Such conforming persons to make oath of Conformity and that he has received the Sacrament.]

[§ V limits Prosecution to three months.]

[§ VI exempts offices of Inheritance from being made void, but requires a non-conforming holder to appoint a deputy.]

VII. And it is hereby further enacted . . . That the Toleration granted to Protestant Dissenters by the Act[1] made in the First Year of the Reign of King William and Queen Mary . . . shall be and is hereby ratified and confirmed and that the same Act shall at all Times be inviolably observed for the exempting of such Protestant Dissenters as are thereby intended from the Pains and Penalties therein mentioned

VIII. And for the rendering the said last mentioned Act more effectual according to the true Intent and Meaning thereof Be it

[1] Sect. A, No. XXIV, p. 63.

further enacted . . . That if any Person dissenting from the Church of England (not in Holy Orders or pretended Holy Orders or pretending to Holy Orders nor any Preacher or Teacher of any Congregation) who should have been entitled to the Benefit of the said last mentioned Act if such Person had duly taken made and subscribed the Oaths and Declaration or otherwise qualified him or herself as required by the said Act and now is or shall be prosecuted upon or by virtue of any of the penal Statutes from which Protestant Dissenters are exempted by the said Act shall at any Time during such Prosecution take make and subscribe the said Oaths and Declaration or being of the People called Quakers shall make and subscribe the aforesaid Declaration and also the Declaration of Fidelity and subscribe the Profession of their Christian Belief according to the said Act or before any Two of Her Majesties Justices of the Peace (who are hereby required to take and return the same to the next Quarter Sessions of the Peace to be there recorded) such Person . . . is hereby entitled to the Benefit of the said Act . . . and shall be thenceforth exempted . . . from all the Penalties and Forfeitures incurred by Force of any the aforesaid penal Statutes

IX. And whereas it is or may be doubted whether a Preacher or Teacher of any Congregation of dissenting Protestants duly in all respects qualified according to the said Act be allowed . . . to officiate in any Congregation in any County other than that in which he so qualified himself altho in a Congregation or Place of Meeting duly certified and registred as is required by the said Act Be it . . . enacted . . . That any such Preacher or Teacher so duly qualified . . . is hereby allowed to officiate in any Congregation although the same be not in the County wherein he was so qualified provided that the same Congregation or Place of Meeting hath been before such officiating duly . . . registred . . . And such Preacher or Teacher shall if required produce a Certificate of his having so qualified himself under the Hand of the Clerk of the Peace for the County or Place where he so qualified himself which Certificate such Clerk of the Peace is hereby required to make and shall also before any Justice of the Peace of such County or Place where he shall so officiate make and subscribe such Declaration and take such Oaths as are mentioned in the said Act if thereunto required.

X. And be it further enacted . . . That on or before the Fifteenth day of June next all Advocates Writers to the Signet Notaries Publick and other Members of the College of Justice within . . . Scotland, . . . are hereby obliged to take and subscribe the Oath appointed by the Act [1] of the Sixth Year of Her Majesties

[1] 6 Anne c. 66.

Reign intituled An Act for the better Security of Her Majesties Person and Government before the Lords of Session of the aforesaid Part of Her Majesties Kingdom except such of the said Persons who have already taken the same And if any of the Persons aforesaid do . . . refuse to take and subscribe the said Oath as aforesaid such Persons shall be ipso facto adjudged . . . disabled in Law to . . . exercise in any Manner his said Employment or Practice

XI. And be it further enacted . . . That in all Time coming no Person . . . shall be admitted to the Employment of Advocate Writer to the Signet Notary Publick or any Office belonging to the said College of Justice until he . . . have taken and subscribed the aforesaid Oath in Manner as is above directed.

XLIV

THE SCHISM ACT,[1] 1714

13 Anne, c. 7.

Whereas by an Act[2] of Parliament made in the Thirteenth and Fourteenth Years of His late Majesty King Charles the Second . . . And whereas notwithstanding the said Act sundry Papists and other Persons dissenting from the Church of England have taken upon them to instruct and teach Youth as Teachers or Schoolmasters and have for such Purpose openly set up Schools and Seminaries whereby if due and speedy Remedy be not had great Danger might ensue to this Church and State For the making of the said recited Act more effectual and preventing the Danger aforesaid . . . Be it enacted . . . That every Person or Persons who shall . . . keep any publick or private School or Seminary or teach and instruct any Youth as Tutor or Schoolmaster within that Part of Great Britain called England the Dominion of Wales or Town of Berwick upon Tweed before such Person or Persons shall have subscribed so much of the said Declaration and Acknowledgement as is before recited and shall have had and obtained a Licence from the respective Archbishop Bishop or Ordinary of the Place under his Seal of Office (for which the Party shall pay One Shilling and no more over and above the Duties payable to Her Majesty for the same) and shall be thereof lawfully convicte, . . . be committed to the Common Goal . . . there to remain without Bail or Mainprize for the Space of Three Months to commence from the Time that such Person or Persons shall be received into the said Goal

[1] Repealed by 5 Geo. I, c. 4.   [2] Sect. A, No. XI, p. 20.

II. Provided always . . . That no Licence shall be granted by any Archbishop Bishop or Ordinary unless the Person or Persons who shall sue for the same shall produce a Certificate of his or their having received the Sacrament according to the Usage of the Church of England in some Parish Church within the Space of One Year next before the Grant of such Lycence under the Hand of the Minister and One of the Church-wardens of the said Parish nor until such Person or Persons shall have taken and subscribed the Oaths of Allegiance and Supremacy and Abjuration as appointed by Law and shall have made and subscribed the Declaration against Transubstantiation contained in the Act . . . intituled An Act [1] for preventing Dangers which may happen from Popish Recusants before the said Archbishop Bishop or Ordinary which said Oaths and Declarations the said Archbishop Bishop or Ordinary are hereby impowered and required to administer and receive and such Archbishops Bishops and Ordinaries are required to file such Certificates and keep an exact Register of the same. . . .

III. And be it further enacted . . . That any Person who shall have obtained a Lycence and subscribed the Declarations and taken and subscribed the Oaths as above appointed and shall at any Time after during the Time of his or their keeping any publick or private School or Seminary or instructing any Youth as Tutor or Schoolmaster knowingly or willingly resort to . . . any Conventicle . . . within England Wales or Town of Berwick upon Tweed for the Exercise of Religion in any other Manner than according to the Liturgy and Practice of the Church of England or shall . . . be present at any Meeting . . . although the Liturgy be there used where Her Majesty (whom God long preserve) and the Elector of Brunswick . . . shall not there be prayed for in express words according to the Liturgy of the Church of England . . . shall . . . thenceforth be incapable of keeping any publick or private School or Seminary or instructing any Youth as Tutor or Schoolmaster

IV. And be it further enacted . . . That if any Person lycensed as aforesaid shall teach any other Catechism than the Catechism set forth in the Book of Common Prayer the License of such Person shall from thenceforth be void and such Person shall be liable to the Penalties of this Act

V. And be it further enacted . . . That it shall . . . be lawful to and for the Bishop of the Diocese or other proper Ordinary to cite any Person or Persons whatsoever keeping School or Seminary or teaching without Licence as aforesaid and to proceed against and punish such Person or Persons by Ecclesiastical Censure

[1] Sect. A, No. XVI, § VIII, p. 42.

subject to such Appeals as in Cases of ordinary Jurisdiction this
Act or any other Law to the contrary notwithstanding. . . .

[§§ VI and VII provide that none shall be punished twice for the
same offence.]

VIII. Provided always That this Act . . . shall not extend
. . . to any Tutor teaching or instructing Youth in any College or
Hall within either of the Universities of . . . England nor to any
Tutor who shall be employed by any Nobleman or Noblewoman
to teach his or her own Children Grand Children or Great Grand
Children only in his or her Family provided such Tutor . . . do
in every respect qualify himself according to this Act except only
in that of taking a Licence from the Bishop

IX. Provided also That the Penalties in this Act shall not
extend to any Foreigner or Alien of the Foreign reformed Churches
allowed . . . by the Queens Majesty Her Heirs or Successors in
England for instructing or teaching any Child or Children of any
such Foreigner or Alien only as a Tutor or Schoolmaster

[§ X. Persons conforming and receiving the Sacrament may be
given a licence.]

[§ XI. Such persons to make oath of Conformity next term.]

XII. Provided always That this Act shall not extend . . . to
any Person who as a Tutor or Schoolmaster shall instruct Youth in
Reading Writing Arithmetick or any Part of Mathematical Learning
only so far as such Mathematical Learning relates to Navigation or
any mechanical Art only and so far as such Reading Writing Arithmetick or Mathematical Learning shall be taught in the English
Tongue only.

[§ XIII extends the provisions of this Act to Ireland.]

XLV

THE RIOT ACT,[1] 1715

1 Geo. I, St. II, c. 5.

*An Act for preventing Tumults and riotous Assemblies, and for
the more speedy and effectual punishing the Rioters.*[2]

" I. Whereas of late many rebellious Riots and Tumults have
been in divers Parts of this Kingdom, to the Disturbance of the
publick Peace, and the endangering of his Majesty's Person and

[1] The text of this Act and of all Acts cited hereafter follows that of the
Statutes at large.

[2] See Vol. II, Sect. B, No. XXIII, p. 201, Sect. C, Nos. VIII-X,
pp. 259-64.

Government, and the same are yet continued and fomented by Persons disaffected to his Majesty, presuming so to do, for that the Punishments provided by the Laws now in being are not adequate to such heinous Offences ; and by such Rioters his Majesty and his Administration have been most maliciously and falsely traduced, with an Intent to raise Divisions, and to alienate the Affections of the People from his Majesty: Therefore for the preventing and suppressing of such Riots and Tumults, and for the more speedy and effectual punishing the Offenders therein ; " Be it enacted . . . That if any Persons to the Number of twelve or more, being unlawfully, riotously, and tumultuously assembled together, to the Disturbance of the Publick Peace . . . and being required or commanded by any one or more Justice or Justices of the Peace, or by the Sheriff of the County, or his Under-sheriff, or by the Mayor, Bailiff or Bailiffs, or other Head-officer, or Justice of the Peace of any City or Town-corporate, where such Assembly shall be, by Proclamation to be made in the King's Name, in the Form hereinafter directed, to disperse themselves and peaceably to depart to their Habitations, or to their lawful Business, shall, to the Number of twelve or more (notwithstanding such Proclamation made) unlawfully, riotously, and tumultuously remain or continue together by the Space of one Hour after such Command or Request made by Proclamation, that then such continuing together to the Number of twelve or more, after such Command or Request made by Proclamation, shall be adjudged Felony without Benefit of Clergy, and the Offenders therein shall be adjudged Felons, and shall suffer Death as in the case of Felony without Benefit of Clergy.

II. And be it further enacted . . . That the Order and Form of the Proclamations that shall be made by the Authority of this Act, shall be as hereafter followeth (that is to say) the Justice of the Peace, or other Person authorized by this Act to make the said Proclamation shall, among the said Rioters, or as near to them as he can safely come, with a loud Voice command, and cause to be commanded Silence to be, while Proclamation is making, and after that shall openly, and with loud Voice make or cause to be made Proclamation in these Words, or like in Effect :

' Our Sovereign Lord the King chargeth and commandeth all Persons, being assembled, immediately to disperse themselves, and peaceably to depart to their Habitations, or to their lawful Business, upon the Pains contained in the Act made in the First Year of King *George*, for preventing Tumults and riotous Assemblies.

God save the King.'

And every such Justice and Justices of the Peace, Sheriff, Under-sheriff, Mayor, Bailiff, and other Head-officer, aforesaid, within the

Limits of their respective Jurisdictions, are hereby authorized, impowered and required, on Notice or Knowledge of any such unlawful, riotous and tumultuous Assembly, to resort to the Place where such unlawful, riotous, and tumultuous Assemblies shall be, of Persons to the Number of twelve or more, and there to make or cause to be made Proclamation in Manner aforesaid.

III. And be it further enacted . . . That if such Persons so unlawfully, riotously, and tumultuously assembled, or twelve or more of them after Proclamation made in Manner aforesaid, shall continue together and not disperse themselves within one Hour, That then it shall be . . . lawful to and for every Justice of the Peace, Sheriff, or Under-sheriff of the County where such Assembly shall be, and also to and for every High or Petty-constable, and other Peace-officer within such County, and also to and for every Mayor, Justice of the Peace, Sheriff, Bailiff, and other Head-officer, High or Petty-constable, and other Peace-officer of any City or Town-corporate where such Assembly shall be, and to and for such other Person and Persons as shall be commanded to be assisting unto any such Justice of the Peace, Sheriff or Under-Sheriff, Mayor, Bailiff, or other Head officer aforesaid, (who are hereby authorized and impowered to command all his Majesty's Subjects of Age and Ability to be assisting to them therein) to seize and apprehend, and they are hereby required to seize and apprehend such Persons . . . in order to their being proceeded against for such their offences according to Law ; and that if the Persons so unlawfully, riotously and tumultuously assembled, or any of them, shall happen to be killed, maimed or hurt, in the dispersing, seizing or apprehending, or endeavouring to disperse, seize or apprehend them, by reason of their resisting the Persons so dispersing, seizing or apprehending, or endeavouring to disperse, seize or apprehend them, that then every such Justice of the Peace, Sheriff, Under-sheriff, Mayor, Bailiff, Head-officer, High or Petty-constable, or other Peace-officer, and all and singular Persons, being aiding and assisting to them, or any of them, shall be free, discharged and indemnified, as well against the King's Majesty, his Heirs and Successors, as against all and every other Person and Persons, of, for, or concerning the killing, maiming, or hurting of any such Person or Persons so unlawfully, riotously and tumultuously assembled, that shall happen to be so killed, maimed, or hurt as aforesaid.

IV. And be it further enacted . . . That if any Persons unlawfully, riotously and tumultuously assembled together, to the Disturbance of the publick Peace, shall unlawfully, and with Force demolish or pull down, or begin to demolish or pull down any Church or Chapel, or any Building for religious Worship certified and registered according to the Statute made in the first Year of the Reign of the late King *William* and Queen *Mary*, . . . or any Dwelling-house, Barn, Stable or other Outhouse, that then every such demolishing, or pulling down, or beginning to demolish, or pull down, shall be adjudged Felony without Benefit of Clergy, and the Offenders therein shall be adjudged Felons, and shall suffer Death as in case of Felony without Benefit of Clergy.[1]

V. Provided always, . . . That if any Person or Persons do, or shall, with Force and Arms, willingly and knowingly oppose, obstruct, or in any manner willfully and knowingly let, hinder, or hurt any Person or Persons that shall begin to proclaim, or go to proclaim according to the Proclamation hereby directed to be made, whereby such Proclamation shall not be made, that then every such opposing, obstructing, letting, hindring or hurting such Person or Persons, so beginning or going to make such Proclamation, as aforesaid, shall be adjudged Felony without Benefit of Clergy, and the Offenders therein shall be adjudged Felons, and shall suffer Death as in case of Felony, without Benefit of Clergy ; and that also every such Person or Persons so being unlawfully, riotously and tumultuously assembled, to the Number of twelve, as aforesaid, or more, to whom Proclamation should or ought to have been made if the same had not been hindred, as aforesaid, shall likewise, in case they or any of them, to the Number of twelve or more, shall continue together, and not disperse themselves within one Hour after such Lett or Hindrance so made, having Knowledge of such Lett or Hindrance so made, shall be adjudged Felons, and shall suffer Death as in case of Felony, without Benefit of Clergy.

. . . . . .

[§ VI provides how damages shall be made good if a church or other building shall be destroyed.]

[§§ VII-VIII. The Act to be read at every quarter sessions, leet, and law-day. Prosecutions to start within twelve months of the offence.]

[§§ IX-X deal with the executive officials in Scotland, and extend the provisions of the Riot Act to all places of religious worship in Scotland tolerated by law.]

XLVI

THE SEPTENNIAL ACT, 1716

1 Geo. I, St. II, c. 38.

' Whereas in and by an Act of Parliament made in the sixth Year of the Reign of their late Majesties King *William* and Queen *Mary*

[1] See Sect. C, No. XII, p. 286, Case of Dammaree.

(of ever Blessed Memory) intituled, *An Act* [1] *for the frequent Meeting and calling of Parliaments*: It was among other Things enacted, That from thenceforth no Parliament whatsoever, that should at any Time then after be called, assembled or held, should have any Continuance longer than for three Years only at the farthest, to be accounted from the Day on which by the Writ of Summons the said Parliament should be appointed to meet: And whereas it hath been found by Experience, that the said Clause hath proved very grievous and burthensome, by occasioning much greater and more continued Expenses in order to Elections of Members to serve in Parliament, and more violent and lasting Heats and Animosities among the Subjects of this Realm, than were ever known before the said Clause was enacted; and the said Provision, if it should continue, may probably at this Juncture, when a restless and Popish Faction are designing and endeavouring to renew the Rebellion within this Kingdom, and an Invasion from Abroad, be destructive to the Peace and Security of the Government;' Be it enacted . . . That this present Parliament, and all Parliaments that shall at any Time hereafter be called, assembled or held, shall and may respectively have Continuance for seven Years, and no longer, to be accounted from the Day on which by the Writ of Summons this present Parliament hath been, or any future Parliament shall be appointed to meet, unless this present, or any such Parliament hereafter to be summoned, shall be sooner dissolved by His Majesty, His Heirs or Successors. [2]

XLVII

AN ACT TO EASE OFFICERS OF CORPORATIONS, 1718

5 Geo. I, c. 6.

[§ I. Indemnity to persons required to take the oath and declaration under 13 Car. II, St. II, c. 1.]

[§ II. Repeal of that oath and declaration.]

' III. And whereas by the said recited Act [3] made in the thirteenth Year of King *Charles* the Second, it is enacted, That no Person or Persons shall be placed, elected or chosen, in or to any of the Offices or Places relating to or concerning the Government of any City, Corporation, Borough, Cinque-port and their Members, and other

[1] See Sect. A, No. XIII, p. 33, and No. XXIX, p. 79, and Vol. II, Sect. A, No. XLII, § 7, p. 143.

[2] See Sect. B, No. XXII, p. 208.   [3] See Sect. A, No. IX, p. 15.

Port-towns, or any other offices in the said recited Act mentioned
or expressed, that shall not have, within one Year next before such
Election or Choice, taken the Sacrament of the Lord's Supper,
according to the Rites of the Church of *England*, and that in Default
thereof every such Placing, Election and Choice shall be void : ' Be
it further enacted by the Authority aforesaid, That all and every
the now Member and Members of any Corporation within this
Kingdom, and all and every Person and Persons now in actual
Possession of any Office, that were required by the said above
recited Act to take the Sacrament of the Lord's Supper according
to the Rites of the Church of *England* within one Year next before
his Election or Choice into such Office, shall be and are hereby
confirmed in their several and respective Offices and Places, notwithstanding their Omission to take the Sacrament of the Lord's
Supper as aforesaid, and shall be indemnified, freed and discharged,
of and from all Incapacities, Disabilities, Forfeitures and Penalties
arising from such Omission ; and that none of their Acts, nor the
Acts not yet avoided, of any who have been Members of any
Corporation, or in Actual Possession of such Offices, shall be
questioned or avoided for or by reason of such Omission ; but that
all such Acts shall be and are hereby declared and enacted to be as
good and effectual as if all and every such Person and Persons had
taken the Sacrament of the Lord's Supper in manner as aforesaid ;
nor shall any Person or Persons, who shall be hereafter placed,
elected or chosen, in or to any the Offices aforesaid, be removed
by the Corporation, or otherwise prosecuted for or by reason of
such Omission ; nor shall any Incapacity, Disability, Forfeiture or
Penalty, be incurred by reason of the same, unless such Person be
so removed, or such Prosecution be commenced, within six Months
after such Person's being placed or elected into his respective Office,
as aforesaid, and that in case of a Prosecution the same be carried
on without wilful Delay.

XLVIII

THE DEPENDENCY OF IRELAND ACT,
1719 [1]
6 Geo. I, c. 5.

' I. Whereas the House of Lords of *Ireland* have of late, against
Law, assumed to themselves a Power and Jurisdiction to examine,

---

[1] Repealed by 22 Geo. III, c. 53. See Sect. A, No. LXI, p. 147.

correct and amend the Judgments and Decrees of the Courts of Justice in the Kingdom of *Ireland*:' Therefore for the better securing of the Dependency of *Ireland* upon the Crown of *Great Britain*, May it please your most Excellent Majesty that it may be declared, and be it declared . . . That the same Kingdom of *Ireland* hath been, is, and of Right ought to be subordinate unto and dependent upon the Imperial Crown of *Great Britain*, as being inseparably united and annexed thereunto ; and that the King's Majesty, by and with the Advice and Consent of the Lords Spiritual and Temporal, and Commons of *Great Britain* in Parliament assembled, had, hath, and of Right ought to have full Power and Authority to make Laws and Statutes of sufficient Force and Validity, to bind the Kingdom and People of *Ireland*.

II. And be it further declared . . . That the House of Lords of *Ireland* have not, nor of Right ought to have any Jurisdiction to judge of, affirm or reverse any Judgment, Sentence or Decree, given or made in any Court within the said Kingdom, and that all Proceedings before the said House of Lords upon any such Judgment, Sentence or Decree, are, and are hereby declared to be utterly null and void to all Intents and Purposes whatsoever.

XLIX

THE USE OF ENGLISH ONLY IN THE LAW COURTS, 1731

4 Geo. II, c. 26.

' Whereas many and great Mischiefs do frequently happen to the Subjects of this Kingdom, from the Proceedings in Courts of Justice being in an unknown Language, those who are summoned and impleaded having no Knowledge or Understanding of what is alledged for or against them in the Pleadings of their Lawyers and Attornies, who use a Character not legible to any but Persons practising the Law ;' To remedy these great Mischiefs, and to protect the Lives and Fortunes of the Subjects of that Part of *Great Britain* called *England*, more effectually than heretofore, from the Peril of being ensnared or brought in danger by Forms and Proceedings in Courts of Justice, in an unknown Language, Be it enacted . . . That . . . all Writs, Process and Returns thereof, and Proceedings thereon, and all Pleadings, Rules, Orders, Indictments, Informations, Inquisitions, Presentments, Verdicts, Prohibitions, Certificates and all Patents, Charters, Pardons, Commissions, Records, Judgments, Statutes, Recognizances, Bonds, Rolls, Entries, Fines and Recoveries, and all Proceedings relating thereunto, and all Proceedings of Courts Leet, Courts Baron and Customary Courts, and all Copies thereof, and all Proceedings whatsoever in any Courts of Justice within that Part of *Great Britain* called *England*, and in the Court of Exchequer in *Scotland*, and which concern the Law and Administration of Justice, shall be in the *English* Tongue and Language only, and not in *Latin* or *French*, or any other Tongue or Language whatsoever, and shall be written in such a common legible Hand and Character, as the Acts of Parliament are usually ingrossed in, and the Lines and Words of the same to be written at least as close as the said Acts usually are, and not in any Hand commonly called *Court Hand*, and in Words at Length and not abbreviated, any Law, Custom or Usage heretofore to the contrary thereof notwithstanding : And all and every Person or Persons offending against this Act, shall for every such Offence forfeit and pay the Sum of fifty Pounds to any Person who shall sue for the same by Action of Debt . . .

L

ACT IMPOSING QUALIFICATIONS ON JUSTICES OF THE PEACE, 1732

5 Geo. II, c. 18.

' Whereas the constituting Persons of mean Estates to be Justices of the Peace may be highly prejudicial to the publick Welfare,' Be it therefore enacted . . . That . . . no Person shall be capable of being a Justice of the Peace . . . within . . . *England* . . . who shall not have an Estate of Freehold or Copyhold to and for his own Use and Benefit, in Possession, for Life, or for some greater Estate . . . of the clear yearly Value of one hundred Pounds, over and above what will satisfy and discharge all Incumbrances that may affect the same.

II. And be it further enacted by the Authority aforesaid, That no Attorney, Solicitor or Proctor in any Court whatsoever shall . . . be capable to continue or be a Justice of the Peace within any County . . . during such Time as he shall continue in the Business and Practice of an Attorney, Solicitor or Proctor.

[§ III. Unqualified persons to forfeit £100.]

IV. Provided always, That this Act, or any Thing herein contained, shall not extend or be construed to extend to any City or Town, being a County of itself, or to any other City, Town, Cinque Port or Liberty having Justices of the Peace within their respective Limits and Precincts by Charter, Commission or otherwise ; . . .

V. Provided always, That nothing in this Act contained shall extend to incapacitate any Peer or Lord of Parliament, or the eldest Son or Heir apparent of any Peer or Lord of Parliament, or of any Person qualified to serve as Knight of a Shire by an Act,[1] intituled, *An Act to secure the Freedom of Parliaments by the further qualifying Members to sit in the House of Commons*, to be a Justice of the Peace for any County, or to act as such ; any Thing herein contained to the contrary thereof in any wise notwithstanding.

VI. Provided also, That nothing in this Act contained shall extend or be construed to extend to incapacitate or exclude the Officers of the Board of Green Cloth from being Justices of the Peace within the Verge of his Majesty's Palaces, or to incapacitate or exclude the Commissioners and principal Officers of the Navy, or the two Under Secretaries in each of the Offices of Principal Secretary of State, from being Justices of the Peace in and for such Maritime Counties and Places where they usually have been Justices of the Peace ; any Thing herein contained to the contrary in any wise notwithstanding.

VII. Provided always, that this Act, nor any Thing herein contained, shall extend or be construed to extend to any of the Heads of Colleges or Halls in either of the two Universities of *Oxford* and *Cambridge*, but that they may be made Justices of the Peace of and in the several Counties of *Oxford*, *Berks* and *Cambridge*, and the Cities and Towns within the same, and execute the Office thereof as fully and freely in all Respects, as heretofore they have lawfully used to execute the same, as if this Act had never been made ; any Thing herein before contained to the contrary notwithstanding.

LI

A PLACE ACT,[2] 1742

15 Geo. II, c. 22.

For further limiting or reducing the Number of Officers capable of sitting in the House of Commons, Be it enacted . . . That from

[1] Sect. A, No. XLII, p. 117.
[2] See also the Act of Settlement, Sect. A, No. XXXVI, p. 92, No. XLI, p. 111, and No. LX, p. 146.

and after the Dissolution, or other Determination of this present Parliament, no Person who shall be Commissioner of the Revenue in *Ireland*, or Commissioners of the Navy or Victualling Offices, nor any Deputies or Clerks in any of the said Offices, or in any of the several Offices following ; that is to say, The Office of Lord High Treasurer, or the Commissioners of the Treasury, or of the Auditor of the Receipt of his Majesty's Exchequer, or of the Tellers of the Exchequer, or of the Chanceller of the Exchequer, or of the Lord High Admiral, or of the Commissioners of the Admiralty, or of the Paymasters of the Army, or of the Navy, or of his Majesty's Principal Secretaries of State, or of the Commissioners of the Salt, or of the Commissioners of the Stamps, or of the Commissioners of Appeals or of the Commissioners of Wine Licences, or of the Commissioners of Hackney Coaches, or of the Commissioners of Hawkers and Pedlars, nor any Persons having any Office, Civil or Military, within the Island of *Minorca*, or in *Gibraltar*, other than Officers, having Commissions in any Regiment there only, shall be capable of being elected, or of sitting or voting as a Member of the House of Commons, in any Parliament which shall be hereafter summoned and holden.

II. And be it further enacted . . . That if any Person hereby disabled . . . shall nevertheless be returned as a Member . . . such Election and Return are hereby enacted and declared to be void to all Intents and Purposes whatsoever : And if any Person disabled, and declared incapable . . . shall . . . presume to sit or vote as a Member of the House of Commons in any Parliament to be hereafter summoned, such Person so sitting or voting, shall forfeit the Sum of twenty Pounds for every Day in which he shall sit or vote in the said House of Commons, to such Person or Persons who shall sue for the same in any of his Majesty's Courts at *Westminster:* . . . and shall from thenceforth be incapable of taking, holding, or enjoying any Office of Honour or Profit under his Majesty, his Heirs or Successors.

III. Provided always, . . . That nothing in this Act shall extend or be construed to extend, or relate to, or exclude the Treasurer or Comptroller of the Navy, the Secretaries of the Treasury, the Secretary to the Chancellor of the Exchequer, or Secretaries of the Admiralty, the Under Secretary to any of his Majesty's Principal Secretaries of State, or the Deputy Paymaster of the Army, or to exclude any Person having or holding any Office or Employment for Life, or for so long as he shall behave himself well in his Office ; any Thing herein contained to the contrary notwithstanding.

LII

PROTECTION OF JUSTICES AND CONSTABLES, 1751 [1]

24 Geo. II, c. 44.

An Act for the rendering Justices of the Peace more safe in the Execution of the Office ; and for indemnifying Constables and others acting in Obedience to their Warrants.

' Whereas Justices of the Peace are discouraged in the Execution of their Office by vexatious Actions brought against them for or by reason of small and involuntary Errors in their Proceedings : And whereas it is necessary that they should be (as far as is consistent with Justice, and the Safety and Liberty of the Subjects over whom their Authority extends) rendered safe in the Execution of the said Office and Trust : And whereas it is also necessary that the Subjects should be protected from all wilful and oppressive Abuse of the several Laws and Statutes committed to the Care and Execution of the said Justices of the Peace ; ' Be it enacted . . . That . . . no Writ shall be sued out against, nor any Copy of any Process, at the Suit of a Subject, shall be served on any Justice of the Peace for any Thing by him done in the Execution of his Office, until Notice in Writing of such intended Writ or Process shall have been delivered to him, or left at the usual Place of his Abode, by the Attorney or Agent for the Party who intends to sue or cause the same to be sued out or served, at least one Calendar Month before the suing out or serving the same ; in which Notice shall be clearly and explicitly contained the Cause of the Action which such Party hath or claimeth to have against such Justice of the Peace ; on the Back of which Notice shall be indorsed the Name of such Attorney or Agent, together with the Place of his Abode, who shall be intitled to have the Fee of twenty Shillings for the preparing and serving such Notice, and no more.

II.   And be it further enacted, That it shall and may be lawful to and for such Justice of the Peace, at any Time, within one Calendar Month after such Notice given as aforesaid, to tender Amends to the Party complaining, or to his or her Agent or Attorney ; and in case the same is not accepted, to plead such Tender in Bar to any Action to be brought against him, grounded on such Writ or Process, together with the Plea of Not Guilty, and any other Plea

---

[1] Sect. C, Nos. XVII and XVIII (B), pp. 295 and 299.

with the Leave of the Court; and if upon Issue joined thereon the Jury shall find the Amends so tendered to have been sufficient, then they shall give a Verdict for the Defendant; . . .

VI. And be it further enacted by the Authority aforesaid, That . . . no Action shall be brought against any Constable, Headborough or other Officer, or against any Person or Persons acting by his Order and in his Aid, for any thing done in Obedience to any Warrant under the Hand or Seal of any Justice of the Peace, until Demand hath been made or left at the usual Place of his Abode, by the Party or Parties intending to bring such Action, or by his, her or their Attorney or Agent, in Writing, signed by the Party demanding the same, of the Perusal and Copy of such Warrant, and the same hath been refused or neglected for the Space of six Days after such Demand; and in case after such Demand and Compliance therewith, by shewing the said Warrant to, and permitting a Copy to be taken thereof by the Party demanding the same, any Action shall be brought against such Constable, Headborough or other Officer, or against such Person or Persons acting in his Aid for any such Cause as aforesaid, without making the Justice or Justices who signed or sealed the said Warrant, Defendant or Defendants, that on producing and proving such Warrant at the Trial of such Action, the Jury shall give their Verdict for the Defendant or Defendants, notwithstanding any Defect of Jurisdiction in such Justice or Justices; and if such Action be brought jointly against such Justice or Justices, and also against such Constable, Headborough or other Officer, or Person or Persons acting in his or their Aid as aforesaid, then on Proof of such Warrant the Jury shall find for such Constable, Headborough or other Officer, and for such Person and Persons so acting as aforesaid, notwithstanding such Defect of Jurisdiction as aforesaid; and if the Verdict shall be given against the Justice or Justices, that in such Case the Plaintiff or Plaintiffs shall recover his, her or their Costs against him or them to be taxed in such Manner by the proper Officer, as to include such Costs as such Plaintiff or Plaintiffs are liable to pay to such Defendant or Defendants for whom such Verdict shall be found as aforesaid. . . .

VIII. Provided also, and be it enacted by the Authority aforesaid, That no Action shall be brought against any Justice of the Peace for any thing done in the Execution of his Office, or against any Constable, Headborough or other Officer, or Person acting as aforesaid, unless commenced within six Calendar Months after the Act committed.

LIII

THE MILITIA ACT,[1] 1757

30 Geo. II, c. 25.

'Whereas a well-ordered and well-disciplined Militia is essentially necessary to the Safety, Peace and Prosperity of this Kingdom : And whereas the Laws in Being for the Regulation of the Militia are defective and ineffectual ; ' Be it enacted . . . That . . . his Majesty, his Heirs and Successors may and shall issue forth Commissions of Lieutenancy for the respective Counties, Ridings and Places herein after mentioned ; and the respective Lieutenants thereby appointed shall have full Power and Authority to call together all such Persons, and to arm and array them at such Times and in such Manner as is herein after expressed ; and such respective Lieutenants shall from Time to Time constitute and appoint such Persons as they shall think fit . . . to be their Deputy Lieutenants ; the Names of such Persons having been first presented to and approved by his Majesty, his Heirs or Successors ; and shall give Commissions to a proper Number of Colonels, Lieutenant Colonels, Majors and other Officers, also qualified as is hereinafter directed, to train and discipline the Persons so to be armed and arrayed, according to the Rules, Orders and Directions herein after provided ; and shall certify to his Majesty, his Heirs and Successors, the Names of such Commission Officers, within one Month after they shall be so appointed, and shall have accepted their respective Commissions. . . .

III. And be it enacted, That his Majesty's Lieutenant of every County, Riding or Place shall have the chief Command of the Militia thereof, which shall be raised by Virtue of this Act ; and in every County, Riding or Place in *England* and *Wales* (except as is herein after excepted) there shall be appointed twenty or more Deputy Lieutenants . . . and each Person so to be appointed a Deputy Lieutenant or Colonel, shall be seised or possessed, either in Law or Equity, for his own Use and Benefit, in Possession of a Freehold, Copyhold or Customary Estate for Life . . . of the yearly Value of four hundred Pounds, or shall be Heir Apparent of some Person who shall be in like Manner seised or possessed of a like Estate as aforesaid, of the yearly Value of eight hundred Pounds ; [and similarly, in decreasing values, property qualification is specified for other officers down to an ensign] ; one Moiety of

[1] See Sect. A, No. X, p. 17, also Vol. II, Sect. A, No. XIV, p. 29, No. XXX, p. 100, and No. XLI, p. 136.

which said Estates, required as Qualifications for each Deputy Lieutenant, Colonel, Lieutenant Colonel, Major, Captain, Lieutenant and Ensign respectively, shall be situate or arising within such respective County or Riding in which he shall be so appointed to serve.

[§§ IV-XI define the conditions of promotion and the oaths to be taken. Officers to be displaced at H.M.'s pleasure. Peers not obliged to serve in the Militia.]

XII. Provided always, and be it enacted, That the Acceptance of a Commission in the Militia shall not vacate the Seat of any Member returned to serve in Parliament.

[§XIII. Officers may be discharged at the end of 4 years.]
[§§ XIV, XV. Adjutants and sergeants to be appointed from the regular army.]

XVI. And be it enacted, That the Number of private Men to be raised by Virtue of this Act, in that Part of *Great Britain* called England, the Dominion of *Wales* and Town of *Berwick* upon *Tweed* (exclusive of the Places herein after excepted) shall be [31,800 listed county by county for England Wales].

[§§ XVII-XLIV. Privy Council may vary the number for any one county. Chief Constables to furnish lists of men between 18 and 50 years of age. Men to be chosen by lot to serve, who may furnish substitutes. Three-year period of service. Militia to be exercised on 16 specified days a year in small formations and as battalions on 4 days in Whit week. The Lieutenants and Colonels may seize arms belonging to the Militia and entrust their keeping to any fit persons. The duties and powers of officers. Penalties for indiscipline in non-commissioned officers. J.P.s to fine absent and disobedient militiamen.]

XLV. And be it enacted, That in case of actual Invasion, or upon imminent Danger thereof, or in case of Rebellion, it may and shall be lawful for his Majesty, his Heirs and Successors (the Occasion being first communicated to Parliament, if the Parliament shall be then sitting, or declared in Council, and notified by Proclamation, if no Parliament shall be then sitting or in Being) to order and direct his Lieutenants . . . with all convenient Speed, to draw out and embody all the Regiments and Battallions of Militia . . . in such Manner as shall be best adapted to the Circumstances of the Danger ; and to put the said Forces under the Command of such General Officers as his Majesty, his Heirs and Successors shall be pleased to appoint over them ; and to direct them to be led by their respective Officers into any Parts of this Kingdom, for the Suppression of such Invasions and Rebellions : And the said Officers of the Militia, and private Militia Men, shall, from the Time of their being drawn out and embodied as aforesaid, and until they shall be returned again, by Order of their Commanding Officers, to their respective Parishes or Places of Abode, remain under the Command of such General Officers, and shall be intitled to the same Pay as the Officers and private Men in his Majesty's other Regiments of Foot receive, and no other ; and the Officers of the Militia shall, during such Time as aforesaid, rank with the Officers of his Majesty's other Forces of equal Degree with them as the youngest of their Rank ; and the Officers of the Militia and private Militia Men, shall be hereby, during such time as aforesaid, subjected and made liable to all such Articles of War, Rules and Regulations, as shall be then by Act of Parliament in Force, for the Discipline and good Government of any of his Majesty's Forces in *Great Britain* ;[1] any Thing herein contained to the contrary notwithstanding ; and when they shall be returned again to their respective Parishes or Places of Abode, they shall be under the same Orders and Directions only, as they were before they were drawn out and embodied as aforesaid : And if any Non-commission Officer of the Militia, or private Militia Man, shall be maimed or wounded in actual Service, he shall be equally entitled to the Benefit of *Chelsea Hospital*, with any Non-commission Officer, or private Soldier, belonging to his Majesty's other Forces : And if any Militia Man so ordered to be drawn out and embodied as aforesaid (not labouring under any Infirmity incapacitating him to serve as a Militia Man) shall not appear and march in pursuance of such Order, every such Militia Man being convicted thereof upon Oath, before two or more Justices of the Peace, shall forfeit and pay the Sum of forty Pounds ; and if such Militia Man shall refuse immediately to pay such Penalty, the Justices of the Peace before whom such Militia Man shall be so convicted, shall, by Warrant, commit such Militia Man to the Common Gaol of the County, Riding or Place, where he shall have been so convicted, there to remain without Bail or Mainprize for the Space of twelve Months, or until he shall have paid the Penalty aforesaid.

XLVI. And be it further enacted, That if at any Time (in case of actual Invasion, or upon imminent Danger thereof, or in case of Rebellion) the Parliament shall happen to be separated by such Adjournment or Prorogation as will not expire within fourteen Days, it shall be lawful for his Majesty, his Heirs and Successors, to issue a Proclamation for the Meeting of the Parliament, upon such Day as he or they shall thereby appoint, giving fourteen Days Notice of such Appointment ; and the Parliament shall accordingly meet upon such Day, and continue to sit and act in like Manner to all Intents and Purposes as if it had stood adjourned or prorogued to the same Day. . . .

[1] See Sect. A, No. XX, § VII, p. 56.

[§§ XLVII-XLVIII. Officers not to sit indiscriminately on trials. Regulations on quartering, impressment of carriages.]
[§§ XLIX-L. The duties of constables.]

LI. Provided always . . . that neither this Act, nor any Matter or Thing herein contained, shall be deemed or construed to extend to the giving or declaring any Power for the transporting any of the Militia of this Realm, or any way compelling them to march out of this Kingdom.

[§§ LII-LXIX. Specia regulations for various specified counties, cities and towns which are counties in themselves.]
[§§ LXX-LXXII. Repeal of former Acts and other provisions.]
[§ LXXIII. The Act to be in force for five years.]

LIV

CROWN REVENUE ACT, 1760

I Geo. III, c. 1.

An Act for the support of his Majesty's Household, and of the Honour and Dignity of the Crown of Great Britain.

May it please your most Excellent Majesty . . .
[Having recited the statutes governing the hereditary revenue of the Crown from taxes, given to former sovereigns, the preamble continues] 'And whereas your Majesty has been graciously pleased to signify your Consent to your faithful Commons in Parliament assembled, That whenever they should enter upon the Consideration of making Provision for your Household, and the Honour and Dignity of your Crown, such Disposition might be made of your Majesty's Interest in the hereditary Revenues of the Crown, as might best conduce to the Utility and Satisfaction of the Publick . . . We your Majesty's most dutiful and loyal Subjects the Commons of *Great Britain* . . . with Hearts full of the warmest Duty and Gratitude, are desirous, That a certain and competent Revenue for defraying the Expences of your Majesty's Civil Government, and supporting the Dignity of the Crown of *Great Britain* during your Life, . . . may be settled on your Majesty . . . have therefore freely and unanimously resolved to grant unto you, . . . a certain Revenue payable out of the aggregate Fund . . . do most humbly beseech your Majesty, that it be enacted.' . . .

[§§ I-III. The hereditary Duties of Excise originally granted by Act 12, Car. 2,[1] to be levied during George III's life, as also the Subsidy of Tonnage and Poundage granted by Act 9 Will. III, and all other

[1] See Sect. A, No. II, § XIV, p. 5, and Vol. II, Sect. A, No. II, p. 2.

duties hitherto payable towards support of the Crown to continue and to be paid into the aggregate Fund.]

[§ IV. A clear yearly sum of £723,000 to be paid to the Crown out of aggregate Fund to be increased to £800,000 on expiry of annuities to the Dowager Princess of Wales, the Duke of Cumberland and Princess Amelia. . . .]

LV

JUDGES AND THE DEMISE OF THE CROWN,[1] 1760

1 Geo. III, c. 23.

[The Preamble cites the provisions in the Act of Settlement[2] relating to the tenure and salaries of the Judges, and then resolves " to enable your Majesty to effectuate the wise, just and generous purposes of your royal heart."]

Be it enacted . . . That the Commissions of Judges for the Time being, shall be, continue, and remain, in full Force, during their good Behaviour, notwithstanding the Demise of his Majesty (whom God long preserve) or of any of his Heirs and Successors ; any Law, Usage, or Practice, to the contrary thereof in any wise notwithstanding.

II. Provided always, and be it enacted by the Authority aforesaid, That it may be lawful for his Majesty, his Heirs, and Successors, to remove any Judge or Judges upon the Address of both Houses of Parliament.

III. And be it enacted by the authority aforesaid, That such Salaries as are settled upon Judges for the Time being, or any of them, by Act of Parliament, and also such Salaries as have been or shall be granted by his Majesty, his Heirs, and Successors . . . shall . . . be paid and payable . . . so long as the Patents or Commissions . . . shall continue and remain in Force.

IV. And be it further enacted by the Authority aforesaid, That such Salaries of Judges as are now or shall become payable out of the annual Rent or Sums granted for the Support of his Majesty's Household . . . shall . . . after the Demise of his Majesty . . . be charged upon, and paid and payable out of, such of the Duties or Revenues granted for the Uses of the Civil Government of his Majesty, . . . until some further or other Provision be made by Parliament for the Expenses of the Civil Government. . . .[3]

[1] See also Sect. A, No. XXXII, p. 84, and Sect. A, No. XLI, § IV, p. 112, and Vol. II, Sect. A, No. XL, p. 136.

[2] Sect. A, No. XXXVI, § III, p. 95.

[3] See Vol. II, Sect. A, No. II, p. 3.

LVI

ELECTORAL QUALIFICATION OF FREEMEN,[1] 1762

3 Geo. III, c. 15.

'Whereas great Abuses have been committed in making Freemen of Corporations, in order to influence Elections of Members to serve in Parliament, to the great Infringement of the Rights of Freemen of such Corporations, and of the Freedom of Elections : To prevent such Practices for the future ; ' Be it enacted . . . That . . . no Person whatsoever claiming as a Freeman to vote at any Election of Members to serve in Parliament for any City, Town, Port or Borough in *England*, *Wales*, and the Town of *Berwick upon Tweed*, where such Voter's Right of voting is as a Freeman only, shall be admitted to give his Vote at such Election, unless such Person shall have been admitted to the Freedom of such City, Town, Port or Borough, twelve Calendar Months before the first Day of such Election : And if any Person shall presume to give his Vote as a Freeman at any Election of Members to serve in Parliament, contrary to the true Intent and Meaning of this Act, he shall for every such Offence forfeit and pay the Sum of one hundred Pounds to him, her or them who shall inform and sue for the same ; and the Vote given by such Person shall be void and of no Effect.

II. Provided always, That nothing herein contained shall extend, or be construed to extend to any Person intitled to his Freedom by Birth, Marriage or Servitude, according to the Custom or Usage of such City, Town, Port or Borough. . . .

LVII

TRIAL OF CONTROVERTED ELECTIONS,[2] 1770

10 Geo. III, c. 16.

'Whereas the present Mode of Decision upon Petitions, complaining of undue Elections or Returns of Members to serve in

[1] See Sect. A, No. XXXI, p. 83, No. XXXIII, p. 85, No. LIX, p. 145, and Vol. II, Sect. A, No. XXII, §§ XXXII and XXXIII, p. 61.

[2] See Sect. B, No. XVII, p. 193, No. XX (B), p. 207, and No. XXXIII (B), p. 229. Also Sect. C, No. IX, p. 278, and Vol. II, Sect. A, No. XXII, § LX, p. 64, and No. XXXIII, p. 107.

Parliament, frequently obstructs publick Business ; occasions much
Expence, Trouble, and Delay to the Parties ; is defective, for want
of those Sanctions and Solemnities which are established by Law
in other Trials ; and is attended with many other Inconveniences :
For Remedy thereof,' be it enacted . . . That . . . whenever a
Petition, complaining of an undue Election or Return of a Member
or Members to serve in Parliament, shall be presented to the House
of Commons, a Day and Hour shall by the said House be appointed
for taking the same into Consideration ; and Notice thereof in
Writing shall be forthwith given, by the Speaker, to the Petitioners
and the Sitting Members, or their respective Agents, accompanied
with an Order to them to attend the House, at the Time appointed,
by themselves, their Counsel, or Agents. . . .

IV. And be it further enacted, That at the Time appointed for
taking such Petition into Consideration, and previous to the reading
the Order of the Day for that Purpose, the Serjeant at Arms shall
be directed to go with the Mace to the Places adjacent, and require
the immediate Attendance of the Members on the Business of the
House ; and that after his Return the House shall be counted, and
if there be less than One hundred Members present, the Order
for taking such Petition into Consideration shall be immediately
adjourned to a particular Hour on the following Day . . . and so,
from Day to Day, till there be an Attendance of One hundred
Members at the Reading the Order of the Day, to take such Petition
into Consideration.

V. And be it further enacted, That if after summoning the
Members, and counting the House as aforesaid, One hundred
Members shall be found to be present ; the Petitioners by themselves,
their Council or Agents, and the Council or Agents of the Sitting
Members, shall be ordered to attend at the Bar ; and then the Door
of the House shall be locked, and no Member shall be suffered to
enter into or depart from the House, until the Petitioners, their
Council, or Agents, and the Council or Agents for the Sitting
Members, shall be directed to withdraw as herein after is mentioned : And when the Door shall be locked as aforesaid, the Order
of the Day shall be read, and the Names of all the Members of the
House, written or printed on distinct Pieces of Parchment or
Paper, being all as near as may be of equal Size, and rolled up in
the same Manner, shall be put in equal Numbers into Six Boxes
or Glasses, to be placed on the Table for that Purpose, and shall
there be shaken together ; and then the Clerk or Clerk Assistant
attending the House shall publickly draw out of the said Six Boxes
or Glasses alternatively the said Pieces of Parchment or Paper, and
deliver the same to the Speaker, to be by him read to the House ;

and so shall continue to do, until Forty-nine Names of the Members then present be drawn.

VI. Provided always, That if the Name of any Member who shall have given his Vote at the Election so complained of as aforesaid, or who shall be a Petitioner complaining of an undue Election or Return, or against whose Return a Petition shall be then depending, or whose Return shall not have been brought in Fourteen Days, shall be drawn; his Name shall be set aside, with the Names of those who are absent from the House.

VII. Provided also, That if the Name of any Member of Sixty Years of Age or upwards be drawn, he shall be excused from serving on the Select Committee, to be appointed as herein after mentioned, if he require it, and verify the Cause of such Requisition upon Oath.

VIII. Provided also, That if the Name of any Member who has served in such Select Committee during the same Session be drawn, he shall, if he requires it, be excused from serving again in any such Select Committee. . . .

XIII. And be it further enacted, That as soon as the said Forty-nine Members shall have been so chosen by Lot, and the Two Members [1] to be added thereunto shall have been so nominated as aforesaid, the Door of the House shall be opened, and the House may proceed upon any other Business; and Lists of the Forty-nine Members so chosen by Lot shall then be given to the Petitioners, their Counsel, or Agents, and the Counsel or Agents for the Sitting Members, who shall immediately withdraw, together with the Clerk appointed to attend the said Select Committee; and the said Petitioners and Sitting Members, their Counsel or Agents, beginning on the Part of the Petitioners, shall alternately strike off One of the said Forty-nine Members, until the said Number shall be reduced to Thirteen; and the said Clerk within One Hour at farthest from the Time of the Parties withdrawing from the House, shall deliver in to the House the Names of the Thirteen Members then remaining; and the said Thirteen Members, together with the Two Members nominated as aforesaid, shall be sworn at the Table, well and truly to try the Matter of the Petition referred to them, and a true Judgment to give according to the Evidence; and shall be a Select Committee to try and determine the Merits of the Return or Election appointed by the House to be that Day taken into Consideration; and the House shall order the said Select Committee to meet at a certain Time to be fixed by the House, which Time shall be within Twenty-four Hours of the Appointment of the said Select Committee. . . .

XVIII. And be it further enacted, That the said Select Com-

[1] Representing the interests of either side.

mittee shall have Power to send for Persons, Papers and Records ;
and shall examine all the Witnesses who come before them upon
Oath ; and shall try the Merits of the Return, or Election, or both ;
and shall determine, by a Majority of Voices of the said Select
Committee, whether the Petitioners or the Sitting Members, or
either of them, be duly returned or elected, or whether the Election
be void ; which Determination shall be final between the Parties
to all Intents and Purposes : And the House, on being informed
thereof by the Chairman of the said Select Committee, shall order
the same to be entered in their Journals, and give the necessary
Directions for confirming or altering the Return, or for the issuing
a new Writ for a new Election, or for carrying the said Determination into Execution, as the Case may require. . . .

XXV. And be it further enacted, That if the said Select Committee shall come to any Resolution other than the Determination
above mentioned, they shall, if they think proper, report the same to
the House for their Opinion, at the same Time that the Chairman of the
said Select Committee shall inform the House of such Determination ; and the House may confirm or disagree with such Resolution,
and make such Orders thereon, as to them shall seem proper. . . .

XXVIII. Provided always, That no such Determination as
aforesaid shall be made, nor any Question be proposed, unless
Thirteen Members shall be present ; and no Member shall have a
Vote on such Determination, or any other Question or Resolu-
tion, who has not attended during every Sitting of the said Select
Committee. . . .

LVIII

THE ROYAL MARRIAGES ACT, 1772

12 Geo. III, c. 11.

Most gracious Sovereign,
Whereas Your Majesty, from Your Paternal Affection to Your
own Family, and from Your Royal Concern for the future Welfare
of Your People, and the Honour and Dignity of Your Crown, was
graciously pleased to recommend to Your Parliament to take into
their serious Consideration, Whether it might not be wise and
expedient to supply the Defect of the Laws now in being ; and, by
some new Provision, more effectually to guard the Descendants of
His late Majesty King George the Second, (other than the Issue
of Princesses who have married, or may hereafter marry, into

Foreign Families) from marrying without the Approbation of Your Majesty, Your Heirs, or Successors, first had and obtained; we have taken this weighty Matter into our serious Consideration; and, being sensible that Marriages in the Royal Family are of the highest Importance to the State, . . . we . . . do humbly beseech Your Majesty, that it may be enacted; . . . That no Descendant of the Body of His late Majesty King *George* the Second, Male or Female, (other than the Issue of Princesses who have married, or may hereafter marry, into Foreign Families) shall be capable of contracting Matrimony without the previous Consent of His Majesty, His Heirs, or Successors, signified under the Great Seal, and declared in Council, (which Consent, to preserve the Memory thereof, is hereby directed to be set out in the Licence and Register of Marriage, and to be entered in the Books of the Privy Council); and that every Marriage, or Matrimonial Contract, of any such Descendant, without such Consent first had and obtained, shall be null and void, to all Intents and Purposes whatsoever.

II. Provided always, . . . That in case any such Descendant of the Body of His late Majesty King *George* the Second, being above the Age of Twenty-five Years, shall persist in his or her Resolution to contract a Marriage disapproved of, or dissented from, by the King, His Heirs, or Successors; that then such Descendant, upon giving Notice to the King's Privy Council, which Notice is hereby directed to be entered in the Books thereof, may, at any Time from the Expiration of Twelve Calendar Months after such Notice given to the Privy Council as aforesaid, contract such Marriage; and his or her Marriage with the Person before proposed, and rejected, may be duly solemnized, without the previous Consent of his Majesty, His Heirs or Successors; and such Marriage shall be good, as if this Act had never been made, unless both Houses of Parliament shall, before the Expiration of the said Twelve Months, expressly declare their Disapprobation of such intended marriage.

III. And be it further enacted . . . That every Person who shall knowingly or wilfully presume to solemnize, or to assist, or to be present at the Celebration of any Marriage with any such Descendant, or at the his or her making any Matrimonial Contract, without such Consent as aforesaid first had and obtained, except in the Case above-mentioned, shall, being duly convicted thereof, incur and suffer the Pains and Penalties ordained and provided by the Statute of Provision and Premunire, made in the Sixteenth Year of the Reign of *Richard* the second.

LIX

A PLACE ACT,[1] (ELECTORS), 1782

22 Geo. III, c. 41.

For the better securing the Freedom of Elections of Members to serve in Parliament, be it enacted. . . . That . . . no Commissioner, Collector, Supervisor, Gauger, or other Officer or Person whatsoever, concerned or employed in the charging, collecting, levying, or managing the Duties of Excise, or any Branch or Part thereof ; nor any Commissioner, Collector, Comptroller, Searcher, or other Officer or Person whatsoever, concerned or employed in the charging, collecting, levying or managing the Customs, or any Branch or Part thereof ; nor any Commissioner, Officer, or other Person concerned or employed in collecting, receiving, or managing any of the Duties on stamped Vellum, Parchment, and Paper, nor any Person appointed by the Commissioners for distributing of Stamps ; nor any Commissioner, Officer, or other Person employed in collecting, levying, or managing, any of the Duties on Salt ; nor any Surveyor, Collector, Comptroller, Inspector, Officer, or other Person employed in collecting, managing, or receiving, the Duties on Windows or Houses ; nor any Postmaster, Postmasters General, or his or their Deputy or Deputies, or any Person employed by or under him or them in receiving, collecting or managing, the Revenue of the Post Office, or any Part thereof, nor any Captain, Master, or Mate, of any Ship, Packet, or other Vessel, employed by or under the Postmaster or Postmasters General in Conveying the Mail to and from foreign Ports, shall be capable of giving his Vote for the Election of any Knight of the Shire, Commissioner, Citizen, Burgess, or Baron, to serve in Parliament . . . or for chosing any Delegate in whom the Right of electing Members to serve in Parliament for that Part of *Great Britain* called *Scotland*, is vested : And if any person, hereby made incapable of voting as aforesaid, shall nevertheless presume to give his Vote, during the Time he shall hold, or within twelve Calendar Months after he shall cease to hold or execute any of the Offices aforesaid, contrary to the true Intent and Meaning of this Act, such Votes so given shall be held null and void . . . and every Person so offending shall forfeit the Sum of one hundred Pounds, one Moiety thereof to the Informer, and the other Moiety thereof to be immediately paid into the Hands of the Treasurer of the County, Riding or

[1] See also Sect. A, No. XXV, p. 67, and No. LX, p. 146. Also Vol. II, Sect. B, No. X, p. 170.

Division, . . . and into the Hands of the Clerk of the Justices of the Peace of the Counties or Stewartries, in that Part of *Great Britain* called *Scotland*, . . . and the Person convicted on any such Suit shall thereby become disabled and incapable of ever bearing or executing any Office or Place of Trust whatsoever under his Majesty, his Heirs and Successors.

[§§ II and III not to extend to Commissioners of Land Tax or to any Office held by Letters Patent for an Estate of Inheritance.]

[§ IV not to apply to Persons who resign Offices before August 1st, 1782.]

[§ V. Prosecution must be brought within twelve months of Offence.]

LX

A PLACE ACT [1] (MEMBERS), 1782

22 Geo. III, c. 45.

For further securing the Freedom and Independence of Parliament, be it enacted . . . That, from and after the End of this present Session of Parliament, any Person who shall, directly or indirectly, himself, or by any Person whatsoever in Trust for him, or for his Use or Benefit, or on his Account, undertake, execute, hold, or enjoy, in the Whole or in Part, any Contract, Agreement, or Commission, made or entered into with, under, or from the Commissioners of his Majesty's Treasury, or of the Navy or Victualling Office, or with the Master General or Board of Ordnance, or with any one or more of such Commissioners, or with any other Person or Persons whatsoever, for or on account of the Public Service ; or shall knowingly and willingly furnish or provide, in pursuance of any such Agreement, Contract, or Commission, which he or they shall have made or entered into as aforesaid, any Money to be remitted abroad, or any Wares or Merchandize to be used or employed in the Service of the Publick, shall be incapable of being elected, or of sitting or voting as a Member of the House of Commons, during the Time that he shall execute, hold, or enjoy, any such Contract, Agreement, or Commission, or any Part or Share thereof, or any Benefit or Emolument arising from the same.

II. And be it further enacted by the Authority aforesaid, That if any Person, being a Member of the House of Commons, shall directly or indirectly, himself, or by any other Person whatsoever

[1] See Sect. A, No. XXXVI, p. 95, No. XLI, § XXV, p. 116, No. LI, p. 131, and No. LIX, p. 145.

. . . enter into, . . . any such Contract, Agreement, or Commission, as aforesaid ; or if any Person, Being a Member of the House of Commons, and having already entered into any such Contract, Agreement, . . . shall, after the Commencement of the next Session of Parliament, continue to hold, execute, or enjoy the same, or any Part thereof, the Seat of every such Person in the House of Commons shall be, and is hereby declared to be void. . . .

LXI

REPEAL OF THE DEPENDENCY OF IRELAND ACT,[1] 1782

22 Geo. III, c. 53.

' Whereas an act was passed in the Sixth Year of the Reign of his late Majesty King George the First, intituled, *An Act for the better securing the Dependency of the Kingdom of* Ireland *upon the Crown of* Great Britain ; ' may it please your most Excellent Majesty that it may be enacted ; and be it enacted . . . That from and after the passing of this Act, the above-mentioned Act, and the several Matters and Things therein contained, shall be, and is and are hereby repealed.

LXII

A CIVIL ESTABLISHMENT ACT,[2] 1782

22 Geo. III, c. 82.

An Act for enabling his Majesty to discharge the Debt contracted upon his Civil List Revenues, and for preventing the same from being in arrear for the future, by regulating the Mode of Payments out of the said Revenues, and by suppressing or regulating certain Offices therein mentioned, which are now paid out of the Revenues of the Civil List.

' Whereas his Majesty, from his paternal Regard to the Welfare of his faithful People, from his Desire to discharge the Debt on his Civil List, without any new Burthen to the Publick, for

[1] See Sect. A, No. XLVIII, p. 128, No. LXIII, p. 150, and Sect. B, No. XXXIX, p. 241. Also Vol. II, Sect. A, No. XII, p. 20, and No. XLIV, p. 145.
[2] 22 Geo. III, c. 81, dealt with economic reforms of the office of Paymaster General, particularly the establishment of an official account at the Bank of England.

preventing the Growth of a like Debt for the future, as well as for introducing a better Order and Oeconomy in the Civil List Establishments, and for the better Security of the Liberty and Independency of Parliament, has been pleased to order, that the Office commonly called or known by the Name of *Third Secretary of State, or Secretary of State for the Colonies*; the Office or Establishment commonly known by the Name and Description of *The Board of Trade and Plantations*;[1] the Offices of Lords of Police in *Scotland*; the principal Officers of the Board of Works: the principal Officers of the Great Wardrobe; the principal Officers of the Jewel Office; the Treasurer of the Chamber; the Cofferer of the Household; the Offices of the six Clerks of the Board of Green Cloth; the Office of Paymaster of the Pensions; the Office of Master of the Harriers and Fox Hounds; and also the Office of Master of the Stag Hounds, should be suppressed:' . . . be it enacted . . . that . . . all and every of the Offices aforesaid, together with certain of the Offices dependent on or connected with the same, . . . shall be, and are hereby utterly suppressed, abolished, and taken away.[2]

[§ II. Any similar Office if established hereafter to be treated as a new Office.] . . .

IV. ' And, whereas a new and œconomical Plan is intended to be adopted . . ., be it therefore enacted, That the Commissioners of the Treasury shall be, . . . authorized and required to direct such Person or Persons as they shall think most fit and capable, to prepare, . . . Methods accommodated to the several Reforms and Alterations in this Act made, and to appoint or continue in Office such Officers as they shall judge most fit and proper for carrying such Plans into Execution, under the Direction of the Lord Steward, Lord Chamberlain, Master of the Horse, and any other principal Officer, to whom the said Officers shall severally be subordinate; and the said Lord Steward, [etc.] . . . shall regularly, . . . make out . . ., an Estimate of all the several Articles of Expence of his Majesty's Civil Government, within their distinct Departments; which shall, after being inspected, and approved by the said Lord Steward, [etc.] . . ., be presented to the said Commissioners of the Treasury; and which Estimate of Expence shall not be exceeded (except as is herein-after excepted and specially provided for) above five thousand Pounds, in any of those Departments in any one Year, without sufficient Reasons, to be produced to the said Commissioners of the Treasury, for increasing the same; and upon the Expiration of the Quarter, the said Commissioners of the

---

[1] See Vol. II, Sect. B, No. VIII, p. 166.
[2] See Sect. B, No. XXXVII, p. 239.

Treasury shall direct so much of the Monies of the Civil List Revenues to be issued at the Receipt of the Exchequer to the said Lord Steward, [etc. ; or to anyone appointed by them and approved by the Treasury Commissioners] . . . as shall be sufficient to satisfy and pay the Whole of the Expence incurred in such Quarter, which shall be by him distributed to and among the several Persons who shall be intitled to receive the same. . . .

[§ VI. An expert Surveyor or Comptroller to be appointed to manage His Majesty's buildings.] . . .

XIX. ' And whereas much Confusion and Expence did arise from having Pensions paid at various Places, and by various Persons ; and a Custom hath prevailed of granting Pensions on a private List during his Majesty's Pleasure, upon a Supposition that in some Cases it may not be expedient for the Public Good to divulge the Names of the Persons in the said List, or that it may be disagreeable to the Persons receiving such Payments to have it known that their Distresses are so relieved, . . .; by Means of which said Usage, secret and dangerous Corruption may hereafter be practised : And whereas it is no Disparagement for any Persons to be relieved by the Royal Bounty in their Distress, or for their Desert, but, on the contrary, it is honourable, on just Cause, to be thought worthy of Reward : ' Be it therefore enacted . . ., That no Pension whatsoever, on the Civil Establishment, shall hereafter be paid but at the Exchequer, and in the same Manner as those Pensions which are now paid and entered at the Exchequer, under the Head, Title, and Description of *Pensions*, and with the Name of the Person to whom, or in Trust for whom, the said Pension is granted. . . .

XXI. Provided also, That it shall and may be lawful for the High Treasurer, or first Commissioner of the Treasury for the Time being, to return into the Exchequer any Pension or Annuity, without the Name of the Person to whom the same is payable, on taking an Oath before the Barons of the Exchequer, or one Baron of the Exchequer, or before the Cursitor Baron, in the Form following :

' I A. B. do swear, That, according to the best of my Knowledge, Belief, and Information, the Pension or Pensions, or Annuity or Annuities, returned without a Name by me into the Exchequer, is or are not, directly or indirectly, for the Benefit, Use, or Behoof, of any Member of the House of Commons, or, so far as I am concerned, applicable, directly or indirectly, to the Purpose of supporting or procuring an Interest in any Place returning Members to Parliament.

' So help me GOD.' . . .

[§ XXIV. Secret Service money not to exceed £10,000 in any one year.] . . .

XXVII. Provided always, That whenever it shall be necessary for the Principal Secretary or Secretaries of State, or First Commissioner of the Admiralty, to make Payment of any Money issued for Foreign Secret Service, or for Secret Service in detecting, preventing, or defeating, treasonable or other dangerous Conspiracies against the State in any Place within this Kingdom, then it shall be sufficient to acquit and discharge the said Secretary [etc.] . . . for such Secretary [etc.] : . . . to make Oath, before the Barons of the Exchequer, or one of them, or before the Cursitor Baron, in the Form following :

' I A. B. do swear, That the Money paid to me for Foreign Secret Service, or for Secret Service in detecting, preventing, or defeating, treasonable, or other dangerous Conspiracies against the State, (mutatis mutandis, as the Case may be,) has been bona fide applied to the said Purpose or Purposes, and to no other ; and that it hath not appeared to me convenient to the State that the same should be paid Abroad.

So help me God.'

. . .

LXIII

THE LEGISLATIVE AND JUDICIAL INDEPENDENCE OF THE IRISH PARLIAMENT AND COURTS, 1783

23 Geo. III, c. 28.

An Act for preventing and removing all Doubts which have arisen, or might arise, concerning the exclusive Rights of the Parliament and Courts of Ireland, in Matters of Legislation and Judicature ; and for preventing any Writ of Error or Appeal from any of his Majesty's Courts in that Kingdom from being received, heard, and adjudged, in any of his Majesty's Courts in the Kingdom of Great Britain.

' Whereas, by an Act of the last Session of this present Parliament, (intituled, *An Act* [1] *to repeal an Act, made in the sixth Year of the Reign of his late Majesty King* George *the First, intituled, An Act* [2] *for the better securing the Dependency of the Kingdom of* Ireland, *upon the Crown of* Great Britain), it was enacted, That the said last-

[1] Sect. A, No. LXI, p. 147.
[2] Sect. A, No. XLVIII, p. 128. See also Vol. II, Sect. A, No. XII, p. 20, and No. XLIV, p. 145.

mentioned Act, and all Matters and Things therein contained, should be repealed : And whereas Doubts have arisen whether the Provisions of the said Act are sufficient to secure to the People of *Ireland* the Rights claimed by them to be bound only by Laws enacted by his Majesty and the Parliament of that Kingdom, in all Cases whatever, and to have all Actions and Suits at Law or in Equity, which may be instituted in that Kingdom, decided in his Majesty's Courts therein finally, and without Appeal from thence : therefore, for removing all Doubts respecting the same, . . . be it declared and enacted. . . . That the said Right claimed by the People of *Ireland* to be bound only by Laws enacted by his Majesty and the Parliament of that Kingdom, in all Cases whatever, and to have all Actions and Suits at Law or in Equity, which may be instituted in that Kingdom, decided in his Majesty's Courts therein finally, and without Appeal from thence, shall be, and it is hereby declared to be established and ascertained for ever, and shall, at no Time hereafter be questioned or questionable.

II. And be it further enacted . . . That no Writ of Error or Appeal shall be received or adjudged, or any other Proceeding be had by or in any of his Majesty's Courts in this Kingdom, in any Action or Suit at Law or in Equity, instituted in any of his Majesty's Courts in the Kingdom of *Ireland* : and that all such Writs, Appeals, or Proceedings, shall be, and they are hereby declared null and void to all Intents and Purposes. . . .

PARLIAMENTARY PROCEEDINGS

(INCLUDING BILLS, RESOLUTIONS, IMPEACHMENTS AND SPEECHES IN EITHER HOUSE)

I

MONEY BILLS,[1] 1661-78

(A)

INITIATION IN COMMONS, 1661

A Bill, sent from the Lords, for Paving, Repairing, and Amending the Streets and Highways of *Westminster*, and Parts adjacent,[2] was this Day read. And this House observing, that the said Bill was to alter the Course of the Law in Part, and to lay a Charge upon the People; and conceiving that it is a Privilege inherent to this House, that Bills of that Nature ought to be first considered here;

Ordered, That the said Bill be laid aside; And that the Lords be acquainted therewith, and the Reasons inducing this House thereunto; and the Lords are to be desired, for the Cause, not to suffer any Mention of the said Bill to remain in the Journals of their House. And the Lords are further to be acquainted, that this House, finding the Matter of their Bill to be very useful, and of publick Concernment, have ordered a Bill of the like Nature to be prepared and brought in To-morrow Morning. . . .

[C.J., viii, 311, July 24, 1661.]

(B)

COMMITTEE OF SUPPLY, 1668

Mr *Pryn* reports from the Committee appointed to inquire into the Order and Method of Proceedings in Parliament, a Resolve of the Committee: Which he read; and, after, delivered it in at the Clerk's Table: Which is as followeth; *viz*. That if any Motion be

[1] See Sect. D, No. VI, p. 326, and Vol. II, Sect. A, No. XLII, § 1 (2), p. 141, and Sect. B, No. XV, p. 187.

[2] See also Sect. B, No. XXI, p. 208.

made in the House for any public Aid, or Charge upon the People, the Consideration and Debate thereof ought not presently to be entered upon ; but adjourned till such further Day as the House shall think fit to appoint ; and then it ought to be referred to the Committee of the whole House ; and their Opinions to be reported thereupon, before any Resolution or Vote of the House do pass therein.

Resolved &c. That the House doth agree with the Committee. . . .

[C.J., ix, 52, Feb. 18, 1668.]

(C)

LORDS NOT TO AMEND MONEY BILLS, 1671

The House then proceeded to the Reading the Amendments and Clauses, sent from the Lords, to the Bill for an Imposition on foreign Commodities : Which were once read :

And the first Amendments, sent from the Lords, being for changing the Proportion of the Impositions on white Sugars from One Peny *per* Pound, to Halfpeny half Farthing, was read the Second Time ; and debated.

Resolved, etc. *Nemine contradicente*, That, in all Aids given to the King, by the Commons, the Rate or Tax ought not to be altered by the Lords.

[C.J., ix, 235, April 13, 1671.]

(D)

COMMONS' RIGHTS,[1] 1678

Mr. Solicitor General reports from the Committee to whom it was, amongst other things, referred, to prepare and draw up a State of Rights of the Commons, in Granting of Money, a Vote agreed by the Committee : Which he read at his Place, and afterwards delivered the same in at the Clerk's Table: Where the same was read; and, upon the Question, agreed ; and is as followeth ; *viz.*

Resolved, etc. That all Aids and Supplies, and Aids to his Majesty in Parliament, are the sole Gift of the Commons : And all Bills for the Granting of any such Aids and Supplies ought to begin with the Commons : And that it is the undoubted and sole right of the Commons, to direct, limit, and appoint, in such Bills, the Ends, Purposes, Considerations, Conditions, Limitations, and Qualifications of such Grants ; which ought not to be changed, or altered by the House of Lords.

[C.J., ix, 509, July 3, 1678.]

[1] See Vol. II, Sect. A, No. XLII, § 1, p. 141.

II

IMPEACHMENT OF CLARENDON,[1] 1667

[On October 26, 1667, Edward Seymour in the House of Commons charged Clarendon with many great crimes. On November 6 the accusations were reduced to Heads, and on November 12 Seymour was deputed by the House to apprize the Lords of the decision of the Commons to proceed to impeachment. This he did in these words : " I do accordingly impeach him of high-treason and other crimes and misdemeanours in the name of the said Commons and of all the Commons of England and they have further commanded me to desire your lordships to sequester him from parliament, and to commit him to safe custody, and in convenient time they will exhibit articles against him." On November 15 the Lords refused to commit Clarendon as the accusation was only of treason in general, without charging anything in particular. In spite of several conferences the Lords reiterated their decision on December 2. The following day the Commons were informed that Clarendon had withdrawn from the Kingdom. The Lords subsequently proceeded against him legislatively, and a Bill of Banishment became law as 19 Car. II, c. 10.]

Articles of Treason exhibited in Parliament

I. That the earl of Clarendon hath designed a standing army to be raised, and to govern the kingdom thereby ; advising the king to dissolve the present parliament ; to lay aside all thoughts of parliaments for the future ; to govern by military power, and to maintain the same by free quarter and contribution.

II. That he hath, in hearing of many of his majesty's subjects, falsely and seditiously said, the king was in his heart a Papist, Popishly affected, or words to that effect.

III. That he hath received great sums of money for passing the Canary Patent, and other illegal patents ; and granting several injunctions to stop proceedings at law against them and other illegal Patents formerly granted.

IV. That he hath advised and procured divers of his majesty's subjects to be imprisoned against law, in remote islands, garrisons, and other places thereby to prevent them from the benefit of the law ; and to introduce precedents for imprisoning of other of his majesty's subjects in like manner.

V. That he hath corruptly sold several offices, contrary to law.

VI. That he hath procured his majesty's customs to be farmed at under rates, knowing the same ; and great pretended debts to be paid by his majesty, to the payment whereof his majesty was not in

[1] Cf. Sect. B, No. VIII, p. 180, and Vol. II, Sect. B, No. IV, p. 159.

strictness bound.   And hath received great sums of money for procuring the same.

VII.   That he hath received great sums of money from the company of Vintners, or some of them, or their agents, for enhancing the
prices of wine, and for freeing them from the payment of legal
penalties which they had incurred.

VIII.   That he had in a short time gained to himself a far greater
estate than can be imagined to be lawfully gained in so short a time :
And contrary to his oath, hath procured several grants under the
great seal from his majesty, to himself and relations, of several of
his majesty's lands, hereditaments, and leases, to the dis-profit of
his majesty.

IX.   That he introduced an arbitrary government in his majesty's
foreign plantations ; and hath caused such as complained thereof,
before his majesty and council, to be long imprisoned for so doing.

X.   That he did reject and frustrate a proposal and undertaking,
approved by his majesty, for the preservation of Nevis and St.
Christopher's, and reducing the French plantations to his majesty's
obedience, after the commissions were drawn for that purpose ;
which was the occasion of such great losses and damages in those
parts.

XI.   That he advised and effected the sale of Dunkirk to the
French king, being part of his majesty's dominions, together with
the ammunition, artillery, and all sorts of stores there, and for no
greater value than the said ammunition, artillery, and stores were
worth.

XII.   That the said earl did unduly cause his majesty's letters
patent under the Great Seal of England (to one Dr. Crowther) to be
altered, and the inrollment thereof to be unduly razed.

XIII.   That he hath, in an arbitrary way, examined and drawn
into question divers of his majesty's subjects concerning their lands,
tenements, goods and chattels, and properties ; determined thereof
at the council-table, and stopped proceedings at law ; and threatened
some that pleaded the Statute [1] of 17 Car. 1.

XIV.   That he had caused Quo Warrantos to be issued out against
most of the corporations of England . . . to the intent he might
receive great sums of money from them for renewing their charters ;
which when they complied withal, he caused the said Quo Warrantos
to be discharged, and prosecution thereon to cease.

XV.   That he procured the bills of settlement for Ireland, and
received great sums of money for the same in a most corrupt and
unlawful manner.

----

[1] See Gardiner, No. 34, p. 179, for 17 Car. I, c. 10, which is clearly the
Statute in question.

XVI. That he had deluded his majesty and the nation, in all foreign treaties and negotiations relating to the late war.

XVII. That he was a principal author of that fatal counsel of dividing the fleet, about June 1666.

[*S.T.*, vi, 395, Nov. 14, 1667.]

III

SKINNER v. THE EAST INDIA COMPANY
1666–70

(A)

Whereas upon the Petition of Thomas Skinner merchant, setting forth his sufferings under the barbarous oppression of the East India Company, his majesty was graciously pleased by order of the 27th of August last, to defer the clearing of the matter for erecting a court to determine affairs of this nature till the second meeting of this board at Whitehall, and in regard the said Company have slighted the orders of this board, and not complied with any references or mediations, designing to wear out the Petitioner's life in tedious attendances ; he did by his Petition this day read at the board, humbly pray that the said court may be now erected, to relieve the Petitioner according to justice, and put a period to his grievances : Whereupon his majesty present in council did order, That his grace the Lord Archbishop of Canterbury, the Lord Chancellor, Lord Privy Seal, and the lord Ashley do send for the Governor and some of the Members of the East India Company, to treat with them, and induce them to give the said Mr. Skinner such reasonable satisfaction, as may in some measure be answerable to the loss and damage he hath suffered under them.

(Signed) JOHN NICHOLAS.

[*S.T.*, vi, 711, March 23, 1666.]

[This Committee of Council eventually reported that they were unable to mediate between the parties. Thereupon the King forwarded on January 19, 1667 all the papers in the case to the House of Lords, recommending them to do justice according to the merits of the case. Skinner sent a petition to the Lords.]

(B)

To the Honourable the Commons of England in Parliament assembled : The humble Petition of the Governor and Company of the Merchants of London, trading to the East Indies.

Humbly sheweth :

That Thomas Skinner lately exhibited a Petition to the right honourable the Lords spiritual and temporal in Parliament assembled, against your Petitioners (many of which are and were members of this honourable House, when the said Petition was exhibited) for injuries pretended to be done by your Petitioners' factors in the East Indies . . . all which matters (excepting what concerns the island) are matters clearly determinable in his majesty's ordinary courts of law, as by the judges attending their lordships, hath been resolved and reported : And for the island the same is parcel of the dominions of a foreign prince, and so the right thereof only determinable by the laws of that prince. That though the Petitioners did humbly tender a plea to their lordships, for that the Petition was in nature of an original complaint (concerning commoners only) and not brought to their lordships by Writ of Error, or Bill of Review, or any way of Appeal, and that the matters therein were relievable in the courts of Westminster Hall . . . Yet their lordships have been pleased not only to give a hearing in all the matters in the said Petition contained, but have denied to grant the Petitioners a commission, or so much as time to send for their witnesses now inhabiting upon the place, where the injuries were pretended to be done, and without whose testimony it was impossible for the Petitioners to make their defence.

That upon the said hearing, their lordships were further pleased to appoint a Committee to assess damages against your Petitioners, which Committee is now proceeding thereon accordingly, whereby several members of this honourable house, who are of the said Company as well as others your Petitioners, may be highly detrimented. All which proceedings, as your humble Petitioners humbly submit to your honourable judgments, are against the laws and statutes of this nation, and custom of Parliament. In tender consideration whereof, and forasmuch as these unusual and extraordinary proceedings of their lordships are not only grievous to your Petitioners at present, but may also be a precedent of ill consequence to all the Commons of England hereafter, and forasmuch as your Petitioners have no way of relief in this case than by making their humble addresses to this honourable house, your Petitioners do therefore most humbly pray, That your honours will be pleased to take the premises into your grave considerations, and to interpose with their lordships for your Petitioners' relief therein, in such way and manner as to your great wisdoms shall seem meet. And your Petitioners, as in duty bound, shall pray, etc.

Signed by the Order, and in the name of the said Governor and Company,   ROBERT BLACKBORNE, *Sec.*

[*S.T.*, vi, 721.]

(C)

Resolutions of the House of Commons

(1) That the proceedings of the House of Lords, upon the Petition of Thomas Skinner, Merchant, against the Governor and Company of Merchants of London trading to the East Indies, Sir William Thompson, and several other Members of the House of Commons, being members of the said Company, are a breach of the Privileges of the House of Commons.

(2) That the House of Lords assuming and exercising a jurisdiction, and taking cognizances of the matters set forth and complained of in the Petition of Thomas Skinner, Merchant . . . and their Lordships over-ruling of the plea of the said Governor and Company, put in to the jurisdiction of the said House of Lords ; the said cause coming before the House originally only upon the complaint of the said Thomas Skinner, and the matters in the said Petition complained of, concerning the taking away of the said petitioner's ship and goods, and assaulting his person, being relievable in the ordinary courts of law ; is contrary to the law of the land, and tends to the depriving of the subject of the benefit of the known law, and the introducing of an arbitrary way of proceeding.

(3) That the House of Lords, in the cause depending before them, upon the Petition of Thomas Skinner . . . allowing of affidavits taken before Masters of the Chancery, and a Judge of the Admiralty, as proof in the said cause, wherein also the Governor and Company had no liberty to cross-examine the said persons making such affidavits ; and the House of Lords not granting a commission to the said Governor and Company for the examination of their witnesses, the same being desired by the said Governor and Company, is illegal, and a grievance to the subject.

[Hatsell, ed. 1818, iii, 369, April 24, 1668.]

(D)

Resolutions of the House of Lords

(1) That the House of Commons entertaining the scandalous petition of the East India Company against the Lords' House of Parliament, and their proceedings, examinations, and votes thereupon had and made, are a breach of the privileges of the House of Peers, and contrary to the fair correspondency which ought to be between the two Houses, and unexampled in former times.

(2) That the House of Lords taking cognizance of the cause of Thomas Skynner, merchant, a person highly oppressed and injured

in East India by the Governor and Company of merchants of London trading thither, and over-ruling the plea of the said Company, and adjudging Five thousand pounds damages thereupon against the said Governor and Company, is agreeable to the laws of the land and well warranted by the law and custom of Parliament, and justified by many parliamentary precedents, ancient and modern.

[H.M.C., viii, App. pt. 1, 172 ff., May 7, 1668.]

(E)

RESOLUTION OF THE HOUSE OF COMMONS

Resolved.—That whosoever should be aiding or assisting in putting the order or sentence of the House of Lords, in the case of Thomas Skinner against the East India Company, in execution, shall be deemed a betrayer of the rights and liberties of the Commons of England, and an infringer of the privileges of this House.

[Hatsell, ed. 1818, iii, 376, May 9, 1668.]

(F)

RESOLUTIONS OF THE HOUSE OF COMMONS

(1) That it is an inherent right of every Commoner of England, to prepare and present petitions to the House of Commons, in case of grievance, and the House of Commons to receive the same.[1]

(2) That it is the undoubted Right and Privilege of the House of Commons, to judge and determine touching the nature and matter of such petitions, how far they are fit or unfit to be received.

(3) That no Court whatsoever hath power to judge or censure any petition prepared for, or presented to the House of Commons, and received by them, unless transmitted from thence, or the matter is complained of by them.

(4) Whereas a petition by the Governor and Company of Merchants trading to the East Indies was presented to the House of Commons by Sir Samuel Barnardiston and others, complaining of grievances therein—which the Lords have censured, under the notion of a scandalous paper or libel — that the said censure and proceeding of the Lords against the said Sir Samuel Barnardiston are contrary to, and in subversion of, the Rights and Privileges of the House of Commons, and Liberties of the Commons of England.

(5) That the continuance upon record of the judgment given by the Lords, and complained of by the House of Commons, in the last session of this Parliament, in the case of Thomas Skinner and the East India Company, is prejudicial to the Rights of the Commoners of England.

[Hatsell, ed. 1818, iii, 387, Dec. 8, 1669.]

[1] See Sect. B, No. XV, p. 191.

(G)

THE KING'S SPEECH

My Lords and Gentlemen,

I did very earnestly recommend to you, the other Day, that you would not suffer any Differences between yourselves to be revived. . . . I remember very well, that the Case of *Skinner* was first sent by Me to the Lords. I have therefore though*t* Myself concerned to offer to you, what I judge the best and safest way to put an End to the Difference; and, indeed, I can find no other. I will myself give present Order to raze all Records and Entries of this Matter, both in the Council Books, and in the Exchequer; and do desire you to do the like in both Houses, that no Memory may remain of this Dispute between you : And then, I hope, all future Apprehensions will be secured.

Resolved, That, in Obedience to His Majesty's Command, in his Speech, a Razure or Vacat be made, in the Journals of this House, of all the Matters therein contained, relating to the Business between the *East India* Company and *Skinner* : Which was accordingly done in the House.

[C.J., ix, 126, Feb. 22, 1670.]

(H)

[Extracts from Serjeant Maynard's argument at a conference with the Lords on behalf of the Commons.]

It hath been already observed to your Lordships, that this cause is not negatively ; to wit, it comes not before your Lordships as matter of evidence to the King, nor as matter of favour, but is brought to you by way of complaint, by one Commoner against another, as supposing your Lordships to be proper judges, *prima instantia*, to hear and determine the cause, as it hath been summarily, and without such legal tryal as by Law ought to have been had in such a case.[1] The Common Law is that which makes your Lordships safe in your honour and estates, by which Justice is to be administered, and whatever is done without this Law, by way of judgment, is done against it. . . .

The grand work of all which I shall farther say is expressed in the vote itself, *viz* that the suit is a common plea, it concerns not the King in his interest, nor any crime ; . . . And "a common person" in this matter is every person under the King, noble or ignoble . . . for there is no person, how great soever, who is a subject, but is concerned in all and every thing he hath and can claim ; and it

[1] See Vol. II, Sect. C, No. XI, at p. 268.

extends to ecclesiastical as well as secular jurisdictions and interests.
. . . This being premised, I say, *non recurritur ad extraordinarium remedium nisi deficiente ordinario.* The Petitioner might have had his ordinary remedy in the inferior Courts as to the ship-goods and assault, . . . and therefore need not, nor ought, to fly to an unusual and extraordinary remedy. . . .

By this way or proceeding, the subject loses that legal and in-different way of tryal, which the Law hath provided for him, by Jurors of his own condition, which is as much his right, yea his birthright and inheritance, as his lands are. . . . This way of tryal is his fence and protection against all storms of power . . . there-fore the Commons are careful (even) to jealousy, that this their liberty and buckler be not taken from them. . . .

But by this way of proceeding before your Lordships all these advantages are lost, for the tryal of fact and of Law, the office of the Judge and Juror, are confounded. . . .

Again ; in case an error be committed in the proceedings, be the same ever so unjust, whether in fact, or in Law . . . yet he is without all remedy in the way of proceeding. . . .

Again ; the way of proceeding summarily by *English* Petition, and without tryal by Jury, is against several Statutes and Declara-tions in Parliament by the Lords themselves.

[Here are examined at length Magna Charta and several other medieval Statutes.]

I next say, this power, now claimed and used in this case by the Lords, is a lessening, or " *emblemissement* " of the King's Royalty, to use the words of the Act, since no command comes from the King . . . nor the name of the King mentioned. . . .

If either party hath cause to complain in Parliament of the Judgment as erroneous, he cannot do it by petition in Parliament, but must bring a writ of error in Parliament in the King's name, and under the King's seal, to authorise the party's complaint, and the jurisdiction of the Lords, and of the Court. . . . This is not a formality only, but the ill inferences and consequences drawn from the neglect of it go farther than at first sight appears, *viz.* that the subject, on original petition to him, should have jurisdiction over the estate and person of his fellow-subject. . . .

The question in the writ of error before the Lords is this regularly, *viz.* admitting all facts to be as they are alleged, whether the Law be as is adjudged in the inferior Courts, or that the proceed-ings have been otherwise than by Law they ought to have been. . . .

It is considerable to the Lords themselves, whether this jurisdic-tion be not as disadvantageous to themselves as to the Com-

moners; let them consider whether it be not most for the interest
and safety of their estates for them to be tried by Jurors sworn . . .
To be tried there, where if injustice be done, redress may be had,
and the injustice be examined, or there, where, if wrong be done, it
shall be to the day of doom. . . . Last of all, it is clear that where
the jurisdiction is changed, the Law is changed, as appears by all
the instances of tryal, appeal, proceeding, judgment, and execution,
fact and law, equity and law, all blended together, and indifferent
and arbitrary.

[Grey's *Debates*, i, 446-62. According to Grey, this speech was
ordered by the Commons on April 15, 1671, to be entered into the
Journals of the House. It does not appear precisely when it was
delivered. Probably during the controversy in the previous session.]

IV

SUSPENDING POWER, 1673 [1]

(A)

RESOLUTIONS OF THE HOUSE OF COMMONS

The House then resumed the Debate of that Part of his
Majesty's Speech, which relates to his Declaration of Indulgence
to Dissenters.

And the Declaration was read. . . .

The main Question being put, That penal Statutes, in Matters
Ecclesiastical, cannot be suspended but by Act of Parliament;

It was resolved in the Affirmative.

Resolved, etc. That an humble Petition and Address, upon
this Vote and the Debate of the House, be forthwith prepared and
drawn up, to be presented to his Majesty; and that it be referred
to . . . [names follow here] . . . to prepare and bring in the
Petition and Address. . . .

[C.J., ix, 251, Feb. 10, 1673.]

(B)

Mr. *Powle* reports from the Committee appointed to prepare
and draw up a Petition and Address to his Majesty, the said
Petition and Address: Which he read, in his Place; and after,
delivered the same in at the Clerk's Table: And the same being
again twice read, is as followeth; viz.

Most Gracious Sovereign,

[1] See Declaration of Indulgence, Sect. D, No. IV, p. 324, and the Seven
Bishops' Case, Sect. C, No. VII, p. 258, and Sect. D, No. XVI (C), p. 346.

We Your Majesty's most loyal and faithful Subjects, the Commons assembled in Parliament, do, in the first place, as in all Duty bound, return your Majesty our most humble and hearty Thanks for the many gracious Promises and Assurances which Your Majesty hath several times, during this present Parliament, given to us, that Your Majesty would secure and maintain unto us the true Reformed Protestant Religion, our Liberties and Properties : Which most gracious Assurances Your Majesty hath, out of Your great Goodness, been pleased to renew unto us more particularly, at the Opening of this present Session of Parliament.

And further we crave Leave humbly to represent, That we have, with all Duty and Expedition, taken into our Consideration several Parts of Your Majesty's last Speech to us, and withal the Declaration therein mentioned, for Indulgence to Dissenters, dated the Fifteenth of *March* last : And we find ourselves bound in Duty to inform Your Majesty, that penal Statutes, in Matters Ecclesiastical, cannot be suspended, but by Act of Parliament.

We therefore, the Knights, Citizens and Burgesses of Your Majesty's House of Commons, do most humbly beseech Your Majesty, that the said Laws may have their free Course, until it shall be otherwise provided for by Act of Parliament : And that your Majesty would graciously be pleased to give such Directions herein, that no Apprehensions or Jealousies may remain in the Hearts of Your Majesty's good and faithful subjects.

Resolved, etc. That this House doth agree with the Committee in the Petition and Address by them drawn up to be presented to his Majesty.

[C.J., ix, 252, Feb. 14, 1673.]

(C)

Mr Secretary *Coventry* reports, and presents, in Writeing, from his Majesty, his Answer to the humble Petition and Address of this House : Which was thrice read ; and the Matter debated ; and is as followeth, *viz.*

Charles R.

His Majesty hath received an Address from you : And He hath seriously considered of it ; and returneth you this Answer : That He is very much troubled, that That Declaration, which He put out for Ends so necessary to the Quiet of His Kingdom, and especially in That Conjuncture, should prove the Cause of Disquiet in His House of Commons, and give Occasion to the Questioning of His Power in Ecclesiasticks : Which He finds not done in the Reigns of any of His Ancestors. He is sure He never had Thoughts of using it otherwise than as it hath been intrusted in Him, to the

Peace and Establishment of the Church of *England*, and the Ease of all His Subjects in general: Neither doth He pretend to the Right of suspending any Laws, wherein the Properties, Rights, or Liberties of any of His Subjects are concerned; nor to alter anything in the established Doctrine or Discipline of the Church of *England*: But His only Design in this was, to take off the Penalties the Statutes inflict upon the Dissenters; and which He believes, when well considered of, you yourselves would not wish executed according to the Rigour and Letter of the Law. Neither hath He done This with any Thought of avoiding or precluding the Advice of His Parliament: And if any Bill shall be offered Him, which shall appear more proper to attain the aforesaid Ends, and secure the Peace of the Church and Kingdom; when tendered in due Manner to Him, He will show how readily He will concur in all Ways that shall appear good for the Kingdom.

[C.J., ix, 256, Feb. 24, 1673.]

(D)

[The House of Commons replied to this royal answer on 26 February as follows:]

Most Gracious Sovereign,

We Your Majesty's most humble and loyal Subjects the Knights, Citizens, and Burgesses, in this present Parliament assembled, do render to Your Sacred Majesty our most dutiful Thanks, for that, to our unspeakable Comfort, Your Majesty hath been pleased so often to reiterate unto us those gracious Promises and Assurances of maintaining the Religion now established; and the Liberties and Properties of Your People: And we do not in the least measure doubt, but that Your Majesty had the same gracious Intentions, in giving Satisfaction to Your Subjects, by Your Answer to our last Petition and Address: Yet upon a serious Consideration thereof, we find, that the said Answer is not sufficient to clear the Apprehensions, that may justly remain in the Minds of Your People, by Your Majesty's having claimed a Power to suspend penal Statutes, in Matters Ecclesiastical; and which Your Majesty does still seem to assert in the said Answer, to be intrusted in the Crown, and never questioned in the Reigns of any of Your Ancestors: Wherein we humbly conceive, Your Majesty hath been very much misinformed; since no such Power was ever claimed or exercised by any of Your Majesty's Predecessors: And if it should be admitted, might tend to the Interrupting of the free Course of the Laws, and Altering the Legislative Power, which hath always been acknowledged to reside in Your Majesty, and Your Two Houses of Parliament. We do therefore, with an unanimous Consent, become again most humble Suitors unto Your Sacred Majesty, That You would be pleased to give us a full and satisfactory Answer to our said Petition and Address : And that Your Majesty would take such effectual Order, that the Proceedings in this Matter may not, for the future, be drawn into Consequence or Example.

[C.J., ix, 257, Feb. 26, 1673.]

(E)

[On 1 March the King referred the matter and the address to the House of Lords. After debate the Lords voted :]

' That the King's Answer to the house of Commons in referring the points now controverted to a parliamentary way, by Bill, is good and gracious : that being a good and natural course for satisfaction therein.'

[On March 7 both Houses agreed to a joint address to the King against the growth of Popery, requesting (1) the issue of a royal Proclamation expelling within thirty days " all Priests and Jesuits " and the execution of the laws against Popish Recusants ; (2) the issue of commissions to the Judge Advocate and Commissaries of the Musters to tender the oaths of supremacy and allegiance to all officers and soldiers ; (3) a requisition that all officers and soldiers should take the oaths of allegiance and supremacy and receive the Sacrament of the Lord's Supper according to the laws and usage of the Church of England ; (4) that similar tests should be applied to officers at sea.
On the same day the King cancelled the Proclamation.]

(F)

[On March 8 the King made a speech to the Lords and Commons, in which he said :]

My Lords and Gentlemen . . . If there be any Scruple remain with you concerning the Suspension of Penal Laws ; I here faithfully promise you, That what hath been done in That Particular, shall not for the future be drawn into Consequence of Example. . . .

[C.J., ix, 266, March 8, 1673.]

(G)

Resolved etc. *Nemine contradicente*, That the humble and hearty Thanks of this House be returned to his Majesty, for his gracious, full, and satisfactory Answer, this Day given to their humble Petitions and Addresses.

[C.J., ix, 266, March 8, 1673.]

V

DISPUTE BETWEEN THE TWO HOUSES OVER SHIRLEY v. FAGG,[1] 1675

[Sir John Fagg, M.P., had successfully proceeded against Dr. Thomas Shirley, physician to the King, in Chancery. Shirley sought to have the decree reversed in the Lords, whose jurisdiction, in Equity and over members of the Commons House, was thereby questioned.]

(A)

Resolved, That a Message be sent to the Lords, to acquaint them, that this House hath received Information, that there is a Petition of Appeal depending before them, at the Suit of *Thomas Shirley*, Esquire, against Sir *John Fagg*, a Member of this House ; to which Petition he is, by Order of the House of Lords, directed to answer on *Friday* next ; and to desire the Lords to have Regard to the Privileges of this House.

[C.J., ix, 330, May 5, 1675.]

The House [of Lords] agreed with the Committee in this Declaration ; and ordered the same to be entered into the Journal Book of this House, as their Declaration ; *videlicet*,

" That it is the undoubted Right of the Lords, in Judicature, to receive and determine, in Time of Parliament, Appeals from Inferior Courts, though a Member of either House be concerned, that there may be no Failure of Justice in the Land."

[L.J., xii, 680, May 6, 1675.]

(B)

By virtue of an Order, made the 12th Day of *May*, 1675, by the Honourable the House of Commons assembled in Parliament, these are to require and authorize you forthwith to apprehend Dr. *Thomas Shirley*, and bring [him] before the said House, to answer his Breach of Privilege, in prosecuting a Suit, by Petition of Appeal, in the Lords House, against Sir *John Fagg*, a Member of this House : And for so doing this shall be your Warrant. Given under my Hand, on *Friday* the 14th Day of *May* in the Seven and Twentieth Year of the Reign of our Sovereign Lord King *Charles* the Second, etc. Annoque Domini 1675.

EDW. SEYMOUR, Speaker

---

[1] See Sect. C, No. X, p. 279.

To Sir *James Northfolk* Knight, One of his Majesty's Serjeants at Arms in Ordinary now attending the Honourable House of Commons, his Deputy or Deputies.

Resolved, That the Appeal brought by Dr. *Sherley* in the House of Lords, against Sir *John Fagg*, a Member of this House, and the Proceedings thereupon, are a Breach of the undoubted Rights and Privileges of this House.

[C.J., ix, 337, May 14, 1675.]

(C)

[On May 14 a Deputy Serjeant went to arrest Shirley in the Lobby. Shirley called upon Lord Mohan for assistance. His Lordship seized the warrant and brought it to the House of Lords.]

Whereas *Thomas Sherley* Esquire, His Majesty's Physician in Ordinary, hath a Cause depending in this House, by Way of Appeal against Sir *John Fagg*, a Member of the House of Commons, and, by Law and Course of Parliament, ought to have Privilege and Freedom from Arrest :

It is Ordered, by the Lords Spiritual and Temporal, in Parliament assembled, That the said *Thomas Sherley* be, and he is hereby, privileged and protected accordingly, by the Authority of this House, during the Depending of his said Cause in this House ; and all Persons whatsoever are hereby prohibited from arresting or otherwise molesting the said *Thomas Shirley* upon any Pretence whatsoever, as they and every of them will answer the contrary to this House.

[L.J., xii, 692, May 14, 1675.]

(D)

The House . . . after a serious Debate, made this Declaration following ; (*videlicet*)

" The Lords do order and declare, That it is the undoubted Right of the Lords, in Judicature, to receive and determine, in Time of Parliament, Appeals from Inferior Courts, though a Member of either House be concerned therein, that there may be no Failure of Justice in the Land ; and from this Right and the Exercise thereof, the Lords will not depart."

[L.J., xii, 694, May 17, 1675.]

The Matter of the Lords' Answer being debated ; *Resolved* &c. That it is the undoubted Right of this House, that none of their Members be summoned to attend the House of Lords during the Sitting or Privilege of Parliament.

[C.J., ix 340, May 18, 1675.]

(E)

Mr. *Powle* reports, from the Conference had with the Lords upon the Subject Matter of the former Conference, upon the Lords Message concerning the Warrant for apprehending Dr. *Shirley*, that the Lords had returned an Answer to the Reasons of this House delivered at the former Conference, and are as follow : *viz.*

The Lords have appointed this Conference, upon the Subject Matter of the last Conference; and have commanded us to give these Answers to the Reasons, and other Matters, then delivered by the House of Commons.

To the First Reason, the Lords conceive, that the most natural Way of being informed, is by way of Question ; and, seeing a Paper here, which did reflect upon the Privileges of the Lords House, their Lordships would not proceed upon it till they were assured it was owned by the House of Commons : But the Lords had no Occasion at that time, nor do they now think fit, to enter into the Debate of the House of Commons being, or not being, proper Judges, in the Case concerning the Privilege of a Member of that House ; their Lordships' necessary Consideration, upon Sight of that Paper, being only how far the House of Commons ordering, if that Paper were theirs, the Apprehension of Dr. *Shirley*, for prosecuting his Appeal before the Lords, did intrench upon their Lordships both Privilege, and undoubted Rights of Judicature, in the Consequence of it, excepting all Members of both Houses from the Judicature of this the highest Court of the Kingdom ; which would cause a Failure of that supreme Justice not administrable in any other Court ; and which their Lordships will never admit.

As to the Second Reason, The Lords answer, That they do not apprehend, how the Matter of this Message is any Reflection upon the Speaker of the House of Commons.

To the Third Reason, The Lords cannot imagine, how it can be apprehended, in the least, to reflect upon the House of Commons, for the House of Peers, upon a Paper produced unto their Lordships, in Form of a Warrant of that House, whereof Doubt was made among the Lords, whether any such thing had been ordered by that House, to enquire of the Commons, whether such Warrant was ordered there or no ; And, without such Liberty used by the Lords, it will be very hard for their Lordships to be so rightly informed, as to preserve a good Correspondence between the Two Houses, which their Lordships shall endeavour, or to know when Warrants, in the Name of that House, are true or pretended : And it is so ungrounded an Apprehension, that their Lordships intended any Reflection in asking that Question, and not taking notice, in their

Message, of the Complaint of the House of Commons owning that Warrant, that the Lords had sent their Message, concerning that Paper to the House of Commons, before the Lords had received the said Commons Complaint.

But their Lordships have great Cause to except against the unjust and strained Reflection of that House upon their Lordships, in asserting, that the Question in the Lord's Message, could not be for Information, as we affirm, but tending to interrupt the mutual Correspondence between the Two Houses ; which we deny, and had not the least thought of.

The Lords have further commanded us to say, That they doubt not, when the House of Commons have received what we have delivered at this Conference, they will be sensible of their Error, in calling our Message strange, unusual, or unparliamentary; though we cannot but take notice, that their Answer to our Message, that they would consider of it, was the first of that kind that we can find to have come from that House.

The Question being put, Whether the House be satisfied with the Reasons delivered by the Lords at the last Conference; It passed in the Negative.

Resolved, &c. That a free Confeıence be desired with the Lords, upon the Matter delivered at the last Conference ; And that the former Managers do attend and manage the free Conference. . . .

[C.J., ix, 344, May 21, 1675.]

(F)

[Fagg was imprisoned in the Tower on May 28 by the Commons for putting in his answer to the appeal of Dr. Shirley in the Lords' House without leave, after he had raised the question of privilege.]

A petition of Sir *John Fagg* was read, submitting himself to the House, and craving their Pardon for his Offence, and praying, he might be released of his imprisonment.

Ordered, That Sir *John Fagg* be released and inlarged from his Imprisonment in the *Tower*. . . .

[C.J., ix, 352, June 3, 1675.]

(G)

Resolved, nemine contradicente, That, as to the Case of Appeal, brought against Sir *John Fagg*, in the House of Lords, Sir *John Fagg* shall have the Protection and the Assistance of this House.

Resolved, nemine contradicente, That, if any Person or Persons shall be aiding or assisting in putting in Execution any Sentence or Judgment that shall be given by the House of Lords, upon the

Appeal brought by Dr. *Shirley*, against Sir *John Fagg*, a Member of this House; such Person and Persons shall be adjudged and taken to be Betrayers of the Rights and Liberties of the Commons of *England*, and the Privileges of this House; and shall be proceeded against accordingly.

[C.J., ix, 356, June 7, 1675.]
[The King prorogued Parliament on June 9 to October 13.]

(H)

Whereas this House hath been informed of several Appeals depending in the House of Lords, from Courts of Equity, to the great Violation of the Rights and Liberties of the Commons of *England*; it is this Day *Resolved*, and *Declared*, That whosoever shall solicit, plead, or prosecute any Appeal against any Commoner of *England*, from any Court of Equity, before the House of Lords, shall be deemed and taken a Betrayer of the Rights and Liberties of the Commons of *England*; and shall be proceeded against accordingly.

Resolved, &c. That Copies of this Resolution and Declaration be forthwith publickly affixed upon the Door of the Lobby of this House, and *Westminster Hall* Gate, and upon the Gates of the Two *Serjeants Inns*, and the Four Inns of Court, and the several Inns of Chancery; to the end all Persons concerned may take Notice thereof: . . .

[C.J., ix, 380, Nov. 19, 1675.]

(I)

It is Ordered, by the Lords Spiritual and Temporal in Parliament assembled, That this House will hear the said Cause (Shirley *v.* Fagg), by Counsel, at the Bar, on *Monday* the 22th Instant, at Ten of the Clock in the Forenoon. . . . The House resumed the Debate concerning the Paper posted up in the Lobby of the House of Commons, and several other Places. And, upon Consideration thereof, Ordered, *Nemine contradicente*, That the Paper, dated " *Veneris*, 19th of *November*, 1675 " and posted up in several Places and signed " Will. Goldsborough, Cler. Dom. Com." against the Judicature of the House of Peers, in Cases of Appeals from Courts of Equity, is illegal, unparliamentary, and tending to the dissolution of the Government."

[L.J., xiii, 32-33, Nov. 20, 1675.]
[On November 22 the King again prorogued Parliament, which did not meet again until February 1677. The prorogation brought the dispute to an end and it was not revived.]

VI

DISPUTE BETWEEN THE TWO HOUSES OVER THE FOUR BARRISTERS, 1675

[This case overlaps in time with that of Shirley *v*. Fagg, as also a similar case of Sir Nicholas Stoughton *v*. Mr. Arthur Winslow, M.P., extracts from which are not here presented.]

(A)

On 12 May, 1675, an appeal was brought to the Lords by Sir Nicholas Crispe, and Mr Thomas and Mr John Crispe against a decree in Chancery obtained by the petitioners of whom Mr Dalmahoy, a member of the House of Commons, was one together with Lady Viscountess Cranbourne, and the Lady Mary Bowyer. On 19 May the Lords agreed to hear the case on the 27th, and Sir John Churchill, Serjeants Pemberton and Peck and Mr Porter were assigned as counsel for the appellants. On 27th May Sir N. Crispe complained to the Lords that his counsel dared not plead his cause for fear of being arrested by order of the Commons. The House of Lords ordered : ' That the said sir John Churchill (and the others) be and are hereby required, to appear at the bar of this house, to-morrow, at three of the clocke in the afternoon, as counsel to plead in the said cause.' On May 28th counsel was heard at the bar on both parts : upon the Petition and Appeal of sir Nicholas Crispe &, and the answer of Diana Viscountess Cranbourne &, and Thomas Dalmahoy esquire put in thereunto, concerning a decree in Chancery : Resolved, the petition and decree be dismissed.

(B)

Mr. Serjeant *Pemberton*, Sir *John Churchill*, Mr. Serj. *Peck*, and Mr. *Porter*, attending at the Door, in Obedience to the Order of this House ; and being severally called in ; Mr. Speaker did severally acquaint them, that they were summoned to give an Account to the House of their appearing as Counsel at the Bar of the House of Lords, in the Prosecution of a Cause depending upon an Appeal, wherein Mr. *Dalmahoy*, a Member of this House, is concerned ; in the manifest Breach of the Order of this House ; and giving up, as much as in them lies, the Rights and Privileges of the Commons of *England*. . . . And being withdrawn ; and the Matter debated. . . . *Ordered*, That Serjeant *Pemberton* be taken into the Custody of the Serjeant at Arms attending this House, for his Breach of the Privilege of this House. [Similar orders concerning the other three.]

[C.J., ix, 349, June 1, 1675.]

(C)

The Lord Privy Seal reported the Draught of the ensuing Order ; which was read as followeth :

" The House of Peers being made acquainted, by Examination of Two Witnesses upon Oath at their Bar, that the Lower House of Parliament had ordered into Custody of their Serjeant, Mr. Serjeant *Pecke*, sir *John Churchill*, Mr. Serjeant *Pemberton*, Counsel assigned by their Lordships in an Appeal heard at their Lordships Bar, for doing their Duty therein ; and judging this to be a great Indignity to the King's Majesty in this His Highest Court of Judicature in this Kingdom, and an unexampled Usurpation, and Breach of Privilege against the whole House of Peers, and tending to the Subversion of the Government of this Kingdom, and a transcendent Breach on the Right and Liberty of the Subject, which is not to be impeached but by due Process of Law ; and being by the Law of the Land concerned in all respects to do themselves and any oppressed Subjects Right ; do order the Gentleman Usher of the Black Rod attending this House to repair to any Place or Prison within the Kingdom of *England* where the said Persons, or any of them, or Mr. *Charles Porter* Counsellor at Law, are, or shall be, detained or held in Custody ; and from any Person or Persons detaining them, or any of them, to demand Delivery of them, without Fees ; and the said Usher of the Black Rod is hereby empowered to call all Persons necessary to his Assistance herein, and to make Return of this Warrant To-morrow Morning, by Eight of the Clock, to this House ; And this shall be a sufficient Authority on that Behalf. . . ."

[The House approved of this Order, and ordered it to be signed by the Clerk of the Parliaments.]

[L.J., xii, 713, June 1, 1675.]

(D)

[On June 2 the Gentleman Usher of the Black Rod took Sir John Churchill from the custody of the Serjeant at Arms, and the same day the four barristers appeared before the Lords and confessed, " that they were all called into the House of Commons and told by the Speaker, that they had invaded and betrayed the liberty of the subjects and privileges of Parliament in pleading for Sir Nicholas Crispe against Mr. Dalmahoy at the bar of the House of Lords ". They were thereupon each given an order of protection by the Lords.

On the same day the Commons arrested their Serjeant at Arms, sent him to the Tower, and requested the King to appoint another Serjeant at Arms.]

Mr. *Vaughan* reports, That the Lord Privy Seal did manage the Conference ; and had delivered the Occasion and Intent of the Conference : Which Mr. *Vaughan* did report to the House, to the Effect following ; viz.

The Lords do take Notice of the House of Commons their ordering into Custody of their Serjeant, Mr. Serjeant *Peck*, sir *John Churchill*, Mr. Serjeant *Pemberton*, and Mr. *Charles Porter*, Counsellors at Law, assigned by their Lordships to be of Counsel in an Appeal, heard at their Lordships Bar, in the Case of Sir *Nicholas Crispe*, against the lady *Bowyer*, Mr. *Dalmahoy*, and others.

The Lords in Parliament, where his Majesty is highest in his Royal Estate, and where the last Resort of judging upon Writs of Error and Appeals in Equity, in all Causes, and over all Persons, is undoubtedly fixed, and permanently lodged.

" It is an unexampled Usurpation, and Breach of Privilege, against the House of Peers, that their Orders or Judgments should be disputed, or endeavoured to be controuled, or the Execution thereof obstructed, by the Lower House of Parliament, who are no Court, nor have any Authority to administer an Oath, or give any Judgment."

" It is a transcendent Invasion on the Right and Liberty of the Subject, and against *Magna Charta*, the Petition of Right, and many other Laws, which have provided, that no Freeman shall be imprisoned, or otherwise restrained of his Liberty, but by due Process of Law."

" This tends to the Subversion of the Government of this Kingdom, and to the introducing of Arbitrariness and Disorder : "

" Because it is in Nature of an Injunction from the Lower House, who have no Authority nor Power of Judicature over inferior Subjects ; much less over the King and Lords, against the Orders and Judgments of the supreme Court."

" We are further commanded to acquaint you, That the Lords have therefore, out of that Justice, which they are Dispensers of, against Oppression, and Breach of Laws, by Judgment of this Court, set at Liberty, by the Gentleman Usher of the Black Rod, all the said Serjeants and Counsellors ; and prohibited the Lieutenant of the *Tower*, and all other Keepers of Prisons, and Gaolers, and all Persons whatsoever, from arresting, imprisoning, detaining, or otherwise molesting or charging the said Gentlemen, or any of them, in this Case : And if any Person, of what Degree soever, shall presume to the contrary, their Lordships will exercise the Authority with them intrusted, for putting the Laws in Execution : And we are further commanded to read to you a Roll of Parliament in the First Year of the Reign of King *Hen.* the Fourth, whereof we have brought the Original with us."

And a Debate arising thereupon ;

Resolved etc., That a Conference be desired with the Lords, upon the Subject Matter of the last Conference. . . .

Ordered, That Mr. Speaker do issue his Warrant to the Serjeant at Arms attending this House, for the apprehending *Charles Porter,* Esquire and bring him to the Bar of this House, to answer the Breach of Privilege objected against him.

[C.J., ix, 352, June 3, 1675.]

(E)

Ordered, that the Thanks of the House be returned to Mr. Speaker, for causing Mr. Serjeant *Pemberton,* formerly committed, by Order of this House, to the Custody of the Serjeant at Arms attending this House, for a Breach of Privilege, to be seized, and taken into Custody, in *Westminster Hall,* for his Breach of Privilege.

The House being informed, That Sir *John Churchill,* Mr. Serj. *Peck,* and Mr. *Charles Porter,* who were ordered to be taken into the Custody of the Serjeant at Arms . . . are now in *Westminster Hall* ; *Ordered,* that the Serjeant at Arms . . . do go with his Mace into *Westminster Hall,* and do execute the Order of this House, and the Warrant of Mr. Speaker thereupon. . . .

The Serjeant returning, gave an Account, That he had executed the Order of this House . . . and had brought the said Serjeant *Peck,* Sir *John Churchill,* and Mr. *Charles Porter,* in Custody, into the Speaker's Chamber. . . .

Ordered that Mr. Serjeant *Peck,* for his Breach of Privilege and Contempt of the Authority of this House, be sent to the Tower.

[Similar orders regarding the other three.]

Ordered, that Mr. Speaker do issue his Warrant to the Lieutenant of the *Tower,* to take into his Custody the Bodies of Sir *John Churchill* (etc), for their Offence in breaking the Privileges, and contemning the Authority of this House ; there to remain in safe Custody during the Pleasure of this House.

[C.J., ix, 353, June 4, 1675.]

(F)

Then instead of putting the Question, it was Ordered, That this House will proceed upon no other Business (except what shall be recommended by His Majesty), till they have received full Satisfaction, and vindicated themselves in this Breach of their Privileges. . . .

Ordered, That the humble Address of this House be presented to His Majesty . . . shewing, " That whereas this House directed the Gentleman Usher of the Black Rod to demand the Persons of Serjeant *Peck*, sir *John Churchill*, Sergeant *Pemberton* and Mr. *Charles Porter* . . . and in Pursuance of that Direction, finding them to be committed Prisoners to *The Tower of London* by Order of the House of Commons, repaired to sir *John Robinson*, His Majesty's Lieutenant of *The Tower*, and demanded them of him, who refused to deliver them otherwise than by Order of the House of Commons : This House humbly desired His Majesty, that He will be pleased to remove the said sir *John Robinson* from that Trust, and to appoint some other Person to be His Lieutenant of *The Tower*.

[L.J., xii, 723, June 4, 1675.]

(G)

Sir *Thomas Lee* reports from the Committee, the Reasons agreed to be offered at the Conference to be had with the Lords, upon the Matters delivered at the last Conference : Which were twice read ; and with some Amendments made at the Table, severally agreed ; and are as followeth, viz.

Your Lordships having desired the last Conference upon Matters of high Importance, concerning the Dignity of the King, and the Safety of the Government ; the Commons did not expect to hear from your Lordships at that Conference, Things so contrary to, and inconsistent with, the Matter upon which the said Conference was desired, as were then delivered by your Lordships.

It was much below the Expectation of the Commons, that, after a Representation in your Lordships Message of Matters of so high Importance, the Particular upon which the Conference was grounded, should be only the Commitment of Four Lawyers to the Custody of their own Serjeant at Arms, for a manifest Violation of the Privileges of their House.

But the Commons were much more surprised, when your Lordships had introduced the Conference, with an Assurance it was in order to a good Correspondency between the Two Houses, that your Lordships should immediately assume a Power to judge the Order of the House of Commons, for the Imprisonment of Mr. Serj. *Peck*, Sir *John Churchill*, Mr. Serj. *Pemberton*, and Mr. *Charles Porter*, to be illegal and arbitrary, and the Execution thereof a great Indignity to the King's Majesty, with many other high Reflections upon the House of Commons, throughout the whole Conference ; whereby your Lordships hath condemned the whole House of Commons as criminal : Which is without Precedent, or Example, or any Ground of Reason so to do.

'Tis not against the King's Dignity for the House of Commons to punish by Imprisonment a Commoner, that is guilty of violating their Privileges, that being according to the known Laws and Custom of Parliament, and the Right of their Privileges, declared by the King's Royal Predecessors in former Parliaments ; and by Himself in this.

But your Lordships claiming to be the supreme Court, and that his Majesty is highest in his Royal Estate in the Court of Judicature there, is a Diminution of the Dignity of the King ; who is highest in his Royal Estate, in full Parliament ; and is derogatory to the Authority of the whole Parliament, by appropriating it to yourselves.

The Commons did not infringe any Privileges of the House of Peers, but only defend and maintain their own ; On the other Side, your Lordships do highly intrench upon the Rights and Privileges of the House of Commons, denying them to be a Court, or to have any Authority or Power of Judicature ; which, if admitted, will leave them without any Authority or Power to preserve themselves.

As to what your Lordships call a transcendent Invasion of the Rights and Liberty of the Subject, and against *Magna Charta*, the Petition of Right, and many other Laws ; the House of Commons presume, that your Lordships know, that neither the Great Charter, the Petition of Right, nor any other Laws, do take away the Law and Custom of Parliament, or of either House of Parliament ; or else your Lordships have much forgotten the Great Charter, and those other Laws, in the several Judgments your Lordships have passed upon the King's Subjects, in Cases of Privilege.

But the Commons cannot find, by *Magna Charta*, or by any other Law or ancient Custom of Parliament, that your Lordships have any Jurisdiction, in Cases of Appeal from Courts of Equity.

We are further commanded to acquaint you, that the Enlargement of the said Persons imprisoned by Order of the House of Commons, by the Gentleman Usher of the Black Rod ; and the Prohibition, with Threats to all Officers and other Persons whatsoever, not to receive or detain them, is an apparent Breach of the Rights and Privileges of the House of Commons : And they have therefore caused them to be retaken into the Custody of the Serjeant at Arms, and hath committed them to the *Tower*.

As to the Parliament Roll of 1st *Hen.* 4, caused to be read by your Lordships at the last Conference, but not applied, the Commons apprehend it doth not concern the Case in Question ; for that this Record was made upon Occasion of Judgments given by the Lords, to depose and imprison their lawful King ; to which the Commons were unwilling to be made Parties ; And therefore the Commons conceived it will not be for the Honour of your Lordships, to make further Use of that Record.

But we are commanded to read to your lordships the Parliament Roll of the 4th of *Edward* the IIId, N⁰. 6 ; which if your Lordships please to consider, they doubt not but your Lordships will find Occasion to apply it to the present Purpose.

[C.J., ix, 354, June 4, 1675.]

(H)

KING'S SPEECH

My Lords and Gentlemen,

You may remember, that at the Meeting of this Sessions I told you, no Endeavours would be wanting to make the Continuance of this Parliament unpracticable ; I am sorry that Experience hath so quickly shewed you the Truth of what I then said : But I hope you are all convinced, that the Intent of all this, in the Contrivers, is to procure a Dissolution. . . . I must tell you plainly My Opinion, that the Means of coming to any Composure betwixt yourselves, cannot be without admitting of such full Conferences as either convince one another by the Reasons then offered ; or enable Me to judge rightly the Differences, when all hath been said upon both Sides, which the Matter will afford : For I am not to suffer these Differences to grow to Disorders in the whole Kingdom, if I can prevent it ; and I am sure, My Judgement shall always be impartial between My Two Houses of Parliament. But I must let you know, that whilst you are in Debate about your Privileges, I will not suffer My own to be invaded.

[C.J., ix, 355, June 5, 1675.]

(I)

Sir *John Robinson*, Lieutenant of the *Tower*, gives an Account to the House, of his receiving the Persons committed to the *Tower*, into his Custody, in Obedience to the Order of this House ; and that the Black Rod, coming afterwards with an Order from the Lords, and demanding them out of his Custody, he denied to deliver them, because they were committed by Order of this House : And that, after he had received the Votes of this House, last Night, relating to the said Persons, . . . Sir *George Charnock*, Serjeant at Arms, attending the Lord Keeper of the Great Seal of *England*, brought him four several Writs of *Habeas Corpus*, under the Great Seal of *England*, for bringing the said several Persons this Morning, at Ten of the Clock, before his Majesty, in his present Parliament at *Westminster* : And that he did, according to the Vote of this House, humbly crave the Advice and Direction of this House, what he should do therein :

And the Matter being debated ;

Mr. Speaker did, by the Direction of the House, intimate to Sir *John Robinson*, Lieutenant of the Tower, that he should forebear to return the said Writs of *Habeas Corpus*; acquainting him, that it was the Opinion of the House, that he could be in no Danger in not returning the same.

[C.J., ix, 356, June 8, 1675.]

(J)

Resolved, *Nemine contradicente*, that no Commoners of *England*, committed by Order or Warrant of the House of Commons for Breach of Privilege or Contempt of that House, ought, without Order of that House, to be by any Writ of *Habeas Corpus*, or other Authority whatsoever, made to appear, and answer, and do and receive a Determination in the House of Peers, during the Session of Parliament, wherein such Person was so committed. . . .

A Message from the King, by Sir *Edward Carterett*, Usher of the Black Rod; Mr Speaker, The King commands this honourable House to attend him immediately in the House of Lords.

And accordingly Mr. Speaker, with the House, went up; where his Majesty was pleased to prorogue both Houses of Parliament,[1] to the Thirteenth Day of *October* next.

[The prorogation brought about the release of the barristers.]

[C.J., ix, 357, June 9, 1675.]

VII

CHARLES II AND ROYAL PREROGATIVE OF PEACE AND WAR,[2] 1677

Gentlemen,

Could I have been silent, I would rather have chosen to be so, than to call to mind Things so unfit for you to meddle with, as are contained in some Part of your Address; wherein you have entrenched upon so undoubted a Right of the Crown, that I am confident it will appear in no Age (when the Sword was not drawn) that the Prerogative of making Peace and War hath been so dangerously invaded. You do not content yourselves with desiring me to enter into such Leagues, as may be for the Safety of the Kingdom; but you tell me what Sort of Leagues they must be, and with whom: And, as your Address is worded, it is more liable to be understood to be by your Leave, than your Request, that I should make such other Alliances as I please with other of the Confederates. Should

---

[1] See Vol. II, Sect. D, No. XLIX (B), p. 436.

[2] See also Sect. D, No. VII, p. 327, No. XIX, p. 354, No. XXX (A), p. 369, and Vol. II, Sect. D, No. LIII, p. 442.

I suffer this fundamental Power of making Peace and War to be so
far invaded (though but once) as to have the Manner and Circumstances of Leagues prescribed to me by Parliament, it is plain, that
no Prince or State would any longer believe, that the Sovereignty
of *England* rests in the Crown ; nor could I think Myself to signify
any more to foreign Princes, than the empty Sound of a King.[1]
Wherefore you may rest assured, That no Condition shall make me
depart from, or lessen, so essential a Part of the Monarchy.

[C.J., ix, 426, May 28, 1677.]

VIII

IMPEACHMENT OF DANBY, 1678-79

[Danby was impeached at the end of 1678. Hoping to save his
minister, Charles II dissolved Parliament on January 24, 1679. The
proceedings were resumed in spite of the Dissolution and the King's
Pardon. But the trial was dropped though Danby remained imprisoned in the Tower.]

(A)

Articles of Impeachment of High Treason, and other High
Crimes and Misdemeanours, and Offences, against Thomas Earl of
Danby, Lord High Treasurer of England

1. That he hath traitorously encroached to himself regal power,
by treating of matters of Peace and War with foreign princes and
ambassadors, and giving Instructions to his majesty's ambassadors
abroad, without communicating the same to the secretaries of state,
and the rest of his majesty's Council; against the express declaration
of his majesty and his parliament ; thereby intending to defeat and
overthrow the provisions which had been deliberately made by his
majesty and his parliament, for the safety and preservation of his
majesty's kingdoms and dominions.

2. That he hath traitorously endeavoured to subvert the ancient
and well established Form of Government in this kingdom ; and
instead thereof to introduce an arbitrary and tyrannical way of
government. And the better to effect this his purpose, he did design
the raising of an Army, upon pretence of a War against the French
king ; and then to continue the same as a Standing Army within this
kingdom : and an army being so raised, and no war ensuing, an act
of parliament having passed to pay and disband the same, and a
great sum of money being granted for that end, he did continue
this army contrary to the said act, and misemployed the said money
given for disbanding, to the continuance thereof ; and issued out of

---

[1] See Sect. D, No. XLV (B), p. 395.

his majesty's revenue divers great sums of money for the said purpose; and wilfully neglected to take security from the paymaster of the Army, as the said act required; whereby the said law is eluded, and the army is yet continued, to the great danger and unnecessary charge of his majesty and the whole kingdom.

3. That he, traitorously intending and designing to alienate the hearts and affections of his majesty's good subjects from his royal person and government, and to hinder the Meeting of Parliaments, and to deprive his sacred majesty of their safe and wholesome councils and thereby to alter the constitution of the government of this kingdom, did propose and negotiate a Peace for the French king, upon terms disadvantageous to the interests of his majesty and his kingdoms : for the doing whereof he did endeavour to procure a great sum of money from the French king, for enabling of him to maintain and carry on his said traitorous designs and purposes, to the hazard of his majesty's person and government.

4. That he is popishly affected; and hath traitorously concealed, after he had notice, the late horrid and bloody Plot and Conspiracy contrived by the Papists against his majesty's person and government; and hath suppressed the evidence, and reproachfully discountenanced the king's witnesses in the discovery of it, in favour of popery; immediately tending to the destruction of the king's sacred person, and the subversion of the Protestant religion.

5. That he hath wasted the king's Treasure by issuing out of his majesty's Exchequer, several branches of his revenue, for unnecessary Pensions and Secret Services, to the value of 231,602l., within two years : and that he hath wholly diverted, out of the known method and government of the Exchequer, one whole branch of his majesty's Revenue to private uses, without any account to be made of it to his majesty in his exchequer, contrary to the express act of parliament which granted the same; and he hath removed two of his majesty's commissioners of that part of the revenue, for refusing to consent to such his unwarrantable actings therein, and to advance money upon that branch of the revenue, for private uses.

6. That he hath by indirect means procured from his majesty for himself, divers considerable Gifts and Grants of inheritance of the ancient Revenue of the crown, even contrary to acts of parliament.

[*Parl. Hist.*, iv, 1067, Dec. 21, 1678.]

(B)

DISSOLUTION DOES NOT INTERRUPT JUDICIAL PROCEEDINGS IN THE LORDS' HOUSE

The House this Day taking into Consideration the Report made from the Lords Committees for Privileges, " That . . . for considering whether Petitions of Appeal, which were presented to this House in the last Parliament, be still in Force to be proceeded on, and for considering of the State of the Impeachments brought up from the House of Commons the last Parliament, and all the Incidents relating thereunto; upon which the Lords Committees were of Opinion, That, in all Cases of Appeals and Writs of Error, they continue, and are to be proceeded on, *in Statu quo*, as they stood at the Dissolution of the last Parliament, without beginning *de novo*; and that the Dissolution of the last Parliament doth not alter the State of the Impeachments brought up by the Commons in that Parliament."

After some Time spent in Consideration thereof : It is Resolved, by the Lords Spiritual and Temporal in Parliament assembled, That this House agrees with the Lords Committees in the said Report.

[L.J., xiii, 466, March 19, 1679.]

(C)

ADDRESS OF COMMONS TO THE LORDS

My Lords,

The Knights, Citizens, and Burgesses, in Parliament assembled, are come up to demand Judgment in their own Names, and the Names of all the Commons of *England*, against *Thomas*, Earl of *Danby*, who stands impeached by them before your Lordships of High Treason, and divers High Crimes and Misdemeanors, to which he has pleaded a Pardon : Which Pardon the Commons conceive to be illegal and void; [1] and therefore they do demand Judgment of Your Lordships accordingly.

[C.J., ix, 612, May 5, 1679.]

(D)

ROYAL PARDON NO BAR TO IMPEACHMENT

The Commons resolved, " That it is the opinion of this house, that the pardon pleaded by the earl of Danby is illegal and void, and ought not to be allowed in bar of the Impeachment of the Commons of England

[May 5.]

" That no Commoner whatsoever should presume to maintain the validity of the Pardon pleaded by the earl of Danby, without the consent of this House; and that persons so doing, shall be accounted betrayers of the liberties of the Commons of England.

[*Parl. Hist.*, iv, 1129, 1130, May 9, 1679.]

[1] See Sect. A, No. XXXVI, § III, p. 95.

IX

THE EXCLUSION BILL, 1680

Whereas James Duke of York is notoriously known to have been perverted from the Protestant to the Popish Religion, whereby not only great encouragement hath been given to the Popish party to enter into and carry on most devilish and horrid plots and conspiracies for the destruction of His Majesty's sacred person and government, and for the extirpation of the true Protestant Religion, but also, if the said Duke should succeed to the Imperial Crown of this Realm, nothing is more manifest than that a total change of Religion within these kingdoms would ensue ; For the prevention whereof, Be it therefore enacted . . . That the said James Duke of York shall be and is by authority of this present Parliament excluded and made for ever incapable to inherit, possess, or enjoy the Imperial Crown of this Realm and of the kingdom of Ireland and the Dominions and Territories to them or either of them belonging, or to have, exercise, or enjoy any Dominion, Power, Jurisdiction, or Authority within the same Kingdoms, Dominions, or any of them. And be it further enacted . . . That if the said James, Duke of York, shall at any time hereafter challenge, claim, or attempt to possess or enjoy or shall take upon him to use or exercise any dominion, power, authority, or jurisdiction within the said kingdoms, dominions, or any of them as King or Chief Magistrate of the same, That then he the said James, Duke of York, for every such offence shall be deemed and adjudged guilty of high treason, and shall suffer the pains, penalties, and forfeitures as in cases of high treason ; And further, That if any person . . . whatsoever shall assist, aid, maintain, abet or willingly adhere unto the said James, Duke of York, in such his challenge . . . or shall of themselves attempt . . . to bring the said James, Duke of York, into the possession or exercise of any regal power . . . or shall by writing or preaching . . . declare that he hath any right . . . to exercise the office of King. . . . That then every such person shall be deemed guilty of high treason and . . . shall undergo the pains, penalties, and forfeitures aforesaid ; And . . . That if the said James, Duke of York, shall . . . come into or within any of the kingdoms or dominions aforesaid, That then he shall be deemed guilty of high treason and . . . suffer the pains, penalties and forfeitures as in cases of high treason. . . . And be it further enacted . . . That the said James, Duke of York or any other person being guilty of any of the treasons aforesaid shall not be

capable of . . . any pardon otherwise than by Act of Parliament . . .
And . . . That it shall and may be lawful to and for all magistrates
. . . and other subjects . . . to apprehend and secure the said
James, Duke of York, and every other person offending in any
of the premises . . . for all which actings and for so doing they
are . . . by virtue of this Act saved harmless and indemnified.
Provided . . . That nothing in this Act contained shall be construed . . . to disable any person from inheriting . . . the Imperial Crown of the Realms and Dominions aforesaid (other than
the said James, Duke of York), but that in case the said James,
Duke of York, shall survive his now Majesty . . . the said Imperial
Crown shall descend to . . . such persons successively . . . as
should have inherited . . . the same in case the said James, Duke
of York were naturally dead. . . . And . . . That during the life
of the said James, Duke of York, this Act shall be given in charge
at every Assizes and General Sessions of the Peace . . . and also
shall be openly read in every Cathedral, Collegiate Church, parish
Church and Chapel . . . by the several and respective parsons . . .
who are hereby required immediately after Divine Service in the
forenoon to read the same twice in every year . . . during the life
of the said James, Duke of York.

[H.M.C.R. MSS., House of Lords, 1678-88, p. 195, Nov. 15,
1680.]

X

PUBLICATION OF VOTES OF THE COMMONS,[1] 1681

(24 March) . . . Sir *John Hotham* : Mr. Speaker, what I am
about to move concerns us all. The last Parliament, when you were
moved to print your Votes, it was for the security of the Nation, and
you found it so ; it prevented ill representations of us to the World
by false copies of our Votes, and none doubted your honour in the
care of it ; and I am confident that this House will be no more
ashamed of their actions than the last was. Printing our Votes will
be for the honour of the King, and the safety of the Nation. . . . I
move, therefore, " That your Votes may be ordered to be printed,
with the rest of your Proceedings ". . . .

Mr. Secretary *Jenkins* : I beg pardon, if I consent not to the
Motion of " printing the Votes, etc." Consider the Gravity of this
Assembly. There is no great Assembly in *Christendom* that does it

[1] See Sect. B, No. XXVII, p. 217, and Vol. II, Sect. B, No. IX, p. 168,
and Sect. C, No. XI, p. 264.

—It is against the Gravity of this Assembly, and it is a sort of Appeal to the People. It is against your Gravity and I am against it.

Mr. *Boscawen* : If you had been a Privy-Council, then it were fit what you do should be kept secret ; but your Journal-Books are open, and copies of your Votes in every Coffee-house, and if you print them not, half Votes will be dispersed, to your prejudice. This printing is like plain *Englishmen*, who are not ashamed of what they do, and the People you represent will have a true account of what you do. You may prevent publishing what parts of your Transactions you will, and print the rest. . . .

Sir *Francis Winnington* : Because what has been said by *Jenkins* is a single Opinion, for he says, " Printing is an Appeal to the People," I hope the House will take notice that printing our Votes is not contrary to Law. But pray who sent us hither ? The Privy-Council is constituted by the King, but the House of Commons is by the choice of the People. I think it not natural, nor rational, that the People, who sent us hither, should not be informed of our actions. In the Long Parliament it was a trade amongst Clerks to write Votes, and it was then said, by a learned Gentleman, " That it was no offence to inform the People of Votes of Parliament, etc., and they ought to have notice of them ". The Long Parliament were wise in their generation to conceal many things they did from the People ; and the Clerk, who dispersed the Votes, was sent away, and nothing done to him. . . .

[Grey, *Debates of the Commons*, viii, 292 f.]

. . . Resolved that the Votes and Proceedings of this House be printed ; And that the Care of the Printing thereof, and the Appointment of the Printers, be committed to Mr. Speaker.

[C.J., ix, 708, March 24, 1681.]

XI

IMPEACHMENT FOR CRIMES COGNIZABLE IN COMMON LAW COURTS,[1] 1681

[Edward Fitzharris, an Irish Catholic, who had resigned his army commission after the passing of the Test Act, published a pamphlet advocating the deposition of Charles II in favour of James, Duke of York.]

The House being informed, That the Lords had refused to proceed upon the Impeachment of the Commons against *Edward*

[1] Cf. Sect. B, No. XIII, p. 188.

Fitzharris; and had directed, That he should be proceeded against at the Common Law ;

And a Debate arising in the House thereupon :

Resolved, That it is the undoubted Right of the Commons in Parliament assembled, to impeach, before the Lords in Parliament, any Peer or Commoner for Treason, or any other Crime or Misdemeanor ; And that the Refusal of the Lords to proceed in Parliament upon such Impeachment is a Denial of Justice, and a Violation of the Constitution of Parliaments.

Resolved, That in the Case of *Edward Fitzharris*, who, by the Commons, had been impeached for High Treason before the Lords, with a Declaration, that in convenient time they would bring up the Articles against him ; for the Lords to resolve, That the said *Edward Fitzharris* should be proceeded with according to the Course of Common Law, and not by Way of Impeachment in Parliament, at this time ; is a Denial of Justice, and a Violation of the Constitution of Parliaments, and an Obstruction to the further Discovery of the Popish Plot, and of great Danger to his Majesty's Person, and the Protestant Religion.

Resolved, That for any inferior Court to proceed against *Edward Fitzharris*, or any other Person, lying under an Impeachment in Parliament for the same Crimes for which he or they stand impeached, is a high Breach of the Privilege of Parliament.

[C.J , ix, 711, March 26, 1681.]
[After the dissolution of Parliament two days later, Fitzharris was convicted in the Court of King's Bench and executed in July 1681.]

XII

SUMMONING THE CONVENTION PARLIAMENT,[1] 1688

(A)

SUMMONS TO THE ASSEMBLY, 1688

Whereas the Necessity of Affairs do require speedy Advice, we do desire all such Persons as have served as Knights, Citizens and Burgesses, in any of the Parliaments that were held during the Reign of the late King *Charles* the Second, to meet us at *St. James's* upon *Wednesday* the Six-and-twentieth of this Instant *December*, by Ten

[1] See Sect. A, No. XIX, p. 54.

of the Clock in the Morning. And we do likewise desire that the Lord Mayor and Court of Aldermen of the City of *London* would be present at the same Time; and that the Common-council would appoint Fifty of their Number, to be there likewise. And hereof we desire them not to fail.

Given at *St. James's*, the three-and-twentieth Day of *December*, 1688.

W. H. Prince of Orange.

By his Highness' special Command

C. Huygens.

[C.J., x, 5.]

(B)

The Letters for Electing of Members for the Convention

Whereas the Lords Spiritual and Temporal, the Knights, Citizens and Burgesses, heretofore Members of the Commons House of Parliament, during the Reign of King *Charles* the Second, residing in and about the City of *London*, together with the Aldermen, and divers of the Common-council of the said City, in this extraordinary Conjuncture, at our Request, severally assembled, to advise us the best Manner how to attain the Ends of our Declaration, in calling a free Parliament, for the Preservation of the Protestant Religion, and Restoring the Rights and Liberties of the Kingdom, and Settling the same, that they may not be in Danger of being again subverted, have advised and desired us to cause our Letters to be written and directed, for the Counties, To the Coroners of the respective Counties . . .; and for the Universities, To the respective Vice-Chancellors; and for the Cities, Boroughs and Cinque Ports, To the chief Magistrate of each respective City, Borough and Cinque Port; containing Directions for the choosing, in all such Counties, Cities, Universities, Boroughs, and Cinque Ports, within Ten Days after the Receipt of the said respective Letters, such a Number of Persons to represent them, as from every such Place is or are of Right to be sent to Parliament; Of which Elections, and the Times and Places thereof, the respective Officers shall give Notice; the Notice for the intended Election, in the Counties, to be published in the Market-towns within the respective Counties, by the Space of Five Days, at the least, before the said Election; and for the Universities, Cities, Boroughs, and Cinque Ports, in every of them respectively, by the Space of Three Days, at the least, before the said Election: The said Letters, and the Execution thereof, to be returned by such Officer and Officers who shall execute the same, to the Clerk of the Crown in the Court of Chancery, so as the

Persons, so to be chosen, may meet and sit at *Westminster* the Two-and-Twentieth Day of *January* next. . . .

Given at *St. James's*, the Nine and twentieth Day of *December*, in the Year of our Lord 1688.

[C.J., x, 7.]

XIII

THE LEGALITY OF IMPEACHMENT FOR TREASON, 1689 [1]

THE CASE OF SIR A. BLAIRE AND OTHERS

[Blaire and his associates were accused of Treason for denying William III's title and in particular publishing a Declaration of James II, dated Dublin, May 8, 1689.]

The Earl of *Rochester* reported what Precedents the Committee have found in the Journals relating to Impeachments and Records in *The Tower* . . .

and, after further Debate, This Question was proposed to be asked the Judges,

" Whether the Lords by this Statute [2] be barred from trying a Commoner upon an Impeachment of the House of Commons ? "

Then this previous Question was put, " Whether that Question shall be put to the Judges ? "

It was Resolved in the Negative.

And, after further Debate,

This Question was put, " Whether this House will proceed upon the Impeachment brought from the House of Commons against Sir *Adam Blaire*, Captain *Henry Vaughan*, Captain *Frederick Mole*, *John Elliott* Doctor in Physic, and *Robert Gray* Doctor in Physic ? "

It was Resolved in the Affirmative.

Leave was given to any Lords, to enter their Dissents ; and these Lords following do enter their Dissents, by subscribing their Names :

[21 names.]

[L.J., xiv, 262, July 2, 1689.]

[*Blaire was brought before the Lords, who on 22 July transmitted his answers to the charges to the Commons. The Commons allowed the matters to drop, and Blaire was finally bailed by the Lords on March 31, 1690.*]

---

[1] Cf. Sect. B, No. XI, p. 185.

[2] Reference is to a record in Rot. Parl. 4 Edw. III in which Parliament held that the Peers were to judge only Peers and not Commoners of Treason. The Judges in the Lords deemed this to be a Statute.

XIV

REFUSAL OF ROYAL ASSENT TO BILLS, 1693

(A)

COMMONS ADDRESS

Resolved, That the said representation, so amended, be agreed unto by the House ; and is as followeth : viz.

' *May it please your Most Excellent Majesty,*

We, your Majesty's most dutiful and loyal Subjects, the Commons in Parliament assembled, think ourselves bound, in Duty to your Majesty, humbly to represent, That the Usage in Parliament in all times hath been, That what Bills have been agreed by both Houses, for the Redress of Grievances, or other publick Good, have, when tendered to the Throne, obtained the Royal Assent ; and that there are very few Instances, in former Reigns, when such Assent, in such Cases hath not been given ; and those attended with great Inconveniences to the Crown of *England* ; especially where the same hath been with-held, by Insinuations of particular Persons, without the Advice of the Privy Council, thereby creating great Dissatisfaction and Jealousies in the Minds of your People.

Your Commons therefore, out of the sincere Desire of the Welfare of Your Majesty, and Your Government ; and that you may always reign, in Prosperity and Happiness, in the Affection of your Subjects ; cannot, without Grief of Heart, reflect, That, since your Majesty's Accession to the Crown, several publick Bills, made by the Advice of both Houses of Parliament, have not obtained the Royal Assent ; and, in particular, one Bill, intituled, An Act touching free and impartial Proceedings in Parliament ; which was made to redress a Grievance, and take off a Scandal relating to the Proceedings of your Commons in Parliament ; after they had freely voted great Supplies for the public Occasions ; Which they can impute to no other Cause than the Insinuations of particular Persons, who take upon them, for their own particular Ends, to advise your Majesty contrary to the Advice of Parliament ; and therefore cannot but look on such as Enemies to your Majesty, and your Kingdom.

Upon these Considerations, we humbly beseech your Majesty to believe, That none can have so great a Concern and Interest in the Prosperity and Happiness of your Majesty, and your Government, as your Two Houses of Parliament: And do therefore humbly pray, That, for the future, your Majesty would be graciously pleased to hearken to the Advice of your Parliament, and not to the secret

Advices of particular Persons, who may have private Interests of their own, separate from the true Interest of your Majesty, and your People.'

Resolved, That the said humble Representation be presented to his Majesty by Mr. Speaker, and the whole House.

Ordered, That such Members of this House that are of his Majesty's most honourable Privy Council, do humbly know his Majesty's Pleasure when he will please to be attended by this House.

[C.J., xi, 72, Jan. 27, 1693.]

(B)

THE KING'S REPLY

Gentlemen,

I am very sensible of the good Affections you have expressed to me upon many Occasions, and of the Zeal you have shewn for our common Interest : I shall make use of this Opportunity to tell you, That no Prince ever had a higher Esteem for the Constitution of the *English* Government than myself ; and that I shall ever have a great Regard to the Advice of Parliaments.   I am persuaded, that nothing can so much conduce to the Happiness and Welfare of this Kingdom, as an entire Confidence between the King and People ; which I shall, by all means, endeavour to preserve : And I assure you, I shall look upon such Persons to be my Enemies, who shall advise any thing that may lessen it.

[C.J. xi, 74, Jan. 31, 1693.]

(C)

THE COMMONS ACQUIESCE

Then the main Question being put, That an humble Application be made to his Majesty, for a further Answer to the humble Representation of this House ;

The House divided : . . .

. . . Yeas . . 88
. . . Noes . . 229

So it passed in the Negative.

[C.J. xi, 75, Feb. 1, 1693.]

XV

THE HOUSE OF COMMONS AND PETITIONS, 1701 [1]

Resolutions of the House of Commons

A Petition from several Gentlemen of the County of *Kent* being offered to the House ;

Ordered, That the said Petition be brought up to the Table.

And it was brought up accordingly.

And the House being informed, That several of the Gentlemen, who signed the said Petition, were at the Door, ready to own the same; They were called in accordingly ; viz.

Mr. *William Colepeper*, Mr. *Thomas Colepeper*, Mr. *David Polhill*, Mr. *Justinian Champneys*, and Mr. *William Hamilton* :

And they, at the Bar, owned the same Petition, and their Hands to the same.

And then they withdrew.

And the Petition was read, intituled, The humble Petition of the Gentlemen, Justices of the Peace, Grand Jury, and other Freeholders, at the General Quarter Sessions of the Peace holden at *Maidston*, in *Kent*, the 29th Day of *April*, in the 13th Year of the Reign of our Sovereign Lord King *William* the Third, over *England*, etc. ; setting forth, That they, deeply concerned at the dangerous Estate of this Kingdom, and of all *Europe* ; and considering, that the Fate of them, and their Posterity, depends on the Wisdom of their Representatives in Parliament ; think themselves bound in Duty humbly to lay before this Honourable House the Consequence, in this Conjuncture, of a speedy Resolution, and most sincere Endeavour, to answer the great Trust reposed in their said Representatives by the Country : And in regard that, from the Experience of all Ages, it is manifest no Nation can be great or happy without Union, they hope no Pretence whatsoever shall be able to create a Misunderstanding among ourselves, or the least Distrust of his Majesty, whose great Actions for this Nation are writ in the Hearts of his Subjects, and can never, without the blackest Ingratitude, be forgot : And praying, That this House will have Regard to the Voice of the People ; that our Religion and Safety may be effactually provided for ; that the loyal Addresses of this House may be turned into Bills of Supply ; and that his Majesty may be enabled powerfully to assist his Allies, before it is too late.

[1] See also Sect. B, No. III (F), p. 160, and Sect. A, No. V, p. 9.

Resolved, That the said Petition is scandalous, insolent, and seditious ; tending to destroy the Constitution of Parliaments, and to subvert the established Government of this Realm.

Resolved, That Mr. *William Colepeper* is guilty of promoting the said Petition.

Ordered That the said Mᴿ *William Colepeper* be, for the said Offence, taken into the Custody of the Serjeant at Arms attending the House [and similarly in respect of the other petitioners].

[C.J., xiii, 518, May 8, 1701.]

XVI

LORDS' PROTESTS AGAINST TACKING,
1700-1702 [1]

(A)

Because (we conceive) the tacking of so many and different Matters to a Money Bill is not only contrary to all the Rules and Methods of Parliament ; but highly dangerous, both to the un-doubted Prerogative of the Crown, and the Right of this House ; putting it (as we conceive) in the Power of the Commons to make any Resolutions of their own as necessary as any Supply given for the Support or Emergencies of State.

[L.J., xvi, 569, April 4, 1700.]

[This is one of the three reasons of a Dissentient, signed by eight Peers, to the Second Reading of a Bill for granting an Aid to the King partly by the sale of forfeited and other Estates and Interests in Ireland. The protesting minority claimed that the titles of private subjects to their estates ought not to be determined in fact by the Commons alone, as was here virtually the case.]

(B)

It is Ordered and Declared, by the Lords Spiritual and Temporal in Parliament assembled, That the annexing any Clause or Clauses to a Bill of Aid or Supply, the Matter of which is foreign to, and different from, the Matter of the said Bill of Aid or Supply, is Unparliamentary, and tends to the Destruction of the Constitution of this Government.

It is Ordered, by the Lords Spiritual and Temporal in Parliament assembled, That this Order and Declaration be added to the Roll of Standing Orders.

[L.J., xvii, 185, Dec. 9, 1702.]

[1] See also Vol. II, Sect. A, No. XLII, § 1 (2), p. 141.

XVII

COMMONS INSISTENCE ON ADJUDICATING ON ELECTORAL MATTERS, 1704

[Ashby, an elector, successfully brought an action for damages against White, Mayor of Aylesbury, for refusing to allow him to vote at an election of burgesses to Parliament. On a motion in Queen's Bench for arrest of judgement, Holt L.C.J. alone supported Ashby's claim. On a writ of error in the Lords, their Lordships sustained Holt and reversed the Queen's Bench judgement. It must be remembered that until the case of O'Connell (Vol. II, Sect. C, No. XIV (p. 278), there was no distinction between the House of Lords in its political and in its judicial capacity.]

(A)

RESOLUTIONS OF THE COMMONS [1]

Resolved . . . That, according to the known Laws and Usage of Parliament, neither the Qualification of any Elector, or the Right of any Person elected, is cognizable or determinable elsewhere, than before the Commons of *England*, in Parliament assembled, except in such Cases, as are specially provided for by Act of Parliament.

Resolved, . . . That the examining, and determining, the Qualification, or Right of any Elector, or any Person elected to serve in Parliament, in any Court of Law, or elsewhere than before the Commons of *England*, in Parliament assembled (except in such Cases as are specially provided for by Act of Parliament) will expose all Mayors, Bailiffs, and other Officers, who are obliged to take the Poll, and make a Return thereupon, to Multiplicity of Actions, vexatious Suits, and insupportable Expenses, and will subject them to different and independent Jurisdictions, and inconsistent Determinations in the same Case, without Relief.

Resolved, . . . That *Matthew Ashby*, having, in Contempt of the Jurisdiction of this House, commenced and prosecuted an Action at Common Law against *William White*, and others, the Constables of *Aylesbury*, for not receiving his vote at an Election of Burgesses, to serve in Parliament for the said Borough of *Aylesbury*, is guilty of a Breach of the Privilege of this House. . . .

Resolved, . . . That whosoever shall presume to commence or prosecute any Action, Indictment, or Information, which shall bring

[1] See also Judgement of Holt, L.C.J., Sect. C, No. IX, p. 278.

the Right of Electors, or Persons elected to serve in Parliament, to the Determination of any other Jurisdiction, than that of the House of Commons (except in Cases specially provided for by Act of Parliament) such Person and Persons, and all Attorneys, Solicitors, Counsellors, Serjeants at Law, soliciting, prosecuting, or pleading in any such Case, are guilty of a high Breach of the Privilege of this House.

Resolved That, according to the known Laws and Usage of Parliament,[1] it is the sole Right of the Commons of *England*, in Parliament assembled (except in Cases otherwise provided for by Act of Parliament) to examine, and determine, all Matters relating to the Right of Election of their own Members

Ordered, That the said Resolutions be fixed upon *Westminster-hall* Gate, signed by the Clerk.

[C.J., xiv, 308, Jan. 26, 1704.]

(B)

RESOLUTIONS OF THE HOUSE OF LORDS IN THE CASE OF ASHBY v. WHITE

" It is Resolved, by the Lords Spiritual and Temporal in Parliament assembled, That, by the known Laws of this Kingdom, every Freeholder, or other Person having a Right to give his Vote at the Election of Members to serve in Parliament, and being willfully denied or hindered so to do by the Officer who ought to receive the same, may maintain an Action in the Queen's Courts against such Officer, to assert his Right, and recover Damages for the Injury."

" It is Resolved, by the Lords Spiritual and Temporal in Parliament assembled, That the asserting, that a Person, having Right to give his Vote at an Election, and being hindered so to do by the Officer who ought to take the same, is without Remedy for such Wrong by the ordinary Course of Law, is destructive of the Property of the Subject, against the Freedom of Elections, and manifestly tends to encourage Corruption and Partiality in Officers who are to make Returns to Parliament, and to subject the Freeholders and other Electors to their arbitrary Will and Pleasure."

" It is Resolved by the Lords Spiritual and Temporal in Parliament assembled, That the declaring *Mathew Ashby* guilty of a Breach of Privilege of the House of Commons, for prosecuting an Action against the Constables of *Aylesbury*, for not receiving his Vote at an Election, after he had, in the known and proper Methods of Law, obtained a Judgement in Parliament for Recovery of his Damages, is an unprecedented Attempt upon the Judicature of

[1] See Sect. C, No. X, at p. 280, and others refs. in note 3.

Parliament, and is in Effect to subject the Law of *England*, to the Votes of the House of Commons."

" It is Resolved, by the Lords Spiritual and Temporal in Parliament assembled, That the deterring Electors from prosecuting Actions in the ordinary Course of Law, where they are deprived of their Right of voting, and terrifying Attornies, Solicitors, Counsellors, and Serjeants at Law, from soliciting, prosecuting, and pleading, in such Cases by voting their so doing to be a Breach of Privilege of the House of Commons, is a manifest assuming a Power to control the Law, to hinder the Course of Justice, and subject the Property of *Englishmen* to the arbitrary Votes of the House of Commons."

[L.J., xvii, 534, March 27, 1704.]

(C)

LORDS' ADDRESS TO THE QUEEN ON COMMONS' CLAIM IN THE CASE OF THE AYLESBURY MEN

". . . We humbly beg Pardon of Your Majesty for this long and melancholy Representation ; which we could not avoid, without being guilty of Treachery to Your Majesty, and to our native Country. The Five Persons immediately concerned are but poor Men ; but, we well know, Your Majesty's Justice and Compassion extends itself to the meanest of Your Subjects.

" The Matters in Dispute are of the highest Consequence : Your Majesty's Prerogative, the Reverence due to Laws, and the Liberties and Properties of all the People of *England*, are concerned, and at Stake, if these Encroachments prevail.

" We do not pretend to solicit Your Majesty to put a Stop to these Innovations : Your own Wisdom will suggest the most proper Methods. We have endeavoured to do our Duty, in laying the whole Matter before You.

" We humbly beg Leave so far to resume what has been said, as to present to Your Majesty a short View of the unhappy Condition of such of Your Subjects as have Right of giving Votes for chusing Members to serve in Parliament ; which has been hitherto thought a great and valuable Privilege, but, by the late Proceedings of the House of Commons, is likely to be made only a dangerous Snare to them, in case they who may be hereafter chosen to serve in Parliament shall think fit to pursue the Methods of this present House of Commons.

" If they refrain from making Use of their Right, in giving their Votes, they are wanting in Duty to their Country, by not doing their Parts towards the chusing such Representatives as will use

their Trust for the Good of the Kingdom, and not for the Oppression
of their Fellow Subjects.

" If the Officer, who has the Right of taking the Suffrages refuse
to admit them to give their Votes, they must either sit down by it,
and submit to be wrongfully and maliciously deprived of their
Rights ; or, if they bring their Actions at Law, in order to assert
their Rights, and recover Damages for the Injury (as all other
injured Men may do in like Cases), they become liable to indefinite
Imprisonment, by incurring the Displeasure of those who are elected.

" If, being thus imprisoned, they seek their Liberty by *Habeas
Corpus* (the known Remedy of all other Subjects), they do not only tie
their own Chains faster, but bring all their Friends and Agents, their
Solicitors and Counsel, into the same Misfortune with themselves.

" If they think themselves to have received Injury by the Judgement upon the *Habeas Corpus*, and seek Relief by Writ of Error
(the known Refuge of those who suffer by any wrong Judgement) ;
all that assist them in that Matter are likewise to lose their Liberties
for it ; and they themselves will be removed to new Prisons, in
order to avoid the Justice of the Law.

" We humbly conclude with acquainting Your Majesty, That we
have been informed, by the Petition of Two of the Prisoners, that
they have been long delayed (though they have made their Applications in due Manner for Writs of Error).   We are under a necessary
Obligation, for the Sake of Justice, and asserting the Judicature of
Parliament, to make this humble Address to Your Majesty, That no
Importunity of the House of Commons, nor any other Consideration whatsoever, may prevail with Your Majesty to suffer a Stop to
be put to the known Course of Justice ; but that You will be pleased
to give effectual Orders for the immediate issuing of the Writs of
Error."

[L.J., xvii, 705, March 13, [N.S.] 1705.]

(D)

THE QUEEN'S ANSWER

To which her majesty was pleased, the same day, to return the
following most gracious answer.

" My Lords : I should have granted the Writ of Error desired
in this Address ; but finding an absolute Necessity of putting an
immediate End to this Session,[1] I am sensible there could have been
no farther proceeding upon that Matter."

[L.J., xvii, 716, March 14, [N.S.] 1705.]

[1] See Sect. B, No. VI (J), p. 179, and Vol. II, Sect. D, No. XLIX *B*,
p. 436.

XVIII

VOTING OF FUNDS FOR THE PUBLIC [1]
SERVICE, 1706

Resolved, That this House will receive no Petitions for any Sum of Money, relating to publick Service, but what is recommended from the Crown.

[C.J., xv, 211, Dec. 11, 1706 : made a Standing Order, June 11, 1713.]

XIX

THE IMPEACHMENT OF HENRY
SACHEVERELL, 1710

ARTICLES OF IMPEACHMENT AGAINST HENRY SACHEVERELL

I. He, the said Henry Sacheverell, in his said Sermon, preached at St. Paul's, doth suggest and maintain, That the necessary means used to bring about the said happy Revolution, were odious and unjustifiable : That his late majesty, in his Declaration, disclaimed the least imputation of Resistance : And that to impute Resistance to the said Revolution, is to cast black and odious colours upon his late majesty and the said Revolution.

II. He, the said Henry Sacheverell, in his said Sermon preached at St. Paul's, doth suggest and maintain, That the foresaid Toleration granted by law is unreasonable, and the allowance of it unwarrantable ; And asserts, That he is a false brother with relation to God, religion, or the Church, who defends Toleration and Liberty of Conscience ; That Queen Elizabeth was deluded by archbishop Grindall, whom he scurrilously calls A False Son of the Church, and a Perfidious Prelate, to the toleration of the Genevian discipline : And that it is the duty of superior pastors to thunder out their ecclesiastical anathemas against persons intitled to the benefit of the said Toleration ; and insolently dares, or defies any power on earth to reverse such sentences.

III. He, the said Henry Sacheverell, in his said Sermon preached at St. Paul's, doth falsely and seditiously suggest and assert, That the Church of England is in a condition of great peril and adversity under her majesty's administration ; and in order to arraign and

[1] See Vol. II, Sect. B, No. XXVIII (D), p. 231.

blacken the said Vote or Resolution of both Houses of Parliament, approved by her majesty as aforesaid, he, in opposition thereto, doth suggest the Church to be in Danger : and, as a parallel, mentions a vote, That the person of king Charles the first was voted to be out of danger, at the same time that his murderers were conspiring his death ; thereby wickedly and maliciously insinuating, that the members of both Houses, who passed the said vote, were then conspiring the ruin of the Church.

IV. He, the said Henry Sacheverell, in his said Sermons and Books, doth falsely and maliciously suggest, That her majesty's administration, both in ecclesiastical and civil affairs, tends to the destruction of the constitution : And that there are men of characters and stations in Church and state who are False Brethren, and do themselves weaken, undermine and betray, and do encourage, and put it in the power of others, who are professed enemies, to overturn and destroy the constitution and establishment : and chargeth her majesty, and those in authority under her, both in Church and state, with a general mal-administration : And, as a public incendiary, he persuades her majesty's subjects to keep up a distinction of factions and parties ; instils groundless jealousies, foments destructive divisions among them, and excites and stirs them up to arms and violence : And that his said malicious and seditious suggestions may make the stronger impression upon the minds of her majesty's subjects, he the said Henry Sacheverell doth wickedly wrest and pervert divers texts and passages of Holy Scripture. . . .

Attorney General (Sir J. Montague). And to shew his little liking of the great work which was begun to be wrought on that day by the arrival of his late majesty, the chief turn of his discourse is, to cry up Non-Resistance and Passive Obedience.

And to make it most evident, that what he said of Non-Resistance, was to cast black and odious colours upon the Revolution ; he lays down a general position, ' That it is not lawful, upon any pretence whatsoever, to make Resistance to the supreme power ' ; which supreme power, by other passages, he explains to be the regal power.

And being apprehensive, that every one that heard him talking in that manner against Resistance, would see plainly he was censuring and condemning the means that brought about the Revolution, and being desirous to cast as heavy reflections as he could upon the memory of king William, he asserts, ' That the Prince of Orange, in his Declaration, utterly disclaimed all manner of Resistance.'

My lords, everybody knows, that knows anything of the Revolution, That the Prince of Orange came over with an armed force ;

and that in several paragraphs of his Declaration, . . . His late Majesty invites and requires all peers of the realm, both spiritual and temporal lords, all gentlemen, citizens, and other commoners, to come in and assist him, in order to the executing that design he had then undertook, against all that should endeavour to oppose him.

Therefore it must be accounted very ridiculous for the Doctor to advance such a position, if he had no further meaning in it, than to give an account of the Prince of Orange's design in coming over here into England.

And this will make it necessary for your lordships to consider what is the true meaning of this assertion : is it not plainly to make the Prince of Orange say one thing, and at the same time do directly another ? And can this be done with any other design, than to asperse the memory of the late king William ? . . .

If what the doctor very frequently asserts in this Sermon be true, That all are false sons of the Church, who assisted in bringing about the Revolution, or that joined in the opposition that was made to the encroachments which were begun by evil ministers in the reign of king James 2, against our religion and liberties ; let the Doctor a little consider, how far his character of a False Brother may be carried !

Everybody knows, that lived in those days, that the body of the clergy of the Church of England made a noble stand against the encroachments which were then making, and appeared as active as any of the laity.

And was it not by their writings, preaching, and example, that the nobility and gentry were animated to maintain and defend their rights, religion and liberties ? . . .

Mr. Lechmere. I crave leave to remind your lordships of the condition of things in both kingdoms immediately preceding the late Revolution : the case is stated and recorded, between the late king James and the subjects of both kingdoms, in the several Declarations of the Rights of both nations made by them at that time.

I shall forbear to aggravate the miscarriages of that unhappy prince, further than by saying, that it is declared in the preamble to the bill passed in England, That by the assistance of evil counsellors, judges and ministers ,employed by him, he did endeavour to subvert and extirpate the Protestant Religion, the laws and liberties of the kingdom, in the several instances there enumerated. . . .

Your lordships, on this occasion, will again consider the ancient legal constitution of the government of this kingdom ; from which it will evidently appear to your lordships, that the subjects of this realm had not only a power and right in themselves to make that Resistance, but lay under an indispensible obligation to do it.

The nature of our constitution is that of a limited monarchy, wherein the supreme power is communicated and divided between Queen, Lords, and Commons, though the executive power and administration be wholly in the crown. The terms of such a constitution do not only suppose, but express an original contract between the crown and the people ; by which that supreme power was [by mutual consent and not by accident] limited and lodged in more hands than one : and the uniform preservation of such a constitution for so many ages without any fundamental change, demonstrates to your lordships the continuance of the same contract.

The consequences of such a frame of government are obvious : that the laws are the rule to both, the common measure of the power of the crown, and of the obedience of the subject ; and if the executive part endeavours the subversion, and total destruction of the government, the original contract is thereby broke, and the right of allegiance ceases : that part of the government thus fundamentally injured, hath a right to save or recover that constitution in which it had an original interest.

Nay, the nature of such an original contract of government proves that there is not only a power in the people, who have inherited its freedom, to assert their own title to it, but they are bound in duty to transmit the same constitution to their posterity also. . . .

That the rights of the crown of England are legal rights, and its power stated and bounded by the laws of the kingdom ; that the executive power and administration itself is under the strictest guard for the security of the people ; and that the subjects have an inheritance in their ancient fundamental constitutions, and the laws of the land, appears from every branch of this government. It is the tenor of all antiquity ; our histories and records afford innumerable proofs of it. . . .

Such was the genius of a people, whose government was built on that noble foundation, not to be bound by laws to which they did not consent : that muffled up in darkness and superstition, as our ancestors were, yet that notion seemed engraven on their minds. . . .

But the Commons think he hath, by his Answer, highly aggravated his crime, by charging so pernicious a tenet, as that of absolute, unlimited Non-Resistance to be a fundamental part of our government, and by asserting this as the doctrine of the Church of England. . . .

My lords, I take the liberty to acquaint your lordships, that the Commons conceive, that the laws and statutes of the realm, and

the order and peace of government, necessarily injoin it as a duty
upon all private subjects, to represent their sense of the nation's
grievances in a course of law and justice, and not otherwise ; and
whenever the oppressions become national or public, they claim it
as the peculiar right of their own body, to pursue the evil instruments of them, till public vengeance be done ; and at the same time
the Commons assure your lordships, that they will account it their
indispensable duty to her majesty and their country to assert the
justice and wisdom of her administration, against the enemies of
both. . . .

Your lordships will consider the necessary consequences of a
position, meant and expounded so as to persuade the world, that
the glorious work of the Revolution was the fruit of rebellion, and
the work of traitors.   Does it not declare the late reign to be one
of continued usurpation ?   And under what better circumstances
does it bring the present ?

Is the Act of Toleration condemned with any other tendency
than to weaken so great a support of the Revolution itself ?   And
I intreat your lordships to consider the certain fatal effects of a universal dissatisfaction of the people, in things that concern them
nearest, the safety of the Church of England, and the Protestant
interest, and the security of themselves and their prosperity.

It is true, my lords, that, considered at a distance, there seems
a repugnancy in this gentleman's system.   How comes it to pass,
that absolute Non-Resistance and the spirit of rebellion stand so
well together, and are made so suitable, in the same discourse ?

But, if your lordships should discern, in any part of his Sermon,
any dark hints, or disguised opinions, of a sole Hereditary Right of
Succession to the crown, that will show your lordships the true
consistency of the whole ; your lordships will find, that in his
opinion, the duty of absolute Non-Resistance is owing to him only
that has the divine commission to govern; and from thence your lordships cannot fail of knowing against what queen, what government,
what establishment, he encourages the taking up the arms of
Resistance. . . .

Mr. Walpole.   My lords, the Commons are now making good
their Charge against Doctor Henry Sacheverell contained in the
first Article, wherein he is accused for suggesting and maintaining,
that the necessary means used to bring about the happy Revolution
were odious and unjustifiable, and that to impute Resistance to the
Revolution, is to cast black and odious colours on his late majesty
and the Revolution. . . .

The great licentiousness of the press, in censuring and reflecting
upon all parts of the government, has of late given too just cause of

offence; but when any pamphlets and common libels are matters of complaint; when none but mercenary scribblers, and the hackney pens of a discontented party, are employed to vent their malice, it is fit to leave them to the common course of the law, and to the ordinary proceeding of the courts below. But, my lords, . . . when the cause of the enemies of our government is called the cause of God, and of the Church; when this bitter and poisonous pill is gilded over with the specious name of loyalty, and the people are taught, for their souls and consciences sake, to swallow these pernicious doctrines: when, instead of sound religion, divinity, and morality, factious and seditious discourses are become the constant entertainments of some congregations; the Commons cannot but think it high time to put a stop to this growing evil, and for the authority of a parliament to interpose, and exert itself, in defence of the Revolution, the present government, and the Protestant succession. All which the Commons think so materially concerned in this question, that if the doctrines advanced by Doctor Sacheverell are not criminal in the highest degree, it will follow that the necessary means used to bring about the Revolution were illegal, and consequently that the present establishment, and Protestant Succession, founded upon that Revolution, are void and of no effect. . . .

The utter illegality of Resistance, upon any pretence whatsoever, is the general position laid down in the Sermon, which, if it be strictly, and in the most extensive manner true, the assuming and exercising a power of dispensing with, and suspending the laws; the commitment and prosecution of the bishops; the erecting a court of commissioners for ecclesiastical causes, the levying money by pretence of prerogative; the raising and keeping a standing army without consent of parliament; the violating the freedom of elections of members to serve in parliament; and all the grievances enumerated in the Bill of Rights, were all mere pretences, and not sufficient to warrant and justify what was then done, in defence of the true, ancient, and indubitable rights and liberties of the people of this kingdom; which are now again enacted, ratified and confirmed, and enjoined to be firmly and strictly holden and observed. By what evasions, or distinctions, the Doctor will explain himself off upon this head, I cannot easily foresee; unless he will be so ingenuous as now to confess, what there is too much reason to believe will be his opinion, if ever a proper time shall serve for declaring, that the acts of parliament made upon, and since the Revolution, are only the effects of a happy usurpation, and no part of the true law of the land.

Resistance is no where enacted to be legal, but subjected, by

all the laws now in being, to the greatest penalties; it is what is
not, cannot, nor ought ever to be described or affirmed, in any
positive law, to be excusable : when, and upon what never-to-be-
expected occasions, it may be exercised, no man can foresee, and
ought never to be thought of, but when an utter subversion of the
laws of the realm threatens the whole frame of a constitution, and
no redress can otherwise be hoped for : it therefore does, and ought
for ever to stand, in the eye and letter of the law, as the highest
offence.   But because any man, or party of men, may not, out of
folly or wantonness, commit treason, or make their own discontents,
ill principles, or disguised affections to another interest, a pretence
to resist the supreme power, will it follow from thence that the utmost
necessity ought not to engage a nation in its own defence for the
preservation of the whole ?   Or, on the other side, because the
greatest and most inexpressible emergencies did sufficiently justify
and warrant the Resistance of the Revolution, will it be a consequence, that therefore, upon every slight pretext or common occasion,
the laws that fence against treason will be of no effect ?   No, my
lords, I hope your just judgment in this case will convince the world,
that every seditious, discontented, hot-headed, ungifted, unedifying
preacher, (the Doctor will pardon me for borrowing one string of
epithets from him, and for once using a little of his own language)
who had no hopes of distinguishing himself in the world, but by a
matchless indiscretion, may not advance, with impunity, doctrines
destructive of the peace and quiet of her majesty's government, and
the Protestant Succession, and prepare the minds of the people for an
alteration, by giving them ill impressions of the present establishment and its administration.

The doctrine of unlimited, unconditional Passive Obedience,
was first invented to support arbitrary and despotic power, and was
never promoted or countenanced by any government that had not
designs some time or other of making use of it : what then can be
the design of preaching this doctrine now, unasked, unsought for,
in her majesty's reign, where the law is the only rule and measure
of the power of the crown, and of the obedience of the people ?   If
then this doctrine can neither be an advantage or security to her
majesty, who neither wants nor desires it, to what end and purpose
must every thinking man conclude it is now set on foot, but to
unhinge the present government, by setting aside all that has been
done in opposition to that doctrine ?   and when, by these means the
way is made clear to another's title, the people are ready instructed
to submit to whatever shall be imposed upon them. . . .

If then there was most undoubtedly Resistance used to bring
about the Revolution, it will follow that all the censures, which are

so freely bestowed upon Resistance in general, must attend, and will be imputed to the Revolution : and if Resistance be utterly illegal, upon any pretence whatsoever ; if it is a sin, which unrepented of, by the doctrine of the Church of England, carries sure and certain damnation ; if, upon repentance, there is no remission of sins without a stedfast purpose to amend the evil we have done, and to make all possible restitution, or at least to do our utmost endeavours for that purpose ; I beg your lordships to consider what a duty is here pressed, upon the peril of damnation, upon every man's conscience, that knows or believes that there was Resistance in the Revolution, and is conscious to himself of being any ways assisting, or even consenting to this damnable sin ; and what must be the consequence if these doctrines, without any reserve or exception, are with impunity preached throughout the kingdom.   All which, my lords, I hope, is sufficient to satisfy your lordships that Dr. Sacheverell is guilty of the charge exhibited against him in the First Article ; and that he is an offender of that nature and malignity, that this Court only could be the proper judges of such high crimes; and from your lordships' justice, the Commons hope, That his punishment will be adequate to the heinousness of his offence. . . .

Sir Simon Harcourt (For the Defence.) . . . Having thus stated to your lordships the question between us, Whether such excepted cases as the Revolution was, are not more proper to be left as implied, than to be expressed, when the general duty of obedience is taught ?   I shall endeavour to satisfy your lordships, first, that the Doctor's assertion of the illegality of Resistance to the supreme power on any pretence whatsoever, in general terms, without expressing any exception, or that any exception is to be made, is warranted by the authority of the Church of England : And secondly, That his manner of expression is agreeable to the law of England. . . .

My lords, is this doctrine of Non-Resistance taught in the Homilies in general terms, in the same manner as doctor Sacheverell has asserted it, without expressing any exception ?   Do the articles of our religion declare the doctrine taught in the homilies to be a godly and wholesome doctrine?   and will your lordships permit this gentleman to suffer for preaching it ?   Is it criminal in any man to preach that doctrine, which it is his duty to read ? . . .

As a further proof that this doctrine of Non-Resistance, as laid down by the Doctor in general terms, without making any exception, is the doctrine of the Church of England, I shall shew your lordships, that it has been so preached, maintained and avowed, and in much stronger terms than the Doctor has expressed himself, by our most orthodox and able divines from the time of the Reformation. It would be endless to offer your lordships all the authorities I might produce on this occasion; but we shall beg your lordships' patience to lay before you some passages out of the learned writings of several reverend fathers of our Church, of nine archbishops, above twenty bishops, and of several other very eminent and learned men. . . .

That your lordships may not think this doctrine died at the Revolution, I shall humbly lay before your lordships the opinions of three archbishops, and eleven bishops, made since the Revolution, which will fully shew the doctrine of Non-Resistance is still the doctrine of our Church. . . . I am sure it is impossible to enter into the heart of man to conceive, that what these reverend prelates have asserted, that any general position they have laid down concerning Non-Resistance, is an affirmance that necessary means used to bring about the Revolution were odious and unjustifiable: why then is Doctor Sacheverell, by having taught the same doctrine, in the same manner as they did, to be charged for having suggested or maintained any such thing?

My lords, I dare not suppose this doctrine, thus established by so many reverend fathers of our Church to be erroneous. . . .

The next thing I beg leave to consider is, the law of England; whether the Doctor's assertion of the utter illegality of Resistance to the supreme power on any pretence whatsoever, in general terms, is agreeable to the law of England. . . . I mean, that as the general rule is always taught and inculcated by the Church, so it has always been declared by the legislature, without making any particular exception. . . .

My lords, I have gone through the several laws I shall lay before your lordships on this occasion; and let me once more humbly beg your lordships, that you will be pleased to compare the Doctor's assertion in his Sermon, concerning the illegality of Resistance, with them; whether it be stronger than the declaration of the undoubted and fundamental law of the kingdom, in the act against the regicides; than the declaration in the Militia Act; than the oath required to be taken by so many acts of parliament; than the declaration in the 25th of Edw. 3. All the Doctor has said is, that Resistance to the supreme power is illegal, on any pretence whatsoever. All the peers and commoners of England, under the characters and employments I have mentioned, have sworn to the truth of it; the 25th of Edw. 3, declares it to be high treason; and your lordships have heard what St. Paul says.

My lords, I began this discourse, relating to the doctrine of the Church and the laws of the land, with the most sincere protestation, that it was far from my intention to offer anything inconsistent with

the justice of the Revolution : I think the justice of it consistent
with our laws, the exceptions to be made being always implied.
And surely none can shew themselves truer friends to the Revolution, than those who prove that the Revolution may stand without
impeaching the doctrines of our Church, or any fundamental law
of the kingdom. . . .

   Mr. Lechmere (in reply). . . . And what light doth it give to the
question now before your lordships, when at your bar, in defence
of a person accused by the Commons, for condemning the necessary
means which brought about the Revolution, you have heard that
original contract, at that time so solemnly declared to be a fundamental principle, publicly denied, ridiculed, and endeavoured (in
what manner it is easy to judge) to have been exploded ?

   My lords, the truth of that position has its foundation in the
nature and essence of the constitution of our government, and it
will stand so long as this remains ; and the sanction it has received
from your lordships, and from that House of Commons, who had
with so much wisdom and bravery asserted the rights of the kingdom
in that extraordinary juncture, and who, pursuant to that Resolution,
settled the crown upon her sacred majesty, ought to render it in-
disputable, so long at least as that establishment is preserved to us.
But yet, could I think it seasonable to enter into it, to consider more
particularly the nature of our government, to draw together some
of the many incontestable evidences of its original freedom, to consider the nature, antiquity and history of the Coronation Oath, and
the Oath of Allegiance, and the mutual obligations and consequences
arising from them to the prince and people : . . . the truth and
certainty of that position of an original contract between the king
and people, might be laid down to your lordships in demonstrative
terms. The gentleman that raised this observation, soon afterwards, in the same discourse, supposed, that by the original contract,
the original constitution was meant ; how strictly proper that
manner of speaking might be found to be, I will not now determine ;
yet thus much may with certainty be concluded, that the denying
the original contract, is not only to disavow the whole proceeding at
the time of the Revolution, but to renounce the constitution itself,
to disclaim those many and undeniable proofs and testimonies of it,
which almost every part of our history, our records, and memorials
of antiquity, will furnish. . . . It must weaken the ancient and just
prerogatives of the crown, subvert the foundations of your lordships' legislative and judicial powers, render the parliamentary
rights of the Commons precarious and uncertain, and terminate at
length, in that absurd, yet dangerous opinion, of the patriarchal
right, which, when together joined with the doctrines of absolute

and unlimited Non-Resistance, and unconditional Obedience of the subject to their prince, completes that fatal system, which has been of late so much contended for towards the enslaving mankind.

[Dr Sacheverell was found guilty by 69-52 votes. He was suspended from preaching for three years and his two sermons, the subject of the impeachment, were ordered to be burnt by the common hangman.]

[*S.T.*, xv, 1/522.]

XX

EXPULSION OF ROBERT WALPOLE,[1] 1712

(A)

The Question being proposed, That *Robert Walpole*, Esquire, a Member of this House, in receiving the Sum of Five hundred Guineas, and in taking a Note for Five hundred Pounds more, on Account of Two Contracts for Forage of her Majesty's Troops quartered in *North Britain*, made by him when Secretary at War, . . . is guilty of a high Breach of Trust, and notorious Corruption. . . .

It was resolved in the Affirmative [205–148].

Resolved, That the said *Robert Walpole*, Esquire be, for the said Offence, committed Prisoner to the *Tower* of *London*, during the Pleasure of this House : . . .

Then a Motion being made, and the Question being put, That the said *Robert Walpole* Esquire be, for the said Offence, also expelled this House. . . .

It was resolved in the Affirmative [170–148].

[C.J., xvii, 30, Jan. 17, 1712.]

(B)

The Question being put, That *Robert Walpole* Esquire, having been, this Session of Parliament, committed a Prisoner to the *Tower* of *London*, and expelled this House, for an high Breach of Trust in the Execution of his Office, and notorious Corruption, when Secretary at War, was, and is, incapable of being elected a Member to serve in this present Parliament ; The House divided. . . .

And so it was resolved in the Affirmative. [202–142] . . .

Ordered, That Mr Speaker do issue his Warrant to the Clerk of the Crown, to make out a new Writ, for the electing a Burgess to serve in this present Parliament for the Borough of *King's Lynn*,

[1] See Sect. B, No. XXXIII, p. 229.

in the County of *Norfolk*, in the room of *Robert Walpole* Esquire;
who is adjudged incapable of being elected a Member to serve in
this present Parliament; and the Election for the said Borough
declared void.

[C.J., xvii, 128, March 6, 1712.]

[Walpole had been re-elected by his constituents after his expulsion
in January. The electors did not again return him.]

XXI

PROCEDURE ON BILLS IMPOSING LOCAL TAXATION,[1] 1716

House of Commons : Resolved

That no Bill be ordered to be brought in for any work proposed
to be carried on by tolls or duties to be levied on the subject in
particular places, till such petition has been referred to a Committee;
and they have examined the matter thereof, and reported the same
to the House.

[Hatsell, ed. 1818, iii, 182, March 11, 1716. Made a Standing
Order, Feb. 28, 1734.]

XXII

PROTEST AGAINST THE SEPTENNIAL ACT,[2] 1716

Dissentient :

" 1. Because we conceive that frequent and new parliaments
are required by the fundamental constitution of the kingdom, and
the practice thereof, for many ages, (which manifestly appears by
our records) is a sufficient evidence and proof of this constitution.

2. Because it is agreed, that the House of Commons must
be chosen by the people, and when so chosen, they are truly the
representatives of the people, which they cannot be so properly
said to be, when continued for a longer time than that for which
they were chosen; for after that time they are chosen by the
parliament, and not the people, who are thereby deprived of the
only remedy which they have against those who either do not under-

---

[1] See also Sect. B, No. I (A), p. 153, and Vol. II, Sect. A, No. XLII,
§ 1 (2), p. 141.
[2] See also Sect. A, No. XLVI, p. 126.

stand or through corruption do wilfully betray the trust reposed in them; which remedy is to chuse better men in their places.

3. Because the reasons given for this bill, we conceive, were not sufficient to induce us to pass it, in subversion of so essential a part of our constitution. 1. For as to the argument that this will encourage the princes and states of Europe to enter into alliances with us, we have not heard any one minister assert, that any one prince or state has asked, or so much as insinuated, that they wished such an alteration. Nor is it reasonable to imagine it: for it cannot be expected that any prince or state can rely upon a people to defend their liberties and interests, who shall be thought to have given up so great a part of their own; nor can it be prudent for them to wish such an experiment to be made, after the experience that Europe has had of the great things this nation has done for them, under the constitution which is to be altered by this bill. But on the other hand, they may be deterred from entering into measures with us, when they shall be informed by the preamble of this bill, that the popish faction is so dangerous, as that it may be destructive to the peace and security of the government; and may apprehend from this bill, that the government is so weak, as to want so extra-ordinary a provision for its safety; which seems to imply, that the gentlemen of Britain are not to be trusted or relied upon; and that the good affections of the people are restrained to so small a number, as that of which the present House of Commons consists. 2. We conceive that this Bill is so far from preventing expences and corruptions, that it will rather increase them; for the longer a parliament is to last the more valuable to be purchased is a station in it, and the greater also is the danger of corrupting the members of it; For if ever there should be a ministry, who shall want a parliament to screen them from the just resentment of the people, or from a discovery of their ill practices to the king, who cannot otherwise, or so truly be informed of them, as by a free parliament, it is so much the interest of such a ministry to influence the elections, (which by their authority, and the disposal of the public money, they, of all others, have the best means of doing) that it is to be feared they will be tempted, and not to fail to make use of them; and even when the members are chosen, they have a greater opportunity of inducing very many to comply with them than they could have if not only the sessions of parliament, but the parliament itself, were reduced to the ancient and primitive constitution and practice of frequent and new parliaments: for as a good ministry will neither practise nor need corruption, so it cannot be any lord's intention to provide for the security of a bad one.

4. We conceive that whatever reasons may induce the Lords to

pass this bill to continue this parliament for seven years, will be at least as strong, and may, by the conduct of the ministry, be made much stronger before the end of seven years, for continuing it still longer, and even to perpetuate it, which would be an express and absolute subversion of the third estate of the realm.

[30 names subscribed.]
[*Parl. Hist.*, vii, 305.]

XXIII

STANDING ARMY,[1] 1717

EXTRACT FROM SPEECH OF SIR THOMAS HANMER

It would certainly be an endless thing, for an House of Commons to enter into the secrets of state, and to debate upon the different views, and interests, and intrigues of foreign courts ; what jealousies there are among them, and what treaties are on foot to reconcile them.   If we take such things into our considerations, to guide us in questions concerning our own guards and garrisons here at home, we shall be in a labyrinth indeed ; and must be compelled at last to put an absolute trust in the Government, because they only know the truth of such matters, and from them we must be content to receive whatsoever account they think fit to give us of them . . . I will venture to say, that during times of peace, no remote fears, . . . have ever yet brought this nation into a concession so fatal to liberty, as the keeping up of standing forces, when there is no other employment for them, but to insult and oppress their fellow-subjects. . . . It may not be taken for granted, that if we dismiss our soldiers, we shall therefore leave ourselves naked, and void of all protection against any sudden danger that may arise. . . . Providence has given us the best protection . . . Our situation is our natural protection ; our fleet is our protection. . . .

[*Parl. Hist.*, vii, 519, Dec. 6, 1717.]

XXIV

PROTEST AGAINST THE MUTINY ACT,[2] 1718

Dissentient :

1st, Because the Number of Sixteen Thousand Three Hundred Forty-Seven Men is declared necessary by this Bill ; But it is not

---

[1] See 1 Geo. I, St. II, c. 9, and 1 Anne, St. II, c. 20, § xxxix.
[2] See Sect. A, No. XX, p. 55.

therein declared, nor are we able, any Way, to satisfy ourselves
from whence that Necessity should arise ; the Kingdom being now
(God be praised) in full Peace, without any just Apprehensions,
either of Insurrections at Home, or Invasions from Abroad.

2d, Because so numerous a Force is near double to what hath
ever been allowed within this Kingdom, by Authority of Parliament, in Times of public Tranquillity ; and being, as we conceive,
no Ways necessary to support, may, we fear, endanger our Constitution, which hath never yet been entirely subverted but by a
Standing Army.

3d, Because the Charge of keeping up so great a Force ought
not unnecessarily to be laid on the Nation, already overburthened
with heavy Debts : And this Charge we conceive to be still more
unnecessarily increased, by the great Number of Officers now kept
on the Establishment, in Time of Peace ; a Number far greater (in
Proportion to that of the Soldiers commanded by them) than hath
ever yet been thought requisite in Times of actual War.

4th, Because such a Number of Soldiers, dispersed in Quarters
throughout the Kingdom, may occasion great Hardships, and
become very grievous to the People, and thereby cause or increase
their Disaffection ; and will probably ruin many of His Majesty's
good Subjects on whom they shall be quartered, and who have been
already by that Means greatly impoverished.

5th, Because such a standing Force, dangerous in itself to a free
People in Time of Peace, is, in our Opinion, rendered yet more
dangerous, by their being made subject to Martial Law ; a Law
unknown to our Constitution, destructive of our Liberties, not
endured by our Ancestors, and never mentioned in any of our
Statutes but in order to condemn it.

6th, Because the Officers and Soldiers themselves, thus subjected to Martial Law, are thereby, upon their Trials, divested of
all those Rights and Privileges which render the People of this
Realm the Envy of other Nations, and become liable to such
Hardships and Punishments as the Lenity and Mercy of our known
Laws utterly disallow : And we cannot but think those Persons best
prepared, and most easily tempted, to strip others of their Rights,
who have already lost their own.

7th, Because a much larger Jurisdiction is given to Courts
Martial, by this Bill, than to us seems necessary for maintaining
Discipline in the Army ; such Jurisdiction extending not only to
Mutiny, Desertion, Breach of Duty, and Disobedience to Military
Commands, but also to all Immoralities, and every Instance of
Misbehaviour, which may be committed by any Officer or Soldier
towards any of his Fellow-subjects : By which Means, the Law of

the Land, in Cases proper to be judged by that alone, may, by the summary Methods of Proceedings in Courts Martial, be obstructed or superseded, and many grievous Offences may remain unpunished.

8th, Because the Officers, constituting a Court Martial, do at once supply the Place of Judges and Jurymen ; and ought therefore, as we conceive, to be sworn, upon their trying any Offence whatsoever : And yet it is provided by this Bill, " That such Officers shall be sworn, upon their trying such Offences only as are punishable by Death : " which Provision we apprehend to be defective, and unwarranted by any Precedent ; there being no Instance, within our Knowledge, wherein the Judges of any Court, having Cognisance of Capital and lesser Crimes, are under the Obligation of an Oath in respect of the one, and not of the other.

9th, Because the Articles of War, thought necessary to secure the Discipline of the Army in Cases unprovided for by this Bill, ought, in our Opinion, to have been inserted therein, in like Manner as the Articles and Orders for regulating and governing the Navy were enacted,[1] in the Thirteenth Year of King *Charles* the Second ; to the End that due Consideration might have been had, by Parliament, of the Duty enjoined by each Article to the Soldiers, and of the Measure of their Punishment ; whereas the Sanction of Parliament is now given, by this Bill, to what they have had no Opportunity to consider.

10th, Because the Clause in the Bill, enabling His Majesty to establish Articles of War and erect Courts Martial,[2] with Power to try and determine any Offences to be specified in such Articles, and to inflict Punishments for the same, within this Kingdom, in Time of Peace, doth, (as we conceive), in all those Instances, vest a sole Legislative Power in the Crown ; which Power, how safely soever it may be lodged with His present Majesty, and how tenderly soever it may be exercised by Him, may yet prove of dangerous Consequence, should it be drawn into Precedent in future Reigns. . . .

[30 names subscribed.]
[L.J., xx, 623, Feb. 24, 1718.]

[1] See Sect. A, No. VII, p. 11.
[2] See Vol. II, Sect. C, No. II, p. 237.

XXV

PEERAGE BILL, 1719

(A)

[Earl Stanhope delivered to the House (of Lords) the following Message from the King:]

G.R.

His Majesty being informed, that the House of Peers have under consideration the state of the Peerage of Great Britain, is graciously pleased to acquaint the House . . . that he is willing his prerogative stand not in the way of so great and necessary a work.

[*Parl. Hist.*, vii, 590, March 2, 1719.]

(B)

THE BILL, 1719

Whereas by the Articles for an Union of the two Kingdoms of England and Scotland, Sixteen of the Peers of Scotland at the time of the Union was declared to be the number to sit and vote in the House of Lords, the same being then considered as a just and necessary proportion of the said Peers of Scotland in the House of Parliament, And whereas the number of the other Peers of Great Britain has been greatly increased since that time, and whereas the Election of the Peers of Scotland to sit and vote in the House of Lords is attended with many bad consequences, and is inconsistent with the true Constitution of Parliament, and whereas it will greatly conduce to the establishing and perpetuating the Freedom of Parliament, and thereby the Rights and Liberties of all his Majesty's Subjects, that the number of the House of Lords may not be arbitrarily increased in a manner detrimental and dangerous to the whole Legislature, To the end therefore that the Peers of Scotland by the enlarging the number of them who are to sit and vote in the House of Lords, and the establishing them on an Independent Foundation, more advantageous to the Peerage of Scotland, and to that part of Great Britain, as well as to the whole United Kingdom, may be in a great measure relieved from the difficulties and disadvantages they now lye under, and that the Freedom and Constitution of Parliament by his Majesty's most gracious indulgence to his People may now receive a lasting Sanction and Security, Be it enacted . . . That instead of the Sixteen elective Peers of Scotland, there shall be Twenty five of the Peers of Scotland at the time of the Union, and of their Successors to their Peerage, who shall have hereditary Seats and Votes in Parliament on the part of the Peerage of Scotland, to be appointed and have continuance and succession and in case of failure supplyd out of the remaining Peers of Scotland, in a manner as is herein after contained (that is to say) that such twenty five Peers of Scotland at the time of the Union or of their successors as his Majesty, his Heirs and Successors shall think fit, shall be nominated declared and appointed by his Majesty, his Heirs and Successors, before the next Session of Parliament, by one or more Instrument or Instruments under the great Seal of Great Britain, to have hereditary seats and votes in Parliament, and that Nine of the said twenty five so to be declared (not being of the number of the Sixteen Peers now sitting in Parliament on the part of the Peerage of Scotland) shall in such Instrument . . . be appointed to have immediate right to such hereditary seats and votes in Parliament ; and such Twenty five Peers . . . and their heirs . . . shall enjoy hereditary seats and votes in Parliament . . . subject nevertheless to the qualifications required of other Lords of Parliament by the Laws in being. . . . And to the end that the extent and continuance of the hereditary seat and vote in Parliament, . . . may be plainly and clearly ascertained, Be it enacted by the Authority aforesaid, That such Declaration or Appointment, and such hereditary right shall extend only to Males . . . and that all Females and all persons claiming through such Females . . . shall be excluded . . . and whenever any such Peerage shall descend or come to a female . . . or shall be utterly extinct then and in every such case the King's Majesty . . . shall make a new Declaration and Appointment . . . That so long as there shall be a sufficient number remaining of the Peers of Scotland at the time of the Union or of their successors, there may instead of the Sixteen elective Peers, be Twenty five Peers . . . who as Peers on the part of the Peerage of Scotland may have hereditary seats and votes in the Parliament of Great Britain in manner and forms aforesaid.

And be it further Enacted by the Authority aforesaid that the number of the Peers of Great Britain to sitt in Parliament on the part of England, shall not at any time hereafter be enlarged (without preceedent right) beyond the number of Six, over and above what they are at Present, but that as any of the Present Peerages or of the Six new Peerages in case they shall be created, or such of them as shall be created shall fail and be extinct, the King's Majesty, his Heirs and Successors, may supply such vacancies or failures by creating new Peers out of Commoners of Great Britain born within the Kingdoms of Great Britain or Ireland or any Dominions thereunto belonging or born of British parents, and in case such new Peerage shall afterward fail or be extinct, the King's Majesty . . . may Re-supply such Vacancies in like manner, and so Toties Quoties as any such failure or vacancy shall happen. And be it further enacted by the Authority aforesaid That whensoever any Peer now living, who so far hath been called up to the House of Lords by Writ, shall depart this life, That then and in such case the King's Majesty . . . may in the roome of every such Peer so dying, make and Create a new Peer out of such Commoners aforesaid, And on the failure or extinction of such new Peerage, may make and Create another Peer out of the persons so as aforesaid described . . . And to the intent and purpose That in all future Grants the Dignity of the Peerage may be confined to the persons meriting and obtaining the same, and to the Issue male of their Bodys, Be it also Enacted by the authority aforesaid That . . . all Creation of Peers shall be by Letters Patent only, and not by Writ, and that no Peerage shall thereafter be granted for any longer or greater Estate than to the new respective Grantees and the heirs male of their bodys begotten. . . . Provided always nevertheless, that no thing in this Act contained shall be taken or construed to lay any restraint upon the King's Majesty . . . from advancing or promoting any Peer, having Vote and Seat in Parliament to any higher Rank or Degree of Dignity or Nobility, nor from creating or making any of the Princes of the Blood Peers of Great Britain or Lords of Parliament, and such Princes of the Blood so created shall not be esteemed to be any part of the number to which the Peers of Great Britain are by this Act restrained.

[Oswald Dykes, *Source Book of Constitutional History*, pub. 1930, p. 185.]

(C)

EXTRACT FROM SPEECH OF SIR ROBERT WALPOLE

". . . The great unanimity with which this Bill has passed the Lords, ought to inspire some jealousy in the Commons; for it must be obvious, that whatever the Lords gain, must be acquired at the loss of the Commons, and the diminution of the regal pre-rogative; and that in disputes between the Lords and Commons, when the House of Lords is immutable, the Commons must sooner or later, be obliged to recede . . . But what is the abuse, against which this bill so vehemently inveighs, and which it is intended to correct? The abuse of the prerogative in creating an occasional number of peers, is a prejudice only to the Lords, it can rarely be a prejudice to the Commons, but must generally be exercised in their favour; and should it be argued, that in case of a difference between the two Houses, the King may exercise that branch of his prerogative, with a view to force the Commons to recede, we may reply, that upon a difference with the Commons, the King possesses his negative, and the exercise of that negative would be less culpable than making peers to screen himself."

[*Parl. Hist.*, vii, 619, Dec. 1, 1719.]

XXVI

THE KING'S COUNCILS, 1738

Mr. Pulteney said :

". . . We have in this kingdom several councils ; we have a privy council ; a cabinet council ; and, for what I know, a more secret and less numerous council still, by which the other two are directed : but the parliament is his Majesty's great and chief council : it is the council which all ministers ought, both for their own sakes and their master's, to advise his Majesty to consult with, upon every affair of great weight and importance ; for, from all our histories we shall find, that those kings have been the most happy and glorious, who have often consulted with their parliaments ; and that those ministers have always gone through their administration with the greatest ease and applause, and have divested themselves of their power with the greatest safety to themselves, which seldom happens to any but those who have advised their masters to depend chiefly upon the advice of their parliaments.

" In our privy council, Sir, in our cabinet council, and in any more secret council, if there be any such, the hon. gentleman may be supposed to have a sway ; nay, it may be even suspected that he has, under his Majesty, the chief direction of each ; and therefore he may, some time hereafter, be made to answer for their determinations ; but it cannot be suspected that he has the direction of either House of Parliament, nor are we to presume that he has any other sway in this House, but that which proceeds either from the solidity and strength of his arguments, or from his superior art of persuasion : For which reason he can never be made to answer for any resolution of parliament, or for any thing that is done pursuant to the advice of Parliament. . . ."

[*Parl. Hist.*, x, 591, March 3, 1738.]

XXVII

PUBLICATION OF PROCEEDINGS OF THE HOUSE OF COMMONS,[1] 1738

The Speaker informed the House, that it was with some concern he saw a practice prevailing, which a little reflected upon the dignity of that House : what he meant was the inserting an Account of their Proceedings in the printed News Papers, by which means the Proceedings of the House were liable to very great misrepresentations. . . .

Mr. Pulteney said : ". . . It is absolutely necessary a stop should be put to the practice which has so justly been complained of : I think no appeals should be made to the public with regard to what is said in this assembly, and to print or publish the Speeches of gentlemen in this House, even though they were not misrepresented, looks very like making them accountable without doors for what they say within. . . ."

. . . It was unanimously resolved :

" That it is an high indignity to, and a notorious breach of the Privilege of, this House, for any News-Writer, in Letters or other Papers, . . . to give therein any Account of the Debates, or other Proceedings of this House, or any Committee thereof, as well during the Recess, as the sitting of Parliament ; and that this House will proceed with the utmost severity against such offenders."

[*Parl. Hist.*, x, 800 ff., April 13, 1738.]

XXVIII

MINISTRY DEPENDENT ON COMMONS, 1739

EXTRACT FROM A SPEECH OF SIR ROBERT WALPOLE

This House and Parliament is his Majesty's greatest, safest, and best council. A seat in this House is equal to any dignity derived from posts or titles, and the approbation of this House is preferable to all that power, or even Majesty itself, can bestow : therefore when I speak here as a minister, I speak as possessing my powers from his Majesty, but as being answerable to this House for the

[1] See Sect. B, No. X, p. 184, XXXIV, p. 236, and Vol. II, Sect. C, No. XVI, at p. 293.

exercise of those powers. I have often on other occasions, professed my readiness to submit to the justice of my country, and shall cheerfully acquiesce in the judgement this House shall form of our negociations. . . .

[*Parl. Hist.*, x, 946, Feb. 1, 1739.]

XXIX

DOUBLE CABINET, 1740

Extract from a Speech by the Duke of Argyle

. . . I shall grant, that there were several lords at that time in the service of the crown, who had been in that service, and some of them perhaps in the administration, in the year 1718; but we are not to suppose, that every lord that is in the service of the crown, is likewise in the administration of the government; for a lord may be in a very high office under the crown, and yet know nothing of what is doing in his majesty's councils : These very instructions to Mr. Vernon, which are now said to contain secrets of such high importance, were made known, I believe, to very few of his majesty's great officers of state ; at least I can answer for myself, that I never saw them ; and yet I was at that time commander in chief of his majesty's forces, and one of his cabinet council. But your lordships must observe, that we have now two cabinet councils in this kingdom; his majesty has one, and the minister has another [1]; and I am afraid it often happens, that his majesty's cabinet council knows little or nothing of what is doing, or intended to be done.

This, my lords, was perhaps the case in the year 1721. . . .

[*Parl. Hist.*, xi, 764, Dec. 1, 1740.]

XXX

LEGISLATION AFFECTING THE CROWN, 1743

The Earl of Ilay, on the Bill for further Quieting Corporations

I hope your lordships will consider, that as the gentlemen of the other House are more particularly the guardians of the liberties

[1] See Sect. D, No. XXXI (B), p. 371.

of the people, so your lordships are more particularly the guardians of the prerogatives of the crown; and as this Bill is certainly an abridgement of the prerogatives of the crown, it would have been more proper to have had it take its rise in the other House. However, since it has been brought in here, I hope, you will give the crown all the indulgence which a private man ought to have, with regard to any Bill, he thinks, may affect any property or privilege he is possessed of. The crown is not, I know, to appear by petition or message against any Bill depending in this House, because the King may refuse his assent, and thereby prevent the Bill being passed into a law, but when those who have the honour to serve the Crown find a Bill brought into this House, which they think the King ought not to give his assent to, it is certainly their duty to oppose the Bill in its progress, and to endeavour to have it rejected by the House, in order to prevent their sovereign's being subjected to the invidious task of refusing the royal assent. This is their duty, and therefore, in justice to the crown, or to those who serve the crown, we ought to give them as much time as a private man ought to have, to consider how the crown may be affected by the Bill.

[*Parl. Hist.*, xviii, 93, March 11, 1743.]

XXXI

ARREST OF JOHN WILKES, M.P., FOR SEDITIOUS LIBEL,[1] 1763

(A)

THE PROCEEDINGS IN THE COMMONS

Mr. Chancellor of the Exchequer informed the House, that he was commanded by the King to acquaint the House, that His Majesty having received Information that *John Wilkes* Esquire, a Member of this House, was the Author of a most seditious and dangerous Libel, published since the last Session of Parliament; He had caused the said *John Wilkes* Esquire to be apprehended, and secured, in order to his being tried for the same by due Course of Law: And Mr. *Wilkes* having been discharged out of Custody by the Court of *Common Pleas*, upon Account of his Privilege as a Member of this House; and having, when called upon by the legal Process of the Court of *King's Bench*, stood out, and declined to appear, and answer to an Information which has since been exhibited against him by His Majesty's Attorney General for the same

[1] See Sect. C, Nos. XV and XVI, pp. 291-95.

Offence: In this Situation, His Majesty being desirous to show all possible Attention to the Privileges of the House of Commons, in every Instance wherein they can be supposed to be concerned; and at the same Time thinking it of the utmost Importance not to suffer the Public Justice of the Kingdom to be eluded, has chosen to direct the said Libel, and also Copies of the Examinations upon which Mr. *Wilkes* was apprehended and secured, to be laid before this House for their Consideration: And Mr. Chancellor of the Exchequer delivered the said Papers in at the Table.

Resolved, Nemine contradicente, That an humble Address be presented to His Majesty, to return His Majesty the Thanks of this House for His most gracious Message, and for the tender Regard therein expressed for the Privileges of this House; and to assure His Majesty that this House will forthwith take into their most serious Consideration, the very important Matter communicated by His Majesty's Message. . . .

Resolved, That the Paper intituled, " The *North Briton* No. 45 " is a false, scandalous, and seditious Libel, containing Expressions of the most unexampled Insolence and Contumely towards His Majesty, the grossest Aspersions upon both Houses of Parliament, and the most audacious Defiance of the Authority of the whole Legislature; and most manifestly tending to alienate the Affections of the People from His Majesty, to withdraw them from their Obedience to the Laws of the Realm, and to excite them to traitorous Insurrections against His Majesty's Government.

Resolved, That the said Paper be burnt by the Hands of the common Hangman.

[C.J., xxix, 667, Nov. 15, 1763.]

(B)

Resolved, That it appears to this House that the said John Wilkes Esquire is guilty of Writing and Publishing the Paper, intituled, " The North Briton, No. 45," which this House has voted to be a false, scandalous and seditious Libel . . .

Resolved, That the said John Wilkes, Esquire be, for his said Offence, expelled this House.

The Question being put, That Privilege of Parliament does not extend to the Case of writing and publishing seditious Libels, nor ought to be allowed to obstruct the ordinary Course of the Laws, in the speedy and effectual Prosecution of so heinous and dangerous an Offence[1] . . . it was resolved in the Affirmative [by 258 votes to 133].

[C.J., xxix, 675, Nov. 24, 1763.]

[1] See Sect. C No. XVIII, at p. 304.

(C)

PROCEEDINGS IN THE LORDS

And it being moved, " To agree with the Commons in the said Resolution : " [1]

The same was objected to.

After long Debate thereupon ;

The Question was put, " Whether to agree with the Commons in the said Resolution ? "

It was resolved in the Affirmative.

" *Dissentient.*

" 1. Because we cannot hear, without the utmost Concern and Astonishment, a Doctrine advanced now for the First Time in this House, which we apprehend to be new, dangerous, and un-warrantable ; *videlicet,* That the Personal Privilege of both Houses of Parliament has never held, and ought not to hold, in the Case of any Criminal Prosecution whatsoever ; by which, all the Records of Parliament, all History, all the Authorities of the gravest and soberest Judges, are entirely rescinded ; and the fundamental Principles of the Constitution, with regard to the Independence of Parliament, torn up, and buried under the Ruins of our most established Rights.

" We are at a Loss to conceive with what View such a Sacrifice should be proposed, unless to amplify in Effect the Jurisdiction of the inferior, by annihilating the ancient Immunities of this superior, Court : The very Question itself proposed to us from the Commons, and now agreed to by the Lords, from the Letter and Spirit of it, contradicts this Assertion ; for, whilst it only narrows Privilege in Criminal Matters, it establishes the Principle.

" The Law of Privilege, touching Imprisonment of the Person of Lords of Parliament, as stated by the Two Standing Orders, declares generally, " That no Lord of Parliament, sitting the Parliament, or within the usual Times of Privilege of Parliament, is to be imprisoned or restrained without Sentence or Order of the House, unless it be for Treason or Felony, or for refusing to give Security for the Peace, and Refusal to pay Obedience to a Writ of *Habeas Corpus.*"

" The first of these Orders was made, after long Consideration, upon a Dispute with the King, when the Precedents of both Houses had been fully inspected, commented upon, reported, and entered in the Journals ; and after the King's Counsel had been heard : It was made in sober Times, and by a House of Peers, not only loyal, but devoted to the Crown ; and it was made by the unanimous Consent of all, not one dissenting. These Circumstances of

[1] *i.e.* the last Resolution in item (B) above.

Solemnity, Deliberation, and Unanimity, are so singular and extraordinary, that the like are scarce to be found in any Instance among the Records of Parliament.

" When the Two Cases, of Surety for the Peace and *Habeas Corpus*, come to be well considered ; it will be found that they both breathe the same Spirit, and grow out of the same Principle.

" The Offences that call for Surety and *Habeas Corpus* are both Cases of present continuing Violence ; the Proceedings in both have the same End, *videlicet*, to repress the Force, and disarm the Offender.

" The Proceeding stops, in both, when that End is attained.

" The Offence is not prosecuted, nor punished in either.

" The Necessity is equal in both ; and, if Privilege was allowed in either so long as the Necessity lasts, a Lord of Parliament would enjoy a mightier Prerogative than the Crown itself is entitled to. Lastly, they both leave the Prosecution of all Misdemeanours still under Privilege ; and do not derogate from that great Fundamental, " That none shall be arrested in the Course of Prosecution for any Crime under Treason and Felony."

" These Two Orders comprise the whole Law of Privilege ; and are both of them Standing Orders, and consequently the fixed Laws of the House, by which we are all bound, till they are duly repealed.

" The Resolution of the other House, now agreed to, is a direct Contradiction to the Rule of Parliamentary Privilege laid down in the aforesaid Standing Orders, both in Letter and Spirit. Before the Reasons are stated, it will be proper to premise Two Observations.

" That, in all Cases where Security of the Peace may be required, the Lord cannot be committed till that Security is refused ; and consequently the Magistrate will be guilty of a Breach of Privilege, if he commits the Offender without demanding that Security.

" Although the Security should be refused ; yet, if the Party is committed generally, the Magistrate is guilty of a Breach of Privilege, because the Party refusing ought only to be committed till he has found Sureties : Whereas, by a general Commitment, he is held fast, even though he should give Sureties ; and can only be discharged by giving Bail for his Appearance.

" This being premised, The First Objection is to the Generality of this Resolution, which, as it is penned, denies the Privilege to the supposed Libeller, not only where he refuses to give Sureties, but likewise throughout the whole Prosecution from the Beginning to the End ; so that, although he should submit to be bound, he may notwithstanding be afterwards arrested, tried, convicted, and punished, sitting the Parliament, and without Leave of the House ;

wherein the Law of Privilege is fundamentally misunderstood, by which no Commitment whatever is tolerated, but that only which is made upon the Refusal of Sureties, or in other excepted Cases, of Treason or Felony, and the *Habeas Corpus*.

" If Privilege will not hold throughout in the Case of a Seditious Libel, it must be, because that Offence is such a Breach of the Peace for which Sureties may be demanded ; and if that be so, it will readily be admitted, that the Case comes within the Exception ; "Provided always, that Sureties have been refused, and that the Party is committed only till he shall give Sureties."

" But this Offence is not a Breach of the Peace ; it does not fall within any Definition of a Breach of the Peace, given by any of the good Writers upon that Subject ; all which Breaches, from Menace to actual Wounding, either alone or with a Multitude, are described to be, Acts of Violence against the Person, Goods, or Possession, putting the Subject in fear by Blows, Threats, or Gestures : Nor is this Case of the Libeller ever enumerated in any of these Writers among the Breaches of Peace ; on the contrary, it is always described as an Act tending to excite, provoke, or produce, Breaches of the Peace. And although a Secretary of State may be pleased to add the inflaming Epithets of treasonable, traitorous, or seditious, to a particular Paper ; yet no Words are strong enough to alter the Nature of Things. To say then that a Libel, possibly productive of such a Consequence, is the very Consequence so produced, is, in other Words, to declare that the Cause and the Effect are the same Thing.

"But, if a Libel could possibly by any Abuse of Language, or has anywhere been, called inadvertently a Breach of the Peace ; there is not the least Colour to say, that the Libeller can be bound to give Sureties for the Peace, for the following Reasons :

" Because none can be so bound unless he be taken in the actual Commitment of a Breach of the Peace, striking, or putting some one or more of his Majesty's Subjects in Fear.

" Because there is no Authority, or even ambiguous Hint, in any Law Book, that he may be so bound.

" Because no Libeller, in Fact, was ever so bound.

" Because no Crown Lawyer, in the most despotic Times, ever insisted he should be so bound, even in the Days when the Press swarmed with the most invenomed and virulent Libels, and when the Prosecutions raged with such uncommon Fury against this Species of Offenders ; when the Law of Libels was ransacked every Term ; when Loss of Ears, perpetual Imprisonment, Banishment, and Fines of Ten and Twenty Thousand Pounds, were the common Judgments in *The Star Chamber* ; and when the Crown had assumed an uncontrollable Authority over the Press

" This Resolution does not only infringe the Privilege of Parliament, but points to the Restraint of the Personal Liberty of every common Subject in these Realms ; seeing that it does in Effect affirm, that all men, without Exception, may be bound to the Peace for this Offence.

" By this Doctrine, every Man's Liberty, privileged as well as unprivileged, is surrendered into the Hands of a Secretary of State : *He* is by this Means empowered, in the first Instance, to pronounce the Paper to be a seditious Libel, a Matter of such Difficulty, that some have pretended it is too high to be intrusted to a Special Jury of the First Rank and Condition : *He* is to understand and decide by himself the meaning of every *Innuendo : He* is to determine the Tendency thereof, and brand it with his own Epithets : *He* is to adjudge the Party guilty, and make him Author or Publisher, as he sees good ; and, lastly, *He* is to give Sentence, by committing the Party.

" All these Authorities are given to One single Magistrate, unassisted by Counsel, Evidence, or Jury, in a Case where the Law says no Action will lie against him because he acts in the Capacity of a Judge.

" From what has been observed, it appears to us, that the Exception of a seditious Libel from Privilege is neither founded on Usage or written Precedents ; and therefore this Resolution is of the First Impression : Nay, it is not only a new Law narrowing the known and ancient Rule, but it is likewise a Law *ex post facto, pendente Lite, et ex Parte,* now first declared to meet with the Circumstances of a particular Case : And it must be further considered, that this House is thus called upon to give a Sanction to the Determinations of the other, who have not condescended to confer with us upon this Point, till they have prejudged it themselves.

" This Method of relaxing the Rule of Privilege, Case by Case, is pregnant with this further Inconvenience, that it renders the Rule precarious and uncertain. Who can foretell where the House will stop, when they have, by One Infringement of their own Standing Orders, made a Precedent, whereon future Infringements may with equal Reason be founded ? How shall the Subject be able to proceed with Safety in this perilous Business ? How can the Judges decide, on these or the like Questions, if Privilege is no longer to be found in Records, and Journals, and Standing Orders ? Upon any occasion, Privilege may be enlarged ; no Court will venture for the future, without trembling, either to recognize or to deny it.

" We manifestly see this Effect of excluding by a general Resolution one Bailable Offence from Privilege To-day; that it will be a Precedent for doing so by another upon some future Occasion, till, instead of Privilege holding in every Case not excepted, it will at last come to hold in none but such as are expressly saved.

"When the Case of the *Habeas Corpus* is relied upon as a Precedent to enforce the present Declaration; the Argument only shews, that the Mischief afore-mentioned has taken Place already; since one Alteration, though a very just one, and not at all applicable to the present Question, is produced, to justify another that is unwarrantable.

"But it is strongly objected, that, if Privilege be allowed in this Case, a Lord of Parliament might endanger the Constitution, by a continual Attack of successive Libels; and, if such a Person should be suffered to escape, under the Shelter of Privilege, with perpetual Impunity, all Government would be overturned; and therefore it is inexpedient to allow the Privilege now, when the Time of Privilege by Prorogations is continued for ever, without an Interval.

"This Objection shall be answered in Two Ways: If Inexpediency is to destroy Personal Privilege in this Case of a Seditious Libel, it is at least as inexpedient that other great Misdemeanours should stand under the like Protection of Privilege: Neither is it expedient that the smaller Offences should be exempt from Prosecution in the Person of a Lord of Parliament. So that, if this Argument of Inexpediency is to prevail, it must prevail throughout, and subvert the whole Law of Privilege in Criminal Matters; in which Method of Reasoning, there is this Fault, that the Argument proves too much.

"If this Inconvenience be indeed grievous, the Fault is not in the Law of Privilege, but in the Change of Times, and in the Management of Prorogations by the Servants of the Crown; which are so contrived, as not to leave an Hour open for Justice. Let the Objection, nevertheless, be allowed in its utmost Extent; and then compare the Inexpediency of not immediately prosecuting on one Side, with the Inexpediency of stripping the Parliament of all Protection from Privilege on the other; Unhappy as the Option is, the Publick would rather wish to see the Prosecution for Crimes suspended, than the Parliament totally unprivileged; although, notwithstanding this pretended Inconvenience is so warmly magnified upon the present Occasion, we are not apprized that any such Inconvenience has been felt, though the Privilege has been enjoyed Time immemorial.

"But the Second and best Answer, because it removes all Pretence of Grievance, is this, that this House, upon Complaint made, has the Power (which it will exert in Favour of Justice) to deliver up the Offender to Prosecution.

" It is a dishonourable, and an undeserved, Imputation upon the Lords, to suppose, even in Argument, that they would nourish an impious Criminal in their Bosoms, against the Call of offended Justice, and the Demand of their Country. It is true however, and it is hoped that this House will always see (as every Magistrate ought that does not betray his Trust) that their Member is properly charged ; but, when that Ground is once laid, they would be ashamed to protect the Offender One Moment. Surely this Trust (which has never yet been abused) is not too great to be reposed in the High Court of Parliament. While it is lodged there, the Publick Justice is in safe Hands, and the Privilege untouched ; whereas, on the contrary, if, for the Sake of coming at the Criminal at once without this Application to the House, Personal Privilege is taken away ; not only the Offender, but the whole Parliament at the same Time, is delivered up to the Crown.

" It is not to be conceived that our Ancestors, when they framed the Law of Privilege, would have left the Case of a Seditious Libel (as it is called) the only unprivileged Misdemeanour : Whatever else they had given up to the Crown, they would have guarded the Case of supposed Libels, above all others, with Privilege, as being most likely to be abused by outrageous and vindictive Prosecutions.

" But this great Privilege had a much deeper Reach ; It was wisely planned, and hath hitherto, through all Times, been resolutely maintained.

" It was not made to screen Criminals, but to preserve the very Being and Life of Parliament ; for, when our Ancestors considered, that the Law had lodged the great Powers of Arrest, Indictment, and Information, in the Crown, they saw the Parliament would be undone, if, during the Time of Privilege, the Royal Process should be admitted in any Misdemeanour whatsoever ; therefore they excepted none : Where the Abuse of Power would be fatal, the Power ought never to be given, because Redress comes too late.

" A Parliament under perpetual Terror of Imprisonment can neither be free, nor bold, nor honest ; and, if this Privilege was once removed, the most important Question might be irrecoverably lost, or carried, by a sudden Irruption of Messengers, let loose against the Members Half an Hour before the Debate.

" Lastly, as it has already been observed, the case of supposed Libels is of all others the most dangerous and alarming to be left open to Prosecution during the Time of Privilege.

" If the Severity of the Law touching Libels, as it hath sometimes been laid down, be duly weighed, it must strike both Houses of Parliament with Terror and Dismay.

" The Repetition of a Libel, the Delivery of it unread to another, is said to be a Publication ; nay the bare Possession of it has been deemed criminal, unless it is immediately destroyed, or carried to a Magistrate.

"Every Lord of Parliament then, who hath done this, who is falsely accused, nay who is, though without any Information, named in the Secretary of State's Warrant, has lost his Privilege by this Resolution, and lies at the Mercy of that Enemy to Learning and Liberty, *the Messenger of the Press.*

" For these, and many other forcible Reasons, we hold it highly unbecoming the Dignity, Gravity, and Wisdom, of the House of Peers, as well as their Justice, thus judicially to explain away and diminish the Privilege of their Persons, founded in the Wisdom of Ages, declared with Precision in our Standing Orders, so repeatedly confirmed, and hitherto preserved inviolable, by the Spirit or our Ancestors ; called to it only by the other House on a particular Occasion and to serve a particular Purpose, *ex post facto, ex Parte, et pendente Lite* in the Courts below."

[17 names subscribed.]

(D)

Resolved, That this House doth agree with the Commons in the said Resolution ; and that the Blank be filled up with [" the Lords Spiritual and Temporal and "].

[L.J., xxx, 426, Nov. 29, 1763.]

XXXII

GENERAL WARRANTS,[1] 1766

(A)

COMMONS' RESOLUTION

A Motion was made, and the Question being proposed, That a General Warrant for seizing and apprehending any Person or Persons being illegal, is, if executed upon a Member of this House, a Breach of the Privilege of this House. . . . An Amendment was proposed to be made to the Question, by inserting, after the Word " illegal," these Words, " except in Cases provided for by Act of Parliament." And the said Amendment was, upon the Question

[1] See Sect. C, No. XVI, p. 294.

put thereupon, agreed to by the House. . . . Then the main Question, so amended, being put ;

Resolved, That a General Warrant for seizing and apprehending any Person or Persons being illegal, except in Cases provided for by Act of Parliament, is, if executed upon a Member of this House, a Breach of the Privilege of this House.

[C.J., xxx, 771, April 25, 1766.]

(B)

Lord Mansfield's Opinion

That, in his opinion, declarations of the law made by either House of parliament were always attended with bad effects : he had constantly opposed them whenever he had an opportunity, and in his judicial capacity thought himself bound never to pay the least regard to them. That, although thoroughly convinced of the illegality of general warrants, which indeed naming no persons, were no warrants at all, he was sorry to see the House of Commons by their vote declare them to be illegal. That it looked like a legislative act, which yet had no force nor effect as a law : for, supposing the House had declared them to be legal, the courts in Westminster would nevertheless have been bound to declare the contrary ; and consequently to throw a disrespect on the vote of the House : but he made a wide distinction between general declarations of law, and the particular decision which might be made by either House, in their judicial capacity, on a case coming regularly before them, and properly the subject of their jurisdiction. That here they did not act as legislators, . . . but as judges, drawing the law from the several sources from which it ought to be drawn, for their own guidance in deciding the particular question before them, and applying it strictly to the decision of that question. That, for his own part, wherever the statute law was silent, he knew not where to look for the law of parliament, or for a definition of the privileges of either House, except in the proceedings and decisions of each House respectively. That he knew of no parliamentary code to judge of questions depending on the judicial authority of parliament, but the practice of each House, moderated or extended according to the wisdom of the House, and accommodated to the cases before them.

[*Parl. Hist.*, xvi, 653, Jan. 9, 1770.]

XXXIII

WILKES AND THE MIDDLESEX ELECTION, 1768–69

(A)

The Question being put, That *John Wilkes*, Esquire, a Member of this House, who hath at the Bar of this House, confessed himself to be the Author and Publisher of what this House has resolved to be an insolent, scandalous, and seditious Libel; and who has been convicted in the Court of King's Bench, of having printed and published a seditious Libel, and Three obscene and impious Libels; and, by the Judgment of the said Court, has been sentenced to undergo Twenty-two Months Imprisonment, and is now in Execution under the said Judgment, be expelled this House. . . . So it was resolved in the Affirmative [219-137].

Ordered, That Mr. Speaker do issue his Warrant to the Clerk of the Crown, to make out a new Writ for the Electing of a Knight of the Shire to serve in this present Parliament for the County of *Middlesex*, in the room of *John Wilkes*, Esquire, expelled this House.

[C.J., xxxii, 178, Feb. 3, 1769.]

(B)

Ordered, That the Deputy Clerk of the Crown do attend this House immediately, with the Return to the Writ for electing a Knight of the Shire to serve in this present Parliament for the County of *Middlesex*, in the room of *John Wilkes*, Esquire, expelled this House.

And the Deputy Clerk of the Crown attending, according to Order; The said Writ and Return were read.

A Motion was made, and the Question being proposed, That *John Wilkes*, Esquire, having been, in this Session of Parliament, expelled this House, was, and is, incapable of being elected a Member to serve in this present Parliament;

The House was moved, That the Entry in the Journal of the House, of the 6th Day of *March*, 1711, in relation to the Proceedings of the House, upon the Return of a Burgess to serve in Parliament for the Borough of *King's Lynn* in the County of *Norfolk*, in the room of *Robert Walpole*, Esquire, expelled the House, might be read.[1]

And the same was read accordingly.

[1] See Sect. B, No. XX, p. 207.

The House was also moved, that the Resolution of the House, of *Friday* the 3rd Day of this Instant *February*, relating to the Expulsion of *John Wilkes*, Esquire, then a Member of this House, might be read.

And the same being read accordingly ;

An Amendment was proposed to be made to the Question, by inserting after the Word " House " these Words, " for having been the Author and Publisher of what this House hath resolved to be an insolent, scandalous, and seditious Libel ; and for having been convicted in the Court of King's Bench, of having printed and published a seditious Libel, and Three obscene and impious Libels ; and having, by the Judgment of the said Court, been sentenced to undergo Twenty-two months Imprisonment, and being in Execution under the said Judgment."

And the Question being put, That those Words be there inserted ;

The House divided. . . .

      . . . Yeas .   . 102
      . . . Noes .   . 228

So it passed in the Negative.

Then the Main Question being put, That *John Wilkes*, Esquire, having been, in this Session of Parliament, expelled this House, was, and is, incapable of being elected a Member to serve in this present Parliament ;

The House divided. . . .

      . . . Yeas .   . 235
      . . . Noes .   . 89

So it was resolved in the Affirmative.

A Motion being made, That the late Election of a Knight of the Shire to serve in this present Parliament for the County of *Middlesex*, is a void Election ;

A Member, in his Place, informed the House, that he was present at the last Election of a Knight of the Shire to serve in this present Parliament for the said County ; that there was no other Candidate than the said Mr. *Wilkes* ; that there was no Poll demanded for any other Person, nor any kind of Opposition to the Election of the said Mr. *Wilkes*.

Resolved, That the late Election of a Knight of the Shire to serve in this present Parliament for the County of *Middlesex*, is a void Election.

Ordered, That Mr. Speaker do issue his Warrant to the Clerk of the Crown, to make out a new Writ for the Electing a Knight of the Shire to serve in this present Parliament for the County of *Middlesex*, in the room of *John Wilkes*, Esquire, who is adjudged incapable of being elected a Member to serve in this present Parliament, and whose Election for the said County has been declared void.

[C.J., xxxii, 228, Feb. 17, 1769.]

(C)

EXTRACT FROM SPEECH OF SERJEANT GLYNN

The disqualification of Mr. Wilkes not being the law of the land, the freeholders of Middlesex were not obliged to take notice of it—that the disqualifications of bodies of men, as clergy, aliens, etc, were all either by express laws, or by implication from the common law, and that the votes of the House to that effect, were only declaratory, but not enacting—that undoubtedly the House had a jurisdiction over its own members, and were judges of the rights of electors, but such judgements must be according to law, a natural consequence of every court of judicature in this kingdom—that the right of the freeholders of Middlesex, as well as the right of every citizen or burgess, was an inherent right in them, not derived from the House of Commons and therefore could not be taken from them by the House, except in cases, where offending against the law, they had forfeited a right to such privileges.[1]

[*Parl. Hist.*, xvi, 587, April 15, 1769.]

(D)

Then the Question being put, That *Henry Lawes Luttrell*, Esquire, ought to have been returned a Knight of the Shire to serve in this present Parliament for the County of *Middlesex*:

The House divided.

The Yeas went forth. [The votes were 197–143.]

So it was resolved in the affirmative.

Ordered, That the Deputy Clerk of the Crown do amend the Return for the County of *Middlesex*, by rasing out the name *John Wilkes* Esquire, and inserting the name of *Henry Lawes Luttrell* Esquire, instead thereof.

And the Deputy Clerk of the Crown, attending according to order, amended the said Return accordingly.

[C.J., April 15, 1769.]

(E)

A Petition of the Freeholders of the County of *Middlesex*, was presented to the House, and read; Setting forth, That the Petitioners being informed by the Votes of the House, that the Return for the said County hath been amended by rasing out the Name of *John*

[1] See Vol. II, Sect. C, No. XIX, at p. 306.

Wilkes, Esquire, and inserting the Name of *Henry Lawes Luttrell*, Esquire, instead thereof, and that Leave was given to petition this House, . . . and representing to the House, that the said *Henry Lawes Luttrell* had not the Majority of legal Votes at the said Election, nor did the Majority of the Freeholders, when they voted for *John Wilkes*, Esquire, mean thereby to throw away their Votes, or to waive their Right of Representation, nor would they by any Means have chosen to be represented by the said *Henry Lawes Luttrell*, Esquire ; the Petitioners therefore apprehend he cannot sit as the Representative of the said County in Parliament, without manifest Infringement of the Rights and Privileges of the Freeholders thereof : . . . *Ordered*, That the Matter of the said Petition, so far as the same relates to the Election of *Henry Lawes Luttrell*, Esquire, be heard at the Bar of this House upon Monday Sevennight, the 8th Day of *May* next.

[C.J., xxxii, 447, April 29, 1769.]

(F)

The House proceeded to the Hearing of the Matter of the Petition of the Freeholders of the County of *Middlesex*. . . . And the Counsel for the Petitioners were heard ; and having proposed to produce Evidence, to shew that the Numbers upon the Poll were for Mr. *Wilkes* 1143 and for Mr. *Luttrell* 296.

The same was admitted by the Counsel for the Sitting Member.

Then the Counsel for the Sitting Member were heard.

And One of the Counsel for the Petitioners having been heard by Way of Reply ; . . . the Question being put, That *Henry Lawes Luttrell*, Esquire, is duly elected a Knight of the Shire . . . for . . . *Middlesex*. . . . So it was resolved in the Affirmative [221-152]

[C.J., xxxii, 451, May 8, 1769.]

(G)

Then it was moved, [in the House of Lords] " To resolve, That the House of Commons, in the Exercise of its Judicature in Matters of Election, is bound to judge according to the Law of the Land, and the known and established Laws and Custom of Parliament, which is Part thereof."

It was resolved in the Negative.

DISSENTIENT

1st, Because the Resolution proposed was in our Judgment highly necessary to lay the Foundation of a Proceeding, which might tend to quiet the Minds of the People, by doing them Justice, at a Time when a Decision of the other House, which appears to us inconsistent with the Principles of the Constitution, and irreconcileable to the Law of the Land, has spread so universal an Alarm, and produced so general a Discontent, throughout the Kingdom.

2ndly, Because, although we do not deny that the Determination on the Right to a Seat in the House of Commons is competent to the Jurisdiction of that House alone, yet when to this it is added, that whatever they, in the Exercise of that Jurisdiction, think fit to declare to be Law, is therefore to be so considered, because there lies no Appeal, we conceive ourselves called upon to give that Proposition the strongest Negative ; for, if admitted, the Law of the Land (by which all Courts of Judicature, without Exception, are equally bound to proceed) is at once overturned, and resolved into the Will and Pleasure of a Majority of One House of Parliament, who, in assuming it, assume a Power to over-rule at Pleasure the fundamental Right of Election, which the Constitution has placed in other Hands, those of their Constituents : and if ever this pretended Power should come to be exercised to the full Extent of the Principle, the House will be no longer a Representative of the People, but a separate Body, altogether independent of them, self-existing and self-elected.

3rdly, Because, when we are told that Expulsion implies Incapacity ; and the Proof insisted upon is, that the People have acquiesced in the Principle, by not re-electing Persons who have been expelled ; we equally deny the Position as false, and reject the Proof offered, as in no Way supporting the Position to which it is applied ; we are sure the Doctrine is not to be found in any Statute or Law-Book, nor in the Journals of the House of Commons, neither is it consonant with any just or known Analogy of Law ; and as not re-electing would, at most, but infer a Supposition of the Electors Approbation of the Grounds of the Expulsion, and by no Means their Acquiescence in the Conclusion of an implied Incapacity : so, were there not One Instance of a Re-election after Expulsion but Mr. *Woolaston's*,[1] that alone demonstrates that neither did the Constituents admit, nor the House of Commons maintain, Incapacity to be the Consequence of Expulsion ; even the Case of Mr. *Walpole*[2] shews, by the first Re-election, the Sense of the People, that Expulsion did not infer Incapacity ; and that Precedent too, (which is the only One of an Incapacity), produced as it was under the Influence of Party Violence in the latter Days of Queen *Anne*, in so far as it relates to the Introduction of a Candidate

[1] Expelled February 20, 1699, because he was a receiver of taxes.
[2] See Sect. B, No. XX, p. 207.

having a Minority of Votes, decides expressly against the Proceedings of the House of Commons, in the late *Middlesex* Election.

4thly, Because, as the Constitution hath been once already destroyed by the Assumption and Exercise of the very Power which is now claimed, the Day may come again when Freedom of Speech may be criminal in that House, and every Member who shall have Virtue enough to withstand the Usurpations of the Time, and assert the Rights of the People, will for that Offence be expelled, by a factious and corrupt Majority, and by that Expulsion rendered incapable of serving the Public : in which Case the Electors will find themselves reduced to the miserable Alternative of giving up altogether their Right of Election, or of choosing only such as are Enemies of their Country, and will be passive at least, if not active, in subverting the Constitution.

5thly, Because, although it has been objected in the Debate, that it is unusual and irregular in either House of Parliament to examine into the judicial Proceedings of the other, whose Decisions, as they cannot be drawn into Question by Appeal, are, it is said, to be submitted to without Examination of the Principles of them elsewhere ; we conceive the Argument goes directly to establish the exploded Doctrine of Passive Obedience and Non-resistance, which, as applied to the Acts of any Branch of the Supreme Power, we hold to be equally dangerous : and though it is generally true, that neither House ought lightly and wantonly to interpose, even an Opinion, upon Matters which the Constitution hath entrusted to the Jurisdiction of the other, we conceive it to be no less true, that where, under Colour of a judicial Proceeding, either House arrogates to itself the Powers of the whole Legislature, and makes the Law which it professes to declare, the other not only may, but ought to assert its own Right and those of the People : That this House has done so in former Instances, particularly in the famous Case of *Ashby* and *White*, in which the First Resolution of the Lords declares, " That neither House of Parliament hath any Power, by any Vote or Declaration, to create to themselves any new Privilege that is not warranted by the known Laws and Custom of Parliament ; " [1] we ought to interfere at this Time, the rather as our Silence on so important and alarming an Occasion, might be interpreted into an Approbation of the Measure, and be a Means of losing that Confidence with the People, which is so essential to the Public Welfare that this House, the hereditary Guardians of their Rights, should at all Times endeavour to maintain.

6thly, Because, upon the Whole, we deem the Power which the House of Commons have assumed to themselves, of creating an

[1] See Sect. C, No. X, at p. 280 and other refs. in note 3.

Incapacity, unknown to the Law, and thereby depriving, in Effect, all the Electors of *Great Britain* of their valuable Right of Free Election, confirmed to them by so many solemn Statutes, a flagrant Usurpation, as highly repugnant to every essential Principle of the Constitution as the Claim of Ship-money by King *Charles* the First, or that of suspending and dispensing Power by King *James* the Second; this being, indeed, in our Opinion, a suspending and dispensing Power assumed and exercised by the House of Commons against the ancient and fundamental Liberties of the Kingdom (signed by 42 peers).

Then the main Question was put, That any Resolution of this House, directly or indirectly, impeaching a Judgment of the House of Commons in a Matter where their Jurisdiction is competent, final, and conclusive, would be a Violation of the Constitutional Rights of the Commons, tends to make a Breach between the Two Houses of Parliament, and leads to general Confusion. It was resolved in the Affirmative.

[L.J., xxxii, 417, Feb. 2, 1770.]

(H)

Resolution of 1769 rescinded, 1782.

The House was moved, That the Entry in the Journal of the House, of the 17th Day of *February* 1769, of the Resolution, " That *John Wilkes*, Esquire, having been in this Session of Parliament expelled this House, was and is incapable of being elected a Member to serve in this present Parliament," might be read. And the same being read accordingly;

A Motion was made, and the Question being put, That the said Resolution be expunged from the Journals of this House, as being subversive of the Rights of the whole Body of Electors of this Kingdom;

The House divided. . . . So it was resolved in the affirmative. . . . [115-47]

Ordered, That all the Declarations, Orders, and Resolutions of this House, respecting the Election of *John Wilkes*, Esquire, for the County of *Middlesex*, as a void Election, the due and legal Election of *Henry Lawes Luttrell*, Esquire, into Parliament for the said County, and the Incapacity of *John Wilkes*, Esquire, to be elected a Member to serve in the said Parliament, be expunged from the Journals of this House, as being subversive of the Rights of the whole Body of Electors of this Kingdom.

And the same was expunged, by the Clerk, at the Table, accordingly.

[C.J., xxxviii, 977, May 3, 1782.]

XXXIV

THE CASE OF BRASS CROSBY, 1771 [1]

(A)

DEBATE ON COMMITTING THE LORD MAYOR AND ALDERMAN OLIVER TO THE TOWER

SERJEANT GLYNN : . . . I do not deny, that the law of parliament [2] constitutes a part of the law of the land ; but then, when the privilege of parliament is repugnant to the known *lex terrae*, to the obvious principles of the constitution, in that case I confidently decide for the supremacy of the latter, and insist, that the immemorial acquiescence of ages or the joint act of the three estates must be necessarily superior to the private resolution of any single branch of the legislative authority.

. . . No court is bound to take notice of our votes ; on the contrary, the judges are bound not to take notice of them, but to act in conformity with the laws ; they are sworn to do justice without any attention whatever to the privy seal, or the great seal ; and, consequently, if they are thus constitutionally placed above the commands of the head, they are placed above the resolutions of the lowest estate in parliament.

If parliamentary privilege were to be once indulged with a superiority over the law, an Englishman would be as insecure in his liberty, as the slaves of the Mogul : because the votes of each House might often be inconsistent . . . In cases of such a kind what line of conduct would be left for the judge ? . . . The inference is obvious, that the law should pay no regard to the resolutions of either House. . . .

The prerogative of the crown is as sacred as our privileges, if we have a right to punish for a contempt of the one, the crown has a right to punish for a contempt of the other. In laying the whole nation, therefore, at our own mercy, we lay it at the mercy of the crown. In our own tyranny, we establish the tyranny of the throne, and while we claim a power of trampling upon Magna Charta, hold out a blessed example for imitation to our sovereign.

[*Parl. Hist.*, xvii, 131, March 25, 1771.]

(B)

Resolved, That *Brass Crosby,* Esquire, Lord Mayor of the City of *London,* having discharged out of the Custody of One of the

[1] See Sect. B, No. XXVII, p. 217, Sect. C, No. XIX, p. 311, and Vol. II, Sect. C, No. XVI, at p. 293.

[2] See Sect. C, No. X, at p. 280 and other refs. in note 3.

Messengers of this House *J. Miller* (for whom the News Paper, intituled, " *The London Evening Post,* from *Thursday, March 7,* to *Saturday, March 9, 1771,*" purports to be printed, and of which a Complaint was made in the House of Commons, on the 12th Day of this Instant *March,* and who, for his Contempt, in not obeying the Order of this House, for his Attendance on this House upon *Thursday* the 14th Day of this Instant *March,* was ordered to be taken into the Custody of the Serjeant at Arms, or his Deputy, attending this House, and who, by Virtue of the Speaker's Warrant, issued under the said Order, had been taken into the Custody of the said Messenger) and having signed a Warrant against the said Messenger, for having executed the said Warrant of the Speaker, and having held the said Messenger to Bail for the same, is guilty of a Breach of the Privilege of this House.

A Motion was made, and the Question being proposed, That *Brass Crosby,* Esquire, Lord Mayor of the City of *London,* and a Member of this House, be, for his said Offence, committed to the Custody of the Serjeant at Arms attending this House.

The Lord Mayor was heard in his Place.

And then he again withdrew.

Then an Amendment was proposed to be made to the Question, by leaving out the Words " Custody of the Serjeant at Arms attending this House," and inserting the Words " Tower of *London* " instead thereof ;

And the Question being put, That the Words " Custody of the Serjeant at Arms attending this House," stand Part of the Question ;

It passed in the Negative.

And the Question being put, That the Words " Tower of *London* " be inserted instead thereof ;

It was resolved in the Affirmative.

Then the main Question, so amended, being put, That *Brass Crosby,* Esquire, Lord Mayor of the City of *London,* and a Member of this House, be, for his said Offence, committed to the Tower of *London ;*

The House divided.

The Yeas went forth. . . .

... Yeas . . 202
... Noes . . 39

So it was resolved in the Affirmative.

Ordered, That Mr. Speaker do issue his Warrants accordingly.

[C.J., xxxiii, 289, March 27, 1771.]

XXXV

THE HOUSE OF LORDS AND THE HOUSE OF COMMONS, 1778

EXTRACT FROM A SPEECH OF THE EARL OF SHELBURNE

It is not the business of this House to call such men to account. That is the duty of the other House. But what is the other House ? Can public justice ever be procured through so foul and corrupt a channel ? Is it possible to obtain justice, while that House is under the immediate controul, and at the devotion of the minister ? Can impeachments be expected to come from pensioners, contractors, and the whole tribe of needy dependents ? . . . I shall never submit to the doctrines I have heard this day from the woolsack, that the other House are the only representatives and guardians of the people's rights . . . I say this House are equally representatives of the people. They hold the balance ; and if they should perceive two of the branches of the legislature unite in oppressing and enslaving the people, it is their duty to interpose to prevent it.

[*Parl. Hist.*, xix, 1048, April 8, 1778.]

XXXVI

COLLECTIVE RESPONSIBILITY OF MINISTERS,[1] 1778

(A)

LORD NORTH IN A DEBATE ON ARMY ESTIMATES

Several gentlemen had likewise called for an inquiry into the conduct of ministers ; and some had pointed their censure directly at the noble lord near him (G. Germain) as the principal author of all our miscarriages. An inquiry into the conduct of ministers, no person in that House more ardently wished for. . . . The measures pursued were his measures, in concert with the rest of the King's servants. He assisted in advising them, and looked upon himself responsible. . . . As to the personal attacks made on the noble lord near him, . . . there, if censure was due, he laid claim for part ; they were measures of state, originating in the King's counsels, and were of course no more the noble Lord's measures than they were

See Vol. II, Sect. B, No. V, p. 160.

of any other member of the cabinet : the crimes or faults, or errors committed there, were imputable to the whole body, and not to a single individual who composed it.

[*Parl. Hist.*, xx, 89, Dec. 14, 1778.]

(B)

LORD NORTH ON A MOTION OF CENSURE ON THE CONDUCT OF THE ADMIRALTY

The present motion was meant to lead to a vote of censure on the first lord of the Admiralty, in his official capacity ; but such a vote . . . would not be a censure merely of the first lord of the Admiralty, but of all his Majesty's confidential servants. He himself was equally criminal with the noble earl ; so was every other efficient member of the cabinet. . . . It was a crime in common, or no crime. Indeed, a case might happen, in which acting merely ministerially, the noble earl might be obliged to execute officially what he had previously disapproved of in council, by being over-ruled by a majority of the King's servants.

[*Parl. Hist.*, xx, 197, March 3, 1779.]

XXXVII

POWER OF THE CROWN, 1780

(A)

Mr. Dunning's Motions—6 April, 1780.

' That it is necessary to declare, that the influence of the crown has increased, is increasing, and ought to be diminished.'

. . . At 12 o'clock the Committee divided : For Mr. Dunning's Motion 233. Against it 215—Majority 18 . . .

' That it is the opinion of this Committee, that it is competent to this House to examine into, and to correct abuses in the expenditure of the civil list revenues, as well as in every other branch of the public revenue, whenever it shall seem expedient to the wisdom of this House so to do ' . . .

The question being called for, the motion was agreed to without a division.

(B)

Mr. Dunning's Motion for securing the Independence of Parliament—10 April, 1780.

' That is it the opinion of this Committee, that, for preserving the independence of parliament, and obviating any suspicion of its purity, there be laid before this House, within seven days after the first day of every session, exact accounts, authenticated by the signature of the proper officers, of every sum and sums of money paid in the course of the preceding year, out of the produce of the civil list, or any other branch of the public revenue, to, or to the use of, or in trust for, any member of either House of Parliament, by way of pension, salary, or on any other account whatsoever ; specifying when, and on what account.' . . . The question was put and carried without a division. . . .

' That it is the opinion of this Committee, that it is incompatible with the independence of parliament, that persons holding the offices of treasurer of the chamber, treasurer of the houshold, cofferer of the houshold and his clerk, comptroller of the houshold and his clerk, master of the houshold, and the clerks of the green cloth, be entitled to hold seats in this House, if such places shall be permitted to exist.' [1]   The Committee divided : Yeas 215 ; Noes 213.

[*Parl. Hist.*, xxi, 340-86.]

XXXVIII

KING'S PREROGATIVE OF CHOOSING MINISTERS, 1782-83 [2]

(A)

LORD SHELBURNE

And it would have been very singular indeed, if he should have given up to them all those constitutional ideas, which for seventeen years he had imbibed from his master in politics, the late earl of Chatham ; that noble earl had always declared, that this country ought not to be governed by any party or faction ; [3] that if it was to be so governed, the constitution must necessarily expire ; with these principles he had always acted ; they were not newly taken up for ambitious purposes ; their lordships might recollect a particular expression that he had used some time ago, when speaking of party, he declared that he would never consent that the " king of England should be a king of the Mahrattas," among whom it was a custom for a certain number of great lords to elect a peshaw, who was the creature of an aristocracy, and was vested with the

---

[1] See Sect. A, No. LXII, p. 147.
[2] Cf. Vol. II, Sect. B, No. I, p. 153, and Sect. D, No. XXV (B), p. 388.
[3] See Sect. D, No. V, p. 325, No. XXIII, p. 359, No. XL, p. 388, and No. XLVI, p. 396.

plenitude of power, while the king was, in fact, nothing more than a royal pageant, or puppet.

These being his principles, it was natural for him to stand up for the prerogative of the crown, and insist upon the King's right to appoint his own servants. If the power which others wished to assume, of vesting in the cabinet the right of appointing to all places, and filling up all vacancies, should once be established, the King must then resemble the king of the Mahrattas, who had nothing of sovereignty but the name : in that case the monarchical part of the constitution would be absorbed by the aristocracy, and the famed constitution of England would be no more.

[*Parl. Hist.*, xxiii, 192, July 10, 1782.]

(B)

MR. FOX

It had been argued again and again, that the King had a right to chuse his own ministers. In that particular, he rested on the spirit of the constitution, and not on the letter of it ; and grounding his opinion on the spirit of the constitution, he ever had, and ever would maintain, that his Majesty, in this choice of ministers, ought not to be influenced by his personal favour alone, but by the public voice, by the sense of his parliament, and the sense of his people. An administration in whom that House did not place confidence, was such an administration as it was unsafe to lodge the government of this country in at this crisis. It was no argument to say, " I am a minister, because his Majesty has made me one."

[*Parl. Hist.*, xxiii, 596, March 6, 1783.]

XXXIX

IRISH AND ENGLISH PARLIAMENTS, 1782 [1]

DEBATE IN THE COMMONS ON THE AFFAIRS OF IRELAND

May 17. The House resolved itself into a Committee of the whole House to take into consideration his Majesty's Message of the 9th of April relative to the State of Ireland. The following Papers, presented to the House by Mr. Secretary Fox on the 1st of May, were referred to the said Committee :

[1] See Sect. A, Nos. LXI, p. 147, and LXIII, p. 150.

MESSAGE to the Houses of Lords and Commons in Ireland, from his Grace the Lord Lieutenant; delivered the 16th April 1782.

" Portland.

" I have it in command from his Majesty, to inform this House, that his Majesty being concerned to find that discontents and jealousies are prevailing among his loyal subjects of this country, upon matters of great weight and importance, his Majesty recommends to this House to take the same into their most serious consideration, in order to such a final adjustment as may give mutual satisfaction to his kingdoms of Great Britain and Ireland.   P."

RESOLUTION of the House of Lords in Ireland, Mercurii, 17° die Aprilis 1782.

" Resolved . . . to represent to his Majesty, that his subjects of Ireland are entitled to a free constitution ; that the imperial crown of Ireland is inseparably annexed to the crown of Great Britain, on which connection the happiness of both nations essentially depends ; but that the kingdom of Ireland is a distinct dominion, having a parliament of her own, the sole legislature thereof : that there is no power whatsoever competent to make laws to bind this nation, except the King, Lords, and Commons of Ireland ; upon which exclusive right of legislation we consider the very essence of our liberties to depend, a right which we claim as the birthright of the people of Ireland, and which we are determined, in every situation of life, to assert and maintain : to represent to his Majesty, that we have seen with concern certain claims, both of legislature and judicature, asserted by the parliament of Great Britain in an Act passed in Great Britain in the sixth year of George I, intituled, ' An Act for the better securing the dependency of Ireland upon the crown of Great Britain : ' that we conceive the said Act, and the powers thereby claimed, to be the great and principal causes of the discontents and jealousies that subsist in this kingdom : to assure his Majesty, that this House considers it as a matter of constitutional right and protection, that all Bills which become law should receive the approbation of his Majesty, under the seal of Great Britain ; but we consider the practice of suppressing our Bills in the council of Ireland, or altering them any where, to be a matter which calls for redress : to represent to his Majesty, that an Act, intituled, ' An Act for the better accomodation of his Majesty's forces,' being unlimited in duration, but which, from the particular circumstances of the times, passed into a law, has been the cause of much jealousy and discontent in this kingdom : . . . that we have the greatest reliance on his Majesty's wisdom, the most sanguine expectations from his virtuous choice of a chief governor, and the greatest con-

fidence in the wise and constitutional council his Majesty has
adopted : that we have moreover a high sense and veneration for the
British character ; and do therefore conceive, that the proceedings
of this country, founded as they are in right, and supported by
constitutional liberty, must have excited the approbation and
esteem of the British nation : that we are the more confirmed in this
hope, inasmuch as the people of this kingdom have never expressed
a desire to share the freedom of Great Britain, without at the same
time declaring their determination to share her fate, standing or
falling with the British nation."

 . . . . . .

As soon as the above Papers had been read by the Clerk, Mr.
Secretary *Fox* rose (to move the resolution that the Act of 6 George I
ought to be repealed).

[*Parl. Hist.*, xxiii, 116, May 17, 1782.]

SECTION C

JUDICIAL PROCEEDINGS

I

BUSHELL'S CASE, 1670

[Edward Bushell, a juryman, had been fined by the Recorder at the Old Bailey sessions, and committed to prison in default for finding a verdict " contra plenam et manifestam evidentiam, et contra directionem curiae in materia legis ".]

IN THE COURT OF COMMON PLEAS

VAUGHAN, L.C.J. : The king's writ of Habeas Corpus, dat. 9 die Novembris, 22 Car. 2, issued out of this court directed to the then Sheriffs of London, to have the body of Edward Bushell, by them detained in Prison, together with the day and cause of his caption and detention, on Friday then next following, before this court, to do and receive as the court should consider ; as also to have then the said writ in court. . . .

In the present case it is returned, That the prisoner, being a juryman, among others charged at the Sessions Court of the Old Bailey, to try the issue between the king, and Penn,[1] and Mead,[2] upon an indictment, for assembling unlawfully and tumultuously, did " contra plenam et manifestam evidentiam," openly given in court, acquit the prisoners indicted, in contempt of the king, etc.

The court hath no knowledge by this return, whether the evidence given were full and manifest, or doubtful, lame, and dark, or, indeed evidence at all material to the issue, because it is not returned what evidence in particular, and as it was delivered, was given. For it is not possible to judge of that rightly which is not exposed to a man's judgment. But here the evidence given to the jury is not exposed at all to this court, but the judgment of the Court of Sessions upon that evidence is only exposed to us ; who tell us it was full and manifest. But our judgment ought to be grounded upon our own inferences and understandings, and not upon theirs.

[1] William Penn, 1644–1718, Quaker and founder of Pennsylvania.
[2] William Mead, 1628–1713, Quaker.

It was said by a learned judge, If the jury might be fined for finding against manifest evidence, the return was good, though it did not express what the evidence particularly was, whereby the court might judge of it, because returning all the evidence would be too long. A strange reason : For if the law allow me remedy for wrong imprisonment, and that must be by judging whether the cause of it were good, or not, to say the cause is too long to be made known, is to say the law gives a remedy which it will not let me have, or I must be wrongfully imprisoned still, because it is too long to know that I ought to be freed ? What is necessary to an end, the law allows is never too long. " Non sunt longa quibus nihil est quod demere possis," is as true as any axiom in Euclid. Besides, one manifest evidence returned had sufficed, without returning all the evidence. But the other judges were not of his mind.

If the return had been, That the jurors were committed by an order of the Court of Sessions, because they did, " minus juste," acquit the persons indicted. Or because they did, " contra legem," acquit the persons indicted. Or because they did, " contra Sacramentum suum," acquit them [sic].

The judges cannot upon the present more judge of the legal cause of their commitment, than they could if any of these causes, as general as they are, had been returned for the cause of their commitment And the same argument may be exactly made to justify any of these returns, had they been made, as to justify the present return, they being equally as legal, equally as certain, and equally as far from possessing the court with the truth of the cause : and in what condition should all men be for the just liberty of their persons, if such causes should be admitted sufficient causes to remand persons to prison. . . .

I would know whether any thing be more common, than for two men students, barristers, or judges, to deduce contrary and opposite conclusions out of the same case in law ? And is there any difference that two men should infer distinct conclusions from the same testimony ? Is any thing more known than that the same author, and place in that author, is forcibly urged to maintain contrary conclusions, and the decision hard, which is in the right ? Is any thing more frequent in the controversies of religion, than to press the same text for opposite tenets ? how then comes it to pass that two persons may not apprehend with reason and honesty, what a witness, or many, say, to prove in the understanding of one plainly one thing, but in the apprehension of the other, clearly the contrary thing ? Must therefore one of these merit fine and imprisonment, because he doth that which he cannot otherwise do, preserving his oath and integrity ? And this often is the case of the judge and jury.

I conclude therefore, That this return, charging the prisoners to have acquitted Penn and Mead, against full and manifest evidence, first and next, without saying that they did know and believe that Evidence to be full and manifest against the indicted persons, is no cause of fine or imprisonment.

And by the way I must here note, That the Verdict of a Jury, and the Evidence of a Witness are very different things, in the truth and falsehood of them : A witness swears but to what he hath heard or seen, generally or more largely, to what hath fallen under his senses. But a juryman swears to what he can infer and conclude from the testimony of such witnesses, by the act and force of his understanding, to be the fact inquired after, which differs nothing in the reason, though much in the punishment, from what a judge, out of various cases considered by him, infers to be the law in the question before him. . . .

We come now to the next part of the Return, viz. " That the jury acquitted those indicted against the direction of the court in matter of law, openly given and declared to them in court." The words, That the jury did acquit, against the direction of the court, in matter of law, literally taken, and *de plano*, are insignificant and not intelligible, for no issue can be joined of matter in law, no jury can be charged with the trial of matter in law barely, no evidence ever was, or can be given to a jury of what is law, or not; nor no such oath can be given to, or taken by, a jury, to try matter in law. . . .

If the meaning of these words, finding against the direction of the court in matter of law, be, That if the judge having heard the evidence given in court (for he knows no other) shall tell the jury, upon this evidence, The law is for the plaintiff, or for the defendant, and you are under the pain of fine and imprisonment to find accordingly, then the jury ought of duty so to do ; Every man sees that the jury is but a troublesome delay, great charge, and of no use in determining right and wrong . . . For if the judge, from the evidence, shall by his own judgment first resolve upon any trial what the fact is, and so knowing the fact, shall then resolve what the law is, and order the jury penally to find accordingly, what either necessary or convenient use can be fancied of juries or to continue trials by them at all ? . . .

But the reasons are, I conceive, most clear, that the judge could not, nor can fine and imprison the jury in such cases.

Without a fact agreed, it is as impossible for a judge, or any other, to know the law relating to that fact or direct concerning it, as to know an accident that hath no subject.

Hence it follows, that the judge can never direct what the law is in any matter controverted, without first knowing the fact ; and then it follows, that without his previous knowledge of the fact, the jury cannot go against his direction in law, for he could not direct.

But the judge, *quâ* judge, cannot know the fact possibly but from the evidence which the jury have, but (as will appear) he can never know what evidence the jury have, and consequently he cannot know the matter of fact, nor punish the jury for going against their evidence, when he cannot know what their evidence is.

It is true, if the jury were to have no other evidence for the fact, but what is deposed in court, the judge might know their evidence, and the fact from it, equally as they, and so direct what the law were in the case, though even then the judge and jury might honestly differ in the result from the evidence, as well as two judges may, which often happens. But the evidence which the jury have of the fact is much other than that : for,

(1) Being returned of the vicinage, whence the cause of action ariseth, the law supposeth them thence to have sufficient knowledge to try the matter in issue (and so they must) though no evidence were given on either side in court, but to this evidence the judge is a stranger.

(2) They may have evidence from their own personal knowledge, by which they may be assured, and sometimes are, that what is deposed in court, is absolutely false : but to this the judge is a stranger, and he knows no more of the fact than he hath learned in court, and perhaps by false depositions, and consequently knows nothing.

(3) The jury may know the witnesses to be stigmatized and infamous, which may be unknown to the parties, and consequently to the court.

(4) In many cases the jury are to have view necessarily, in many, by consent, for their better information ; to this evidence likewise the judge is a stranger.

(5) If they do follow his direction, they may be attainted and the judgment reversed for doing that, which if they had not done, they should have been fined and imprisoned by the judge, which is unreasonable.

(6) If they do not follow his direction, and be therefore fined, yet they may be attainted, and so doubly punished by distinct judicatures for the same offence, which the common law admits not. . . .

(7) To what end is the jury to be returned out of the vicinage, whence the cause of action ariseth ? To what end must hundredors be of the jury, whom the law supposeth to have nearer knowledge of the fact than those of the vicinage in general : To what end are

they challenged so scrupulously to array and pole ? To what end must they have such a certain freehold, and be " probi et legales homines," and not of affinity with the parties concerned ? To what end must they have in many cases the view, for their exacter information chiefly ? To what end must they undergo the heavy punishment of the villainous judgment, if after all this they implicitly must give a verdict by the dictates and authority of another man, under pain of fines and imprisonment, when sworn to do it to the best of their own knowledge ?

A man cannot see by anothers eye, nor hear by anothers ear, no more can a man conclude or infer the thing to be resolved by anothers understanding or reasoning ; and though the verdict be right the jury give, yet they being not assured it is so from their own understanding, are forsworn, at least *in foro conscientiæ.*

(9) It is absurd a jury should be fined by the judge for going against their evidence, when he who fineth knows not what it is, as where a jury find without evidence, in court of either side, so if the jury find, upon their own knowledge, as the course is if the defendant plead solvit ad diem, to a bond proved, and offers no proof. The jury is directed to find for the plantiff, unless they know payment was made of their own knowledge, according to the plea. . . .

That Decantatum in our books, ' Ad quæstionem facti non respondent Judices, ad quæstionem legis non respondent Juratores', literally taken is true ; for if it be demanded, What is the fact ? the Judge cannot answer it : if it be asked, What is the law in the case, the Jury cannot answer it [1] . . .

The Chief Justice delivered the Opinion of the Court, and accordingly the Prisoners [Bushell and his fellows] were discharged.

[*S.T.*, vi, 999.]

II

THOMAS *v.* SORRELL, 1674

In Exchequer Chamber

[Sorrell was a member of the Vintner's Company and as such sold wine retail without a licence under a dispensation granted to members of that Company by James I by letters patent.]

VAUGHAN, L.C.J. : I observed not that any steddy rule hath been drawn from the cases cited to guid a mans judgment, where the King may or may not dispence in penal laws, excepting that old rule

[1] See Vol. II, Sect. A, No. IV, p. 6 ; Sect. C, No. VI, p. 233.

taken from the case of 11 H. 7. That with malum prohibitum by stat. the King may dispence, but not with malum per se. But I think that rule hath more confounded mens judgments on that subject, than rectified them. Yet I conceive that case, and the instances given in it, rightly understood, to be the best key afforded by our books, to open this dark learning (as it seems to me) of dispensations.[1]

I agree, that with malum prohibitum by stat. indefinitely understood the king may dispense. But I deny that the king can dispense with every malum prohibitum by statute, though prohibited by statute only. . . . So it is generally true, that malum per se cannot be dispensed with ; but thence to inferr (as many do) that every malum which the King cannot dispense with is malum per se, is not true. . . . When the suit is only the Kings for breach of a law, which is not to the particular damage of any third person, the King may dispense ; but where the suit is only the Kings, but for the benefit and safety of a third person, and the King is intitled to the suit by the prosecution and complaint of such third person, the King cannot release, discharge or dispense with the suit, but by consent and agreement with of the party concern'd . . . and by the same reason other penal laws, the breach of which are to mens particular damage, cannot be dispens'd with. . . . Nor see I any reason why the King may not dispense with these nusances by which no man hath right to a particular action, as well as he may with any other offence against a penal law, by which no third person hath cause of action. . . . Therefore I may conclude those things to be mala in se, which can never be made lawful. . . . And the reason why the king cannot dispense in such cases, is, not only as nusances are contra bonum publicum, but because if a dispensation might make it lawful to do a nusance . . . the person damaged by it would be deprived of his action. . . . No non obstante can dispense in these cases, and many the like, for that were to grant that a man should not have lawful actions brought against him . . . which the king cannot grant. . . . As to the second question ; admitting King James might have dispens'd with particular persons for selling wine by retail . . . whether he could dispense with a corporation or with this Corporation of Vinters, and their successors, as he hath done, having no possible knowledge of the persons themselves, or of their number ? . . . First, that the nature of the offence is such as may be dispens'd with, seems clear in reason of law, and by constant practice of licencing particular persons. 2. Where the King can dispense with particular persons, he is not confined to number or place, but may licence as many, and in such places, as he thinks

[1] See Sect. C, No. VI, p. 256.

fit. . . . I must say, as my brother Atkins observed before, that in
this case the plaintiff's council argue against the King's prerogative,
for the extent of his prerogative is the extent of his power, and the
extent of his power is to do what he hath will to do, according to
that, ut summæ potestatis Regis est posse quantum velit sic magni-
tudinis est velle quantum potest; if therefore the King have a will
to dispense with a corporation, as it seems K James had in this
case, when the patent was granted, but by law cannot, his power, and
consequently his prerogative, is less than if he could.   Malum Prohibitum is that which is prohibited per le statute : Per le Statute is
not intended only an Act of Parliament, but any obliging law of
constitution, as appears by the case.

[Vaughan 330.]

III

THE CASE OF ANTHONY, EARL OF SHAFTESBURY,[1] 1677

[Shaftesbury had been committed to the Tower by order of the
House of Lords, February 16, 1677, " during his majesty's pleasure,
and the pleasure of this House, for high contempts committed against
this House ".   On June 27, 1677, Shaftesbury was brought to the King's
Bench on an Habeas Corpus.]

Sir *Tho. Jones*, Justice : Such a commitment by an ordinary
Court of Justice, would have been ill and uncertain, but the cause
is different when it comes before this High Court, to which so
much respect has been paid by our predecessors, that they have
deferred the determination of doubts conceived on an act of
parliament, until they have received the advice of the Lords : and
now, instead thereof, it is demanded of us to control the judgment
of all the Peers, given on a member of their own House, and during
the continuance of the same session.   The cases where the Courts
of Westminster have taken cognizance of privilege, differ from this
case : for in those it was only an incident to the case before them,
which was of their cognizance ; but the direct point of the matter is
now the judgment of the Lords . . .

It has not been affirmed, That the usage of the House of Lords
has used to express the matter more particularly on commitments
for contempts, and therefore I shall take it according to the course
of parliament . . . It is said that the judges are assistants to the
Lords, to inform them of common law ; but they ought not to
judge of any law, custom, or usage of parliament. . . . I shall not

[1] See Sect. C, No. X, at p. 280 and other refs. in note 3.

say what would be the consequence (as to this imprisonment) if the session were determined, for that is not the present case : but as the case is, the Court can neither bail nor discharge the Earl.

Wild, Justice : The return, no doubt, is illegal ; but the question is a point of jurisdiction, Whether it may be examined here ? This Court cannot meddle with the transactions of the most High Court of Peers in parliament during the session, which is not determined ; and therefore the certainty or uncertainty of the return is not material, for it is not examinable here : but if the session had been determined, my opinion would be, that he ought to be discharged.

Rainsford, Chief Justice . . . The consequence would be very mischievous, if this Court should deliver a member of the House of Peers and Commons who are committed, for thereby the business of parliament may be retarded ; for it may be commitment was for evil behaviour, or indecent reflections on other members, or the disturbance of the affairs of parliament.

The commitment in this case is not for safe custody, but it is in execution of judgment given by the Lords for the contempt ; and therefore if he should be bailed, he would be delivered out of execution ; for a contempt *in facie curiae* there is no other judgment or execution.

This Court has no jurisdiction, and therefore he ought to be remanded.

[Shaftesbury remained in prison until a new session, when after submitting himself he was discharged.]

[*S.T.* vi,, 1296, June 27, 1677.]

IV

THE COMMON LAW AND THE PRESS, 1680 [1]

(A)

THE CASE OF BENJAMIN HARRIS
AT GUILDHALL, LONDON

[Harris was accused of selling a pamphlet entitled, ' An Appeal from the Country to the City for the Preservation of his Majesty's Person, Liberty, Property and the Protestant Religion '.]

SCROGGS, L.C.J. : Because my brother shall be satisfied with the opinion of all the judges of England, what this offence is, which they would insinuate, as if the mere selling of such a book was no offence : it is not long since, that all the judges met, by the king's

---

[1] See also Sect. A, No. XII, p. 29, Sect. C, No. XI, p. 285, and Nos. XVI-XVIII, pp. 294-310, and cf. Vol. II, Sect. C, No. XVI, p. 287.

command : as they did some time before too : and they both times
declared unanimously, that all persons that do write, or print, or
sell any pamphlet, that is either scandalous to public, or private
persons ; such books may be seized, and the person punished by
law : that all books, which are scandalous to the government may be
seized : and all persons so exposing them, may be punished. And
further, that all writers of news, though not scandalous, seditious,
nor reflective upon the government or the state ; yet if they are
writers (as there are few others) of false news, they are indictable and
punishable on that account. So that your hopes of any thing of that
kind will be vain ; for all the judges have declared this offence, at
the common law, to be punishable in the seller, though in the way of
his trade : the books may be seized, and the person punished. As
for this book, in particular : you can hardly read a more base, and
pernicious book, to put us all into a flame. . . . Except the writer
of it, there cannot be a worse man in the world . . . And, Mr.
Harris, if you expect any thing in this world, of this kind of favour,
you must find out the author : for he must be a rebellious, and
villainous traitor. . . . You (the Jury) have nothing more to do, but
to give your verdict : If there be any thing in law, let me know it
because you go out.

Then one of the Jury asked my lord, if they might not have the
book with them, which was then in the court, and it was answered
in the negative. . . .

And being, as is usual, asked if they were agreed on their verdict,
they answered Yes . . . he was Guilty of selling the book. At
which there was a great and clamorous shout. Lord Chief Justice
said, that was not their business, they were only to determine whether
barely Guilty, or not Guilty . . . they all unanimously cried out, they
were all agreed, and then the foreman gave the verdict again, Guilty.

[Fined £500, pillory for one hour, sureties for good behaviour for
three years.]
[*S.T.*, vii, 929.]

(B)

THE CASE OF HENRY CARR
AT GUILDHALL, LONDON, ON NISI PRIUS

SCROGGS, L.C.J. : The present case it stands thus : Mr. Carr,
here is an information brought against him for publishing a printed
pamphlet called, The Pacquet of Advice from Rome . . . The
question is, Whether he was the author or publisher of this. . . .
As for those words, *illicite*, *maliciose*, unlawful : for that I must
recite what Mr. Recorder (Sir Geo. Jefferies) told you of at first,
what all the judges of England have declared under their hands.

The words I remember are these : When, by the king's command, we were to give in our opinion what was to be done in point of the regulation of the press ; we did all subscribe, that to print or publish any news-books or pamphlets of news whatsoever, is illegal : that it is a manifest intent to the breach of the peace, and they may be proceeded against by law for an illegal thing. Suppose now that this thing is not scandalous, what then ? If there had been no reflection in this book at all, yet it is *illicite*, and the author ought to be convicted for it. And that is for a public notice to all people, and especially printers and booksellers, that they ought to print no book or pamphlet of news whatsoever, without authority. So as he is to be convicted for it as a thing *illicite* done, not having authority. And I will assure you, if you find any of those papers, I shall be more merciful in the consideration of their punishment, if it be inoffensive. But if so be they will undertake to print news foolishly, they ought to be punished, and shall be punished if they do it without authority, though there is nothing reflecting on the government as an unlawful thing. . . . Therefore this book, if it be made by him to be published, it is unlawful, whether it be malicious or not. . . . If you find him guilty, and say what he is guilty of, we will judge whether the thing imports malice or no. . . . Now there only remains one thing, that is, Whether or no he was the publisher of this book ? . . . If you are satisfied in your consciences that you believe he is not the author, you must acquit him. If you are satisfied it is not he, you must find him Not guilty. . . .

[The Jury went from the bar and nigh an hour after returned, and brought him in Guilty.]

[*S.T.*, vii, 1126.]

V

QUO WARRANTO : TO THE CHARTERS OF THE CITY OF LONDON, 1681-83 [1]

[An information by *Quo Warranto* was brought against the City on two grounds : (i) the City had exceeded its powers by imposing a toll on certain goods sold in the City Markets, and (ii) the Common Council was guilty of a misdemeanour in petitioning the King in 1679. The object of the Crown in bringing this and many other actions against the boroughs was the forfeiture of Charters and the grant of new instruments by which the Crown could exercise control over the Borough officers.]

[1] See Sect. A, No. XXVII, p. 75, and Sect. D, Nos. XII, XIII, pp. 332-39, and XVII, p. 347.

IN THE COURT OF KING'S BENCH

SAUNDERS, *L.C.J.*: But this is one thing, Mr. Pollexfen, that I would say to you upon your argument, what a grievous thing would it be, if so be, the being of a corporation might be forfeited or dissolved, because say you, it is possible that all the corporations in England may be dissolved because they have committed such things that may be forfeitures. We must put the scales equal on both sides. Let us then consider the other side, whether, if so be that it should be taken for law, that a corporation is indissoluble or cannot be dissolved for any crime whatsoever, then those two things do not follow; First, you will shut out the king's Quo Warranto, let him have what reason he can for it, or let them do what they will: And in the next place, you have set up so many independent commonwealths. For if a corporation may do nothing amiss whatsoever, what else does follow, for now I am not upon the point whether this corporation has done any act that is amiss, but considering your argument in general, when you make it a thing of such ill consequence that a corporation should be forfeited by any crime; but I say now, to put in the other scale the mischiefs that would follow, if so be by law a corporation might not be dissolved for one fault or another: But let them do what they would, it should still remain a corporation. Then it is plain, they are so many commonwealths independent upon the king, and the king's Quo Warranto is quite shut out, that is mighty considerable. For a man to make an argument and to say it would be very mischievous, inconvenient, or worse to the city of London, if a judgment should be given against it, is not to govern us . . . what we are to look at principally is what the law is, for that way the law goes, we must go . . . and that the way the law has settled has the least inconvenience in it. . . .

Jones, J. We are all unanimously agreed in one and the same opinion in this whole matter. . . . First, Then as to the great preliminary point, Whether a corporation aggregate such as the city is, may be forfeited or seized into the king's hands. We are of opinion that it may, upon breach of that condition which the law annexes to it which is a trust for the good government of the King's subjects. . . . And this seems evident beyond all contradiction . . . by the statute of 28 Edward III. cap. 10. . . . And as to a forfeiture it seems to me plain, by the general act of oblivion, by which all bodies corporate and politic as well as persons natural are pardoned. . . . It is likewise plain by the very act for regulating corporations . . . And if the law should be otherwise it would erect as many independent republics in the kingdom as there are corporations aggregate, which, how fatal that might prove to the crown and the government now established, every man may easily conceive. To the Second point, we are of opinion that the assuming a power by the mayor, commonalty and citizens of London, to make by-laws, to levy money upon the subject, and the levying vast sums of money thereby is a great oppression upon the people . . . and so a just cause of forfeiture. Thirdly, We are of opinion, that the charge touching the ordering, exhibiting and printing the Petition, so scandalous to the king and government, so dangerously tending to the seduction of his subjects, to a dislike of his person and government, and so evidently tending to sedition thereby and rebellion, is another just cause of forfeiture. Fourthly; we are of opinion, that these acts are the acts of the corporation, being so alleged by the replication, and not sufficiently answered by the rejoinder. . . . And it is the judgment of this Court : That the franchise and liberty of London be taken into the king's hands. . . . And it is the opinion of the whole Court.

[*S.T.*, viii, 1039.]

VI

GODDEN *v.* HALES, 1686

[Hales, already a Colonel, became a Roman Catholic in 1685. James II, by letters patent under the Great Seal, dispensed him from the obligations imposed by 25 Car. II, c. 2. By a collusive action he was convicted at the Assizes : but on appeal it was held that the royal dispensation was a bar to the action.]

IN THE COURT OF KING'S BENCH

HERBERT, L.C.J. : This is a case of great consequence, but of as little difficulty as ever any case was, that raised so great an expectation : for if the king cannot dispense with this statute he cannot dispense with any penal law whatsoever.

As to the first point. . . .

As to the second point, whether the king can dispense with the act or no, I think it a question of little difficulty. There is no law whatsoever but may be dispensed with by the supreme lawgiver ; as the laws of God may be dispensed with by God himself ; as it appears by God's command to Abraham, to offer up his son Isaac : So likewise the law of man may be dispensed with by the legislator, for a law may either be too wide or too narrow, and there may be many cases which may be out of the conveniencies which did induce the law to be made ; for it is impossible for the wisest lawmaker to foresee all the cases that may be, or are to be remedied, and therefore there must be a power somewhere, able to dispense with these laws. But as to the case of simony, that is objected by the other side, that is against the law of God, and a special offence, and therefore *malum in se*, which I do agree the king cannot dispense with. And as to the cases of usury and non-residence, those cases do come in under that rule, that the king cannot dispense with them, because the subject has a benefit by them ; for in case of usury the bond is made void by the statute, and therefore if the king should dispense with it, the subject would lose the benefit of the avoiding the bond. And as to the cases of buying and selling of offices, which are objected, there is no need of resolving, whether the king could dispense with that statute or no, because the party was disabled to take any such office by the contract, and the disability was attacked by force before the office was vested, so that the king could not remove the disability ; and so I do agree that it would have been in this case, if the defendant had by his neglect or refusal to take the oaths, rendered himself incapable before he had taken the king's dispensation ; for the king's dispensation coming before the disability attacked, it does prevent it. . . .

On Monday the 21st of June, after having consulted with all the judges, his lordship delivered their opinions in open court, thus :

" In the case of Godden and Hales, wherein the defendant pleads a dispensation from the king ; it is doubted, whether or no the king had such a prerogative ? Truly, upon the argument before us, it appeared as clear a case as ever came before this court : but because men fancy I know not what difficulty, when really there is none, we were willing to give so much countenance to the question in the case, as to take the advice of all the judges of England. They were all assembled at Serjeant's-Inn, and this case was put to them ; and the great case of the sheriffs was put, whether the dispensation in that case were legal ? because upon that depended the execution of all the law of the nation : and I must tell you, that there were ten upon the place, that clearly delivered their opinions, That the case of the sheriffs [1] was good law ; and that all the attainders grounded upon indictments found by juries returned by such sheriffs, were good, and not erroneous ; and consequently that men need not have any fears or scruples about that matter. And in the next place, they did clearly declare, that there was no imaginable difference between that case and this ; unless it were, that this were the much clearer case of the two, and liable to the fewer exceptions.

" My brother Powell said, he was inclined to be of the same opinion ; but he would rather have some more time to consider of

---

[1] In 1487 it was held that the King could dispense with the statutory limitation to one year of the tenure of office by a Sheriff. See Holdsworth, iv, 205.

it : but he has since sent by my brother Holloway, to let us know, that he does concur with us.   To these eleven judges there is one dissenter, brother Street, who yet continues his opinion, That the king cannot dispense in this case : but that's the opinion of one single judge, against the opinion of eleven.   We were satisfied in our judgments before, and having the concurrence of eleven out of twelve, we think we may well declare the opinion of the court to be, that the king may dispense in this case : and the judges go upon these grounds ;

" 1. That the kings of England are sovereign princes.

" 2. That the laws of England are the king's laws.

" 3. That therefore 'tis an inseparable prerogative in the kings of England, to dispense with penal laws in particular cases, and upon particular necessary reasons.

" 4. That of those reasons and these necessities, the king himself is sole judge : and then, which is consequent upon all,

" 5. That this is not a trust invested in, or granted to the king by the people, but the ancient remains of the sovereign power and prerogative of the kings of England ; which never yet was taken from them, nor can be.   And therefore such a dispensation appearing upon record to come time enough to save him from the forfeiture, judgment ought to be given for the defendant."

[*S.T.*, xi, 1195.]

VII

THE SEVEN BISHOPS' CASE,[1] 1688

In the Court of King's Bench

Serj. *Levinz* (for the defence).   Now, my lord, if your lordship pleases, the charge is a charge for a libel, and there are two things to be considered.

First, Whether the bishops did deliver this paper to the king ? But that we leave upon the evidence that has been given ; only we say, there has been no direct proof of that.

In the next place, supposing they did deliver this petition to the king, Whether this be a libel upon the matter of it, the manner of delivering it, or the persons that did it ?

And with submission, my lord, this cannot be a libel, although it be true that they did so deliver it.

First, my lord, there is little disingenuity offered to my lords the bishops, in only setting forth part, and not the whole ; in only reciting the body, and not the prayer.

But, my lord, with your lordship's favour, taking the petitionary

[1] See Sect. C, No. XV (B), p. 291, and Sect. D, No. XVI, p. 343.

part, and adding it to the other, it quite alters the nature of the thing; for it may be, a complaint without seeking redress might be an ill matter; but here taking the whole together, it appears to be a complaint of a grievance, and a desire to be eased of it.

With your lordship's favour, the subjects have a right to petition the king in all their grievances, so say all our books of law, and so says the statute [1] of the thirteenth of the late king; they may petition, and come and deliver their petition under the number of ten, as heretofore they might have done, says the statute; so that they all times have had a right so to do, and indeed if they had not, it were the most lamentable thing in the world, that men must have grievances upon them, and yet they not to be admitted to seek relief in an humble way.

Now, my lord, this is a petition setting forth a grievance, and praying his majesty to give relief. And what is this grievance? It is that command of his, by that order made upon my lords the bishops, to distribute the declaration, and cause it to be read in the churches: and pray, my lord, let us consider what the effects and consequences of that distribution and reading is: it is to tell the people, that they need not submit to the Act of Uniformity, nor to any act of parliament made about ecclesiastical matters, for they are suspended and dispensed with. This my lords the bishops must do, if they obey this order; but your lordship sees, if they do it, they lie under an Anathema by the statute of 1 Eliz., for there they are under a curse if they do not look to the preservation and observation of that act: but this command to distribute and read the declaration, whereby all these laws are dispensed with, is to let the people know, they will not do what the act requires of them.

Now, with your lordship's favour, my lords the bishops lying under this pressure, the weight of which was very grievous upon them, they by petition apply to the king to be eased of it, which they might do as subjects: besides, my lord, they are peers of the realm, and were most of them sitting as such in the last parliament, where, as you have heard, it was declared, such a dispensation could not be; and then in what a case should they have been, if they should have distributed this declaration,[2] which was so contrary to their actings in parliament? What could they have answered for themselves, had they thus contributed to this declaration, when they had themselves before declared, that the king could not dispense?

And that this was no new thing, for it had been so declared in a parliament before, in two sessions of it, in the late king's reign within a very little time one of another; and such a parliament that were

[1] Sect. A, No. V, p. 9.
[2] James II's Second Declaration of Indulgence, cf. Sect. D, No. XVI, p. 343.

so liberal in their aids to the crown, that a man would not think they should go about to deprive the crown of any of its rights. It was a parliament that did do as great services for the crown as ever any did, and therefore there is no reason to suspect, that if the king had had such a power, they would have appeared so earnest against it.

But, my lord, if your lordship pleases, these are not the beginnings of this matter ; for we have shewed you from the fifteenth of Richard the second, that there was a power granted by the parliament to the king to dispense with a particular act of parliament, which argues, that it could not be without an act of parliament : and in 1662, it is said expressly, that they could not be dispensed with but by an act of parliament. It is said so again in 1672.[1] The king was then pleased to assume to himself such a power as is pretended to in this declaration ; yet upon information from his houses of parliament, the king declared himself satisfied that he had no such power, cancelled his declaration, and promised that it should not be drawn into consequence or example. And so the Commons, by their protestation, said in Richard the second's time, that it was a novelty, and should not be drawn into consequence or example.

Now, my lord, if your lordship pleases, if this matter that was commanded the bishops to do, were something which the law did not allow of, surely then my lords the bishops had all the reason in the world to apply themselves to the king, in an humble manner to acquaint him why they could not obey his commands : and to seek relief against that which lay so heavy upon them.

Truly, my lord, Mr. Attorney was very right in the opening of the cause at first, that is, That the government ought not to receive affronts, no, nor the inferior officers are not to be affronted ; a justice of the peace, so low a man in office, is not. For a man to say to a justice of the peace, when he is executing his office, that he does not right in it, is a great crime, and Mr. Attorney said right in it : but suppose a justice of the peace were making of a warrant to a constable, to do something that was not legal for him to do, if the constable should petition this justice of the peace, and therein set forth, Sir, you are about to command me to do a thing which, I conceive, is not legal ; surely that would not be a crime that he was to be punished for : for he does but seek relief, and shew his grievance in a proper way, and the distress he is under.

My lord, this is the bishops' case with submission ; they are under a distress being commanded to do a thing which they take not to be legal, and they with all humility, by way of petition acquaint the king with this distress of theirs, and pray him, that he will please to give relief.

[1] See Sect. B, No. IV, p. 163. (The date is Feb. 14, 1673, not as here stated 1672.)

My lord, there is no law but is either an act of parliament, or the common law ; for an act of parliament there is none for such a power ; all that we have of it in parliamentary proceedings is against it ; and for the common law, so far as I have read it, I never did meet with anything of such a nature, as a grant or dispensation that pretended to dispense with any one whole act of parliament ; I have not so much as heard of any such thing mentioned by any of the king's counsel ; but here, my lord, is a dispensation that dispenses with a great many laws at once, truly I cannot take upon me to tell how many, there may be forty or above, for aught I know.

Therefore, my lord, the bishops lying under such a grievance as this, and under such a pressure, being ordered to distribute this declaration in all their churches, which was to tell the people they ought to be under no law in this case, which surely was a very great pressure, both in point of law and conscience too, they lying under such obligations to the contrary as they did ; with submission to your lordship, and you gentlemen of the jury, if they did deliver this petition (publishing of it I will not talk of, for there has been no proof of a publication, but a delivering of a petition [1] to his majesty in the most secret and decent manner that could be imagined), my lords the bishops are not guilty of the matter charged upon them in this information. . . .

Mr. Somers. My lord, I would only mention the great case of Thomas and Sorrel in the Exchequer-chamber, upon the validity of a dispensation of the statute of Edward the 6th, touching selling of wine. There it was the opinion of every one of the judges, and they did lay it down as a settled position, that there never could be an abrogation, or a suspension (which is a temporary abrogation) of an act of parliament, but by the legislative power. That was a foundation laid down quite through the debate of that case. Indeed it was disputed how far the king might dispense with the penalties in such a particular law, as to particular persons ; but it was agreed by all, that the king had no power to suspend any law : and, my lord, I dare appeal to Mr. Attorney General himself, whether, in the case of Godden and Hales, which was lately in this court, to make good that dispensation, he did not use it as an argument then, that it could not be expounded into a suspension : he admitted it not to be in the king's power to suspend a law, but that he might give a dispensation to a particular person, was all that he took upon to justify him at that time.

My lord, by the law of all civilised nations, if the prince does require something to be done, which the person who is to do it takes it to be unlawful, it is not only lawful, but his duty, *rescribere principi.* This is all that is done here, and that in the most humble

[1] See Sect. A, No. V, p. 9.

manner that could be thought of. Your lordship will please to observe how far it went, how careful they were that they might not any way justly offend the king ; they did not interpose by giving advice, as peers ; they never stirred till it was brought home to themselves. When they made their petition, all they beg is, that it may not so far be insisted upon by his majesty, as to oblige them to read it. Whatever they thought of it, they do not take upon them to desire the declaration to be revoked.

My lord, as to matters of fact alleged in the said petition, that they are perfectly true, we have shewn by the journals of both houses. In every one of those years which are mentioned in the petition, this power of dispensation was considered in parliament, and, upon debate, declared to be contrary to law : there could be no design to diminish the prerogative, because the king hath no such prerogative. Seditious, my lord it could not be, nor could possibly stir up sedition in the minds of the people, because it was presented to the king in private and alone : false it could not be, because the matter of it is true : there could be nothing of malice, for the occasion was not sought : the thing was pressed upon them ; and a libel it could not be, because the intent was innocent, and they kept within the bounds set by the act of parliament, that gives the subject leave to apply to his prince by petition, when he is aggrieved. . . .

The Solicitor-General, for the Crown. . . . Then, my lord, let us take this case as it is, upon the nature of the petition, and the evidence that they have given, and then consider whether it will justify all that is done : for the business of petitioning, I would distinguish and inquire, whether my lords the bishops out of parliament can present any petition to the king ? I do agree, that in parliament the lords and commons may make addresses to the king, and signify their desires, and make known their grievances there ; and there is no doubt but that is a natural and proper way of application : for in the beginning of the parliament, there are receivers of petitions appointed, and upon debates, there are committees appointed to draw up petitions and addresses ; but to come and deduce an argument, that because the lords in parliament have done thus (there being such methods of proceedings usual in parliament) therefore my lords the bishops may do it out of parliament, that is certainly a *non sequitur*, no such conclusion can be drawn, from those premises.

My lord, I shall endeavour to lay the fact before you as it really is, and then consider what is proper for the court to take notice of as legal proof or evidence : and I take it, all those precedents that they have produced of what the lords did, and what the commons did in parliament, is no warrant for them to shelter themselves under, against the information here in question.

[Here Mr. Justice Powell spoke aside to the Lord Chief Justice thus.]

Mr. Just. Powell. My Lord, this is strange doctrine! Shall not the subject have liberty to petition the king but in parliament? If that be law, the subject is in a miserable case.

L.C.J. Brother, let him go on, we will hear him out, though I approve not of his position.

Sol. Gen. The Lords may address to the king in parliament, and the commons may do it, but therefore that the bishops may do it out of parliament, does not follow. . . .

I dare say it will not be denied me, that the king may, by his prerogative royal, issue forth his proclamation; it is as essential a prerogative as it is to give his assent to an act of parliament to make it a law. And it is another principle, which I think cannot be denied, that the king may make constitutions and orders in matters ecclesiastical; and that these he may make out of parliament, and without the parliament. If the king may do so, and these are his prerogatives, then suppose the king do issue forth his royal proclamation (and such in effect is this declaration under the great seal) in a matter ecclesiastical, by virtue of his prerogative royal; and this declaration is read in the council, and published to the world, and then the bishops come and tell the king, Sir, you have issued out an illegal proclamation or declaration, being contrary to what has been declared in parliament, when there is no declaration in parliament; is not this a diminishing the king's power and prerogative in issuing forth his proclamation or declaration, and making constitutions in matters ecclesiastical? Is not this a questioning his prerogative? Do not my lords the bishops in this case raise a question between the king and the people? Do not they, as much as in them lies, stir up the people to sedition? For who shall be judge between the king and the bishops? Says the king, I have such a power and prerogative to issue forth my royal proclamation, and to make orders and constitutions in manners ecclesiastical, and that without the parliament, and out of parliament. Say my lords the bishops, you have done so, but you have no warrant for it. Says the king, every prince has done it, and I have done no more than what is my prerogative to do. But this, say the bishops, is against law. How shall this be tried? Should not the bishops have had the patience to have waited until a parliament came and complained there, and sought redress. The question in this case is not whether the king may dispense with the law, but whether he may issue out his proclamation in matters ecclesiastical. . . .

Now my lord, I come to that which is very plain from the case of De Libellis Famosis,[1] in lord Coke's Reports: if any person have slandered the government in writing, you are [? not] to examine the

[1] In 1606. See Holdsworth, v, 208.

truth of that fact in such writing, but the slander which it imports to the king or government ; and be it never so true, yet if slanderous to the king or the government, it is a libel, and to be punished : in that case, the right or wrong is not to be examined, or if what was done by the government be legal or no ; but whether the party have done such an act.   If the king have a power (for still I keep to that) to issue forth proclamations to his subjects, and to make orders and constitutions in matters ecclesiastical, if he do issue forth his proclamation, and make an order upon the matters within his power and prerogative ; and if any one would come and bring that power in question otherwise than in parliament, that the matter of that proclamation be not legal, I say that is sedition, and you are not to examine the legality or illegality of the order or proclamation, but the slander and reflexion upon the government, and that, I think, is very plain upon that case, in the fifth Report De Libellis Famosis : for it says, If a person do a thing that is libellous, you shall not examine the fact, but the consequence of it ; whether it tended to stir up sedition against the public, or to stir up strife between man and man, in the case of private persons : as if a man should say of a judge, he has taken a bribe, and I will prove it ; this is not to be sent in a letter, but they must take a regular way to prosecute it according to law.

If it be so in the case of an inferior magistrate, what must it be in the case of a king ?   To come to the king's face, and tell him, as they do here, that he has acted illegally, doth certainly sufficiently prove the matter to be libellous.   What do they say to the king ? They say and admit, that they have an averseness for the declaration, and they tell him from whence that averseness doth proceed : and yet they insinuate that they had an inclination to gratify the king, and embrace the dissenters, that they were averse to them as could be, with due tenderness, when it should be settled by parliament and convocation.   Pray what hath their convocation to do in this matter?

L.C.J.   Mr. Solicitor General, I will not interrupt you ; but pray come to the business before us.   Shew us that this is in diminution of the king's prerogative, or that the king ever had such a prerogative.

Sol. Gen.   I will, my lord, I am observing what it is they say in this petition—They tell the king it is inconsistent with their honour, prudence and conscience, to do what he would have them to do : And if these things be not reflective upon the king and government, I know not what is.   This is not in a way of judicature ; possibly it might have been allowed to petition the king to put it into a course of justice, whereby it may be tried ; but alas ! there is no such thing in this matter.

It is not their desire to put it into any method for trial, and so it comes in the case de Libellis Famosis ; for by this way they make themselves judges, which no man by law is permitted to do. My lords the bishops have gone out of the way, and all that they have offered does not come home to justify them ; and therefore I take it, under favour, that we have made it a good case for the king : We have proved what they have done, and whether this be warrantable or not, is the question, gentlemen, that you are to try. The whole case appears upon record ; the declaration and petition are set forth, and the order of the king and council. When the verdict is brought in, they may move anything what they please in arrest of judgment. They have had a great deal of latitude, and taken a great deal of liberty ; but truly, I apprehend, not so very pertinently. But I hope we have made a very good case of it for the king, and that you, gentlemen, will give us a verdict.

Just. *Holloway*. Mr. Solicitor, there is one thing I would fain be satisfied in : You say the bishops have no power to petition the king.

Sol. Gen. Not out of parliament, Sir.

Just. *Holloway*. Pray give me leave, Sir : Then the king having made such a declaration of a general toleration and liberty of conscience, and afterwards he comes and requires the bishops to disperse this declaration ; this, they say, out of a tenderness of conscience, they cannot do, because they apprehend it is contrary to law, and contrary to their function : What can they do, if they may not petition ?

Sol. Gen. I'll tell you what they should have done, Sir. If they were commanded to do anything against their consciences, they should have acquiesced till the meeting of the parliament. [At which some people in the court hissed.] . . .

Wright, L.C.J. Gentlemen, thus stands the case : it is an information against my lords the bishops, his grace my lord of Canterbury, and the other six noble lords ; and it is for preferring, composing, making, and publishing, and causing to be published, a seditious libel : the way that the information goes is special, and it sets forth, that the king was graciously pleased, by his royal power and prerogative, to set forth a declaration of indulgence for liberty of conscience, in the third year of his reign ; and afterwards upon the 27th of April, in the fourth year he comes and makes another declaration ; and afterwards in May, orders in council that this declaration should be published by my lords the bishops in their several dioceses ; and after this was done, my lords the bishops come and present a petition to the king in which were contained the words which you have seen.

Now, gentlemen, the proofs that have been upon this, you will see what they are. The two declarations are proved by the clerks of the council, and they are brought here under the great seal. . . .

The next question that did arise was about the publishing of it, whether my lords the bishops had published it ? . . .

Gentlemen, after this was proved, then the defendants came to their part ; and these gentlemen that were of counsel for my lords, let themselves into their defence, by notable learned speeches, by telling you that my lords the bishops are guardians to the church, and great peers of the realm, and were bound in conscience to take care of the church. They have read you a clause of a statute made in queen Elizabeth's time, by which they say, my lords the bishops were under a curse, if they did not take care of that law : . . . Then they shew you some journals of parliament; first in the year 1662, where the king had granted an indulgence, and the house of commons declared it was not fit to be done, unless it were by act of parliament : . . . and so likewise that in 1672, which is all nothing but addresses, or orders of the house, or discourses . . . what is a declaration in parliament is a law, and that must be by the king, lords, and commons ; . . . but a vote of the house . . . cannot be said to be a declaration in parliament. Then they come to that in 1685, where the commons take notice of something about the soldiers in the army that had not taken the test, and make an address to the king about it : but in all these things (as far as I can observe) nothing can be gathered out of them one way or the other ; it is nothing but discourses. Sometimes this dispensing power has been allowed, as in Richard the 2nd's time, and sometimes it has been denied, and the king did once waive it ; Mr. Solicitor tells you the reason, there was a lump of money in the case ; but I wonder indeed to hear it come from him.

Sol. Gen.   My lord, I never gave my vote for money, I assure you.

L.C.J.   But those concessions which the king sometimes makes for the good of the people, and sometimes for the profit of the prince himself (but I would not be thought to distinguish between the profit of the prince and the good of the people, for they are both one ; and what is the profit of the prince is always for the good of the people), but I say, those concessions must not be made law, for that is reserved in the king's breast, to do what he pleases in it at any time.

The truth of it is, the dispensing power is out of the case, it is only a word used in the petition ; but truly, I will not take upon me to give my opinion in the question, to determine that now, for it is not before me : the only question before me is, and so it is before you, gentlemen, it being a question of fact, whether here be a certain proof of a publication? And then the next question is a question of law indeed, whether, if there be a publication proved, it be a libel?

Gentlemen, upon the point of the publication, I have summed up all the evidence to you; and if you believe that the petition which these lords presented to the king was this petition, truly, I think, that is a publication sufficient: if you do not believe it was this petition, then my lords the bishops are not guilty of what is laid to their charge in this information, and consequently there needs no inquiry whether they are guilty of a libel? but if you do believe that this was the petition they presented to the king, then we must come to inquire whether this be a libel.

Now, gentlemen, any thing that shall disturb the government, or make mischief and a stir among the people, is certainly within the case of " Libellis Famosis "; and I must in short give you my opinion, I do take it to be a libel. Now, this being a point of law, if my brothers have anything to say to it, I suppose they will deliver their opinions.

Just. *Holloway*. Look you, gentlemen, it is not usual for any person to say anything after the Chief Justice has summed up the evidence; it is not according to the course of the court: but this is a case of an extraordinary nature, and there being a point of law in it, it is very fit that everybody should deliver their own opinion. The question is, Whether this petition of my lords the bishops be a libel or no. Gentlemen, the end and intention of every action is to be considered; and likewise, in this case, we are to consider the nature of the offence that these noble persons are charged with; it is for delivering a petition, which, according as they have made their defence, was with all the humility and decency that could be: so that if there was no ill intent, and they were not (as it is not, nor can be pretended they were) men of evil lives, or the like, to deliver a petition cannot be a fault, it being the right of every subject to petition. If you are satisfied there was an ill intention of sedition, or the like, you ought to find them guilty: but if there be nothing in the case that you find, but only that they did deliver a petition to save themselves harmless, and to free themselves from blame, by shewing the reason of their disobedience to the king's command, which they apprehended to be a grievance to them, and which they could not in conscience give obedience to, I cannot think it is a libel: it is left to you, gentlemen, but that is my opinion.

L.C.J. Look you, by the way, brother, I did not ask you to sum up the evidence (for that is not usual) but only to deliver your opinion, whether it be a libel or no.[1]

[1] See Vol. II, Sect. A, No. IV, p. 6.

Just. *Powell.* Truly I cannot see, for my part, any thing of sedition, or any other crime, fixed upon these reverend fathers, my lords the bishops.

For, gentlemen, to make it a libel, it must be false, it must be malicious, and it must tend to sedition. As to the falsehood, I see nothing that is offered by the king's counsel, nor any thing as to the malice : It was presented with all the humility and decency that became the king's subjects to approach their prince with.

Now, gentlemen, the matter of it is before you ; you are to consider of it, and it is worth your consideration. They tell his majesty, it is not out of averseness to pay all due obedience to the king, nor out of a want of tenderness to their dissenting fellow subjects, that made them not perform the command imposed upon them ; but they say, because they do conceive that the thing that was commanded them was against the law of the land, therefore they do desire his majesty, that he would be pleased to forbear to insist upon it, that they should perform that which they take to be illegal.

Gentlemen, we must consider what they say is illegal in it. They say, they apprehend the declaration is illegal, because it is founded upon a dispensing power, which the king claims, to dispense with the laws concerning ecclesiastical affairs.

Gentlemen, I do not remember, in any case in all our law (and I have taken some pains upon this occasion to look into it), that there is any such power in the king, and the case must turn upon that. In short, if there be no such dispensing power in the king, then that can be no libel which they presented to the king, which says, that the declaration, being founded upon such a pretended power, is illegal.

Now, gentlemen, this is a dispensation with a witness : it amounts to an abrogation and utter repeal of all the laws ; for I can see no difference, nor know of none in law, between the king's power to dispense with laws ecclesiastical, and his power to dispense with any other laws whatever. If this be once allowed of, there will need no parliament ; all the legislature will be in the king, which is a thing worth considering, and I leave the issue to God and your consciences.

Just. *Allybone.* The single question that falls to my share is, to give my sense of this petition, whether it shall be in construction of law a libel in itself, or a thing of great innocence. I shall endeavour to express myself in as plain terms as I can, and as much as I can, by way of proposition.

And I think, in the first place, that no man can take upon him to write against the actual exercise of the government, unless he have leave from the government, but he makes a libel, be what he writes true or false; for if once we come to impeach the government by way of argument, it is the argument that makes it the government or not the government. So that I lay down that, in the first place, the government ought not to be impeached by argument, nor the exercise of the government shaken by argument; because I can manage a proposition in itself doubtful, with a better pen than another man : this, say I, is a libel.

Then I lay down this for my next position, that no private man can take upon him to write concerning the government at all ; for what has any private man to do with the government, if his interest be not stirred or shaken ? It is the business of the government to manage matters relating to the government ; it is the business of subjects to mind only their own properties and interests. If my interest is not shaken, what have I to do with matters of government ? They are not within my sphere. If the government does come to shake my particular interest, the law is open for me, and I may redress myself by law : and when I intrude myself into other men's business that does not concern my particular interest, I am a libeller.

These I have laid down for plain propositions ; now then, let us consider further, whether, if I will take upon me to contradict the government, any specious pretence that I shall put upon it shall dress it up in another form, and give it a better denomination ? And truly I think it is the worse, because it comes in a better dress ; for by that rule, every man that can put on a good vizard, may be as mischievous as he will to the government at the bottom : so that whether it be in the form of a supplication, or an address, or a petition, if it be what it ought not to be, let us call it by its true name, and give it its right denomination—it is a libel.

Then, gentlemen, consider what this petition is : this is a petition relating to something that was done and ordered by the government. Whether the reasons of the petition be true or false, I will not examine that now, nor will I examine the prerogative of the crown, but only take notice that this relates to the act of the government. The government here has published such a declaration as this that has been read, relating to matters of government ; and shall, or ought anybody to come and impeach that as illegal, which the government has done ? Truly, in my opinion, I do not think he should, or ought : for by this rule may every act of the government be shaken, when there is not a parliament *de facto* sitting.

I do agree, that every man may petition the government, or the king, in a matter that relates to his own private interest, but to meddle with a matter that relates to the government, I do not think my lords the bishops had any power to do more than any others. When the house of lords and commons are in being, it is a proper way of applying to the king : there is all that openness in the world for those that are members of parliament, to make what addresses they please to the government, for the rectifying, altering, regulating, and making of what law they please ; but if every private man shall come and interpose his advice, I think there can never be an end of advising the government. I think there was an instance of this in king James' time, when by a solemn resolution it was declared to be a high misdemeanour, and next to treason, [to petition] the king to put the penal laws in execution.

Just. *Powell.* Brother, I think you do mistake a little.

Just. *Allybone.* Brother, I dare rely upon it that I am right : it was so declared by all the judges.

Sol. Gen. The Puritans presented a petition to that purpose, and in it they said, if it would not be granted, they would come with a great number.

Just. *Powell.* Aye, there it is.

Just. *Allybone.* I tell you, Mr. Solicitor, the resolution of the judges is, That such a petition is next door to treason, a very great misdemeanour.

Just. *Powell.* They accompanying it with threats of the people's being discontented.

Just. *Allybone.* As I remember . . . the resolution of the judges is, That to frame a petition to the king, to put the penal laws in execution, is next to treason ; for, say they, no man ought to intermeddle with matters of government without leave of the government.

Serj. *Pemberton.* That was a petition against the penal laws.

Just. *Allybone.* Then I am quite mistaken indeed, in case it be so.

Serj. *Trinder.* That is not material at all which it was.

Mr. *Pollexfen.* They there threatened, unless their request were granted, several thousands of the king's subjects would be discontented.

Just. *Powell.* That is the reason of that judgment, I affirm it.

Just. *Allybone.* But then I'll tell you, brother, again, what is said in that case that you hinted at, and put Mr. Solicitor in mind of ; for any man to raise a report that the king will or will not permit a toleration, if either of these be disagreeable to the people, whether he may or may not, it is against law ; for we are not to measure things from any truth they have in themselves, but from that aspect they have upon the government ; for there may be

every tittle of a libel true, and yet it may be a libel still : so that I
put no stress upon that objection, that the matter of it is not false ;
and for sedition, it is that which every libel carries in itself ; and as
every trespass implies *vi & armis*, so every libel against the government carries in it sedition, and all the other epithets that are in the
information. This is my opinion as to the law in general.[1] I will
not debate the prerogatives of the king, nor the privileges of the
subject ; but as this fact is, I think these venerable bishops did
meddle with that which did not belong to them : they took upon
them in a petitionary, to contradict the actual exercise of the government, which I think no particular persons, or singular body, may do.

[Verdict of the jury : Not Guilty, June 30, 1688.]
[*S.T.*, xii, 183-433.]

VIII

THE BANKERS' CASE, 1696–1700

(A)

IN THE EXCHEQUER-CHAMBER

LORD KEEPER SOMMERS : Robert Williamson comes before the
barons, and exhibits letters patent under the great seal, dated 30 April,
29 Car. 2 [1678], granting to sir Robert Vyner, his heirs and assigns,
the yearly rent or sum of 25,003£. 9s. 4d. to be yearly paid, received,
and taken, of the rents, revenues, and profits arising to the king, his
heirs and successors, out of the duty of excise, by virtue of the act[2]
made 12 Car. 24 for taking away the court of wards and liveries, &c,
and settling a revenue in lieu thereof ; and prays that these letters
patent may be inrolled of record.

The barons cause them to be read and inrolled ; and the letters
patent are set forth at large in the record.

The effect of them is :

The king takes notice, that he had been constrained to postpone
the payment of monies due to the goldsmiths, and others, upon
tallies and orders registered.

That he could not spare such a sum, as would satisfy those
debts ; but was willing to grant to the persons to whom he was
indebted, an annual sum answerable to the interest of their debts, after
the rate of 6£. per cent.

To that end he had commanded the accounts to be stated to the
first of January, 1676 ; whereupon there appeared due to sir Robert

[1] See Vol. II, Sect. C, No. I, especially Lord Mansfield's judgement,
p. 235. Also Vol. II, Sect. A, No. IV, p. 6.
[2] See Sect. A, No. II, § XIV, p. 5.

Vyner, 416,724£. 13s. 1½d.   In satisfaction whereof, the king resolved to grant him 25,003£. 9s. 4d. per annum. . . .

Then Williamson sets forth, that by virtue of the letters patent sir Robert Vyner was seized *ut de feodo et jure*, and was indebted unto him in 1,000£. And that the 9th of April, 32 Car. 2 [1680], by deed of assignment (which he brings into court) reciting that he had delivered up his securities to sir Robert Vyner, and had discharged him, the said sir Robert Vyner, grants and assigns to him and his heirs 60£. part of the said yearly sum, being his proportionable part, in satisfaction of the said debt, under the condition in the letters patent ; and prays the assignment may be read and inrolled ; which is ordered, and the tenor is entered. . . .

. . . and that the principal sum is not paid ; and that the arrears of the yearly sum of 60£. were paid to Lady-day 35 Car. 2, and that from that time 405£. is due for six years and three quarters, ending at Christmas last.   Then he prays the letters patent and assignment may be allowed, and the arrears paid, and the yearly sum paid for the future ; . . .

To this the Attorney General demurs ; and Williamson joins in demurrer.

Whereupon the barons of the exchequer give this judgment : that the letters patent to sir Robert Vyner, and the assignment to Williamson, 'juxta tenorem et effectum earundem eidem Roberto Williamson allocentur : ' and that the sum of 405£. being the arrears to and for Christmas 1 W. & M. so as aforesaid in arrear, be paid to him at the receipt of the exchequer, . . . And that the said yearly sum of 60£. from Christmas 1 W. & M. be paid to Williamson and his heirs, at the receipt of the exchequer, . . .

Upon this Judgment the Writ of Error is brought.

There have been two principal questions made in the arguments upon these cases.

1st.   Whether the grants, made by king Charles 2, of the several annual sums out of the hereditary excise,[1] to the goldsmiths, their heirs and assigns, be effectual in law, and do charge this revenue in the time of his successors ?

2dly.   Whether the remedies which the parties have pursued in this case be proper, and such as are warranted by law, or justified by the course of the court of exchequer ? . . .

The first general question has been divided, as well by the counsel at the bar, as by my lords the judges, who argued this case, into two points.

1st.   If this revenue of excise be such an inheritance, that the king could alien the whole, or any part of it, in perpetuity from the crown ?

---

[1] See Sect. A, No. II, § XIV, p. 5.

2dly. Admitting that he might, whether it be effectually done by the grants to the goldsmiths?

My lords the judges, who have argued these cases upon the writs of error, have all agreed in opinion, that the letters patent are good in law to pass an interest to the patentees and their heirs, and to bind king Charles 2, and his successors.

Mr. baron Lechmere was of another opinion in the court of exchequer. . . .

I shall not speak at all at this time to either part of the first question.

As to the second general question, whether this manner of suit, and the proceedings in it, be warranted by the course of the exchequer; so that the parties here can come immediately to the barons, and demand their annuities, and thereupon the barons by their judgment, can in a regular course prescribe to the treasurer and chamberlains to issue money out of the receipt?—this is what I cannot hitherto be convinced of, either by what I have heard in the debate of this matter, or by what I have been able to observe upon the best endeavours I could use to inform myself, in which I have spared no pains.

I take this to be a point of as great moment as ever came to be discussed in Westminster-hall: not so much in respect of the value of what is in demand, and of what does depend upon the same question, (though that amounts to about 42,385£. 17s. 6d. per annum, besides the arrears;) as because it does in so high a degree concern the government, and disposal of the public revenue, and the treasure of the crown; whereof the law has always had a superlative care, as that upon which the safety of the king and kingdom must, in all ages, depend. . . .

No man can be more tender of property, and careful to preserve it than I have always, and always shall be: but I freely own, that we, who are concerned in judicature in this reign, ought to ascribe less merit to ourselves for our care of property, than most of those who went before us. We run no hazard in doing of it: no man has cause to think he shall be ill looked upon for giving his judgment for the subject according to law, though it be against the interest of the crown. . . .

But I think the word property could hardly be brought into any case less aptly than it is into this.

There has been no difference of opinion, as to the interest and property which the subject takes by the letters patent, amongst the judges who have argued in this court.

We are all agreed that the subject has, in this case, all the same remedies for recovering his right, which in any such case the common law of England did ever allow, or which are given to him by any statute ; so that the subject is as safe in his property, and as secure in the method of coming at it, if it be detained from him, as by the English constitution he ought to be.

The only question is, whether this be such a remedy as the law allows, for recovering from the king the arrears, and growing payments of the annual sums in question ?

If it be not, I am sure none of us ought to make the parties case better than the law has made it. We must judge of property according to the rules which the law has fixed, and can make no new ones, nor invent new remedies, however compassionate the case may appear, or however popular it may seem to attempt it.

The question then is, if an annual sum be granted by the king, under the great seal, out of any branch of the revenue, to a subject and his heirs, in the manner of these grants, and the annual payments happen to be in arrear ; whether by any law, now in force, the party may come to the barons of the exchequer immediately, and they upon prayer to them, may inroll and allow the letters patent, and may thereupon order the treasurer and chamberlains to pay out of the Exchequer the arrears and also the growing payments for the future ?

I think it may be proper to premise, that we are not now speaking of the Exchequer in general, as it comprehends that great college of the revenue made up of all the officers of the upper and lower Exchequer ; nor of the jurisdiction of the Exchequer-chamber before the lord treasurer and chancellor ; nor of the court of equity before the treasurer, chancellor, and barons ; but only of the authority of the court of pleas holden before the barons : nor is the question now of the barons' power over the receivers, collectors, and other officers of the revenue ; but of their power over the king's treasure, when it is lodged in the receipt of the exchequer, and over the treasurer and chamberlains, in whose custody it is.

In speaking to this matter, I shall proceed by these steps :

First, to observe that no authors ancient or modern, who have wrote of the jurisdiction and business of the court of Exchequer, have mentioned any such power to be lodged in the barons of the Exchequer, as will be sufficient to warrant the judgments in these cases.

Secondly, that these judgments cannot be defended by any thing which I can find, upon the best search I can make, in any records or acts of parliament :

Nor 3rdly, by any authorities in our books. . . .

Having insisted thus far in shewing that I have met with nothing in the authors, who have wrote upon the jurisdiction of the Exchequer, or in the law books, or in the records, which countenance such a power as is assumed by the barons of the Exchequer in these cases; I shall mention a fourth thing which confirms my opinion, viz. that in the oath of the barons, there is nothing expressed which does relate to any such trust lodged in them.

And, perhaps, there is not a better measure to be taken of what is the natural and proper business of these antient officers, than what is compendiously and significantly expressed in the oaths, which have with great care and wisdom been formed and instituted for them to take. . . .

In the fifth place I shall observe, that to suppose a power lodged in the barons to issue writs requiring the lord treasurer, or the treasurer of the Exchequer to do their duty, is to suppose a direct absurdity in the original institution of the Exchequer; since it is to invest the barons, who are subordinate, with a right of commanding their superior officers. . . .

I have been too long already; but I will add one consideration more, which does arise from the inconvenience; no considerable argument in law: which is that if the king's treasure be so far subject to the administration of an ordinary court of justice, as that it must be regularly issued upon the application of the subject, who has a demand thereupon for an annuity, or any other debt, (for I do not see but the reason is the same :) this may turn to the weakening of the public safety to a very high degree.

The barons of the Exchequer cannot, as such, be conusant of the necessities of the state; and if they were, and knew them to be ever so pressing, they must act according to one rule; and must order a pension, granted upon no consideration, or perhaps, upon a very ill one, and for a pernicious end, to be paid with the very money, which ought to be employed, and possibly was provided by parliament, for suppressing a rebellion, or resisting an invasion, or setting out a fleet.

For they, as a court of justice, have no judgment of discretion allowed them: whenever the party comes to pray it, the grant must be inrolled and allowed, and the judgment given, and the writ go.

And what is the treasurer to do in such a case? Is he to obey the great or privy seal, which requires the money for the uses of the war, and the necessary defence of the realm; or the Exchequer seal, which requires it to be paid for the use of a private subject?

He would be under a great difficulty; especially if there be ground to think, that such a writ would be the foundation of an action against him, which if I did not misapprehend, was affirmed by one. . . .

It must be presumed the crown will pay its just debts. But to say the king is not to have the ordering the course of payments, when the money is in his own coffers, is to deny him that, which is in every subject's power. It is to take from him the judgment of public necessities, or, at least, the means of relieving them.

I have shewn the reasons for which I cannot give my opinion for the affirming of these judgments. But much the greater part of my lords the judges having delivered their opinions for the affirmance of them, I shall defer doing any thing further, till I hear the opinion of the judges upon the point referred to them,

' Whether, as this court is constituted, judgment ought to be given according to the opinion of the great number of the judges, who are called by the lord chancellor and lord treasurer to their assistance, notwithstanding they themselves are of a different opinion ? '

[*S.T.*, xiv, 39.]

(B)

HOLT'S JUDGEMENT IN EXCHEQUER CHAMBER [1]

Holt, C.J. In this case, here have been two points made :
1. Whether this grant be good
2. Whether here be a proper course taken by the patentees.

. . . As to the first question, I hold the grant to be good ; and all, that have argued here, have concurred in the same opinion. I do confess this is the great point of the case . . . I hold that King Charles 2 might change this branch of his revenue, and my reason for my opinion is but short. It is, because the king was seised of an estate in fee of this revenue ; for to such an estate a power of alienation is incident . . . I come now to the second point . . . And I hold they have taken a very proper and legal remedy. We are all agreed that they have a right ; and if so, then they must have some remedy to come at it too. The remedies at common law, to recover against the king, were by petition, or ' monstrans de droit ' . . . But first, a petition of right is not necessary in this case . . . for two reasons ; 1. Because a petition of right is grounded always upon a naked matter of fact suggested and not of record . . . But here the title is derived by letters patents which are of record . . . 2. The patentees do not endeavour to destroy the king's title : but petitions of right do so, and are generally inconsistent with the king's title . . . I take this remedy to be by a ' monstrans de droit ' ; and this remedy is to be sued at common law, when the party's title appeared of record . . . ' Monstrans de droit ', or

[1] This judgement, contrary to that of Sommers (above), was delivered before that of Sommers, but is printed in this place in order that the student may grasp the facts related by the Lord Keeper.

' ouster le maine ', (which is all one in effect) always lies where the title or right of the subject appears as well by matter of record as the king's title . . . Also it is plain, that a ' monstrans de droit ' lies in the Exchequer : I think there is no doubt of that.

. . . So that upon the whole I am of opinion that the Judgment given by the Barons ought to be affirmed

[S.T., xiv, 29.]

(C)

Afterwards, on Tuesday, November 24, 1696, the Lord Keeper came again into the Exchequer-chamber, and declared, That he had received a Paper from the lord chief justice Holt, containing the Opinion of the Judges upon the question referred to them : and that three Judges were of opinion, ' That the Lord Keeper was bound to give Judgment in these cases, according to opinions of the majority of the Judges by him called to his assistance : ' but that seven Judges were of opinion, ' That he was not bound by such a majority of opinions, but was at liberty to give judgment according to his own : ' and declared, ' That as to this question, he himself concurred in opinion with the seven Judges.' And accordingly pronounced Judgment, ' That the Judgments given in these causes, by the court of Exchequer, be reversed.' . . .

[S.T., xiv, 105.]

(D)

JUDGMENT OF REVERSAL REVERSED [1]

Whereas, by virtue of his majesty's writ of error, returnable into the House of Peers in parliament assembled, a record of the court of Exchequer was brought into this House, the 4th day of April, 1699, wherein a Judgment given by the barons of the said court, in Hilary term, 1691, for Robert Williamson, against his majesty's Attorney General, for the payment of an annual sum of 60 £. and the arrears thereof, out of the hereditary revenue of excise, was in Michaelmas term, 1696, reversed in the Exchequer chamber, by the Lord Keeper of the great seal of England, now Lord Chancellor :

After hearing counsel several days, to argue the errors assigned upon the said writ of error ; and due consideration of what was offered on either side ; It is this day ordered and adjudged, by the Lords spiritual and temporal in parliament assembled, That the

[1] The grounds of their Lordships' judgements were at that time not published.

said Judgment of Reversal shall be, and is hereby, reversed; and
that the said Judgment, given by the barons of the Exchequer for
the said Robert Williamson, shall be, and is hereby, affirmed.

[*S.T.*, xiv, 111.]

IX

ASHBY *v*. WHITE AND OTHERS,[1] 1704

[Ashby brought an action against White, Mayor of Aylesbury and
others for damages in refusing his vote at an election. Ashby was
successful and was awarded £5 damages. Holt alone gave a dissentient
judgement on a motion in Queen's Bench in arrest of judgement. The
judgement against Ashby in Queen's Bench was set aside by the
House of Lords.]

In the Court of Queen's Bench

HOLT, L.C.J. : The Case is truly stated, and the only question
is, whether or not, if a Burgess of a Borough that has an undoubted
right to give his vote for the chusing a Burgess of Parliament for
that Borough, is refused giving his vote, has he any remedy in the
King's Courts for this Wrong against the Wrong-doer ? All my
Brothers agree that he has no Remedy ; but I differ from them, for I
think the Action well maintainable, that the Plaintiff had a Right to
vote, and that in consequence thereof the Law gives him a Remedy,
if he is obstructed ; and this Action is the proper Remedy. By the
Common Law of England, every Commoner hath a Right not to be
subjected to Laws, made without their Consent ; and because it
cannot be given by every individual Man in Person, by Reason of
Number and Confusion, therefore that Power is lodged in the Representatives, elected by them for that purpose, who are either Knights,
Citizens or Burgesses : and the Grievance here is, that the Party not
being allowed his Vote, is not represented. The Election of Knights
of Shires is by Freeholders ; and a Freeholder has a Right to vote by
Reason of his Freehold, and it is a real Right. . . . In Boroughs . . .
they have a right of voting *Ratione Burgagii* and *Ratione Tenurae* ;
and this like the Case of a Freeholder before mentioned is a real
Right, annexed to the Tenure in Burgage. . . . This is a noble
Franchise and Right, which entitles the subject in a Share of the
Government and Legislature. And here the Plaintiff having this
Right, it is apparent that the Officer did exclude him from the
enjoyment of it, wherein none will say he has done well, but Wrong
to the Plaintiff ; and it is not at all material whether the Candidate,

[1] See Sect. B, No. XVII, p. 193, and also Vol. II, Sect. C, No. V, p. 247.

that he would have voted so, were chosen, or likely to be, for the Plaintiff's Right is the same, and being hindered of that, he has Injury done him, for which he ought to have Remedy. It is a vain Thing to imagine, there should be Right without a Remedy; for Want of Right and Want of Remedy are Convertibles:[1] If a Statute gives a Right, the Common Law will give Remedy to maintain it; and wherever there is Injury, it imposts a Damage. And there can be no Petition in this Case to the Parliament, nor can they judge of this Injury, or give Damages to the Plaintiff. And although this Matter relates to the Parliament, yet it is an injury precedaneous to the Parliament; and where Parliamentary Matters come before us, as incident to a Cause of Action concerning the Property of the Subject, which we in Duty must determine, though the Matter be Parliamentary, we must not be deterred, but are bound by our Oaths to determine it. The Law consists not in particular Instances, but in the Reason that rules them; and if where a Man is injured in one Sort of Right, he has a good Action, why shall he not have it in another? And though the House of Commons have Right to decide Elections, yet they cannot judge of the Charter originally, but secondarily in the Determination of the Election; and therefore where an Election does not come in Debate, as it doth not in this Case, they have nothing to do: and we are to exert and vindicate the Queen's Jurisdiction, and not to be frightened because it may come in Question in Parliament; and I know nothing to hinder us from judging of Matters depending on Charter or Prescription. He concluded for the Plaintiff.

[Holt's Reports: (ed. 1737), p. 524.]

X

CASE OF THE AYLESBURY MEN[2]

(A)

In the Court of Queen's Bench

[The five Aylesbury men, following the decision of the Lords in the case of Ashby, brought similar actions. They were thereupon committed to Newgate by the Commons for breach of privilege.]

Mr. Justice Powell. That this is a case of the highest consequence, for it concerns the privileges of the House of Commons, the liberty of the subject, and the jurisdiction of this court; it is the first case of this nature, for the lord Shaftesbury was a member of

[1] See Vol. II, Sect. C, No. XIX, at p. 305.
[2] See Sect. C, No. XIX, p. 311, and Vol. II, Sect. C, No. V, p. 247.

the House,[1] and there may be a greater jurisdiction in some cases over their own members, than over strangers ; however, they had not any authority upon the return, for they [the Aylesbury men] are committed by another law than we proceed by : and to be committed by one law, and to judge of the commitment here by another law, would be a strange thing : for the House do not commit by the authority of the common law, but by another law, ' Legem et Consuetudinem Parliamenti ' ; for there are in England several other laws, besides the common law, viz. the ecclesiastical law, the admiralty law, etc., and there is the law and customs of parliament, where they have particular laws and customs for their directions.

To state judicature will help to clear this case. The House of Lords have a power to judge by the common law, but not originally, but a dernier resort upon Writs of Error and Appeals ;[2] and for that reason it is provided by the constitution, for the judges to give their assistance, which they are bound to do. But they have another law, viz. ' Lex et Consuetudo Parliamenti,'[3] which the judges are not to assist in, or give any opinion ; and I dare say, the House of Lords would take it ill, should they meddle or advise therein, for they have their privileges in their own rolls and books.

That the Commons have also a judicature, not by the common law, but do judge of breaches of privileges, and contempts to their House, ' secundum Legem et Consuetudinem Parliamenti,' and by this law these persons are committed, and are now brought to be discharged by the common law. The Resolution of the Commons upon the breach of privileges is a judgement, and the commitment an execution of it, which cannot be controuled ; for this would be to draw it *ad aliud Examen*, and then the Commons would not be supreme judges of their own privileges.

That the Resolution in the House of Lords, in the case of Ashby and White, does not bind the House of Commons, nor determine their privileges ; for they judged of the privileges of the Commons as an incident to the action, and one court may judge of a matter within the jurisdiction of another court, when without it they cannot determine the case before them ; as this court may of admiralty, or ecclesiastical jurisdiction, if the question arises in an action depending in this court. But such a determination will not bind another court, which has an original cognizance of that matter, as in [a case] now depending in the Common Pleas . . . ; the

---

[1] See Sect. C, No. III, p. 251. ' House '=House of Lords.

[2] See Sect. B, No. V (H), p. 171.

[3] See also Sect. C, No. III, p. 251, and No. XIX, at p. 312, and Sect. B, No. XVII (A), at p. 194, No. XXXIII (G), at p. 234, and XXIV (B), at p. 237. Also Vol. II, Sect. C, No. V, p. 243, No. XI, at p. 268, and No. XIX, at p. 301.

question there is, If a Quaker's marriage be good? Now if it should be held in that court a void marriage, and the judgment should be affirmed in this court, and upon a Writ of Error in the House of Lords, it should be reversed, this would not bind the ecclesiastical court, but they might proceed there for incontinency; and if they should proceed there to excommunication, finding it a void marriage and the party taken by the *Excommunicato Capiendo* should bring his Habeas Corpus upon the return of it, we could not discharge him. But this [case we are deciding] is a matter originally arising in parliament.

That this court may keep other inferior courts within their jurisdictions, but not the House of Commons; for no prohibition was ever granted to that court, though they exceeded jurisdiction; so if the House of Lords do exceed, or take cognizance of matters in the first instance, no prohibition would lie; for no inferior court can prohibit a superior: and no prohibition was moved here, nor could we have granted it; for the House of Commons is superior to all ordinary Courts of law.

Lord Chief Just. Holt. That this case does depend upon the vote that is recited in the Speaker's Warrant of commitment, which was to this effect:

That it did appear to that honourable House, that John Paty of Aylesbury has been guilty of commencing and prosecuting an action at common law, against W. White and others, late constables of Aylesbury, for not allowing his vote in an election of members to serve in parliament, contrary to the declaration, in high contempt of the jurisdiction, and in breach of the known privileges of this House.

That he owned himself to lie under two disadvantages: one, That all the rest of the judges do agree with his three brethren, from whom he had the misfortune to dissent. The other, That he opposed the votes of the House of Commons, and did begin to think he might justify himself in resigning his opinion to the rest; but that he valued more the dictates of his own conscience, than anything he could suffer in this world, and by that and his judgement (though it were but weak) he would be guided.

That this was not such an imprisonment as the freemen of England ought to be bound by. And that it did highly concern the people of England, not to be bound by a declaration of the House of Commons in a matter that before was lawful.

That neither House of Parliament has a power separately to dispose of the liberty or property of the people, for that cannot be done but by the Queen, Lords, and Commons; and this is the security of our English constitution, which cannot be altered but by act of parliament.

That there is a crime charged by the vote for commencing an action ; but sure that cannot be a breach of privilege, for an original may be filed against a member of parliament during the time of privilege, so that you do not molest him, and it is no breach of privilege : . . . for otherwise, by lapse of time in several actions, he may be barred by the statute of limitations ; so that if it be not a breach of privilege to commence an action against a member of parliament, then how can it be so to commence an action against the constable of Aylesbury ?

But then the vote goes further, and says, for commencing and prosecuting an action : but prosecuting may not be a breach of privilege neither ; for entering and continuing is prosecuting, which may be done without a breach of privilege.

That it does not appear, that the constable of Aylesbury has any privilege above another person, for no man is presumed to be privileged, unless it be shewn ; and he has no privilege as constable.

That the vote goes yet further, and says, for not allowing his vote in an election of members to serve in this present parliament : but this can be no crime.

That he admitted they were judges of their own privileges ; but the law must also be observed. . . .

That when subjects have such a right to bring actions, it cannot be stopt by privilege of parliament, for no privilege of parliament can intend so far as to destroy a man's right.

That it has been adjudged a good action by the law of the land, and that damages may be recovered for the injury, in not allowing his vote ; and this action is the same as Ashby and White, which lies before us ; and if we consult the Records, we shall find it to be the same.

That the latter part of this vote is, That the prosecuting this action is contrary to the declaration, in high contempt of the jurisdiction, and in breach of the known privileges of this House.

That the privileges of the House of Commons are limited, for there is no privilege in case of treason, or felony, or breach of the peace ; for a justice of the peace may commit a member for breach of the peace, and if he should be indicted for it, his plea of privilege would not be allowed.

That nothing can make a privilege that was not so before, (for the breach of which a man shall lose his liberty) but an act of parliament.

That each House is judge of their own privileges, because they are more conversant with the privileges of their own House ; so the judges decline it ; but if they come incidently before the courts of law, they must determine it there.

That suppose the House of Commons had not meddled in this matter, but the defendants in this action had pleaded to the jurisdiction of this court, that this was a matter examinable only in parliament, and the plaintiff had demurred, we must then have determined it, and be judges then of their privileges.

Coke's 1 Inst. 'Lex et Consuetudo Parliamenti ab omnibus querenda, a multis ignorata, a paucis cognita;'[1] and the reason it is known by so few is, because they do not seek for it. We are bound to take notice of the customs of parliament, for they are part of the law of the land; and there are the same methods of knowing it, as the law in Westminster-hall. [After quoting from Clarendon's History as to privileges of parliament, the Chief Justice proceeded] That if bringing an action is a breach of privilege, why was not Ashby laid hold on? He prosecuted to judgement and execution; but these persons are committed for commencing an action.

How can the bringing an action in one court be a contempt to another?

If a man that has a privilege in one court is sued in another, he shall have his privilege: but it is no contempt in a plaintiff that sues in another court, and there is no punishment for it; much less can it be a contempt to the House of Commons, where no action can be brought.

That he admitted, the House of Commons may commit any person, and for any crime, because they may impeach any person for any crime whatsoever; but that course is seldom taken, unless where the crime requires a strict prosecution, and much concerns the public.

That the lord Shaftesbury's case[2] is not like this; for he was a member of the House, and it was for a contempt in the House.

The House may at any time commit a man for a contempt in the face of the House; whereas the prisoners are committed not for a breach of privilege or contempt, but because they have brought their actions which are legal, and so adjudged by the Lords in the Writ of Error.

That he did not question but that the warrant was a good warrant.

That 'lex et consuetudo parliamenti' is as much the law of the land as any other law. It is the law gives the queen her prerogative: It is the law gives jurisdiction to the House of Lords; and it is the law limits the jurisdiction of the House of Commons.

That if the ecclesiastical court exceed their jurisdiction, a prohibition will lie; and even the king's acts, if contrary to law, are void.

[1] See Sect. C, No. XIX, p. 313.   [2] See Sect. C, No. III, p. 251.

He insisted that the lord Banbury's case was a great authority for him.

He petitioned the House of Lords to sit, and also to have the king's leave. The lords determined he was not a lord ; yet when he was brought upon an indictment by the name of Charles Knowles, esq. he here pleaded and insisted, that he was a peer ; which plea was allowed and he was not tried.

Though the Lord Chief Justice was so clear in his judgement, yet the other three judges being of a contrary opinion, the majority prevailed ; and the prisoners were remanded to Newgate.

[*S.T.*, xiv, 854.]

(B)

Opinion of the Judges on granting of Writ of Error

May it please your majesty ;

In obedience to your majesty's command, we have considered of the Petition [1] hereunto annexed ; and we are humbly of opinion that a Writ of Error in this case ought to be granted of right, and not of grace. But we give no opinion whether a Writ of Error does lie in the case ; because it is proper to be determined in parliament, where the writ of error and record are returned and certified.

Holt	Powis
Trevor	Blencowe
Ward	Gold
Nevill	Tracey
Powell	Bury.

May it please your majesty ;

In obedience to your majesty's command, we have considered of the petition hereunto annexed ; and we are humbly of opinion that your majesty is not of right and justice obliged to grant a Writ of Error in this case.

Price	Smith.

(C)

The judges all attended the queen at the cabinet on the 25th February, and delivered these their several resolutions to her majesty, in the presence of the prince and many of the principal members of the Council.

[The Queen then prorogued Parliament. The end of the Session meant the release of the imprisoned men. The matter then dropped.]
[*S.T.*, xiv, 862.]

[1] Petition from John Paty, one of the Aylesbury men, to the Queen for a Writ of Error.

XI

THE CASE OF JOHN TUTCHIN,[1] 1704

AT THE SESSIONS COURT, GUILDHALL, LONDON

HOLT, L.C.J. : Gentlemen of the jury, this is an information that is preferred by the queen's Attorney General against Mr. Tutchin, for writing and composing, and publishing, or causing to be writ, composed or published, several libels [2] against the queen and her government . . . So that now you have heard this evidence, you are to consider whether you are satisfied that Mr. Tutchin is guilty of writing, composing, and publishing these libels. They say they are innocent papers, and no libels, and they say nothing is a libel but what reflects upon some particular person. But this is a very strange doctrine, to say, it is not a libel reflecting on the government, endeavouring to possess the people that the government is mal-administered by corrupt persons, that are employed in such or such stations either in the navy or army. To say that corrupt officers are appointed to administer affairs, is certainly a reflection on the government. If people should not be called to account for possessing the people with an ill opinion of the government, no government can subsist. For it is very necessary for all governments that the people should have a good opinion of it. And nothing can be worse to any government, than to endeavour to procure animosities, as to the management of it ; this has always been looked upon as a crime, and no government can be safe without it be punished.

Now you are to consider, whether these words I have read to you, do not tend to beget an ill opinion of the administration of the government ? To tell us, that those that are employed know nothing of the matter, and those that do know are not employed. Men are not adapted to offices, but offices to men, out of a particular regard to their interest, and not to their fitness for the places : this is the purport of these papers. . . . Gentlemen, I must leave it to you ; if you are satisfied that he is guilty of composing and publishing these papers at London, you are to find him guilty.

[The jury found him guilty of composing and publishing, but not guilty of writing. Subsequently on technical grounds judgement was not given against him.]

[S.T., xiv, 1125.]

---

[1] See Sect. C, No. IV, p. 252, and Vol. II, Sect. A, No. IV, p. 6, and Sect. C, No. I, p. 233.

[2] Alleging peculation in the navy, etc. in a paper entitled ' The Observator '.

XII

THE CASE OF DAMMAREE,[1] 1710

[Dammaree was indicted for high treason on the ground that an avowed intention to destroy lawful dissenting chapels generally was constructively an attempt to levy war against the Queen.]

THE SESSIONS COURT, OLD BAILEY

L.C.J. Parker. Give me leave to take notice what the law is in this case. For it has been insisted on by the counsel for the prisoner (and I must do them right, they have taken into consideration all the cases that relate to this matter)—They insist that this is not levying war ; and on this ground, that he was not proved to be at the meeting-house in Drury-lane, but only at the fire at Dr. Burgess's ; and if he was only at one place, one instance would not make it levying war. If, say they, there had been a general intention, it would have gone hard with him ; there was an intention the night before, and Mr. Burgess's was only mentioned ; and it is not certain that there was a general design to pull down the rest. Nay, he was not there, and it was by accident he came to Lincoln's-inn-fields, and he was but at that one place ; and they take notice of some cases, especially that about the bawdy-houses, and that the lord-chief-justice Hale differed from the rest of the judges.[2]

This is a matter that has been often under consideration : the act of the 25th Edward the 3rd, which is the great law for declarations of treason, declares what shall be adjudged treason : compassing or imagining the death of the king, and levying war against the king, are two distinct species of treason. Now they say, that nothing was designed against the queen. If the levying war against the queen, was there meant only of a war against the queen's person it would have been idle to maintain it in that act, because they had before made the compassing her death to be treason.

Now he that levies war, does more than compass or imagine the king's death ; therefore it has been always ruled, that where there is an actual levying of war, which concerns the person of the king, they lay the treason to be the compassing the death of the king, and give a proof of it by levying war. But there is another levying of war, which is not immediately against the person of the king, but only between some particular persons. There is a vast difference between a man's going to remove an annoyance to himself,

[1] See Sect. A, No. XLV, § IV, p. 125.
[2] See Rex *v.* Messenger and others (1668), *S.T.*, vi, 879.

and going to remove a public nuisance, as the case of the bawdy-houses : and the general intention to pull them all down is the treason : for if those that were concerned for them would defend them, and the others would pull them down, there would be a war immediately.

In the case of inclosures, where the people of a town have had a part of their common inclosed, though they have come with a great force to throw down that inclosure, yet that is not levying of war ; but if any will go to pull down all inclosures, and make it a general thing to reform that which they think a nuisance, that necessarily makes a war between all the lords and the tenants. A bawdy-house is a nuisance, and may be punished as such ; and if it be a particular prejudice to any one, if he himself should go in an unlawful manner to redress that prejudice, it might be only a riot ; but if he will set up to pull them all down in general, he has taken the queen's right out of her hand : he has made it a general thing, and when they are once up, they may call every man's house a bawdy-house ; and this is a general thing, it affects the whole nation.

Now to come to this instance. If you believe the evidence, Dammaree was concerned in pulling down two meeting-houses : he was not present at Drury-lane, that is, he was not proved to be there : but if he set others on to do it, it is his doing, and he as much pulled down that meeting-house in Drury-lane, as if he had pulled it down with his own hands. Besides, they tell you his declaration, that he would have all of them down. Again, these gentlemen do not seem to deny, but if the intention were general, it would be levying war : if it were general, where would it end ? And it is taking on them the royal authority ; nay, more, for the queen cannot pull them down till the law is altered : therefore he has here taken on him not only the royal authority, but a power that no person in England has. It concerns all that are against the meeting-houses on one side, and all that are for them on the other, and therefore is levying war.

They [counsel for the prisoner] said, they would desire this point to be reserved to them on the account of the opinion of the lord chief justice Hale ; But I believe this matter has been so often settled, that it would be strange for us to depart from such a settled rule of law ; for these are only the same arguments that were offered by the lord-chief-justice ; and he offered the same arguments that were used in queen Elizabeth's reign ; but it was then held to be treason, and has been held so ever since. His objection made them consider it then, and they did so ; and I suppose they will not expect that it should have more weight out of their mouths than out of his. It was then settled, and has been taken for law at all times since, so that it is not a matter now to be called in question. And as to the statute of 13 Eliz. the intention to levy war surely is not an intention to do a thing, which when it is done, is not levying war.

Thus the matter stands in point of law : I take it to be clear that it is levying war, if you take him to be guilty of being at one of the meeting-places, and leading them, and tempting them to another. Whether that is true, or not, is what must be left to your consideration. You have heard what has been said, and what difficulties arise in point of time, and on the other proofs : If you are of opinion, that he was present at Lincoln's-inn-fields, and did encourage them, and acted any otherwise than by force ; if you believe he led, or invited them to another place, and pulled down that, then you will find him guilty of high treason. If you think he was not there, or was under a compulsion, then he will not be guilty.

[Dammaree was found guilty and sentenced to be hung, drawn and quartered. He was reprieved and subsequently pardoned by the Queen.]

[*S.T.*, xv, 605.]

XIII

THE KING AGAINST THE CHANCELLOR, MASTERS, AND SCHOLARS OF THE UNIVERSITY OF CAMBRIDGE, 1724

[Richard Bentley, D.D., Master of Trinity College, Cambridge, was summoned in 1718 for a debt of £4 : 6s. by Dr. Middleton before the Vice-Chancellor's Court. Bentley, served with a decree by an esquire bedel to appear at the next court, refused to obey. On October 3 he was suspended by the Vice-Chancellor from all his degrees and 14 days later was deprived of his degrees by a Grace of Congregation. As the University failed to allege that there was any Visitor to whom Bentley might have appealed, the Court of King's Bench held in Trinity Term 1723 that a mandamus would lie. The merits of the case were argued in Hilary Term 1724 when the following judgement was delivered.]

In the Court of King's Bench

Lord chief justice Pratt delivered the opinion of the court, viz. of himself, Powys, Fortescue and Raymond Justices, that the return was ill ; because since it is not shewn in the return, that the proceedings in the vice-chancellor's court or the congregation are according to the rules of the civil law, they must be intended to be agreeable to the rules of the common law ; and if so, it not appearing the party has any redress by applying to another Court, this Court will relieve him, if he has been proceeded against and degraded, without being heard, which is contrary to natural justice. This case therefore will fall under the rules for the removing of members of corporations which cannot be done, without summoning the party, and giving him an opportunity of being heard. The cases determined upon that head are so numerous, and the rule so well settled and known, that it cannot now be disputed ; for want of doing which, this suspension or degradation cannot be supported. And therefore a peremptory mandamus was granted.

[Lord Raymond's Reports, ii, 1347.]

XIV

REX *v*. BROADFOOT, 1743 [1]

AT THE SESSIONS OF GAOL DELIVERY, BRISTOL

FOSTER, J., The Recorder: The only question at present is, whether mariners, persons who have freely chosen a sea-faring life . . . may not be legally pressed into the service of the crown, whenever the public safety requireth it. . . . For my part, I think they may. . . . And as for the mariner himself, he when taken into the service of the crown only changeth masters for a time : his service and employment continue the very same ; with this advantage, that the dangers of the sea and enemy are not so great in the service of the crown, as in that of the merchant. . . .

According to my present apprehension, (and I have taken some pains upon myself) the right of impressing mariners for the public service is a prerogative inherent in the crown, grounded upon common law, and recognized by many acts of parliament.

A general immemorial usage not inconsistent with any statute, especially if it be the result of evident necessity, and withal tendeth to the public safety, is, I apprehend, part of the common law of England. If not, I am at a loss to know what is meant by common law, in contradistinction to statute-law. And therefore it is a great mistake in this case, as indeed it would be in any other, to conclude that there is no law, because perhaps there may be no statute that expressly and in terms impowereth the crown to press. For the rights of the crown, and the liberties of the subject too, stand

---

[1] See Sect. C, No. XXI, p. 316, and Vol. II, Sect. A, No. VI, p. 8.

principally upon the foot of common law ; though both have been in many cases confirmed, explained, or ascertained by particular statutes.

As to the point of usage in the matter of pressing, I have met with a multitude of commissions and mandatory writs to that purpose conceived in various forms ; and from time to time directed to different officers, as the nature of the service required.

. . . And now, when I consider these precedents, not fetched from dark, remote, and unsettled times, but running uniformly through a course of many ages, all, as I conceive, speaking to the same purpose, though in different forms of expression ; some for making choice of, others, and those the much greater number and of the latest date, for making choice of and taking up, or of arresting, pressing and taking up, mariners, and putting them on board for the public service : when I consider these precedents, with the practice down to the present time, I cannot conceive otherwise of the point in question, than that the crown hath been always in possession of the prerogative of pressing mariners for the public service. Which prerogative hath been carried into execution, as well by virtue of special commissions, issued as the exigency of affairs required, as by the persons who from time to time have been intrusted with the whole admiralty-jurisdiction. . . . I come now to the statutes which speak of this matter.

And I do admit, that I know of no statute now in force, which directly and in express terms impowereth the crown to press mariners into the service : and admitting that the prerogative is grounded on immemorial usage, I know of no necessity for any such statute ; for let it be remembered, that a prerogative grounded upon immemorial usage not inconsistent with any statute, nor repugnant to the public utility, is as much part of the law of England, as statute law. You will be pleased to carry this observation too along with you, that the statutes which mention pressing as a practice then subsisting and not disallowed, are at least an evidence of the usage, if they go no farther, I mean if they do not amount to a tacit approbation of it. . . .

For rights of every kind, which stand upon the foot of usage, gradually receive new strength in point of light and evidence from the continuance of that usage ; as it implieth the tacit consent and approbation of every successive age, in which the usage hath prevailed. But when the prerogative hath not only this tacit approbation of all ages, the present as well as the former on its side, but is recognized, or evidently presupposed, by many acts of parliament, as in the present use I think it is, I see no legal objection that can be made to it.

[*S.T.*, xviii, 1323.]

XV

WILKES v. LORD HALIFAX,[1] 1763

[A writ of Habeas Corpus was moved for, following the arrest of John Wilkes, M.P. on a warrant issued by Halifax, a Secretary of State, after the publication of No. 45 of *The North Briton*.]

(A)

THE WARRANT OF COMMITMENT IN QUESTION

' Charles earl of Egremont and George Dunk earl of Halifax, lords of his majesty's most honourable privy council, and principal secretaries of state : these are in his majesty's name to authorize and require you to receive into your custody the body of John Wilkes, esq. herewith sent you, for being the author and publisher of a most infamous and seditious libel, intitled, The North Briton, No 45, tending to inflame the minds and alienate the affections of the people from his majesty, and to excite them to traitorous insurrections against the government, and to keep him safe and close, until he shall be delivered by due course of law ; and for so doing this shall be your warrant. Given at St. James's the 30th day of April 1763, in the third year of his majesty's reign.

' EGREMONT, DUNK HALIFAX.'

' To the right honourable John lord Berkley of Stratton, constable of his majesty's Tower of London, or to the lieutenant of the said Tower, or his deputy.'

(B)

THE JUDGEMENT. IN THE COURT OF COMMON PLEAS

PRATT, L.C.J., said :

There are two objections taken to the legality of this warrant, and a third insisted on for the defendant, is privilege of parliament.

The first objection is, that it does not appear to the Court that Mr. Wilkes was charged by any evidence before the secretaries of state, that he was the author or the publisher of the North Briton No. 45. In answer to this, we are all of opinion, that it is not necessary to state in the warrant that Mr. Wilkes was charged by any evidence before the secretaries of state, and that this objection has no weight. Whether a justice of peace can, *ex officio*, without any evidence or information, issue a warrant for apprehending for a crime, is a different question. If a crime be done in his sight, he may commit the criminal upon the spot ; but where he is not

[1] See Sect. B, No. XXXI, p. 219.

present, he ought not to commit upon discretion. Suppose a magistrate hath notice, or a particular knowledge that a person has been guilty of an offence, yet I do not think it is a sufficient ground for him to commit the criminal; but in that case he is rather a witness than a magistrate, and ought to make oath of the fact before some other magistrate, who should thereupon act the official part, by granting a warrant to apprehend the offender; it being more fit that the accuser should appear as a witness, than act as a magistrate. But that is not the question upon this warrant. The question here is, whether it is an essential part of the warrant, that the information, evidence or grounds of the charge before the secretaries of state should be set forth in the warrant? And we think it is not . . . we think it not requisite to set out more than the offence, and the particular species of it. It may be objected, if this be good, every man's liberty will be in the power of a justice of peace. But Hale, Coke and Hawkins, take no notice that a charge is necessary to be set out in the warrant. In the case of the Seven Bishops,[1] their counsel did not take this objection, which no doubt but they would have done, if they had thought there had been any weight in it. I do not rely upon the determination of the judges who then presided in the King's-bench. I have been attended with many precedents of warrants returned into the King's-bench; they are almost universally like this; . . . And Hawkins, . . . says, " It is safe to set forth that the party is charged upon oath; but this is not necessary; for it hath been resolved, that a commitment for treason, or for suspicion of it, without setting forth any particular accusation, or ground of suspicion, is good " . . .

The second objection is, that the libel ought to be set forth in the warrant in *hæc verba*, or at least so much thereof as the secretaries of state deemed infamous, seditious, etc. that the Court may judge whether any such paper ever existed; or if it does exist, whether it be an infamous and seditious libel, or not. But we are all of a contrary opinion. A warrant for commitment for felony must contain the species of felony briefly, " as for felony for the death of J. S. or for burglary in breaking the house of J. S. etc. and the reason is, because it may appear to the judges upon the return of an Habeas Corpus, whether it be felony or not." The magistrate forms his judgement upon the writing, whether it be an infamous and seditious libel or not at his peril; and perhaps the paper itself may not contain the whole of the libel; innuendoes may be necessary to make the whole out. There is no other word in the law but libel whereby to express the true idea of an infamous writing. We understand the nature of a libel as well as a species of felony. It is said that the libel ought to be stated, because the court cannot judge whether it is a libel or not without it ; but that is matter for the judge and jury to determine at the trial. If the paper was here, I should not be afraid to read it. We might perhaps be able to determine that it was a libel, but we could not judge that it was not a libel, because of the innuendoes, etc. It may be said, that without seeing the libel we are not able to fix the quantum of the bail ; but in answer to this, the nature of the offence is known by us. It is said to be an infamous and seditious libel, it is such a misdemeanor as we should require good bail for, (moderation to be observed) and such as the party may be able to procure.

The third matter insisted upon for Mr. Wilkes is, that he is a member of parliament, (which has been admitted by the king's serjeants) and intitled to privilege to be free from arrests in all cases except treason, felony, and actual breach of the peace ; and therefore ought to be discharged from imprisonment without bail ; and we are all of opinion that he is intitled to that privilege, and must be discharged without bail. In the case of the Seven Bishops,[1] the Court took notice of the privilege of parliament, and thought the bishops would have been intitled to it, if they had not judged them to have been guilty of a breach of the peace ; for three of them, Wright, Holloway, and Allybone, deemed a seditious libel to be an actual breach of the peace, and therefore they were ousted of their privilege most unjustly. If Mr. Wilkes had been described as a member of parliament in the return, we must have taken notice of the law of privilege of parliament, otherwise the members would be without remedy, where they are wrongfully arrested against the law of parliament. We are bound to take notice of their privileges as being part of the law of the land. 4 Inst. 25, says, the privilege of parliament holds unless it be in three cases, viz. treason, felony, and the peace : these are the words of Coke. . . . We are all of opinion that a libel is not a breach of the peace. It tends to the breach of the peace, and that is the utmost, . . . But that which only tends to the breach of the peace cannot be a breach of the peace. Suppose a libel be a breach of the peace, yet I think it cannot exclude privilege ; because I cannot find that a libeller is bound to find surety of the peace, in any book whatever, nor ever was, in any case, except one, viz. the case of the Seven Bishops, where three judges said, that surety of the peace was required in the case of a libel. Judge Powell, the only honest man of the four judges, dissented ; and I am bold to be of his opinion, and to say, that case is not law. But it shews the miserable condition of the state at that time. Upon the whole, it is absurd to require surety of the peace or bail in the

[1] Sect. C, No. VII, p. 258.

case of a libeller, and therefore Mr. Wilkes must be discharged from his imprisonment.

[Whereupon there was a loud huzza in Westminster-hall. He was discharged accordingly.]

[*S.T.*, xix, 987.]

XVI

WILKES *v*. WOOD,
CASE OF GENERAL WARRANTS,[1] 1763

(A)

THE GENERAL WARRANT IN QUESTION

' George Montague Dunk, earl of Halifax, viscount Sunbury and baron Halifax, one of the lords of his majesty's most honourable privy council, lieutenant general of his majesty's forces, and principal secretary of state :[2] these are in his majesty's name to authorize and require you (taking a constable to your assistance) to make strict and diligent search for the authors, printers and publishers of a seditious and treasonable paper, intitled, The North Briton, No. 45, Saturday April 23, 1763, printed for G. Kearsley in Ludgate-street, London, and them, or any of them, having found, to apprehend and seize, together with their papers, and to bring in safe custody before me, to be examined concerning the premises, and further dealt with according to law : and in the due execution thereof, all mayors, sheriffs, justices of the peace, constables, and all other his majesty's officers civil and military, and loving subjects whom it may concern, are to be aiding and assisting to you, as there shall be occasion ; and for so doing this shall be your warrant. Given at St. James's the 26th day of April, in the third year of his majesty's reign.

DUNK HALIFAX.'

' To Nathan Carrington, John Money, James Watson, and Robert Blackmore, four of his majesty's messengers in ordinary.

(B)

THE JUDGEMENT.   IN THE COURT OF COMMON PLEAS

PRATT, L.C.J. : . . . It was action of tresspass, . . . He then went through the particulars relating to the justification, the king's speech, the libel No. 45 ; information given, that such a libel was published, Lord Halifax granting a warrant ; messengers entering

---

[1] See Sect. B, No. XXXII, p. 227.

[2] See Sect. A, No. XII, § XIV, p. 32, and Sect. D. No. XLIII, p. 393.

Mr. Wilkes house; Mr. Wood directed to go thither only with a message, and remaining altogether inactive in the affair. . . .

His lordship then went upon the warrant, which he declared was a point of the greatest consequence he had ever met with in his whole practice. The defendants claimed a right, under precedents, to force persons' houses, break open escrutores, seize their papers, &c. upon a general warrant, where no inventory is made of the things thus taken away, and where no offenders' names are specified in the warrant, and therefore a discretionary power given to messengers to search wherever their suspicions may chance to fall. If such a power is truly invested in a secretary of state, and he can delegate this power, it certainly may affect the person and property of every man in this kingdom, and is totally subversive of the liberty of the subject.

And as for the precedents, will that be esteemed law in a secretary of state which is not law in any other magistrate of this kingdom? If they should be found to be legal, they are certainly of the most dangerous consequences; if not legal, must certainly aggravate damages. . . . I still continue of the same mind, that a jury have it in their power to give damages for more than the injury received . . . It is my opinion the office precedents, which had been produced since the Revolution, are no justification of a practice in itself illegal, and contrary to the fundamental principles of the constitution; though its having been the constant practice of the office, might fairly be pleaded in mitigation of damages.

[The jury found a general verdict for the plaintiff, Wilkes, with £1000 damages.]

[*S.T.*, xix, 1166.]

XVII

LEACH [1] *v.* JOHN MONEY, JAMES WATSON, AND ROBERT BLACKMORE, THREE OF THE KING'S MESSENGERS, 1765

In the Court of King's Bench

Lord Mansfield : . . . The three material Questions are—1st, " Whether a secretary of state acting as a conservator of the peace by the common law, is to be construed within the statutes of James the first, and of the last king." [2]

The protection of the officers, if they have acted in obedience to

---

[1] Dryden Leach, the plaintiff, was arrested as the presumed printer of No. 45 of *The North Briton* under the General Warrant. Sect. C, No. XVI, p. 294.   [2] Sect. A, No. LII, p. 133.

the warrant, is consequential, in case a secretary of state is within these statutes. As to the arrest being made in obedience to the warrant, or only under colour of it and without authority from it—this question depends upon the construction of the warrant ; whether it must not be construed to mean ' such persons as are under a violent suspicion of being guilty of the charge ; ' (for they cannot be conclusively considered as guilty, till after trial and conviction). The warrant itself imparts only suspicion ; for, it says,—" to be brought before me, and examined, and dealt with according to law " : and this suspicion must eventually depend upon future trial. Therefore the warrant does not seem to me, to mean conclusive guilt ; but only violent suspicion. If the person apprehended should be tried and acquitted, it would shew ' that he was not guilty ' ; yet there might be sufficient cause of suspicion.

Mr. Dunning, [of Counsel for Wilkes] says, very rightly, that, ' to bring a person within 24 G. 2,[1] the act must be done in obedience to the warrant.'

The last point is, ' whether this general warrant be good.' One part of it may be laid out of the case : for, as to what relates to the seizing his papers, that part of it was never executed ; and therefore it is out of the case.

It is not material to determine, whether the warrant be good or bad ' ; except in the event of the case being within 7 J. 1, but not within 24 G. 2.

At present—as to the validity of the warrant, upon the single objection of the incertainty of the person, being neither named nor described—the common law, in many cases, gives authority to arrest without warrant ; more especially, where taken in the very act : and there are many cases where particular acts of parliament have given authority to apprehend, under general warrants ; as in the case of writs of assistance, or warrants to take up loose, idle, and disorderly people.   But here, it is not contended, that the common law gave the officer authority to apprehend ; nor that there is any act of parliament which warrants this case.

Therefore it must stand upon principles of common law.

It is not fit, that the receiving or judging of the information should be left to the discretion of the officer. The magistrate ought to judge ; and should give certain directions to the officer. This is so, upon reason and convenience.

Then as to authorities—Hale and all others hold such an uncertain warrant void : and there is no case or book to the contrary.

It is said, ' that the usage hath been so ; and that many such have been issued, since the Revolution, down to this time.'

---

[1] See Sect. A, No. LII, p. 133.

But a usage, to grow into a law, ought to be a general usage, *communiter usitata et approbata*; and which, after a long continuance, it would be mischievous to overturn.

This is only the usage of a particular office, and contrary to the usage of all other justices and conservators of the peace.

There is the less reason for regarding this usage; because the form of the warrant probably took its rise from a positive statute; and the former precedents were inadvertently followed, after that law[1] was expired.

Mr. Justice *Wilmot* declared, that he had no doubt, nor ever had, upon these warrants: he thought them illegal and void.

Neither had the two other judges, Mr. Justice Yates, and Mr. Justice Ashton, any doubt (upon this first argument) of the illegality of them: for no degree of antiquity can give sanction to a usage bad in itself. And they esteemed this usage to be so. They were clear and unanimous in opinion, that this warrant was illegal and bad. . . .

[On Nov. 8.] Lord *Mansfield* . . . Where the justice cannot be liable, the officer is not within the protection of the act. . . . For, here the warrant is to take up the author, printer or publisher; but they took up a person who was neither author, printer, nor publisher . . . the judgment[2] must be affirmed. The other judges assenting, the rule of the Court was, ' that the judgment be affirmed.'

[*S.T.*, xix, 1026.]

XVIII

ENTICK *v.* CARRINGTON AND OTHERS, CASE OF SEARCH WARRANTS
1765

(A)

The Search Warrant in Question

' George Montagu Dunk, earl of Halifax, viscount Sunbury, and baron Halifax, one of the lords of his majesty's honourable privy council, lieutenant general of his majesty's forces, lord lieutenant general and general governor of the kingdom of Ireland, and principal secretary of state, &c. these are in his majesty's name to authorize and require you, taking a constable to your assistance,

---

[1] See Sect. A, No. XII, p. 29 (the Licensing Act, especially § XIV).

[2] Mansfield's judgement was delivered in proceedings in error on an action of false imprisonment tried originally in Common Pleas before Pratt, L.C.J.

to make strict and diligent search for John Entick, the author, or one concerned in writing of several weekly very seditious papers, intitled the Monitor, or British Freeholder, No 357, 358, 360, 373, 376, 378, 379, and 380, London, printed for J. Wilson and J. Fell in Pater Noster Row, which contain gross and scandalous reflections and invectives upon his majesty's government, and upon both houses of parliament ; and him, having found you are to seize and apprehend, and to bring, together with his books and papers, in safe custody before me to be examined concerning the premisses, and further dealt with according to law ; in the due execution whereof all mayors, sheriffs, justices of the peace, constables, and other his majesty's officers civil and military, and loving subjects whom it may concern, are to be aiding and assisting to you as there shall be occasion ; and for so doing this shall be your warrant. Given at St. James's the 6th day of November 1762, in the third year of his majesty's reign, Dunk Halifax. To Nathan Carrington, James Watson, Thomas Ardran and Robert Blackmore, four of his majesty's messengers in ordinary.'

(B)

The Judgement.   In the Court of Common Pleas

Lord Camden (Pratt), L.C.J. : This record hath set up two defences to the action, on both of which the defendants have relied.

The first arises from the facts disclosed in the special verdict ; whereby the defendants put their case upon the statute of 24 Geo. 2, insisting, that they have nothing to do with the legality of the warrants, but that they ought to have been acquitted as officers within the meaning of that act.

The second defence stands upon the legality of the warrants ; for this being a justification at common law, the officer is answerable if the magistrate has no jurisdiction.

These two defences have drawn several points into question, upon which the public, as well as the parties, have a right to our opinion.

Under the first, it is incumbent upon the officers to shew, that they are officers within the meaning of the act of parliament, and likewise that they have acted in obedience to the warrant.

The question, whether officers or not, involves another ; whether the secretary of state, whose ministers they are, can be deemed a justice of the peace,[1] or taken within the equity of the description ; for officers and justices are here co-relative terms : therefore either both must be comprised, or both excluded.

[1] See Sect. D, No. XLIII, p. 393.

The question leads me to an inquiry into the authority of that minister, as he stands described upon the record in two capacities, viz. secretary of state and privy counsellor. And since no statute has conferred any such jurisdiction as this before us, it must be given, if it does really exist, by the common law; and upon this ground he has been treated as a conservator of the peace.

The matter thus opened, the questions that naturally arise upon the special verdict, are ;

First, whether in either of the characters, or upon any other foundation, he is a conservator of the peace.

Secondly, admitting him to be so, whether he is within the equity of the 24th Geo. 2.[1]

These points being disposed of, the next in order is, whether the defendants have acted in obedience to the warrant.

In the last place, the great question upon the justification will be, whether the warrant to seize and carry away the plaintiff's papers is lawful.

First Question

The power of this minister, in the way wherein it has been usually exercised, is pretty singular.

If he is considered in the light of a privy counsellor, although every member of that board is equally entitled to it with himself, yet he is the only one of that body who exerts it. His power is so extensive in place, that it spreads throughout the whole realm ; yet in the object it is so confined, that except in libels and some few state crimes, as they are called, the secretary of state does not pretend to the authority of a constable.

To consider him as a conservator. He never binds to the peace, or good behaviour, which seems to have been the principal duty of a conservator ; at least he never does it in those cases, where the law requires those sureties. But he commits in certain other cases, where it is very doubtful, whether the conservator had any jurisdiction whatever.

His warrants are chiefly exerted against libellers, whom he binds in the first instance to their good behaviour, which no other conservator ever attempted, from the best intelligence that we can learn from our books.

And though he doth all these things, yet it seems agreed, that he hath no power whatsoever to administer an oath or to take bail.

This jurisdiction, as extraordinary as I have described it, is so dark and obscure in its origin, that the counsel have not been able to form any certain opinion from whence it sprang.

[1] See Sect. A, No. LII, p. 133.

Sometimes they annex it to the office of secretary of state, sometimes to the quality of privy counsellor; and in the last argument it has been derived from the king's royal prerogative to commit by his own personal command.

Whatever may have been the true source of this authority, it must be admitted, that at this day he is in the full legal exercise of it; because there has been not only a clear practice of it, at least since the Revolution, confirmed by a variety of precedents; but the authority has been recognized and confirmed by two cases in the very point since that period: and therefore we have not a power to unsettle or contradict it now, even though we are persuaded that the commencement of it was erroneous. . . . [His Lordship then discussed the history and powers of the office of Secretary of State.]

Having thus shewn, not only negatively that this power of committing was not annexed to the secretary's office, but affirmatively likewise that he was notifier or countersigner of the king's personal warrant acting *in alio jure* down to the times of the 16th of Charles the first, and consequently to the Restoration. . . . I have but little to add on this head. . . . [His Lordship then examines whether a privy councillor has a power of commitment.]

There cannot be a stronger authority than this [1] I have now cited for the present purpose. The whole body of the law, if I may use the phrase, were as ignorant at that time of a privy counsellor's right to commit in the case of a libel, as the whole body of privy counsellors are at this day.

The counsel on both sides in that cause were the ablest of their time, and few times have produced abler. They had been concerned in all the state-cases during the whole reign of Charles the second, on the one side or the other; and to suppose that all these persons could be utterly ignorant of this extraordinary power, if it had been either legal or even practised, is a supposition not to be maintained.

This is the whole that I have been able to find, touching the power of one or more privy counsellors to commit . . .

I have now finished all I have to say upon this head; and am satisfied, that the secretary of state hath assumed this power as a transfer, I know not how, of the royal authority to himself; and that the common law of England knows no such magistrate. . . .

However, I will for a time admit the Secretary of State to be a conservator, in order to examine, whether in that character he can be within the equity of this act [of 24th of Geo. 2]

---

[1] Seven Bishops' Case. The warrant in that case had been signed by thirteen Privy Councillors, but separately and not in Council.

SECOND QUESTION

. . . And now give me leave to ask one question. Will the secretary of state be classed with the higher or the lower conservator ? If with the higher, such as the king, the chancellor, etc. he is too much above the justice to be within the equity. If with the lower, he is too much below him. And as to the sheriff and the coroner, they cannot be within the law; because they never grant such warrants as these. So that at last, upon considering all the conservators, there is not one who does not stand most evidently excluded, unless the secretary of state himself shall be excepted.

But if there wanted arguments, to confute this pretension, the construction that has prevailed upon the seventh of James the First, would decide the point. That is an act of like kind to relieve justices of the peace, mayors, constables, and certain other officers, in troublesome actions brought against them for the legal execution of their offices ; who are enabled by that act to plead the general issue. Now that law has been taken so strictly, that neither church-wardens, nor overseers, were held to be within the equity of the word ' constables,' although they were clearly officers, and acted under the justice's warrants. Why ? Because that act, being made to change the course of the common law, could not be extended beyond the letter. If then that privilege of giving the special matter in evidence upon the general issue is contrary to the common law, how much more substantially is this act an innovation of the common law, which indemnifies the officer upon the production of the warrant, and deprives the subject of his right of action ?

It is impossible, that two acts of parliament can be more nearly allied or connected with one another, than that of 24 George 2, and the 7th of James 1. The objects in both are the same, and the remedies are similar in both, each of them changing the common law for the benefit of the parties concerned. The one, in truth, is the sequel or second part of the other. The first not being an adequate remedy in case of the several persons therein mentioned, the second is added to complete the work, and to make them as secure as they ought to be made from the nature of the case. If by a contrary construction any person should be admitted into the last that are not included in that first, the person, whoever he is, will be without the privilege of pleading the general issue, and giving the special matter in evidence, which the latter would have certainly given by express words, if the parliament could have imagined he was not comprised in the first.

Upon the whole, we are all of opinion, that neither secretary of state, nor the messenger, are within the meaning of this act of parliament. . . .

THIRD QUESTION

. . . It behoved the messenger to shew, that they have acted in obedience to the warrant. . . . The late decision of the Court of King's-bench in the Case of General Warrants [1] [Leach v. Money & others] was ruled upon this ground, and rightly determined. This part of the case is clear, and shall be dispatched in very few words.

First, the defendants did not take with them a constable, which is a flat objection. . . .

Secondly, they did not bring the papers to the Earl of Halifax. . . .

FOURTH AND LAST QUESTION

. . . I come in my last place to the point, which is made by the justification ; for the defendants, having failed in the attempt made to protect themselves by the statute of the 24th of Geo. 2, are under a necessity to maintain the legality of the warrants, under which they have acted, and to shew that the secretary of state in the instance now before us, had a jurisdiction to seize the defendant's papers. If he had no such jurisdiction, the law is clear, that the officers are as much responsible for the trespass as their superior.

This, though it is not the most difficult, is the most interesting question in the cause ; because if this point should be determined in favour of the jurisdiction, the secret cabinets and bureaus of every subject in this kingdom will be thrown open to the search and inspection of a messenger, whenever the secretary of state shall think fit to charge, or even to suspect, a person to be the author, printer, or publisher of a seditious libel.

The messenger, under this warrant, is commanded to seize the person described, and to bring him with his papers to be examined before the secretary of state. In consequence of this, the house must be searched ; the lock and doors of every room, box, or trunk must be broken open ; all the papers and books without exception, if the warrant be executed according to its tenor, must be seized and carried away ; for it is observable, that nothing is left either to the discretion or to the humanity of the officer.

This power so assumed by the secretary of state is an execution upon all the party's papers, in the first instance. His house is rifled ; his most valuable secrets are taken out of his possession, before the paper for which he is charged is found to be criminal by any competent jurisdiction, and before he is convicted either of writing, publishing, or being concerned in the paper.

This power, so claimed by the secretary of state, is not supported by one single citation from any law book extant. It is claimed by

---

[1] See Sect. C, No. XVII, p. 295.

no other magistrate in this kingdom but himself : the great executive hand of criminal justice, the lord chief justice of the court of the King's-bench, chief justice Scroggs excepted,[1] never having assumed this authority.

The arguments, which the defendant's counsel have thought fit to urge in support of this practice, are of this kind.

That such warrants have issued frequently since the Revolution, which practice has been found by the special verdict ; though I must observe, that the defendants have no right to avail themselves of that finding, because no such practice is averred in their justification.

That the case of the warrants bears a resemblance to the case of search for stolen goods.

They say too, that they have been executed without resistance upon many printers, booksellers, and authors, who have quietly submitted to the authority ; that no action hath hitherto been brought to try the right ; and that although they have been often read upon the returns of Habeas Corpus, yet no court of justice has ever declared them illegal.

And it is further insisted, that this power is essential to government, and the only means of quieting clamours and sedition.

These arguments, if they can be called arguments, shall be all taken notice of ; because upon this question I am desirous of removing every colour or plausibility.

Before I state the question, it will be necessary to describe the power claimed by this warrant in its full extent.

If honestly exerted, it is a power to seize that man's papers, who is charged upon oath to be the author or publisher of a seditious libel ; if oppressively, it acts against every man, who is so described in the warrant, although he be innocent.

It is executed against the party, before he is heard or even summoned ; and the information, as well as the informers, is unknown.

It is executed by messengers with or without a constable (for it can never be pretended, that such is necessary in point of law) in the presence or the absence of the party, as the messengers shall think fit, and without a witness to testify what passes at the time of the transaction ; so that when the papers are gone, as the only witnesses are the trespassers, the party injured is left without proof.

If this injury falls upon an innocent person, he is as destitute of remedy as the guilty : and the whole transaction is so guarded against discovery, that if the officer should be disposed to carry off a bank-bill, he may do it with impunity, since there is no man capable of proving either the taker or the thing taken.

[1] See Sect. C, No. IV, p. 252.

It must not be here forgot, that no subject whatsoever is privileged from this search ; because both Houses of Parliament have resolved, that there is no privilege in the case of a seditious libel.[1]

Nor is there pretence to say, that the word ' papers ' here mentioned ought in point of law to be restrained to the libellous papers only. The word is general, and there is nothing in the warrant to confine it ; nay, I am able to affirm, that it has been upon a late occasion executed in its utmost latitude : for in the case of Wilkes against Wood,[2] when the messengers hesitated about taking all the manuscripts, and sent to the secretary of state for more express orders for that purpose, the answer was, " that all must be taken, manuscripts and all." Accordingly, all was taken, and Mr. Wilkes' private pocket-book filled up the mouth of the sack.

I was likewise told in the same cause by one of the most experienced messengers, that he held himself bound by his oath to pay an implicit obedience to the commands of the secretary of state ; that in common cases he was contented to seize the printed impressions of the papers mentioned in the warrant ; but when he received directions to search further, or to make a more general seizure, his rule was to sweep all. The practice has been correspondent to the warrant.

Such is the power, and therefore one should naturally expect that the law to warrant it should be clear in proportion as the power is exorbitant.

If it is law it will be found in our books. If it is not to be found there, it is not law.

The great end, for which men entered into society, was to secure their property. That right is preserved sacred and incommunicable in all instances, where it has not been taken away or abridged by some public law for the good of the whole. The cases where this right of property is set aside by positive law, are various. Distresses, executions, forfeitures, taxes, etc., are all of this description ; wherein every man by common consent gives up that right, for the sake of justice and the general good. By the laws of England, every invasion of private property, be it ever so minute, is a trespass. No man can set his foot upon my ground without my licence, but he is liable to an action, though the damage be nothing ; which is proved by every declaration in trespass, where the defendant is called upon to answer for bruising the grass, and even treading upon the soil. If he admits the fact, he is bound to shew by way of justification, that some positive law has empowered or excused him. The justification is submitted to the judges, who are to look into the

---

[1] See Sect. B, No. XXXI (B), p. 220.
[2] See Sect. C, No. XVI, p. 294.

books ; and if such a justification can be maintained by the text of the statute law, or by the principles of common law. If no such excuse can be found or produced, the silence of the books is an authority against the defendant, and the plaintiff must have judgement.

According to this reasoning, it is now incumbent upon the defendants to shew the law, by which this seizure is warranted. If that cannot be done, it is a trespass. . . .

What would the parliament say, if the judges should take upon themselves to mould an unlawful power into a convenient authority, by new restrictions ? That would be, not judgement, but legislation.

I come now to the practice since the Revolution, which has been strongly urged, with this emphatical addition, that an usage tolerated from the æra of liberty, and continued downwards to this time through the best ages of the constitution, must necessarily have a legal commencement. . . .

If the practice began then, it began too late to be law now. If it was more ancient the Revolution is not to answer for it ; and I could have wished, that upon this occasion the Revolution had not been considered as the only basis of our liberty.

The Revolution restored this constitution to its first principles. It did no more. It did not enlarge the liberty of the subject ; but gave it a better security. It neither widened nor contracted the foundation, but repaired, and perhaps added a buttress or two to the fabric ; and if any minister of state has since deviated from the principles at that time recognized, all that I can say is, that, so far from being sanctified, they are condemned by the Revolution.

With respect to the practice itself, if it goes no higher, every lawyer will tell you, it is much too modern to be evidence of the common law ; and if it should be added, that these warrants ought to acquire some strength by the silence of those courts, which have heard them read so often upon returns without censure or animadversion, I am able to borrow my answer to that pretence from the Court of King's-bench, which lately declared with great unanimity in the Case of General Warrants,[1] that as no objection was taken to them upon the returns, and the matter passed *sub silentio*, the precedents were of no weight. I most heartily concur in that opinion ; and the reason is more pertinent here, because the Court had no authority in the present case to determine against the seizure of papers, which was not before them ; whereas in the other they might, if they had thought fit, have declared the warrant void, and discharged the prisoner *ex officio*.

This is the first instance I have met with, where the ancient

[1] See Sect. C, No. XVII, p. 295.

immemorable law of the land, in a public manner, was attempted
to be proved by the practice of a private office.

The names and rights of public magistrates, their power and
forms of proceeding as they are settled by law, have been long since
written, and are to be found in books and records. Private customs
indeed are still to be sought from private tradition. But whoever
conceived a notion, that any part of the public law could be buried
in the obscure practice of a particular person ?

To search, seize, and carry away all the papers of the subject
upon the first warrant : that such a right should have existed from
the time whereof the memory of man runneth not to the contrary,
and never yet have found a place in any book of law ; is incredible.
But if so strange a thing could be supposed, I do not see, how we
could declare the law upon such evidence.

But it is still insisted, that there has been a general submission,
and no action brought to try the right.

I answer, there has been a submission of guilt and poverty to
power and the terror of punishment. But it would be strange
doctrine to assert that all the people of this land are bound to
acknowledge that to be universal law, which a few criminal booksellers have been afraid to dispute. . . .

It was very evident, that the Star-Chamber, how soon after the
invention of printing I know not, took to itself the jurisdiction
over public libels, which soon grew to be the peculiar business of
that court. Not that the courts of Westminster-hall wanted the
power of holding pleas in those cases ; but the Attorney-general for
good reasons chose rather to proceed there ; which is the reason,
why we have no cases of libels in the King's-bench before the
Restoration.

The Star-Chamber from this jurisdiction presently usurped a
general superintendance over the press, and exercised a legislative
power in all matters relating to the subject. They appointed
licencers ; they prohibited books ; they inflicted penalties ; and
they dignified one of their officers with the name of the messenger
of the press, and among other things enacted this warrant of search.

After that court was abolished, the press became free, but
enjoyed its liberty not above two or three years ; for the Long
Parliament thought fit to restrain it again by ordinance. Whilst
the press is free, I am afraid it will always be licentious, and all
governments have an aversion to libels. This parliament, therefore, did by ordinance restore the Star-Chamber practice ; they
recalled the licences, and sent forth again the messenger. It was
against the ordinance, that Milton wrote that famous pamphlet
called Areopagitica. Upon the Restoration, the press was free once

more, till the 13th and 14th of Charles 2, when the Licensing Act [1] passed, which for the first time gave the secretary of state a power to issue search warrants ; but these warrants were neither so oppressive, nor so inconvenient as the present. The right to enquire into the licence was the pretence of making the searches ; and if during the search any suspected libels were found, they and they only could be seized.

This act expired on the 32nd year of that reign, or thereabouts. It was revived again in the 1st year of king James 2, and remained in force till the 5th of King William, after one of his parliaments had continued it for a year beyond its expiration.

I do very much suspect, that the present warrant took its rise from these search-warrants, that I have been describing ; nothing being easier to account for than this engraftment ; the difference between them being no more than this, that the apprehension of the person in the first was to follow the seizure of the papers, but the seizure of the papers in the latter was to follow the apprehension of the person. The same evidence would serve equally for both purposes. If it was charged for printing or publishing, that was sufficient for either of the warrants. Only this material difference must always be observed between them, that the search-warrant only carried off the criminal papers, whereas this seizes all.

When the Licensing Act expired at the close of king Charles 2's reign, the twelve judges were assembled at the king's command,[2] to discover whether the press might not be as effectually restrained by the common law, as it had been by that statute.

I cannot help observing in this place, that if the secretary of state was still invested with a power of issuing this warrant, there was no occasion for the application to the judges : for though he could not issue the general search-warrant, yet upon the least rumour of a libel he might have done more, and seized everything. But that was not thought of, and therefore the judges met and resolved :

First, that it was criminal at common law, not only to write public seditious papers and false news ; but likewise to publish any news without a licence from the king, though it was true and innocent.

Secondly, that libels were seizable. This is to be found in the State Trials ; and because it is a curiosity, I will recite the passage at large. . . .

[Lord Camden here quoted the judgment of Chief Justice Scroggs in the case of *Harris*.[2]]

---

[1] See Sect. A, No. XII, p. 29.
[2] See Sect. C, No. IV (A), p. 252.

These are the opinions of all the twelve judges of England ; a great and reverend authority.

Can the twelve judges extrajudicially make a thing law to bind the kingdom by a declaration, that such is their opinion ?—I say No.—It is a matter of impeachment for any judge to affirm it. There must be an antecedent principle or authority, from whence this opinion may be fairly collected ; otherwise the opinion is null, and nothing but ignorance can excuse the judge that subscribed it. Out of this doctrine sprang the famous general search-warrant, that was condemned by the House of Commons ; and it was not unreasonable to suppose, that the form of it was settled by the twelve judges that subscribed the opinion.

The deduction from the opinion to the warrant is obvious. If you can seize a libel, you may search for it : if search is legal, a warrant to authorize that search is likewise legal : if any magistrate can issue such a warrant, the chief justice of the King's-bench may clearly do it.

It falls here naturally in my way to ask, whether there by any authority beside this opinion of these twelve judges to say, that libels may be seized ?   If they may, I am afraid, that all the inconveniences of a general seizure will follow upon a right allowed to seize a part.   The search in such cases will be general, and every house will fall under the power of a secretary of state to be rummaged before proper conviction. . . .

I can find no other authority to justify the seizure of a libel, than that of Scroggs and his brethren.

If the power of search is to follow the right of seizure, everybody sees the consequence. He that has it or has had it in his custody ; he that has published, copied, or maliciously reported it, may fairly be under a reasonable suspicion of having the thing in his custody, and consequently become the object of the search warrant.   If libels may be seized, it ought to be laid down with precision, when, where, upon what charge, against whom, by what magistrate, and in what stage of the prosecution.   All these particulars must be explained and proved to be law, before this general proposition can be established.

As therefore no authority in our books can be produced to support such a doctrine, and so many Star Chamber decrees, ordinances, and acts have been thought necessary to establish a power of search, I cannot be persuaded, that such a power can be justified by the common law.

I have now done with the argument, which has endeavoured to support this warrant by the practice since the Revolution.

It is then said, that it is necessary for the ends of government to lodge such a power with a state officer ; and that it is better to prevent the publication before than to punish the offender afterwards. I answer, that if the legislature be of that opinion they will revive the Licensing Act. But if they have not done that, I conceive they are not of that opinion. And with respect to the argument of state necessity, or a distinction which has been aimed at between state offences and others, the common law does not understand that kind of reasoning, nor do our books take notice of any such distinctions.

Sergeant Ashley was committed to the Tower in the 3rd of Charles 1st, by the House of Lords only for asserting in argument, that there was a ' law of state ' different from the common law ; and the Ship-Money judges were impeached for holding, first, that state-necessity would justify the raising money without consent of parliament ; and secondly, that the king was judge of that necessity.

If the king himself has no power to declare when the law ought to be violated for reason of state, I am sure we his judges have no such prerogative.

Lastly, it is urged as an argument of utility, that such a search is a means of detecting offenders by discovering evidence. I wish some cases had been shown, where the law forceth evidence out of the owner's custody by process. There is no process against papers in civil causes. It has been often tried, but never prevailed. Nay, where the adversary has by force or fraud got possession of your own proper evidence, there is no way to get it back but by action.

In the criminal law such a proceeding was never heard of ; and yet there are some crimes, such for instance as murder, rape, robbery, and house-breaking, to say nothing of forgery and perjury, that are more atrocious than libelling. But our law has provided no paper-search in these cases to help forward the conviction.

Whether this proceedeth from the gentleness of the law towards criminals, or from a consideration that such a power would be more pernicious to the innocent than useful to the public, I will not say.

It is very certain, that the law obligeth no man to accuse himself, because the necessary means of compelling self-accusation, falling upon the innocent as well as the guilty, would be both cruel and unjust ; and it should seem that search for evidence is disallowed upon the same principle. There too the innocent would be confounded with the guilty.

Observe the wisdom as well as the mercy of the law. The strongest evidence before a trial, being only *ex parte*, is but suspicion ; it is not proof. Weak evidence is a ground of suspicion, though in a lower degree ; and if suspicion at large should be a ground of search, especially in the case of libels, whose house would be safe ?

If, however, a right search for the sake of discovering evidence ought in any case to be allowed, this crime above all others ought to be excepted, as wanting such a discovery less than any other. It is committed in open daylight, and in the face of the world ; every act of publication makes new proof ; and the solicitor of the treasury, if he pleases, may be the witness himself.

The messenger of the press, by the very constitution of his office, is directed to purchase every libel that comes forth, in order to be a witness.

Nay, if the vengeance of government requires a production of the author, it is hardly possible for him to escape the impeachment of the printer, who is sure to seal his own pardon by his discovery. But suppose he should happen to be obstinate, yet the publication is stopped, and the offence punished. By this means the law is satisfied, and the public secured.

I have now taken notice of everything that has been urged upon the present point ; and upon the whole we are all of opinion, that the warrant to seize and carry away the party's papers in the case of a seditious libel, is illegal and void.

Before I conclude, I desire not to be understood as an advocate for libels. All civilized governments have punished calumny with severity ; and with reason ; for these compositions debauch the manners of the people ; they excite a spirit of disobedience, and enervate the authority of government ; they provoke and excite the passions of the people against their rulers, and the rulers oftentimes against the people.

After this description, I shall hardly be considered as a favourer of these pernicious productions. I will always set my face against them, when they come before me ; and shall recommend it most warmly to the jury always to convict when the proof is clear. They will do well to consider, that unjust acquittals bring an odium upon the press itself, the consequences whereof may be fatal to liberty ; for if kings and great men cannot obtain justice at their hands by the ordinary course of law, they may at last be provoked to restrain that press, which the juries of their country refuse to regulate. When licentiousness is tolerated, liberty is in the utmost danger ; because tyranny, bad as it is, is better than anarchy, and the worst of governments is more tolerable than no government at all.

[*S.T.*, xix, 1044.]

XIX

THE CASE OF BRASS CROSBY,[1] 1771

[Brass Crosby, Lord Mayor of London and a member of the House of Commons, had been committed by the authority of the House for breach of privilege. The Lord Mayor had discharged Miller, a printer who had been arrested by order of the House for printing and publishing their debates, and had committed the messenger of the House for assault.]

IN THE COURT OF COMMON PLEAS

JUDGEMENT OF DE GREY, L.C.J., If either myself or any of my brothers on the bench, had any doubt in this case, we should certainly have taken some time to consider, before we had given our opinions ; but the case seems so very clear to us all, that we have no reason for delay.

The writ by which the lord mayor is now brought before us, is a Habeas Corpus at common law, for it is not signed *per statutum*. It is called a prerogative writ for the king ; or a remedial writ : and this writ was properly advised by the counsel for his lordship, because all the judges (including Holt) agreed, that such a writ as the present case required, is not within the statute. This is a writ by which the subject has a right of remedy to be discharged out of custody, if he hath been committed, and is detained contrary to law ; therefore the Court must consider, whether the authority committing, is a legal authority. If the commitment is made by those having authority to commit, this Court cannot discharge or bail the party committed ; nor can this Court admit to bail, one charged or committed in execution. Whether the authority committing the lord mayor, is a legal authority or not, must be adjudged by the return of the writ now before the Court. The return states the commitment to be made by the House of Commons, for a breach of privilege, which is also stated in the return ; and this breach of privilege or contempt is, as the counsel has truly described it, three-fold ; discharging a printer in custody of a messenger by order of the House of Commons ; signing a warrant for the commitment of the messenger, and holding him to bail ; that is, treating a messenger of the House of Commons as acting criminally in the execution of the orders of that House. . . . The House of Commons, without doubt, have power to commit persons examined at their bar touching elections, when they prevaricate or speak falsely ; so they have for breaches of privilege ; so they have in many other cases. . . . This power of committing must be inherent in the House of Commons, from the very nature of its institution, and therefore is part of the

[1] See Sect. B, No. XXXIV, p. 236, and Vol. II, Sect. C, No. V, p. 248.

law of the land. They certainly always could commit in many cases. In matters of elections, they can commit sheriffs, mayors, officers, witnesses, etc. and it is now agreed that they can commit generally for all contempts. All contempts are either punishable in the Court contemned, or in some higher court. Now the parliament has no superior court ; therefore the contempts against either house can only be punished by themselves. The stat. 1 Jac. 1, cap. 13. sect. 3, sufficiently proves that they have power to punish : it is in these words : viz. ' Provided always, that this act, or anything therein contained, shall not extend to the diminishing of any punishment to be hereafter by censure in parliament inflicted upon any person which hereafter shall make, or procure to be made, any such arrest as is aforesaid.' So that it is most clear the legislature have recognized this power of the House of Commons.

In the case of the Aylesbury men,[1] the counsel admitted, lord chief justice Holt owned, and the House of Lords acknowledged, that the House of Commons had power to commit for contempt and breach of privilege. Indeed, it seems, they must have power to commit for any crime, because they have power to impeach for any crime. When the House of Commons adjudge anything to be a contempt, or a breach of privilege, their adjudication is a conviction, and their commitment in consequence, is execution ; and no court can discharge or bail a person that is in execution by the judgement of any other court. The House of Commons therefore having an authority to commit, and that commitment being an execution, the question is, what can this court do ? It can do nothing when a person is in execution by the judgement of a court having a competent jurisdiction : in such case, this court is not a court of appeal.

It is objected, 1. That the House of Commons are mistaken, for they have not this power, this authority ; 2. That supposing they have, yet in this case they have not used it rightly and properly ; and, 3. That the execution of their orders was irregular. In order to judge, I will consider the practice of the courts in common and ordinary cases. I do not find any case where the courts have taken cognisance of such execution, or of commitments of this kind : there is no precedent of Westminster-hall interfering in such a case. . . .

How then can we do anything in the present case, when the law by which the lord mayor is committed, is different from the law by which he seeks to be relieved ? He is committed by the law of parliament, and yet he would have redress from the common law. The law of parliament is only known to parliament men, by experi-

---

[1] Sect. C, No. X, at p. 280 and other refs. in note 3.

ence in the House. Lord Coke says, every man looks for it, but few can find it.[1] The House of Commons only know how to act within their own limits. We are not a court of appeal. We do not know certainly the jurisdiction of the House of Commons. We cannot judge of the laws and privileges of the House, because we have no knowledge of those laws and privileges. We cannot judge of the contempts thereof : we cannot judge of the punishment thereof.

I wish we had some code of the law of parliament ; but till we have such a code, it is impossible we should be able to judge of it. Perhaps a contempt in the House of Commons, in the Chancery, in this court, and in the court of Durham, may be very different ; therefore we cannot judge of it, but every court must be sole judge of its own contempts. Besides, as the court cannot go out of the return of this writ, how can we inquire as to the truth of the fact, as to the nature of the contempt ? We have no means of trying whether the lord-mayor did right or wrong. This court cannot summon a jury to try the matter. We cannot examine into the fact. Here are no parties in litigation before the court. We cannot call in any body. We cannot hear any witnesses, or depositions of witnesses. We cannot issue any process. We are even now hearing *ex parte*, and without any counsel on the contrary side. Again, if we could determine upon the contempts of any other court, so might the other courts of Westminster-hall ; and what confusion would then ensue ! none of us knowing the law by which persons are committed by the House of Commons. If three persons are committed for the same breach of privilege, and applied severally to different courts, one court perhaps would bail, another court discharge, a third re-commit.

Two objections have been made, which I own have great weight ; because they hold forth, if pursued to all possible cases, consequences of most important mischief. 1st, It is said, that if the rights and privileges of parliament are legal rights, for that very reason the Court must take notice of them, because they are legal. And 2ndly, If the law of parliament is part of the law of the land, the judges must take cognizance of one part of the law of the land, as well as of the other. But these objections will not prevail. There are two sorts of privileges which ought never to be confounded ; personal privilege, and the privilege belonging to the whole collective body of that assembly. . . .

At present, when the House of Commons commits for contempt, it is very necessary to state what is the particular breach of privilege ; but it would be a sufficient return, to state the breach of privilege generally. This doctrine is fortified by the opinion of

[1] See Sect. C, No. X, p. 283.

all the judges, in the case of lord Shaftesbury,[1] and I never heard this decision complained of till 1704. Though they were times of heat, the judges could have no motive in their decision, but a regard to the laws. The houses disputed about jurisdiction, but the judges were not concerned in the dispute. As for the present case, I am perfectly satisfied, that if Lord Holt himself were to have determined it, the lord-mayor would be remanded. . . . Courts of justice have no cognizance of the acts of the houses of parliament, because they belong ' ad aliud examen.' I have the most perfect satisfaction in my own mind in that determination. Sir Martin Wright, who felt a generous and distinguished warmth for the liberty of the subject; Mr. Justice Denison, who was so free from connexions and ambition of every kind; and Mr. Justice Foster, who may truly be called the Magna Charta of liberty of persons, as well as fortunes; all these revered judges concurred in this point: I am therefore clearly and with full satisfaction of opinion, that the lord-mayor must be remanded.

[*S.T.*, xix, 1146.]

XX

SOMMERSETT'S CASE,[2] 1772

In the Court of King's Bench

LORD MANSFIELD : I shall recite the return to the writ of Habeas Corpus, as the ground of our determination; omitting only words of form. The captain of the ship on board of which the negro was taken, makes his return to the writ in terms signifying that there have been, and still are, slaves to a great number in Africa; and that the trade in them is authorized by the laws and opinions of Virginia and Jamaica; that they are goods and chattels; and, as such, saleable and sold. That James Sommersett is a negro of Africa, and long before the return of the king's writ was brought to be sold, and was sold to Charles Steuart, esq., then in Jamaica, and has not been manumitted since; that Mr. Steuart, having occasion to transact business, came over hither, with an intention to return; and brought Sommersett to attend and abide with him, and to carry him back as soon as the business should be transacted. That such intention has been, and still continues; and that the negro did remain till the time of his departure in the service of his master, Mr. Steuart, and quitted it without his consent; and thereupon, before the return

---

[1] Sect. C, No. III, p. 251.
[2] See Vol. II, Sect. C, No. VII, p. 257.

of the king's writ, the said Charles Steuart did commit the slave on board the Anne and Mary, to safe custody, to be kept till he should set sail, and then to be taken with him to Jamaica, and there sold as a slave. And this is the cause why he, captain Knowles, who was then and now is, commander of the above vessel, then and now lying in the river of Thames, did the said negro, committed to his custody, detain; and on which he now renders him to the orders of the Court. We pay all due attention to the opinion of Sir Philip Yorke, and lord chancellor Talbot, whereby they pledged themselves to the British planters, for all the legal consequences of slaves coming over to this kingdom or being baptized, recognized by lord Hardwicke, sitting as chancellor on the 19th of October, 1749, that trover would lie; that a notion had prevailed, if a negro came over, or became a Christian, he was emancipated, but no ground in law; that he and lord Talbot, when attorney and solicitor general, were of opinion, that no such claim for freedom was valid; that though the statute of tenures had abolished villeins regardant to a manor, yet he did not conceive but that a man might still become a villein in gross, by confessing himself such in open court. We are so well agreed, that we think there is no occasion of having it argued . . . before all the judges, as is usual, for obvious reasons, on a return to a Habeas Corpus. The only question before us is, whether the cause on the return is sufficient? If it is so, the negro must be remanded; if it is not, he must be discharged. Accordingly the return states, that the slave departed and refused to serve; whereupon he was kept, to be sold abroad. So high an act of dominion must be recognized by the law of the country where it is used. The power of a master over his slave has been extremely different, in different countries. The state of slavery is of such a nature, that it is incapable of being introduced on any reasons, moral or political, but only by positive law, which preserves its force long after the reasons, occasion, and time itself from whence it was created, is erased from memory. It is so odious, that nothing can be suffered to support it, but positive law. Whatever inconveniences, therefore, may follow from the decision, I cannot say this case is allowed or approved by the law of England; and therefore the black must be discharged.

[*S.T.*, xx, 80.]

XXI

REX *v.* TUBBS,[1] 1776

[Tubbs was a certified waterman of the City of London who had been impressed for the Navy. He claimed that his certificate exempted him from impressment.]

IN THE COURT OF KING'S BENCH

LORD MANSFIELD : The power of pressing is founded upon immemorial usage allowed for ages : if it be so founded and allowed for ages, it can have no ground to stand upon, nor can it be vindicated or justified by any reason but the safety of the State : and the practice is deduced from that trite maxim of the constitutional law of England, " that private mischief had better be submitted to, than that public detriment and inconvenience should ensue." . . . Being founded on immemorial usage, there can be no doubt but there may be an exception out of it, on the same foundation ; upon immemorial usage.   I therefore lay out of the case all that has been said about the necessity of an Act of Parliament to create an exemption ; and likewise all that has been mentioned relative to the doubt stated of the power of the Crown to exempt by charter. . . . The only question . . . is, " whether, in fact, there is evidence of such usage as a matter of right ? " . . . In the first place, it does not appear from any law book, it does not appear from any history, it has not been suggested at the Bar, that there is, throughout the whole kingdom, any other exemption by the common law. . . . Persons liable, must come purely within the description of seamen, sea-faring men &c. . . . The commission is not to press landsmen, or persons of any other description of life. . . . It is a very strong circumstance, therefore, that there is in fact no other exemption stated or alluded to, which rests upon the common law.   There are many exemptions by statute ; but they are grounded upon considerations of public policy . . . But the exemption of those called the watermen of the City of London, is to be found in no statute or common law book whatever. . . . There is no instance of any officer upon the impress service ever having paid any regard to a water-bailiff's certificate, nor any case produced where the city had taken it up as a matter of right, or insisted upon it as such in a Court of Justice.   Therefore to give my opinion upon the case as at present stated, and upon the mere fact whether this exemption as here claimed is, or is not, warranted by immemorial usage, I cannot say it is.

[Cowper, ii, 517.]

[1] See Sect. C, No. XIV, p. 289, and Vol. II, Sect. A, No. XIV, § XLIII, p. 31.

SECTION D

MISCELLANEA

I

A FIRST MINISTER,[1] 1660–67

(A)

The Chancellor . . . desired wholly to be left to the Discharge of his Office, and that all other Officers might diligently look to their own Provinces, and be accountable for them ; and detested Nothing more than that Title and Appellation, which He saw He should not always be able to avoid, of principal Minister or Favourite, and which was never cast on him by any Designation of the King, (who abhorred to be thought to be governed by any single Person) but by his preferring his Pleasures before his Business, and so sending all Men to the Chancellor to receive Advice. And hereby the Secretaries of State, not finding a present Access to him when the Occasions pressed, resorted to the Chancellor, with whom his Majesty spent most Time, to be resolved by him ; which Method exceedingly grieved him, and to which He endeavoured to apply a Remedy, by putting all Things in their proper Channel, and by prevailing with the King, when He should be a little satiated with the Divertisements He affected, to be vacant to so much of his Business, as could not be managed and conducted by any Body else.

[*The Continuation of the Life of Edward, Earl of Clarendon* (ed. 1759), ii, 77.]

(B)

[Clarendon had told the King during his exile that]

" England would not bear a Favourite, nor any one Man, who should out of his Ambition engross to himself the Disposal of the publick Affairs." He said, " He was more now of the same Mind, and was confident that no honest Man, of a competent Understanding, would undertake that Province." . . . " Whilst He kept the

[1] See Sect. D, No. XXIX, p. 369, No. XXXIX, p. 387, and No. XLVII, p. 398.

Office He had . . . the King felt not the Burden of it; because little of the Profit of it proceeded out of his own Purse, . . . Whereas if He gave over that Administration, and had Nothing to rely upon for the Support of himself and Family, but an extraordinary Pension out of the Exchequer, under no other Title or Pretence but of being First Minister (a Title so newly translated out of *French* into *English*, that it was not enough understood to be liked, and every Man would detest it for the Burden it was attended with[1]); the King himself . . would be quickly weary of so chargeable an Officer, and be very willing to be freed from the Reproach of being governed by any (the very Suspicion whereof He doth exceedingly abhor) at the Price and Charge of the Man, who had been raised by him to that inconvenient Height above other Men."

[*The Continuation of the Life of Edward, Earl of Clarendon*, ii, 88.]

II

THE PRIVY COUNCIL[2] AND ITS COMMITTEES, 1660-67

(A)

MEMBERSHIP

The Members of that Board [the Privy Council] had been always those great Officers of State, and other Officers, who in Respect of the Places They held had a Title to sit there, and of such others who, having great Titles and Fortunes and Interest in the Kingdom, were an Ornament to the Table. That there were at present too many already, and the Number lessened the Dignity of the Relation.

[*The Continuation of the Life of Edward, Earl of Clarendon*, iii, 565.]

(B)

ITS AUTHORITY

For by the Constitution of the Kingdom, and the very Laws and Customs of the Nation, as the Privy Council and every Member of it is of the King's sole Choice and Election of him to that Trust (for the greatest Office in the State, though conferred likewise by the King himself, doth not qualify the Officer to be of the Privy Council, or to be present in it, before by a new Assignation that Honour is bestowed upon him, and that He be sworn of the Council); so the

[1] Cf. Vol. II, Sect. D, No. XXIX, p. 391.
[2] See Sect. A, No. XXXVI, § III, p. 95, and Sect. D, No. XXII, p. 358, and Vol. II, Sect. D, No. XL, p. 409.

Body of it is the more sacred, and hath the greatest Authority in the Government of the State, next the Person of the King himself, to whom all other Powers are equally subject : And no King of *England* can so well secure his own just Prerogative, or secure it from Violation, as by a strict defending and supporting the Dignity of his Privy Council.

[*The Continuation of the Life of Edward, Earl of Clarendon*, iii, 676.]

(C)

THE COMMITTEE

As soon as it pleased God to bring his Majesty into *England*, He established his Privy Council, and shortly out of them a Number of honourable Persons of great Reputation, who for the most Part are still alive, as a Committee for foreign Affairs, and Consideration of such Things as in the Nature of them required much Secrecy ; and with these Persons He vouchsafed to join me. And I am confident this Committee never transacted any Thing of Moment, his Majesty being always present, without presenting the same first to the Council-Board. . . .

[*The Continuation of the Life of Edward, Earl of Clarendon*, iii, 874.]

(D)

A COMMITTEE

. . . We to a Committee of the Council to discourse concerning pressing of men ; but, Lord ! how they meet ; never sit down : one comes, now another goes, then comes another ; one complaining that nothing is done, another swearing that he hath been there these two hours and nobody come. At last it come to this, my Lord Annesly, says he, " I think we must be forced to get the King to come to every committee ; for I do not see that we do any thing at any time but when he is here." And I believe he said the truth : and very constant he is at the council table on council-days . . .

[Pepys, *Diary*, ed. H. B. Wheatley, iv, 362, February 27, 1665.]

(E)

THE " CABINET "

. . . Home and eat something, and then shifted myself, and to White Hall, and there the King being in his Cabinet Council (I desiring to speak with Sir G. Carteret), I was called in, and demanded by the King himself many questions, to which I did give him full answers. There were at this Council my Lord

Chancellor, Archbishop of Canterbury, Lord Treasurer, the two
Secretarys, and Sir G. Carteret. . . .

[Pepys, *Diary*, iv, 285, Nov. 9, 1664.]

(F)

The " Cabinet "

. . . and then Sir W. Pen and I by coach to White Hall, and
there staid till the King and Cabinet were met in the Green
Chamber, and then we were called in ; and there the King began with
me, to hear how the victualls of the fleete stood. I did in a long
discourse tell him and the rest (the Duke of Yorke, Lord Chancellor,
Lord Treasurer, both the Secretarys, Sir G. Carteret, and Sir W.
Coventry,) how it stood, . . .

[Pepys, *Diary*, v, 411, Aug. 26, 1666.]

(G)

What could the Chancellor say ? ". . . That he would be ready
to confer with the *Portugal* Ambassadour [1] when He came, and then
He should entertain his Majesty farther upon that Subject." The
Ambassadour came to him, repeated what he said and proposed to
the King . . . of all which the Chancellor gave his Majesty a
faithful Account, without presuming to mingle with it a Word of
his own Advice. The King appeared abundantly pleased, and
willing to proceed farther ; and asked " what was next to be done : "
To which He answered, " that it was a Matter of too great Importance for him to deliver any Opinion upon ; indeed too great for
his Majesty to resolve, upon the private Advice of any one Man.
. . ." And therefore He desired him " that He would call to him
four or five Persons, whom He thought to be the most competent
Considerers of such an Affair, and consult it very maturely with
them. . . ." The King appointed that the Lord Treasurer, the
Marquis of *Ormond*, the Lord Chamberlain, and Secretary *Nicholas*,
should be together at the Chancellor's House, where his Majesty
would likewise be and propose the Business to them.

[*The Continuation of the Life of Edward, Earl of Clarendon*, ii, 150.]

(H)

Upon the whole Matter,[2] the King thought not fit to make
any further Exceptions, but resolved to assemble his whole Privy
Council, and to communicate the Matter to them ; for it did remain
a Secret yet, no Man knowing or speaking of it. The Council was

[1] Treating of the Marriage Alliance, 1662.
[2] The Portuguese Marriage proposals, 1662.

so full, that there was only one Counsellor that was absent. The King informed them of all that had passed in that Affair. . . . He commanded then the particular Propositions, which were offered by the Ambassadour, to be reported. And thereupon He commanded and conjured all the Lords severally to give him their Advice ; for He said " He had not yet so firmly resolved, but that He might change his Mind, if He heard Reasons to move him : And therefore They would not deal faithfully with him, if They did not with all Freedom declare their Judgment to him." In short, every Man delivered his Opinion, and every One agreed in the Opinion, " that it was very fit for his Majesty to embrace the Propositions . . . and that their Advice was, " that He should speedily and without more Delay conclude the Treaty."

[*The Continuation of the Life of Edward, Earl of Clarendon*, ii, 178.]

(I)

And after several Debates [1] the King thought it so counsellable a Thing, that He resolved to have it debated before that Committee which He trusted in his most secret Affairs ; and the Chancellor being then lame of the Gout, He commanded that all those Lords should attend him at his House. Besides his Majesty himself and the Duke of *York*, there appeared the Lord Treasurer, the General, the Earl of *Sandwich*, the Vice-Chamberlain Sir *George Carteret*, who had been a great Commander at Sea, and the two Secretaries of State . . . Upon these Reasons, urged and agreed upon by those who could not but be thought very competent Judges, in Respect of their several Professions and great Experience, the King resolved to ease himself of the insupportable Burden of maintaining *Dunkirk* . . . Upon this full Deliberation, his Majesty inclined rather to give it up to *France* than to *Spain* ; but deferred any positive Resolution till He had imparted the whole Matter to the Council-Board, where the Debate was again resumed. . . . After a long Debate of the whole Matter at the Council Board, where all was averred concerning the Uselessness and Weakness of the Place, by those who had said it at the Committee ; there was but one Lord of the Council who offered his Advice to the King against parting with it. . . . In Conclusion, his Majesty resolved to put it into the Hands of *France*, if that King would comply with his Majesty's Expectation in the Payment of so much Money as He would require for it. . . .

[*The Continuation of the Life of Edward, Earl of Clarendon*, ii, 384 *sqq.*]

[1] On the question of the sale of Dunkirk, 1662. The ' Debates ' were between the Treasurer, the General, the Duke of York, and the King.

III

MANAGEMENT OF THE COMMONS,[1] 1663

(A)

The House of Commons was upon the Matter not the same :
Three Years sitting, for it was very near so long since They had
been first assembled, had consumed very many of their Members ;
and in the Places of those who died, great Pains were taken to have
some of the King's menial Servants chosen : so that there was a
very great Number of Men in all Stations in the Court, as well
below Stairs as above, who were Members of the House of Commons.
And there were very few of them, who did not think themselves
qualified to reform whatsoever was amiss in Church or State, and
to procure whatsoever Supply the King would require. . . . They,
according to the Comprehension They had of Affairs, represented
their Advice to him for the conducting his Affairs. . . . They
brought those, who appeared to them to be most zealous for his
Service . . . to receive his Majesty's Thanks, and from himself his
immediate Directions how to behave themselves in the House ;
when the Men were capable of no other Instruction, than to follow
the Example of some discreet Man in whatsoever He should vote,
and behave themselves accordingly.

To this Time, the King had been content to refer the Conduct
of his Affairs in the Parliament to the Chancellor and the Treasurer ;
who had every Day Conference with some select Persons of the
House of Commons, who had always served the King, and upon
that Account had great Interest in that Assembly, and in Regard of
the Experience They had and their good Parts were hearkened to
with Reverence. And with those They consulted in what Method
to proceed in disposing the House, sometimes to propose sometimes to consent to what should be most necessary for the Publick ;
and by them to assign Parts to other Men, whom They found
disposed and willing to concur in what was to be desired : And all
this without any Noise, or bringing many together to design, which
ever was and ever will be ingrateful to Parliaments. . . .

[*The Continuation of the Life of Edward, Earl of Clarendon*, ii, 343-45]

(B)

The King very much desired to have him [Sir Henry Bennet]
elected a Member in the House of Commons, and commanded the

[1] Cf. Sect. D, No. XXXVIII, p. 385.

Chancellor to use his Credit to obtain it upon the first Opportunity.
. . . [Sir William Coventry] had sate a Member in the House of
Commons, from the Beginning of the Parliament, with very much
Reputation of an able Man . . . and was one of those with whom
They, who were trusted by the King in conducting his Affairs in
the lower House, consulted frequently; but not so much, nor
relied equally upon his Advice, as upon some few others who had
much more Experience . . . and so did not think himself to be
enough valued and relied upon, and only to be made Use of to the
celebrating the Designs and Contrivance of other Men, without
being signal in the Managery, which He aspired to be. Nor did
any Man envy him the Province, if He could indeed have governed
it, and that others who had more useful Talents would have been
ruled by him. . . .

When those two Persons, Sir *Henry Bennet* and Mr. *Coventry*
. . . came now to sit together in the House of Commons ; . . . They
thought they should have the greatest Wrong imaginable, if They
did not entirely govern it, and if the King took his Measures or
what should be done there from any Body but themselves. They
made Friendships with some young Men, who spake confidently and
often . . . Sir *Harry Bennett* . . . believed He understood the
House and what was to be done there, as well as any Man in *England*.

He recommended those Men to the King " as Persons of sublime
Parts, worthy of his Majesty's caressing : That He would undertake
to fix them to his Service ; and when They were his own, He
might carry what He would in the House of Commons." The Men
had Parts indeed and good Affections, and often had resorted to
the Chancellor, received Advice from him, and thought themselves
beholden to him ; being at that Time entirely governed by Sir
Hugh Pollard, who was himself still advised by the Chancellor (with
whom He had a long and fast Friendship) how He should direct
his Friends, having indeed a greater Party in the House of Commons willing to be dispensed of by him, than any Man that ever
sate there in my Time. But now these Gentlemen had got a
better Patron ; the new Courtier had raised their Value, and talked
in another Dialect to them, of Recompenses and Rewards, than
They had heard formerly.

[*The Continuation of the Life of Edward, Earl of Clarendon*, ii, 347-
351, *passim*.]

IV

THE DECLARATION OF INDULGENCE,[1]
1672

Our care and endeavours for the preservation of the rights and interests of the church, have been sufficiently manifested to the world, by the whole course of our government, since our happy Restoration, and by the many and frequent ways of coercion that we have used for reducing all erring or dissenting persons, and for composing the unhappy differences in matters of religion, which we found among our subjects upon our return : But it being evident by the sad experience of twelve years, that there is very little fruit of all those forcible courses, we think ourselves obliged to make use of that supreme power in ecclesiastical matters, which is not only inherent in us, but hath been declared and recognized to be so by several statutes and acts of parliament : And therefore we do now accordingly issue out this our royal Declaration, as well for the quieting the minds of our good subjects in these points, for inviting strangers in this conjuncture to come and live under us, and for the better encouragement of all to a chearful following of their trades and callings, from whence we hope, by the blessing of God, to have many good and happy advantages to our government ; as also for preventing for the future the danger that might otherwise arise from private meetings, and seditious conventicles. And in the first place, we declare our express resolution, meaning and intention to be, That the Church of England be preserved, and remain entire in its doctrine, discipline and government, as it now stands established by law : And that this be taken to be, as it is, the basis, rule and standard of the general and public worship of God, and that the orthodox conformable clergy do receive and enjoy the revenues belonging thereunto ; and that no person, though of different opinion or persuasion, shall be exempt from paying his tythes, or other dues whatsoever. And further, we declare, That no person shall be capable of holding any benefice, living, or ecclesiastical dignity or preferment of any kind in this kingdom of England, who is not exactly conformable. We do in the next place declare our will and pleasure to be, That the execution of all and all manner of penal laws in matters ecclesiastical, against whatsoever sort of non-conformists, or recusants, be immediately suspended, and they are hereby suspended. And all judges of assize and gaol-delivery, sheriffs, justices of the peace, mayors,

[1] See Sect. B, No. IV, p. 163.   See also Sect. D, No. XVI, p. 343.

bailiffs, and other officers whatsoever, whether ecclesiastical or civil, are to take notice of it, and pay due obedience thereunto. And that there may be no pretence for any of our subjects to continue their illegal meetings and conventicles, we do declare, That we shall from time to time allow a sufficient number of places, as shall be desired, in all parts of this our kingdom, for the use of such as do not conform to the Church of England, to meet and assemble in, in order to their public worship and devotion ; which places shall be open and free to all persons.   But to prevent such disorders and inconveniences as may happen by this our indulgence, if not only regulated, and that they may be better protected by the civil magistrate, our express will and pleasure is, That none of our subjects do presume to meet in any place, until such place be allowed, and the teacher of that Congregation be approved by us.   And lest any should apprehend, that this our restriction should make our said allowance and approbation difficult to be ordained, We do further declare, That this our indulgence, as to the allowance of public places of worship, and approbation of teachers, shall extend to all sorts of nonconformists and recusants, except the recusants of the Roman catholic religion, to whom we shall no ways allow in public places of worship, but only indulge them their share in the common exemption from the executing the penal laws, and the exercise of their worship in their private houses only.   And if after this our clemency and indulgence, any of our subjects shall presume to abuse this liberty, and shall preach seditiously, or to the derogation of the doctrine, discipline, or government of the established church, or shall meet in places not allowed by us ; we do hereby give them warning, and declare, we will proceed against them with all imaginable severity: And we will let them see, we can be as severe to punish such offenders, when so justly provoked, as we are indulgent to truly tender consciences.

[*Parl. Hist.*, iv, 515, March 15, 1672.]

V

PARTY ORIGINS AND PARLIAMENT,[1] 1673

This began to weigh heavy upon the country, and to make them repine, which stirred up some gentlemen in both Houses to oppose this currant (which was called the Country party in opposition to those others, whom they called the Court party).   The first of thes

[1] See Sect. B, No. XXXVIII, p. 240, Sect. D, No. XXIII, p. 359, and No. XLVI, p. 396.

pretended to protect the country from being overburdened in their estates, in their privileges and liberty as Englishmen and to stand by the religion and government as established by law. The other declared for that too, but at the same time for the King to have a sufficient revenue and power for the exercize of his regall authority, without too much depending upon the people, since it had prooved of soe ill consequence in the exemple of his father.

This difference made gentlemen more active to come into Parlament as oppertunity offered, as their inclinations led them to one side or the other, which was the caus of great competitions in elections, and of great charges [1] to thos that stood, insoemuch as it did cost some persons from one or two hundred pounds to two thousand. This was not all the reason of some mens soe eager endeavours to be Parlament men neither. Such as were in debt found protection by it (this Parlament haveing sitt soe long, and meeting soe often) and others had gotten great places and presents from Court to stand by that interest. Soe that it was noe wonder, when I offered myselfe to stand at Audbrough, if I had noe fewer than five competitours. . . .

The way that had been used time out of mind in that borough for chooseing Parlament men was only by nine electours, the owners of nine bourgage houses. But Mr. Wentworth, lord of the mannour, pretended that long since ther were twenty-four houses that had right to elect, which being at this time in his own possession, he had given and his predicessours but one voat for them all, and therfore pretended to alien and sell them now to create soe many more voats. Thes Mr. Wentworth gave to Mr. Benson. Mr. Long stood by the popularity, or the houshoulders at large that paid scot and lot. I stood by the only known way of electing, which was the nine (of which I had the majority), and all the rest desisted before the time of election ; soe that the sheriff made a double return of Mr. Benson and me, but did not return Mr. Long.

[*Memoirs of Sir John Reresby*, ed. A. Browning, 1936, p. 89.]

VI

MONEY BILLS: LORDS AND COMMONS, 1677 [2]

My Lord Treasurer sent for me among others that evening, and desired us to assist what we could to reconcile a difference likely to

---

[1] See Sect. D, No. XXVII, p. 366, No. XXXV, p. 377, No. L, p. 399. Also Sect. A, No. XXXI, p. 83, and other refs. in note 3 at p. 83.

[2] See also Sect. B, No. I, p. 153, and Vol. II, Sect. A, No. XLII, p. 141.

happen between the two Houses about frameing the bill for the 600,000l. to be given the King, which might endanger the loss of the bill.

The thing was this—the Commons had made a claus in the bill that the officers of the Exchequer should give an account to that Hous of the laying out of that money to the uses to which it was given. The Lords had added another to that, which was that thos officers should be accountable to both Houses. The Commons would not allowe of this, saying the Lords could neither add to nor deminish in bils for money ; as it was peculiar to the Commons to give mony, soe it was only proper to them to have an account of its laying forth. The Lords replyed that to deny them to call the officers of the Exchequer to an account was to deny them their privilege of judicature which they had as the supreme court ; and were possessed of it in the very like case, for when mony was given by the Convention for disbanding the army, an account of laying it out was ther enacted to be given to their Hous as well as the other. In fyne, both adhering to their point, the King prevailed with the Lords to rase their claus out of the bill, and the other continuing it passed after in that method ; soe the Commons gott the better.

[*Memoirs of Sir John Reresby*, p. 116, April 12, 1677.]

VII

CROWN AND FOREIGN POLICY,[1] 1677

May 21. The Parlament met at Westminster the 21, according to adjournment. The King, speaking to both Houses, acquainted them that he could not make such alliances as they desired without they would first give him mony to make preparations for warr. The Commons, upon the debate concerning the Kings speech, would not consent to give mony, but voted the contrary, till his Majesty had first entered into alliances ; and at the same time that an addresse should be humbly made to him to enter into a league offensive and defensive with Holland, and the rest of the United Provinces, for the safety of thes kingdoms, for the recovery of Flanders, and to abate the power of the French King.

May 28. The said address being presented to the King, he returned this answer to it : that we had exceeded the methods of Parlament in that address, that we had entrenched on his prerogative by not only directing him to make alliances, but by pointing out to

[1] See Sect. B, No. VII, p. 179, Sect. D, No. XIX, p. 354, and No. XXX (A), p. 369, and Vol. II, Sect. B, No. XXVIII (C), at p. 228, Sect. D, No. LIII, p. 442.

him what thos alliances should be, and with whom they should
be made ; that the power of makeing peace or warr only belonged to
himselfe, and if that was taken from him he should only have the
name of a King, and then what states or princes would treat with
him ; for which reason, as well as want of mony, he should not
comply with their address.   However, he should doe that which
became him for the good of his kingdomes, and ordered the Parlament to be adjourned till the 16 of July following.

The Speaker (which was Mr. Seamur) returning to the Hous did
adjourn the Hous, but without putting the question, by the Kings
order or command.   This (as was mooved) being without president
did soe discompose the Hous that some were offering to hold the
Speaker in the chair ; but he leaped from it very nimbly, for he was
in fear that many being dissatisfyed with his Majesty's speech would
have made some mutinous speeches before he could adjourn, and
with good reason.   I was of thos that thought the Commons outwent
their due limits in wording their address, in nameing the countrys
with which he was to make his alliances and the manner of them
(viz., offensive and defensive) ;   for besides the undecencys of it,
the Secretarys of State then of the Hous tould us the thing would
be granted if we did not loos it in the manner of asking it.

[*Memoirs of Sir John Reresby*, p. 123, May 21 and 28, 1677.]

VIII

KING'S APPROVAL OF THE SPEAKER,[1] 1679

The Commons began to be angry with the Treasurer for the
Speaker[2] they had a mind to being refused by the King, saying he
was the occasion of it, bycaus he was not his lordship's friend.
The dispute continued between the King and the Commons till
at last they addressed the King, beseeching him not to invade their
undoubted privilege to choos their Speaker.   The King still
insisted upon it as his to allowe their choice, without which he was
noe Speaker.   It was the opinion of all the moderate men in the
Hous that such punctillios did not deserve to occasion delays when
ther laid business of such importance before them, but the angry
party would not submitt ;   soe that by way of expedient the King
did proroague the Parlament from the 11th to the 15th instant ;
then Sergiant Gregory was chosen Speaker, which all sides agreed to.

[*Memoirs of Sir John Reresby*, p. 171, March 7, 1679.]

[1] See also Vol. II, Sect. D, No. XXVIII, p. 391.   [2] Seymour.

IX

CHARLES II AND TEMPLE'S SCHEME FOR A PRIVY COUNCIL,[1] 1679

His Ma^{ty} gives You all thanks for Your Service to Him here, and for all the Good Advices You have given him, wch might have been more frequent, If the great Number of this Councill had not made it unfit for the Secrecy & dispatch that are necessary in many great Affaires. This forced Him to use a smaller Number of you in a forreigne Committee, and sometimes the Advices of some few among them (upon such occasions) for many yeares past. Hee is sorry for the ill success He has found in this Course, and sensible of the ill posture of affaires from that, and, some unhappy accidents wch have raised great jealousyes and dissatisfaction among His Good Subjects & thereby left the Crowne & Government in a Condition too weake for those Dangers we have reason to feare both at home & abroad.

These His Ma^{ty} hopes may be yet prevented by a Course of wise & steady Councells for the future. . . . To this End Hee hath resolved to lay aside the Use he may have hitherto made of any Single Ministry or private advices, or forreigne Committees for the general direction of His affaires, and to constitute such a Privy Councell, as may not only by its Number be fit for the Consultation and Digestion of all business both Domestique & forreigne but also by the choise of them out of the Severall parts this State is composed of, may be the best informed in the true Constitutions of it, And thereby the most able to Councell him in all the Affaires and Interests of this Crowne & Nation, And by the Constant advice of such a Councell, His Ma^{ty} is resolved hereafter to govern His Kingdomes, together with the frequent Use of his great Councill of Parliament, wch he takes to be the true ancient Constitution of this State & Government.

Now for the greater dignity of this Councill His Ma^{ty} resolves their Constant Number shall be limited to that of Thirty, and for their greater authority there shall be fifteen of His chief Officers, who shall be Privy Councellours by their places, and for the other fiveteen Hee will choose ten out of the Severall Ranks of the Nobility, and five Commoners of the Realme, whose knowne Abilityes Interest & Esteeme in the Nation, shall render them without any suspition of either mistakeing or betraying the true Interests of the Kingdome and consequently of advising Him ill.

[1] See also Vol. II, Sect. B, No. V, p. 163.

In the first place therefore and to take care of the Church His Ma^ty will have the Archbishop of Canterbury, and Bishop of London for the time being; and to Informe Him well in what concernes the Lawes, the Lord Chancellour, and one of the Lord Chief Justices: for the Navy & Stores (wherein consists the chiefe strength and safety of this Kingdom) the Admirall & Master of the Ordnance: For the Treasury the Treasurer & Chancellour of the Exchequer (or, whenever any of these charges are in Commission, then the first Com^r to serve in their roome), the rest of the fifteen shall be the Lord Privy Seale, the M^r of the Horse, Lord Steward, and Lord Chamberlain of His Household, the Groome of the Stole, and the two Secretaryes of State. And these shall be all the Offices of his Kingdome, to wch the Dignity of a Privy Councellor shall be annexed. The other (15) His Ma^ty has resolved, and hopes he has not chosen ill. His Ma^ty intends besides to have such Princes of His Blood as he shall at any time call to this Board, being here in Court, a President of the Councill whenever he shall find it necessary, and the Secretary of Scotland, when any suit shall be here. But these, being uncertain, Hee reckons not of the constant number of thirty wch shall never be exceeded.

. . . His Ma^ty was also pleased to declare that he would have all his affairs here debated freely, of what kind soever they were and therefore absolutely [in] secrecy.

His Ma^ty was also pleased to declare that he would communicate this alteration of the Councill unto both Houses of Parliament in a few words.

[Privy Council Register, Charles II, xv, April 21, 1679.]
[Quoted by H. W. V. Temperley in *E.H.R.*, xxvii, 684.]

X

THE CABINET, *circa* 1680

He [Guildford] begins with the state of the Cabinet Council,[1] that consisted of those few great officers, and courtiers, whom the king relied upon for the interior dispatch of his affairs. And as offices of the law, out of clerkships, spawn other offices, so this council was derived from the Privy Council, which, originally, was the same thing, and derived out of the *magnum concilium*, by that name, mentioned in the rolls of parliament; and the same, out of parliament, authorized by King Henry VII. was known by the place where it sat, viz. the Star-chamber. Assemblies, at first, reasonably constituted of a due number and temper for dispatch of

See Vol. II, Sect. B, No. V, p. 160.

affairs committed to them, by improvident increase, came to be formal and troublesome, the certain consequence of multitude, and thereby a new institution becomes necessary : whereupon it is found easier and safer to substitute than to dissolve. Thus the cabinet council, which, at first, was but in the nature of a private conversation, came to be a formal council, and had the direction of most transactions, of the Government, foreign and domestic.

[The Hon. Roger North, *Life of Lord Keeper Guildford*, etc., ed. 1826, ii, 50.]

XI

THE POWERS OF THE PRIVY COUNCIL, 1681

We had this day at Council an Experiment, we had such an other this time twelvemonth, how necessary it is, that some of My Lords that His Ma^{ty} does principally rely on, sh^d be allwayes present where there is Council-sitting. . . .

My Lord Privy Seal . . . was pleased to fall upon the Sec^{rys} of State, for that they did not communicate to the Council those matters of importance, that the Peace of the Kingdomes and the Repose of Christendom did depend upon, or to that effect, saying that they came thither to hear news and causes.

Thereupon I took the liberty to assert, that it was the Duty of the Sec^{rys} soe to manage those correspondencies that his Ma^{ty} should direct, that he should have a constant and punctual account of it ; but that they were not at liberty to carry any part of their Intelligences to the Council, unless His Majesty directed it specially soe to be done ; [1] that I for my part had allwayes governed myself by that Rule, because I thought it a Duty that lay indispensably upon me.

My Lord was pleased to reply, that Mr. Sec^{ry}'s answer was such an Answer as never was offer'd by a Sec^{ry} to a Privy Council before ; however that he could not find fault with the answer, for it was constant to the practice of later years. My Lord Faulconberg likewise was pleas'd to allow of what I had answered ; but found fault with the present Constitution of the Council, and confess'd, that this was not a Debate proper for this Council. There was nothing resolv'd on, but that those who found themselves aggrieved with the Constitution of the Council, as now it is, might complaine to his Ma^{ty} when he Return'd. . . .

[Secretary Jenkins to Earl Conway, October, 5, 1681, S.P.D., E.B., lxii, 327-30 (quoted by H. W. V. Temperley, *E.H.R.*, xxviii, 130).]

[1] See Sect. D, No. XLIII, p. 393, and No. XLIX, p. 399.

XII

SURRENDER BY BRISTOL CORPORATION TO CHARLES II OF ITS CHARTERS, 1683

A Writ of Quo Warranto [1] being brought against the Old Charter by Sir Robert Sawyer, Attorney-General, in Hill. Term in the 34th and 35th year of King Charles II the following Resignation of the Governing Part of the Charter was made as follows :

To the King's Most Excellent Majesty

We, the Mayor, Burgesses, and Commonalty, of your Majesty's City of *Bristol*, reflecting upon our selves, That for several Years last past, we have negotiated all the principal Affairs of this City, made all the *Elections of our Mayor*, Recorder, Town-Clerk, Sheriffs, Common-Council-Men, and all other Officers whatsoever, amongst us, by a *supernumerary* Common-Council, *contrary* to the Institution of this City, by your Majesty's Royal Progenitors, in our Charters, and *contrary to the Usage and Custom* ever since that Time, till of late Years ; and that we may have been faulty in that Particular, which might justly offend your Sacred Majesty, and for that there are some Defects in the Model of the Government among us, which renders it not so useful to your Sacred Majesty, or to Our selves as we could wish, we do therefore (with all Humility) beseech your Majesty to accept, and we have Granted, Surrendered, and Yielded up ; and we do hereby, Grant, Surrender, and Yield up, unto your most Gracious Majesty, your Heirs and Successors, all and singular the Powers, Franchises, Liberties, Privileges, and Authorities whatsoever, and howsoever, heretofore granted to, or used, or exercised by the said Mayor, Burgesses, and Commonalty, in, for, or concerning the Electing, Nominating, Constitutions, Being, or Appointing, of any Person or Persons, into, or for the several respective Offices . . . of the Mayor, Aldermen, Sheriffs, Recorder, Town-Clerk, Steward of the Sheriffs Court, and Coroners of the said City . . . or into, or for the Exercise or Execution of them, or any of them ; with the Offices and Authorities, Place and Places of Justices of the Peace, and Common-Council-Men, within the City of *Bristol*, and County of the same City ; and all the Right, Title, Interest, Claim, and Demand, whatsoever, of us, the said Mayor [etc] of Electing [etc] the said Officers and Members . . . by Force and Virtue of any Letters Patent, Charters, Prescriptions,

[1] See Sect. C, No. V, p. 254, and Sect. A, No. XXVII, p. 75. Also Sect. D, No. XIII, p. 333, and No. XVII (A) and (B), p. 347.

Customs, or other Ways or Means whatsoever : And we, the said
Mayor [etc] do hereby humbly beseech your Majesty to accept of
this our Surrender, and do . . . implore your Grace and Favour,
to Confirm our Charter, as to all other Privileges, and to Re-grant
unto the Citizens of this your Ancient City of *Bristol*, the said
Liberties and Franchises, or so many of them, and in such Manner,
as your Majesty (in your great Wisdom) shall judge most conducing
for the better Government of your City of *Bristol*. In *Witness*
whereof, we the said Mayor, Burgesses, and Commonalty, of the
City of *Bristol*, have hereunto set our Common Seal, this 9th day
of *November*, in the 35th Year of the Reign of our Sovereign Lord,
King Charles the Second, by the Grace of God, of *England* &c.

[*Bristol: The City Charters*, sold by F. Farley and others, 1736.]

XIII

CHARLES II's NEW CHARTER TO THE CITY OF BRISTOL,[1] 1685

Know ye, That We the bettering of our City of Bristol, and
County of the same City, graciously desiring and willing, That
for ever hereafter, in the same City, and County thereof, there may
continually be had one sure and undoubted Manner for the keeping
of our Peace, and for the good Rule and Government of our People
there ; . . . and hoping that the Citizens of the same City, and
their Successors, by our Grant, may have and enjoy greater Liberties,
Profits and Privileges ; and that then they would think themselves
more especially and strongly oblig'd to the Service of us, our
Heirs and Successors, of our especial Grace, certain Knowledge
and mere Motion ; and at the humble Petition of the late Mayor,
Burgesses, and Commonalty, of the City aforesaid, we have
Willed . . . and by these Presents, for us, our Heirs and Successors,
do Will . . . That the aforesaid City of Bristol, from henceforth,
may be and remain, for ever, a City Incorporate, and County of
itself, such and in as ample and large Bounds, Circuits, and Precincts,
bounded and limited, as the same City and County at any Time
within the Space of Twenty Years now last past, was bounded and
limited ; and that the Citizens and Inhabitants of the said City,
and their Successors, from henceforth, for ever, be, and shall be,
One Body Corporate, and Politick, in Deed, Fact, and Name, by

[1] See Sect. D, No. XII, p. 332, and No. XVII (A) and (B), p. 347, and
No. XXIV, p. 362.

the Name of Mayor, Burgesses, and Commonalty, of the City
of Bristol . . . and that they . . . shall be for ever hereafter,
Persons able, and in Law capable to have, receive, and to possess
Lands, Tenements, Liberties, Privileges, Jurisdictions, Franchises,
Hereditaments of what Kind or Sort soever . . . and also Goods,
Credits, and Chattles . . . and that by the same Name they may
and can plead and be impleaded, . . . in all Courts and Places . . .
in all Manner of Actions, Suits, Plaints . . . as other our Liege
People . . . and that the Mayor, Burgesses, and Commonalty of
the City aforesaid, and their Successors, may, for ever, have a
Common Seal to serve for all Causes and Businesses whatsoever
. . . and it shall be lawful for them . . . that Seal, at their
Pleasure, from Time to Time, to break, change, and also to make a
new from Time to Time, as to them shall seem good . . . And
farther we Will . . . that there shall be, within the City aforesaid,
one Mayor, of the Citizens of the City aforesaid, in form hereunder
specified and expressed : And for the better Execution of this our
Will in this Point, we have assigned . . . our well-beloved Sir
William Clutterbuck, Knight, to be our First and Present Mayor,
. . . until the 15th Day of *September* next following ; . . . and
that as well the said Sir *William Clutterbuck*, as every succeeding
Mayor of the same City, may and shall have such and the same
Power and Authority, Perquisites and Profits, in and by all Things,
to the said Office in any Manner whatsoever belonging or appertaining, as any other preceding Mayor heretofore had or enjoyed . . .
he the aforesaid Sir *William Clutterbuck*, and every other succeeding
Mayor of the same City, at the Time of his respective Admission
into the Office . . . taking the Corporal Oath of Allegiance, and
the Oaths, by a certain Act of Parliament, entitled, *An Act for
Regulating Corporations*, appointed : and also, all other Oaths,
usually administered to the Mayor . . . *openly* and *publickly*, and
with the Solemnity in these Cases accustomed, in the *Guildhall* of
the same City, . . . *And further*, we Will . . . That for ever
hereafter, there be . . . Two Sheriffs, who . . . the same Power
and Authority, Priviledge, Profit, and Jurisdiction, may have, in,
and to all Things, as other Sheriffs of the said City . . . had and
enjoyed.   And . . . we have assigned . . . our well-beloved
Nathaniel Driver, and *Edmund Arundel*, Esqrs. to be our first and
present Sheriffs of the City . . . until the said 1st Day of *September*
. . . [oath to be taken before the Mayor].

    Moreover we Will, . . . That there shall be in the City aforesaid,
so many, and such of the better and more discreet Burgesses and
Inhabitants of the City aforesaid, who with the Mayor and Aldermen
of the same City, may not exceed the Number of *Forty and Three*,

and with them shall be, and shall be called and named a Common-
Council of the said City, . . . at all Times to be aiding and
assisting to the Mayor of the said City, . . . in all Causes and
Matters . . . And we have assigned . . . our well-beloved Sir
John Churchill, [and 41 others] to be, and that they shall be, and
be called, The *Common-Council of the City* aforesaid, to continue
in the said Office of the Common-Council of the City aforesaid,
during their Natural Lives, respectively : [oaths of Allegiance, and
oaths in Corporations Act to be taken and other usual oaths] And
we Will . . . That whensoever, and as often as it shall happen,
any one or more of the Common-Council-Men of the City . . .
shall die or from the Office . . . be removed, That then, and so
often the Common Council of the City aforesaid, at the Meeting of
the Common-Council next following, after such Death or Removal
or the Major Part of them . . . one or more, of the *Better* and
more *Discreet Burgesses*, and Inhabitants . . . into the Place or
Places of him or them, so dead or removed, . . . shall and may
elect and make, and by perpetual Succession, continue the Number
of *Forty and Two*, besides the Mayor of the said City, for the
Time being. *And further*, we Will, . . . That the Common-
Council . . . shall have full Power and Authority of Constituting,
Ordaining, Making, and Establishing, from Time to Time, Laws,
Statutes, Constitutions, Decrees, and Ordinances . . . which to
them, or the Major Part of them . . . shall seem to be good . . .
for the Good Rule and Government of the City . . . and for
declaring in what Manner and Order the said Common-Council
. . . and all and singular the Artificers, Inhabitants, and Residents
. . . in their Offices, Functions, Mysteries, Arts and Businesses
in the said City . . . shall behave Themselves, for the further
publick Good, common Profit, and good Rule, of the said City . . .
yet so, that the Laws, Ordinances, Constitutions . . . be reasonable,
and be not repugnant or *contrary* to the *Laws, Statutes, Customs*, or
Rights of this our Kingdom of *England* . . . *Provided always* ; and
we Will, That the Laws, Statutes . . . to be made as aforesaid . . .
shall not continue or be *Valid* above the Space of *One Year*, next
after the making the same, unless our Chancellor, or the Keeper
of our Great Seal of *England*, for the Time being, or the Chief
Justice of either Bench at *Westminster*, or any Two of them, shall
approve such Laws, Statutes, and Constitutions, . . . to be *legal*,
and in Law *valid*, such their Approbations under their Hands and
Seale, in Writing to be signified.

And Moreover, we Will . . . That the Mayor and Common-
Council aforesaid . . . for ever hereafter in and upon the 15th
Day of *September*, yearly may assemble in the Chapel of St. *George*

in the *Guildhall* of the said City, . . . or some other convenient
Place . . . to elect and name, by the Majority of Voices, One out
of the Common-Council . . . to be Mayor . . . for One Year,
next following; and also, . . . to elect Two Burgesses, . . . of
the Common-Council . . . or not, to be Sheriffs . . . for One
Year, next following; and to elect and name all other Officers or
Ministers . . .

   And we Will . . . That such Elections as aforesaid, made, or
to be made by the Common-Council . . . be, and shall be, as
sound and effectual as any Election or Elections heretofore made.
And further, we Will . . . That every Person, for ever, hereafter
elected to the Office of Mayor before his admission . . . in and
upon the Feast of St. *Michael* the Arch-Angel, the Corporal Oath,
called *The Oath of Allegiance*; and also, all other Oaths . . .
publickly shall take, as in these Presents in that part above is
appointed. [Sheriffs to be sworn by the Mayor: Provision for
special elections necessitated by death or other voidance of a Mayor
or of Sheriffs].

   And further we do Grant, to the Mayor, Burgesses, and
Commonalty, of the said City . . . That they . . . may, and shall
have in the said City, an honest and discreet Man, skilled in the
Laws of *England*, and a Barrister by the Space of five Years at the
least, in Form hereafter in these Presents mentioned to be chosen,
who shall be . . . called the Recorder of the said City. [Appoint-
ment of Sir John Churchill as First Recorder, during his Natural
Life with all Power and Authority, Wages and Profits as former
Recorders. He and his successors to take Oaths.] *And further* we
Will . . . That in case of the Death or Removal of the said Sir
John Churchill or any other Recorder . . . That then, it shall and
may be lawful for the Mayor and Common-Council . . . to elect
and name, One honest and discreet Man, learned in the Laws of
England, and by the Space of Five Years, a Barrister, to succeed
such Recorder, so dead or removed, as aforesaid. *Provided always*:
and we Will, That he so elected shall not be admitted . . . until
we, our Heirs, or Successors . . . shall signify the Approbation
. . . of such Person. *We Will also* . . . That . . . there be . . .
Twelve Aldermen in the said City . . . who may, and shall be
Conservators, and Justices of the Peace, . . . And that they . . .
shall have, hold, and enjoy . . . the same, and such Sort of Powers
and Authorities, as the Aldermen of the said City at any Time
before the Date of these Presents . . . enjoyed. . . . The said
John Churchill . . . shall be the First Alderman of the said City
. . . [Eleven others named as Aldermen]

   We Will also . . . That if any one or more of the Aldermen

. . . die or . . . be removed, it shall be lawful for the Mayor . . .
to summon all the Aldermen . . . to assemble in the *Guildhall* . . .
and there the Mayor and Aldermen . . . shall choose and name,
One or More of the Common-Council . . . to succeed. [Aldermen
to take the oaths] *And also*, we Will, That all the Aldermen . . .
shall be resident in the said City, the Suburbs, Liberties, and
Precints of the same. [Refusal of Office of Mayor, Sheriff etc
punishable by fine not exceeding £500 or prison in default]
Provided always, and we Will, That if any Person elected . . . shall
voluntarily before the Mayor, and Two of the Aldermen . . .
swear That he hath not, or doth not, *Bona Fide*, possess Riches,
Real and Personal, to the Value of *Two Thousand Pounds*, of lawful
Money of *England*, (he) shall be . . . exempted from the Penalty Fine
and Imprisonment.

And further we Will, . . . That the Mayor and Aldermen . . .
shall be Justices of us . . . to enquire . . . of all Treasons,
Murders, Rapes of Women, and other Felonies; of whatsoever
Trespasses, Riots, Routs, unlawful Conventicles, Embraceries,
Maintenances, Ambidexters, Regratings and Forestallings . . .
And also, of those who . . . lie in wait to maim or kill our People
. . . [etc] within the County of the City, the Liberties and Precints of *Bristol* . . . And also, to enquire of all Sheriffs, Bailiffs,
Constables, and Gaol-keepers, who . . . in the Execution of their
Offices against Artificers, Servants, Labourers, Victuallers, Hostlers,
Beggars, and Vagabonds . . . who . . . unduly have behaved themselves . . . shall happen to be cold, remiss, or negligent . . . And
that the Mayor, Burgesses, and Commonalty, of the said City
. . . may have all Manner of Fines, Ransoms, Issues, Forfeitures,
and Amerciaments, before the said Justices . . . to be made,
assessed, forfeited, and adjudged. *And we Will*, That the Mayor
. . . the Recorder . . . and the said Aldermen . . . or Three of
them (whereof the Mayor or Recorder, if he shall be in the City,
or the Senior Aldermen . . . we Will to be One) . . . may and
shall have and hold, *Four Sessions* of the Peace . . . and all and
singular those Things, within the same City . . . to do, exercise,
and execute . . . as any other Justices of Gaol-Delivery have,
exercise, and do execute . . . whereof, in such Case, the Mayor
and Recorder of the said City, for the Time being, we Will to be
Two. *Saving* always, to Our selves . . . all the Fines, Issues, and
Amerciaments, Forfeitures, and other Profits, before the Justices
of Gaol-Delivery [J.P.s to be sworn]. *And we Will* . . . That
they . . . shall have . . . One fit and honest Man, who is, and
shall be called, The Town-Clerk of the said City. And . . . we
do assign nominate . . . and make, our well-beloved *John Romsey*,

Esq: to be our First and Present Town-Clerk . . . [He and successors to enjoy usual emoluments. Mayor and Common-Council to choose future Town-Clerks]. *Provided* always, and we Will, That no one to the Office of Town-Clerk . . . shall be elected, unless he be skilled in the Laws of *England*, and a Barrister by the Space of Three Years at the least; and that no Person so elected . . . shall be admitted . . . before we . . . shall signify our Approbation of him so elected . . . under the Royal Hand . . . [Person thus approved to be sworn by the Mayor] *Provided* also: and we Will, That no Town-Clerk . . . during the Continuance in the said Office, be, or shall be, an Alderman, or Sheriff, of the City or County aforesaid. *We Will* also, . . . That they . . . shall have . . . One Steward of the Court of the Sheriffs . . . and we make . . . *John Robins* to be the First Steward [to enjoy usual emoluments after being sworn. Mayor and Common-Council thereafter to elect successors, being Barrister of three years standing, to be sworn and admitted after receipt of royal approval].

We Will further, That they . . . shall have Two Coroners . . . and we make . . . *George Lymell*, and *Rowland Searchfield* to be our first Coroners . . . [to take oaths. Mayor and Common-Council thereafter to elect successors, sworn and admitted after receipt of royal approval.]

And further we Will, and do command That the Mayor, Sheriffs, and Common-Council-Men, Aldermen, Justices of the Peace, Town-Clerk, Steward of the Court of the Sheriffs, and Coroners . . . shall take the Oath of Allegiance, and the Oaths by the said Act of Parliament appointed: and other Oaths, their Offices touching, . . . before our most beloved and very faithful Counsellor, *Francis*, Baron of *Guilford*, Keeper of our Great Seal of *England*, our most beloved, and very faithful Cousin and Counsellor, *Henry*, Duke of *Beaufort*, our most beloved, and very faithful Cousin, *Charles*, Marquess of *Worcester*, Son and Heir apparent of the before-mentioned Duke of *Beaufort*, our most beloved and very faithful Counsellor, Sir *Leoline Jenkins*, Kt. (and four others), or any Three of them, . . . *Provided always*, and full Power and Authority, to us, our Heirs and Successors, by these Presents, we do reserve, from Time to Time, and at all Times hereafter, the Mayor, Recorder, and any one or more of the Aldermen or Sheriffs, and any one or more of the Common-Council, or Town-Clerk, Steward of the Sheriffs Courts, or Coroners of the said City . . . at the Will and Pleasure of us, our Heirs, or Successors, in Privy-Council, made, . . . to remove, and to declare him or them to be removed.

We Will also . . . That all Bread, Corn, and Grain . . .

brought by Land, shall be sold and bought at the Ancient Market-Place in *Wine-Street* . . . *We Will further* . . . That they . . . may and shall have, hold, and keep *One Market*, for the Buying and Selling all, and all Manner of Grain, imported by Water, to the Key of the City . . . at the Place commonly called *Aldworth-Slip* . . . yet *we Will*, That the said Market shall be regulated, and reasonable Toll thence proceeding, . . . shall be paid in such Manner and Quantities, as to the Mayor and Aldermen . . . shall seem convenient and expedient. *We Will also* and . . . do grant That they . . . may keep *Three Fairs*, or Markets, for Buying and Selling all, and all Manner of Wool, Wollen Cloth and Wollen Workmanship, on the Days hereafter mentioned viz [18th April for two days, 10th June for two days, first Thursday after Michaelmas for one day, in King-Street] *And also* . . . *Five Fairs*, or Markets, for Buying and Selling all, and all Manner of Horses, Mares, and Colts on . . . [25 January in Temple-Street, 25 & 26 March at Redcliff-Hill, 25 & 26 May at Broad-Mede, 25, 26, 27 September in Temple-Street, 25, 26, 27 November on Redcliff Hill] The aforesaid several Fairs or Markets, in the several Places and Days aforesaid, unless any of the Days shall happen to be the Lord's Day, and then in and upon *Monday* next following, to be held and kept yearly ; . . . together with the Courts of Pypowder there, at the Time of the same several Fairs or Markets, to be held. . . . Yet so, that the several said Markets, or Fairs, . . . be not to the Hurt of neighbouring Markets, or Fairs. *We Will further* and . . . do Grant . . . That the same Mayor, Burgesses, and Commonalty, and the Citizens of the said City, and their Successors, for ever hereafter, may have, hold, use and enjoy, . . . all Gifts, Grants, Courts, Liberties, Exemptions, Franchises, Freedoms, Articles, Immunities and Customs, as well in these Presents, as in any other our Charters or Letters Patent, of us, or any of our Progenitors or Predecessors, late Kings or Queens of *England*, contained, declared, explained, specified, and confirmed : . . . which, by these Presents, are not changed . . . yielding, and paying to us, our Heirs, or Successors yearly, so many, the like, the same and such Rents, Services, Sums of Money, and Demands, whatsoever, as ought to be yielded or paid for the Premises, or any of them ; . . . *In Witness* whereof, We have caused these our Letters to be made Patents. *Witness* Our self at *Westminster*, the Second Day of *June*, in the 36th Year of our Reign

PIGOTT

By Writ of the Private Seal, for a Fine in the Haniper 6£. 13ˢ. 4ᵈ.

GUILFORD, C.S.

[*Bristol: The City Charters.*]

XIV

A BALANCED CONSTITUTION, 1685

(A)

We in England, by a happy use of this controversy, conclude them both in the wrong, and reject them from being our pattern, taking the words in their utmost extent, which is—Monarchy, a thing that leaveth men no liberty ; and a Commonwealth, such a one as alloweth them no quiet. We think that a wise mean [1] between these two barbarous extremes is that which self-preservation ought to dictate to our wishes, and we may say that we have attained to this mean in greater measure than any nation now in being, or perhaps any we have read of, though never so much celebrated for the wisdom or the felicity of their constitutions. We take from one the too great power of doing hurt, and yet leave enough to govern and protect us ; we take from the other the confusion of parity, the animosities and the licence, and yet reserve a due care of such a liberty as may consist with men's allegiance. But it being hard, if not impossible, to be exactly even, our government hath much the stronger bias towards monarchy, which by the more general consent and practice of mankind seemeth to have the advantage in the dispute against a commonwealth. The rules of a common-wealth are too hard for the bulk of mankind to come up to ; that form of Government requireth such a spirit to carry it on as doth not dwell in great numbers, but is restrained to so very few, especially in this age, that, let the methods appear never so reasonable in paper, they must fail in practice, which will ever be suited more to men's nature as it is than as it should be. Monarchy is liked by the people for the bells and the tinsel, the outward pomp and gilding ; and there must be milk for babes, since the greatest part of mankind are, and ever will be, included in that list. And it is approved by wiser and more thinking men as the best when com-pared with others, all circumstances and objections impartially considered.

(B)

Our Trimmer admireth our blessed constitution, in which dominion and liberty are so happily reconciled. It giveth to the Prince the glorious power of commanding freemen, and to the subjects the satisfaction of seeing that power so lodged as that their liberties are secure. . . . And though in some instances the King is restrained, yet nothing in the government can move without him.

[1] Cf. Vol. II, Sect. B, No. I, at p. 154.

Our laws make a true distinction between vassalage and obedience, between devouring prerogatives and a licentious ungovernable freedom ; and as, of all the orders of building, the composite is the best, so ours, by a happy mixture and a wise choice of what is best in others, is brought into a form that is our felicity who live under it, and the envy of our neighbours that cannot imitate it. The Crown hath power sufficient to protect our liberties. The people have so much liberty as is necessary to make them useful to the Crown. Our government is in a just proportion—no tympany, no unnatural swellings either of power or liberty. And whereas, in all overgrown monarchies, reason, learning, and inquiry are banished and hanged in effigy for mutineers ; here they are encouraged and cherished, as the surest friends to a government established upon the foundation of law and justice.

(C)

Our Trimmer is a friend to Parliaments, notwithstanding all their faults and excesses, which of late have given such matter of objection to them. He thinketh that though they may at some times be troublesome to authority, yet they add the greatest strength to it under a wise administration. He believeth no government is perfect except a kind of omnipotency reside in it, to be exercised upon great occasions. Now this cannot be attained by force alone upon the people, let it be never so great. There must be their consent, too, or else a nation moveth only by being driven—a sluggish and constrained motion, void of that life and vigour which is necessary to produce great things ; whereas the virtual consent of the whole being included in their representatives, and the King giving the sanction to the united sense of the people, every act done by such an authority seemeth to be an effect of their choice as well as a part of their duty ; and they do, with an eagerness of which men are uncapable whilst under a force, execute whatsoever is so enjoined, as their own will better explained by Parliament, rather than from the terror of incurring the penalty of the law for omitting it. And by the means of this political omnipotency,[1] whatever sap or juice there is in a nation may be to the last drop produced, whilst it riseth naturally from the root, whereas all power exercised without consent is like the giving wounds and gashes and tapping of a tree at unseasonable times for the present occasion, which in a very little time must needs destroy it. Our Trimmer believeth that by the advantage of our situation there can hardly any such sudden disease come upon us but that the King may have time enough left to consult with his physicians in Parliament. Pretences, indeed may be

[1] Cf. Sect. D, No. XLV (A), p. 395.

made, but a real necessity so pressing that no delay is to be admitted is hardly to be imagined, and it will neither be easy to give an instance of any such thing for the time past, or reasonable to presume it will ever happen for the time to come. But if that strange thing should fall out, our Trimmer is not so strait-laced as to let a nation die or be stifled rather than it should be helped by any but the proper officers. The cases themselves will bring the remedies along with them, and he is not afraid to allow that, in order to its preservation, there is a hidden power in government which would be lost if it was defined, a certain mystery by virtue of which a nation may at some critical times be secured from ruin. But then it must be kept a mystery ; it is rendered useless when touched by unskilful hands, and no government ever had or deserved to have that power which was so unwary as to anticipate their claim to it.

[From the *Character of a Trimmer*, by George Saville, Marquis of Halifax, December 1684-January 1685, quoted from H. C. Foxcroft, *Life and Letters of Sir George Saville*, vol. ii.]

XV

AN ELECTION : CITY OF YORK,[1] 1685

March 10. . . . I found I was to use all diligence and to spare no charge, if I expected success ; and therefore went about the streets from house to house (the aldermen attending upon me) to ask the votes of the citizens ; and on the 13th I made a general entertainment throughout the town, viz., in three or four houses in every street, for those to entertain themselves with good liquor that had promised to be for me ; though my competitors had begun that custom long before, to gain friends. . . .

March 16. All the candidates went into the streets to gather their party to them, where it was presently seen I had a greater number of followers than any of the rest. At eight of the clock the poll began at the common hall, and lasted till six at night, when the books being cast up, there appeared that Sir Metcalfe Robinson had polled 781 ; Mr. Moyser, 770 ; Colonel Jenkins, 502 ; and Sir John Reresby had polled 937. So that the sheriffs published me and Sir Metcalfe Robinson duly elected for burgesses to serve in the next Parliament for that city. The charge[2] I was at in this election came to 350 £., though it cost them more that lost it.

[*Memoirs of Sir John Reresby*, p. 320, 1685.]

[1] See also Sect. D, No. XXVIII, p. 367, and No. XXXV, p. 377.
[2] See Sect. D, No. V, p. 325, No. XXVII, p. 366, and No. L, p. 399.

XVI

THE DECLARATION OF INDULGENCE,[1] 1687

(A)

His Majesty's gracious declaration to all his loving subjects for liberty of conscience.

James R.

It having pleased Almighty God, not only to bring us to the imperial crowns of these kingdoms through the greatest difficulties, but to preserve us by a more than ordinary Providence, upon the throne of our royal ancestors, there is nothing now that we so earnestly desire, as to establish our government on such a foundation as may make our subjects happy, and unite them to us by inclination as well as duty; which we think can be done by no means so effectually, as by granting to them the free exercise of their religion for the time to come, and add, that to the perfect enjoyment of their property, which has never been in any case invaded by us since our coming to the crown; which being the two things men value most, shall ever be preserved in these kingdoms during our reign over them, as the truest methods of their peace and our glory. We cannot but heartily wish, as it will easily be believed, that the people of our dominions were members of the Catholic church; yet we humbly thank Almighty God, it is, and has of long time been our constant sense and opinion (which upon divers occasions we have declared) that conscience ought not to be constrained, nor people forced in matters of mere religion. It has ever been directly contrary to our inclination, as we think it is to the interest of government, which it destroys by spoiling trade, depopulating countries, and discouraging strangers, and finally, that it never obtained the end for which it was employed. And in this we are the more confirmed by the reflections we have made upon the conduct of the four last reigns. For after all the frequent and pressing endeavours that were used in each of them, to reduce these kingdoms to an exact conformity in religion, it is visible the success has not answered the design; and that the difficulty is invincible. We therefore, out of our princely care and affection unto all our loving subjects, that they may live at ease and quiet, and for the increase of trade, and encouragement to strangers, have thought fit by virtue of our royal prerogative, to issue forth this our declaration of indulgence, making no doubt of the

[1] See also Sect. D, No. IV, p. 324, for Charles II's Declaration of Indulgence, and Sect. C, No. VII, p. 258, for the Seven Bishops' Case arising from the reissue of this Declaration on April 27, 1688. The Second Declaration contained a promise to call a Parliament in November.

concurrence of our two houses of parliament, when we shall think it convenient for them to meet.

In the first place we do declare, that we will protect and maintain our archbishops, bishops, and clergy, and all other our subjects of the church of England in the free exercise of their religion, as by law established, and in the quiet and full enjoyment of all their possessions, without any molestation or disturbance whatsoever.

We do likewise declare, that it is our royal will and pleasure, that from henceforth the execution of all and all manner of penal laws in matters ecclesiastical, for not coming to church, or not receiving the sacrament, or for any other non-conformity to the religion established, or for or by reason of the exercise of religion in any manner whatsoever, be immediately suspended and the further execution of the said penal laws, and every of them is hereby suspended.

And to the end that by the liberty hereby granted, the peace and security of our government, in the practice thereof, may not be endangered, we have thought fit, and hereby streightly charge and command all our loving subjects, that as we do freely give them leave to meet and serve God after their own way and manner, be it in private houses, or places purposely hired or built for that use, so that they take special care that nothing be preached or taught amongst them which may any ways tend to alienate the hearts of our people from us or our government, and that their meetings and assemblies be peaceably, openly and publicly held, and all persons freely admitted to them ; and that they do signify and make known to some one or more of the next justices of the peace, what place or places they set apart for those uses. And that all our subjects may enjoy such their religious assemblies with greater assurance and protection—we have thought it requisite, and do hereby command, that no disturbance of any kind be made or given to them, under pain of our displeasure, and to be further proceeded against with the uttermost severity.

And forasmuch as we are desirous to have the benefit of the service of all our loving subjects, which by the law of nature is inseparably annexed to, and inherent in our royal person, and that none of our subjects may for the future be under any discouragement or disability (who are otherwise well inclined and fit to serve us) by reason of some oaths or tests that have been usually administered on such occasions, we do hereby further declare, that it is our royal will and pleasure, that the oaths commonly called the oaths of supremacy and allegiance, and also the several tests and declarations mentioned in the acts of parliament made in the twenty-fifth and thirtieth years of the reign of our late royal brother king Charles the second,[1] shall not at any time hereafter be required to

[1] Sect. A, No. XVI, p. 39, and No. XVII, p. 43.

be taken, declared, or subscribed by any person or persons whatsoever, who is or shall be employed in any office or place of trust, either civil or military, under us, or in our government. And we do further declare it to be our pleasure and intention, from time to time hereafter, to grant our royal dispensations under our great seal, to all our loving subjects so to be employed, who shall not take the said oaths, or subscribe or declare the said tests or declarations in the above-mentioned acts, and every of them.

And to the end that all our loving subjects may receive and enjoy the full benefit and advantage of our gracious indulgence hereby intended, and may be acquitted and discharged from all pains, penalties, forfeitures, and disabilities by them or any of them incurred or forfeited, or which they shall or may at any time hereafter be liable to, for or by reason of their nonconformity, or the exercise of their religion; and from all suits, troubles or disturbances for the same; we do hereby give our free and ample pardon unto all nonconformists, recusants, and other our loving subjects for all crimes and things by them committed or done, contrary to the penal laws formerly made relating to religion, and the profession or exercise thereof; hereby declaring, that this our royal pardon and indemnity shall be as good and effectual to all intents and purposes, as if every individual person had been therein particularly named, or had particular pardons under the great seal, which we do likewise declare shall from time to time be granted unto any person or persons desiring the same; willing and requiring our judges, justices, and other officers, to take notice of, and obey our royal will and pleasure herein-before declared.

And although the freedom and assurance we have hereby given in relation to religion and property, might be sufficient to remove from the minds of our loving subjects all fears and jealousies in relation to either; yet we have thought fit further to declare, that we will maintain them in all their properties and possessions, as well of church and abbey lands, as in any other their lands and properties whatsoever.

Given at our Court at Whitehall the 4th day of April, 1687, in the third year of our reign.

[*S.T.* xii, 234.]

(B)

Order in Council

At the Court at Whitehall, May 14, 1688

By the King's most Excellent Majesty, and the Lords of his Majesty's most Honourable Privy-Council.

It is this day ordered by his majesty in council, That his majesty's late gracious Declaration, bearing date the 27th of April last, be read at the usual time of divine service, upon the 20th and 27th of this month, in all churches and chapels within the cities of London and Westminster, and ten miles thereabout; and upon the 3rd and 10th of June next, in all other churches and chapels throughout this kingdom. And it is hereby further ordered, That the right reverend the bishops cause the said Declaration to be sent and distributed throughout their several and respective dioceses, to be read accordingly.   W. BRIDGMAN.

[*S.T.* xii, 278.]

(C)

PETITION OF THE BISHOPS

To the KING's most excellent Majesty.

The humble Petition of William Archbishop of Canterbury, and of divers of the suffragan Bishops of that Province, now present with him, in behalf of themselves and others of their absent brethren, and of the Clergy of their respective Dioceses,

Humbly sheweth ; That the great averseness they find in themselves to the distributing and publishing in all their churches your majesty's late Declaration for Liberty of Conscience, proceedeth neither from any want of duty and obedience to your majesty (our holy mother, the Church of England, being both in her principles and in her constant practice unquestionably loyal ; and having, to her great honour, been more than once publicly acknowledged to be so by your gracious majesty), nor yet from any want of due tenderness to Dissenters, in relation to whom they are willing to come to such a temper as shall be thought fit, when the matter shall be considered and settled in parliament and convocation ; but amongst many other considerations, from this especially, because that Declaration is founded upon such a Dispensing power as hath been often declared illegal in parliament, and particularly in the years 1662, and 1672, and in the beginning of your majesty's reign ; and is a matter of so great moment and consequence to the whole nation, both in church and state, that your Petitioners cannot in prudence, honour or conscience, so far make themselves parties to it, as the distribution of it all over the nation, and the solemn publication of it once and again, even in God's house, and in the time of his divine service, must amount to, in common and reasonable construction.

Your Petitioners therefore most humbly and earnestly beseech your majesty, that you will be graciously pleased not to insist upon

their distributing and reading your majesty's said Declaration :—
And your Petitioners (as in duty bound) shall ever pray, &c.
Signed :

W. CANT.	THO. BATH & WELLS.
W. ASAPH.	THO. PETRIBURGENS.
FRAN. ELY.	JON. BRISTOL.
JO. CICESTR.	

[*S.T.* xii, 318. Presented May 18, 1688.]

XVII

JAMES II AND BOROUGH CORPORATIONS, 1688

(A)

AT THE COURT AT *WHITEHALL*, JANUARY 13, 1687–88

By the King's Most Excellent Majesty, and the Lords of His
Majesty's Most Honourable Privy-Council

Whereas, by the Charter granted to the City of *Bristol*,[1] a Power
is reserved to his *Majesty*, by his Order in Council, to remove from
their Imployments any Officers in the said City, His *Majesty* in
Council is pleased to Order, and it is hereby Ordered, That *Richard
Lawe*, Mayor, *William Swymmer*, Esq ; (and 5 others) Aldermen
Samuel Wallis and *John Sandford*, Sheriffs, *John Romsey*, Esq ;
Town-Clerk ; *Edmund Arundell* (and 17 others) Common-Council-
Men, be, and they are hereby removed and displaced from their
aforesaid Offices in the said City of *Bristol*

WILLIAM BRIDGEMAN.

[*Bristol: the City Charters.*]

(B)

JAMES REX

Trusty and well-beloved, we Greet you well.

Whereas We have, by our Order in Council, thought fit to
remove *Richard Lawe* from being Mayor of that our City of *Bristol*
(and the others as above) We have thought fit hereby to Will and
Require you, forthwith, to Elect and Admit our Trusty and Well-
beloved *Thomas Day*, to be Mayor (and others in the places of the
deprived Officers) in the Room of the Persons above-mentioned,
without administring unto them any Oath, or Oaths, but the usual
Oath for the Execution of their respective Places, with which we

[1] See Sect. D, No. XIII, p. 333. See also No. XXIV, p. 362.

are pleased to dispense in His Behalf ; and for so doing, this shall
be your Warrant ; and so We bid you farewell.

Given at our Court at Whitehall the 14th Day of January, 1687-8,
in the Third Year of our Reign

By His Majesty's Command

SUNDERLAND, P.

To our Trusty and Well-
beloved, the Aldermen
and Corporation of our
City of *Bristol.*

[*Bristol : The City Charters.*]

(C)

CONSEQUENCES OF CROWN'S CONTROL OF MUNICIPALITIES : YORK

September 1. I writt several letters to the Lord Maior of
Yorke, Mr. Rains, to the aldermen and severall citizens declareing
my intention to stand for cittizen ther in the next Parlament, and to
desire their voats. The next post after I recieved for answer from
his lordship that a court of aldermen had been called the day before
he received my letter, and that they had ressolved, as most of the
twenty-four and commons had done, to choos two of the bench
for their members, viz. Mr. Prickit, their deputy-recorder, and
Sir Stiphen Thomson. The Maior, as he had ever been my
adversary, had done this purpasly to prevent my admission. I
had encouragement, however, from other cittizens that I might
succeed. . . .

September 6. I went to Windser, and acquainted the King
with my letters and their answers, desireing three things of him.
One was, if, since the contest was like to be both chargeable and
difficult, and the success doubtfull, it were yet his pleasure I should
stand, to which he said positively I should. Secondly, that in case
I miscarryed, he would not, the opposition being so strong against
me, impute it to my fault, which he promessed me he would not.
Thirdly, that he would assist me in all he could not to be bafled
in the contest, by such means as I should propose, with which he
complyed, and gave orders to the lords for the purgeing of corporations (as my lord Marquis of Powis tould me and Mr. Brent), that
whatever change or alteration I desired in that citty, it should be
complyed with, and that they should putt in or out amongst the
magistrates and officers as I pleased (which the King, it seems,
had reserved power to doe by the last charters).

I was very carefull to act in this matter, considering, if I putt out none, it would showe I had noe power, and they would dispise me ; if too many, it might exasperate and make the citty jealous that I was too deep in the Court interest, which might prevent my successe. I therefore only desired that the Lord Maior might be laid aside and Sir Stiphen Thomson be made Maior, (which would prevent his being a member of Parlament) ; and that two, viz., Mr. Edward Thomson and Mr. Ramsden, who had been my principal friends in the former election of me for Yorke, and were turned out afterwards partly on my account, might be putt into their places.

[*Memoirs of Sir John Reresby*, p. 50, Sept. 1688.]

(D)

RESTORATION OF ANCIENT CHARTERS [1]

By the King
A Proclamation
For Restoring Corporations to their Ancient Charters,
Liberties, Rights, and Franchises.

James Rex.

Whereas, We are informed, that several Deeds of Surrender which have been lately made by several Corporations, and Bodies Corporate, of, and in our Cities and Towns, within our Kingdom of *England*, and Dominion of *Wales*, of the Charters, Franchises, and Privileges, are not yet *recorded* or *enrolled* ; and that upon the Proceedings and Rules for Judgment, which have lately been had upon the *Quo Warranto's*, or Informations in Nature of a *Quo Warranto*, Judgments are not yet entered upon Record ; whereupon, notwithstanding new Charters have been granted in the Reign of our late dear Brother, and in our Reign, which said Deeds (being not *enrolled* or *recorded*) do not amount unto, or in Law make any Surrender of the Charters, Franchises, or Liberties, therein mentioned ; and such of the said Corporations, or Bodies Politick, against which Rules for Judgments have been made in the Life-time of our late dear Brother, or since, in our Court of *King's-Bench*, (but no Judgments entred upon *Record*) are not discorporate or dissolved ; and that it is in our Power to leave such Corporations in the same Estate and Condition they were in, to discharge all further Proceedings and Effects that may be of such Rules for Judgments, and Deeds of Surrender. We do hereby publish and declare, That upon due Search and Examination made, We have Satisfaction that the Deeds of Surrender made by Corporations, and Bodies

[1] See also Sect. A, No. XXV, § III, p. 74.

Publick, of the said Cities and Towns, except the Corporations following; *that is to say, Retford, Nottingham,* (and 27 others including *Exeter, Winchester, Plymouth, Doncaster* and *Colchester*) are not *enrolled* or *recorded* in any of our Courts; and that though Rules for Judgments have passed upon Informations in Nature of a *Quo Warranto,* against the Corporations, and Bodies Politick, of several Cities and Towns in our said Kingdom and Dominions, yet no Judgments have been, or are entered upon *Record,* upon any such Informations, except against the City of *London, Chester, York* [and 6 other places]: *And We,* of our mere Grace and Favour, being resolved to restore, . . . into the same State and Condition they were, and was, in our late dear Brother's Reign, before any Deed of Surrender . . . or Proceedings against them . . . upon any *Quo Warranto* . . .

We do hereby, therefore, publish, declare, direct and require, That the said Corporation . . . of all the said Cities, Towns . . . and the Mayors, Bailiffs, Sheriffs [etc] . . . take on them, and proceed to act as a Corporation, or Body Politick, and where Places are vacant by Death, or otherwise, to make Elections . . . And We do also, by this our *Proclamation,* made with the Advice of our said Council, discharge, remove, and dismiss, all and every Person or Persons, of and from all Offices . . . which they claim only by Charter . . . since the Dates of the respective Deeds of Surrender or Rules for Judgment, . . .

And We do hereby . . . declare, That We have caused all and every the said Deeds of Surrender, which can be found, to be delivered and put into the Hands of our Attorney-General, to be by him *cancelled* and *returned* to the Corporations . . . And have also given to our said Attorney Authority . . . to enter upon the respective Records, *Noli Prosequis,* and legal Discharges thereof . . .

And We do hereby likewise declare . . . as far and concerning the restoring to such of our Cities, Corporations, and Boroughs, . . . which have made Deeds of Surrender, or have had Judgments given against them, (which Surrenders and Judgments are entered of *Record,*) That our Chancellor, Attorney-General and Solicitor-General, without Fees to any Officer or Officers whatsoever, . . . are hereby required to prepare and pass Charters, Instruments [etc] for the Incorporating, Regranting, Confirming, and Restoring, to all and every the said Cities, Corporations and Boroughs, their respective Charters, Liberties, Rights, Franchises, and Privileges, and for restoring the respective Mayors, Bailiffs [etc] as were of such Cities [etc] at the Time of such Deeds of Surrender, or Judgments, respectively given or had.

And *whereas* divers Boroughs, that were not heretofore Corporations, have since the Year 1679, had Charters of Incorporation granted and passed unto them, We . . . determine and annul the said last mentioned Charters and Corporations ; . . . And We do hereby promise and declare, That We will do, and consent to all such Acts, Matters, and Things, as shall be necessary to render these our Gracious Intentions and Purposes effectual, it being our Gracious Intention to call a Parliament as soon as the General Disturbance of our Kingdom, by the intended Invasion, will admit of.

Given at our Court at Whitehall the 17th Day of October 1688, in the Fourth Year of our Reign

God Save the King

[*Bristol : The City Charters.*]

(E)

CONFUSION IN NOTTINGHAM

Whereas the Burgesses have lately Chosen severall persons to bee of the Councell of this towne, who refuise to act therein upon ye accountt of ye old Charter, they Lookeing upon itt to bee still in force, from whence they conclude yat they ought not to joyne with or act under any other Authority then what is grounded upon yat Charter ; therefore ye Councell, taking occation from them, doe thinke fitt, for there owne vindication and others' satisfaction, to assert and declare yat they are and ever were for ye said old Charter, and ever did and does looke upon ye pretended Surrender of yat Charter to bee fraudalant and sureptitious ; and yat ye new Charter, obtained there upon, was Illegal and unjust ; and they ever did and doe highly approve, owne, and commend all those who stood for ye old charter, as they themselves in their private Stations and capacitys ever did, nor would they have accepted of ye late King's Mandates, but to serve the towne, and to free them from a company of ill men, who had no Legall right to there places, and who had very much oppressed, enslaved, and abuised the Town ; And for these reasons and ends, and to prevent those men from coming in againe, and to secure the government till the old charter should bee restored, they, upon the *Quo Warranto*, procured a new Charter, not out of any dislike to the old one, but out of necessity, they being advised to itt, and ye time then not permitting the restoration of that Charter ; by which new Charter they have hithertoo, to the servise of the Towne, keept out the new-Charter men, and have acted as much as they could under itt, according to the rulls of the old Charter, and to the servise and interest of all those yat were friends to itt ; soe that, in truth, the old charter ever since ye new-Charter men was turned out, hath biene vertually amongst us ; for they have done all they can to haisten and have itt, till when they must either act by the authority they have, or dissert ye goverment ; but yat they may not, must not, nor dare not doe, and therefore they must doe ye first ; and who ever Blames them for itt, or will not assist them in itt, are, they thinke, very much to blame.

[Nottingham Borough Records, Minute of the Common Council, v, 359, Aug. 30, 1689.]

XVIII

INVITATION TO WILLIAM, PRINCE OF ORANGE, JUNE 30, 1688

We have great satisfaction to find by 35 [Mr. Russell], and since by Mons. Zulestein, that your Highness is so ready and willing to give us such assistances as they have related to us. We have great reason to believe, we shall be every day in a worse condition than we are, and less able to defend ourselves, and therefore we do earnestly wish we might be so happy as to find a remedy before it be too late for us to contribute to our own deliverance ; but although these be our wills, yet we will, by no means, put your Highness into any expectations which may misguide your own councils in this matter ; so that the best advice we can give, is to inform your Highness truly both of the state of things here at this time, and of the difficulties which appear to us. As to the first, the people are so generally dissatisfied with the present conduct of the government, in relation to their religion, liberties and properties (all which have been greatly invaded) and they are in such expectation of their prospects being daily worse, that your Highness may be assured, there are nineteen parts of twenty of the people throughout the kingdom, who are desirous of a change ; and who, we believe, would willingly contribute to it, if they had such a protection to countenance their rising, as would secure them from being destroyed, before they could get to be in a posture able to defend themselves ; it is no less certain, that much the greatest part of the nobility and gentry are as much dissatisfied, although it be not safe to speak to many of them before hand ; and there is no doubt but that some of the most considerable of them would venture themselves with your Highness at your first landing, whose interests would be able to draw great numbers to them, whenever they could protect them and the raising and drawing men together ; and if such a strength could be landed as were able to defend itself and them, till they could be got together into some order, we make no question but that strength would quickly be increased to a number double to the army here, although their army should all remain firm to them ; whereas we do upon very good grounds believe, that their army then would be very much divided among themselves ; many of the officers being so discontented that they continue in their service only for a subsistence, (besides that, some of their minds are known already), and very many of the common soldiers do daily shew such an aversion to the Popish religion, that there is the greatest probability imaginable of great numbers of deserters which would come from them, should there be such an occasion ; and amongst the seamen, it is almost certain there is not one in ten who would do them any service in such a war. Besides all this, we do much doubt, whether this present state of things will not yet be much changed to the worse before another year, by a great alteration which will probably be made both in the officers and soldiers of the army, and by such other changes as are not only to be expected from a packed parliament, but what the meeting of any parliament (in our present circumstances) may produce against those, who will be looked upon as principal obstructers of their proceedings there ; it being taken for granted, that if things cannot then be carried to their wishes in a parliamentary way, other measures will be put in execution by more violent means ; and although such proceedings will then heighten the discontents, yet such courses will probably be taken at that time, as will prevent all possible means of relieving ourselves.

These considerations make us of opinion that this is a season in which we may more probably contribute to our own safeties than hereafter (although we must own to your Highness there are some judgments differing from ours in this particular), in so much that if the circumstances stand so with your Highness, that you believe you can get here time enough, in a condition to give assistances this year sufficient for a relief under these circumstances which have been now represented, we who subscribe this, will not fail to attend your Highness upon your landing, and to do all that lies in our power to prepare others to be in as much readiness as such an action is capable of, where there is so much danger in communicating an affair of such a nature, till it be near the time of its being made public. But as we have already told your Highness, we must also lay our difficulties before your Highness, which are chiefly ; that we know not what alarum your preparations for this expedition may give, or what notice it will be necessary for you to give the

States before hand, by either of which means their intelligence or suspicions here, may be such, as may cause us to be secured before your landing; and we must presume to inform your Highness, that your compliment upon the birth of the child (which not one in a thousand here believes to be the Queen's) hath done you some injury; the false imposing of that upon the Princess and the nation, being not only an infinite exasperation of people's minds here, but being certainly one of the chief causes upon which the declaration of your entering the kingdom in a hostile manner, must be founded on your part, although many other reasons are to be given on ours. If, upon a due consideration of all these circumstances, your Highness shall think fit to adventure upon the attempt, or at least to make such preparations for it as are necessary, (which we wish you may), there must be no more time lost, in letting us know your resolution concerning it, and in what time we may depend that all the preparations will be ready, as also whether your Highness does believe the preparations can be so managed as not to give them warning here, both to make them increase their force, and to secure those they shall suspect would join with you. We need not say anything about ammunition, artillery, mortar pieces, spare arms, &c. because if you think fit to put any thing in execution you will provide enough of these kinds, and will take care to bring some good engineers with you; and we have desired Mr. H.[1] to consult you about all such matters, to whom we have communicated our thoughts in many particulars too tedious to have been written, and about which no certain resolutions can be taken, till we have heard again from your Highness.

25.	24.	27.	29.	31.
Sh[rewsbury]	Dev[onshire]	Danby	Lumley	London [Bp. of]

35.	33.
Russel	Sydney

[Sir John Dalrymple, *Memoirs of Great Britain and Ireland*, vol. ii, Appendix Part the First, p. 228.]

XIX

LOCKE ON "FEDERATIVE POWER", 1689

145. . . . So that under this consideration the whole community is one body in the state of Nature in respect of all other states or persons out of its community.

---

[1] Rear-Admiral Arthur Herbert, later Earl of Torrington.

146. This, therefore, contains the power of war and peace,[1] leagues and alliances, and all the transactions with all persons and communities without the commonwealth, and may be called federative if any one pleases. So the thing be understood, I am indifferent as to the name.

147. These two powers, executive and federative, though they be really distinct in themselves,[2] yet one comprehending the execution of the municipal laws of the society within itself upon all that are parts of it, the other the management of the security and interest of the public without with all those that it may receive benefit or damage from, yet they are always almost united. And though this federative power in the well or ill management of it be of great moment to the commonwealth, yet it is much less capable to be directed by antecedent, standing, positive laws than the executive, and so must necessarily be left to the prudence and wisdom of those whose hands it is in, to be managed for the public good. For the laws that concern subjects one amongst another, being to direct their actions, may well enough precede them. But what is to be done in reference to foreigners depending much upon their actions, and the variation of designs and interests, must be left in great part to the prudence of those who have this power committed to them to be managed by the best of their skill for the advantage of the commonwealth.

[John Locke, *Second Treatise on Civil Government*, 1689, ch xii.]

XX

THE CABINET,[3] 1694

(A)

SHREWSBURY TO WILLIAM III

By her majesty's directions, I suppose, Mr. Secretary Trenchard, upon Wednesday last, writ letters to my lord keeper, lord Portland, privy seal, lord Sydney, and myself, to meet at his office to consult about the two services that are now expected from the fleet, viz. that of the Mediterranean and the attempt upon Brest. This being at Mr. Secretary's office, where many people came in upon business, could not be such a secret, but the marquis of Normanby hearing of it, came to me yesterday morning, and so positively assured me, that

---

[1] See Sect. B, No. VII, p. 179 ; Sect. D, No. VII, p. 327 ; and No. XXX (A), p. 369.   [2] See Sect. D, No. XXXVI, p. 378.

[3] See Sect. D, No. XXXI (A), p. 371.

your majesty had, in express terms, promised him to be called to all councils, when any, in what place soever, should be summoned, that he could not believe but this proceeding of the queen, in leaving him out in any consultations, must proceed from a mistake, and therefore desired me to go to her majesty, and to acquaint her, how he understood himself to be left here, entrusted with your majesty's business of the most secret concerns. I waited upon the queen accordingly, and she was pleased to permit me to tell my lord again, that your majesty's instructions to her were, that there should be no cabinet council; but lords should be summoned, sometimes one, and sometimes another, as they should be judged most proper for the business they were to advise about; only some whose employments belong to the crown, made it necessary they should not be excluded.

[Coxe, *Correspondence of Shrewsbury*, p. 34, May 11/21, 1694.]

(B)

WILLIAM III TO SHREWSBURY

It is true, that I did promise my lord Normanby, that when there was a cabinet council, he should assist at it; but surely this does not engage either the queen or myself, to summon him to all meetings, which we may order, on particular occasions, to be attended solely by the great officers of the crown, namely, the lord keeper, the lord president, the lord privy seal, and the two secretaries of state. I do not know the reason why lord Sydney was summoned to attend, unless it was on account of some business relative to the artillery, which, however, might have been communicated to him. I do not see that any objection can be made to this arrangement, whenever the queen summons the aforesaid officers of the crown, to consult on some secret and important affair. Assuredly that number is fully sufficient, and the meeting cannot be considered as a cabinet council, since they are distinguished, by their offices, from other counsellors of state, and therefore no one can find fault if they are more trusted and employed than others.

I entirely agree with you, that if Lord Normanby is admitted, all those who have ever attended any cabinet council, should likewise have a seat. Doubtless the queen communicates to him the dusiness, that is to be discussed, and places confidence in him, with which he ought to be contented; but if he forces us to have a regular cabinet council, merely that he may attend, and when we do not deem it advantageous for the welfare of our service, it is assuming too much.

[Coxe, *Correspondence of Shrewsbury*, p. 38, May 22/June 1, 1694.]

XXI

THE CONVOCATION CONTROVERSY,[1] 1697

. . . I will lay down some *General Rules*, by which we may the better Judge, at what *Times*, and in what *Cases*, it may be either *necessary*, or *expedient* for a *Prince* to call a *Convocation*. . . .

It has, I think been generally agreed, that the main *End* for which *Synods* are necessary to be Assembled, is either to *establish* the *Faith*, and to declare the *Unity*, of the *Church*, in *matters* of *Doctrine*: or to *advise*, and *assist* the *Civil Magistrate*, in things pertaining to the *Discipline* of it. . . . The Exercise of *Ecclesiastical Jurisdiction* . . . is commonly provided for by some more *Ordinary* Means: So that, except in a few *Cases* of an *Extraordinary Nature*, there is seldom any Occasion for a *Synod* to meet, upon such an Account.

. . . And (1st) Because in *Clear*, and *Evident Cases*, where both the *Truth* is *Manifest*; and the *Consent* of the *Church Constant* and *Out* of *doubt*; there is no need of any *Definitions*, either to declare its Sense, or to testifie its Agreement: therefore neither can there be any Need to Assemble a *Convocation*, to *Judge* or *Determine* in such *Cases*.

If, in a *Christian Country*, where the *Gospel* is profess'd, and its Truth establish'd, and Men have, for many Ages, been Bred up in the Knowledge and Belief of it; A sort of *Libertines* should arise, to deny not only the truth of *Christianity*, but the very *Being* of a *God* . . . it would be not only *Needless*, but *Absurd*, for a *Synod* to be call'd to debate over again the *Fundamentals* of *Piety*. . . . In such Cases as this, the *Christian Magistrate* ought to take upon him the *Protection* of *Religion*. . . . *Civil Authority* may Restrain such bold Men; but 'tis Ridiculous to think that all the *Synods* in the World, should ever be able to Perswade Them.

Again (2dly) Upon the same Grounds I affirm, that neither is there any need of a *New Synod* to declare the *Doctrine*, and *Consent* of the *Church*, in such Points, in which it has, by as *Great*, Or even *Greater Authority*, been before Declared. . . .

But (3dly) If a Convocation ought not to be called without need, then neither can it be *Necessary*, or even *fitting*, to Assemble it for such *Matters*, as not only may be Equally provided for, by *Ordinary Means* but which fall, more properly, under the Cognizance of some Other *Authority* . . .

Where the *Discipline*, and *Authority* of the Church itself is

[1] Convocation was prorogued in 1717, and was not allowed by the Crown to resume its functions until 1852.

Defective; and Irregularities both in the *Clergy*, and *Laity* abound for want of a Power sufficient to suppress them; a *Convocation* may be needful, to consider, How a *Remedy* may be *provided* for this *Defect*; and the *Church* be enabled, more successfully, both to *Guard* the *Faith*, and to *Reform* the *Manners*, of its *Members*. . . . But I am afraid our *Distemper* is become too Great to be *healed*: And that we are Uncapable of such a *Discipline*, as, above all things, We the most Want. And therefore (4thly) . . . As in such *Cases*, as I have hitherto mentioned, it is *needless* to Call a *Convocation*, so would it be in Vain to Assemble it for such purposes in which there were no notable Expectation of Success, or *hope*, that any Good would be done by it. This, as for ought I know, it may be One Great Reason why a Convocation is not called, to Review some of our *Publick Offices*; to *Improve* our *Discipline*; And to *Reform* many *Disorders* in the Exercise of the *Ecclesiastical Jurisdiction*.

But (5thly) And to have done: As there are many *Cases* for which it would be improper to call a *Convocation*; so may there be some *Times* too, in which it would be altogether *Unadvisable* to *Assemble* it.

When Mens *Passions* are let loose, and their *Minds* disorder'd: When their *Interests*, and *Designs*; their *Friends* and their *Parties*; nay, their very *Judgments*, and *Principles*, lead them *different Ways*; and they Agree in nothing so much, as in being Very *Peevish*, and *Angry*, with One Another; When their very *Reason* is depraved; and they judge not according to *Truth*, or *Evidence*, but with *Respect* of *Persons*; and Every One Opposes, what Another of a *different Perswasion* either *Moves*, or *Approves* of: What Good can the *Prince* propose to Himself, or any *Wise Man* hope for, from an *Assembly* than can be brought together under the unhappy Influence of These, and the like *Prepossessions*.

[William Wake (later Archbishop of Canterbury), *The Authority of Christian Princes over their Ecclesiastical Synods asserted*, 1697, p. 305.]

XXII

THE PRIVY COUNCIL,[1] 1701

And here it may be observed, that an Error has formerly Crept into this Part of our Constitution; and that is, *By Determining Matters of the highest Importance without Advising with any of the Established Councils*. The original of which, in the late Reigns, seems to be derived from the Precedent of *France*, where it was

[1] See Sect. A, No. XXXVI, § III, p. 95, and Sect. D, No. II, p. 318.

first invented as an Introduction to an Arbitrary Government; and 'tis to be doubted, that they were no true Friends to the Constitution of this Government, who first brought that evil Custom into *England*.

'Tis true, former Princes did sometimes Advise with particular Persons, before they offered a Matter to the Council to be Debated and Determined; but it's an Innovation by Evil Ministers, that War and Peace, and Matters of the highest Consequences, should be finally Concluded in a *Secret Cabal*, and only pass through the *Privy-Council* for Forms sake, as a Conduit-Pipe, to Convey those Resolutions with Authority to the People.

All Proclamations, for Declaring War, &c are constantly set forth in the Name of the *King*, with *Advice of his* Council, (which shews that it ought to be so) when, perhaps, the War was Resolved in a *Private Cabal*, and only Declared in a *Privy-Council*, and Published with that Authority to the People; which is an Abuse of the Constitution.

'Tis therefore a Noble Resolution in His Majesty, to Restore to *England* the Practice of their Ancient Constitution, to Repair the Breaches and Innovations brought in upon them in the late Reigns, and not only to Declare, but Debate and Transact all Matters of State in the *Privy-Council*.

[Sir H. Mackworth, *A Vindication of the Rights of the Commons of England*, 1701, p. 16.]

XXIII

PARTY GOVERNMENT,[1] 1706–14

(A)

QUEEN ANNE TO GODOLPHIN

Besides, I must own freely to you, I am of the opinion, that making a party man secretary of state, when there are so many of their friends in employment of all kinds already, is throwing myself into the hands of a party, which is a thing I have been desirous to avoid. Maybe some may think I would be willing to be in the hands of the tories . . . but . . . I am not inclined, nor never will be, to employ any of the violent persons, that have behaved themselves so ill towards me. All I desire is, my liberty in encouraging and employing all those that concur faithfully in my service, whether they are called whigs or tories not to be tied to one, nor the other; for if I should be so unfortunate as to fall into the hands of

[1] See Sect. B, No. XXXVIII, p. 240; Sect. D, No. V, p. 325, No. XL, p. 388, No. XLVI, p. 396.

*Anne afraid
of faction*

either, I shall not imagine myself, though I have the name of queen, to be in reality but their slave, which as it will be my personal ruin, so it will be the destroying all government; for instead of putting an end to faction, it will lay a lasting foundation for it. You press the bringing lord Sunderland into business, that there may be one of that party in a place of trust, to help carry on the business this winter; and you think if this is not complied with, they will not be hearty in pursuing my service in parliament. But is it not very hard that men of sense and honour, will not promote the good of their country because everything in the world is not done that they desire! when they may be assured lord Sunderland shall come into employment as soon as it is possible. Why, for God's sake, must I, who have no interest, no end, no thought, but for the good of my country, be made so miserable, as to be brought into the power of one set of men?

[Coxe, *Memoirs of John, Duke of Marlborough*, ed. 1818, ii, ch. 51, p. 137, Aug. 30/Sept. 10, 1706.]

(B)

DUKE OF MARLBOROUGH TO QUEEN ANNE

I am no ways concerned for the power that the whigs may have with you, but the great concern that I must always have for your quiet and safety; for if you are served to your satisfaction and security, I am very indifferent who the persons are . . . I am persuaded that if you continue in the mind, that I think you now are, and will not suffer those who have the honour to serve you, to manage your affairs agreeably to the circumstances of the times, your business must inevitably run into confusion; and, consequently, make it impossible for my lord treasurer to serve; for if he is thought to have the power, when he has not, both parties will be angry with him. . . . If I were with your majesty, I believe I could let you see the trouble and distraction you are like to be in this winter, which you must prevent, before the meeting of parliament, or it will be too late.

[Coxe, *Memoirs of John, Duke of Marlborough*, ed. 1818, ii, 344, Sept. 15, 1707.]

(C)

LORD COWPER TO GEORGE I

Having thus stated to your Majesty the practices and dispositions of the parties, I shall only add, that 'tis not to be doubted but your Majesty's known goodness and experienced wisdom will necessarily incline you to such moderate counsels as will render you King of all your divided people. But I humbly conceive it not possible so to distribute your royal favours, but that one or other of the parties will appear to have a superior degree of trust reposed in them : and if such a perfect equality was possible to be observed, perhaps it would follow that an equal degree of power, tending at the same time different ways, would render the operations of the government slow and heavy, if not altogether impracticable.

It remains therefore, in my humble opinion, for your Majesty to determine which of these shall have the chief share in your Majesty's confidence, as most likely to support your title to the Crown with the greatest zeal and most untainted affection to it. For as to their power to do it, give me leave to assure your Majesty, on repeated experience, that the parties are so near an equality, and the generality of the world so much in love with the advantages a King of Great Britain has to bestow, without the least exceeding the bounds of law, that 'tis wholly in your Majesty's power, by showing your favour in due time (before the elections) to one or other of them, to give which of them you please a clear majority in all succeeding parliaments.

It is needless to suggest to your Majesty, but, for method's sake, it ought just to be touched upon, that whichsoever party shall have the lower degree of your Majesty's trust, it ought nevertheless to be used by those in power with very great tenderness and affection while obedient to your Majesty and the laws, and as a father would a child whom he dearly loves, though he does not totally approve, and, to be more particular, should, in my humble opinion, be admitted to a fair share of such places and employments of trust, according to their several qualifications, as are during the pleasure of the Crown, and not attended with the chief dependences. . . .

I have but one thing more humbly to represent to your Majesty, as the only, and, if I mistake not, a sure means to extinguish the being and the very name of party amongst us, that your Majesty would be pleased to use the utmost caution not to prefer any of those ecclesiastics whose known principles lead them to scruple the validity of a limitation of the right to the Crown by act of parliament. There is a sufficient number of the clergy of the Church of England, of the most learned and best livers, out of whom your Majesty may choose for all preferments that shall fall vacant, who are not the least tainted with those notions which, while they continue, will ever find matter for discontents and divisions in your Majesty's kingdoms. But when once it is discerned that, by a steady and uninterrupted administration, no man who is known to hold opinions inconsistent with the very foundation of your Majesty's government can get into any of the Crown preferments in the Church, they who find themselves troubled with these inconvenient scruples will soon apply their thoughts and studies in good earnest to satisfy themselves, and then others, of the weakness of those errors, which will afterwards, in a little time, be confined to a few melancholy Nonjurors, who are the less dangerous for being known ; and when the clergy are brought to be of one mind as to your Majesty's title, all differences in opinion among the laity on that head will soon vanish. But that part of the clergy who have always violently contended against excluding the next successor, though a Papist, will never own themselves to have been in the wrong while they find they have a fair chance for the best of the Church preferments without disavowing those errors, otherwise than by taking the oaths in form.

[*Campbell's Lives of the Chancellors*, iv, 428 *sqq.*, written between Aug. 1 and Sept. 18, 1714.]

XXIV

QUEEN ANNE'S CHARTER TO THE CITY OF BRISTOL,[1] 1711

[Confirms in their offices the existing Mayor, Recorder, Aldermen, Sheriffs, and Common-Council Men until the usual election day—September 15. Town Clerk, Steward of the Sheriffs' Court, and the Coroners also nominated.]

And whereas, by the Death of some of the Common-Council of the City aforesaid, and by Reason of the Contemptuous Refusal of some of the Burgesses of the City aforesaid, to be of the Common-Council of the City aforesaid, to which Office, respectively, they were duly elected, *Seven Persons* are now wanting to compleat the aforesaid Number of *Forty and Two* of the Common-Council of the said City, besides the Mayor of the said City ; *Know ye*, therefore, That We Will . . . That the Mayor . . . and the Persons before Named and Constituted Common-Council-Men . . . before the 15th Day of *September* . . . Assemble Themselves, and . . . Choose and Prefer so many Burgesses . . . to be Common-Council-Men . . . as . . . fill up the Number of *Forty Two* . . . And We do Require and Command, That . . . the Common-Council . . . shall immediately . . . make . . . reasonable Laws and Ordinances in Writing, with such Pains, Fines, Amerciaments, and Penalties, as to them . . . shall seem expedient to compel and coerce every Person into the Office of a Common-Council-Man, or into any other Office . . . to which he shall be

[1] See Sect. D, No XIII, p. 333, and No. XVII (A) and (B), p. 347.

respectively Elected. *And We further Will* . . . That the Common-
Council . . . may and shall have Full Power and Authority . . . of
Making and Establishing, from Time to Time, such *reasonable Laws*,
Ordinances, Constitutions, in Writing, as to them . . . shall seem
good, wholesome, profitable, necessary, and *honest* for the good Rule
and Government of the City aforesaid, Suburbs, Liberties, and
Precincts of the same . . . And that the Common-Council . . . as
often as they shall Frame, Make, Ordain, or Establish such Laws
. . . shall Make, Ordain, Impose, Limit and Provide, such and
the like Pains, Punishments, Penalties, by Fines and Amerciaments,
. . . as shall seem fit and necessary . . . *Provided*, That such
Laws . . . be *reasonable*, and be not *contrary*, nor *repugnant* to the
Laws, Statutes, Customs or Rights of our Kingdom of Great-Britain.

[Mayor and Aldermen to fill up vacancy caused by death or
removal of an Alderman from among existing Common-Council-Men.
Common-Council to elect to other vacant offices, but the Recorder
must be a Barrister of 5 years' standing, Town-Clerk and Steward of
Sheriffs' Court, barristers of 3 years' standing.]

We Will also . . . That every Recorder, Alderman, Common-
Council-Man, Common-Clerk, Steward of the Sheriffs' Court, and
Coroners of our City of *Bristol* . . . shall continue in his Office . . .
as long as he respectively shall demean himself well in the same.

[Mayor, Recorder, and Aldermen to be Justices of the Peace, of
Oyer and Terminer and general Gaol Delivery. Profits of Justice
granted to the City. Quarter Sessions to be held four times a year.
Quorum to be the Mayor, or Recorder, or two of the five Senior
Aldermen. Oath of Aldermen and J.P.s to be taken before the
Recorder, or Mayor.]

And Know ye farther, That We, of our especial Grace, certain
Knowledge, and mere Motion, have Pardoned, Remised, and
Released, . . . to the Mayor, Burgesses, and Commonalty of our
City of *Bristol* aforesaid, and their Successors ; as also to all and
singular Mayors, Recorders, Aldermen, Sheriffs, Common-Clerks,
Stewards of the Sheriffs' Court and Coroners of our City of *Bristol*
who do now exercise, or heretofore have exercised the Offices
aforesaid . . . all Manner of Offences, Trespasses, Crimes,
Negligencies . . . committed and perpetrated . . . in, of, for, or
concerning, the taking of the Oath to their respective Offices . . .
or concerning . . . their Admissions, to the Execution of their
Offices . . . without our approbation, or without the Approbation
of any of our Predecessors . . . first signified under the Royal
Hand, contrary to the Proviso, Tenor, and True Intention of certain
Letters Patents, bearing Date at Westminster the 2nd Day of *June*,
in the 36th Year of the Reign of the late King CHARLES the
Second . . . And out of our more abundant especial Grace, and

of our certain knowledge, and mere Motion, We have Remised,
and Released, and by these Presents, We do, for Us, our Heirs
and Successors, Remise and Release, to the Mayor, Burgesses, and
Commonalty of our City of *Bristol* aforesaid, and their Successors,
all, and all Manner of Power and Authority reserved to the said late
King CHARLES the Second, his Heirs and Successors, in and by
the aforesaid Letters Patents bearing date the 2nd Day of *June*,
in the 36th Year of the Reign of the aforesaid late King CHARLES
the Second, in, of, for or concerning, the Approbation of the
Mayor (etc) . . . to be signified under his Royal Hand, or under
the Royal Hand of his Heirs and Successors : And also, all, and all
Manner of Powers, and Authority to the aforesaid late King
CHARLES the Second, his Heirs and Successors, also reserved in
the said Letters Patents from Time to Time, and at all Times, to
Remove and Amove, any Mayor (etc) . . . at the Will and Pleasure
of the said King CHARLES the Second, or of his Heirs and
Successors, to be made in Privy-Council, and under the Seal of
the Privy-Council aforesaid, to be signified to them respectively, to
be Amoved, and to be declared Amoved and Removed.

[Power in Common Council to alter times and places of Markets
which the Common Council by By-laws are to regulate. General
confirmation of all Franchises and Liberties.]

In *Testimony* whereof, We have caused these our Letters to be
made Patents. *Witness* Ourself, at *Westminster*, the 24th Day of
July, in the Ninth Year of our Reign.

By Writ of the Privy Seal
COCKS.

Twenty Marks Sterling to be paid as a Fine in the Queen's
Haniper.

COWPER, Chancellor.

[*Bristol: The City Charters.*]

XXV

ADMINISTRATION BY JUSTICES, 1724

RATE FOR REPAIRING THE HIGHWAYS OF THE TOWN

Whereas his Majesties Justices of the Peace for this Town and
County of the Town of Nottingham now present here in Court
(upon the representation and application of Marmaduke Pennell
Gent. Henry Morris Gent. George Oldfield and Michael Cowle
the present Surveyors of the Highways within the Parish of St.

Mary in this Town and County of the Town of Nottingham) are fully satisfyed and it being otherwise notorious to them that the Common Highways within the said Parish are so far out of Order that they cannot be otherwise sufficiently amended repaired paved cleansed and Supported as they ought to be by means of the Laws now in force without the help of the Act of Parliament made in the third and fourth Years of the Reign of their late Majesties King William and Queen Mary Intituled An Act for the better repairing and amending the Highways and for setling the rates of Carriage of goods. It is therefore ordered by this Court That an Assessment shall be forthwith made for this present Year after the rate of Sixpence in the Pound of the yearly value of all and Singular Lands houses . . . and after the Rate of Sixpence for every twenty pounds in personal Estate usually rateable to the Poor upon all and every the respective Inhabitants . . . by the said Surveyors of the Highways which being allowed by the Mayor of this Town . . . and one of the Aldermen thereof shall be levyed . . . And . . . imployed for and towards the repairing amending paving cleansing and Supporting the said Highway in such Manner as the said Marmaduke Pennell shall order and direct rendering an Account thereof to the said Justices . . . And . . . the like Assessment shall be made in every of the four next and immediate succeeding Years . . .

[Sessions Record Books, Nottingham Borough Records, vi, 93, June 1, 1724.]

XXVI

THE INDEPENDENT MEMBER AND THE MINISTRY, 1729

Saturday, 25 [Jan.] . . . Col. Negus [1] stayed an hour or two after the rest, and I complained to him of the uneasiness Philipson [2] gives us on the Corporation ; that we never set up a man that he does not oppose by setting up another, and I was sure he must have some great support behind the curtain, nay, that I was sure an injury had been done me with the King, who, though I went down to my election with his consent and approbation, received me very coolly at my return. Negus said there was no doubt of it, I had applied first to the King and not to the Ministers ; and that they very probably told him the Post Office being at his command, it ought

[1] M.P. for Ipswich. Invented negus in Anne's reign.
[2] Agent of the Packets at Harwich, for which borough Lord Egmont sat in the Commons.

to govern Harwich, and so he would be master of electing there, whereas I was uniting an interest against the Post Office there to render elections independent. I told him every one knew Philipson to be a disaffected man, and that I thought it dangerous to let him have the command in a seaport town, and the common passage to foreign countries. Negus said the Ministry had rather see little fellows in Parliament than others of better figure and independent men, for they were surer of them. I told him, I thought to complain to the Ministry. He said it were better go myself to the King. I said they had told their story so possibly I should not be heard. He said it might be so. He complained the Ministry deserted every gentleman in like manner, and left them to spend their own money and tire themselves out ; that they gave him no assistance at Ipswich.

[H.M.C., *Diary of Lord Egmont*, iii, 333.]

XXVII

THE COURT—THE MEMBER—THE CONSTITUENTS, 1732

Saturday, 28 [Oct.]—Paid my Court at Kensington, where my reception was gracious, and the Prince said to me in private a thousand kind and obliging things. He inquired after every one of my family, and my brother Parker,[1] and entered into the detail of all our concerns. He wished my brother Parker would set up for the county of Suffolk next Parliament, at least that he would be in Parliament, as it became men of his great estate. Asked me who I would set up at Harwich. I told him I intended to recommend my son if the Government liked of him and would give their assistance. He replied, that to be sure the King would like of it, but said I wanted no assistance, the borough being at my devotion. I answered, though I could bring him in, there might be a great expense attend it, if any rich citizen or neighbouring Tory should resolve to spend much money there ; that I was not such a Don Quixote as to spend my money when there was no occasion, the last election having cost [2] me near 1,000 *l.* He asked whether I did not design myself to stand. I said I was growing old, and had rather leave it to younger men ; but whoever his Majesty pleased should be chosen. . . . I returned and dined at home, and spent the evening in writing and

[1] Sir Philip Parker, Egmont's brother-in-law, member with Egmont for Harwich in the last Parliament.

[2] See Sect. D, No. V, p. 325, No. XV, p. 342, No. XXXV, p. 377, and No. L, p. 399.

answering letters, one of which was to Clements,[1] Mayor of Harwich, who acquainted me by letter that Cockerill, one of our Common Council men, was dead beyond the sea, and that he would set up his brother Clements unless I had any other in view. I answered nothing could please me more than to see his brother chose, and therefore enclosed a letter to him for him to show all my friends, to desire them to vote for his brother. I also writ a strong worded letter to Mr. Sanson, wherein I gave him in civil terms to understand how ill I took it of the Post Office [2] to be still firm in a body against my interest.

[H.M.C., *Diary of Lord Egmont*, i, 293.]

XXVIII

HARWICH ELECTION,[3] 1734

(A)

I look on the election as lost, since Sir Robert would not let Mr. Leathes [4] know after the tricks he plays that he should not have the Government's interest, since also he would not order any of the Government's voters to come up, and lastly, since Charles Stanhope is gone down, who being the Secretary of State's brother will undoubtedly by promises secure all our enemies to him, if not gain some of our friends, for *Harwichiæ omnia venalia*.

However, I writ to Mr. Ven, rector of St. Antholin's, to write this night to some friends he had to influence those he could for my son, which he promised to do. My friends have seen this game long ago, and are extremely angry with Sir Robert, and will not allow him to have acted a sincere part, for they say Mr. Leathes is his creature, with whom he might do what he pleased, and since he had put him upon me by asking my consent, he ought in honour to support my son, which he has not done to the utmost of his power, and it is certain his suffering Mr. Leathes to depart from his engagement whereby he promised not to oppose Clements being Mayor, which yet he did to the utmost, and his continuing his friendship to him even after, and giving Sam Philips the *Walpole* sloop, are marks

[1] Clements was the leader of the pro-Egmont faction in the Corporation, and a bitter enemy of Philipson.

[2] The Post Office controlled the Packets plying from Harwich to Holland.

[3] See also Sect. D, No. XV, p. 342, and No. XXXV, p. 377.

[4] Leathes, a henchman of Sir R. Walpole, had been put up with Egmont's son for the Parliamentary representation of Harwich. At the last moment Charles Stanhope stood as a third candidate.

that Mr. Leathes was still to be preferred to me, though I have
acted so handsomely by the Court, and wrote for them, as also my
son had done more than once.   But Mr. Leathes is a Norfolk man,
and useful to Sir Robert at this time in the impending election, and
present services are to be regarded more than past by him, although
I was so well at Court, and had, as you see, the King's desire that
my son should be chosen, so all the base tricks used by Leathes are
passed by, which any other than Sir Robert would have scorned to
countenance.

My friends say this is never to be forgiven, and are angry with
me for not being as openly furious in my discourse against Sir
Robert as they are.   They say if Sir Robert uses his friends so, what
must others expect, and if independent men of large fortunes and
remarkably attached to the Government are to be debarred entering
the Parliament, what bad designs must not the minister have,
what work to do in the ensuing Parliament ?   They say that it is
not enough that independent gentlemen vote with the Court out of
a principle, for if they have no other attachment but their judgement, they may happen to be of a different judgement from the
Court measures in a following Parliament. . . .

[H.M.C., *Diary of Lord Egmont*, ii, 95, April 25, 1734.]

(B)

He [Dr. Courage] told me he saw Mr. Charles Stanhope two
days ago, who is chosen at Harwich.

He told him that he had a letter from thence signed by twenty,
to desire him to stand, if not, that the same express was to find out
Mr. Heath and offer him the borough.   That he had no acquaintance
with Mr. Leathes nor any thought of standing there, until the
Corporation sent to him.   That the reason they rejected my son
was that I had put a person into the agency of the packets who was
odious to them all, meaning James Clements, and had represented
several there to be Jacobites.   That he had not the assistance of
the Government ; Sir Robert Walpole, indeed, had sent down to
recommend my son, but left the Government's servants to do as
they pleased.   This was confirmed to me by Lord Wilmington,
who told me Sir Robert said he was for my son until Lord Harrington
put up his brother, and then he concerned himself no more in the
matter.   That my son had six Government's servants, and himself
but five.   That as soon as the election was over, five or six of the
voters cried out, " Liberty ! we are free from the tyranny we were
under fourteen years past."

[H.M.C., *Diary of Lord Egmont*, ii, 99, May 3, 1743.]

XXIX

A PRINCIPAL MINISTER,[1] 1733

His [George II's] design at his first accession to the throne was certainly, as Boileau says of Louis XIV.,—

> Seul, sans ministre, à l'exemple des dieux,
> Faire tout par sa main et voir tout de ses yeux.

He intended to have all his ministers in the nature of clerks, not to give advice, but to receive orders ; and proposed, what by experiment he found impracticable, to receive applications and distribute favours through no principal channel, but to hear from all quarters, and employ indifferently in their several callings those who by their stations would come under the denomination of ministers. But it was very plain, from what I have just now related from the King's own lips, as well as from many other circumstances in his present conduct, that the Queen had subverted all his notions and schemes, and fully possessed His Majesty with an opinion that it was absolutely necessary, from the nature of the English Government, that he should have but one minister ; and that it was equally necessary, from Sir Robert's superior abilities, that he should be that one.

[John, Lord Hervey, *Memoirs of the Reign of King George II*, ed. Sedgwick, 1931, i, 151.]

XXX

THE KING'S INFLUENCE, 1735-37

(A)

IN FOREIGN AFFAIRS[2]

. . . His Majesty declared, a little before the Parliament rose, his intention of visiting, as soon as it should rise, his foreign dominions. His Ministers in England were one and all extremely desirous to divert His Majesty from this resolution, but did not succeed. It is certain it would have been much for the despatch as well as for the convenience of foreign negotiations, which were

[1] See Sect. D, No. I, p. 317, No. XXXIX, p. 387, and No. XLVII, p. 398.
[2] See Sect. B, No. VII, p. 179, Sect. D, No. VII, p. 327, No. XIX, p. 354, No. XLIII, p. 393, and Vol. II, Sect. D, No. LIII, p. 442.

likely to be the chief business of this summer, that the King should have remained in England, in order to prevent every paper, which in that case might be regulated by a short journey only from Sir Robert Walpole's house at Chelsea to the King's palace at Kensington, being obliged to make a voyage or two from England to Hanover before it could be settled. . . .

The English Ministers apprehended, too, that if the King went into Germany, his German Ministers, being all of them Imperialists, might make the difficulties of keeping his Majesty out of the war, in case the proposition for peace did not take place, still more troublesome and harder to be surmounted than they had hitherto found them, which might be of fatal consequence when the English Ministers, by experience, knew their influence was barely a match for such difficulties even in their former degree, and combated on this side of the water.

[John, Lord Hervey, *ibid*. ii, 456.]

(B)

IN THE ARMY

Sir Robert Walpole said ". . . But here, my Lord, lies the disagreeable difficulty of my situation : when I tell them if they will arm me with power I will conquer and humble their son, I receive such a flow of grace and good words, such a flood of promises and favour, that I could dictate nothing stronger ; yet, whenever I propose anything particular, I am answered short by the King, ' I will not do that.' How many people there are I could bind to me by getting things done in the army you may imagine, and that I can never get any one thing done in it you perhaps will not believe ; but it is as true as that there is an army, that I never ask for the smallest commission by which a Member of Parliament may be immediately or collaterally obliged, that the King's answer is not ' I won't do that ; you want always to have me disoblige all my old soldiers ; you understand nothing of troops ; I will order my army as I think fit ; for your scoundrels of the House of Commons you may do as you please ; you know I never interfere, nor pretend to know anything of them, but this province I will keep to myself.' . . ."

[John, Lord Hervey, *ibid*. iii, 771.]

XXXI
THE CONDUCT OF ADMINISTRATION,
1740

(A)
INNER CABINET
CHANCELLOR HARDWICKE TO THE DUKE OF NEWCASTLE

As to bringing the affair of either of the intended Expeditions before the Cabinet,[1] I think we should not depart from what has been the usual practice in like cases. I have allways been told that it was not the custom to bring matters, which require such absolute Secrecy, before such a number of persons. To propose it there in general only, without explaining the destination and other essential particulars, will give more offence, and be liable to more objections than not proposing it at all.

[Add. MSS., 32,692, f. 538, Dec. 27, 1739.]

(B)
PRIVY COUNCIL, CABINET AND INNER CABINET

To day his Magisty had a Counsell at St. James' and gave his aprobation of severall Irish bills and for passing a prive sele upon the representations of the Commiss[r]. of the Admiralty upon aplication to them for the selling old stores and sum ships : and an order of Counsell was sined to direct the L[d] Mayor of Londen with the Aldermen and Justises of the peace to put an anchiant Law in Exsicution ; that was maid perpetuale in King William and queen mary time ; against the Exorbitant price of Coles in the sittys of London and Westminster which is so nessesary in this sevear seson that the cold has never been more sevear at any time in these parts ; and by those laws if the sellors of Coles wont conforme to the orders of the sittys the magistrates are to order the Counstable with assistance to deliver out those cole to the buyer leveing the money with the owner of them when the King went from Counsell[2] the Duke of Newcastle desired the Lords of the Cabinett that were present with my selfe ; to hear him read Tow letters of intelligence that came from Mr van der muir[3] at Madrid ; dated in Jan[ry] ; which related that the Court of Spaine had ordered a number of Forces with about a hundred pecis of Cannon ; to be gott redy at Barsolona to be transported to Mayor and had named the

[1] See Sect. D, No. XX, p. 355.
[2] See Sect. B, No. XXIX, p. 218.
[3] Vandermeer, Dutch Minister in Spain.

Genrale officers to command the Exspedetion which could only be with a desine to attack Mahone. . . . upon these intelligence, the Duke has drawn an order to be sent to Mr. Haddock to send such a detachment of his ships as should be suffitiant to prevent the Spaniard makeing any transportation from Barsolona to Mayork or Minyork ; and according to such further intelligence as he mout receive to be at Liberty to go him selfe with all his force if nessesary ; to prevent the said Transportation ; and protect our Iland of Minorka. when this order was agreed to his Grace was to send it to plymouth To Tow men of warr that was redy to saile from thence with a slave ship to Mr. Hadock and if they should be sailed then the pakett at falmouth should be ordered to carry the orders directly to Mr. Haddock. when this was over I told the Duke of Newcastle privately, if this became a reale desine of the Spaniard : it would be well for us who youse to mete at Sr Roberts to consider what could farther be dun towards the protection of Minyorka ; and if that should be I had drafts to show where the Enemy mout probably land and to consider what methods could be taken to prevent it and like wise how by sea ; we mout be most yousefull ; his Grace said, he would speke to Sr Robert and as I had the honor of being in those private meteing ; [1] I thought it was incumbent upon our honor to take utmost causion and resoning to preserve the honor of our Country and avoyed any disgrace.

[Diary of Admiral Sir John Norris : Add. MSS., 28,132, ff. 149-51, Feb. 14, 1739/40.]

(C)

DIFFICULTIES DURING A REGENCY

CHANCELLOR HARDWICKE TO THE DUKE OF NEWCASTLE

It is my firm opinion that, more especially whilst the King is abroad (who when here was a kind of centre of unity, at least his final opinion concluded everybody else [? s]), the utmost endeavours should be used to preserve harmony and good agreement. This general proposition inclines me to think that every point, wherein we are likely to differ, and which is not necessary to be determin'd *at present*, should be studiously avoided being brought on the carpet. At least, sure I am, that such points should be avoided, which we have not authority to determine. Now I take the proportion in which the captures ought to be divided and disposed to be one of those . . .

Consider then, my dear Lord, what must be the consequences, if this point should now be brought on again. We must previously transmit our opinion and advice to the King and desire his orders

[1] Cf. Vol. II, Sect. D, No. XV (A), p. 367.

upon it. Those, who shall differ in opinion from the majority, will undoubtedly (privately at least) transmit theirs with their reasons —attended probably with complaints of others ; and thus we shall be drawn into complaints, justifications and incriminations, instead of concurring to carry on the public business. What a figure shall we make at Hanover ? What a figure shall we make here ?—and how will the Government be carried on under such a Regency ?

[Yorke, *Life of Hardwicke*, i, 238, June 8, 1740.]

(D)

The Cabinet and the King

The Duke of Newcastle to Chancellor Hardwicke

His Majesty afterwards in a formal set speech or declaration, but not in ill-humour, said to my Lord Harrington and I : " As to the business in Parliament, I don't value the Opposition, if all those in my service act together and are united ; but if they thwart one another and create difficulties in the carrying on the public business, then indeed—or to that purpose—it would be another case." I easily saw from whom this came. (Sir Robert had been in the Closet near an hour and came out in high spirits and humour.) I answered his Majesty that to be sure all his servants would unite in doing him the best service they could. I found Sir Robert in the outward room and after mentioning to him in the presence of Lord Harrington that the King was quite altered from the day before as to writing to Vienna and Berlin, I told him his Majesty had made a pretty extraordinary speech to us and I then repeated it, saying, " I have heard this language often before." He replied, " I know you mean from me ", and indeed I did, for I can almost swear to the words. " However " (says Sir Robert) " agreeable it may be to my own way of thinking, and true in itself,"—and then muttered something—" I have said nothing to the King (*or*) nothing *now* to that purpose." (It might have been the day before when he acquainted the King with our difference in Council.) I said then to him, Lord Harrington present, " When measures are agreed amongst us, it is very right that everybody should support them, but not to have the liberty of giving one's opinion before they are agreed, is very wrong." He said shortly, " What do you mean. This war is yours, you have had the conduct of it, I wish you joy of it." I contented myself with denying that fact and so we parted. Now, my dear Lord, how can business go on this way ? What is agreed amongst us is often equally overhauled afterwards, both by Lord Harrington and Sir Robert, if it is not quite agreeable to their own inclinations.   And when we have reason to fear that our united credit with the King may hardly be sufficient to induce his Majesty to do quite right in this great conjecture, *one* will govern all and fill the King's head with complaints and unreasonable jealousies of part of his servants.

[Yorke, *Life of Hardwicke*, i, 250, Oct. 25, 1740.]

XXXII

DUTY OF A CABINET MINISTER, 1742

The Duke of Richmond[1] to the Duke of Newcastle

. . . In the first place I am delighted to see things go so well in the house of comons.   then as to the house of Lords I take for granted any attendance will be unnecessary.   & as for Cabinet Counsels they are quite out of fashion, so that all the business I can possibly have in town is waiting upon my Royal Master, which I ever was and ever shall be ready to do, when there is any real duty that calls me . . . butt I own I cant help preferring foxhunting, being with my family, to what may be called fiddle-faddle waiting.   so I could wish to be excused going up till after Christmas. . . .

[Add. MSS. 32,699, f. 539, Goodwood, Nov. 28, 1742.]

XXXIII

MINUTES OF A CABINET MEETING,[2] 1743

Whitehall, Novr. 24th: 1743

Lord Chancellor [Earl of Hardwicke]
Lord President [Earl of Harrington]
Lord Steward [Duke of Dorset]
Lord Chamberlain [Duke of Grafton]
Duke of Richmond [Master of the Horse]
Duke of Bolton [Lord Lieutenant of Southampton]
Duke of Montague [Master-general of the Ordnance]
Duke of Argyle [Keeper of the Great Seal of Scotland]
Duke of Newcastle [Secretary of State for Southern Dept.]

[1] The Duke of Richmond was Master of the Horse.
[2] See Vol. II, Sect. D, No. XXXII, p. 398, and No. XLVI, p. 429.

Marq^{ss}. Tweeddale [Secretary of State for Scotland]
Earl Winchelsea [First Lord of the Admiralty]
Lord Carteret [Secretary of State for Northern Dept.]
Mr Pelham [First Lord of the Treasury]

A Convention, between His Majesty, and the Queen of Hungary, signed by Lord Carteret, and Monsr Wasner, at Worms, on $\frac{3rd}{14}$ of October ; and the necessary Papers relating thereto, were read.   And their Lordships, in pursuance of His Majesty's Commands, took the said Convention into Consideration ; And My Lord Chancellor, My Lord President, My Lord Steward, My Lord Chamberlain, the Duke of Richmond, the Duke of Montague, the Duke of Newcastle, and Mr Pelham, were of Opinion, humbly to advise His Majesty, not to ratify the said Convention ; But that His Majesty would be pleased to cause proper Instances to be made, at the Court of Vienna, to substitute, in lieu thereof, another Treaty, or Convention, for paying the Queen of Hungary a Subsidy of 300,000£, for the ensuing year.   And the Duke of Argyle was of Opinion, That this Convention should not be ratified, without Explanations, And The Duke of Bolton, The Marquess of Tweeddale, The Earl of Winchelsea, and My Lord Carteret, were of Opinion that the Convention should be ratified.

[Add. MSS. 33,004, f. 57, Nov. 24, 1743.]

XXXIV

THE KING AND THE MINISTRY, 1744-46

(A)

Notes of Audience

Chancellor. But, Sir, there still remains something very material behind ; how this situation may be best improv'd and the advantages of it not to be lost.

King. I have done all you ask'd of me.   I have put all power into your hands and I suppose you will make the most of it.

Ch. The disposition of places is not enough, if your Majesty takes pains to shew the world that you disapprove of your own work.

K. My work! I was forc'd : I was threatened.

Ch. I am sorry to hear your Majesty use those expressions.   I know of no force : I know of no threats.   No means were us'd but what has been us'd in all times, the humble advice of your servants,

supported by such reasons as convinc'd them that the measure was
necessary for your service.

K. Yes, I was told that I should be opposed.

Ch. Never by me, Sir, nor by any of my friends. How others
might misrepresent us, I don't pretend to know; but, whatever
had been our fate, and though your Majesty had determin'd on
the contrary side to what you did, we would never have gone into
an opposition against the necessary measures for carrying on the
war and for the support of your Government and family. For
myself, I have serv'd your Majesty long in a very laborious station,
and am arrived at a length of service which makes me very indifferent as to personal considerations. Taking your money only
is not serving you, and nothing can enable one to do that but being
put into a possibility and capacity of doing so by your gracious countenance and support.

But, Sir, to return to what I was mentioning, of making the
proper use and advantage of your present situation.

K. The changes might have been made by bringing in properer
persons and not those brought in, who had most notoriously distinguish'd themselves by a constant opposition to my Government.

Ch. If changes were to be made in order to gain strength, such
persons must be brought in as could bring that strength along with
them : otherwise it would have been useless. On that account it
was necessary to take in the leaders and that with the concurrence
of their friends : and, if your Majesty looks round the House of
Commons, you will find no man of business or even of weight left,
capable of heading or undertaking an opposition.

Pause—the King silent.

Sir, permit me to say the advantage of such a situation is a real
advantage gain'd to the Crown. Ministers may carry their points
in Parliament, and frequently do so by small narrow majorities,
and in this way they may struggle on long : but by the same way
the Crown always loses both its lustre and its strength. But when
things are put upon a national foot by a concurrence of the heads
of all parties, and yet so as not to overbear or discourage your old
friends, then a real solid strength is gain'd to the Crown, and the
King has both more power to carry his present measures for the
support of his Government and is more at liberty to choose and act
as he pleases. Your Ministers, Sir, are only your instruments of
Government.

K. (smiles). <u>Ministers are the Kings in this Country.</u>

Ch. If one person is permitted to engross the ear of the
Crown and invest himself with all its power, he will become so in

effect ; but that is far from being the case now, and I know no one now in your Majesty's service that aims at it.

Sir, the world without doors is full of making schemes of an administration for your Majesty for the future ; but whatever be your intention for the future, I humbly beg that you would not spoil your own business for the present.

[Yorke, *Life of Hardwicke*, i, 380, Jan. 5, 1744.]

(B)

FROM THE HON. CHARLES YORKE TO COL. THE HON. JOSEPH YORKE

But the *Great Person* has been talked to as if he were King of France and not the King of a free country. The notion of the Constitution is this that ministers are accountable for every act of the King's government to the people. If that be so, they have a right to his confidence in preference to all others, else they are answerable for measures not their own. Here is the security both of the King and of his people. The next great policy of the constitution is this, that whatever the King does, should seem to come *ex mero motu*, the result of his own wisdom and deliberate choice. This gives a grace to government in the eyes of the people, and here is the dignity of the monarchy. Now suppose the confidence to be separated from the ministers, they have no other part to take in justice to themselves than that of resigning, and the King himself is exposed to the odium of changing for worse measures and more suspected men, so that the security both of him and his people is gone. Again, suppose that *Great Person* reduced into circumstances of seeming constraint by any unhappy accident or advice and this [? thus] exposed of necessity to the people, the grace of his government and the dignity of the Crown is gone.

[Yorke, *Life of Hardwicke*, i, 504, Feb. 15, 1746.]

XXXV

COUNTY ELECTION,[1] 1747

HON. PHILIP YORKE TO THE LORD CHANCELLOR

I am very glad everything passed off so well on Friday, with so much harmony and good humour. The meeting was a very numerous one. . . . Yesterday was spent in signing the printed circular letters, which several of the gentlemen have taken home with them to distribute, and in walking the town to canvass. This

[1] See Sect. D, No. V, p. 325, No. XV, p. 342, Nos. XXXVII and XXXVIII, pp. 366-67, and No. L, p. 399.

is a compliment which has always been paid to the voters who live in Cambridge only, and took us up 7 hours and a half to go through. As we walked the whole time, I was heartily footweary when I got home. Most gave us favourable answers. . . . One particular I will mention to your Lordship now. It was formerly the custom to treat all the electors, but the last time the entertainment was confined to the gentlemen, and the common freeholders had a largess given them to bear their expenses viz. a guinea to those that come out of the Isle and half a guinea to those of the County. It was paid to those entitled to it on their producing a ticket. Mr. Shepard and Mr. Jenyns both say they found it not only the cheapest method, but most liked by the people, because they put the best part of it in their pockets. . . .

[Yorke, *Life of Hardwicke*, ii, 161, June 21, 1747.]

XXXVI

DE LA CONSTITUTION D'ANGLETERRE,[1]
1748

Il y a dans chaque État trois sortes de pouvoirs : la puissance législative, la puissance exécutrice des choses qui dépendent du droit des gens, et la puissance exécutrice de celles qui dépendent du droit civil.[2]

Par la première, le prince ou le magistrat fait des lois pour un temps ou pour toujours, et corrige ou abroge celles qui sont faites. Par la seconde, il fait la paix ou la guerre, envoie ou reçoit des ambassades, établit la sûreté, prévient les invasions. Par la troisième, il punit les crimes ou juge les différends des particuliers. On appellera cette dernière la puissance de juger ; et l'autre, simplement la puissance exécutrice de l'État.

La liberté politique, dans un citoyen, est cette tranquillité d'esprit qui provient de l'opinion que chacun a de sa sûreté ; et, pour qu'on ait cette liberté, il faut que le gouvernement soit tel qu'un citoyen ne puisse pas craindre un autre citoyen.

Lorsque dans la même personne ou dans le même corps de magistrature la puissance législative est réunie à la puissance exécutrice, il n'y a point de liberté, parce qu'on peut craindre que le même monarque ou le même sénat ne fasse des lois tyranniques pour les exécuter tyranniquement.

[1] Cf. Vol. II, Sect. B, No. V, at p. 162, and No. XXVIII, pp. 220 and 229 ; also Sect. D, No. XLII (A), p. 411.
[2] See Sect. D, No. XIX, p. 354.

Il n'y a point encore de liberté si la puissance de juger n'est pas séparée de la puissance législative et de l'exécutrice. Si elle était jointe à la puissance législative, le pouvoir sur la vie et la liberté des citoyens serait arbitraire ; car le juge serait législateur. Si elle était jointe à la puissance exécutrice, le juge pourrait avoir la force d'un oppresseur.

Tout serait perdu si le même homme, ou le même corps des principaux, ou des nobles, ou du peuple, exerçait ces trois pouvoirs ; celui de faire des lois, celui d'exécuter les résolutions publiques, et celui de juger les crimes ou les différends des particuliers. . . .

Comme dans un État libre tout homme qui est censé avoir une âme libre doit être gouverné par lui-même, il faudrait que le peuple en corps eût la puissance législative ; mais comme cela est impossible dans les grands États, et est sujet à beaucoup d'inconvénients dans les petits, il faut que le peuple fasse par ses représentants tout ce qu'il ne peut faire par lui-même.

L'on connaît beaucoup mieux les besoins de sa ville que ceux des autres villes, et on juge mieux de la capacité de ses voisins que de celle de ses autres compatriotes. Il ne faut donc pas que les membres du corps législatif soient tirés en général du corps de la nation, mais il convient que dans chaque lieu principal, les habitants se choisissent un représentant.

Le grand avantage des représentants, c'est qu'ils sont capables de discuter les affaires. Le peuple n'y est point du tout propre : ce qui forme un des grands inconvénients de la démocratie.

Il n'est pas nécessaire que les représentants, qui ont reçu de ceux qui les ont choisis une instruction générale, en reçoivent une particulière sur chaque affaire,[1] comme cela se pratique dans les diètes d'Allemagne. Il est vrai que de cette manière la parole des députés serait plus l'expression de la voix de la nation ; mais cela jetterait dans des longueurs infinies, rendrait chaque député le maître de tous les autres ; et, dans les occasions les plus pressantes, toute la force de la nation pourrait être arrêtée par un caprice.

Quand les députés, dit très-bien M. Sidney, représentent un corps de peuple comme en Hollande, ils doivent rendre compte à ceux qui les ont commis : c'est autre chose lorsqu'ils sont députés par des bourgs, comme en Angleterre. . . .

Il y a toujours dans un État des gens distingués par la naissance, les richesses ou les honneurs ; mais s'ils étaient confondus parmi le peuple, et s'ils n'y avaient qu'une voix comme les autres, la liberté commune serait leur esclavage, et ils n'auraient aucun intérêt à la défendre, parce que la plupart des résolutions seraient contre eux. La part qu'ils ont à la législation doit donc être proportionnée aux

[1] See Sect. D, No. XLII, p. 392.

autres avantages qu'ils ont dans l'État : ce qui arrivera s'ils forment un corps qui ait droit d'arrêter les entreprises du peuple, comme le peuple a droit d'arrêter les leurs.

Ainsi la puissance législative sera confiée, et au corps des nobles, et au corps qui sera choisi pour représenter le peuple, qui auront chacun leurs assemblées et leurs délibérations à part, et des vues et des intérêts séparés.

Des trois puissances dont nous avons parlé, celle de juger est en quelque façon nulle. Il n'en reste que deux ; et, comme elles ont besoin d'une puissance réglante pour les tempérer, la partie du corps législatif qui est composée de nobles est très-propre à produire cet effet.

Le corps des nobles doit être héréditaire. Il l'est premièrement par sa nature ; et d'ailleurs il faut qu'il ait un très-grand intérêt à conserver ses prérogatives, odieuses par elles-mêmes, et qui, dans un État libre, doivent toujours être en danger.

Mais, comme une puissance héréditaire pourrait être induite à suivre ses intérêts particuliers et à oublier ceux du peuple, il faut que dans les choses où l'on a un souverain intérêt à la corrompre, comme dans les lois qui concernent la levée de l'argent, elle n'ait de part à la législation que par sa faculté d'empêcher, et non par sa faculté de statuer. . . .

La puissance exécutrice doit être entre les mains d'un monarque, parceque cette partie du gouvernement, qui a presque toujours besoin d'une action momentanée, est mieux administrée par un que par plusieurs ; au lieu que ce qui dépend de la puissance législative est souvent mieux ordonné par plusieurs que par un seul.

Que s'il n'y avait point de monarque, et que la puissance exécutrice fût confiée à un certain nombre de personnes tirées du corps législatif, il n'y aurait plus de liberté, parce que les deux puissances seraient unies ; les mêmes personnes ayant quelquefois et pouvant toujours avoir part à l'une et à l'autre.

Si le corps législatif était un temps considérable sans être assemblé, il n'y aurait plus de liberté. Car il arriverait de deux choses l'une : ou qu'il n'y aurait plus de résolution législative, et L'État tomberait dans l'anarchie ; ou que ces résolutions seraient prises par la puissance exécutrice, et elle deviendrait absolue. . . .

Si la puissance exécutrice n'a pas le droit d'arrêter les entreprises du corps législatif, celui-ci sera despotique ; car, comme il pourra se donner tout le pouvoir qu'il peut imaginer, il anéantira toutes les autres puissances.

Mais il ne faut pas que la puissance législative ait réciproquement la faculté d'arrêter la puissance exécutrice ; car l'exécution ayant ses limites par sa nature, il est inutile de la borner ; outre que la

puissance exécutrice s'exerce toujours sur des choses momentanées.
. . . Mais si, dans un État libre, la puissance législative ne doit
pas avoir le droit d'arrêter la puissance exécutrice, elle a droit, et
doit avoir la faculté d'examiner de quelle manière les lois qu'elle a
faites ont été exécutées ; . . .

Il pourrait encore arriver que quelque citoyen, dans les affaires
publiques, violerait les droits du peuple, et ferait des crimes que
les magistrats établis ne sauraient ou ne voudraient pas punir. Mais,
en général, la puissance législative ne peut pas juger ; et elle le
peut enclore moins dans ce cas particulier, où elle représente la partie
intéressée, qui est le peuple. Elle ne peut donc être qu'accusatrice.
Mais devant qui accusera-t-elle ? Ira-t-elle s'abaisser devant les
tribunaux de la loi, qui lui sont inférieurs, et d'ailleurs composés de
gens qui, étant peuple comme elle, seraient entraînés par l'autorité
d'un si grand accusateur ? Non : il faut, pour conserver la dignité
du peuple et la sûreté du particulier, que la partie législative du
peuple accuse devant la partie législative des nobles, laquelle n'a ni
les mêmes intérêts qu'elle ni les mêmes passions.

C'est l'avantage qu'a ce gouvernement sur la plupart des
républiques anciennes, où il y avait cet abus, que le peuple était en
même temps juge et accusateur.

La puissance exécutrice, comme nous avons dit, doit prendre
part à la législation par sa faculté d'empêcher ; sans quoi, elle sera
bientôt dépouillée de ses prérogatives. Mais si la puissance
législative prend part à l'exécution, la puissance exécutrice sera
également perdue.

Si le monarque prenait part à la législation par la faculté de
statuer, il n'y aurait plus de liberté. Mais comme il faut pourtant
qu'il ait part à la législation pour se défendre, il faut qu'il y prenne
part par la faculté d'empêcher. . . .

Voici donc la constitution fondamentale du gouvernement dont
nous parlons. Le corps législatif y étant composé de deux parties,
l'une enchaînera l'autre par sa faculté mutuelle d'empêcher. Toutes
les deux seront liées par la puissance exécutrice, qui le sera elle-même
par la législative.

Ces trois puissances devraient former un repos ou une inaction.
Mais, comme par le mouvement nécessaire des choses elles sont
contraintes d'aller, elles seront forcées d'aller de concert.

La puissance exécutrice ne faisant partie de la législative que
par sa faculté d'empêcher, elle ne saurait entrer dans le débat des
affaires. Il n'est pas même nécessaire qu'elle propose, parce que,
pouvant toujours désapprouver les résolutions, elle peut rejeter les
décisions des propositions qu'elle aurait voulu qu'on n'eût pas faites.

Dans quelques républiques anciennes, où le peuple en corps

avait le débat des affaires, il était naturel que la puissance exécutrice les proposât et les débattît avec lui ; sans quoi, il y aurait eu, dans les résolutions, une confusion étrange.

Si la puissance exécutrice statue sur la levée des deniers publics autrement que par son consentement, il n'y aura plus de liberté, parce qu'elle deviendra législative dans le point le plus important de la législation.

Si la puissance législative statue, non pas d'année en année, mais pour toujours, sur la levée des deniers publics, elle court risque de perdre sa liberté, parce que la puissance exécutrice ne dépendra plus d'elle, et quand on tient un pareil droit pour toujours, il est assez indifférent qu'on le tienne de soi ou d'un autre. Il en est de même si elle statue, non pas d'année en année, mais pour toujours, sur les forces de terre et de mer qu'elle doit confier à la puissance exécutrice. . . .

Si l'on veut lire l'admirable ouvrage de Tacite sur les mœurs des Germains, on verra que c'est d'eux que les Anglais ont tiré l'idée de leur gouvernement politique. Ce beau système a été trouvé dans les bois.

[Montesquieu, *De l'Esprit des Lois*, livre xi, ch. vi.]

XXXVII

FORMATION OF A MINISTRY, 1754

(A)

Chancellor Hardwicke to Archbishop of Canterbury

In the several audiences, which I have had of the King, His Majesty has declared that " he has no favourite for this succession, that he shall be for the best man, who can carry on the public service in the best manner ; that he would have it considered by the Lords of his Cabinet Council, and know their opinion. But he hoped they would not think of recommending to him any person who has flown in his face." The meaning of this is plain, and I have seen Mr. Fox through it, though His Majesty has never named him to me. Your Grace knows his great supporter [1] at Court, and from that quarter the prepossession comes. I have thrown out several considerations to His Majesty from day to day, and so have others. These have made an impression upon him, and he has been more *deliberative*. He begins to find that all the world is not for Mr. Fox, as he had been told ; for in truth it is a

[1] The Duke of Cumberland, the King's younger son and Commander-in-Chief.

very narrow clique, and many of them of the worst sort. If he should succeed to the plenitude of power, which Mr. Pelham had, there is an end of this administration, and of all that you and I wish well to in that respect. He would also, by his connection in a certain place, have another power added to it, which Mr. Pelham had not for several years, the army. So here would be the *Treasury*, the *House of Commons* and the *Sword* joined together.

[Yorke, *Life of Hardwicke*, ii, 206, March 11, 1754.]

(B)

Minute [1] of such of the King's servants, as are of the Cabinet Council, who met, in obedience to His Majesty's commands, to consider of filling up the vacancies happening by Mr. Pelham's death.

N.B. I delivered this minute on Wednesday, March 13th, to the King in his Closet, who read it over deliberately, and entirely approved thereof. His Majesty was afterwards pleased to deliver the same back to me to keep . . .

Powis House, March 12th, 1754.

Lord President	Duke of Argyll
Lord Steward	Marquis of Hartington
Lord Chamberlain	Earl of Holderness
Duke of Devonshire	Lord Anson

Lord Chancellor.

The Lords above-mentioned met in obedience to His Majesty's commands, and were acquainted by the Lord Chancellor that the King had been pleased to order such of his servants, as are of the Cabinet Council, together with the Duke of Devonshire, to be summoned to deliberate upon the most proper and advisable methods of filling up the vacancies, happening in consequence of the great loss, which His Majesty has sustained by the death of so able and faithful a servant as Mr. Pelham.

The Lord Chancellor further acquainted the Lords that His Majesty had been graciously pleased to open to him his own ideas as to what might be proper to be done on this occasion, and to direct him to communicate them to their Lordships, in order to His Majesty's being informed of their sentiments thereupon ; (viz.) that His Majesty's first idea was that it might be for his service, in the present circumstances, to divide the two offices of First Commissioner of the Treasury and Chancellor of the Exchequer, and to fill the former with some peer of great rank and character, and the latter with some gentleman of the House of Commons of proper

[1] See also Vol. II, Sect. D, No. XXXII, p. 398.

talents for it. That, for the first, His Majesty had cast his eyes upon the Duke of Newcastle, who had long served him with ability and integrity, and greatly to his satisfaction, in the office of Secretary of State, and that, for the office of Chancellor of the Exchequer, His Majesty had thought of Mr. Legge.

That, as by this means, a vacancy would be made in the office of Secretary of State for the Northern Province, his Majesty had thoughts of laying his commands upon the Earl of Holderness, from whose services he had received great satisfaction, to change his department of the Southern Province for the Northern.

That to fill up the department of the Southern Province, His Majesty had cast his eyes upon Mr. Fox, who had served him a great while, and much to his satisfaction, in the employment of Secretary at War.

Their Lordships took these several matters into their serious consideration, and expressed the most dutiful sense of the King's great goodness and condescension in being willing to know their sentiments upon an affair of this nature and high importance.[1] And their Lordships do unanimously lay their humble sentiments before His Majesty that the ideas, which he has been graciously pleased to communicate to them, are the most prudent and wise that could be formed upon the present occasion ; and they humbly offer their opinion to His Majesty that (if he shall be so pleased) they may be carried into execution, as the most advisable plan for His Majesty's service in this critical conjuncture. . . .

[Yorke, *Life of Hardwicke*, ii, 191, March 12, 1754.]

(C)

CHANCELLOR HARDWICKE TO WILLIAM PITT

His Majesty seemed to be unresolved, professed to have no favourite for the important employment vacant, and declared that he would be advised by his Cabinet Council with the Duke of Devonshire added to them; and yet I could plainly discern a latent prepossession in favour of a certain person, who, in a few hours after Mr. Pelham's death, had made strong advances to the Duke of Newcastle and myself. I gained no further ground for four days and remained in a state of utmost anxiety, as well for the King's dignity, as for the event. To poll in a Cabinet Council for his first minister, which should only be decided in his closet, I could by no means digest, and yet I saw danger in attempting to drive it to a personal determination.

[Yorke, *Life of Hardwicke*, ii, 211, April 2, 1754.]

[1] See also Vol. II, Sect. D, No. XVI, p. 369.

XXXVIII

THE MINISTRY AND THE COMMONS,[1]
1754–55

(A)

THE DUKE OF NEWCASTLE TO CHANCELLOR HARDWICKE

Mr. Legge replied, the day was good, but that he would not deceive me . . . He came plainly to his old point, that Pitt and Fox must be satisfied, and then made (as from himself only) the following proposal in form; that he had had a discourse with Mr. Pitt; that he found he would no longer insist upon being Secretary of State, *since the King did not like it*; nay, that he (Legge) believed now, that if it was offered him, he would not take it, but that *if the King would take notice of him, and he was treated with confidence*, that *that* would do, and that Pitt, (he believed) would then act an active part. But, continued Mr. Legge, " Mr. Fox *must be Secretary of State*." As to Mr. Pitt, I said I was glad to hear he was *now* in that disposition; that when *I* flung out that very thing to him, he treated it as *words* and *mere amusement*; but that, if he would be satisfied with that, one might endeavour to bring that about. As to Mr. Fox's being Secretary of State, I did not know who would advise the removal of Sir Thomas Robinson; but if they did, I was sure the King would not do it. " No," says Legge, " that I believe, but something may be found for Lord Holderness, and Sir Thomas Robinson be made a peer and remain Secretary of State in the House of Lords, and Mr. Fox in the House of Commons." I contented myself with saying only *to him*, that it was too great and too difficult a thing for me to say anything upon, and did not in the least give in to it. He said remarkably, *he left it with me to consider*, and repeated his nonsense of uniting by that means *the Whigs*, and of his two dear friends, Mr. Fox and Mr. Pitt. It is plain to me that this proceeds, first from their seeing that they are *beat*, then from a most thorough combination in the *three* to get at once the House of Commons and consequently the whole administration, into their hands.

[Yorke, *Life of Hardwicke*, ii, 219, Nov. 17, 1754.]

(B)

THE DUKE OF NEWCASTLE TO CHANCELLOR HARDWICKE

. . . your Lordship and I took that opportunity to represent to the King in the strongest manner, the necessity of forming a system

---

[1] Cf. Sect. D, No. III, p. 322, and Vol. II, Sect. D, No. XIV (A), p. 364.

for the House of Commons, and of engaging and enabling him (Mr. Pitt) to take an active part in support of the King's measures there; that his Majesty, in answer, had been pleased, not only most graciously to approve what my Lord Chancellor and I had thus offered to his consideration, but had been pleased also to authorise us to assure Mr. Pitt of his gracious acceptance of his service, and of his Majesty's countenance, and also, as a mark of it, that the King was willing to call him to the Cabinet Council. He then began his reply, and with great decency said that the King's countenance was more to him than any other consideration; but that, if it was expected that he should take an *active part* in support of measures, he must be enabled to do it, which he could not think the calling him to the Cabinet Council would, in any degree, do; that the House of Commons was now an assembly of atoms, that the great wheels of the machine were stopped, that this could not be thought sufficient to put them in motion; that if nothing was required of him but what related to himself, he would very readily, in his present employment, acquiesce in measures, if he approved them, but that I did not know the state of the House of Commons which, he might say without vanity, he did better than anybody. He then repeated, word for word, the same plan and system which Mr. Legge proposed to me, the last year, viz :—that the business of the House of Commons could not go on without there was a minister, (a subordinate one perhaps), which should go directly between the King and them; that if there was any objection to him, he was far from desiring it himself, that any other person might be thought of; but that he could not, and would not, take an *active part* in the House of Commons without he had an *office of advice* as well as of *execution*, and that was the distinction he made throughout the whole conversation, that he would support the measures which he *himself* had advised, but would not, like a lawyer, talk from a *brief*.

[Yorke, *Life of Hardwicke*, ii, 238, Sept. 3, 1755.]

(C)

CHANCELLOR HARDWICKE TO DUKE OF NEWCASTLE

The first is the *general* principle, that there must be a minister *with the King* in the House of Commons. The other is the *personal* one, that Mr. Pitt must be Secretary of State. They are neither of them new. The former we heard much of, even before this Parliament set down, but notwithstanding all the awkwardnesses of the last session, none of us thought that the principle made much way in general. 'Tis espoused by a few who are, or would be, leading men there, and they sound it high in order to make it popular.

When they say a *subordinate minister*, 'tis what they don't mean ; and *younger brothers* as they are, their meaning is to be in the place of Sir Robert Walpole or Mr. Pelham. If the King would give sufficient confidence and authority to his first minister to confine it to this *subordinate* character, possibly there might be no great hurt in it ; for I have long been convinced that,whoever your Grace shall make use of as your first man and man of confidence in the House of Commons, you will find it necessary if he be a man of reputation and ability, accompanied with the ambition naturally incident to such a character, I say, your Grace under these circumstances will find it necessary to invest him with more power, than from the beginning you thought fit to impart, either to Mr. Legge or Sir Thomas Robinson.

[Yorke, *Life of Hardwicke*, ii, 245, Sept. 4, 1755.]

XXXIX
DEPARTMENTAL MINISTERS, 1755
CHANCELLOR HARDWICKE TO DUKE OF NEWCASTLE

I . . . said that I thought it my duty to mention to His Majesty that, though I had not seen your Grace, I had received a letter from you last night, by which I found you were under the greatest concern that His Majesty should interpret the opinion you gave him for suspending the disposition of the Groom of the Stole for the present, as proceeding from any other motive than the real one, a desire that it might be further considered by His Majesty. The King grew warm, and said, " The Duke of Newcastle meddles in things he has nothing to do with. He would dispose of my Bedchamber, which is a personal service about myself, and I won't suffer anybody to meddle in." . . . that the Treasury was the Duke of Newcastle's department, and that was business enough etc. ; that your Grace had begun at the wrong end, and proposed Lords of the Bed-chamber to him before there was any vacancy there. To this I said that the head of his Treasury was indeed an employment of great business, very extensive, which always went beyond the bare management of the revenue ; that it extended through both Houses of Parliament, the members of which were naturally to look thither ; that there must be some principal person [1] to receive applications, to hear the wants and the wishes and the requests of mankind, with the reasons of them, in order to lay them before His Majesty for his determination ; that it was impossible for the King

[1] See Sect. D, No. I, p. 317, No. XXIX, p. 369, No. XLVII, p. 398 and Vol. II, Sect. B, No. XIII, p. 182.

to be troubled with all this himself.   This he in part admitted, but there were some things nobody should meddle in etc.   I said it was only a method of laying things before him, and the absolute final decision was in *him* ;[1] that it had been always the usage in this Country, and I supposed was so in others ; that without it no administration could be enabled to serve him, that ministers bore all the blame and resentment of disappointed persons, and they could never carry on his affairs without having some weight in the disposition of favours.   The King said, he had seen too much of that in this Country already, and it was time to change it in some degree.   I then asked his pardon for presuming so far ; that I only thought it my duty and a point of justice.   The King said the thing was over, and he had determined it ;   " But I know how you are connected (I am not sure whether he did not say linked) together." I answered that it was far from my intention to argue for altering *the thing*, but only to shew him the reasons why a suspension had been proposed ; that as to connections I had none, but what were very consistent with his service and tended to the real support of it ; and here my audience ended.   One thing I forgot that, in the course of what I said, I let him know that such things would materially create appearances and interpretations in the world that, by weakening his administration, might give rise to disturbance in Parliament, and alter that state of ease and quiet, which his Majesty and his servants under him had been endeavouring to bring about; that people would be looking different ways, and every question upon an election might become a contest between different sides of the Court.   But the King seemed to despise such fears at present.

[Yorke, *Life of Hardwicke*, ii, 224, Jan. 3, 1755.]

XL

OPPOSITION, 1757

(A)

THE EARL OF HARDWICKE TO THE DUKE OF NEWCASTLE

I am inclined to think that the right and honest way will be to take some proper method of informing the King that no solid plan of administration can be made for him by anybody, that will give him ease and comfort for the remainder of his days,—ease at home or procure peace abroad, but such a one as may, if possible, unite the whole Royal Family and bring *the succession* to support

[1] Cf. Vol. II, Sect. D, No. IX (C), p. 355.

and give quiet to *the possession*. Everything else will be perpetual contest. . . .

What part our friends should act in the meantime? This is certainly attended with difficulties. For my own part, I am determined not to go into a formed general opposition.[1] I have seen so much of them that I am convinced they are the most wicked combinations that men can enter into;—worse and more corrupt than any administration that I ever yet saw, and so they have appeared in the conclusion. Therefore I see no other way at present but to keep off from any absolute engagement with either party (unless some new system should arise out of these overtures), and to oppose wrong measures and concur in right ones, as particular questions shall arise or be foreseen. I am sensible that this is not the political way to keep a party[2] together, but that is not an objection against doing what I think in my own conscience to be right.

[Yorke, *Life of Hardwicke*, ii, 392, April 9, 1757.]

(B)

The Earl of Hardwicke to Lord Anson

. . . The King then said, " But why then will not the Duke of Newcastle promise me his support. . . . Will he go into opposition? "—" He will never do anything contrary to his duty and zeal for your Majesty's service."—" But tell me your opinion, if the Duke of Newcastle should go into *opposition, would the Whigs of the House of Commons follow him?* "—" Since your Majesty commands me to tell you my opinion, I think they would."[3]—That was a strong answer indeed and must have an effect. H.M. made no reply. . . .

[Yorke, *Life of Hardwicke*, ii, 394, April 9, 1757.]

XLI

COMMISSION OF THE PEACE

George the second by the grace of God, of Great Britain, France, and Ireland, king, defender of the faith, and so forth. To A. B. C. D. etc. greeting.

[1] See Vol. II, Sect. B, No. VIII, p. 166, and Sect. D, No. VII, p. 352.
[2] See Sect. D, No. V, p. 325, No. XXIII, p. 359, No. XLVI, p. 396, and Sect. B, No. XXXVIII, p. 240.
[3] But, at the beginning of the next reign, much to Newcastle's chagrin, this proved a false prophecy.

Know ye that we have assigned you, jointly and severally, and every one of you, our justices to keep our peace in our county of W. And to keep and cause to be kept all ordinances and statutes for the good of the peace, and for preservation of the same, and for the quiet rule and government of our people made, in all and singular their articles in our said county (as well within liberties as without) according to the force, form, and effect of the same; And to chastise and punish all persons that offend against the form of those ordinances or statutes, or any one of them, in the aforesaid county, as it ought to be done according to the form of those ordinances and statutes; And to cause to come before you, or any of you, all those who to any one or more of our people concerning their bodies or the firing of their houses have used threats, to find sufficient security for the peace, or their good behaviour, towards us and our people; and if they shall refuse to find such security, then them in our prisons until they shall find such security to cause to be safely kept.

We have also assigned you, and every two or more of you (of whom any one of you the aforesaid A. B. C. D. etc. we will shall be one) our justices to inquire the truth more fully, by the oath of good and lawful men of the aforesaid county, by whom the truth of the matter shall be the better known, of all and all manner of felonies, poisonings, inchantments, sorceries, art magick, trespasses, forestallings, regratings, ingrossings, and extortions whatsoever; and of all and singular other crimes and offences, of which the justices of our peace may or ought lawfully to inquire, by whomsoever and after what manner soever in the said county done or perpetrated, or which shall happen to be there done or attempted; And also of all those who in the aforesaid county in companies against our peace, in disturbance of our people, with armed force have gone or rode, or hereafter shall presume to go or ride; And also of all those who have there lain in wait, or hereafter shall presume to lay in wait, to maim or cut or kill our people; And also of all victuallers, and all and singular other persons, who in the abuse of weights or measures, or in selling victuals, against the form of the ordinances and statutes, or any one of them therefore made for the common benefit of England and our people thereof, have offended or attempted, or hereafter shall presume in the said county to offend or attempt; And also of all sheriffs, bailiffs, stewards, constables, keepers of gaols, and other officers, who in the execution of their offices about the premisses, or any of them, have unduly behaved themselves, or hereafter shall presume to behave themselves unduly, or have been, or shall happen hereafter to be careless, remiss, or negligent in our aforesaid county; And of all and singular articles, and circumstances, and all other things whatsoever, that concern the premisses or any of them, by whomsoever, and after what manner soever, in our aforesaid county done or perpetrated, or which hereafter shall there happen to be done or attempted in what manner soever ; And to inspect all indictments whatsoever so before you or any of you taken or to be taken, or before others late our justices of the peace in the aforesaid county made or taken, and not yet determined ; and to make and continue processes thereupon, against all and singular the persons so indicted, or who before you hereafter shall happen to be indicted ; until they can be taken, surrender themselves, or be outlawed : And to hear and determine all and singular the felonies, poisonings, inchantments, sorceries, arts magick, trespasses, forestallings, regratings, ingrossings, extortions, unlawful assemblies, indictments aforesaid, and all and singular other the premisses, according to the laws and statutes of England, as in the like case it has been accustomed, or ought to be done ; And the same offenders, and every of them for their offences, by fines, ransoms, amerciaments, forfeitures, and other means as according to the law and custom of England, or form of the ordinances and statutes aforesaid, it has been accustomed, or ought to be done, to chastise and punish.

Provided always, that if a case of difficulty, upon the determination of any the premisses, before you, or any two or more of you, shall happen to arise ; then let judgment in no wise be given thereon, before you, or any two or more of you, unless in the presence of one of our justices of the one or other bench, or of one of our justices appointed to hold the assizes in the aforesaid county.

And therefore we command you and every of you, that to keeping the peace, ordinances, statutes, and all and singular other premisses, you diligently apply yourselves ; and that at certain days and places, which you, or any such two or more of you as is aforesaid shall appoint for these purposes, into the premisses ye make inquiries ; and all and singular the premisses hear and determine, and perform and fulfil them in the aforesaid form, doing therein what to justice appertains, according to the law and custom of England : Saving to us the amerciaments, and other things to us therefrom belonging.

And we command by the tenor of these presents our sheriff of W. that at certain days and places, which you, or any such two or more of you as is aforesaid, shall make known to him, he cause to come before you, or such two or more of you as aforesaid, so many and such good and lawful men of his bailiwick (as well within liberties as without) by whom the truth of the matter in the premisses shall be the better known and inquired into.

Lastly, we have assigned you the aforesaid A. B. keeper of the rolls of our peace in our said county. And therefore you shall cause to be brought before you and your said fellows, at the days and places aforesaid, the writs, precepts, processes, and indictments aforesaid, that they may be inspected, and by a due course determined as is aforesaid.

In witness whereof we have caused these our letters to be made patent.   Witness our self at Westminster etc.

[Burns, *Justice of the Peace*, fifth edition, 1758, p. 426.]

XLII

REPRESENTATIVE THEORY [1]

Every Member, as soon as he is chosen, becomes a representative of the whole body of the Commons, without any distinction of the place from whence he is sent to Parliament. Instructions, therefore, from particular constituents to their own Members, are or can be only of information, advice, and recommendation (which they have an undoubted right to offer, if done decently ; and which ought to be respectfully received, and well considered) but are not absolutely binding upon votes, and actings, and conscience, in Parliament. That every Member is equally a Representative of the *whole* (within which, by our particular constitution, is included a Representative, not only of those who are electors, but of all the other subjects of the Crown of Great Britain at home, and in every part of the British empire, except the Peers of Great Britain) has, as I understand, been the constant notion and language of Parliament.

[Note of Arthur Onslow, Speaker (1728–61), quoted by J. Hatsell, ii, 76, edit. 1818.]

[1] Cf. Burke's Speech to the Electors of Bristol, Nov. 3, 1774 : " But *authoritative* instructions, *mandates* issued, which the member is bound blindly and implicitly to obey. . . . these are things utterly unknown to the laws of this land, and which arise from a fundamental mistake of the whole order and tenor of our constitution." Cf. also, Vol. II, Sect. B, No. XXVIII, at p. 222, and Sect. C, No. XXIV, p. 320.

XLIII
SECRETARY OF STATE, 1761

The Busyness of Secretary of State consists of two Parts :—

Domestic, Foreign.

The Domestic Busyness relates to Instruments of various Sorts for the King's signature, which are carried or sent by the Secretary of State to the King. . . .

Another part of the Domestic Busyness of a Secretary of State relates to his Correspondence with the different Boards or with the several subordinate Ministers for the King's Information, either in Matters of Fact or of Law. . . .

Another part of the Domestic Busyness of the Secretary of State is, when He acts as a Magistrate, being in Right of His Office a *Conservator of the Peace*[1] and has thereby in many respects the same powers as a Justice of the Peace ; In consequence of this He apprehends such Criminals as are worthy the Attention of Government, Persons guilty of Treason, Spies etc. When these are apprehended by a warrant,[2] directed to a Messenger, there is a Law Clerk belonging to the Office, to take their Depositions ; and they are disposed of according to the Discretion of the Secretary of State, with the advice of His Majesty's Ministers, which belong to the Law.

The other parts of the Domestic Busyness of the Secretary of State consist of such Correspondence as may occasionally arise from Domestic Occurrences which in peaceable times are very few, and when they do arise, are of the Nature of every other Correspondence, where the King's Commands are to be transmitted.

The Foreign Part of the Busyness of Secretary of State relates to the different kind of Correspondence, which He carries on with all, who bear His Majesty's Commission in Foreign Parts, whether Ministers, Generals, etc. The General Intent of this is to convey the King's Commands to them, and to receive from them such Intelligence, as they can supply. . . .

It consists of Letters and Instructions, *sent* or *received*.

Before any Letter or Instruction is sent, the Secretary of State takes the Commands of His Majesty,[3] and consults upon it such of His Majesty's Confidential Ministers as He thinks proper. In consequence of this the Draught of the Letter is formed either by Himself or by one of His Under-Secretaries. . . . When the Draught is

[1] See Sect. C, No. XVIII, p. 297.
[2] *e.g.* Sect. C, No. XVI (A), p. 294.
[3] See Sect. D, No. XI, p. 331, and No. XLIX, p. 399.

settled in proportion to its Importance it is circulated or not to any other of the Confidential Ministers ; and after it has received their Corrections, it is sent to the King ; . . . and being then transmitted to the Secretary of State for His Signature, it is afterwards returned to the Office to be dispatched . . .

The Letters received are brought always first to the Office ; When They arrive either by Mail or Messenger, They are first opened by an Under Secretary, who dockets them ; if the Secretary of State is in the Way, he sends them first to Him, who after having perused them, transmits them to the King ; But if the Secretary of State is at the House of Lords, or any otherwise engaged they are then sent immediately to the King, and after that they are put into a Course of Circulation as is agreed on among the Ministers. Each Secretary always sends His Dispatches to the other Secretary, before He sends them to any other Minister ; the dispatches out of Cypher are always sent up from the Office first with a Schedule of such as are in Cypher ; and as soon as these last can be decyphered, They are sent up also. . . .

[Memorandum by Charles Jenkinson, Under-Secretary of State in 1761 ; M. S. North, c. 3, ff. 284-86. Quoted by N. S. Jucker in the " Jenkinson Papers ", 1949.]

XLIV

LOCAL GOVERNMENT :[1] *AD HOC* BODIES

The Lighting of the Town

(A)

Agreed unanimously that this Corporation shall give the Sum of One Hundred Pounds towards the obtaining an Act of Parliament for the Lighting of the Public Streets Lanes and Passages of this Town and the Purchasing of the Lamps intended to be set up and towards the Expences of fixing up the said Lamps as soon as a Sum of money shall be raised by Subscription which with the Said Sum of One Hundred Pounds shall be sufficient for Paying the Expences of obtaining the said Act purchasing the said Lamps fixing them up and all other Expences attending the same.

[Nottingham Borough Records, vol. vii, Dec. 18, 1761.]

(B)

Agreed that the Trustees for the Lighting of this Town with Lamps shall have the Cellar under the Town Hall Steps for placing

[1] See Sect. D, No. LIII, p. 404.

Oyl there and also the use of the Garrett over the Hall for the
Depositing the Lamps so long as this Corporation shall agree
thereto paying annually the sum of one Shilling.

[Nottingham Borough Records, vol. vii, Aug. 6, 1762.]

XLV

BLACKSTONE ON PARLIAMENT AND PREROGATIVE

(A)

The power and jurisdiction of parliament, says Sir Edward
Coke, is so transcendent and absolute, that it cannot be confined,
either for causes or persons, within any bounds.   And of this high
court he adds, it may be truly said " *si antiquitatem spectes, est
vetustissima ; si dignitatem, est honoratissima ; si jurisdictionem,
est capacissima.*"   It hath sovereign and uncontrolable authority in
making, confirming, enlarging, restraining, abrogating, repealing,
reviving, and expounding of laws, concerning matters of all possible
denominations, ecclesiastical, or temporal, civil, military, maritime,
or criminal : this being the place where that absolute despotic power,
which must in all governments reside somewhere, is entrusted by
the constitution of these kingdoms.   All mischiefs and grievances,
operations and remedies, that transcend the ordinary course of the
laws, are within the reach of this extraordinary tribunal.   It can
regulate or new model the succession to the crown ; as was done
in the reign of Henry VIII and William III.   It can alter the
established religion of the land ; as was done in a variety of instances,
in the reigns of king Henry VIII and his three children.   It can
change and create afresh even the constitution of the kingdom and
of parliaments themselves ; as was done by the act of union, and
the several statutes for triennial and septennial elections.   It can,
in short, do every thing that is not naturally impossible ; and therefore some have not scrupled to call it's power, by a figure rather
too bold, the omnipotence [1] of parliament.

[Blackstone, *Commentaries* (1765-9), Bk. I, ch. 2.]

(B)

After what has been premised in this chapter, I shall not (I
trust) be considered as an advocate for arbitrary power, when I lay

[1] Cf. Sect. D, No. XIV (C), p. 341.

it down as a principle, that in the exertion of lawful prerogative, the king is and ought to be absolute : that is, so far absolute, that there is no legal authority that can either delay or resist him.   He may reject what bills, may make what treaties, may coin what money, may create what peers, may pardon what offences he pleases : unless where the constitution hath expressly or by evident consequence, laid down some exception or boundary ; declaring, that thus far the prerogative shall go and no farther.   Foi otherwise the power of the crown would indeed be but a name and a shadow,[1] insufficient for the ends of government, if, where its jurisdiction is clearly established and allowed, any man or body of men were permitted to disobey it, in the ordinary course of law.

[Blackstone, *Commentaries* (1765–69), Bk. I, ch. 7.]

XLVI

BURKE ON PARTY,[2] 1770

That connexion and faction are equivalent terms is an opinion which has been carefully inculcated at all times by unconstitutional statesmen.   The reason is evident.   Whilst men are linked together, they easily and speedily communicate the alarm of any evil design. They are enabled to fathom it with common counsel, and to oppose it with united strength.   Whereas, when they lie dispersed, without concert, order, or discipline, communication is uncertain, counsel difficult, and resistance impracticable.   Where men are not acquainted with each other's principles, nor experienced in each other's talents, nor at all practised in their mutual habitudes and dispositions by joint efforts in business ; no personal confidence, no friendship, no common interest, subsisting among them ; it is evidently impossible that they can act a public part with uniformity, perseverance, or efficacy.   In a connexion, the most inconsiderable man, by adding to the weight of the whole, has his value, and his use ; out of it, the greatest talents are wholly unserviceable to the public.   No man, who is not inflamed by vain-glory into enthusiasm, can flatter himself that his single, unsupported, desultory, unsystematic endeavours are of power to defeat the subtle designs and united cabals of ambitious citizens.   When bad men combine, the

[1] See Sect. B, No. VII, p. 179, and Vol. II, Sect. D, No. XLII (G), p. 422, No. XLV, p. 428.

[2] See Sect. D, No. V, p. 325, No. XXIII, p. 359, No. XL, p. 389, and Sect. B, No. XXXVIII, p. 240, and Vol. II, Sect. D, No. III, p. 347, and No. XLII (D), at p. 419.

good must associate ; else they will fall, one by one, an unpitied sacrifice in a contemptible struggle.

It is not enough in a situation of trust in the common-wealth, that a man means well to his country ; it is not enough that in his single person he never did an evil act, but always voted according to his conscience, and even harangued against every design which he apprehended to be prejudicial to the interests of his country. This innoxious and ineffectual character that seems formed upon a plan of apology and disculpation falls miserably short of the mark of public duty. That duty demands and requires that what is right should not only be made known, but made prevalent ; that what is evil should not only be detected, but defeated. When the public man omits to put himself in a situation of doing his duty with effect, it is an omission that frustrates the purposes of his trust almost as much as if he had formally betrayed it. It is surely no very rational account of a man's life, that he has always acted right, but has taken special care to act in such a manner that his endeavours could not possibly be productive of any consequence. . . .

Party is a body of men united for promoting by their joint endeavours the national interest upon some particular principle in which they are all agreed. For my part, I find it impossible to conceive, that any one believes in his own politics, or thinks them to be of any weight, who refuses to adopt the means of having them reduced into practice. It is the business of the speculative philosopher to mark the proper ends of government. It is the business of the politician, who is the philosopher in action, to find out proper means towards those ends, and to employ them with effect. Therefore every honourable connexion will avow it is their first purpose, to pursue every just method to put the men who hold their opinions into such a condition as may enable them to carry their common plans into execution, with all the power and authority of the state. As this power is attached to certain situations, it is their duty to contend for these situations. Without a pro-scription of others, they are bound to give to their own party the preference in all things ; and by no means, for private considerations, to accept any offers of power in which the whole body is not included ; nor to suffer themselves to be led or to be controlled, or to be overbalanced, in office or in council, by those who contradict the very fundamental principles on which their party is formed, and even those upon which every fair connexion must stand. Such a generous contention for power, on such manly and honourable maxims, will easily be distinguished from the mean and interested struggle for place and emolument.

[Burke, *The Present Discontents*, O.U.P., ii, 78.]

XLVII

PRIME MINISTER,[1] 1778

LORD NORTH TO GEORGE III

. . . There are two points, which Lord North has the honour of submitting to his Majesty's consideration, which he conceives very important for the government of this country.

The first is, That the Public business can never go on as it ought, while the Principal most efficient offices are in the hands of persons who are either indifferent to, or actually dislike their situation.

The second is, That in critical times, it is necessary that there should be one directing Minister, who should plan the whole of the operations of government, control all the other departments o administration so far as to make them co-operate zealously actively with his designs even tho contrary to their own. . . .

[Fortescue, *Correspondence of George III*, iv, 215, Nov. 10, 1778.]

XLVIII

SUPREMACY OF COMMONS, 1782

LORD NORTH TO GEORGE III

. . . Your Majesty is well apprized that, in this country, the Prince on the Throne, cannot, with prudence, oppose the deliberate resolution of the House of Commons : Your Royal Predecessors (particularly King William the Third and his late Majesty) were obliged to yield to it much against their wish in more instances than one : They consented to changes in their Ministry which they disapproved because they found it necessary to sacrifice their private wishes, and even their opinions to the preservation of public order, and the prevention of these terrible mischiefs, which are the natural consequence of the clashing of the two branches of the Sovereign Power in the State. . . . The Parliament have altered their sentiments, and as their sentiments whether just or erroneous, must ultimately prevail, Your Majesty . . . can lose no honour if you yield at length, as some of the most renowned and most glorious of your Predecessors have done, to the opinion and wishes of the House of Commons.

[Fortescue, *Correspondence of George III*, v, 395, March 18, 1782.]

[1] See Sect. D, No. I, p. 317, No. XXIX, p. 369, No. XXXIX, p. 387, and Vol. II, Sect. D, No. XXIX, p. 391.

XLIX

THE KING AND THE CABINET, 1782

(A)

LORD SHELBURNE TO GEORGE III

. . . I must take that, or some opportunity of stating what I conceive the natural course of business to be, first for the Department to submit any business to Your Majesty, and to be consider'd afterwards by the Cabinet under Your Majesty's Reference. . . .

[Fortescue, *Correspondence of George III*, v, 503, April 29, 1782.]

(B)

GEORGE III TO LORD SHELBURNE

. . . Certainly it is quite new for business to be laid before the Cabinet and consequently advice offered by the Ministers to the Crown unasked; the Minister of the Department used always to ask the permission of the King to lay such a point before the Cabinet,[1] as he cldnt chuse to venture to take the direction of the Crown upon without such sanction; then the Advice came with propriety. . . .

[Fortescue, *Correspondence of George III*, v, 504, April 29, 1782.]

L

THE TREASURY AND ELECTION EXPENSES,[2]
1782

LORD NORTH TO GEORGE III

As to the election acc^{ts}, Ld. N. never received it (sic) till he sent it to his M——y on the 27th of March last. He had for some months past pressed Mr. R. to let him see it (sic), but Mr. R. was not able to give him a compleat state of it before. If Ld. N. had thought that the expence attending elections and re-elections in the years 1779, 1780, and 1781 would have amounted to 72,000 *l.*, he certainly would not have advis'd his Majesty to have embark'd in any such expence. He begs, however, a few moments of his

[1] See Sect. D, No. XI, p. 331.
[2] See also Sect. D, No. V, p. 325, No. XV, p. 342, No. XXVII, p. 366, No. XXXV, p. 377, and Vol. II, Sect. D, No. X, p. 356.

M——y's attention to state some circumstances which may in a degree account for the largeness of the sum in the election acc^t.

That acc^t contains, besides the expences attending the general election, the expence of the Hampshire contest in the year 1779, and of the elections of *Bristol, Coventry,* and *Gloucestershire,* together with about 2000 *l.* for sundry smaller elections. The 2000 *l.* sent to the Duke of Chandos and Sir R. Worsley in Hampshire bore, as Ld. North fears, a very small part of this expence. Mr. Chester, in the great contest for *Gloucestershire,* has, as it is said, spent from 20 to 30,000 *l.,* but nevertheless left at his death from 3 to 4000 *l.* unpaid. This debt was great prejudice to the friends of Governm^t in the contest which follow'd upon Mr. Chester's death ; to assist in removing it 2000 *l.* was paid.

The sitting members for Coven^{ty} had stood three contested elections, two trials before the Committee, and a long examination at the Bar of the House, in the course of a year and half before they made any application. They then rec'd 2000 *l.*

The general elect^n at Bristol cost but 1000 *l.* to Governm^t ; but Mr. H. Lippingcot's death bringing on a fresh contest on the back of the former, the merchants of Bristol, who had contributed largely to the first contest, as well as to many loyal subscriptions, thought they might without impropriety apply for assistance. They rec^d at different times 5000 *l.* Ld. N. encloses an abstract of their expences, and of the assistance they received.

Expences in the account not incurred at the general election :—

	£
Hampshire	2000
Gloucestershire	2000
Coventry	2000
Bristol	5000
Sundry re-elections	2000
	£13,000

Ld. N. was very unwillingly drawn into the contest for Westminster, Surrey, and the City of London : but the necessity of strengthening the Government at that time, and weakening the Opposition, and the importance of a victory in those places with the fair prospect of success, prevailed upon him to advise the beginning, which drew on the subsequent expence.

The expence of the Westmin^r amounted to more than 8000 *l.* ; Surrey to 4000 *l.* ; the City, to 4000 *l.* ; the amount of all the three to more than 16,000 *l.* These three contests were unhappily not successful, and therefore the expence is the greater grievance ; but Ld. N. must, in justice to the Members who were assisted to come in to Parliament, say that they all behaved with very steady attachment to the end. Ld. N. will just add that he was disappointed of some contribution-money as he had every reason to expect. Ld. N. does by no means intend by this state to propose to his M——y to add more (than) 13,000 *l.* to the 40,000 *l.* already issued, which undoubtedly is a very large sum, but only to lay fully and fairly before his M——y the principal causes of the acc^t of (which) his M——y complains. If Ld. N. remembers correctly, the last gen^l election cost near 50,000 *l.* to the Crown, beyond which expence there was a pension of 1000 *l.* a-year to Ld. Montacute and 500 *l.* a-year to Mr. Selwyn for their interest at Midhurst and Luggershall. The elections in 1779 and 1780 and 1781 will cost 53,000 *l.*; but then there has been no additional pensions promised; nay, Ld. Montagu's pension is struck off because two friends of Government, Mr. Sampson Gideon and Mr. Drummond, purchas'd with their own money, at Ld. N.'s recommendation, the two seats at Midhurst, so that, all things considered, this elect^n will not in the end have been so burthensome to his M——y as the last.

[Donne, *Correspondence of George III with Lord North,* ii, 424.]

LI

THE KING SEEKS A GOVERNMENT,[1] 1783

(A)

EARL TEMPLE [2] TO W. W. GRENVILLE [3]

I believe that Lord Shelburne cannot stand alone. I know the King will not hear of Fox, and I think that neither His Majesty nor Lord North will venture to reunite the old opposition by restoring all as they stood in March. The solution therefore is plain; that Lord North and his friends will have a share of *office,* and will have, either avowedly or not, a share of *government.* . . . I did not come here for the sake of Lord Shelburne, nor is it necessary for me to decorate his exit. . . . I cannot bring my mind to that old system of corruption on the one hand, or of faction on the other, . . . to which we shall owe the total overthrow of our Constitution unless the property and weight of the nobility save it. Whatever therefore is the event I will not join an Opposition while the form of law and government continue to leave me a free man . . . I wish most truly to support an Administration who will make head against the frenzy of reform;

[1] Cf. Vol. II, Sect. D, No. XLII B, p. 414.
[2] Lord Lieutenant of Ireland.
[3] Chief Secretary, and brother of Temple.

for I must freely own that I fear more from that reform than from
the power of the Crown, which this convulsion in the empire will
have truly weakened. . . (Dublin, Feb. 11, 1783.)

(B)

W. PITT TO EARL TEMPLE

. . . In different parts of his conversation [i.e. Thurlow's] he
expressed very strongly the necessity of stable government; but,
at the same time threw out doubts whether objections to particular
persons being brought forward, might not be in the way of it.   He
also dropped, in a passing way, and at separate times, that the King
had no insight into the means of forming a government; that his
directly turning out his Ministers was different from their resigning
or being pressed in Parliament; and that the King had *gone through
the worst*, in the struggle which ended in bringing them in.   Yet he
said, when I hinted that they might succeed in their endeavours to
reconcile the King to them, that the King could never forgive their
conduct. . . .

I reminded him how much I was personally pledged to Parliamentary reform . . . I treated as out of the question any idea of
measures being taken to extend influence, though such means as
are fairly in the hands of Ministers would undoubtedly be to be
exerted. . . . (July 22, 1783.)

(C)

EARL TEMPLE TO W. PITT

. . . We cannot be too explicit in our refusal to engage in
government upon the avowed or implied system of replacing in
the hands of the Crown that influence which has already been taken
from it; excepting . . . where an improper new arrangement may
make a change necessary, not for influence, but for the proper
administration of each department . . . The idea of the change
originating in an offer or in eagerness from us cannot be allowed;
nor do I see the necessity of it, as I think it clear that the King is in
earnest. . . . (July 21 [? 31], 1783.)

[H.M.C., 13th Rep., App. pt. iii, vol. i (Fortescue of Dropmore),
p. 192 *sqq.*]

LII

THE KING INTERVENING TO DEFEAT A MINISTRY, 1783

(A)

MEMORANDUM BY LORD TEMPLE,[1] DECEMBER 1ST, 1783

. . . We profess to wish to know whether this Bill[2] appear to His Majesty in this light : a plan to take more than half the royal power, and by that means disable [the King] for the rest of the reign. There is nothing else in it which ought to call for this inter-position.

Whether any means can be thought of, short of changing his Ministers, to avoid this evil.

The refusing the Bill, if it passes the Houses, is a violent means. The changing his Ministers[3] after the last vote of the Commons, in a less degree might be liable to the same sort of construction.

An easier way of changing his Government would be by taking some opportunity of doing it, when, in the progress of it, it shall have reached more discountenance than hitherto.

This must be expected to happen in the Lords in a greater degree than it can be hoped for in the Commons.

But a sufficient degree of it may not occur in the Lords, if those whose duty to His Majesty would excite them to appear are not acquainted with his wishes, and that in a manner which would make it impossible to pretend a doubt of it, in case they were so disposed.

By these means the discountenance might be hoped to raise difficulties so high, as to throw it [out], and leave his Majesty at perfect liberty to choose whether he will change them or not.

This is the situation which it is wished his Majesty should find himself in.

[Buckingham, *Courts and Cabinets George III*, i, 288.]

(B)

MR. FITZPATRICK TO LORD OSSORY, MONDAY, DECEMBER 15TH, 1783

LORD TEMPLE had a long audience on Thursday last, and is said to have come out declaring himself authorised to say that the

---

[1] Partly in Lord Temple's handwriting but mainly in a hand scarcely legible and believed to be that of Lord Thurlow.

[2] Fox's India Bill. [3] Cf. Vol. II, Sect. D, No. XXIII, p. 383.

King disapproved of the Bill,[1] as unconstitutional, and subversive of the rights of the Crown, and that he should consider all who voted for it as his enemies. Lord Temple has not dared to avow this, but continues to insinuate it. The Bishops waver, and *the Thanes fly from us* ; in my opinion, the Bill [1] will not pass ; the Lords are now sitting, and the debate will certainly be too late to send you an account of the division ; the proxies of the King's friends are arrived against the Bill. The public is full of alarm and astonishment at the treachery as well as the imprudence of this unconstitutional interference. No body guesses what will be the consequence of a conduct that is generally compared to that of Charles the First in 1641. I hope you will come to town, for it will be certainly impossible to send you satisfactory accounts, and some measures must, of course, be immediately taken in the House of Commons. I consider the Ministry as over.

(C)

SAME TO SAME, DECEMBER 16TH, 1783

Tuesday morning, 3 o'clock
ADMINISTRATION were beat by eight. The Commons do not meet till Wednesday, when it is agreed they must not acquiesce tamely. We shall depend upon seeing you ; the left wing of the Coalition is stout and in good spirits. The Prince of Wales voted in the minority. We shall certainly have a question on Wednesday.

[Lord J. Russell, *Memorials and Correspondence of C. J. Fox*, ii, 220.]

LIII

LOCAL GOVERNMENT,[2] 1783

STREET PAVING AND CLEANING

A Requisition to the Mayor from the Committee appointed by the Inhabitants of this Town to prepare Plans and Estimates of the Expence attending the appointing a Regular Watch Watch [*sic*] and Paving and cleaning the Streets and other things for the Improvement of this Town desiring that the Mayor would Call a Common Hall to take the Sentiments of that Hall what may have been the Medium of this Corporations Annual expence towards Paving the Streets of this Town and the like Medium of their Annual expence of cleaning the Streets for the last Fifteen Years

---

[1] Fox's India Bill.
[2] See Sect. D, No. XLIV, p. 394.

and to know what this Corporation woud be willing to allow Annually in future towards the paving and Cleaning of the Streets in this Town and that the Mayor be also desired to Request of the Hall that a Committee of the Hall or some other Person or Persons from them on behalf of this Corporation might be appointed to meet that Committee at their next Meeting with the Corporations Answer to the above Particulars being now read in Council In answer thereto It is the Sentiments of this Hall that the Annual Expence to this Corporation of Cleaning the Streets has amounted to Fifty pounds per Annum and that the Annual Expence of Paving is quite Uncertain but that Fifty Pounds more would be as much as this Corporation would be inclined to give in case they should be satisfyed with the intended Scheme of Improving the Town and that the same can be done without laying too large a Burthen on the Town And this Hall do appoint the Town Clerk to Represent this their Sentiments to the Committee in Answer to their Request.

[Nottingham Borough Records, vol. vii, Dec. 16, 1783.]

GLOSSARY

ACTION OF DEBT
An action which lies for the recovery of a certain sum of money owed, *e.g.* on a deed or contract or judgement, as opposed to a sum of money which is assessed by the jury.

ACTION OF RAVISHMENT OF WARD
An action which lay for the guardian holding land by knight service or in socage (*q.v.*) against a person who took from him the body of his ward.

ADVOCATION
The process by which, in Scotland, an action was carried from an inferior to a superior court; appeals were substituted by 31 & 32 Vict., c. 100.

ADVOWSON
The right, belonging to a patron, of presentation to a church or benefice.

AGGREGATE FUND
Fund created by consolidating the produce of various taxes into one fund, which became known as the Consolidated Fund by the Act of 27 Geo. III, c. 13.

AIDE (1) PUR FILE MARRIER, (2) PUR FAIER FITZ CHIVALIER
Incidents of feudal obligation whereby tribute was rendered by a tenant to his superior or lord on the occasion (1) of the marriage of the eldest daughter, and (2) the knighting of the eldest son, of the lord.

AMBIDEXTERS
Double dealers.

AMERCIAMENT
Pecuniary punishment of offenders against King or other lord in his Court, differing from fines, which are mainly statutory and certain, whereas amerciaments are arbitrarily imposed.

ANCIENT DEMESNE, TENURE IN

Tenure of land—either by charter or copy of court roll (*q.v.*)—which was recorded as Crown land in Domesday Book ; it carried with it certain exemptions from tolls and jury service, and from the jurisdiction of courts other than those of the ancient demesne, unless the issue was between lord and tenant, when the courts at Westminster had jurisdiction.

ASSIGNS

Persons to whom an interest, *e.g.* a lease or a right under a contract, has been assigned, *i.e.* transferred, particularly by a testator.

ASSISTANTS OF THE HOUSE OF PEERS

Judges and Law Officers of the Crown summoned personally to attend the House of Lords (*e.g.* as advisers) but who are not active members thereof.

AUDITOR OF THE RECEIPT

Officer of Exchequer responsible for all receipts.

AVERMENT

A formal offer to prove a plea ; the plea thus offered.

BAILIFFS

Chief magistrates of various towns.

BAILIWICK

The town or district over which a Bailiff has jurisdiction.

BAR, TRIAL AT

Trial before a full court consisting of several judges, distinguished from trial at Nisi Prius (*q.v.*) before one judge at the assizes or at the sittings in London and Middlesex.

BARON, COURT. *See* COURT

BARONS OF EXCHEQUER OF DEGREE OF COIF

Judges of the Court of Exchequer who had been admitted to the highest degree of the Common Law, a serjeant-at-law or degree of coif (*q.v.*). In former times when the Barons of the Exchequer were mainly financial officers they might not be men of legal training. (On this last point *see also* CURSITOR BARON.)

BENEFIT OF CLERGY. *See* CLERGY

BILL

When used in judicial proceedings is a declaration in writing expressing some fault committed against some law or statute of the realm, addressed to the proper jurisdiction. It was the normal way of starting an action at Common Law, and served the purpose of a statement of claim. It always assumed the existence of an original writ, the service of which, however, in order to avoid complications, was as a matter of fact dispensed with. It was the invariable way of starting a suit in equity before the Chancellor.

BILL OF REVIEW

A declaration the object of which is to procure the examination and reversal of a decree in Chancery, made upon a former Bill, and signed by the person holding the Great Seal, and enrolled.

BOARD OF GREEN CLOTH

Court of justice of King's household composed of lord steward, treasurer of household, comptroller, and other officers, to which is committed *inter alia* the government and oversight of King's Court.

BURGAGE

An ancient form of tenure similar to socage whereby houses or lands in an ancient borough are held of some lord in common socage by a certain established rent.

CANARY PATENT

A licence for a monopoly of importation of Canary wine.

CASE, SPECIAL

A method of obtaining a judicial decision, by the full Court in Banc, on points of law. At the trial, instead of taking a special verdict (*q.v.*) the parties took a general verdict (*q.v.*) for the plaintiff or the defendant, to which they attached a statement of the facts agreed on between them and approved by the trial judge. This special case was then submitted to the full court for final decisions on the points of law involved.

CASSET=CASCHET, CASHET or CATCHETT

A facsimile of the King's signature used in legal processes in Scotland before, but especially since, 1603, when the seat of Scottish government was transferred to London.

CERTIORARI, WRIT OF

A writ of, and returnable to, either Chancery or King's Bench, directing the officers of an inferior court to return the record of a case before them; used to remove cases to Westminster or to a judge at Nisi Prius (*q.v.*) when there is reason to doubt the capacity of the inferior court to give justice. Also, and in later times mainly, in order to examine the proceedings and see whether the decision of the inferior court should or should not be quashed.

CESS, PARISH

A parish assessment or tax.

CESTUI QUE TRUST

When property is given to a trustee in trust for another person who is the beneficiary of the trust, the latter is called " Cestui que Trust ".

CESTUI QUE TRUST IN POSSESSION

When " Cestui que Trust " and not the trustee is actually possessed of the property.

CHAMBERLAINS (OF EXCHEQUER)

Officers of the Exchequer who until 1826 were chiefly concerned with the preparation and custody of tallies.

CINQUE PORTS

Those ports which lie towards France and therefore have been considered by the King to be especially in need of protection. They were granted a peculiar jurisdiction and include the five towns of Dover, Sandwich, Romney, Winchelsea, and Rye.

CLERGY, BENEFIT OF

Ancient privilege of Clerks in Orders of exemption from certain penalties of law for the first offence (though a fine or branding might be imposed instead). The class of persons who could claim it was extended (and, from 1692, included women), upon a test of literacy by the so-called " neck verse " from the Psalms. Its operation, however, was much narrowed in course of time by statutory exceptions and abolished by Peel's Acts, 7 & 8 Geo. IV, cc. 27-29.

CLERK OF THE CROWN

An officer in the King's Bench whose function is to frame, read, and record all indictments against offenders arraigned or indicted of any public crimes.

COFFERER OF THE HOUSEHOLD

A principal officer of King's house next under the Controller with special charge and oversight of other officers of the household.

COIF, DEGREE OF

Title given the serjeants-at-law from the lawn worn under the caps at their creation. They were the highest class of pleaders at Common Law, and had a monopoly of pleading before the Common Pleas. All judges until the Judicature Act (1873) were first made serjeants.

COLLATE
To bestow a benefice upon; to appoint to a benefice.

COLLEGE
A corporation with privileges founded by royal or papal licence.

COLLEGIATE CHURCH
Church built and endowed for a society, or body corporate, of a dean or other president and secular priests, as canons or prebendaries in the said church.

COMMENDAM
A benefice or church living which, being vacant, is commended to the charge of an adequate clerk who for a period enjoys the profits, though not instituted.

COMMISSARY
Title in ecclesiastical law belonging to one who exercises the jurisdiction and office of a bishop on his behalf.

CONSERVATOR OF THE PEACE
All who have a special charge to see the King's peace kept, whether generally throughout the realm as the judges of the High Court or locally within a jurisdiction as a coroner or sheriff.

CONVOCATION
Assembly of the Bishops and representatives of the clergy of the province of Canterbury or of York to consult on ecclesiastical matters in time of parliament.

COPY OF COURT ROLL, TENURE BY. *See* COPYHOLD

COPYHOLD
A form of tenure (abolished in 1925) in which the tenant had no evidence of title but the copy of an entry in the roll made by the steward of the lord's court.

COUNTY COURT
(1) Before 1846 the old County Court (or shiremote) presided over by the sheriff; it had originally jurisdiction over all pleas, except pleas of the Crown (*q.v.*), but was gradually restricted by statute and by the growth of the assize system to petty cases. Knights of the Shire were elected in the County Court.

(2) From 1846 local and inferior courts of record for the trial of claims to debt and damage not exceeding £100 and to equity claims not exceeding £500 (*see* Vol. II, Sect. A, No. XXVIII, p. 94). These courts have no relation to the county, and the name is therefore

misleading : " local civil courts " would have been a more accurately descriptive name.

COUNTY OF ITSELF (TOWN OR CITY)

Borough which possessed the attribute of the ancient county, particularly sheriffs' court and quarter-sessions. To be distinguished from the modern county boroughs established at the same time as the administrative counties by the Act of 1888.

COUNTY PALATINE

Counties of Chester, Durham, and Lancaster, in which their owners had the full jurisdiction which the King had in the Kingdom. Notably the King's writ did not run within these counties.

COURT BARON

A court of civil jurisdiction which every lord of a manor held for the freeholders of his manor. (*See* CUSTOMARY COURTS.)

COURT LEET

An ancient court for criminal jurisdiction hardly distinguishable in practice from the manorial court in which its jurisdiction was exercised. Nevertheless sixteenth-century lawyers insisted that it was a franchise court (*i.e.* one based upon privilege from the King) exercising the criminal authority of the sheriff's tourn. It was purely local and was presided over by the steward of the lord of the manor or by borough officers. It undertook administrative as well as judicial work, *e.g.* police control.

COURT OF RECORD

King's courts in right of his crown and royal dignity ; all courts of whose proceedings public records are kept, which can be cited as authoritative in legal proceedings.

COURT OF SESSION

The highest civil court in Scotland : it includes both the Inner and the Outer House, the former a court of appeal sitting in two divisions, the latter a number of Lords Ordinary who sit singly and try cases at first instance.

COURT OF WARDS AND LIVERIES

Established by 32 Hen. VIII, c. 46 (abolished 1660) for settlement of matters concerning wardships.

CURSITOR BARON

An official of the Court of Exchequer whose duty it was to know the " cursus " or course of the Exchequer. When the Barons of the Exchequer had become purely judicial officers, the cursitor

Baron grew in importance on account of his technical knowledge. Until 1834 he had duties to perform as an auditor.

CUSTOMARY COURTS

Courts which exercised jurisdiction over copyholders and administered the custom of the manor. (*See* COURT BARON.)

CUSTOMARY TENANTS

Those holding land by custom of the manor, or copyholders. (Sometimes called customary freeholders to distinguish them from those holding purely by the will of the lord of the manor. Their claim, under this name, to vote as freeholders at elections disallowed by 31 Geo. 2, c. 14.)

DEGREE OF THE COIF. *See* COIF

DEMUR

To put a stop to any action upon a point of legal difficulty, which must be determined by the court before any further proceedings can be had therein. Demurrer is a means of deciding a matter of law. It implied an admission of the truth of the facts alleged by the other side.

DISPENSATION BY NON OBSTANTE

Licence from King to do a thing which at Common Law might be done lawfully but was restrained by Act of Parliament.

DROITS OF ADMIRALTY

Enemy goods seized in time of war go to the Crown as Droits of Admiralty ; also in former times shipwreck and wreckage on the high seas were Droits of Admiralty.

EMBRACERY

Unlawful influencing a jury by fear or favour.

ENGLISH PETITION

A bill in Chancery praying in aid the " extraordinary " equitable jurisdiction of this court—called an English Bill by way of distinction from proceedings in the " ordinary " jurisdiction of the court (consisting mainly of the preparation of writs for use at common law) which were entered and enrolled in French or Latin. From earliest time all Chancery procedure was in English, while Common Law Courts used Latin or French.

ERROR, WRIT OF

A writ directed to the chief justice of the court whose record is being attacked calling upon him to produce the record of the case before a superior court, so that it might consider the errors in the record alleged by the appellant. Only errors of law and not of fact could be dealt with and it only applied to Common Law courts.

ESCUAGE (SCUTAGE)
An incident of tenure by Knight Service, originally entailing military service for forty days but later commuted to a fixed money payment.

ESSOINE
A valid excuse, such as sickness, absence, etc., for not appearing before a court to answer an action.

ESTREAT
To take out record of fine, bail, etc., and return it to the Court of Exchequer to be prosecuted.

EXCHEQUER CHAMBER, COURT OF
A court set up by Statute in 1358 to determine causes upon writs of error (*q.v.*) from the Common Law side of the Court of Exchequer ; in 1588–89 a second Court of Exchequer Chamber was set up to determine any causes of particular difficulty which had been begun in the court of King's Bench. Both these Courts of Exchequer Chamber were abolished in 1830 (along with the jurisdiction of King's Bench to hear error from Common Pleas) and a new Court of Exchequer Chamber was established to hear cases in error from all three courts, composed of the judges of the two courts other than the one from which error was being brought. But in addition to these formal functions it was the practice of the Common Law judges, sitting in banc when a point of exceptional difficulty arose, to adjourn it to be further argued in Exchequer Chamber before a meeting of the judges of all three courts. In strictness this was an informal meeting, but some famous cases (*e.g.* Godden *v.* Hales) were thus argued before the twelve judges. This custom had died out by the middle of the eighteenth century.

(DE) EXCOMMUNICATO CAPIENDO
A writ issued to a sheriff to apprehend an excommunicated person who had not submitted within forty days and to keep him in prison until submission. Abolished in 1813, but some of the rules applicable to it transferred to the writ " de contumace capiendo ". The whole of the law concerning it is now, in effect, obsolete.

EX OFFICIO INFORMATION. *See* INFORMATION
EX OFFICIO OATH, *see* OATH

FELONY
Every species of crime which occasioned the forfeiture of land or goods and which were capital offences. (Distinguished from Treason and Misdemeanour.)

FORESTALLING, INGROSSING AND REGRATING

Buying or bargaining for any corn, cattle, or other merchandise, by the way, as they come to fairs or markets to be sold with a view to profit, obtained by cornering the market. Ingrossing and regrating were similar crimes.

FRANK ALMOIGN

Tenure by spiritual service, where an ecclesiastical person or corporation holds land for itself and successors of some lord and his heirs; free from secular services or incidents to the donor and his heirs. Abolished 1925.

FREEHOLD FOR LIFE OR LIVES

Freehold estates (unlike leasehold estates which are for a definite period, *e.g.* for five years or from year to year) are for an indefinite period. Among freehold estates are (*a*) Estates in fee simple, (*b*) Estates in tail, (*c*) Life Estates. (*a*) is limited to a man and his heirs; this means that if he dies intestate the estate will go to his nearest heir whether that person is a descendant or collateral; it is also freely alienable. In effect the fee simple is now a perpetual interest and, for all except technical purposes, amounts to absolute ownership. (*b*) is to a man and the heirs of his body, that is to say it could only go to his descendants and not to collaterals; but, under certain circumstances, it can be barred, *i.e.* turned into a fee simple. (*c*) can be either for the life of the holder himself, or for the life of another, or for the lives of several persons to continue until the death of the survivor. Life estates, though commonly called leases for lives, were not leasehold but freehold estates. Freehold for life or lives may apply to land or to offices.

GAOL DELIVERY

This is a commission which is a patent in form of a letter from the King to certain persons, appointing them his justices and authorizing them to clear his gaol at such a place of its prisoners and bring them to trial.

GENERAL ISSUE

As opposed to " special pleading ". In all proceedings the plaintiff or prosecutor had to set out all his allegations in detail. Then if the defendant was required to plead " special " he had to deal with each of these allegations one by one. If, on the other hand, he was allowed to plead the " general issue " he could in effect just say that he did not accept the allegations as a whole as a correct statement. An example is a plea of NOT GUILTY in criminal cases, and in civil suits various pleas according to the action, *e.g.* in trespass the plea not guilty, or in an action for breach of contract the plea *non assumpsit*. The general issue in civil cases was abolished in 1834.

GENERAL VERDICT. *See* VERDICT

GENTLEMAN USHER OF THE BLACK ROD
The chief gentleman usher to the King. His duties are various but include attendance on the House of Lords when sitting.

GRAND JURY. *See* JURY

GRAND SERJEANTY
A tenure similar to Knight Service. Its main incident was personal service to the King, usually within the realm, and consisting of some duty such as carrying his banner or sword, etc.

GREAT WARDROBE
A branch of the King's wardrobe which looked after the storage of bulky articles, *e.g.* clothing. Distinguished from the Privy Wardrobe in the Tower of London which had control of arms and armour.

HABEAS CORPUS
Habeas Corpus is one of the prerogative writs demanding the production of a prisoner to enable the court to determine the legality of his imprisonment. If the first writ had no effect upon the custodian a second (alias) or third (pluries) was issued.

HANIPER (OR HANAPER)
A department of the wardrobe into which were paid the profits of the great seal. (From old French *hanapier*, case for goblet. Hence hamper = basket.)

HEADBOROUGH
A kind of constable similar to a tything man (*q.v.*) and inferior to a constable proper.

HEREDITAMENT
Real property that can be inherited, *i.e.* would go to the heir-at-law on the tenant's death intestate. Therefore it did not include a life estate or a leasehold, which was personal property and went to the next of kin.

HERIOT
The best beast, whether horse, ox, or cow, sometimes other articles, that a customary tenant dies possessed of, due and payable to the lord of the manor.

HIGH CONSTABLE
Constable of the Hundred or franchise constituted for the keeping of the King's peace. (*See* HUNDRED.)

HOMILIES
See Article XXXV of the Articles of Religion, 1562.

HONOURS
More noble sort of lordship on which other inferior lordships or manors depend, by performance of some customs or services to those who are lords over them.

HUNDRED
A part or division of a shire for jurisdictional and other purposes.

IMPARLANCE
A petition in a court of Common Law for a day to consider or advise what answer the defendant shall make to the action of the plaintiff, or to a criminal charge.

INFORMATION
Accusation or complaint exhibited against a person for some criminal offence. Information is only the allegation of the officer who exhibits, hence it differs from indictment which is an accusation found by oath of twelve men.

INFORMATION, *EX OFFICIO*
Accusation filed on behalf of the King by his own immediate officer, the Attorney-General. Usually employed against crimes which endanger public safety or order.

JEWEL OFFICE
Office administering the custody of the royal jewels in the Tower of London.

JUDGE ADVOCATE OF THE FLEET
An officer who conducts prosecutions in naval court-martial.

JUDICIALLY NOTICED
Recognized as true by the courts without the need of any formal evidence to prove the existence or nature of some fact or law. Thus the judge may require information from counsel about some local custom or Private Act, but of Acts of general application, of matters of common knowledge, etc., he should have cognizance.

JURY, COMMON (OR PETTY)
Twelve freeholders chosen by lot (challengeable by either party) from the panels of jurors returned by the sheriff.

JURY, GRAND

Body of twenty-four good and lawful men to examine charges or indictment before the justices of the peace in quarter-sessions or before the King's justices to decide whether there is a prima facie case for trial. Abolished in 1933.

JURY, SPECIAL

Juries introduced in trials where the issues are of too great nicety for ordinary freeholders, or when the impartiality of the sheriff is suspect. By 3 Geo. 2, c. 25, either party may demand a special jury if he is prepared to meet the extra cost in the event of the judge not seeing the necessity of such a jury. Abolished in 1949 except for the trial of Commercial cases in the City of London.

KINGS-OF-ARMS (GARTER, CLARENCEUX, NORROY, LYON)

Garter is the principal, Clarenceux the second, Norroy (North of Trent) third of the Chief Heralds of the College of Arms. Lyon is the Scottish King-of-Arms.

KNIGHT SERVICE IN CAPITE

A form of tenure whereby those holding land directly (in chief) from the King had to perform personal military service—this was later commuted to a money payment. (*See* ESCUAGE.)

LEET, COURT. *See* COURT

LETTERS PATENT

Open authorization under the King's Great Seal for the enjoyment of some privilege or the commission of some act. Patents for the development of inventions are still granted in this way.

LIBERTIES (OR FRANCHISES)

A royal privilege or branch of the King's prerogatives, normally conferred by a charter upon, and subsisting in the hands of, a subject. They are of various kinds (*e.g.* the Franchise of the City of London).

MAINPRIZE

The giving of security for the appearance of some person, who otherwise might be committed to prison, at a time stated. When a prisoner is bailed he is actually put in the custody of the person who has given bail for him so that technically he is still in prison. If mainprize has been given he is not in custody at all but someone has given sureties for his appearance. But this distinction early became obscured.

MALUM PROHIBITUM AND MALUM PER SE

Crimes used to be regarded as of two classes. All offences at Common Law were generally regarded as *mala per se* (wrong in themselves—wrong by Natural Law), but others, generally statutory offences (*e.g.* playing at unlawful games, and frequenting of taverns etc.), are only *mala prohibita* to some persons and at certain times and not *mala per se*.

MANDAMUS

Prerogative writ issued by the King's Bench to compel an inferior court to execute its jurisdiction, or to compel a subject or corporation to perform some ministerial duty. Only issued when there is no other convenient remedy, *e.g.* action for damages.

MARTIAL LAW

The law of war, that depends upon the prerogative power of the King. Formerly used to cover not only what is now called martial law, *i.e.* the peculiar situation created by a rebellion, but also what is now called military law, *i.e.* the internal law of the armed forces.

MASTERS OF CHANCERY

Assistants to the Court of Chancery concerned with the issue of certain writs and reporting on matters referred to them. Their chief was the Master of the Rolls, who later became the regular Chancery judge at first instance, and at the present day is President of the Court of Appeal.

MESSENGERS OF HIS MAJESTY'S CHAMBER

Officers employed in apprehending state prisoners, under the control of the Lord Chamberlain. Sixteen Messengers in 1772 were made dependent on the Secretaries of State and employed in conveying dispatches to foreign courts and also in arresting persons alleged to be guilty of libel on the government, etc.—called in consequence " Messengers of the Press ".

MISDEMEANOUR

Any crime or indictable offence not amounting to a felony, such as perjury, battery, libel, conspiracy, or public nuisance; generally punishable at Common Law by fine and imprisonment with or without hard labour. Modern statutes have often attached special punishments to specific misdemeanours, which may be crimes even more serious than many felonies.

MISPRISION OF TREASON

A crime consisting of the bare knowledge and concealment of treason without any degree of assent thereto.

MITTIMUS

Writ for removing and transferring of records from one court to another.

MONSTRANS DE DROIT

A Chancery writ to be restored to lands and tenements that are claimed to be a man's in right, though by some inquest found to be in the possession of one lately dead and to which the King was entitled. It was enacted in 1362 that a claimant to lands seized by the King, as a result of a verdict of an inquest taken *ex officio* by a royal officer, could obtain a writ to the escheator to certify the cause of his seisin into Chancery. There the finding at the inquest could be traversed or he could show his right " monstrer son droit ". Hence derived the Chancery writ of *Monstrans de Droit*. It was one of the remedies against the Crown virtually superseded by the Petition of Right Act 1860 and abolished by the Crown Proceedings Act 1947.

MORTMAIN

Lands held by a corporation (particularly the Church) are said to be held in Mortmain (in the dead hand). Medieval statutes (*e.g.* the Statute of Mortmain, 1279) attempted to prevent alienation of land to the Church. By 7 & 8 Will. III, a licence from the Crown dispenses from such statutes (thus regularizing previous prerogative practice). By 34 Vict., c. 13, various charitable gifts are exempted from the statutes.

NISI PRIUS

The commission to the Judge on Assize giving him civil jurisdiction. In the writ to the sheriff he is ordered to send a jury to Westminster " *unless* the judge comes *before* " on assize. As distinguished from Trial at Bar (*q.v.*) it is trial before a single judge either on Assize or at the sittings for the same purpose held in London and Middlesex.

NON VULT ULTERIUS PROSEQUI

Method of staying prosecution by the Crown, usually called " Nolle Prosequi ". It can be entered by the Attorney-General and operates to stop all proceedings without any need for the consent of the court.

NOTARY PUBLIC

A person publicly authorized to attest contracts, etc. An officer common in Scots law : in England mainly concerned with foreign business.

NOTICED. *See* JUDICIALLY NOTICED

OATH, EX OFFICIO

A Canon Law procedure, consisting of a series of interrogations both comprehensive and precise, to which a suspected person was bound to answer on oath.

ORDINARY

Civil and Common Law term for one who has, of his own right and not by deputation, immediate jurisdiction in ecclesiastical causes, as the archbishop in a province or the bishop or the bishop's deputy in a diocese.

ORDINARY LORDS OF SESSION

Members of the Court of Session (*q.v.*), the highest civil tribunal in Scotland, other than the Lord President and the Lord Justice Clerk.

OUSTER-LE-MAIN

A delivery of possession of land from the King, on a judgement given in Chancery for a person suing a *monstrans de droit* (*q.v.*), that the King's hand be amoved (*ouster le main*).

OUTLAWRY

Being put out of the law and hence out of the King's protection. The penalty for refusing to be amenable to the justice of a King's court. No longer important since judgement by default was made possible in the nineteenth century.

OYER AND TERMINER

A commission directed to the judges on assize by virtue of which they have power to hear and determine criminal matters.

PARISH CESS. *See* CESS

PATENT. *See* LETTERS PATENT

PATRON

He who has the power of appointment to an ecclesiastical benefice.

PETITION OF RIGHT

Procedure by which the subject may sue the Crown for illegal seizure of goods or for breach of contract (provided the Attorney-General or, since 1860, the Home Secretary endorses the petition " fiat justitia ") despite the royal prerogative not to be sued by writ. By the Crown Proceedings Act, 1947, an ordinary action is substituted.

PETTY CONSTABLE

or Constable of the vill, village, or township, as opposed to Constable of the hundred or High Constable.

PETTY TREASON

Treason of a lesser kind. Crime against the security of the commonwealth, though not expressly, *e.g.* where servant killed his master or wife her husband, etc.

PLAINT

The exhibiting any action in writing. The party making his plaint is the plaintiff.

PLEA

The reply to a plaint ; a mode of defence by contesting the facts.

PLEAS OF THE CROWN

Offences *contra pacem Domini Regis, coronam et dignitatem suam* which could be tried only in the King's courts ; a term for criminal prosecutions.

POPISH RECUSANTS

Roman Catholics who wilfully absented themselves from their parish church, and on whom heavy fines and other penalties were imposed by various statutes.

PRAEMUNIRE

The name of a writ, or the crime for which it is granted, which though not capital is most serious as immediately affecting the King or his government. Originally the offence consisted in asserting the authority of a foreign (*i.e.* Papal) jurisdiction in the land. Other crimes were subsequently brought by statute within its ambit.

PREBENDARY

The holder of a prebend which is the portion of the revenues of a cathedral or collegiate church granted to a canon or the member of a chapter as his stipend.

PRECEPT

A command in writing by a justice of the peace, or other officer, for bringing a person or records before him, *e.g.* the order of the sheriff addressed to chief officers of boroughs in his shire to return to him the names of burgesses duly elected to serve in Parliament. In modern usage also a statutory order by a superior local authority to a subordinate one for the levy of a rate to cover the expenditure of the superior authority (*e.g.* a county council issues precepts to the district and borough councils in its area to levy rates for general county purposes).

PRIMER-SEISINS

The right of the King to first possession of land (that is, the entire profits of it for a year) of which a tenant-in-chief died possessed, until the heir did homage or reached the age of 21.

PROCTOR (PROCURATOR)

He who undertakes to manage another man's cause in any court of civil or ecclesiastical law for his fee.

PROHIBITION

A writ issuing out of a superior court of law directing the judge and parties in an inferior court to cease from the prosecution of a cause as not belonging to that jurisdiction.

PROTECTION

Protection of the King is an act of Grace, by writ issued out of Chancery, giving a subject immunity from lawsuits for a certain time, and for s)me reasonable cause.

PUISNE JUDGE

The Common Law judges and barons not being chiefs. (From French *puissant* = powerful.)

PURVEYANCE (or POURVEYANCE)

Right enjoyed by the Crown, of buying up provisions and other necessaries, for the use of the royal household, at an appraised valuation, in preference to others and even without the owner's consent.

PYPOWDER, COURT OF

Incident to the franchise of a fair, this court administered the Law Merchant. From *pied poudré*, dusty foot of merchants on their travels.

QUAM DIU SE BENE GESSERINT

Translation—As long as they shall behave themselves well in their office. A clause often inserted in letters patent of the grant of offices—particularly judgeships. Ultimately distinguished from tenure at the King's pleasure (*bene placito*).

QUARTER SEAL

A minor seal used in Scottish law for ordinary business such as the authentication of Chancery Precepts. It consists of the upper part of the Great Seal, obverse and reverse.

QUO WARRANTO

A writ which lies against any person or corporation alleged to have usurped or unwarrantably to have extended any franchise or liberty against the King without good title, and is brought against them to show by what right or title they hold or claim such franchise or liberty.

RAVISHMENT OF WARD. *See* ACTION OF RAVISHMENT OF WARD

RECOGNIZANCE

An obligation exacted and put on record by some court of record or magistrate, to perform some particular act, such as appearing at the Assizes, paying a debt, or keeping the peace.

RECORD, COURT OF. *See* COURT

RECORDER

Generally a qualified barrister appointed for a city or borough to preside over a court of record (almost always quarter-sessions) established by Crown grant giving jurisdiction to the mayor and other magistrates.

REGRATING. *See* FORESTALLING

REVERSION

Reversion is the return of land (according to Coke) to the grantor or his heirs at the end of the period of the grant. Offices, other than judicial offices, may be granted in reversion ; judicial offices may not, for fear that the grantee may be incapable, whereas for other offices it is assumed that in such case the duties will be performed by a deputy.

RIDING (CORRUPTION OF TRITHING)

Parts or divisions of Yorkshire—namely East, West, and North.

RULE OF COURT

Either (1) an order of the court in a case between parties, or (2) a rule to regulate the practice of the court.

RULES OF PRACTICE

The same as the second meaning of Rule of Court above.

SCANDALUM MAGNATUM

Statutory offence, created in thirteenth and fourteenth centuries and finally abolished in 1888, of defaming the reputation of magnates and aimed at safeguarding the peace of the Kingdom.

SCOT AND LOT

One who pays scot and bears lot contributes to the local rates.

SERVITUDE

A subjection or subserviency of property either (1) to some definite person other than its owner, (2) to some definite property other than that of its owner for the benefit of the other property, *e.g.* a right of way which the owner of one piece of land enjoys as such over an adjoining piece of land.

SESSION, COURT OF. *See* COURT

SIGNET

A seal kept by the Keeper of the Signet, used to authenticate and give effect to summonses in the Court of Session, *i.e.* a writ by which proceedings are commenced in that court.

SIGNET, WRITERS TO THE. *See* WRITERS

SIGN MANUAL

The superscription of the King at the top of grants or letters patent.

SIMONY

Corrupt presentation of any one to an ecclesiastical benefice for money, gift, or reward.

SOCAGE IN CAPITE

A form of tenure whereby the tenant performed certain non-military services to the King.

SPECIAL CASE. *See* CASE

SPECIAL JURY. *See* JURY

SPECIAL VERDICT. *See* VERDICT

STANNARIES

The mines and works where tin is mined and purified as in Cornwall and Devonshire, which had their own courts and jurisdiction.

STEWARTRIES

A parcel of land in Scotland enjoying a regal jurisdiction, generally parts of a county, but sometimes, *e.g.* in the case of Kirkcudbright, a county of itself.

SUMMONS, WRIT OF

The first step in an action; a process issued in the High Court at the plaintiff's instance to give the defendant notice of the claim made against him, and compelling him to appear and answer if he does not admit it; it also contains the name of the court, etc. where appearance is to be made.

SUSPENSION, PLEAS IN

were those in which some temporary incapacity to proceed with the action or suit was set forth.

TABLER
One who gets his meals at another's table for payment.

TELLERS OF THE EXCHEQUER
The four officers of the Exchequer who were formerly charged with receipt and payment of moneys.

TENANT IN ANCIENT DEMESNE. *See* ANCIENT DEMESNE

TESTE
Witness (so and so). Beginning of attestation clause which ended with the date.

TITHE
A tenth part of the produce of the land, originally devoted to the maintenance of the parochial clergy.

TORT
Wrong arising out of conduct (other than breach of contract) for which compensation or damages will be given in a civil action; *e.g.* trespass, libel, nuisance, negligence.

TOWN BEING A COUNTY OF ITSELF. *See* COUNTY

TREASURER OF THE CHAMBER
A chief officer of the Exchequer of Receipt.

TREASURER OF THE HOUSEHOLD
A court office, of a political nature before 1924.

TRIAL AT BAR. *See* BAR

TROVER
A special form of action which originally lay for damages against one who had found (hence the word *trover* = *trouver*) and converted to his own use the goods of another. The allegation of finding rapidly became fictitious and the need to plead it ceased to be necessary in the nineteenth century. Now the normal action for the recovery of goods or their value.

TUTORY
Custody of a ward.

TYTHINGMAN
A kind of petty constable elected by parishes; constable's deputy.

VACAT
Cancellation and erasure of an entry on a roll.

VERDICT, GENERAL

The answer of the jury on the matters committed to trial before them, *e.g.* verdict for the plaintiff for £500.

VERDICT, SPECIAL

In cases where the jury had doubt as to the law involved they might find a Special verdict, stating the facts as they found them, and referring the law thereon to the decision of the court. Or the judge might ask them for a special verdict.

VICAR-GENERAL

An ecclesiastical officer appointed by a bishop as his representative in matters of jurisdiction or administration.

VICINAGE

Neighbourhood or near dwelling.

VILLEIN IN GROSS

Bondman or servant being bound to a lord irrespective of any other property owned by him.

VILLEIN REGARDANT TO A MANOR

Bondman or servant, being bound to a lord, as a member belonging and annexed to a manor whereof the lord was owner.

WAGER OF LAW

An offer to make an oath of innocence or non-indebtedness, to be supported by the oaths of eleven compurgators who would swear to like effect—especially used in cases of debt. It became a form of licensed perjury and therefore other forms of action were gradually substituted.

WAPENTAKE

Synonym for HUNDRED (*q.v.*). Generally of northern shires owing to Danish influence.

WAST(E)

Actionable damage to real property by tenant or guardian.

WRITERS TO THE SIGNET

A corporation in Edinburgh whose members had the exclusive privilege (until it was modified in 1868 and abrogated in 1933) of signing summonses in the Court of Session (*q.v.*), and as, without such a signature a summons could not be signeted, they had a monopoly of work in the Court. It remains a Society of solicitors of the highest standing in Scotland.

WRITS

of advocation, certiorari, error, etc. (*see under* appropriate name, *e.g. under* Certiorari).

INDEX

Action :
  of debt, *see* Debt
  against J.P., *see* J.P.
  in Ireland, to be finally decided
    there, 151
  concerning electoral matters, 193-
    194, 279
  against the Crown, 276
  of trespass, 294
Admiral, Lord High :
  to stay in office on Sovereign's
    demise, 113
  power to give commissions for
    courts martial, 12
  Lord Justice under Regent Act,
    114
  Clerks in office of, not to sit in
    Commons, 132
  on Temple's Privy Council,
    330
Admiralty :
  jurisdiction in Scotland, 102
  Commissioners of : Deputies and
    Clerks of, not to sit in Com-
    mons, 132
  Secretaries of : eligible for the
    Commons, 132
  First Commissioner of, 150, 239
  Judge of, 159-60
  Law, 280
Advocates, 120
Africa :
  Scottish company, 101
  slavery in, 314
Aid :
  pur file marrier and pur faier fitz
    Chivalier, abolished, 2
  public : not to be altered by
    Lords, 154, 192 ; motion for,
    to be debated in committee
    of whole House, 154 ; sole
    gift of Commons, 154
Aldborough, 326
Aldermen :
  to take various oaths, 15

Aldermen—(*contd.*)
  of London :
    to allow petitions, 10
    to be J.P.s for purposes of
      Second Conventicle Act, 39
    members of Assembly of Con-
      vention Parliament, 187
  of Bristol, 332, 336, 347, 363
  of York, 348-9
  of Nottingham, 365
Aliens :
  religious rights of, 25, 62, 91, 123
  not to be made Privy Councillors,
    95
  not to sit in the Commons, 231
Allegiance, *see* Oaths
Allybone, Sir Richard, Judge of
  King's Bench, in Case of
  Seven Bishops, 268-71, 293
Ambassador, servant of, 62
Amelia, Princess, daughter of Geo.
  III, annuity to, 139
Anne, Queen :
  place in the Succession, 72, 92,
    98
  dissolves Parliament, 196
  party government under, 233,
    359-62
  charter of, to Bristol, 362-4
Anne and Mary, ship, 315
Annesley, Arthur, Earl of Anglesey,
    319
Annuity :
  oath of Treasurer concerning, 149
  whether payment of, by the Crown,
    can be enforced, 273
Anson, George, Baron Anson, Ad-
  miral, 383, 389
Appeals :
  Commissioners of : Deputies and
    Clerks of, not to sit in
    Commons, 132
  not to lye from Irish to English
    courts, 151
  by writ of error, *see* Writ

427

Appeals—(*contd.*)
  of Shirley from Chancery to the
    Lords, 167-71
  of Sir Nicholas Crispe and others
    from Chancery to Lords,
    172-9
  to the people: publication of votes,
    185
Ardran, Thomas, a King's Messen-
    ger, 298
Argyle, John Campbell, Second
    Duke of, 218, 374, 383
Arms, Kings of (Garter, Clarenceux,
    Norroy) :
  to license books on heraldry, 30
  (Lyon), 105
Army :
  discipline of, 56, 212
  officers not debarred from the
    Commons, 116
  legalization of standing, 55, 68, 69
  Commissioners of Accounts of,
    115
  to provide adjutants and sergeants
    for the Militia, 136
  fear of standing, 68, 155, 180, 210
  officers and soldiers to take oaths
    and receive sacrament, 40,
    166, 256
  misuse of, by Danby, 180
  estimates, 238
  a source of grievance in Ireland,
    242
  control of, by George II, 370
  interest of Cumberland and Fox
    in, 383
Articles, XXXIX :
  heads of colleges to subscribe to,
    26
  partial subscription to, by dis-
    senters, 65
Articles of Naval Discipline, 11-12
Articles of War, 212
Arundel, Edmund, Sheriff of Bristol,
    334
Ashby, M., an elector of Aylesbury,
    193-6, 234, 278-9, 283
Ashley, Baron, *see* Shaftesbury
Ashley, Serjeant, 309
Assent, royal, to legislation, 7, 189-
    190, 219, 396, 403-4
Assizes :
  Habeas Corpus Act, 53
  Exclusion Bill to be read at, 184

Association, to defend William III
    and the Succession, 88
Attainder, 96, 257
Attorney :
  not to be a J.P. where in practice,
    130
  to give notice of a writ against a
    J.P. and constables, 133, 134
  breach of privilege to act in an
    election case, 194
Attorney-General :
  (Sir J. Montague) in Sacheverell's
    Impeachment, 198-9
  in Wilkes' Case, 220
  Noli Prosequis, 350
Auditor of the Receipt :
  Deputy and Clerks of, not to sit
    in Commons, 132
Aylesbury :
  election at, 193
  Aylesbury men, 279-84, 312

Bail, 222
  excessive, 68
Bailey, Old, 245, 286
Bailiffs :
  to take oaths of supremacy and
    allegiance, etc., 15
  election returns, 193
  answerable to J.P.s, 390
Banishment, 223
  Bill of, against Clarendon, 155
  of James, Duke of York, 183
Bank of England, established, 77
Bankers' case, 271-8
Baptists, under Toleration Act, 65
Barcelona, 371
Barnardiston, Sir Samuel, member
    of East India Company, 160
Baron of the Exchequer :
  duties under Habeas Corpus Act,
    47 *sqq.*
  to administer oath under the Civil
    Establishment Act, 149-50
Bath and Wells, Thomas, Bishop of,
    347
Beaufort, Henry Somerset, first Duke
    of, 338
Bedchamber, Lords of, 387
Benefices :
  patronage of, 23
  conditions of holding, 22 ff., 60,
    324
Benefit of Clergy, 126

Bennett, Sir Henry (later first Earl
    of Arlington) :
    elected M.P. at desire of Charles
        II, 322
    a leading member of the Com-
        mons, 323
Benson, candidate at Aldborough,
    326
Bentley, Dr. Richard, Master of
    Trinity College, Cambridge,
    288-9
Berkley of Stratton, John Baron,
    Constable of the Tower, 291
Berlin, 373
Berwick-upon-Tweed, 40, 51, 82,
    117, 122, 136, 140
Bills of Exchange, Bank of England
    dealings in, 79
Bishops :
    to license schoolmasters, 24, 121,
        122
    to administer Coronation Oath, 58
    to take oaths of supremacy and
        allegiance, 60-61
    a dissenting meeting-place to be
        certified to, 67
    support of non-resistance, 205
    Case of Seven, 258-71, 292, 300,
        346-7
Blackborne, Robert, secretary to
    East India Company, 158
Blackmore, Robert, a Messenger,
    294-7
Black Rod, Usher of the :
    ordered to release four barristers,
        173
    sent to require attendance of Com-
        mons, 179
Blackstone, Sir William, on Parlia-
    ment and Prerogative, 395-6
Blaire, Sir Adam, impeached 1689,
    188
Board :
    of Works (q.v.)
    of Trade and Plantations (q.v.)
    of Green Cloth (q.v.)
Bohemia, Elizabeth, late Queen of,
    93
Boileau, 369
Bolingbroke, Henry St. John, Vis-
    count, Property Qualification
    Act, 117
Bolton, Charles Paulet, third Duke
    of, 374

Bonds, to be in English, 130
Borough, Elections for, 86
    See also Corporations
Boscawen, Mr., M.P. urged publica-
    tion of Commons' votes, 185
Bowyer, Lady Mary, concerned in
    Four Barristers' Case, 172-9
Breach of Privilege :
    for proceeding against an M.P.,
        167-71, 172-9, 282
    for courts to proceed against an
        impeached man, 186
    for bringing an action concerning
        elections in the ordinary
        courts, 193, 279
    for publishing proceedings of the
        Commons, 217
    for committing a lord before he
        has refused to give surety, 222
    for arresting an M.P., 227
    for arresting a Messenger of the
        Commons, 236, 311
Breach of the Peace :
    seditious libel as, 223
    no Parliamentary privilege in case
        of, 282, 293
Brent, Mr., 348
Brest, 355
Bristol :
    Earl and Countess of, 42
    city, charters of, 332-9, 362-4
    city, officers of, removed, 347
    city, election expenses, 400
    John, Bishop of, 347
    sessions of, 289
    Burke's speech to electors of, 392
Broadfoot, Rex v., 289-90
Brunswick, Elector of, 122
Burgage, tenure in, franchise of,
    278, 326
Burgess, Rev. Dr. Daniel, his meet-
    ing-house burnt down, 286
Burghs, Scotland, 103
Burke, Edmund :
    speech to electors of Bristol, 392
    on representation, 394
    on party, 396-7
Bushell, Edward, juryman, case of,
    1680, 245-9

Cabinet :
    under Charles II, 317, 330-31 ;
        William III, 355-6, 359 ;
        Anne, 284

Cabinet—(*contd.*)
  in time of Walpole, 216, 218, 369,
    371, 372
  origin of, 330
  and the Crown, 240-41, 373, 386,
    399
  collective responsibility of, 238-9,
    372
  duties of ministers in, 374
  minutes, 374-5, 383-4
  consulted on ministerial appoint-
    ments, 382-4
  the King and the Agenda, 399
Cambridge :
  Rex *v.* University of, 288
  election, 377-8
Canons, of 1640, not confirmed, 14
Canterbury, Archbishop of :
  to license books, 30
  a Lord Justice under the Regency
    Act, 114, 115
  to hold one instrument of Regency,
    115
  in Privy Council Committee, 157
  in Cabinet Council of Charles II,
    320
  on Temple's Privy Council, 330
  petitions, James II, 346
  consulted on formation of a Minis-
    try, 382
Caroline, Queen, supports Walpole,
    369
Carr, Henry, Case of, 253-4
Carrington, Nathan, a Messenger,
    294-5, 297-310
Carteret, Sir Edward, Usher of the
    Black Rod, 179
Carteret, Sir George, Vice-Chamber-
    lain and Treasurer of the
    Navy, 320, 321
Carteret, John, second Baron (later
    Earl Granville), Secretary of
    State, 375
Catechism, 122
Catherine, Queen, Consort of
    Charles II, her servants pro-
    tected, 46, 62
Certificate :
  under First Test Act, 41
  under Toleration Act, 64
  of conviction of a popish priest,
    90
  for a Noncomformist minister, 120
  to be in English, 130

Certificate—(*contd.*)
  of a waterman of the City of Lon-
    don, 316
Chamber, office of Treasurer of,
    suppressed, 148
Chamberlain, Lord :
  to direct reforms in royal house-
    hold, 148
  advises Charles II on foreign
    affairs, 320
  in Temple's Privy Council, 330
  in Cabinet, 383
Chamberlains, of the Exchequer, 273
Champneys, Justinian, presented
    Kentish Petition, 191
Chancellor, Lord (*see also* Clarendon,
    Cowper and Hardwicke) :
  duties under Licensing Act, 30
  duties under Habeas Corpus Act,
    47 ff.
  issue of election writs, 85
  to remain in office at Sovereign's
    demise, 113
  duties under the Regency Act, 115
  on council committee in Skinner's
    Case, 157
  in Temple's Privy Council, 330
Chancellor (of University) :
  duties under Licensing Act, 30
  Rex *v.* Chancellor, etc., of Cam-
    bridge University, 288-9
Chancellor of the Exchequer, 219
  Clerks of, not to sit in Commons,
    132
  Secretary to : eligible to sit in
    Commons, 132
  in Temple's Privy Council, 330
  and First Lord of the Treasury,
    383
Chancery, Court of :
  to hear and enrol oaths of su-
    premacy and allegiance, 40,
    91
  also to hear declaration on sacra-
    ments, 44, 46
  to issue election writs, 45
  to issue writs of habeas corpus, 51
  Masters of, 159
  Fagg *v.* Shirley in, 167
  Four Barristers' Case, 172
  Clerk of Crown in : election writs
    returns, 187, 207, 229
Chandos, James Brydges, first Duke
    of, 400

Channel Islands : Habeas Corpus
Act concerning, 51
officers in, subject to Test Act, 40
to remain in office on demise of
Crown, 113
Chapters, to keep a Prayer Book, 28
Charles II :
speech to Parliament on Skinner's
Case, 161
Declaration of Indulgence, 163-6,
324-5
speech to Parliament on Four
Barristers' Case, 178
speech on royal prerogative of war
and peace, 179
tried to save Danby, 180
deposition of : urged by Fitzharris, 185
policy towards boroughs, 254,
332-9, 364
habits of business, 317, 319-21,
331
foreign policy, 320-21
and Temple's scheme for a Privy
Council, 329-30
Charter :
of corporation, 15, 131
granted before 23 Oct. 1689, confirmed, 74
of London, 75, 254-6
to be in English, 130
power of Crown to exempt by, 316
of Bristol, 332-9, 347, 362-4
of York, 348-9
of Nottingham, 351-2
Chatham, William Pitt, Earl of, 240,
384-7
Chelsea Hospital :
militiamen entitled to benefits of,
as well as regulars, 137
Chester, city, 350
Chester, Mr., 400
Chichester, John, Bishop of, 347
Church of England (see Prayer Book,
Liturgy, etc.) :
protected against criticism, 29
in Coronation Oath, 59
dissent from, allowed, 64
dissenters not allowed to escape
its dues, 65
king to be in communion with, 94,
108
legislation concerning, at Act of
Union, 108

Church of England—(contd.)
Occasional Conformity Act, 118 ff.
maintenance of, by Crown, 164-5,
324, 344
and Dr. Sacheverell, 197-207
and non-resistance, 197-207
and convocations, 357-8
Churchill, Sir John, Alderman and
Recorder of Bristol, 335, 336
one of the Four Barristers, 172-9
Churchwarden :
to issue certificates of taking the
sacraments, 41, 122
to give information concerning
conventicles, 38
exempted from First Test Act,
42
dissenting ministers exempt from
serving as, 66
Cinque ports, writ of Habeas Corpus
to men in, 51 ; also 117, 127
Civil List :
certain offices supported out of,
abolished, 148
reformed and controlled, 148
secret payments from, regulated,
149
power of Commons over, 239
Clarendon, Edward Hyde, Earl of :
impeachment of, 155-7
his history, 283
as " first minister ", 317-18
and Privy Council, 318-21
and management of Commons,
322-3
Clements, James, Mayor of Harwich,
367, 368
Clergy :
Temporal jurisdiction of, 9
to use Prayer Book, 22
to be episcopally ordained, 25
attitude of, to James II, 199
disqualified from becoming members of the Commons, 231
Clerk of the House, duties during
determination of controverted
elections, 141
Clerk of the Peace :
to issue certificates to Nonconformist ministers, 120
to receive part of fines inflicted on
voters being ineligible, 146
Clerks : of the Board of Green Cloth,
suppressed, 148, 240

Clerks—(*contd.*)
of the Crown in Court of Chancery, 187, 207, 229
of comptroller and of cofferer, of the household, 240
Clutterbuck, Sir William, Mayor, of Bristol, 334
Cockerill, Grey, of Harwich, 367
Coffee-House, centre of political discussion, 185
Cofferer, of the household, suppressed, 148, 240
Coinage, same for England and Scotland, 101
Coke, Sir Edward, L.C.J., 292, 293, 313, 395
Colchester, 350
Colepeper, William and Thomas, presented Kentish Petition, 191
Collector :
of Excise, of Customs, of duties on windows and houses, deprived of the vote, 145
College of Justice (Scotland), 102
Colleges (in Universities) :
heads of : oaths of allegiance and supremacy, 23-4, 60
eligible as J.P.s, 131
use of Prayer Book in, 26
use of Latin in services allowed, 26
abjuration oath imposed, 47
Scottish, 106
Colonies :
Secretary of State for, suppressed, 148
Clarendon and, 156
Commander-in-Chief (Duke of Argyle), 218
Commissions :
to administer Corporation Act, 15-17
not to expire on death of king, 89
judges', 95, 139
to negotiate with Scotland, 99
to be in English, 130
of the Peace and property qualification, 131, 389
in the Militia, 18, 135
of impressment, 316
statutory : for town improvements, 394-5

Commissioners :
various, not to be members of Commons' House, 115, 132
not to vote in elections, 146
not to make contracts with members, 146
of Navy, may be J.P.s, 131
not to be increased, 116
Committees :
of Houses of Parliament, 8
select, to decide disputed elections, 142
of the whole House, 153-4, 239, 241
use of, in Commons, 154, 163, 208, 239
use of, in Lords, 158, 188
of Commons : proceedings of, not to be published, 217
of Privy Council, 319, 321, 329
of burgesses, 404
Common Council :
of London :
to allow petitions, 10
to take prescribed oaths, 15
to send 50 to Assembly of Convention Parliament, 187
guilty of petitioning Charles II in 1679, 254
of Bristol, 332, 335, 347, 362
of Nottingham, 351, 404
Common Law :
and the press, 252-4, 307
gives no ground for suspending a law, 261
to secure property, 273-4
remedies against the king, 276
right in, not to be subject to laws made without consent, 278
impressment of sailors grounded in, 289, 316
and general warrants, 296-7
the power of the Secretary of State in, 299-300
altered by statute, 301
Common Pleas, Court of :
to grant writs of habeas corpus, 51
discharged Wilkes as an M.P., 219, 291-4
Bushell's Case before, 245-9
Case of General Warrants, 294-5
Entick v. King's Messengers, 298-310
Case of Brass Crosby, 311-14

Common Prayer, Book of, *see* Prayer
Commons, House of :
  declaration against transubstantiation, 43
  the oaths and declaration, 45, 55, 97-8, 104
  freedom of election of, 68, 69, 83, 140, 145, 146
  election procedure, 86, 187, 193
  to adhere to association, 89
  independence of the Crown, 95, 116, 132, 149, 322
  Scottish members, 103, 145
  incapacity of persons to sit, 45, 115, 116, 131, 146
  re-election to, after taking office, 116
  property qualifications of, 117
  petitions to, 9, 157, 160, 191, 231
  controverted elections, 140, 193, 231, 233, 278-9
  and government contracts, 146, 207
  summoned to Convention Parliament of 1688, 186
  and money bills, 153, 154, 192, 197, 208, 322, 326
  right of impeachment, 155-7, 180-82, 185-6, 188, 197-207, 238, 283, 312
  privileges of, 153, 154, 159, 160, 167-71, 172-9, 220-27, 237, 279-84, 293-4, 313, 326, 328
  conflicts with Lords, 153, 154, 159, 161, 167-71, 172-9, 185-6, 193-6, 215, 326-7
  conferences with Lords, *see* Conferences
  petition of, to Crown, 163-5, 176, 189
  right to commit, 170, 176, 191, 207, 236, 279, 283, 311
  publication of votes of, and proceedings, 184-5, 217, 311
  relation of, to the people, 185, 208, 218, 233, 392
  right to expel, 207-8, 229
  and local bills, 153, 208, 394
  responsibility of a ministry to, 217, 238, 241
  declaring the law, 228
  royal management of, 322-3, 326, 361, 365-6, 386, 387, 398, 399-401
  and control of expenditure, 239, 327

Commons, House of—(*contd.*)
  appointment of the Speaker, 328
  theory of representation, 392
  supremacy of, 398
Communion, *see* Sacrament of
Comptroller :
  of the accounts of the Army, not to be M.P., 115
  of the Navy : eligible to sit in the Commons, 132
  of Customs : deprived of the vote, 145
  of Duties on Windows or Houses : deprived of the vote, 145
  of Royal Buildings : to be appointed, 149
  of the Household, 240
Conferences, of both Houses, 8, 155, 161, 168, 170, 174, 175, 176
Congregation, of Cambridge, 288-9
Conservator of the Peace, 297, 393
Conspiracy :
  Secret Service money to be used against, 150
  of Titus Oates, 181
  of papists, 183
Constables :
  duties under Second Conventicle Act, 38
  exempted from First Test Act, 42
  and Habeas Corpus Act, 50
  duties under Riot Act, 125
  statutory protection of, 134, 301
  Chief : duties under Militia Act, 136, 137 ; of Aylesbury in Ashby *v.* White, 193 ; to assist Royal Messengers, 297 ; J.P.s to supervise, 390
Constitution of the Kingdom, 193-196, 198-207, 233, 237, 240-241, 281, 295
  nature of, 200, 340-42
  frequency of Parliaments, 208
  and the Army, 211
  and the Revolution, 305
  place of Privy Council in, 318-19, 329, 358-9
  place of ministers under the, 377
  Montesquieu's opinions on, 378-382
Contempt :
  of Lords, 251-2, 314
  of Commons, 179, 193, 236-7, 312
  of Court, 313

Contracts :
  M.P.s not to take government,
    146, 238
  made by Walpole, 207
Conventicles, 324
  and Five Mile Act, 34
  penalties on those preaching at,
    35
  Second Conventicle Act, 36
  those holding office not to attend,
    119
  schoolmasters not to attend, 122
Convention Parliament, 1, 10, 54,
    74, 186, 187
Convocation, 21
  use of Latin services, 26
  controversy concerning, 357-8
Copyhold, 3
Coroners :
  to procure elections of county
    M.P.s, 187
  of Bristol, 332, 338, 363
Corporations, Municipal :
  conditions of holding office in, 15-
    17, 119, 127, 218
  affected by quo warranto proceed-
    ings, 76, 156
  dissenters gravitate to, 35
  multiplication of freemen in, to in-
    fluence elections, 140
  legal position of, 255
  removal of members of, 289
  of Bristol, 332-9, 362-4
  and James II, 347-52
  York, 348-9, 350
  Nottingham, 351-2, 394-5, 404-5
Corrupt elections :
  act against, 83
  multiplication of freemen, 140
  cause of, 194
Corruption :
  Walpole guilty of, 207
  Parliamentary, 209, 238, 240, 322-
    323
  alleged by John Tutchin, 285
Country party, its principles, 325-
    326
Courage, Dr., 368
Court :
  The : members of, in House of
    Commons, 322 ; and elec-
    tions to Parliament, 365-8
  Party : principles of, 325
Court, Baron, 130

Court, County :
  for election of Knights of the
    Shire, 86
  Ecclesiastical, 13-14
Court of, see under King's Bench, etc.
Court hand, abolished, 130
Court martial :
  power of Lord High Admiral, 12
  power of Lords Lieutenant, 19
  set up by the Mutiny Act, 56
  protest against, 211-12
Court of Session, 102
Court of Wards and Liveries, 2
Courts leet, 130
Courts of Common Law :
  to preserve authentic copies of
    Prayer Book, 28
  not to have jurisdiction in Scot-
    land, 102
  proceedings to be in English, 129
  Irish, independence of, 150
  side-tracked in Skinner's Case,
    158-63
  not to proceed in matters subject
    to impeachment, 186
  not to proceed in matters concerning
    Parliamentary elections, 193-6
  relations to the Houses of Parlia-
    ment, 193 ff., 228, 237, 251-2,
    278 ff., 311 ff.
Coventry, Sir William, Secretary of
    State :
  communicates royal message to
    Commons, 164
  member of Cabinet of Charles
    II, 320
  aspired to manage the Com-
    mons, 323
  city, elections, 400
Cowle, Michael, 364
Cowper, William, Earl, Lord
    Chancellor, 360-62, 364
Coxe, Archdeacon William, 356, 360
Cranbourne, Viscountess, 172-9
Crispe, Sir Nicholas, Mr. Thomas
    and Mr. John, 172
Crosby, Brass, Lord Mayor of Lon-
    don, M.P., 236-7, 311-14
Crown Lands :
  only to be granted to a British-
    born subject, 95
  Clarendon obtained grants of, 156
  Danby obtained grants of, 181
Crowther, Dr., 156

Cumberland, William Augustus, Duke of, 139, 382

Customary Courts, proceedings to be in English, 130

Customs :
English rates extended to Scotland, 100
officers, deprived of the vote, 145
farm of, 155

Dalmahoy, Thomas, M.P., 172 ff.

Dammaree, rioter, 286 ff.

Danby, Thomas Osborne, Earl of, 180 ff., 354

Debt :
imprisonment for, not affected by Habeas Corpus Act, 50
action of, 79, 130
paid by Charles II, 155
National, 211
and privilege of members, 326

Declaration :
under the Act of Uniformity, 31
under the First Test Act, 42
under the Second Test Act, 43, 62, 64, 73, 83, 94, 104
for those scrupling the taking of an oath, 66
of right, 67, 199
of indulgence, see Indulgence
of James II, treason to publish a, 188

Delegate, for election of Scottish members, 145

Demise of the king :
continuance of Parliament on, 84
judges' commissions, 139
special provisions for death of William III, 84-5; of Anne, 111 ff.

Denison, Mr. Justice, 314

Denmark, Princess Anne of, 92, 98

Devonshire :
William, first Duke of, 354
William, third Duke of, 383

Dispensing power, 235
illegal, 68, 69, 74, 259, 346
by non obstante, 74
on behalf of Vintner's Company, 249
Godden v. Hales, 256-8, 261
Case of Seven Bishops, 258-71

Dissenters, see also Recusants :
Corporation Act, 15
relaxation of disabilities, 127

Dissenters—(contd.)
deprived under Act of Uniformity 22-7
ministers expelled from corporate towns, 34 ff.
conventicles of, illegal, 36 ff.
Toleration Act, 53 ff., confirmed, 119
schoolmasters, 121
declarations of indulgence (1673), 163-6, 324-5 ; (1687), 343-7
chapels of, treason to destroy, 286-8

Dissents, of minorities in the Lords, 188, 192, 208-10, 210-12, 221-227, 232-5

Dissolution :
of Parliament, 55, 186
advice of Clarendon on, 155
not to interrupt judicial proceedings in the Lords, 181

Divine right, 201

Doncaster, 350

Dorset, Sackville, Lionel Cranfield, first Duke of, Lord Steward, 374

Driver, Nathaniel, Sheriff of Bristol, 334

Drummond, Mr., M.P. for Midhurst, 401

Dublin, 188

Dunkirk, 156, 321

Dunning, John, Baron Ashburton (1782), 239, 296

Durham, court of, 313

Duties :
on beer, etc., 5, 77, 271
Bill of Rights and, 68
tunnage, 77
Act of Union and Scottish, 100
carried to Aggregate Fund, 138, 139
Commons' rights, 153, 154, 208
See also Excise, Taxation, Revenue

Earl Marshall, duties under Licensing Act, 30

East India Company, case of Thomas Skinner against, 157-63

Ecclesiastical courts, spiritual jurisdiction of, 13-14, 357
not to prosecute for mere nonconformity, 64
jurisdiction in tithe, 65
court of commissioners for ecclesiastical causes, 68, 69

Ecclesiastical persons, temporal jurisdiction of, 9
abjuration oath imposed on, 97
injunctions of Act of Uniformity concerning, 20 ff.
See also Ministers, Bishops, etc.
Edinburgh, 111
Egmont, Sir John Perceval, Earl of, and Harwich elections, 365 ff.
Egremont, Charles Wyndham, Earl of, 291
Elections :
  against corruption in, 68, 69, 83, 85, 140, 145, 209
  procedure of, 86, 187
  of those accepting office, 116
  expenses of, 127, 209, 342, 366, 399-402
  freedom of, 68, 69, 233, 235
  controverted, 140, 193, 229-35, 278
  Walpole and King's Lynn, 207
  Wilkes and Middlesex, 229-35
  to Commons under Charles II, 322, 326
  to Commons under James II, 342, 348-9
  to Commons under George II, 367-8, 377-8
Elizabeth, Queen :
  legislation of, 6, 20
  and toleration : remarks of Sacheverell, 197
Elliott, Dr. John, 188
Ely, Francis, Bishop of, 347
Enclosures, 287
Entick, John, 297-310
Equity :
  Irish suits in, to be decided in Ireland, 151
  the Jurisdiction of the Lords in, 167-71, 172-9, 182
  Exchequer Court of, 274
Escuage (Scutage), abolished, 2
Estimates :
  of expense in royal household, 148
  Army, 238
Exchequer, Court of :
  to grant writs of habeas corpus, 51
  to proceed against popish recusants, 88
  established in Scotland, 102, 130
  records of Skinner v. East India Company to be razed, 161
  Thomas v. Sorrell before, 249-51

Exchequer, Court of—(*contd.*)
  Bankers' Case, 271-8
  appeal to House of Lords from, 277-8
Exchequer Chamber, 271, 276
Exchequer, Royal :
  Auditor of the Receipt of, *see* Auditor
  tellers of, *see* Tellers
  Chancellor of, *see* Chancellor
  to issue revenues on Treasury warrant, 149
  pensions to be paid at, 149
  Danby's irregularities, 181
  monies to be paid at receipt of the, 272
  relation to barons of, 273
  officers of : accountable to Commons for expenditure, 327
Excise :
  provisions under Act of Union, 100
  given to Charles II, 5
  given to George III, 138
  officers of, deprived of the vote, 145
  grants by letters patent out of, 271-8
Exclusion, Bill of, 183
Excommunicato capiendo, 281
Exeter, 350

Fagg, Sir John, M.P., 167-71
Fairs, in Bristol, 339
Falmouth, 372
Faulconberg, Thomas Belasyse, Earl, 331
Federative power, 355
Fell, J., publisher, 298
Felony :
  position of persons accused of, under Habeas Corpus Act, 47-8, 50
  under the Riot Act, 124
  riotously pulling down buildings, 125
  M.P.'s not privileged in case of, 221, 282, 293
  warrant of commitment for, 292
Feudal Tenures, Abolition of, 2
Fines :
  for alienation, 2
  excessive, by James II, 68
  to be in English, 130
Fitzharris, Edward, 185-6
Fitzpatrick, Richard, 403

Five Mile Act, 34
Foreign Affairs :
  Clarendon's part in, 157, 319, 320
  control of, 95, 179, 210, 327-8, 355, 393
  errors of Danby in, 180
  Kentish petition, 191-2
  and the Septennial Act, 209
  Walpole and, 218
  committee of Privy Council for, 319, 320
  and Charles II, 320-21, 327-8
  and George II, 369-70, 371-2, 375
Forfeitures :
  promises of, granted, 68
  for treason, 183
  of charters of corporations, 255
Foster, Sir Michael, Recorder of Bristol and Judge of King's Bench, 289, 314
Fox, Charles James, 241-3, 401, 403
Fox, Henry, 382, 384, 385
France :
  Dunkirk sold to, 156, 321
  Clarendon refused to attack plantations of, 156
  relations of Danby with, 181
  Commons wish to check power of (1677), 327
  arbitrary government of, 358-9, 369
Franchise :
  freeholders, 86, 278
  disqualifications, 87, 89, 145
  freemen, 140
  controlled by Commons, 193
  burgesses, 278
Frankalmoin, 3
Freeholders :
  as electors, 86, 231
  to form jury in trials for high treason, 70
  took part in Kentish Petition, 191
  right to claim damages from an officer refusing to record a vote, 144
Freemen, franchise restricted, 140
Fundamental Laws :
  Solemn League and Covenant against, 7
  the Act of Union, 99
  theory of, 200-7

Gaol delivery, justices of, 50, 53

Gaolers, 174
  and the Habeas Corpus Act, 47 ff.
Gauger of Excise, deprived of the vote, 145
George I, message to Lords on the Peerage Bill, 213
George II :
  and his ministers, 369, 370-74, 375-7, 382-4, 385-8
  and elections, 365-8
  his influence on foreign affairs, 369-70 ; on the Army, 370
George III :
  arrest of Wilkes, 219-27
  opposition to, 239
  and Ireland, 241
  and the Cabinet, 399
  seeks a government, 401-2
  defeats Fox's India Bill, 403-4
Germain, Lord George, 238
Gibraltar, those holding office in disqualified for election to Commons, 132
Gideon, Sampson, 401
Gloucester, William, Duke of, death of, 93
Gloucestershire, election expenses in, 400
Glynn, Serjeant John, 231, 237
Godden, 256-8, 261
Godolphin, Sidney, Earl of, 359-60
Goldsborough, William, Clerk of the House of Commons, 171
Goldsmiths Company, 271-8
Governor of plantation disqualified for election to Commons, 115
Grafton, Charles Fitzroy, Duke of, 374
Gray, Dr. Robert, 188
Great Britain :
  established by Act of Union, 99
  Crown of, inseparable from Kingdom of Ireland, 129
Green Cloth, Board of :
  officers of, as J.P.'s, 131
  abolished, 148
Gregory, Sir William, Serjeant, Speaker, 328
Grenville, William Wyndham, Baron, 401
Grey, William de, Baron Walsingham, Chief Justice of Common Pleas, 311-14
Grindall, Edmund, Archbishop of Canterbury, 197

Groom of the Stole :
  in Temple's Privy Council, 330
  appointment of, 387
Guildford, Francis Lord, 330, 338

Habeas Corpus Act, 46
  writ of, 47, 178, 179, 196, 221 ff., 245,
    251, 281, 291, 292, 303, 311,
    314 ; Clarendon avoids, 155
Haddock, Nicholas, Admiral, 372
Hale, Sir Matthew, L.C.J., 286, 292,
    296
Hales, Sir Edward, 256-8, 261
Halifax, George Montagu Dunk,
    Earl of, 291, 294, 297-8
  George Savile, Marquis of, 340-42
Hamilton, William, presented Kent-
    ish Petition, 191
Hampshire, election expenses, 400
Haniper, 339, 364
Hanmer, Sir Thomas, 210
Hanover, Sophia, Electress and
    Duchess Dowager, 93, 98, 99
Hanover, town of, 370, 373
Harcourt, Sir Simon, 204-6
Hardwicke, Philip York, Earl of,
    Chancellor :
  on slavery, 315
  on the Inner Cabinet, 371
  on difficulties of a Regency, 372-3
  audience with George II, 375-7
  and choice of a ministry, 382-4
  on Pitt's claims to office, 386-7
  on departmental ministers, 387-8
  on Opposition, 388-9
Harrington, William Stanhope, first
    Earl of, 368, 373, 374
Harris, Benjamin, 252-3, 307
Hartington, William Cavendish, Mar-
    quis of, 383
Harwich, 365-8
Hawkins, Justice, 292
Head Boroughs :
  duties under Second Conventicle
    Act, 38
  actions against, for the execution
    of their duties, 134
Heath, Thomas, 368
Herbert, Rear-Admiral Arthur, Lord
    Torrington, 354
Herbert, Sir Edward, L.C.J., Judge-
    ment in Godden v. Hales,
    256-8
Heriots, 3

Hervey, John Lord, 369-70
High Commission :
  abolition confirmed, 14, 69
  under James II, 68
Highways, improvement, 153, 364-5,
    404
Holderness, Robert D'Arcy, Earl of,
    Secretary of State, 383-5
Holland, 327
Holloway, Sir Richard, Judge, 257,
    265-7, 293
Holt, Sir John, L.C.J. :
  in case, Ashby v. White, 193, 278-9
  in Bankers' Case, 276-7
  in Case of Aylesbury Men, 281-4,
    311, 312
  in Case of John Tutchin, 285
Homage, 2
Homilies, and doctrine of non-
    resistance, 204
Horse, Master of the :
  and reform of royal household, 148
  in Temple's Privy Council, 330
Hotham, Sir John, M.P., 184
Hounds, masters of the stag, and of
    the fox, suppressed, 148
Household, Royal :
  officers of, to continue on demise
    of sovereign, 113
  revenue for, 138
  cofferer of, office suppressed, 148,
    240
  reforms in, 148
  Comptroller of, 240
  Master of, 240
Houses, officers of Duties on, de-
    prived of vote, 145
Hungary (Maria Theresa), Queen of,
    375
Huygens, Christian, 187

Ilay, Archibald Campbell, Earl of,
    218
Impeachment, 238, 312
  not affected by Treason Act, 83
  no pardon under the Great Seal, 95
  of Clarendon, 155-7
  of Danby, 180-82
  not affected by Dissolution, 182
  of Edward Fitzharris, 185-6
  of Blaire and others, 188
  of Henry Sacheverell, 197-207
Imposition, bill for, on foreign
    commodities, 154

Impressment :
  of sailors, 289-90
  of Tubbs, 316
  discussed by committee of Privy
    Council, 319
Indemnity :
  of Charles II, 5, 7
  by statute, 184
India Bill, 403-4
India Company (Scotland), 101
Indictment, 226, 245, 391
  in cases of high treason, 81
  to be in English, 129
  concerning electoral matters, 193
  found by juries, 257
Indulgence, Declarations of, 163 ff.,
    259, 260, 324-5, 343-5
Informations, 226
  to be in English, 129
  concerning electoral matters, 193
  against Wilkes, 219
  against Henry Carr, 253
  by quo warranto, 254
  against seven bishops, 265
Informer :
  under Five Mile Act, 35
  under Second Test Act, 44
  under Act against Popery of
    1698-99, 90
  under Occasional Conformity Act,
    119
  under Place Acts, 132, 145
Inheritance, offices of, 102, 119,
    146
Injunctions :
  to stop proceedings at law against
    patents, 155
  of the Commons, 174
Inquisitions, to be in English, 129
Inspector of Duties on Windows or
    Houses : deprived of the
    vote, 145
Ipswich, 366
Ireland :
  capital offenders in, 53
  schoolmasters in, 123
  peers of, 44
  dependency of, 128, 147, 242,
    371
  commissioner of the revenue in,
    see Commissioner
  legislative and judicial independ-
    ence of, 150, 242
  bills of settlement for, 156

Ireland—(contd.)
  exclusion from throne of James II,
    183
  forfeited estates in, 192

Jacobites, 368
Jamaica, 314
James I, 40, 93, 249, 295, 301
James II, misdeeds of, 68, 199, 235,
    352
  abdication of, 69, 88
  a declaration of, 188
  dispensing power, 256
  his ecclesiastical policy, 258-71
  his policy towards boroughs, 347-
    352
  declaration of indulgence, 259,
    343-7
  See also York, James, Duke of
Jefferies, Sir George, 253
Jenkins, Sir Leoline, Secretary of
    State, 184, 338
Jenkins, Colonel, candidate for York,
    342
Jenkinson, Charles, 393-4
Jenyns, Mr., 378
Jesuit :
  English subject, not to be a royal
    servant, 63
  reward for conviction, 90
  expulsion of, demanded, 166
Jewel office, principal officers of, sup-
    pressed, 148
Jones, Sir Thomas, Chief Justice of
    Common Pleas :
  judgement in Shaftesbury's Case,
    251-2
  judgement in Quo Warranto Case,
    255
Judge Advocate :
  to administer oaths in Navy, 12
  to administer oaths at court mar-
    tials, 57
  to administer oaths of supremacy
    allegiance, 166
Judgements, to be in English, 130
Judges :
  misused by James II, 68
  their commissions, 95, 139
  duties under Habeas Corpus Act,
    47 ff.
  manner of removal, 95, 139
  salaries of, 139
  consultation of, by the Lords, 188

Judges—(*contd.*)
  not bound by resolutions of either
    House, 237
  relations with jury, 245-9, 253
  consulted by Lord Keeper, 277
  consulted by queen, 284
Jury :
  Grand : in treason cases, 82
    and petitions, 10, 191
  Petty : and James II, 68, 70
    dissenting ministers exempt
      from service on, 66
    and protection of J.P.s and con-
      stables, 133-4
    commoners to be tried by,
      162
    in libel cases, 224
    independence established by
      Bushell's Case, 245-9
    in Press cases, 253
    relations to judges, 245-9, 253
    returned by sheriff, 257
    at Quarter Sessions, 390-91
Justice, College of (Scotland), 102,
  120, 121
Justice, Lords Chief :
  duties under Licensing Act, 30
  of Queen's Bench : Lord Justice
    under Regency Act, 114
  one in Temple's Privy Council,
    330
Justices :
  of oyer and terminer, 50, 363
  of gaol-delivery, 50, 337, 363
  of assize, 50, 391
Justices of the Peace :
  two to enforce Five Mile Act,
    36
  one or more to enforce Second
    Conventicle Act, 37, 38
  under Habeas Corpus Act, 50, 54
  to expel popish recusants from
    London, 61-2
  to tender oaths to dissenters, 64,
    120
  to authorize dissenting meeting-
    places, 67, 344
  set up in Scotland, 110
  to break up riots, 124, 337
  three may allow petitions, 10
  property qualification, 130
  attorneys, solicitors, proctors dis-
    qualified, 130
  protection of, 133, 301

Justices of the Peace—(*contd.*)
  their warrant protects constables,
    134
  duties under Militia Act, 136-7
  to arrest James, Duke of York,
    184
  and Kentish Petition, 191
  not to be affronted, 260
  powers of committee, 291-2
  of Bristol, 337 (list of duties),
    363
  care of highways, 364-5
  commission of the peace, 389-92
  Secretaries of State as, 297, 393

Kearsley, G., publisher, 294
Keeper, Lord :
  duties under Licensing Act, 30
  duties under Habeas Corpus Act,
    47 ff.
  to issue writs for elections, 85
  to remain in office on sovereign's
    demise, 113
  Lord Justice under Regency Act,
    114
  in Four Barristers' Case, 178
  See also Rolls
Kent :
  papists to be expelled from, 61
  general Quarter Sessions of :
    origin of Kentish Petition,
      191
King's Bench, Court of :
  to hear and enrol oaths of suprem-
    acy and allegiance, 40, 91
  misused by James II, 68
  quo warranto proceedings in, 75,
    255-6, 349-51
  and habeas corpus procedure, 48,
    51
  Fitzharris convicted in, 186
  heard Ashby *v.* White, 193, 278-
    279
  Wilkes before, 219, 229
  Shaftsbury before, 251-2
  Godden *v.* Hales, 256-8
  Case of Seven Bishops, 258-71
  The Aylesbury men, 279-84
  the king against Cambridge Uni-
    versity, 288-9
  Leach *v.* King's Messengers, 295-
    297
  Sommersett's Case, 314-15
  Rex *v.* Tubbs, 316

King's Lynn, 207, 229
King's Person, safety of, 6, 43, 82, 88, 111, 181, 183, 186, 252
  slander against, 6-7, 88, 111
  oath of allegiance, 16
  not to be papist, 6, 72, 94, 99, 183
  controlled by Parliament, 95
  Act to preserve, 5, 60, 62
King's Speeches and Messages, 161, 178, 179, 190, 213
Knight of the Shire :
  qualifications for serving as, 117
  may be a J.P., 131
Knight Service, 2
Knowles, Captain, detained Sommersett on board *Anne and Mary*, 315

Land Tax :
  Anglo-Scottish proportion, 100
  commissioners of : eligible to vote, 146
Lawyers :
  Abjuration Oath imposed on, 97
  Scottish, to take oath, 120
Leach, Dryden, 295-7
Leathes, Carteret, 367-8
Lechmere, Sir Nicholas, Baron of the Exchequer, 199-201, 206-207, 273
Lecturer : control of,
  by Act of Uniformity, 27, 34
  by Five Mile Act, 35
Lee, Sir Thomas, M.P., 176
Legge, Henry Bilson, Chancellor of Exchequer, 384, 385, 387
Letters Patent, 332
  Clarendon altered, 156
  creation of peers by, 215
  dispensations by means of, 249, 256
  grant of money by, 271
Levinz, Sir Creswell, Serjeant (formerly Judge of Common Pleas), defence of Seven Bishops, 258-61
Libel :
  seditious : Wilkes arrested for 219-27, 229 ff., 291-4, 294-295
  seven bishops accused of, 258
  de libellis famosis, 263-5
  John Tutchin accused of, 285

Libel—(*contd.*)
  rights of Secretary of State in cases of, 299-310
  privilege of M.P.s in case of seditious, 304
  history of libel, 306 ff.
Licence :
  to schoolmasters, 24, 121
  of books, 30
  to sell wine retail, 249
Licensing Act, 29, 297, 307
Licensers :
  to license books for printing, 30
  appointed by Star Chamber, 306
Lighting of Nottingham, 394-5
Lippingcot, Mr. H., M.P. for Bristol, 400
Liturgy, of the Church of England, 11, 20 ff.
  enforced on holders of office, 119
  enforced on schoolmasters, 122
Local Government :
  statute for improvements, 153, 394, 404
  procedure for money bills concerning, 208
  finance, 256, 365
  by-laws, 256
  of Bristol, 332-9, 362-4
  James II and, 347-52
  of Nottingham, 351-2, 344-5, 364-5, 404-5
Locke, John, 354-5
London :
  Charles II and Duke of York's servants in, 40
  popish recusants in, 61-2
  quo warranto against, 75, 254-6, 350
  authorities of, to allow petitions, 10
  trades in, protected, 62
  and Convention Parliament of 1688, 187
  Lord Mayor of (Brass Crosby), 236-7, 311-14
  finance of, 256
  by-laws, 256
  issued certificates to watermen, 316
  coal in, 371
  election for, 400
  Bishop of : and Licensing Act, 30
    member of Privy Council, 330
    invites William of Orange, 354

Long, Mr., candidate for Aldborough,
    326
Lords, House of :
    Scottish peers, 103
    of Ireland : rights to hear appeals,
        129, 242
    and money bills, 153, 154, 192,
        326-7
    impeachment before, 155-7, 180-
        182, 185-6, 188, 197-207
    petition to : by Skinner, 157
    judicial powers of, 158-63, 167-
        171, 172-9, 193-6, 223-7, 228,
        277-8, 280-84, 327
    gives judgement for Skinner, 158
    privileges of, 159, 173, 174, 221
    conflicts with Commons, 153, 154,
        159-60, 167-71, 172-9, 185-6,
        193-6, 215, 326-7
    conferences with Commons, 8, 155,
        161
    writ of error, see Writ
    discussion on declaration of indul-
        gence, 166
    orders of protection from arrest by
        Commons, 168, 173, 174
    appeals in equity to, 167-71, 172-
        179, 182
    right to deliver prisoners, 173
    committee of privileges, 181
    part in Convention Parliament,
        187
    address to Crown, 195
    right of minority to dissent, see
        Dissents
    Peerage Bill, 213-16
    guardians of prerogative, 219
    Wilkes' Case, 221-7
    position of, vis-à-vis the people,
        234, 238
    right to imprison, 251
    Fox's India Bill defeated in, 403-
        404
Lords Justices under Regency Act,
    115
Lords Lieutenant :
    duties and powers under Militia
        Acts, 18, 135
    deputy : property qualification,
        135
    of Ireland, 242
Lords of Police in Scotland, sup-
    pressed, 148
Lord's Supper, see Sacraments

Louis XIV, 369
Luggershall, 401
Lumley, Richard, first Earl of Scar-
    borough, 354
Luttrell, Henry Lawes, 231-2, 235

Mackworth, Sir Henry, 358-9
Madrid, 371
Magna Charta, 162, 174, 237
Mahon, Port, 372
Mahrattas, King of, 240
Maidstone, 191
Malt Tax, 101
Malum per se, 249-51, 257
Malum prohibitum, 249-51
Mansfield, William Murray, first
    Earl of :
    on general warrants, 228
    judgement in Leach v. King's
        Messengers, 295-7 ; in Som-
        mersett's Case, 314-15 ; in
        Rex v. Tubbs, 316
Markets, in Bristol, 339, 364
Marlborough, John Churchill, Duke
    of, 360
Marriages :
    royal, 143
    determined by ecclesiastical courts,
        281
    alliance with Portugal by, 320
Martial Law, see Courts Martial
Mary, Queen, and the Cabinet, 355-6
Master :
    of the Harriers and Fox Hounds,
        of the Stag Hounds, sup-
        pressed, 148
    of the Horse (q.v.)
    of the Household, 240
    and slave, 314-15
Master-General of the Ordnance,
    146, 330
Maynard, Sir John, Serjeant, 161-3
Mayor :
    to break up riots, 124
    to take oaths of supremacy and
        allegiance and make declara-
        tions, 15
    of Aylesbury, a Returning Officer,
        193
    protected against troublesome ac-
        tions for executing duty, 301
    of Bristol, 332, 334, 336, 362-4,
        347

Mayor—(contd.)
  of York, 348-9
  of Nottingham, 365, 404
Mayor, Lord :
  of London :
    to sanction petitions, 10
    member of Assembly of Conven-
      tion Parliament, *ex officio*, 187
    (Crosby), 236-7, 311-14
Mead, William, Quaker, 245
Members of Parliament, *see* Commons, House of
Messengers :
  of King's Chamber to search by
    warrant, 32, 393
  in Wilkes' Case, 226, 294-7
  in Entick *v.* Carrington, 297-310
  of House of Commons, in Brass
    Crosby's Case, 236, 311
Middlesex :
  papists expelled from, 61
  Wilkes' election in, 229-35
Middleton, Dr., 288
Midhurst, 401
Militia (*see* Army) :
  control vested in king, 17
  issue of commissions, 18, 135
  levy of troops, 18-19
  powers of Lords Lieutenant, 19
  to help break up conventicles,
    38
  not affected by Mutiny Act, 56
  Act of 1757, 135 ff.
Miller, J., publisher, 236, 311
Milton, John, 306
Ministers of the Crown :
  advice to sovereign, 216, 217, 372,
    375-7
  responsible to Parliament, 217,
    377, 398
  collective responsibility of, 238-9
  chosen by Crown, 240-41, 369,
    382-4, 401-2
  and king's decisions, 369-70, 399
  duties of, 374
  in Commons, 385-6
Ministers of Religion :
  assent to the Prayer Book, 21 ff.,
    34
  conditions of holding a benefice,
    22-3
  oath of allegiance and supremacy,
    24
  episcopal ordination of, 25, 34

Ministers of Religion—(contd.)
  subject to Five Mile Act, 35
  to issue certificates of taking the
    sacrament, 41, 122
  dues to, payable by Nonconform-
    ists, 65
  Nonconformist, freedom for, 65,
    120, 325, 343
Ministry :
  responsible to Commons, 217,
    241, 377, 398
  and independent members, 365-
    366
  relation to king, 375-7, 385-6
  formation of a, 382-4
Minorca, 132, 372
Mint, English and Scottish coinage,
    101
Misprision of treason, 81
Mohan, Lord, 168
Mole, Captain Frederick, 188
Money, John, a messenger, 294-7
Money bills :
  initiation in Commons, 153-4
  to be debated in a committee of
    the whole House, 154
  not to be amended by Lords, 154
  tacking, 192
  to be recommended by the Crown,
    197
  local taxation, 153, 208
  control of expenditure, 326-7
  See also Duties, Excise, Revenue
Monitor, or British freeholder, 298
Monk, George, Duke of Albemarle,
    Captain-General, 321
Monstrans de droit, 276
Montagu, George Brudenell, Duke
  of, 401
Montagu(e), Sir James (Attorney-
  General), 198-9
Montagu(e), John, second Duke of,
  Master-General of the Ordi-
  nance, 374
Montesquieu, 378-82
Morris, Henry, of Nottingham, 364
Motions :
  on expenditure to be referred to
    the whole House, 153-4
  of censure, 239
Moyser, Mr., candidate for York,
    342
Musters, Commissaries of, 166
Mutiny Act, 55, 210-12

Natural justice, 289
Nature, state of, 354
Naval Discipline, Articles and Orders of, 11-12, 212
Navy :
    officers allowed to be M.P.s, 116 ; and also J.P.s, 131
    Commissioners of the, see Commissioner
    Treasurer of, see Treasurer
    Comptroller of, see Comptroller
    Houses want officers to take tests, 166
    the protection of England, 210
    impressment for, 289-90, 316
    victuals of, 320
Negus, Colonel Francis, 365-6
Nevis, 156
Newcastle, Pelham-Holles, Sir Thomas, Duke of, 374
    the Inner Cabinet, 371, 373
    conduct of war against Spain, 372-373
    First Lord of the Treasury, 384, 385-8
    a party leader, 389
News Letters, Newspapers, see Press
Nicholas, Sir Edward, Secretary of State, 320
Non-Jurors, 361-2
Non obstante, 74, 250
Non-residence, 257
Non-resistance, see Sacheverell, Norfolk, 368
Normanby, John Sheffield, Marquis of (later Duke), of, 355
Norris, Sir John, Admiral, 371-2
North, Frederick, Lord :
    collective responsibility of ministers, 238-9
    on the position of Prime Minister, 398
    on supremacy of Commons, 398
    and election expenses, 399-401
North Briton, No. 45, 220, 291, 294
Northfolk, Sir James, Serjeant-at-Arms, 167
Notary Public, 120
Nottingham :
    charters of, 350-52
    lighting of, 394-5
    repairing highways of, 364-5
    paving, 404

Oates, Titus, his conspiracy, 181
Oath, ex officio illegal, 14
    power of Judge Advocate to administer, 12, 57, 166
    of allegiance and supremacy, 16, 40, 43, 55 (new oaths), 60, 64, 71, 82, 88, 104, 166, 206, 334-5, 344
    of ministers and the Prayer Book, 22
    against Solemn League and Covenant (q.v.)
    against taking arms against the king, 16, 34, 35
    coronation, 57 ff., 44, 206
    those who scruple to take, 66
    abjuration, 97, 104
    for M.P.s re property qualification, 118
    of conformity, 119
    at courts martial, 56-7
    of witnesses before a select committee, 143
    regarding undisclosed pensions, 149
    regarding genuine Secret Service expenditure, 150
    of a Baron of the Exchequer, 275
    of borough officers, 334-5, 363
Occasional Conformity Act, 118
Office(rs) :
    conditions of, religious tests under the Crown, 40-42, 45-6, 60, 89, 95, 97, 115, 118, 345
    not to lapse at sovereign's demise, 113
    to proclaim new sovereign, 114
    not to be held by M.P.s, 95, 115, 116, 131, 312
    in corporations, see Corporations
    for life, 132
    hereditary, 102, 119, 146
    suppressed by Parliament, 148
    sale of, 155, 257
    returning, 193-6
    great, of state : place in sovereign's councils, 218, 318, 329-30, 356
    corruption in, 285
Oldfield, George, 364
Oliver, Richard, Alderman, 237
Onslow, Arthur, Speaker, 392
Opposition, 373, 376, 388, 389, 401

Orange, William, Prince of, 70, 187, 198, 199, 352. *See also* William III

Orders :
  judicial : to be in English, 129
  of the House of Commons, 153, 167-71, 172-9
  of the House of Lords, 167-71, 172-9, 192, 221-2
  in Council, 265, 346, 347
Ordnance, Board of, 146
Original contract, 200
Ormond, James Butler, Marquis (later Duke) of, 320
Ossory, James Butler, Earl of, 403
Ouster-le-mains, abolished, 2
Outlawry, 81
Overseer of the Poor, 38, 66
Oyer and Terminer, 50

Pamphlets, 6, 29, 185, 202, 252, 253
  See also Press
Papists, *see* Recusants (Popish)
Pardon :
  of Charles II, general, 5, 7
           particular, 8, 182
  to be in English, 130
  pleaded in bar by Danby, 182
Parker, Sir Philip, 366
Parker, Sir Thomas (later first Earl of Macclesfield), judgement in Dammaree's Case, 286-8
Parliament :
  Convention Parliaments : status of, 1, 11, 54, 74, 186
  Long Parliament, 1, 7, 9, 13-14, 33, 185, 306
  dissolution, 1, 7, 55, 113
  prorogation, 171, 179, 196
  demise of sovereign, 84, 112
  duration, 33-4, 79, 126, 208
  privileges, 8, 70, 237, 293, 313
  royal speeches, *see* King's Speeches
  royal assent to Bills of, 7, 189, 403
  law and custom of, 177, 193-6, 232, 234, 280, 283, 312
  aliens excluded, 95
  impeachment (q.v.)
  parties (q.v.)
  management of, 373, 376, 383, 387
  balance of, 340 ff., 378 ff.
  His Majesty's Great and Chief Council, 216, 217, 329

Parliament—(*contd.*)
  sovereignty of, 395
  control over :
    Militia, 17, 55, 135
    Army, 55, 68, 69, 210-12
    religious affairs, 9, 13, 20, 36, 39, 43, 63, 68, 69, 98, 118, 121, 127, 163-4, 263, 324, 343-5
    succession to the Crown, 54-55, 70, 74, 92, 96, 99, 112, 183
    taxation, 5, 68, 69, 77, 101, 138, 139, 147
    foreign affairs, 95, 179, 180, 181, 327-8, 354
    judges, 95, 139
    supremacy over Ireland, 129, 147, 150, 241
    Acts of, suspended and dispensed, 68, 69, 163-4, 259-271
Party :
  under Queen Anne, 233, 359-62
  theories of government by, 240-41, 396-7
  origins of, 325-6
  opposition (q.v.)
Passive obedience, 197-207, 234
Patents :
  to be in English, 130
  Clarendon and illegal, 155
Paty, John, of Aylesbury, 281
Paving :
  statutory provision for, 153, 404
  J.P.s may order a rate for, 364-365
Paymasters :
  of Navy and Army : clerks of, not to sit in Commons, 132
  deputy, of the Army : eligible for the Commons, 132
  of the pensions, suppressed, 148
Peck, Sergeant, 172-9
Peers :
  privileges of, 8, 33, 38-9, 104, 262
  Test Act applied to, 43-4
  must take oaths and declaration, 45, 55, 104
  trial of, for treason, 82
  Abjuration Oath, 98, 104
  Scottish, 44, 103, 213
  peerage not forfeit, 7
  houses of, exempt from search, 33, 38

Peers—(*contd.*)
  Irish, 44
  not subject to property qualifica-
    tions for J.P.s., 131
  not obliged to serve in the Militia,
    136
  in Convention Parliament, 187
  right to enter dissents in Lords'
    Journal, *see* Dissents
  Peerage Bill, 213-16
  bishops as, 9, 259
Pelham, Henry, First Lord of the
    Treasury, 375, 383, 386
Pemberton, Sir Francis, Serjeant,
    Judge and L.C.J. (1679–83),
    then again practised at the
    Bar:
  one of the Four Barristers, 172-
    179
  in Seven Bishops' Case, 270
Penn, Sir William, Admiral, in
    Cabinet, 320
Penn, William, Quaker, son of Sir
    William, 245
Pennell, Marmaduke, 364
Pension :
  M.P.s and, 95, 116, 238, 240
  Paymaster of the, office sup-
    pressed, 148
  public payment of, at the Ex-
    chequer, 149
  Danby's use of, 181
Pepys, Samuel, *Diary*, 319-20
Peterborough, Thomas, Bishop of,
    347
Petition :
  restrictions on right of, 9-10
  of the Seven Bishops, 68, 258,
    346-7
  right to, 69, 157, 160, 259, 262,
    267, 269-70
  to Commons, 140, 157, 191, 197,
    231, 279
  to the Crown, 157, 262, 284
  procedure by English, 162
  to the Lords, 167-71, 196
  of Right, 174, 276
  of City of London in 1679,
    256
Philips, Sam, of Harwich, 367
Philipson, of Harwich, Packet Agent,
    365
Pitt, William, Earl of Chatham, *see*
    Chatham

Pitt, William (later First Lord of the
    Treasury), 401-2
Place Acts, 131, 145, 146
Plantations :
  governors of, not to sit in Com-
    mons, 115
  Board of Trade and, suppressed,
    148
  Clarendon introduced arbitrary
    government in, 156
  Clarendon refused to reduce
    French, 156
Pleadings to be in English, 129
Plymouth, 350, 372
Polhill, David, 191
Police :
  Lords of, in Scotland : sup-
    pressed, 148
  See Constables
Pollard, Sir Hugh, 323
Pollexfen, Sir Henry, Barrister (later
    Chief Justice of Common
    Pleas), 270
Pope, the, 43, 55, 71
Popery, 39, 43, 69, 90
  See Recusants
  See Popish priests
  joint address against growth of,
    166
  Danby's help to, 181
  encouraged by James, Duke of
    York, 183
  importance under George I, 209
Popish priests :
  to be apprehended, 90
  expulsion proposed, 166
  plot, 186
  See Oates, Titus
  See Recusants
Porter, Sir Charles (later Irish Lord
    Chancellor), Barrister, 172-
    179
Portland, William Bentinck, first
    Earl of, 355
Portland, William Henry Cavendish,
    third Duke of, 242
Portugal :
  subjects of King of, 46, 62
  negotiations *re* marriage alliance
    with (1662), 320
Post Office :
  employees of : deprived of the
    vote, 145
  influence in elections, 365-6, 367

Powell (or Powle), Henry, M.P. for Cirencester, later Master of the Rolls, 163, 168
Powell, Sir John, Judge :
in Godden v. Hales, 257
in Case of Seven Bishops, 263-70, 293
in Case of Aylesbury Men, 279-281
Powis, William Herbert, first Marquis of, 348
Praemunire :
for purveyance, 5
for upholding Long Parliament, 7
for illegal transportation, 52
for denying the king's title, 88, 112
for failing to carry out Regency Act, 115
for officiating at a royal marriage not consented to by the king, 144
Pratt, Sir Charles, first Earl Camden, Chief Justice of Common Pleas, 1761, Lord Chancellor, 1766-70 :
judgement in King v. Cambridge University, 288-9
judgement in Wilkes v. Lord Halifax, 291-4
judgement in Wilkes v. Wood, 294-5
judgement in Entick v. King's Messengers, 298-310
Prayer, Book of Common :
use in Navy of, 11
compulsory use of, 20 ff.
revision of, 21
authentic copies to be reserved in Courts of Record, 28
dissenters from, 34, 36, 63, 119, 122
schoolmasters to use Catechism in, 122
Preacher :
at a conventicle, 37
dissenting, under Toleration Act, 65
Precept, Sheriff's, 85
Pre-emption abolished, 4
Prerogative, 192, 237, 319, 341-2, 395-6
of pardon, 8, 95, 182, 345, 396
legislative, 7, 189, 213, 219, 258, 268, 396, 403-4

Prerogative—(contd.)
and the Armed Forces, 17, 68, 69, 135-6, 212, 370
of assembling and dissolving Parliaments, 1, 34, 54-5, 85, 112-13, 186-7
of dispensing and suspending laws, 68, 163-6, 249-51, 256-8, 259-271, 324, 343-7
of taxation, 68, 69
of war and peace, 95, 179, 180, 181, 327-8, 355, 359, 369, 378, 396
coinage, 396
of appointing certain officers, 174, 176
of appointing Ministers and Privy Councillors, 240-41, 318, 320-321, 329-30, 331, 359-62, 369, 375, 382-4, 385-9
Sacheverell's doctrine of non-resistance to, 202, 206
of creating peers, 213-16, 396
of creating and dissolving corporations, 333, 347 ff., 362
of issuing proclamations, 263
of impressing sailors, 289, 316
of approval of the Speaker, 328
Presbyterian Church established in Scotland, 99, 106
Presentments to be in English, 129
President of the Council, Lord, 330, 374, 383
to remain in office at sovereign's demise, 113
a lord justice under Regency Act, 114
Press (see also Pamphlets), 29
activities of the, 201, 223
and the Common Law, 252-4, 268-9, 307
and the government, 285
under Star Chamber, 306-7
and Parliamentary proceedings, 184-5, 217, 236-7, 311-14
North Briton, No. 45, 220, 291, 294
London Evening Post, 236
Monitor, or British Freeholder, 298
Pretender :
attainder of, 96
See Wales : pretended Prince of
Prickit, Deputy Recorder of York, 348

" Prime " Minister :
Walpole as, 216, 218, 369
Clarendon as a First Minister,
317-18
Hardwicke and, 385, 387
North as, 398
Primer seizin, abolished, 2
Printers :
Licensing Act to regulate, 29
and publication of Commons'
votes and proceedings, 184-
185, 217, 236, 311-14
and search warrants, 303
Privy Council :
function of, 95, 216, 318-19, 320-
321, 358-9, 371
of Great Britain, 110
to continue on sovereign's death,
113
to proclaim successor, 114
instruments of Regency to be
opened at, 115
may vary Militia quotas for the
counties, 136
royal marriages to be entered into
books of, 144
books of : proceedings in Skinner's
Case to be erased, 161
not consulted by Danby, 180
secrecy, 185
constituted by king, 185, 318,
330
advice to sovereign, 95, 331
composition of, 318, 329
orders in, 345, 347, 364
Privy Councillor :
legal powers of, 299-300
committees of, 157, 319, 321, 329
Privy Seal, Lord :
to remain in office at sovereign's
demise, 113
Lord Justice under Regency Act,
114
on Council committee in Skinner's
Case, 157
reports draught of order to release
four barristers, 173
manages conference (over four
barristers), 174
in Temple's Privy Council, 330
criticizes Secretaries of State, 331
Prizes, officers of, not to be M.P.,
115
Prohibitions, to be in English, 130

Property :
Crown's duty to protect, 164-5,
343, 352
Parliament's rights to alter titles
to, 192, 195, 281
Parliamentary vote, a species of,
194
protection of, by courts, 273
and the origin of society, 304
Property qualification :
for J.P.s, 130
for M.P.s, 117, 131
for Militia officers, 135
for Aldermen of Bristol, 337
Protestant religion :
James II's efforts to upset, 68, 183,
199
in Scotland, 106-8
maintenance of, 164, 187, 191
Danby's subversion of, 181
danger to, 39-46, 68, 72-3, 87, 90,
94, 186, 252
Proxy, in Lords, 45
Pryn, William, M.P. for Bath, 153
Pulteney, Sir William (later Earl of
Bath), 216, 217
Purveyance, Abolition of, 4
Pypowder, Court of, 339

Quakers, and oaths and declarations,
36, 66, 89, 120
Quarter Sessions :
to hear and enrol oaths, 40, 91
popish recusants to register at, 62
Riot Act to be read at, 126
Exclusion Bill to be read at, 184
Kentish Petition formulated at,
191
extent of jurisdiction, 390, 391
Quartering of soldiers, 68, 137, 155,
211
Quo Warranto :
against London, 75, 254-6
Clarendon issued, against corporations, 156
against Bristol Charter, 332
reversal of proceedings by, 349-
351
against Nottingham Charter ,351

Rains, Mayor of York, 348
Rainsford, Sir Richard, Judge,
judgement in Shaftesbury's
Case, 252

Rate, 364-5
Raymond, Sir Robert, later Baron and L.C.J., 289
Recognizances, 48 ff., 130
Recorders, 15, 245, 253
of Bristol, 289-90, 332, 336, 363
Records :
to be in English, 130
power of a select committee to send for, 143
in the Tower, 188
Recoveries, 130
Recusants (Popish) :
and wardship rights, 4
and right to hold offices, 39 ff., 185
penalty under the First Test Act, 41
disabled from sitting in Parliament, 43, 55
to be removed from London, 61-62
not relieved by Toleration Act, 67
armed by James II, 68
king never to be, 73, 94, 99
all to be treated as, unless oaths taken, 88
penalty for not taking oaths and declaration, 91
peers and M.P.s as, 44
joint address that laws be enforced against, 166
and Declarations of Indulgence to, 324, 343-5
Regency Act (Anne), 111
Reresby, Sir John :
and elections at Aldborough, 326, at York, 342
extracts from memoirs of, 325-8, 348-9, 342
Resolution :
on election matters, 193-4
on supply, 154, 197, 208
on Lord's action, in Skinner v. East India Company, 159-160
on Lord's action in Shirley v. Fagg, 167-71
in obedience to King's command, 161
on suspending power, 163
on impeachment, 186
on Kentish Petition, 192

Resolution—(contd.)
on publishing of proceedings, 217
on privilege of Parliament, 220, 280
on general warrants, 228
of the Lords, 280
on Commons' action in Skinner v. East India Company, 159
on Commons' pretensions over election matters, 194
Retford, 350
Revenue :
in lieu of purveyance and wardships, 5, 271
to be paid to the Bank of England, 77
Customs and Excise unified for England and Scotland, 100
Land Tax, 100
Commissioner of the, see Commissioner
Crown, 138, 147
officers engaged in : deprived of the vote, 145
misused by Danby, 180-81
control of Commons, see Commons
and Court of Exchequer, 273
Revolution :
Sacheverell's impeachment: views expressed on, 197-207
its importance, 305
Richmond and Gordon, Charles Lennox, second Duke of, Master of the Horse, 374
Rights and liberties :
of the country and its subjects, 71, 96, 160, 165, 170, 173, 174, 182, 187, 195, 213, 224, 231, 281, 340-41, 352
Bill of, 67, 202
Riots, 123, 245
Robinson, Sir John, lieutenant of the Tower, 176, 178
Robinson, Sir Metcalfe, Member for York, 342
Robinson, Sir Thomas, Secretary of State, 385, 387
Rochester, Laurence Hyde, first Earl of, 188
Rolls :
to be in English, 130
of 1 Hen. IV, 175
of 4 Ed. III, No. 6, 178
Keeper of, 392

Rome, Church of, *see* Pope, Popery,
    Recusants
Rules to be in English, 129
Russell, Edward (later Earl of Or-
    ford), 352
Russell, William, fifth Earl (later
    first Duke of Bedford), 354

Sacheverell, Henry, impeached, 197-
    207
Sacraments :
  of holy communion : a condition
    of office in corporations, 17,
    119, 127
  Act of Uniformity, 20 ff.
  condition of office under the
    Crown, 40, 119, 166
  declaration regarding, 42, 43
  sovereign to join in, 94
  schoolmasters to take, 122
  of baptism, 65
St. Antholin's, London, 367
St. Asaph, Bishop of, 347
St. Bartholomew's Day, 25
St. Christopher's, 156
St. James's, 187, 371
St. Mary, Nottingham, 365
St. Paul's, 197
Salt :
  Commissioners of the : clerks of,
    not to sit in Commons, 132
  clerks of, deprived of the vote,
    145
Sancroft, William, Archbishop of
    Canterbury, 346 ff.
Sandwich, Edward Montagu, first
    Earl of, 321
Sanson, a Corporator of Harwich,
    367
Saunders, Sir Edmund, L.C.J., judge-
    ment in Quo Warranto, 255
Sawyer, Sir Robert, Attorney-
    General, 332
Schism Act, 121
Schoolmasters :
  oaths of supremacy and allegiance,
    23-4, 35-6, 122
  to be licensed, 24, 121
  penalties for Roman Catholic, 90,
    121
  abjuration oath imposed, 97, 122
  Scottish, 106
  not to attend Conventicles, 122
Scot and lot, 326

Scotland :
  capital offenders in, 53
  Act of Union, 98 ff.
  peers of, 44, 213
  elections to Parliament in, 145
Scroggs, Sir William, L.C.J., judge-
    ments on the press, 252-4,
    303, 307-8
Seal, Great :
  no pardon under, for impeach-
    ment, 95
  commissioners nominated under,
    99
  of Great Britain, 105, 214
  to be continued in use after
    sovereign's demise, 113
  royal consent to royal marriages
    given under, 144
  letters patent under, 156, 256,
    271
Searcher of Customs : deprived of
    the vote, 145
Secretary :
  of Chancellor of the Exchequer,
    see Chancellor
  of Admiralty, *see* Admiralty
  of Treasury, *see* Treasury
  at War : corruption of Walpole
    as, 207
Secretary of State :
  duties under Licensing Act, 30
  his subordinates, except Under-
    Secretary, ineligible for Com-
    mons, 132
  third—or for the Colonies, sup-
    pressed, 148
  to swear oath concerning Secret
    Service money, 150
  not consulted by Danby, 180
  powers of arrest, 224, 291, 244-5
  legal position of, 299-300, 301-10,
    393
  resorted to Clarendon instead of
    Charles II, 317, 320
  members of council of Charles II,
    320, 331
  to advise Charles II on foreign
    affairs, 321
  in Temple's Privy Council, 330
  duties of a, 393-4
Secret Service :
  disbursements on, controlled, 149,
    150
  misuse of, by Danby, 181

Selwyn, George Augustus, M.P. for
    Luggershall, 401
Septennial Act, 126, 208
Serjeant-at-Arms :
    to require attendance of M.P.s for
        the business of the House, 141
    to arrest by order of Commons,
        167, 172, 175, 236
    sent to Tower, 173-4
    employed by Lord Keeper, 178
    to hold in custody authors of
        Kentish Petition, 192
Serjeants-at-Law, 194
Serjeanty, Grand, abolished, 3
Session, Court of (Scotland), 102
Settlement, Act of, 92
    Bills of, in Ireland, 156
Seymour, Sir Edward, fourth
    Baronet :
    charged Clarendon in the Com-
        mons, 155
    Speaker, 167, 328
Shaftesbury, Anthony Ashley Cooper,
    Baron Ashley, Earl of :
    member of Council Committee, 157
    committed to Tower, 251-2, 283,
        314
Shelburne, Sir William Petty, second
    Earl of (later first Marquis of
    Lansdowne), 238, 240, 399,
    401
Shepard, of Cambridgeshire, 378
Sheriff :
    must obey writ of habeas corpus,
        47, 245
    to forward copies of the panel of
        jurors in treason cases, 82
    to execute writs calling for the
        election of M.P.s, 85, 342
    to pay those securing the convic-
        tion of popish priests, 90
    to break up riots, 124
    to suppress conventicles, 38
    case of the, 257
    to return juries, 257
    of Bristol, 332, 334, 336, 347
    answerable to J.P.s, 390
Ship-money, 235, 309
Ships :
    Scottish become British, 100
    used by the Post Office : officers
        on, 145, 367
Shirley, Dr. Thomas, physician to
    the king, 167-71

Shrewsbury, Charles Talbot, twelfth
    Earl and only Duke of, 354,
    355-6
Sidney, Algernon, 379
Sidney, Henry, Viscount (later Earl
    of Romney), younger brother
    of Algernon, 354, 355
Simony, 257
Skinner, Thomas, 157-63
Slavery, Sommersett's Case, 314-15
Socage, Tenure in, 3
Solemn League and Covenant, 7, 16,
    24-5
Solicitor :
    not to be a J.P. while in practice,
        130
    breach of privilege to prosecute an
        action on election returns, 194
Solicitor-General, 154, 262-70
Sommers (or Somers), John, Baron,
    Lord Keeper (later Lord
    Chancellor) :
    in Seven Bishops' Case, 261-2
    judgement in Bankers' Case, 271-
        277
Sommersett, James, an African
    negro, 314-15
Sophia Electress, Duchess of Han-
    over, 93, 98, 99
Sorrell, a Vintner, Case of Thomas
    v. Sorrell, 249-51, 261
Southwark, papists expelled from, 61
Spain, 321, 371
Speaker :
    duty in controverted elections, 141
    issues warrant for a writ of elec-
        tion, 45, 207, 229
    issues warrants of arrest, 167, 237,
        281
    and publication of Commons pro-
        ceedings, 185, 217
    to adjourn the Commons, 328
    appointment of, 328
Stanhope, James, first Earl, and
    Peerage Bill, 213
Stanhope, Charles, brother of
    William, first Earl of Harring-
    ton, elected at Harwich, 367-
    368
Stanneries, 5
Stamps :
    Commissioners of the, Clerks of :
        not to sit in Commons, 132
        deprived of the vote, 145

Star Chamber, 223, 306, 330
Stationer's Company, functions of, under Licensing Act, 30-32
Statutes to be in English, 130
Steuart, Charles, slave owner, 314-315
Steward, Lord :
    to reform royal household, 148
    in Temple's Privy Council, 330
    in the Cabinet, 374, 383
Stewartry, 146
Stoughton, Sir Nicholas, 172
Street, Sir Thomas, Judge, in Godden v. Hales, 258
Streets, improvement of, 153, 394-5, 404-5
Succession :
    established by Parliament, 54, 70, 74, 92 ff., 96, 99, 183
    safeguarded, 84, 88, 89, 112
    as opposed to " possession ", 388
Suffolk, 366
Sugar, imposition on, 154
Sunday observance, 67
Sunderland, Charles Spencer, third Earl of, 360
Supervisor, of Excise, deprived of the vote, 145
Supply, Committees of, 153
Supremacy :
    royal, in ecclesiastical affairs, 14, 21, 39, 60, 164-6, 259-71, 324-5, 343-7, 357-8
    Oath of, see Oath
Surety for the peace, 222
Surrey, papists expelled from, 61
    election for, 400
Surveyor :
    of Duties on Windows or Houses : deprived of the vote, 145
    to manage royal buildings, 149
    of highways, 364-5
Suspending Power :
    illegal, 68, 69, 235
    resolution of the Commons concerning, 163
    not to apply to laws touching properties, rights, liberties, 165
    by Declaration of Indulgence, 259, 324, 343 ff.
Seven Bishops' Case, 258-71
Sussex, papists expelled from, 61
Sydney, see Sidney, Henry

Tacitus, " Germania ", 382
Talbot, Charles, Baron Talbot of Hensol, Lord Chancellor, 315
Tallies, 271
Tangier, 51
Taxation :
    prerogative challenged, 68, 69
    hereditary revenues from, 138
    See also Duties, Excise, Revenue
Tellers of the Exchequer, clerks of : not to sit in Commons, 132
Tenures, Feudal, abolition of, 2, 315
Temple, George Nugent-Temple-Grenville, Earl, Lord Lieutenant of Ireland (later Marquis of Buckingham), 401-4
Temple, Sir William, scheme for reforming Privy Council, 329-30
Test Act, First, 39 ; Second, 43
    effects of, 185, 256
Thomas, Case of, v. Sorrell, 249-51, 261
Thompson, Edward, citizen of York, 349
Thompson, Sir Stephen, candidate for York, 348
Thompson, Sir William, M.P. and member of East India Company, 159
Thurlow, Edward, first Baron, Lord Chancellor, 402
Tithes :
    Toleration Act does not exempt dissenters from, 65
    Declaration of Indulgence does not exempt dissenters from, 324
Tithingmen : to assist J.P.s under Second Conventicle Act, 38
Toleration :
    for dissenters, 63 ff., 119, 127
    Declarations of Indulgence, 163-6, 258-71, 324, 343-7
    attacked by Sacheverell, 197-207
Tolls, 208, 339
Tonnage and Poundage, given to George III, 138
Tories, 359, 366
Tower of London :
    Lieutenant of, 174, 175
    records kept in the, 188
    imprisonment in, Brass Crosby, 236-7 ; Danby, 180 ; Shaftsbury, 251 ; Walpole, 207

Town-Clerks :
  to take oaths of supremacy and
    allegiance, 15
  of Bristol, 332, 337, 347, 363
  of Nottingham, 405
Trade :
  protection of, in London, 62
  pursuit of, prohibited to Bank of
    England, 79
  between England and Scotland,
    100
  Board of, and plantations, sup-
    pressed, 148
  and Declaration of Indulgence,
    324, 343
Transubstantiation, declaration
  against, 42
Treason, High, legislation concerning, 6, 80 ff.
  and habeas corpus, 47, 89
  special provision, 50
  juries to try, 68, 70
  Pretender attainted of, 96
  to correspond with the Pretender,
    96
  to compass Anne's death, 98
  to dispute succession established
    by Parliament, 112
  not to proclaim lawful successor,
    114
  impeachment of Clarendon for,
    155-7
  impeachment of Danby for, 180-
    182
  for James to accede and for those
    helping him, 183
  impeachment of Fitzharris for,
    185-6
  to deny title of William III, 188
  and resistance, 203
  no privilege of Parliament in case
    of, 221, 282, 293
  Dammaree accused of, 286-8
  misprision of, 80 ff.
Treasurer :
  of the Navy : eligible to sit in
    Commons, 132
  of the County, 145
  of the Chamber : office sup-
    pressed, 148, 240
  of the Household, 240
Treasurer, Lord High :
  to remain in office at sovereign's
    demise, 113

Treasurer, Lord High—(contd.)
  a Lord Justice under Regency
    Act, 114
  not to sit in Commons, 132
  oath regarding pensions to be
    sworn before, 149
  Danby : impeached, 180
  position vis-à-vis Court of Ex-
    chequer, 273-8
  member of Cabinet Council of
    Charles II, 320
  to advise Charles II on foreign
    affairs, 320-21
  manages House of Commons,
    322
  in Temple's Privy Council, 330
Treasury :
  to repay sheriffs under act against
    popery, 90
  Commissioners of : Clerks of, not
    to sit in Commons, 132
  Secretaries of : eligible for the
    Commons, 132
  Commissioners of : not to make
    contracts with M.P.s, 146 ; to
    reform royal household, 148 ;
    oath regarding pensions to be
    sworn before, 149
  extent of functions of, 387, 399-
    401
  First Lord, 383
Trenchard, Sir John, Secretary of
  State, 355
Triennial Acts, 33, 79
Trimmer, 340-42
Trinder, Serjeant, 270
Trinity, Doctrine of, 67
Tubbs, waterman of London, 316
Tutchin, John, case of, 285
Tweeddale, John Hay, fourth Mar-
  quis of, Secretary of State for
  Scotland, 375

Under - Secretary of State to be
  eligible as J.P., 131 ; and also
  as M.P., 132
Uniformity, Act of, 20-9, 108, 259
  use of Prayer Book in the Navy, 11
  disregard of, 34
  enforced, 36
  and Toleration Act, 63
  repeal of, not to be consented to
    by Lords Justices, 115
  suspension of, 259

Union of England and Scotland,
    98 ff., 213
Unitarians not relieved by Tolera-
    tion Act, 67
United Kingdom, 100
Universities (*see also* Colleges) :
    oaths of allegiance and supremacy,
        23-4, 60
    compulsory use of Prayer Book, 26
    special circumstances of lectures
        in, 27
    Licensing Act not to infringe the
        privileges of, 33
    Abjuration Oath imposed, 97
    Scottish, 106
    M.P.s for, unaffected by property
        qualifications, 117
    tutors in, 123
    heads of colleges in, *see* Colleges
    election of M.P.s for, 187
    Rex *v.* Cambridge, 288-9
Usury, 257

Vacation, operation of habeas corpus
    during, 49
Vaughan, Sir Henry, M.P. for Car-
    marthenshire, 174
Vaughan, Captain Henry, impeached,
    1689, 188
Vaughan, Sir John, Lord Chief
    Justice :
    judgement on freedom of jury
        (Bushell's Case), 245-9
    judgement on royal prerogative
        of dispensation (Thomas *v.*
        Sorrell), 250-51
Ven, Richard, Rector of St. Antho-
    lin's, London, 367
Verdicts :
    to be in English, 129
    in actions against J.P.s and con-
        stables in pursuit of their
        duties, 134
    jury's immunity for, 248-9
Vernon, Edward, Admiral, instruc-
    tions to, 218
Vice-Chancellor :
    to license books printed within the
        university, 30
    to receive a copy of every book
        printed, 33
    to receive orders for election of
        M.P.s, 187
    holds a court, 288

Victualling Office :
    Commissioners of : not to be
        M.P.s, 132 ; not to make
        contracts with M.P.s, 146
Vienna, 373
Villeins, 315
Vintners, Company of :
    Clarendon's illegal dealings with,
        156
    dispensation granted to, by
        James I, 249
    Sorrell, a member of, 249
Virginia, 314
Visitor, 288
Votes :
    of the Commons : to be pub-
        lished, 184
    See Franchise
Vyner, Sir Robert : in Bankers'
    Case, 271-8

Wake, William (later Archbishop of
    Canterbury) on Convocation,
    357-8
Wales :
    Prayer Book to be in Welsh, 28
    pretended Prince of, 88, 96, 97,
        112, 354
    Dowager Princess of : annuity to,
        139
    Frederick, Prince of, 366
    George, Prince of (later George
        IV), 404
Walpole, Robert :
    speech against Sacheverell, 201-4
    expelled from the Commons, 1712,
        207-8, 229, 233
    speech against Peerage Bill, 215-
        216
    principal Minister, 216, 218, 369,
        370-74, 386
    dependence of a ministry on the
        Commons, 217
    the Harwich election, 1734, 367-
        368
War, levying, against the Crown,
    286-8
Wardrobe, Great, principal officers
    of, suppressed, 148
Wardship and liveries, Court of,
    abolished, 2-3, 271
Warrant :
    search, 32-3, 297-8, 306-10
    for forcible entry in conventicles, 38

Warrant—(*contd.*)
issued by Speaker for a new election, 45, 207, 229
of commitment, 48, 281, 291-4
of J.P.s protect constables, 134
of arrest, issued by Speaker, 167, 175, 236
of Lords to Black Rod, 173
of Secretary of State, 227, 291
general, 227-8, 294-5, 295-7, 302
Watson, James, a messenger, 294-7
Weights and Measures for England and Scotland, 101
Wentworth, Lord of Manor at Aldborough, 326
Westminster :
bill for paving streets, 153
meeting-place of Parliament, 178, 187
servants of king and Duke of York in, subject to Test Act 40
papists expelled from, 61
coals for poor, 371
election at, 400
Whigs, 359-60, 385, 389
White, W., Mayor of Aylesbury, sued by Ashby, 193-6, 278-9, 281
Wild, John, Chief Baron, judgement on Lord's commitment of Shaftesbury, 252
Wilkes, John :
arrest of, 219-27
the Middlesex Election, 229-35
Wilkes *v.* Lord Halifax, 291-4
Wilkes *v.* Wood, 294-5
William III, *see also* Orange
declared king, 69 ff.
alone to exercise royal power, 70
association to defend, 88
and the succession, 92
his rights reasserted, 97
summons Convention Parliament, 186
treason to deny title of, 188
refuses assent to bills, 189
Kentish Petition on behalf of, 191
Sacheverell's opinion of, 197-207
finance of, 271
invitation to, 352-4
and Cabinet, 355-6
Williamson, Robert, 271-8

Wilmington, Spencer Compton, Earl of, 368
Wilmot, Sir John Eardley-, Judge in King's Bench, later L.C.J. of Common Pleas, 297
Wilson, J., publisher, 298
Winchester, 350
Winchilsea, Daniel, seventh Earl of, First Lord of the Admiralty, 375
Wine :
royal rights, 5
licences, Commissioners of, *see* Commissioner
Clarendon raised price of, 156
licences, 249, 261
Winnington, Sir Francis, M.P., 185
Winslow, Arthur, M.P., 172
Witnesses :
two required, 8, 37, 48, 81
defendant may produce, if charged with high treason, 81
before a select committee, 143
Wood, Wilkes *v.*, 294-5
Woolaston, Mr., expelled from Commons, 233
Worcester, Marquis of, 338
Works, Board of : principal officers suppressed, 148
Worsley, Sir Richard, M.P. for Newport, Isle of Wight, 300
Wright, Sir Martin, 314
Wright, Sir Robert, L.C.J., in Seven Bishops' Case, 265-7, 293
Writ :
of summons, 1, 34, 45, 54, 80, 85, 207, 229
of habeas corpus (*q.v.*), 47
of error, 5, 82, 151, 158, 162, 174, 182, 196, 272, 277, 280-84
to be in English, 129
only to be served on a J.P. after one month's notification, 133
of summons to House of Lords, 215
of mandamus, 288
of assistance, 296
prerogative, 311
of Quo Warranto, 75, 254 ff., 332, 349-51
Writer to the Signet, 120

York, City of :
1685 election, 342